Sex and Morality in the U.S.

Sex and Morality in the U.S.

An Empirical Enquiry under the Auspices of The Kinsey Institute

Albert D. Klassen
Colin J. Williams
Eugene E. Levitt

Edited and with an Introduction by
Hubert J. O'Gorman

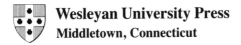

Wesleyan University Press
Middletown, Connecticut

All inquiries and permissions requests should be addressed to the Publisher, Wesleyan University Press, 110 Mt. Vernon Street, Middletown, Connecticut 06457.

Library of Congress Cataloging-in-Publication Data

Klassen, Albert D.

Sex and morality in the U.S. : an empirical enquiry under the auspices of the Kinsey Institute / Alfred D. Klassen, Colin J. Williams, Eugene E. Levitt ; edited and with an introduction by Hubert J. O'Gorman. — 1st ed.

p. cm.

Bibliography: p.

Includes index.

ISBN 0-8195-5224-0

1. Sex customs—United States. 2. Sex customs—Moral and ethical aspects. 3. Sexual behavior surveys—United States. 4. Married people—United States—Attitudes. I. Williams, Colin J. II. Levitt, Eugene E. III. O'Gorman, Hubert J. IV. Alfred C. Kinsey Institute for Sex Research. V. Title.

HQ18.U5K64 1989

306.7′0973—dc20 89-5751
CIP

Manufactured in the United States of America

First Edition

Contents

Tables

Figures

Preface

When I assumed the directorship of the Kinsey Institute in the fall of 1982, among the many problems which lay before me was the complex of unresolved issues surrounding the 1970 survey of sexual attitudes and behavior that has now emerged as *Sex and Morality in the U.S.* In discussions with the authors and others associated with their work, I was made aware of the professional difficulties among the authors, the many bruised feelings that these disputes had engendered, and the consequent delays in bringing this material to publication. Rather than tackle this maze of interpersonal disputes which had defied resolution for many years, I lay the matter aside to focus on more immediately pressing priorities. It was necessary to revitalize the Institute's virtually extinct research efforts, to rebuild its deteriorated physical plant, and to preserve the endangered treasures of its library and collections. Within three years, as it became evident that behavioral data were essential in determining and understanding factors affecting the transmission and spread of the AIDS virus, we began to search the Institute's extensive data bases, from Kinsey's time to the present, for any as yet untapped resources that could shed some light on this critical public health problem. In the course of this search, we recognized the potential value of the unpublished 1970 survey data, derived from a random sample of interviews on sexual attitudes and norms and self-administered questionnaires on sexual behavior. As a consequence, I began the task of trying to mediate a resolution of the long-standing problems that had held this important work in limbo. A comprehensive report on the design and the data collection procedures needed to be made available to the scholarly and biomedical communities and to others who might wish to extend the use of the dataset. In addition, in response to outside inquiries regarding the 1970 survey, we released the dataset to several qualified scholars.

As Tennyson wrote, "Science moves, but slowly, slowly, creeping on from point to point." I recognize, of course, that scholarly works based on extensive, multidimensional bodies of data often involve rather long periods from inception to final publication. Kinsey's own interview surveys extended over more than ten years from initiation to the publication of the first comprehensive volume. The works of Bell and Weinberg (1978) required a similar period. But by 1986 there was increasing urgency to bring the unique data from the 1970 survey into the scientific arena in a more fully realized form. In spite of the time that had elapsed, no comparable body of information had been developed assessing the sexual attitudes and behavior of the American public, so directly relevant to our efforts to stem the AIDS epidemic.

Detailed examination of the 1970 data made clear its singular significance, as well as some of its shortcomings. While the information on sexual attitudes and norms had been developed on the basis of face-to-face interviews conducted by trained interviewers from the National Opinion Research Center, the data on personal sexual behavior had been gathered through a self-administered questionnaire, because the interviewers and the respondents were apparently uncomfortable with the behavioral questions to be posed in the interview format. But despite any limitations occasioned by this procedure, the unprecedented representative national sample upon which the data were based provided a desperately needed data foundation upon which to examine sexual attitudes and behavior in the 1980s. Whatever difficulties had stalled publication, I was determined to enlist the full energies and good will of the original authors in overcoming these problems. Only then would we be able to fulfill the authors' and the Institute's responsibility to bring the material into the scientific arena.

Deeply felt personal differences are not easily reconciled, particularly when so much time, emotion, and professional energy have been invested in an important work of science. Nonetheless, after repeated discussions with the original authors, the Institute was successful in resolving the issues that had delayed publication. It was later agreed that a distinguished sociologist would be recruited to evaluate independently and restructure the material for publication. We were most fortunate in enlisting the objective and sensitive assistance of Professor Hubert J. O'Gorman of Wesleyan University in accomplishing this task; it was further agreed that he would make the final decisions on the editing and contents of the volume.

To be sure, not all the disagreements have been laid to rest, but with the cooperation of everyone concerned, Professor O'Gorman has accomplished the task of preparing this volume for publication with protean skill and herculean effort. On behalf of the Institute and of the scientific and general public, I applaud the authors, Albert Klassen, Colin Williams, and Eugene Levitt, for their untiring efforts. They have provided a vitally needed and unparalleled body of data that will continue to contribute to the studies of sexual behavior and norms in American society, both in the struggle to cope with the AIDS epidemic and in the continued efforts to understand the forces that shape our morality and behavior in this significant and ubiquitous aspect of human life.

February 1989

June Machover Reinisch
Director
The Kinsey Institute for Research in Sex, Gender, and Reproduction,
Indiana University

Acknowledgments

A study as broad and lengthy as this one obviously required the help of a great many people. First among them is Dr. Stanley Yolles, in whose wisdom and vision this project had its origin. As director of the National Institute of Mental Health, Dr. Yolles inspired the creation of the NIMH Taskforce on Homosexuality and its recommendations for encouraging and supporting major projects concerned with issues of homosexuality. We wish to acknowledge our gratitude to the NIMH for the grant to the Institute for Sex Research, Indiana University, that made this study possible (Contract No. R01 MH-16979).

As members of Yolles's staff, his assistant, Jon Meyer, and Jane Lynch, executive secretary of the NIMH, played major roles in implementing the commitment to this project. Jack Wiener, of the NIMH Center for Studies of Mental Health and Social Problems, lent special support throughout the life of the funding. In addition, various members of the NIMH Taskforce on Homosexuality contributed to the study design: Evelyn Hooker, John Money, Edwin M. Schur, and especially Judd Marmor. Other experts in the fields of human sexuality and survey research whom we consulted during the initial stages of our work were Frank Beach, Irving Bieber, Bruce P. Dohrenwend, Laud Humphries, Ira Reiss, Edward Sagarin, Joseph Satten, and George Serban.

Over the years we have also received a great deal of assistance from colleagues in the Indiana University Departments of Sociology at Bloomington and Indianapolis—George Bohrnstedt, Sue Kiefer Hammersmith, Elton Jackson, Samuel Mueller, James Norton, Sheldon Stryker, Brian Vargus, and James Wood were always generous with their help. Special thanks go to David Knoke, Karl Schuessler, and David Ford, who advised and encouraged our uses of factor and path analytic techniques in general and relative to the stereotyping of homosexuals, offering various useful criticisms and suggestions. Several members of the Indiana University administration helped negotiate knotty bureaucratic tangles, especially two associate deans of research and advanced studies, Richard Curtis and Rex Stockton, with contributions from Ray Martin, Clifford Travis, Alvin York, and Jack Getman.

Since our data were collected by the National Opinion Research Center (NORC), we of course worked closely with a number of people at that organization. Norman Bradburn was executive director there at the time of our initial contact and remained until September of 1970; he was followed by Paul B. Sheatsley, acting director until September of 1971 and director of the Survey Research Service throughout the time of the project, and then by James A. Davis. In addition, we worked closely with Robert McDonald, treasurer; Shelby Orrell, business manager; and Seymour Sudman and, later, Benjamin King, as directors of sampling. Other assistance came from Pat Bova, NORC librarian; Frances Harris, coding supervisor; and Winona Atkins, computer programmer in charge of data editing and cleaning operations.

From the NORC Field Department came the efforts of Eve Weinberg, director; Fan Calloway, her assistant director; and Ruth Nepon, senior field supervisor. Jeanne Schwartz, field supervisor for Chicago, had immediate responsibility for the entire field operation. Our consultant in developing the training program was Dr. Anthony G. Banet. We extend our particular appreciation to the more than fifty NORC field supervisors who attended our Chicago training sessions. The results in this book show how successfully they shared their Chicago experience and the challenge of the study with their interviewing staffs all over the country. Those interviewers bore the ultimate responsibility for sensitive yet rapid-fire data gathering from over 3,000 respondents.

Beyond the actual survey, most of the work was naturally done at the Institute for Sex Research at Indiana University, and we benefited from the unique resources the Institute provides. To Paul H. Gebhard, who was director of the Institute, we extend our appreciation for his general support. For library assistance we thank Joan Brewer, Rebecca Dixon, Helen Hofer, Susan Matusak, and their diligent staff. Expert secretarial assistance was provided in the early days of the project by Lenora Key, Sue Williams, and Jane Wines, and later by Stephanie Penoff Molitor, Elizabeth Ann ("E. A.") Shelby, Marianne Sigmund, and Karen Ruse Strueh. We are especially grateful to Stephanie Huddle Schaeffer for tirelessly typing draft after draft. The initial computer work was done by Robert Dean and Jason Sachs. For the bulk of the computer production required throughout the years we are indebted to Lois Downey, an indispensable member of our research team. Many work-study students and a graduate assistant performed those mundane and tedious tasks so essential to a project of this magnitude; we specifically acknowledge Robert E. Dargitz, graduate research assistant, and Teresa Farrell Bottoms, Gerald P. Downey, Jeanne Inlow, Jan Ranck, Laura Sherfey, Steve Snyder, and Lou Anne White, who served as student clerical assistants. Eric Klassen did early path analysis computer runs and helped his father weigh the pros and cons of beta versus partial correlation coefficients. Other Institute members due special thanks are Alan Blaine Johnson, who handled many administrative details, and Alan P. Bell, as much a warm friend as Institute colleague, who gave us continuing support and encouragement.

We wish also to acknowledge the contributions of our two project coordinators, without whom this book would not have been completed. In the first several years, Jan Shipps organized many aspects of data collection, including the preliminary consultations, the training of interviewer supervisors, the organization and writing up of results from two major pretests of the questionnaire, and the preparation of the data codebook. In general, she capably imposed order on all the burgeoning aspects of a complex study. From 1975 to 1981, and then in our 1988 editing for publication, Linda DuPlantis contributed enormously to the successful completion of the project, analyzing data, constructing tables, writing and editing drafts, and in general seeing to the myriad of demanding details that ensure a sound report.

More recently, great appreciation is owed to the University of North Dakota, the UND School of Medicine, and the UND departments of sociology and neuroscience, without whose support the final editing and its negotiation would have been impossible. More specifically, the gracious support of Professor Sharon C. Wilsnack, principal investigator of the National Institute on Alcohol Abuse and Alcoholism project, "Problem Drinking in Women: A National Survey" (Grant No. R01 AA04610; the senior author as project director), made possible over two months of final editorial effort and underwrote the expense of uncounted and lengthy phone calls to Middletown, Indianapolis, and Bloomington, to bring the manuscript to fruition as a book.

To all of these people whose efforts went into this project, we express our appreciation and gratitude.

February 1989

Albert D. Klassen
Colin J. Williams
Eugene E. Levitt

I wish to acknowledge my gratitude to June M. Reinisch, director of the Kinsey Institute, without whose initiative and support this book would not have been published. I would also like to thank Jeannette Hopkins, Eliza Childs, and Jan Fitter of the Wesleyan University Press for their valuable help and advice.

March 1989

Hubert J. O'Gorman

Introduction

Sex and Morality in the U.S. presents the major findings from a unique national survey of American sexual norms and experiences. The survey was conducted in 1970 under the auspices of the Institute for Sex Research[1] at Indiana University and is based on interviews with more than 3,000 adults. This book incorporates the data, and interpretations of the data, from those interviews. This extensive statistical analysis represents an important contribution to the literature on human sexuality, a field that still reflects, as Dr. Alfred C. Kinsey once put it, our "absorbing interest and astounding ignorance." By using the findings of this 1970 survey to identify the moral rules applied to sexual behavior and thus to view behavior in its normative context, *Sex and Morality in the U.S.* seeks to extend and expand the type of research represented by the pioneering work of Dr. Kinsey and his associates.

After describing the degree to which the survey's respondents judged sexual activities like prostitution, masturbation, premarital sex, extramarital sex, and homosexuality to be morally right or wrong, *Sex and Morality in the U.S.* examines the extent to which these normative judgments were altered by sexual experiences, as reported by the individuals in self-administered questionnaires, and by their personal, social, and demographic characteristics.

As in the earlier Kinsey volumes (Kinsey, Pomeroy, Martin, and Gebhard, 1953; Kinsey, Pomeroy, and Martin, 1948), the data reported in this book are based on personal information provided by many individuals. However, this work differs importantly from earlier ones in method and purpose. There is, for example, a critical difference in the sampling techniques used to select individuals to be interviewed. Although Kinsey and his associates interviewed large numbers of males and females, their sampling procedures make it difficult to determine what larger population their volunteer subjects represented (Cochran, Mosteller, and Tukey, 1954). In contrast, those respondents who agreed to participate in the 1970 survey constituted a national sample carefully designed to represent the adult population of the United States.

There is, in addition, a major difference in research goals between this study and the earlier Kinsey reports.[2] For members of the early Kinsey team the primary objective was to describe human sexual behavior. They were emphatically not interested in the moral norms that guided the reported conduct. The 1970 survey, on the other hand, not only attempted to depict patterned sexual experiences, but it also took the further and significant step of asking respondents for their moral judgments about certain sexual activities. Indeed, it was the first and, as far as can be ascertained, it remains the only national survey centered wholly on the sexual experiences and the sexual norms of a representative sample of the adult American population. If the results of Kinsey's own published research provided a provisional taxonomy of human sexual behavior, the results of the 1970 survey now provide, just as provisionally, the much needed national data base for studying the moral context of sexual conduct. It is these national data that the authors of *Sex and Morality in the U.S.* drew on to prepare their analysis of the sociology and the social psychology of sexual norms. Although collected in 1970 and analyzed in the next eight years, these data are demonstrably relevant for an understanding of how Americans then and now define and respond to sexual situations.[3]

Sex and Morality in the U.S. had its origins in a research project that was conceived as a national sample survey of the public images of homosexuality. The envisioned survey was part of a proposal drafted in 1968 by Albert Klassen, a sociologist who at the time was a research associate at Indiana University's Institute for Sex Research, in response to a suggestion made by the National Institute of Mental Health's (NIMH) Task Force on Homosexuality.[4] Recognizing that it would be extremely difficult to assess reactions to homosexuality without a comparison with reactions to other kinds of sexual conduct, Klassen expanded the plan for the survey to cover a wide variety of sexual behaviors, attitudes, norms, and experiences. As the planning for this study evolved, the Institute, in response to a recommendation from the NIMH that a psychologist or psychiatrist be added to the project, recruited Eugene Levitt, a clinical psychologist from Indiana University's School of Medicine, as a part-time participant. In 1968 the Institute formally submitted the more elaborate proposal for a national survey on sexual deviance to the NIMH, listing Klassen and Levitt as coprincipal investigators. The award was granted in May 1969 for a three-year period ending April 30, 1972.[5]

The Institute then contracted with the National Opinion Research Center (NORC) at the University of Chicago to carry out the study. After about twelve months of preliminary work, including special training for the NORC interviewers and pretesting of the questions, the national survey was completed in the fall of 1970. In the process, it became evident that the cost of conducting each interview was far greater than either NORC or the Institute had anticipated; the question of who should pay for the resulting cost overrun became a major source of contention between the two institutions. After months of protracted negotiation, the dispute was resolved. Some time late in 1971 or early in 1972 NORC turned the data it had collected over to the Institute. To compensate, in part, for this unanticipated delay, the NIMH complied with the Institute's request for a supplementary grant to run through April 1973.

What happened in the years after 1972, that is, after the survey data were in the hands of the Institute, is still a matter of controversy. The following account attempts to reconstruct the major events based on the often conflicting versions provided by the participants. After 1972 the analysis of the 1970 survey data apparently proceeded slowly, though Klassen and Levitt did present some of their findings at two professional meetings in 1973 and in an article published a year later (Klassen and Levitt, 1974). In April 1973 the NIMH funds had run out. While Klassen's salary was then terminated he continued to work on the project, supporting himself with part-time work outside of the Institute.

Impatient with what they perceived to be the lack of progress and the increasingly fragile working relationship between Klassen and Levitt, the trustees of the Institute in 1975 placed Colin Williams, himself one of the trustees and a sociologist on the Institute staff, in charge of the project. To expedite matters, Williams was instructed to work with and to coordinate the efforts of Klassen and Levitt to prepare a manuscipt summarizing the project's work. Initially, Williams did not expect to do much of the writing, enough perhaps to qualify him as a third author. In due course, however, he found himself writing far more than he had anticipated. The three authors worked together tolerably well under these new arrangements, although there were occasions of serious personal and professional conflict. By late 1979, Williams, with the help of Klassen and Levitt, finished the manuscript.

In early 1980, as the long-awaited manuscript was being considered for publication, an intense dispute broke out about whose name should appear first on the title page. By this time, Williams, still an Institute trustee, had written so much of the manuscript that he felt he was entitled to be listed as its first author, and he asked the trustees to designate him as the senior author in place of Klassen. They did so without, according to Klassen and Levitt, discussing the matter with the other authors. More was at stake than the listing of names. Klassen was also disturbed because he strongly disagreed with certain editorial decisions made by Williams regarding both the title and content of the manuscript. After a lengthy discussion of the controversy, the Institute's trustees again voted that Williams be listed as the first author and Klassen as the second, but that Klassen was to receive the largest share of any royalties. Klassen and Levitt both objected strenuously to this arrangement. Under the circumstances, of apparently unresolved dispute, publishers lost interest in the book.

The authors resumed their careers elsewhere. The Institute, meanwhile, became engaged in a reassessment of its institutional future; the outcome was a new board of trustees, and in 1982 they installed June M. Reinisch as director to replace Paul Gebhard, who retired. For the next four years nothing was done about the manuscript.

In 1986, Charles Turner, a sociologist with the National Academy of Sciences, heard of the national survey that NORC had done in 1970 for the Kinsey group. As study director of the Academy's committee on AIDS research and the social sciences, Turner was eager to look at the survey's findings. He contacted Klassen, asked to see the data, and urged him to publish the work. Since both the data and the manuscript belonged to the now renamed The Kinsey Institute for Research in Sex, Gender, and Reproduction, Turner and Klassen called Reinisch in late 1986 to see what could be done. Reinisch, who had been making an independent effort to resolve the controversy, made the data available to Turner and others. By the spring of 1987 she had persuaded the authors to settle their differences. After they signed an agreement stipulating that Klassen was to be the first-named author, that Williams was to act as the official spokesman for the book, and that they would share equally in the royalties, Reinisch began to look for a publisher. In March 1988 the history of the manuscript was reviewed in *Science* magazine,[6] the first public acknowledgment that the 1970 survey had been done and that most of the results were still unpublished. Several months later, the Wesleyan University Press contracted to publish the results of what *Science* had dubbed "The Long, Lost Survey on Sex."

However unfortunate the long delay in its publication, *Sex and Morality in the U.S.* merits serious attention. It identifies some of the important patterns of sexual morality and behavior that prevailed in this country in 1970. Certainly anyone with more than a passing interest in what happened in the United States during the 1960s and the 1970s, and particularly anyone who believes that during those decades the nation experienced a transformation of sexual values and norms, will recognize the importance of some of the findings reported here. If, as conventional wisdom has it, there was a sexual revolution of the 1960s, it apparently was not experienced by the great majority of women and men interviewed in the 1970 survey.

Another and perhaps more important reason why this book deserves careful reading is the general contribution it makes to the systematic study of the patterned ways in which human beings assess sexual activities. As the book makes abundantly clear, and the doubts of some sex researchers notwithstanding, it is possible and it is fruitful to investigate in a national sample survey the moral norms that individuals apply to sexual conduct, to elicit from them accounts of their own sexual experiences, and to measure the reciprocal relationship between sexual norms and sexual experience.

Given the psychological and social significance of sexual behavior, its symbolic value in American culture, and the widespread use of survey research by social scientists, it is remarkable that no such comprehensive study was done before 1970. It seems even more remarkable that, by the late 1980s, the 1970 Kinsey survey still remains the only study with a sample that provides a statistically sound basis for characterizing the American adult population's sexual standards and experiences. There have been, of course, numerous investigations of sexual activities and a more limited number of investigations of sexual morals. But for the most part, such studies used severely restricted samples of subjects. When national samples have occasionally been used, the questions put to respondents have been few in number and limited in scope.[7]

Because the 1970 Kinsey survey has had no immediate counterpart to date, the findings and analyses of this book provide an essential benchmark for sex researchers. They do so in two closely related ways. First, by establishing a set of national baseline data, they allow for more accurate measurements of large-scale changes in sexual mores than would otherwise be possible. When similar national surveys are conducted in the future—five, ten, twenty, or fifty years from now—their value as comparative instruments will obviously be substantially enhanced by the data that appear in *Sex and Morality in the U.S.* In particular, because they were collected well before the epidemic became evident, these data will probably be indispensable to any attempt to describe the effects of AIDS on American sexual morality and behavior. The second way in which the 1970 findings serve as a benchmark is that, until they are modified by the results from similar later surveys, they contribute an approximate and much needed national frame of reference for sex studies. By analyzing studies of more circumscribed samples against the 1970 data, it will be possible to judge the degree to which plausible inferences about sexual behavior can be drawn from them and applied to the adult population as a whole.

Beyond serving as a social chronicle and a significant point of reference for other related research, this book presents a rich array of intrinsically interesting findings drawn from the respondents' answers to questions in the 1970 survey.[8] These findings emerge as the authors, relying heavily on the statistics of path analysis, describe and explain, among other things, variations in their respondents' sexual norms, their reported involvement in premarital sex, their perception of changes in sexual norms, and the formal and informal sanctions they would like to see applied to violators of sexual norms. Additional and related findings appear in the four chapters that focus on the respondents' perception of and reactions to homosexuality. Since all of this material is spelled out by the authors in great detail, there is no need to review it here, except to note one point. Because 90% of the respondents in the 1970 survey were married or had been married, these reported findings incorporate the pertinent views and experiences of the majority of adults whose opinions and behavior largely define the standards of sexual morality in the United States.

The book raises two other issues that are worth commenting on. It reminds us, and we apparently do need to be occasionally reminded, how critically important norms are in any attempt to comprehend human conduct, sexual or otherwise. And it draws to our attention the significant but neglected question of how members of a society come to acquire a reasonably accurate knowledge of the operative norms prevailing in the social world around them. As the authors correctly insist, sexual behavior cannot be adequately understood divorced from its normative context.[9] That is to say, the meaning of such behavior to the participants—what they do and how they think and feel about what they are doing—can only be grasped if we know whether or not they conceive of their behavior as complying with a relevant set of norms. Although the authors repeatedly allude to the cultural and social implications of this normative conception of sexual behavior, they are never expressly discussed.

A norm is, of course, a behavior-regulating rule that individuals, as members of a society, share and believe they share with others. It is a morally binding rule that ordinarily elicits both external social and internal psychological sanctions. Sexual norms, then, are shared conceptions stipulating what sexual conduct is culturally prescribed, preferred, permitted, or proscribed. In most social situations there is usually a substantial but varying degree of consensus about what is right and what is wrong. More often than not, this variation in consensus reflects diverse patterns of acceptance, interpretation, and application of the norms by individuals located in different parts of the social structure, as indicated, for example, by their different marital, gender, and age statuses. In addition, because individuals are located by themselves and by others in terms of different statuses, there will be, in most social situations, patterned variation in the rates of compliance with these norms and patterned variation in the rates of publicly known compliance. And both of these rates will influence the viability of the norms as reflected in the external and internal sanctions applied to their violations. Frequently, observable variations in sexual behavior lead observers and participants to exaggerate the extent of moral violations or to underestimate the strength of differently perceived norms.

One of the noteworthy aspects of this book is the skill with which its authors tacitly employ this normative formulation in their analysis. Thus we are able to understand the reasonably coherent moral consensus among the persons interviewed, despite their varying social characteristics and personal experiences. At the same time, we are able to understand how that normative consensus varied, nonetheless, in predictable ways in terms of their age, gender, religion, and marital status as well as by the regions of the country and the type of community in which they lived. Similarly, how the variation in respondents' reported sexual experiences affected their moral interpretation of certain sexual activities seems equally clear. And we are also able to see as a bonus how respondents' moral judgments were affected by the social characteristics of others. The authors, for example, in a particularly insightful analysis, show that respondents' moral evaluation of the premarital sexual behavior of others depends not only on their own gender and premarital experience, but on the age, gender, and emotional attachment of those they are judging.

Equally impressive is the evidence of normative constraints on sexual experience. This appears, perhaps predictably, in the persistent effects of past and present religious commitment in shaping sexual behavior and morality. But it also shows up, and less predictably, in the thoughtful analysis of the regret expressed by many respondents about their normative digressions. The impact of normative restraints even appears among those who said they were sexually inexperienced. They were asked how they thought they *would* have reacted had they engaged in particular sexual activities. The honest expression of negative sentiments by respondents over a norm violation that they did not commit is fitting testimony to the strength of any moral code.

To talk of norms is, as we noted, to assume that individuals share and believe they share moral rules with others. This, in turn, assumes that there is public recognition of the prevailing state of sexual morality, and that this public awareness is an accurate reflection of the actual state of affairs. One of the principal contributions of *Sex and Morality in the U.S.* is that it calls this last assumption into question, at least for sexual norms in the United States in the 1960s and 1970s. During those years it was widely and firmly believed that American society was experiencing a sexual revolution.[10] There seemed to be little doubt among commentators on the passing scene that the moral rules of sexual conduct were being rapidly transformed. But the term *sexual revolution* is, as the authors point out, too ambiguous to be conceptually useful. More to the point, and they stress this throughout their book, is the absence of any empirical evidence from their survey suggesting that a major change in sexual morals had taken place. To be more concrete, the majority of the respondents in the 1970 survey considered, for example, prostitution, homosexuality, extramarital sex, and premarital sex among adolescents to be always or almost always wrong. Understandably, the authors regard these responses as quite conventional and conservative, and not at all what one would expect if a sexual revolution had actually occurred.

The implication seems clear. Insofar as the data in the 1970 survey can be viewed as an endorsement of traditional sexual morality, and insofar as the belief that there had been a marked change in that morality was widely accepted as true, then a state of pluralistic ignorance surely existed. Generally speaking, pluralistic ignorance refers to erroneous cognitive beliefs shared by some individuals about other individuals (O'Gorman, 1988). In this case, the prevailing norms governing sexual conduct were mistakenly believed by many to be far more liberal than they in fact were. According to the authors, this radical bias in public perception was facilitated by the change in legal norms that allowed for increasing explicitness in the handling of sexual matters in the arts and the mass media. And it was greatly strengthened, they believe, by the proliferation of well-publicized studies of sexual behavior based on samples of individuals that could by no stretch of the imagination be considered representative of the population.

Whatever the sources of pluralistic ignorance regarding sexual morality, the evidence for its existence is in this instance not restricted to the discrepancy between the prevailing conventional wisdom and the data collected in the 1970 survey. It is in fact documented by the survey: 40% of the individuals interviewed, for example, mistakenly thought they were more conservative about premarital and extramarital sex than most other adults. It remains to be seen whether, as Alfred Kinsey thought, human sexuality is more likely to generate and maintain patterns of pluralistic ignorance than are other areas of social life. In any event, there is no reason to believe that the members or observers of American society are today any better informed about the sexual norms endorsed by most other individuals around them than they were in 1970.

For all of this book's distinct merits, it would be unrealistic to ignore some of the problems that readers will confront herein. A number of these difficulties concern the validity and reliability of the survey. Aside from their comments made in reference to the pretesting of the questionnaire, the authors never address this important issue. This is, of course, a problem that all researchers routinely face; but in a study of sexual morality in which respondents are queried at length about their own sexual histories and values, the validity and reliability of their replies are of more than routine significance. To be sure, these issues were not ignored in the execution of the study. The questions were constructed and pretested with commendable care (Appendix C); the NORC interviewers received special training (Appendix B); and that part of the questionnaire that dealt with the respondents' sexual experiences was self-administered (Appendix F). Nonetheless, the book would have been greatly strengthened had it included a detailed examination of the technical quality of the data. The lack of a summary of the patterns of nonresponse to different kinds of questions among respondents of diverse social and personal characteristics is particularly disconcerting. As matters stand, we do not know what the authors think about the ways in which the respondents' answers may have been shaped by fallible memories, by the wording of the questions, by the order in which the questions were presented, and by the desire to appear morally decent in the eyes of NORC's predominantly white, female, middle-class interviewers. Moreover, in reporting the results of a study as innovative, elaborate, and ambitious as the 1970 national survey, it would have been useful for the authors to have reminded their readers that survey data, no matter how valid and reliable, necessarily reflect the content of the questions put to the respondents. Such a caveat would have been especially appropriate in their extensive discussion of public conceptions of homosexuality.

Still other problems exist in this book. There are sections where the writing style, the reasoning, and the interpretation of data will probably try some readers' patience. Furthermore, no attempt has been made in the book to assess its findings and analysis in the light of more recent research bearing directly on the topics discussed by the authors. By and large, with but a few deletions, the book is as it was prepared and written, a research report from the late 1970s.[11] This decision to publish the book without major revisions and without an attempt to bring it up-to-date was made by the editor and the publisher. In arriving at this decision, we carefully weighed the factors responsible for the ten-year lag in publication, the Kinsey Institute's desire to see the book in print as soon as possible, and the persisting differences among the authors. But the most important consideration was our conviction that the findings reported in this book are, as they stand, of substantial value to the research community and should be made quickly available. In our judgment, the hard core of this book's contribution is to be found in the 1970 baseline data regarding the sexual norms and experiences reported by a national sample of American adults. The study remains, after all these years of neglect, the only one of its kind. No one with a serious interest in the exploration of the interplay between sexual norms and experiences can afford to ignore its findings. That is no small achievement.

February 1989

Hubert J. O'Gorman
Wesleyan University

NOTES

1. In 1982 the Institute was renamed The Kinsey Institute for Research in Sex, Gender, and Reproduction.
2. There were, of course, other differences between the 1970 survey and the Kinsey reports. All of the Kinsey data were collected in face-to-face interviews by Kinsey and his small staff. In the 1970 study the data concerning the respondents' beliefs, norms, and attitudes were gathered in personal interviews by professional interviewers employed by a university-affiliated research organization, while information about their sexual experiences was obtained from them on a self-administered questionnaire provided by the interviewers.
3. For two recent publications that use the 1970 national sample data for estimating the size of the population at risk for AIDS, see Fay, Turner, Klassen,

and Gagnon (1989) and Klassen, Williams, Levitt, Rudkin-Miniot, Miller, and Gunjal (1989).

4. The Task Force on Homosexuality, appointed in 1967 by Stanley F. Yolles, director of the National Institute of Mental Health, included among its members Paul Gebhard, director of the Institute for Sex Research. By the late 1960s the Institute for Sex Research was devoting a substantial proportion of its resources to studies of homosexuality. The history and design of the 1970 survey are discussed in Appendix A.
5. NIMH supported the project entitled "Attitudes Toward Selected Forms of Deviant Behavior" from May 1, 1969, to April 30, 1973, with grants totaling $369,327. During this same period the Institute received another large grant from the NIMH to study the social and psychological adjustment of homosexuals living in the San Francisco Bay area. The published results are in Bell and Weinberg (1978) and Bell, Weinberg, and Hammersmith (1981).
6. *Science* 239, (March 4, 1988). For comments by Klassen and Reinisch, see their letters to *Science* in the April 22 and May 14 issues.
7. In 1963, for example, NORC at the University of Chicago conducted an amalgam national survey that included, among other items, a set of questions asking for adult respondents' attitudes toward certain premarital sexual behavior (Reiss, 1967). Since 1972 NORC has frequently included some of the questions first asked in the 1970 Kinsey survey as part of its annual General Social Surveys. For the results of a 1967 national sample survey of sexual conduct among college students, see Gagnon and Simon, 1987.
8. All of the items used in the 1970 survey questionnaire and the percentages of male and female responses to each question are reproduced in Appendix F.
9. Nor can social control of sexual behavior be effective apart from a normative framework. The futility of moral exhortation as a solution to social problems is well known among researchers who attempt to apply their knowledge to control some of the undesired effects of sexual activities. But it hardly follows, as is sometimes suggested, that normative considerations are not an essential part of the problem. Illegitimate births and sexually transmitted diseases, to cite only two highly publicized examples, only occur in a culturally transmitted context of shared norms and values.
10. Putative signs of the so-called sexual revolution were readily identified before the 1960s. They were clearly detected in the 1950s with characteristic pessimism by Pitirim Sorokin (1956) and in 1949 with sober optimism by Wilhelm Reich (1961). Both authors assured their readers that the moral sexual revolution had been going on for several decades.
11. The deleted material included an introduction that seemed unnecessarily defensive about the application of survey research and statistical techniques to the study of sex and a chapter on sex education based on the recollections of a relatively small proportion of the respondents. Also not included in this book were two chapters submitted after the manuscript was received. One was entitled, "The Undersocialized Conception of Woman," the other, "Salient Sexual Behavior Patterns in the U.S.: Across 20th Century Decades," subsequently rewritten and published in Klassen et al., 1989. Although each of these chapters contained some pertinent material, they appeared, as written and organized, to be in need of substantial revision.

Sex and Morality in the U.S.

Chapter 1

The Notion of the "Sexual Revolution"

Among the popular rubrics describing changes in the United States from the end of World War II through the 1970s, few have been so succinct and seemingly appropriate as that of the "sexual revolution." On the surface, such a label appears quite warranted. For example, never before in our society have the public representation and discussion of sexual matters been so extensive. Magazines with pictures of full frontal nudity are available at corner drug stores; movie theaters show films that depict almost every kind of sexual behavior; best-selling books often include down-to-earth advice on sexual performance and relationships; and even television, which enters most homes, is gradually expanding the erotic content of both its documentary and entertainment offerings. People's behaviors seem different as well. Premarital cohabitation among the young is no longer extraordinary; jokes about sex have come out of the locker room; the revealing bathing suit has lost its shock value; "singles bars" are to be found in any city of size.

Such sexual openness was simply nonexistent, except among a small avant-garde, as recently as the 1950s in most places in the United States. So much seems to have happened since then that some commentators see the sexual revolution as successfully completed. As one journalist (Greene) noted in 1975:

> For a revolution to be worthy of its name it must struggle fiercely against the accepted values and customs of a society. By that standard, the sexual revolution became tame and toothless some time ago. Male pros-

titutes are now convivial guests on the daytime talk shows. Paperback copies of "The Joy of Sex" are tossed into the grocery shopping bag with the asparagus. Wife swapping and group sex are . . . old topics of suburban patio conversation. It's kind of difficult for a revolution to keep up a head of steam in a culture that has long ceased to put up even a token show of resistance.

As this quotation suggests, the notion of a sexual revolution was widely accepted by many as a way of summing up what they believed to be going on in the sexual life of contemporary America. We have doubts that such a revolution occurred, and in this book we present a large number of findings, taken from our national sample conducted in 1970, to substantiate our doubts. But first we need to address the question: Why did the idea of a sexual revolution become so widely accepted in the United States?

One reason seems apparent. The idea that a sexual revolution has occurred or that sexual morality has broken down is not unique to present-day society but has enjoyed a vogue at various times not only in our past but in the histories of other societies. Such an idea seems to emerge in conjunction with unsettling social changes, for example, during and after wars.[1] It should not be surprising, therefore, that the idea surfaced again in the United States in the late 1960s, a time of domestic turmoil over the war in Asia, civil rights battles, political assassinations, the renewal of feminism, Vatican II, experimentation with drugs, and so on. Amid all these convulsions in the social fabric, the idea of radical ("revolutionary") changes in the sexual sphere seemed logical enough. Thus the sexual revolution joined the "black revolution," "women's revolution," and "youth revolution" as social labels that served to make sense of what seemed at the time to presage a radical reconstruction of American society.

Although a major reason why the idea of a sexual revolution caught on, this is not the only explanation. Such an interpretation is also liable to serve other needs and interests. Weinberg (1971) suggested the following: the mass media, who popularized the term, exploit sexuality for their own purposes; "moral entrepreneurs" have a vested interest in the scare value of the idea, which can gain them supporters and a platform; many of the liberal avant-garde perceive change—any change, but especially revolution—as desirable; people who have difficulty accepting their own sexual desires may project them onto others; and finally, many gullible people indiscriminately accept popular notions of the social scene.

Whatever the reason(s), there is no doubt that the notion became a powerful cultural reality. Its immediacy, plausibility, and contemporaneity meant that it entered the realm of public discourse so that each mention served to sustain it further. Indeed, Gagnon and Simon (1970) suggested that this increased openness about sex allowed people to engage more in *public* talk about it, a situation that added to the belief that change was occurring, insofar as people often assume that public talk reflects private practice.

So influential did the sexual revolution idea become that some social scientists, treating it as an objective description of events, engaged in heated discussions not so much about whether or not the revolution had occurred as about the exact nature of the revolution they presumed to surround them. This focus was unfortunate, because the sexual revolution idea itself was far too imprecise to use in analyzing what had been going on in the sexual realm in the recent past. Consequently the notion of a sexual revolution produced confusion rather than enlightenment among social commentators.

Still, it is important to evaluate these usages and consider what they tell us. The first point is that the idea of revolution, in the sense that it is conventionally used—of radical (usually violent) change—does poorly as a concept in analyzing sexual behavior. As Petras (1978:211–212) pointed out: "In no other area of behavior and attitudes would the term revolution be used to describe nonviolent changes." It is no surprise, then, that the term often remains poorly defined or, as is usually the case, not defined at all. For example, Walsh (1978:298), after commenting that ". . . it is a very rare article that even tries to define the concept of 'sexual revolution,' " failed to do so himself, yet cheerfully concluded his review of recent sex research by claiming to have observed a "sexual revolution" in women's greater use of erotic imagery, an increase in female masturbation, people openly living together, and so on and so forth. This, of course, begs the question of why *these* changes could be considered revolutionary and not others.

In other words, for the notion to be worthwhile, some clear definition of *sexual revolution* needed to be established *prior* to dealing with evidence. This task was more difficult than it seemed.

To fully address it, the following issues would have to be confronted: What, among all the phenomena considered sexual, should be examined in evaluating change, and what would be the grounds for inclusion and exclusion? What aspects of these behaviors and attitudes should be studied—their incidence? frequency? social location? emotional context? How much of the population has to be affected? In what parts of the population must these changes occur—why are some groups singled out for special attention and not others? When did such changes begin? Were they continuous or sporadic? How rapidly did they happen? And what other changes in society were occuring at the same time?[2]

These are important questions, yet they really do not depend upon the notion of revolution for their utility. To simply ask what changes in sexual behavior had occurred over a specified time would have been more accurate and less subjective, otherwise we would have been faced with issues such as whether one type of sex behavior is more revolutionary than another, how much change in incidence, frequency, or whatever constitutes a revolutionary change, and so forth. We should not be surprised to find that, in practice, investigators dispensed with such a framework. As Petras (1978:213) commented, "Currently, the most popular approach to the question of the sexual revolution is through the use of scientific data concerning changes in the frequencies of certain types of behavior and changes in attitudes. One especially popular method is to compare studies that deal with premarital sex in order to determine whether or not it has been increasing." Most of these attempts focused on the unmarried, middle-class, college-going, young, white female (e.g., Luckey & Nass, 1969; Bell & Chaskes, 1970; Christensen & Gregg, 1970; Kaats & Davis, 1970). These studies reported an increase in the *incidence* of premarital coitus for such females since the early or mid-1960s. Other studies of younger, noncollege females documented a similar increase (Zelnik & Kantner, 1972, 1977; Miller & Simon, 1974). Many of these studies also considered the relationships among those involved in premarital sex. Findings showed that most women who had had premarital coitus had it with one partner only, the man they eventually would marry (Bell & Blumberg, 1959) or, increasingly, one to whom they had a strong emotional commitment (Bell & Chaskes, 1970; Simon et al., 1972; Lewis & Burr, 1975). Zelnik and Kantner (1972) found the same for their noncollege sample of females in

1971. In their 1977 study, they reported that unmarried teenage females in 1976 had had *more* partners than those surveyed in 1971; but they provided no data on respondents' relationships with these males.

It was often concluded from such studies that coitus had remained part of the established courtship system and had not become casual or "promiscuous" for most college females. Thus the term *evolution* sometimes replaced *revolution* as a descriptive summary of events. Again, however, the precise meaning of *evolution* received scant attention.

The study of premarital sexual behavior has been quite extensive but, even so, is far from complete. Few studies have looked at young men, few have looked at noncollege youth, and many have ignored crucial questions such as frequency of sex,[3] noncoital sexuality, homosexuality, and the meaning of behavior other than its relational significance. Despite these drawbacks, such studies remain outstanding compared with the data we have on sexual behavior among adults (with the exception of the work of Kinsey and his colleagues, 1948, 1953). For example, most heterosexuality occurs within the context of marriage, yet there has not been a single broadly based study of marital sex since Kinsey's that would allow us to gauge changes in this realm. The same can be said for other relatively common forms of adult sexual behavior, such as masturbation and postmarital sex (Goode & Troiden, 1974). What have appeared instead are mainly studies of unconventional sex, such as mate swapping or "swinging" (Bell & Silvan, 1970; Bartell, 1971; Denfeld & Gordon, 1974; Gilmartin, 1974; Smith & Smith, 1974). The great attention given by researchers to this minority form of sexual expression, we feel, has added further strength to the notion of a sexual revolution.

Simplifying the complex issues that underlie the concept of a sexual revolution is quite well suited to research strategies that attempt to consider changes in sexual *behavior* over time. Behaviors appear to be unambiguous, so that quantitative differences between two time periods are readily apparent. Hence the popularity of such work.

It is in the use of quantification, however, that a principal difficulty with studying "revolution" arises: How big is a "major" change, and compared to what? For example, suppose we take as a conservative estimate that in past times, no more than 25% of the population thought premarital sex was acceptable. If we find that now 50% approve of it, we might cite this as a "major" change in sexual norms. But if we find that 35% approve, does this fail to constitute a large enough difference from our 25% figure, or might it mean that 25% was too high an estimate? If we say that the 35% figure denotes not revolutionary but "evolutionary" change, as some have done, we run into further problems: another term to define and an arbitrary distinction to defend.[4] It is here that the problem becomes evident: how to *interpret* the data, given that definitions receive little consideration beforehand and that the methodology employed is so simplistic. Thus, Reiss (1976:169), one of the foremost researchers in this tradition, acknowledged the debate about "whether or not there has been a sexual revolution," did not bother to define any criteria, and concluded not that there has or hasn't been one but that there has been "a *significant change* in premarital sexual relationships since 1965" (1976:181). He estimated that the number of female nonvirgins at marriage had gone up from 50% in 1965 to 75% in the 1970s.

The crux of the matter is that crude behaviorism will not do. Research in this tradition does acknowledge this dictum, usually in one or two ways: (a) by considering the emotional meaning of premarital sex to be implicit in the nature of the relationship or (b) by considering the moral meaning of premarital sex to be indicated by the guilt or remorse of the females involved (e.g., Christensen & Carpenter, 1962; Christensen, 1966). In other words, changes in behavior per se are difficult to interpret unless their cultural context and social meaning can be ascertained. As Petras (1973:108) noted, "sexual behavior in society is the result of the peculiar cultural and social conditions existing at any one time." To believe otherwise would be to consider sexual behavior as a mere biological act divorced from the social context that produces it, something no sociologist would entertain. Gagnon and Simon (1970:107) summed this up as follows: "The [sexual] revolution would occur when the context of values and meanings attached to acts changes, not when there are small scale differences in rates or incidences . . . it is the social psychological context that provides meaning for sexual expression and not the latter for the former."

There have been few studies expressly concerned with the meanings of sexuality and the question of whether these meanings (or the proportion of the population who hold them) have changed over time. Further, most of these studies usually have dealt only with the question of premarital sex, with college students again being the major focus. The most extensive and sophisticated study of the moral meanings of premarital sex was conducted by Reiss (1967). Using a probability sample of the general population (data gathered in 1963) as well as student samples, he was able to delineate four major standards—abstinence, double standard, permissiveness with affection, and permissiveness without affection—that describe how Americans interpret premarital sex among the young. This work gives a good basis from which to evaluate change in one area of sexuality during the 1960s and 1970s. It is thus asserted with good reason that America has moved from a position in which premarital sex norms were abstinence or double-standard to one in which permissiveness with affection is generally accepted (Walsh, 1978:301), or in which there is a "variety of sexual codes" from which an individual can choose (Reiss, 1976:185). Noteworthy here is that the idea of a sexual revolution is unnecessary in detailing important social changes.

No study can do all the things required to give a complete picture of changes in American sexual patterns. However, the 1970s Kinsey study attempted, as far as possible, to provide basic data from which a fuller picture will emerge. In collecting and analyzing the data we were guided by the following ideas:

1. We dispensed with the notion of sexual revolution as too imprecise and subjective a term for analytical use. Rather, we attempted to gain an accurate picture of the sexual situation in America in 1970 to gauge what changes appear to have occurred or to be occurring. Whether these changes are important can only be ascertained in light of a sociological argument that takes the total social context into consideration.

2. We retained one idea implicit in the notion of a sexual revolution—that we should look for important changes not in ephemeral matters concerning sex (e.g., increases in the consumption of pornography) but in the basic underpinnings of sexual patterns. Thus our main focus in this study is on what we refer to as *sexual norms*, that set of moral strictures that give social meaning to sexual acts. These represent the cultural framework within which the individual acts and which determines the nature of his or her

sexual expression. It is this basic normative framework that we must look to first for any radical changes in sexuality, in that such changes would represent what has been called a "paradigm change" (Walsh, 1978:298), whereby the basic interpretations of sexuality in our society have been altered.[5]

For these reasons, our research focused on *public* moralities—the sexual norms people verbalize and support in public. That is, we do not accept as a criticism that people may hold different sexual standards in private or behave differently from the public norms they profess. These are important issues (and are dealt with in Chapter 11), yet they do not impinge on our central question. Many people think and behave differently from prevailing norms and always have: we do not see people as "cultural dopes" (Garfinkel, 1967). The most important indicant of widespread sexual change, we believe, would be people *publicly* expressing standards quite different from what is referred to as traditional sexual morality. If this were widespread it would suggest that community norms were changing and that the symbolic environment in which sex was learned and expressed had also significantly altered. We hope, therefore, to have established a criterion of important change that, if not agreed upon by others, is at least objective and measurable.

3. In formulating our study, we also considered many aspects of the moral meanings of sex—not only norms toward particular behaviors such as premarital sex, extramarital sex, masturbation, and so on, but also how such evaluations differ when the age and gender of those involved vary. Mainly, we were looking at what we call *ordinary sex*—what most adults do sexually—because these behaviors should be where changing interpretations would be most evident. Homosexuality is a special case. Not only is it not rare among unconventional sexualities, but it has long had an important symbolic meaning in the minds of most Americans. We believe that the moral meanings surrounding homosexuality represent a touchstone for understanding American sexual norms. In fact, our national study of sexual morality began as an effort to understand public conceptions of homosexuality, and Chapters 7–10 of this book are devoted to that topic. As well as studying sexual norms directly, we studied people's reactions to violators of sexual morality. In this way we hope to provide a fuller understanding of sexuality in the United States. Finally, the breadth of our study is

also evident in our examination of a great many possible determinants of sexual norms.

4. The temporal nature of changes in sexual standards posed some difficult problems for us. Ideally, only a longitudinal study could demonstrate a change in norms. In such a case we could consider important changes to have taken place if, compared to an earlier survey, the same respondents now believed that the morality of any given sexual behavior depended entirely on the immediate context rather than anything intrinsically "wrong" or "right" about the behavior. Or if people were hesitant to condemn a conventional behavior such as heterosexual coitus and did not qualify their judgments on such bases as the gender, age, or relationship of the actors. Our survey only gathered data at one point in time, so such a comparison is impossible. We are thus left with making statements about possible change based on the following three inferences.

First, on historical grounds we "know" many important things about the moral meanings of sex in the past. Logically, it would follow, as argued above, that certain outcomes in our data may reflect important changes.[6] We are also fortunate that our data were collected in 1970, in the middle of the so-called sexual revolution, so that any change in a liberal direction should be maximized.

Second, we did collect three kinds of retrospective data, which other studies rarely do. We asked our entire sample about actual sexual experience occurring in childhood, adolescence, and early adulthood (both hetero- and homosexual relationships, as well as masturbation to climax). In addition, we asked respondents how they had changed their various standards and also how their norms compared with their parents'. We are aware of the problems of distortion with retrospective data, yet we feel that data on the same individuals do constitute a more than acceptable base on which to approach the study of perceived change. At least, if radical sexual change has taken place during the lifetimes of the current population, such an approach should be able to detect it. For example, the extent to which our respondents were aware of any conflict between so-called *old* and *new* moralities could be reflected in the proportion saying they did not know or could not say whether a given behavior is always, usually, sometimes, or never wrong. Or from their retrospective evaluations of their own premarital activities, we can infer, for example, whether the supposedly permissive climate of 1970 led many to regret that they did not have more extensive sexual experiences before marriage. Our findings on these issues are so interesting and in some ways unexpected that we devote Chapter 5 to *perceived changes* in sexual norms.

Third, we are aware that certain *relationships* hold from past research. These we consider to be the traditional social structural anchors of sexual standards. For example, we would expect religiosity to be a strong predictor of sexual standards. If this did not appear in our analyses, then important changes could be said to have occurred. Similarly, older people have been shown to be more conservative than younger people. If we found the relationship between age and conservatism to be weak or reversed, this again would constitute an important change.

5. Finally, our study overcomes the biggest stumbling block that has previously prevented an accurate evaluation of the American sexual scene—the lack of representative samples. The early 1970s produced a variety of studies that appeared to give empirical support to the idea that something like a sexual revolution had taken place, regardless of how ill-defined that idea might have been. Even though they were not conducted by social scientists, these studies have often been cited in the academic literature, the "respectability" thus given them adding strength to the notion that the sexual revolution is an accomplished fact.

Two frequently quoted studies are surveys conducted for magazines. The first was done through *Psychology Today*, which included a 100-item questionnaire in its July 1969 issue. Results were published in the July 1970 issue (Athanasiou et al., 1970). Over 20,000 readers responded, a large sample. Size of sample, however, does not guarantee lack of bias, and this sample was very biased indeed, the respondents tending to be young, and well educated, with high incomes. Of course, this was because they were all *Psychology Today* readers, an extremely selective group. Even within this group, we should also take note that response was voluntary and that we do not know anything about the nonrespondents. Presumably the nonrespondents would be persons either more conservative about sex or more uncomfortable in dealing with it. Such liberal bias is evident in that 32% of the sample rated their attitudes as "very liberal" and another 45% as "somewhat liberal." Not surprisingly, this study showed people to be very tolerant—for example, only 9% thought that premarital intercourse was wrong and that couples should wait till they are married, and only 22% stated that extramarital sex was wrong.

Larger than the *Psychology Today* study was one conducted by *Redbook* magazine. A questionnaire was included in the October 1974 issue, and results were published in subsequent issues and also in book form (Tavris & Sadd, 1977). The questionnaire was completed by over 100,000 women, but again this sample cannot be considered representative of American women in general. As with the *Psychology Today* study, respondents were limited to those readers of a specific magazine who voluntarily completed and returned the questionnaire. Although only 2,278 respondents out of the huge sample constituted the base *N* for most of the analyses reported, this subsample still overrepresented young, white, affluent, highly educated, and politically liberal women, a bias that probably accounts for the positive relationship expressed between religious devoutness and enjoyment of sex, for the vast majority reporting that they like engaging in oral-genital contact with their husbands, and for similar findings. Such bias precludes inferences about American women in general.

A third study that included both males and females was Sorensen's (1973) investigation of adolescents. This study purported to show wide participation in sex and liberal attitudes toward it among a representative sample of American teenagers. However, apart from the fact that many of these findings seemed based on methodologically dubious subgroups of respondents (see Bell, 1973; Goldsmith, 1973) rather than the total sample, it is questionable whether the final sample really was representative. Although the pool of *potential* respondents was randomly drawn, only those whose parents allowed it (60% of those in this pool) could complete the questionnaire, and among those about one-quarter of the adolescents refused, with the result that fewer than half of the potential respondents eventually provided usable data; the sample was thus most likely biased in the direction of sexual liberalism, as adolescents from more conservative families would not have participated. The small size (411) of the final sample further increases the probability of sampling error.

Finally, there was Morton Hunt's book, *Sexual Behavior in the 1970s*, published in 1974. Although Hunt made strong claims for the validity of the data he relied on, they were not drawn from a national sample representative of the population. The sample for the Hunt study, which was commissioned by the Playboy Foundation in an effort to replicate Kinsey's earlier work, was supposed to be representative (1974:16)—that is, to include respondents of varying characteristics in proportion to their numbers in the population at large, so that findings could be generalized to Americans everywhere. However, the representativeness of the sample can be seriously questioned. Among groups entirely excluded were people living in rural areas, small towns, and small to medium-sized cities. Nor was the sample, as claimed (1974:16), really random (in a random sample, every member of the study population has an equal chance of being asked to participate). The Research Guild, the organization that drew the sample and collected the data for the Hunt study, used techniques that tended to underrepresent the poor, the less educated, the young, and the conservative.

The important point about sampling, technical or finicky as these objections may seem, is that when the sample is *not* properly representative or random, findings simply *cannot* be said to apply more generally to the public at large. Thus, as interesting as these four studies may be, they do not accurately portray American moralities.

The aim of our 1970 study was to achieve a national sample that was representative of the adult, noninstitutionalized population of the United States. Our sampling and interviewing were done by the National Opinion Research Center (NORC), a highly regarded survey research organization located at the University of Chicago. The NORC interviewers received special training in collecting sensitive information before they went into the field, and in fall 1970 they interviewed 3,018 respondents. Further details about the design of the study, the training of interviewers, pretesting the interviews, and characteristics of the sample are provided in Appendices A, B, C, and D.

To summarize the foregoing points: previous attempts to investigate or delineate U.S. sexual patterns—often described as having undergone a sexual revolution—have met with several notable difficulties, which we tried to deal with in this study. First, there has been the questionable application of the term *revolution* to a phenomenon that was neither demonstrably violent nor swift nor widely influential upon other (nonsexual) aspects of American life. In this presentation of our study, we therefore dispense with the notion and describe our findings without such a label. Second has been both the overemphasis on discrete sexual behaviors and the problems of interpreting percentage differences in rates. Here we argue for the utility of studying the moral meanings publicly ascribed to various forms of sexuality as a most crucial indicant of change and basis for interpreting data within a sociological framework. Third, the analysis of what produces and sustains sexual norms has been limited. This presentation deals with our study's multiplicity of variables said to impinge on sexual norms, evaluates them, and delineates their complex causal structures. Fourth, any assertion of change begs comparison with some earlier data base if we are not simply to reify selected popular assumptions. Although our 1970 study gave us no such base, we did obtain retrospective data to assess perceived changes among the individuals who made up our sample. Finally, most past work has suffered from inadequate samples. This work is the first broadly based study of American sexual standards to have employed a national representative sample. Not only will our findings stand as a sound basis on which comparison can be made using post-1970s data, but they will permit us now to state confidently what heretofore has only been speculated: the general configuration of sexual morality in the United States.

NOTES

1. See DeLora and Warren (1977:546), who say, "The same theme of sexual revolution has been repeated in every decade of the twentieth century and undoubtedly earlier. . . . Any change is threatening to the values of some section of the population and may be seen by them as a major revolution."
2. The clearest attempt at a definition has come not from a social scientist but from a journalist, Morton Hunt (1974:36–37), who asserted that we could say there had been a sexual revolution if there were (1) the *displacement* of *vaginal coitus* by nonvaginal sex acts violating biological and/or psychological criteria of normality, such as sexual connection with animals, sadomasochistic acts, and homosexuality; or (2) a *major* increase in sexual acts that fundamentally alter the connection between sex and marriage, such as mutually sanctioned extramarital affairs, mate-swapping, and "swinging"; or (3) a *growing* preference for sex acts devoid of emotional significance or performed with strangers. The italicized words illustrate the researcher's dilemma in applying behavioral

criteria. What comparative incidence figures constitute "displacement"? How big an increase is a "major" one; and what size is a "growing" preference? Two other difficulties also inhere in such an approach. First, any such data usually can be compared only with what one *presumes* about earlier patterns, given the absence of representative data from the past. Second, Hunt's particular criteria clearly illustrate that so potent a term as *revolution* can be defined so as to allow the commentator's own values to determine whether or not such an "event" has occurred.

3. Most of these studies rarely have distinguished between respondents reporting a solitary episode and those who engage in frequent coitus. The few exceptions have reported *low* frequencies (see Zelnik & Kantner, 1972, 1977).
4. In addition we eventually encounter the "ceiling effect" (Walsh, 1978): there is so little variance in some variables—e.g., the incidence of male masturbation, which generally exceeds 90% regardless of the date or sample of a particular study—that any percentage difference among various studies is substantively meaningless.
5. Following Kuhn (1962), Walsh (1978:298) defines "paradigm change" as "a whole new model of reality or way of looking at things . . . everything is now evaluated in a new light, from different ground rules." Like his use of the concept of *sexual revolution*, however, this idea is left undeveloped until the end of his review, where he claims that many of the present generation judge sexuality by a situational ethic rather than absolute standards, supposedly allowing new behaviors or a new absence of guilt.
6. We can also use data gathered before our study. For example, Reiss (1967:29) showed that 80% of an adult representative sample surveyed in 1963 disapproved of premarital coitus for both males and females who are in love. We can assume that for premarital sex under less personal conditions, as well as for extramarital sex and homosexuality, the number would be as high or higher.

Chapter 2

Sexual Norms in the United States: An Overview

This chapter provides an overview of our sample survey findings in terms of simple percentages and relationships involving basic sociological variables. In this way we hope to introduce the reader to our national data and to illustrate the broad parameters of sexual norms in the United States.

Our data demonstrate one striking fact: with regard to many forms of sexual expression, our respondents were extremely conservative (Table 2-1). A majority disapproved of homosexuality, prostitution, extramarital sex, and most forms of premarital sex.[1] Even masturbation, a near-universal behavior among males, was disapproved by 48% of our respondents. Furthermore, except for masturbation and for premarital sex between people who are in love, our data suggest that a majority of Americans are "moral absolutists" in that they see these behaviors as *always* wrong.

Extramarital coitus and homosexual relations without affection received the most disapproval (87% and 88% responded "always wrong" or "almost always wrong," respectively). Even with love involved, homosexual relations were still disapproved by 79% of our respondents. Love does have a mitigating effect, however, with regard to premarital sex, as do the age and gender of those involved. Teenage girls having premarital sex without love were more disapproved than were boys engaging in similar behavior (82% as against 73%). Less disapproval, and less of a gender differential, was found in the case of adult premarital sex (70% vs. 65%). Still less disapproval, although with the same gender differential, appeared for people involved in premarital sex who are in love. Thus,

TABLE 2-1 Moral Response to Selected Sexual Behaviors

Response	Extramarital sex	Homosexuality between two persons who have no special affection for each other	Homosexuality between two persons who love each other	Premarital sex by a teenage boy with a girl he doesn't love
Always wrong	72.3%	77.8%	70.5%	53.3%
Almost always wrong	14.3	8.5	8.5	19.5
Wrong only sometimes	10.8	6.4	7.2	17.0
Not wrong at all	2.2	5.7	11.5	9.4
Don't know	0.4	1.7	2.3	0.7
Column total	100.0%	100.1%	100.0%	99.9%
Base *n*	3,016	3,016	3,009	3,015
No answer	2	2	9	3
Total sample	3,018	3,018	3,018	3,018

Response	Premarital sex by a teenage boy with a girl he loves	Premarital sex by an adult man with a woman he doesn't love	Premarital sex by an adult man with a woman he loves
Always wrong	37.3%	50.1%	33.3%
Almost always wrong	19.1	15.2	14.2
Wrong only sometimes	20.5	17.2	18.4
Not wrong at all	22.3	16.7	33.3
Don't know	0.8	0.8	0.9
Column total	100.0%	100.0%	100.0%
Base *n*	3,017	3,018	3,018
No answer	1	0	0
Total sample	3,018	3,018	3,018

Response	Premarital sex by a teenage girl with a boy she doesn't love	Premarital sex by a teenage girl with a boy she loves	Premarital sex by an adult woman with a man she doesn't love
Always wrong	68.0%	46.0%	55.3%
Almost always wrong	14.4	17.5	15.0
Wrong only sometimes	11.3	17.3	15.4
Not wrong at all	5.8	18.6	13.7
Don't know	0.6	0.6	0.6
Column total	100.1%	100.0%	100.0%
Base *n*	3,015	3,016	3,016
No answer	3	2	2
Total sample	3,018	3,018	3,018

Response	Premarital sex by an adult woman with a man she loves	Masturbation	Prostitution
Always wrong	36.4%	27.0%	57.1%
Almost always wrong	15.1	21.0	14.8
Wrong only sometimes	17.3	29.8	16.3
Not wrong at all	30.5	18.8	11.1
Don't know	0.7	3.4	0.7
Column total	100.0%	100.0%	100.0%
Base *n*	3,017	3,014	3,017
No answer	1	4	1
Total sample	3,018	3,018	3,018

TABLE 2-2 Subjective Assessment of Perceived Moral Stability

Response	Have you always felt the same way about . . . premarital and extramarital sex?	sex acts between persons of the same sex?	masturbation?
Always felt this way	65.7%	81.6%	73.0%
Used to be more approving	9.3	2.0	4.3
Used to be less approving	23.9	16.2	22.2
Both kinds of change	1.0	0.2	0.5
Column total	99.9%	100.0%	100.0%
Base *n*	3,011	3,004	2,978
No answer	7	4	40
Total sample	3,018	3,018	3,018

64% of our sample disapproved of teenage girls so involved, as compared with 56% for teenage boys. The corresponding percentages for adults were 52% for women and 48% for men.

There seems little doubt, therefore, that many respondents still cherished the ideal of love as a basis for sexual behavior. On the average, 15% fewer respondents disapproved of a given act if love was involved. Looking at individual acts, this difference is more than 15% in every instance except homosexuality, where the difference is only 7%. Apparently, people have more difficulty in associating love with homosexuality, or else they consider homosexuality so repugnant as to be unjustifiable even when those involved love each other.[2] Age considerations are somewhat less influential: there were 10% more disapproving responses, on the average, for behavior involving teenagers rather than adults. Gender considerations show only a 6% average difference in greater disapproval for females than for males engaging in the same behavior, which suggests that the "double standard" is less important than age and affection.

It should be stressed, however, that of all the behaviors evaluated, only masturbation and an adult man's premarital involvement with someone he loves were disapproved by fewer than half our respondents, and indeed these two behaviors were disapproved by nearly half.

Our results further show that the national sexual morality is perceived to be stable over time (Table 2-2). A large majority of our respondents reported that they have always held the same standards. A much smaller number stated that they were less ap-

TABLE 2-3 Subjective Comparisons of Own Norms with Others'

	Do you feel you are more or less approving of . . .			
Response	premarital and extramarital sex than your parents were when you were a child?	premarital and extramarital sex than most of your friends?	premarital and extramarital sex than most American adults?	sex relations between persons of the same sex than your parents were when you were a child?
More approving	45.7%	16.7%	22.0%	25.5%
About the same	44.2	52.3	31.8	61.7
Less approving	7.2	28.0	40.0	4.7
Don't know	2.9	3.1	6.1	8.1
Column total	100.0%	100.1%	99.9%	100.0%
Base *n*	3,008	3,014	3,014	3,012
No answer	10	4	4	6
Total sample	3,018	3,018	3,018	3,018

proving at one time, and very few said that they had ever been *more* approving. Norms involving homosexuality were reported to be the most stable, those toward premarital and extramarital sex the least so.

Perceived moral stability (as well as change) can be greatly influenced by subjective comparison with the attitudes perceived to be held by various others (Festinger, 1954; Mirande, 1968). About half our respondents believed that their views on the morality of premarital sex (whether they viewed it as wrong or not wrong) were "about the same" as their parents' and their friends', but only one-third thought their views were "about the same" as most American adults' (Table 2-3). Among those reporting dissimilarity, it is most evident in the case of their parents, compared with whom 46% saw themselves as *more* approving, and most American adults, compared with whom 40% felt they were *less* approving. They also tended to feel *less* approving of premarital and extramarital sex than they believed their friends to be.

Regarding homosexuality, a clear majority (62%) saw themselves as having about the same moral stance as their parents, and about one-quarter reported that they were more approving. Few were less approving than their parents. Comparisons with friends and with other American adults were not asked regarding this behavior.

Futhermore, our respondents were quite consistent in their normative standards when asked about specific formal actions toward sexual behaviors. That is, a majority favored laws against prostitution (62%), homosexuality (59%), and extramarital sex (52%). Indeed, over a quarter (29%) approved of outlawing premarital sex. The severity of the penalty advocated by those opting for legal control, however, seems unrelated to the proportion desiring it. Table 2-4 shows that 14% believed a person convicted of a homosexual act should be sentenced to at least a year in prison, and 12% chose this penalty for extramarital sexual activity. But only 6% said they would be so punitive with a prostitute on her first conviction. Moreover, there seems to be much more faith in "treatment": in all cases, this option for dealing with offenders was the most popular choice.

Considering something one dislikes in the abstract can produce a stereotyped, unduly punitive reaction. Thus we also included questions asking our respondents what they would do if a good friend of theirs engaged in premarital sex, extramarital sex, or homosexuality. Between one-quarter and one-third of the respondents said they would still remain friends but admitted it would be a problem (Table 2-5). Premarital sex would present the least problem, with 70% saying that their friendship would be unaffected. The corresponding figure in the case of extramarital sex was 51%. It is homosexuality that takes the greatest toll on friendship: only about one-fifth said they would be unaffected by such knowledge. Concerning homosexuality, the most common response was to have nothing more to do with the person—36% reacting this way to a female friend and 40% to a male friend.[3] (Respondents were not asked to differentiate between male and female friends on the premarital or extramarital items.)

Such data, with their air of stern moralism (three-quarters of our sample described themselves as "pretty much" or "very much" serious and moral about sex), might predispose us to expect an avoidance or lack of enjoyment in sexual life.[4] However, this does not seem to be the case. For example, over 75% of our respondents stated that they avoided sex "little" or "not at all"; 44% said they regarded themselves as "very much" or "pretty much" a "sexual person"; and, when asked how much they enjoyed sex, 40% said "just about every time," with an additional 39% claiming that they did "most of the time."

This preliminary view of our data must call into question the

TABLE 2-4 Preferred Legal Disposition for People Guilty of ''Illegal'' Sex

Response	Which action should be taken if a person is convicted of . . .							
	adultery?		homosexuality?		prostitution, and it's her first conviction?		visiting a prostitute, and it's his first conviction?	
Given a prison term of at least a year	5.9%	11.5%[a]	8.3%	14.1%[a]	4.0%	6.3%[a]	4.3%	6.8%[a]
Given a lesser punishment, like jail or a fine	6.8	13.2	4.3	7.4	5.1	8.0	8.7	13.9
Put on probation, with threat of jail if probation is violated	17.2	33.4	7.3	12.4	17.2	27.2	23.1	36.8
Assigned to a rehabilitation or treatment program for help	19.5	38.0	38.2	64.8	36.1	57.1	23.8	38.0
Don't know	2.1	4.0	0.8	1.4	0.8	1.3	2.9	4.6
Should not be illegal[a]	48.5		41.1		36.9		37.2	
Column total	100.0%	100.1%	100.0%	100.1%	100.1%	99.9%	100.0%	100.1%
Base n	2,999	1,543	2,995	1,765	3,012	1,901	2,984	1,873
No answer, legality	3	3	11	11	1	1	1	1
No answer, penalty	16	16	12	12	5	5	33	33
Should not be illegal		1,456		1,230		1,111		1,111
Total sample	3,018	3,018	3,018	3,018	3,018	3,018	3,018	3,018

[a] Respondents who oppose outlawing the given behavior were not asked this question; thus the actual distribution of responses is given in the second column for each behavior.

TABLE 2-5 Hypothetical Effects of Friends' Sexual Behaviors

	What would you do if you found out that a good friend . . .			
Response	had had extramarital sex?	who is female had had homosexual sex?	who is male had had homosexual sex?	had had premarital sex?
Not want to have anything more to do with the person	5.7%	35.8%	40.5%	2.9%
Still be in touch, but no longer be friends	9.4	15.3	14.7	4.9
Stay friends, but it would be a problem	33.4	28.2	25.1	22.0
Still be friends, no problem	50.6	19.4	18.5	69.5
Don't know	0.9	1.4	1.3	0.7
Column total	100.0%	100.1%	100.1%	100.0%
Base *n*	3,017	3,013	3,017	2,984
No answer	1	5	1	34
Total sample	3,018	3,018	3,018	3,018

belief that America in 1970 had undergone a tremendous change in sexual morality. Unless we are to assume that there was a 100% disapproval in the past toward the sexual behaviors we have discussed or that the change was from a more *permissive* to a more restrictive stance—two assumptions that no proponent of the sexual revolution has made—these data must be supportive of an alternate view. This view is one in which the public moral meanings of sexuality in 1970 were quite conservative and perceived to be stable over time. That is, such phenomena as sexually explicit films, cohabitation, and so on, do not connote "revolutionary" change if people's publicly professed moralities do not accord with the sexual liberality these phenomena imply.[5] Where change may be evident from our data, it is gradual and not extensive, the most notable example being the decline of the double standard. Our data show that despite the sternness of their standards, however, most Americans do not avoid sex and report a great deal of enjoyment in it.

We next examine how sexual norms are distributed across standard population categories. In this way we are able to consider important subgroups in the population—for example, Jews, blacks, midwesterners—and to allow the reader to compare a subgroup with the overall population percentages in Table 2-1. Also we can begin to present relationships instead of discrete percentages and offer gamma as a measure of the strength of association between our variables. Note that in our bivariate tables we do not provide levels of statistical significance: our sample is so large that a difference of only 5% will be significant at the .001 level. In addition, because we wish merely to "map" the distribution of American sexual norms, we do not yet introduce any control variables.[6] Our more detailed findings follow in later chapters.

Age. Our data support the findings of many investigators that younger people tend to be less conservative than their elders. Table 2-6 shows that for every behavior examined, older people were more likely to express an opinion of "always wrong" and less likely to say "not wrong at all." Older respondents also bore out the tendency of the population as a whole to be somewhat more lenient when people involved in a given behavior are in love with each other and to be more conservative concerning females' behavior than males'; and despite the mitigating influence of a person being male or in love, a majority of older respondents disapproved of all the behaviors in the table. In contrast, a majority of those under 35 said that only 5 of the 13 behaviors are always wrong. Whether these findings represent "aging" or generational influences is considered later. We would note here, however, that this seemingly simple relationship can involve more complex issues (see Glenn, 1974).

Gender. Table 2-7 illustrates that females tend to be more conservative in their sexual norms than males, another finding that traditionally has held (see Nunn et al., 1978). When love is involved in premarital sex, the difference between men and women in responding "always wrong" is somewhat reduced. It is interesting to note, however, that our findings show women to be especially conservative with regard to their own gender: they condemned teenage girls' or adult women's participation in premarital sex more than they did that of teenage boys or adult men, and they more roundly condemned prostitution than male respondents did, although for three behaviors where the sex of the actor was not specified—homosexuality without affection, homosexuality with affection, and masturbation—differences between males' and females' responses are sharply reduced.[7] Note that, as with age,

TABLE 2-6 Moral Response to Sexual Behaviors, by Age

Item/response	Under 35	35 to 64	65 or older
Prostitution (gamma = −.19)			
Always wrong	50.3%	58.6%	71.5%
Almost always wrong	18.2	14.0	9.8
Wrong only sometimes	19.0	15.8	12.3
Not wrong at all	12.5	11.6	6.4
Column total	100.0%	100.0%	100.0%
Base *n*[a]	1,060	1,496	438
Premarital sex by teenage boy, not in love (gamma = −.30)			
Always wrong	42.2%	57.5%	69.0%
Almost always wrong	20.3	20.1	16.8
Wrong only sometimes	23.4	14.6	10.6
Not wrong at all	14.1	7.8	3.7
Column total	100.0%	100.0%	100.1%
Base *n*[a]	1,061	1,494	435
Premarital sex by teenage boy, in love (gamma = −.29)			
Always wrong	24.9%	42.7%	51.5%
Almost always wrong	18.1	20.7	17.2
Wrong only sometimes	26.7	17.6	16.2
Not wrong at all	30.3	19.0	15.1
Column total	100.0%	100.0%	100.0%
Base *n*[a]	1,060	1,498	431
Premarital sex by adult man, not in love (gamma = −.27)			
Always wrong	38.7%	54.1%	67.4%
Almost always wrong	17.7	14.3	13.4
Wrong only sometimes	23.1	15.7	9.3
Not wrong at all	20.5	16.0	10.0
Column total	100.0%	100.1%	100.1%
Base *n*[a]	1,066	1,494	432
Premarital sex by adult man, in love (gamma = −.29)			
Always wrong	20.5%	38.5%	48.8%
Almost always wrong	14.3	14.3	14.4
Wrong only sometimes	23.0	16.0	16.3
Not wrong at all	42.1	31.2	20.5
Column total	99.9%	100.0%	100.0%
Base *n*[a]	1,063	1,495	430

TABLE 2-6 (*Continued*)

Item/response	Under 35	35 to 64	65 or older
Premarital sex by teenage girl, not in love (gamma = −.36)			
Always wrong	56.4%	72.5%	83.4%
Almost always wrong	16.6	14.4	9.7
Wrong only sometimes	18.2	8.4	4.6
Not wrong at all	8.7	4.7	2.3
Column total	99.9%	100.0%	100.0%
Base *n*[a]	1,065	1,495	435
Premarital sex by teenage girl, in love (gamma = −.34)			
Always wrong	31.0%	52.4%	62.2%
Almost always wrong	17.5	18.6	14.1
Wrong only sometimes	23.9	14.2	12.9
Not wrong at all	27.6	14.8	10.8
Column total	100.0%	100.0%	100.0%
Base *n*[a]	1,063	1,497	434
Premarital sex by adult woman, not in love (gamma = −.29)			
Always wrong	43.0%	59.9%	72.4%
Almost always wrong	18.9	13.2	12.2
Wrong only sometimes	21.4	13.6	7.1
Not wrong at all	16.6	13.2	8.3
Column total	99.9%	99.9%	100.0%
Base *n*[a]	1,064	1,497	434
Premarital sex by adult woman, in love (gamma = −.31)			
Always wrong	22.8%	41.2%	55.2%
Almost always wrong	15.9	15.7	11.8
Wrong only sometimes	21.5	15.4	14.5
Not wrong at all	39.8	27.7	18.5
Column total	100.0%	100.0%	100.0%
Base *n*[a]	1,064	1,497	433
Extramarital sex (gamma = −.29)			
Always wrong	63.8%	75.1%	85.8%
Almost always wrong	19.2	13.2	6.6
Wrong only sometimes	14.8	9.3	5.9
Not wrong at all	2.2	2.3	1.6
Column total	100.0%	99.9%	99.9%
Base *n*[a]	1,065	1,500	437
Homosexuality without affection (gamma = −.27)			
Always wrong	72.9%	80.5%	89.7%
Almost always wrong	10.6	8.1	5.1
Wrong only sometimes	9.3	5.6	2.8
Not wrong at all	7.2	5.7	2.3
Column total	100.0%	99.9%	99.9%
Base *n*[a]	1,055	1,479	428

TABLE 2-6 (*continued*)

Item/response	Under 35	35 to 64	65 or older
Homosexuality with affection (gamma = −.27)			
Always wrong	63.8%	74.6%	84.0%
Almost always wrong	10.7	8.0	6.1
Wrong only sometimes	10.2	6.4	4.0
Not wrong at all	15.3	11.0	5.9
Column total	100.0%	100.0%	100.0%
Base n^a	1,046	1,465	426
Masturbation (gamma = −.25)			
Always wrong	18.9%	30.2%	43.2%
Almost always wrong	21.4	21.5	23.1
Wrong only sometimes	35.7	29.2	24.5
Not wrong at all	24.0	19.1	9.2
Column total	100.0%	100.0%	100.0%
Base n^a	1,049	1,448	412

[a] Excluded are 3 respondents who did not give their current age, as well as those who responded "don't know" or failed to answer the given item (see Table 2-1).

TABLE 2-7 Moral Response to Sexual Behaviors, by Gender

Item/response	Male	Female
Prostitution (gamma = −.43)		
Always wrong	45.3%	68.9%
Almost always wrong	15.7	14.1
Wrong only sometimes	21.9	11.2
Not wrong at all	17.0	5.8
Column total	99.9%	100.0%
Base n^a	1,450	1,547
Premarital sex by teenage boy, not in love (gamma = −.31)		
Always wrong	45.5%	61.5%
Almost always wrong	19.5	19.8
Wrong only sometimes	21.0	13.5
Not wrong at all	13.9	5.3
Column total	99.9%	100.1%
Base n^a	1,454	1,539
Premarital sex by teenage boy, in love (gamma = −.28)		
Always wrong	30.5%	44.4%
Almost always wrong	17.0	21.3
Wrong only sometimes	23.2	18.2
Not wrong at all	29.3	16.1
Column total	100.0%	100.0%
Base n^a	1,451	1,541

TABLE 2-7 (*Continued*)

Item/response	Male	Female
Premarital sex by adult man, not in love (gamma = −.32)		
Always wrong	41.8%	58.7%
Almost always wrong	14.5	16.1
Wrong only sometimes	20.5	14.4
Not wrong at all	23.2	10.8
Column total	100.0%	100.0%
Base *n*[a]	1,451	1,544
Premarital sex by adult man, in love (gamma = −.26)		
Always wrong	27.5%	39.3%
Almost always wrong	12.4	16.1
Wrong only sometimes	18.8	18.2
Not wrong at all	41.3	26.3
Column total	100.0%	99.9%
Base *n*[a]	1,449	1,542
Premarital sex by teenage girl, not in love (gamma = −.48)		
Always wrong	56.6%	79.4%
Almost always wrong	17.3	11.9
Wrong only sometimes	16.2	6.8
Not wrong at all	10.0	1.9
Column total	100.1%	100.0%
Base *n*[a]	1,454	1,544
Premarital sex by teenage girl, in love (gamma = −.32)		
Always wrong	37.2%	54.7%
Almost always wrong	17.1	18.1
Wrong only sometimes	20.5	14.5
Not wrong at all	25.2	12.6
Column total	100.0%	99.9%
Base *n*[a]	1,454	1,543
Premarital sex by adult woman, not in love (gamma = −.43)		
Always wrong	43.6%	67.0%
Almost always wrong	15.0	15.2
Wrong only sometimes	20.5	10.7
Not wrong at all	20.9	7.1
Column total	100.0%	100.0%
Base *n*[a]	1,451	1,547
Premarital sex by adult woman, in love (gamma = −.30)		
Always wrong	28.7%	44.1%
Almost always wrong	13.2	17.0
Wrong only sometimes	19.2	15.8
Not wrong at all	38.9	23.0
Column total	100.0%	99.9%
Base *n*[a]	1,451	1,546

TABLE 2-7 *(Continued)*

Item/response	Male	Female
Extramarital sex (gamma = −.28)		
Always wrong	66.5%	78.4%
Almost always wrong	17.0	11.9
Wrong only sometimes	12.9	8.8
Not wrong at all	3.6	0.8
Column total	100.0%	99.9%
Base *n*[a]	1,456	1,549
Homosexuality without affection (gamma = −.23)		
Always wrong	75.1%	82.9%
Almost always wrong	9.1	8.1
Wrong only sometimes	7.7	5.4
Not wrong at all	8.1	3.6
Column total	100.0%	100.0%
Base *n*[a]	1,439	1,526
Homosexuality with affection (gamma = −.18)		
Always wrong	68.4%	75.7%
Almost always wrong	8.8	8.5
Wrong only sometimes	7.9	6.9
Not wrong at all	14.8	8.9
Column total	99.9%	100.0%
Base *n*[a]	1,424	1,516
Masturbation (gamma = −.10)		
Always wrong	26.2%	29.6%
Almost always wrong	20.6	22.8
Wrong only sometimes	31.0	30.7
Not wrong at all	22.1	16.9
Column total	99.9%	100.0%
Base *n*[a]	1,424	1,488

[a] Excluded are respondents who said ''don't know'' or failed to answer the given item (see Table 2-1).

complex issues emerge when gender is included in a multivariate analysis of morality.

Race. Although whites are commonly supposed to be more conservative than blacks, Table 2-8 shows that this is not always so. Only on the four items concerning premarital sex when love is involved did the whites show much more conservatism, which is consistent with Reiss's (1967) findings. In addition, blacks tended to be *less* approving of prostitution, homosexuality, and masturbation than were whites, although the percentage differences are

TABLE 2-8 Moral Response to Sexual Behaviors, by Race

Item/response	White[a]	Black
Prostitution (gamma = −.14)		
Always wrong	55.9%	65.8%
Almost always wrong	16.1	8.4
Wrong only sometimes	16.7	14.9
Not wrong at all	11.3	10.9
Column total	100.0%	100.0%
Base *n*[b]	2,520	477
Premarital sex by teenage boy, not in love (gamma = .04)		
Always wrong	53.4%	55.7%
Almost always wrong	21.1	11.8
Wrong only sometimes	17.1	17.1
Not wrong at all	8.4	15.4
Column total	100.0%	100.0%
Base *n*[b]	2,519	474
Premarital sex by teenage boy, in love (gamma = .38)		
Always wrong	39.8%	26.1%
Almost always wrong	20.7	11.6
Wrong only sometimes	21.2	17.4
Not wrong at all	18.2	45.0
Column total	99.9%	100.1%
Base *n*[b]	2,516	476
Premarital sex by adult man, not in love (gamma = .07)		
Always wrong	50.6%	50.1%
Almost always wrong	16.4	9.8
Wrong only sometimes	17.2	18.0
Not wrong at all	15.8	22.1
Column total	100.0%	100.0%
Base *n*[b]	2,516	479
Premarital sex by adult man, in love (gamma = .44)		
Always wrong	36.4%	18.8%
Almost always wrong	15.4	8.5
Wrong only sometimes	19.2	15.0
Not wrong at all	29.0	57.7
Column total	100.0%	100.0%
Base *n*[b]	2,511	480

TABLE 2-8 (*Continued*)

Item/response	White[a]	Black
Premarital sex by teenage girl, not in love (gamma = .10)		
Always wrong	68.7%	66.2%
Almost always wrong	15.3	10.5
Wrong only sometimes	11.4	11.1
Not wrong at all	4.6	12.2
Column total	100.0%	100.0%
Base *n*[b]	2,521	477
Premarital sex by teenage girl, in love (gamma = .38)		
Always wrong	48.8%	32.7%
Almost always wrong	18.8	11.5
Wrong only sometimes	17.9	11.5
Not wrong at all	14.6	40.9
Column total	100.1%	100.0%
Base *n*[b]	2,520	477
Premarital sex by adult woman, not in love (gamma = .12)		
Always wrong	56.5%	51.1%
Almost always wrong	15.3	14.0
Wrong only sometimes	15.5	15.0
Not wrong at all	12.6	19.8
Column total	99.9%	99.9%
Base *n*[b]	2,519	479
Premarital sex by adult woman, in love (gamma = .42)		
Always wrong	39.4%	22.2%
Almost always wrong	16.5	8.4
Wrong only sometimes	17.8	15.7
Not wrong at all	26.3	53.8
Column total	100.0%	100.1%
Base *n*[b]	2,519	478
Extramarital sex (gamma = .18)		
Always wrong	73.6%	67.6%
Almost always wrong	15.3	9.4
Wrong only sometimes	9.6	17.3
Not wrong at all	1.5	5.6
Column total	100.0%	99.9%
Base *n*[b]	2,526	479
Homosexuality without affection (gamma = −.09)		
Always wrong	78.5%	82.6%
Almost always wrong	9.7	3.0
Wrong only sometimes	6.4	7.2
Not wrong at all	5.5	7.2
Column total	100.1%	100.0%
Base *n*[b]	2,495	470

TABLE 2-8 (*Continued*)

Item/response	White[a]	Black
Homosexuality with affection (gamma = −.04)		
Always wrong	71.6%	75.1%
Almost always wrong	9.6	3.9
Wrong only sometimes	7.7	5.8
Not wrong at all	11.1	15.3
Column total	100.0%	100.1%
Base n[b]	2,475	465
Masturbation (gamma = −.06)		
Always wrong	26.8%	34.1%
Almost always wrong	22.8	16.1
Wrong only sometimes	30.9	30.7
Not wrong at all	19.5	19.1
Column total	100.0%	100.0%
Base n[b]	2,452	460

[a] The "white" group includes 19 respondents of Oriental or "other" race.
[b] Excluded are respondents who said "don't know" or failed to answer the given item (see Table 2-1).

small. This too is in accord with what we know about black sexuality: that blacks consider sexual behaviors other than affectionate coitus "abnormal" (Staples, 1972).

Marital Status. Because marital status is a discrete rather than an ordinal variable, Table 2-9 does not present gamma coefficients. Inspection of the table, however, does reveal that our widowed respondents were most conservative and our single (never married) ones the least so (the obvious age controls are discussed in the next chapter). On most of the items, the married and the divorced respondents look very much alike, although the latter were more likely to accept premarital sex among people in love. In the case of extramarital sex, the married and the widowed were more disapproving than the other two groups—a finding that might be expected—but a large majority of all the groups said it is either always wrong or almost always wrong.

Education. Table 2-10 again shows a finding supported by much previous research (see Lipset, 1959a)—that more-educated respondents are generally not as conservative as those with less education. Once again, however, this difference is reduced when people engaging in premarital sex are in love. The more-educated respondents were considerably less condemning of homosexuality,

TABLE 2-9 Moral Response to Sexual Behaviors, by Marital Status

Item/response	Married	Widowed	Divorced, separated	Single
Prostitution				
Always wrong	56.5%	74.7%	60.0%	43.1%
Almost always wrong	16.0	7.7	11.9	14.2
Wrong only sometimes	16.9	11.1	13.8	20.3
Not wrong at all	10.5	6.5	14.3	22.3
Column total	99.9%	100.0%	100.0%	99.9%
Base *n*[a]	2,329	261	210	197
Premarital sex by teenage boy, not in love				
Always wrong	53.1%	73.2%	51.2%	37.8%
Almost always wrong	21.3	13.0	15.3	13.8
Wrong only sometimes	16.9	10.7	19.1	26.5
Not wrong at all	8.7	3.1	14.4	21.9
Column total	100.0%	100.0%	100.0%	100.0%
Base *n*[a]	2,327	261	209	196
Premarital sex by teenage boy, in love				
Always wrong	38.1%	54.2%	28.8%	19.7%
Almost always wrong	21.0	15.8	13.7	9.1
Wrong only sometimes	21.0	14.6	18.9	26.3
Not wrong at all	19.9	15.4	38.7	44.9
Column total	100.0%	100.0%	100.1%	100.0%
Base *n*[a]	2,322	260	212	198
Premarital sex by adult man, not in love				
Always wrong	50.2%	66.8%	48.3%	34.3%
Almost always wrong	16.3	11.5	12.0	13.6
Wrong only sometimes	17.7	10.3	16.7	23.2
Not wrong at all	15.8	11.5	23.0	28.8
Column total	100.0%	100.1%	100.0%	99.9%
Base *n*[a]	2,326	262	209	198
Premarital sex by adult man, in love				
Always wrong	34.2%	48.1%	23.2%	18.3%
Almost always wrong	15.3	13.1	9.0	9.6
Wrong only sometimes	19.5	13.5	16.1	16.8
Not wrong at all	31.0	25.4	51.7	55.3
Column total	100.0%	100.1%	100.0%	100.0%
Base *n*[a]	2,323	260	211	197

TABLE 2-9 (*Continued*)

Item/response	Married	Widowed	Divorced, separated	Single
Premarital sex by teenage girl, not in love				
Always wrong	68.5%	87.0%	65.6%	44.9%
Almost always wrong	15.6	6.1	14.0	16.7
Wrong only sometimes	10.9	4.6	15.8	20.2
Not wrong at all	5.0	2.3	7.7	18.2
Column total	100.0%	100.0%	100.1%	100.0%
Base *n*[a]	2,329	262	209	198
Premarital sex by teenage girl, in love				
Always wrong	47.1%	64.0%	34.1%	25.3%
Almost always wrong	18.6	14.2	17.1	11.1
Wrong only sometimes	18.0	10.3	16.6	21.2
Not wrong at all	16.3	11.5	32.2	42.4
Column total	100.0%	100.0%	100.0%	100.0%
Base *n*[a]	2,327	261	211	198
Premarital sex by adult woman, not in love				
Always wrong	55.7%	73.3%	51.9%	36.4%
Almost always wrong	16.2	10.7	11.4	12.6
Wrong only sometimes	15.3	8.8	19.0	22.2
Not wrong at all	12.9	7.3	17.6	28.8
Column total	100.1%	100.1%	99.9%	100.0%
Base *n*[a]	2,328	262	210	198
Premarital sex by adult woman, in love				
Always wrong	37.3%	54.2%	25.1%	18.7%
Almost always wrong	16.4	13.0	10.9	8.1
Wrong only sometimes	18.2	11.1	16.1	18.7
Not wrong at all	28.1	21.8	47.9	54.5
Column total	100.0%	100.1%	100.0%	100.0%
Base *n*[a]	2,326	262	211	198
Extramarital sex				
Always wrong	73.0%	85.1%	68.4%	56.1%
Almost always wrong	15.1	6.9	9.9	20.2
Wrong only sometimes	9.7	6.5	18.4	21.7
Not wrong at all	2.2	1.5	3.3	2.0
Column total	100.0%	100.0%	100.0%	100.0%
Base *n*[a]	2,333	262	212	198
Homosexuality without affection				
Always wrong	79.1%	90.6%	77.8%	65.6%
Almost always wrong	9.0	3.5	8.7	10.3
Wrong only sometimes	6.2	3.1	7.2	13.8
Not wrong at all	5.7	2.7	6.3	10.3
Column total	100.0%	99.9%	100.0%	100.0%
Base *n*[a]	2,308	255	207	195

TABLE 2-9 (*Continued*)

Item/response	Married	Widowed	Divorced, separated	Single
Homosexuality with affection				
Always wrong	72.0%	84.4%	69.6%	60.4%
Almost always wrong	9.3	5.5	7.4	6.8
Wrong only sometimes	7.7	3.5	6.4	10.4
Not wrong at all	11.0	6.6	16.7	22.4
Column total	100.0%	100.0%	100.1%	100.0%
Base *n*[a]	2,288	256	204	192
Masturbation				
Always wrong	26.9%	40.5%	29.4%	22.4%
Almost always wrong	22.7	20.6	15.9	18.2
Wrong only sometimes	31.1	26.7	29.4	34.9
Not wrong at all	19.3	12.1	25.4	24.5
Column total	100.0%	99.9%	100.1%	100.0%
Base *n*[a]	2,272	247	201	192

[a] Excluding respondents who said "don't know" or failed to answer the given item (see Table 2-1).

masturbation, and extramarital sex as well. (These relationships remain regardless of the cutting points used for educational level.)

Socioeconomic Status.[8] There is some confusion as to which direction we can expect in the relationship between social class and sexual norms. Kinsey et al. (1948, 1953) found that low-status people are rather high on premarital permissiveness, as indicated through sexual *behaviors*. Reiss (1967), however, was unable to find much of a relationship at all for his adult sample when it came to sexual *norms*. He noted a weak curvilinear relationship, with the middle class being the least permissive. We find the same relationship with regard to our premarital items involving the presence of love (Table 2-11). (This curvilinear relationship cannot be evaluated by gamma coefficients.) On the other hand, for those premarital items where love is not involved, as well as those concerning homosexuality, we find a positive relationship between social class and permissiveness. Thus, social class seems to produce different effects, depending on which particular sexual behavior is at issue.

Geographic Region. The region of the United States in which one lives is traditionally associated with liberal or conservative views, as different regions have different historical and cultural traditions (Glenn, 1967; Glenn & Simmons, 1967). In an effort to

TABLE 2-10 Moral Response to Sexual Behaviors, by Education

Item/response	8th grade or less	Part or all of high school	Beyond high school
Prostitution (gamma = .27)			
Always wrong	67.3%	53.6%	35.7%
Almost always wrong	9.9	17.7	22.3
Wrong only sometimes	14.0	17.6	21.0
Not wrong at all	8.9	11.1	21.0
Column total	100.1%	100.0%	100.0%
Base *n*[a]	1,254	1,419	319
Premarital sex by teenage boy, not in love (gamma = .24)			
Always wrong	62.7%	49.5%	37.3%
Almost always wrong	16.4	22.1	21.3
Wrong only sometimes	13.1	18.3	27.9
Not wrong at all	7.8	10.1	13.5
Column total	100.0%	100.0%	100.0%
Base *n*[a]	1,250	1,419	319
Premarital sex by teenage boy, in love (gamma = .05)			
Always wrong	40.9%	37.2%	27.6%
Almost always wrong	16.8	20.8	21.6
Wrong only sometimes	17.9	21.2	28.2
Not wrong at all	24.4	20.8	22.6
Column total	100.0%	100.0%	100.0%
Base *n*[a]	1,248	1,420	319
Premarital sex by adult man, not in love (gamma = .29)			
Always wrong	61.8%	45.0%	30.8%
Almost always wrong	13.0	17.2	16.2
Wrong only sometimes	12.2	19.2	29.3
Not wrong at all	13.0	18.6	23.7
Column total	100.0%	100.0%	100.0%
Base *n*[a]	1,246	1,423	321
Premarital sex by adult man, in love (gamma = .14)			
Always wrong	39.2%	31.3%	22.2%
Almost always wrong	13.7	15.6	10.3
Wrong only sometimes	15.5	19.6	25.9
Not wrong at all	31.6	33.5	41.6
Column total	100.0%	100.0%	100.0%
Base *n*[a]	1,245	1,421	320

TABLE 2-10 (*Continued*)

Item/response	8th grade or less	Part or all of high school	Beyond high school
Premarital sex by teenage girl, not in love (gamma = .29)			
Always wrong	76.3%	66.7%	45.1%
Almost always wrong	11.4	15.4	22.3
Wrong only sometimes	7.3	12.1	23.5
Not wrong at all	5.0	5.8	9.1
Column total	100.0%	100.0%	100.0%
Base n^a	1,252	1,422	319
Premarital sex by teenage girl, in love (gamma = .11)			
Always wrong	51.0%	45.4%	31.6%
Almost always wrong	15.0	19.1	21.3
Wrong only sometimes	14.6	18.0	25.9
Not wrong at all	19.4	17.6	21.3
Column total	100.0%	100.1%	100.1%
Base n^a	1,250	1,422	320
Premarital sex by adult woman, not in love (gamma = .30)			
Always wrong	66.6%	51.0%	34.3%
Almost always wrong	12.4	16.9	17.1
Wrong only sometimes	10.8	16.9	27.4
Not wrong at all	10.2	15.2	21.2
Column total	100.0%	100.0%	100.0%
Base n^a	1,250	1,422	321
Premarital sex by adult woman, in love (gamma = .15)			
Always wrong	42.9%	34.3%	23.1%
Almost always wrong	13.7	17.1	12.5
Wrong only sometimes	14.3	18.3	25.9
Not wrong at all	29.0	30.3	38.6
Column total	99.9%	100.0%	100.1%
Base n^a	1,248	1,423	321
Extramarital sex (gamma = .30)			
Always wrong	79.9%	72.3%	45.6%
Almost always wrong	8.8	15.4	31.9
Wrong only sometimes	9.4	9.9	20.6
Not wrong at all	2.0	2.4	1.9
Column total	100.1%	100.0%	100.0%
Base n^a	1,256	1,424	320
Homosexuality without affection (gamma = .37)			
Always wrong	85.8%	79.0%	53.0%
Almost always wrong	6.5	9.0	15.0
Wrong only sometimes	4.9	6.3	17.6
Not wrong at all	3.6	5.7	14.4
Column total	99.9%	100.0%	100.0%
Base n^a	1,241	1,406	313

TABLE 2-10 (*Continued*)

Item/response	8th grade or less	Part or all of high school	Beyond high school
Homosexuality with affection (gamma = .32)			
Always wrong	79.5%	71.7%	45.1%
Almost always wrong	7.0	8.8	14.9
Wrong only sometimes	5.0	8.2	13.6
Not wrong at all	8.5	11.3	26.3
Column total	100.0%	100.0%	99.1%
Base *n*[a]	1,230	1,397	308
Masturbation (gamma = .30)			
Always wrong	37.4%	23.2%	12.6%
Almost always wrong	21.1	23.7	15.8
Wrong only sometimes	28.5	32.9	30.9
Not wrong at all	13.0	20.2	40.7
Column total	100.0%	100.0%	100.0%
Base *n*[a]	1,196	1,394	317

[a] Excluded are 5 respondents who did not give their educational level, as well as those who responded "don't know" or failed to answer the given item (see Table 2-1).

reflect these differences, we considered the following four areas to be roughly homogeneous culturally: (1) New England, the Mid-Atlantic states, and the east north central region (Wisconsin, Michigan, etc.); (2) the Southwest and Rocky Mountain states; (3) the "Deep South" and the Midwest region (Oklahoma, Iowa, etc.), often called the Bible Belt; and (4) the Pacific coast states. Table 2-12 shows respondents' sexual norms in terms of the part of the country where they were living at the time of the interview. (The region in which one grew up, and mobility from one region to another, is discussed in the next chapter.) The first and fourth regions in the table are commonly supposed to be less conservative than inland areas, and the table generally bears this out.

Community Size. Table 2-13 demonstrates that residents of small towns or rural areas are clearly more conservative in their moralities than are their counterparts in metropolitan America. This finding has previous support (see Glenn & Alston, 1967; Willets et al., 1973). Taken together with the above finding on region, it throws doubt on those theories claiming that America is becoming generally liberalized through increased education and the spread of mass communications, and that a singularly liberal sexual ethic, a generally liberal one, will emerge (see DeLora & Warren, 1977).

TABLE 2-11 Moral Response to Sexual Behaviors, by Socioeconomic Status

Item/response	Lower	Middle	Upper
Prostitution (gamma = .15)			
Always wrong	64.5%	58.7%	50.5%
Almost always wrong	12.2	15.0	17.2
Wrong only sometimes	14.0	16.9	17.4
Not wrong at all	9.2	9.4	14.9
Column total	99.9%	100.0%	100.0%
Base *n*[a]	662	1,176	1,013
Premarital sex by teenage boy, not in love (gamma = .13)			
Always wrong	59.3%	54.9%	48.0%
Almost always wrong	18.5	20.1	20.8
Wrong only sometimes	13.6	16.4	20.3
Not wrong at all	8.6	8.6	10.9
Column total	100.0%	100.0%	100.0%
Base *n*[a]	661	1,174	1,013
Premarital sex by teenage boy, in love (gamma = .03)			
Always wrong	36.3%	40.2%	36.2%
Almost always wrong	15.6	20.0	21.1
Wrong only sometimes	20.2	19.4	22.2
Not wrong at all	27.9	20.4	20.5
Column total	100.0%	100.0%	100.0%
Base *n*[a]	662	1,173	1,012
Premarital sex by adult man, not in love (gamma = .14)			
Always wrong	56.0%	53.5%	43.0%
Almost always wrong	14.2	15.0	16.4
Wrong only sometimes	15.1	16.3	20.6
Not wrong at all	14.7	15.2	20.0
Column total	100.0%	100.0%	100.0%
Base *n*[a]	661	1,169	1,019
Premarital sex by adult man, in love (gamma = .02)			
Always wrong	32.2%	36.8%	31.0%
Almost always wrong	14.1	15.4	13.8
Wrong only sometimes	17.8	17.7	20.1
Not wrong at all	35.9	30.1	35.1
Column total	100.0%	100.0%	100.0%
Base *n*[a]	658	1,171	1,016

TABLE 2-11 (*Continued*)

Item/response	Lower	Middle	Upper
Premarital sex by teenage girl, not in love (gamma = .12)			
Always wrong	71.1%	70.6%	62.7%
Almost always wrong	12.6	14.2	16.1
Wrong only sometimes	10.6	9.6	14.8
Not wrong at all	5.7	5.6	6.4
Column total	100.0%	100.0%	100.0%
Base *n*[a]	661	1,176	1,016
Premarital sex by teenage girl, in love (gamma = −.02)			
Always wrong	45.0%	48.7%	44.1%
Almost always wrong	15.3	17.3	20.2
Wrong only sometimes	15.5	16.9	19.2
Not wrong at all	24.2	17.1	16.6
Column total	100.0%	100.0%	100.1%
Base *n*[a]	660	1,776	1,017
Premarital sex by adult woman, not in love (gamma = .13)			
Always wrong	60.8%	57.5%	49.6%
Almost always wrong	14.1	14.9	16.0
Wrong only sometimes	12.7	15.3	17.5
Not wrong at all	12.4	12.3	16.9
Column total	100.0%	100.0%	100.0%
Base *n*[a]	661	1,173	1,018
Premarital sex by adult woman, in love (gamma = .03)			
Always wrong	36.2%	39.8%	33.5%
Almost always wrong	13.8	16.5	15.1
Wrong only sometimes	17.4	15.8	19.6
Not wrong at all	32.6	27.9	31.8
Column total	100.0%	100.0%	100.0%
Base *n*[a]	660	1,174	1,017
Extramarital sex (gamma = .17)			
Always wrong	76.4%	76.9%	65.4%
Almost always wrong	12.8	11.1	19.9
Wrong only sometimes	8.7	9.6	12.7
Not wrong at all	2.1	2.4	2.0
Column total	100.0%	100.0%	100.0%
Base *n*[a]	664	1,176	1,018
Homosexuality without affection (gamma = .27)			
Always wrong	84.3%	82.8%	70.5%
Almost always wrong	6.7	8.0	10.9
Wrong only sometimes	5.5	4.3	10.4
Not wrong at all	3.5	5.0	8.2
Column total	100.0%	100.1%	100.0%
Base *n*[a]	656	1,166	1,001

TABLE 2-11 (*Continued*)

Item/response	Lower	Middle	Upper
Homosexuality with affection (gamma = .21)			
Always wrong	77.0%	75.9%	63.4%
Almost always wrong	7.9	8.0	10.6
Wrong only sometimes	6.2	6.1	10.2
Not wrong at all	9.0	9.9	15.8
Column total	100.1%	99.9%	100.0%
Base *n*[a]	647	1,160	992
Masturbation (gamma = .15)			
Always wrong	32.2%	30.0%	22.1%
Almost always wrong	21.0	24.1	19.8
Wrong only sometimes	30.8	30.4	31.8
Not wrong at all	16.0	15.6	26.3
Column total	100.0%	100.1%	100.0%
Base *n*[a]	643	1,138	998

[a] Excluded are 113 respondents who reported no main earner in their households and 34 with unclassifiable occupations, as well as those who responded "don't know" or failed to answer the given item (see Table 2-1).

Religious Affiliation. Table 2-14 shows that religious creed affects moral beliefs. This is in line with previous research, even though findings have often been inconsistent (see Dittes, 1969). Our respondents were allied with a variety of religious traditions, but for this analysis we have grouped them in rather broad categories. We have divided the sample into Catholics, Jews, and three groups of Protestants—Reformation (e.g., Presbyterian, Congregationalist, Episcopalian); Pietistic (e.g., Methodist, United Brethren, American Baptist); and Fundamentalist (e.g., Southern Baptist, Pentecostal, conservative Lutheran synods)—with a separate category for those who reported no religious affiliation. We find respondents who are Fundamentalist Protestants to be the most conservative and those who are Jewish or do not have a religious affiliation to be the least so. The other two Protestant groups are much alike on all the measures, never differing from each other by as many as 10 percentage points in the "always wrong" category. Interestingly, the Roman Catholics in our sample responded much more like the more liberal Protestant groups than like the Fundamentalists, even though the maxims of Catholicism are well known for their conservatism (see also on this point Glock & Stark, 1966).[9]

TABLE 2-12 Moral Response to Sexual Behaviors, by Geographic Region

Item/response	Northeast	Rockies-Southwest	Midwest-South	Pacific Coast
Prostitution				
Always wrong	50.5%	60.7%	70.7%	44.9%
Almost always wrong	16.9	16.5	10.8	16.3
Wrong only sometimes	20.2	13.3	11.4	19.7
Not wrong at all	12.4	9.5	7.1	19.2
Column total	100.0%	100.0%	100.0%	100.1%
Base *n*[a]	1,275	399	942	381
Premarital sex by teenage boy, not in love				
Always wrong	47.0%	60.0%	63.2%	46.4%
Almost always wrong	20.5	24.8	15.8	21.1
Wrong only sometimes	21.3	11.1	12.7	20.6
Not wrong at all	11.2	4.1	8.4	11.9
Column total	100.0%	100.0%	100.1%	100.0%
Base *n*[a]	1,280	395	939	379
Premarital sex by teenage boy, in love				
Always wrong	31.0%	42.6%	46.7%	32.4%
Almost always wrong	20.7	23.4	16.0	18.2
Wrong only sometimes	23.5	20.1	15.1	25.3
Not wrong at all	24.8	14.0	22.2	24.2
Column total	100.0%	100.1%	100.0%	100.1%
Base *n*[a]	1,278	394	940	380
Premarital sex by adult man, not in love				
Always wrong	43.9%	58.5%	60.9%	38.4%
Almost always wrong	15.1	18.3	13.7	17.1
Wrong only sometimes	20.5	14.1	12.6	22.1
Not wrong at all	20.5	9.0	12.8	22.4
Column total	100.0%	99.9%	100.0%	100.0%
Base *n*[a]	1,278	398	939	380
Premarital sex by adult man, in love				
Always wrong	26.2%	40.7%	43.9%	25.2%
Almost always wrong	14.4	19.9	12.2	1[illegible].3
Wrong only sometimes	21.8	17.2	14.7	18.6
Not wrong at all	37.6	22.2	29.2	43.0
Column total	100.0%	100.0%	100.0%	100.1%
Base *n*[a]	1,277	396	941	377

TABLE 2-12 (*Continued*)

Item/response	Northeast	Rockies-Southwest	Midwest-South	Pacific Coast
Premarital sex by teenage girl, not in love				
Always wrong	64.5%	73.9%	74.1%	61.3%
Almost always wrong	15.2	15.6	12.0	17.4
Wrong only sometimes	13.5	8.8	8.4	13.9
Not wrong at all	6.8	1.8	5.5	7.4
Column total	100.0%	100.1%	100.0%	100.0%
Base *n*[a]	1,279	398	941	380
Premarital sex by teenage girl, in love				
Always wrong	40.6%	52.1%	54.3%	38.9%
Almost always wrong	19.9	18.9	14.0	17.6
Wrong only sometimes	19.5	17.6	12.9	21.6
Not wrong at all	20.1	11.3	18.8	21.8
Column total	100.1%	99.9%	100.0%	99.9%
Base *n*[a]	1,279	397	941	380
Premarital sex by adult woman, not in love				
Always wrong	49.2%	63.7%	64.8%	46.4%
Almost always wrong	15.7	17.1	12.8	16.9
Wrong only sometimes	19.0	11.6	11.5	17.2
Not wrong at all	16.1	7.6	10.9	19.5
Column total	100.0%	100.0%	100.0%	100.0%
Base *n*[a]	1,281	397	941	379
Premarital sex by adult woman, in love				
Always wrong	29.7%	44.7%	46.1%	28.1%
Almost always wrong	15.8	19.6	13.3	13.0
Wrong only sometimes	19.9	15.6	13.6	20.7
Not wrong at all	34.5	20.1	27.0	38.2
Column total	99.9%	100.0%	100.0%	100.0%
Base *n*[a]	1,281	398	941	377
Extramarital sex				
Always wrong	67.1%	81.4%	78.4%	67.8%
Almost always wrong	16.8	13.1	10.2	18.1
Wrong only sometimes	13.9	4.5	8.9	11.8
Not wrong at all	2.3	1.0	2.5	2.4
Column total	100.0%	100.0%	100.0%	100.1%
Base *n*[a]	1,281	397	945	382
Homosexuality without affection				
Always wrong	74.5%	85.8%	86.4%	69.9%
Almost always wrong	10.4	8.7	5.5	10.3
Wrong only sometimes	7.9	3.8	3.9	11.3
Not wrong at all	7.3	1.8	4.3	8.4
Column total	100.1%	100.1%	100.1%	99.9%
Base *n*[a]	1,261	393	932	379

TABLE 2-12 *(Continued)*

Item/response	Northeast	Rockies-Southwest	Midwest-South	Pacific Coast
Homosexuality with affection				
Always wrong	67.6%	74.0%	81.3%	62.8%
Almost always wrong	9.7	13.0	5.4	8.8
Wrong only sometimes	8.4	7.0	5.1	10.4
Not wrong at all	14.3	6.0	8.3	17.9
Column total	100.0%	100.0%	100.1%	99.9%
Base *n*[a]	1,252	384	930	374
Masturbation				
Always wrong	23.0%	32.0%	35.4%	21.9%
Almost always wrong	21.1	22.2	22.4	21.7
Wrong only sometimes	33.1	32.5	27.3	30.5
Not wrong at all	22.7	13.4	14.9	25.9
Column total	99.9%	100.1%	100.0%	100.0%
Base *n*[a]	1,244	388	906	374

[a] Excluded are respondents who said "don't know" or failed to answer the given item (see Table 2-1).

TABLE 2-13 Moral Response to Sexual Behaviors, by Community Size

Item/response	Rural area, small town	25,000 to 1 million	More than 1 million
Prostitution (gamma = .30)			
Always wrong	77.4%	57.3%	47.0%
Almost always wrong	14.5	15.1	13.9
Wrong only sometimes	6.0	16.7	21.5
Not wrong at all	2.1	10.9	17.6
Column total	100.0%	100.0%	100.0%
Base *n*[a]	283	2,222	489
Premarital sex by teenage boy, not in love (gamma = .24)			
Always wrong	66.3%	54.1%	44.7%
Almost always wrong	22.7	19.8	17.2
Wrong only sometimes	10.3	17.0	21.9
Not wrong at all	0.7	9.1	16.2
Column total	100.0%	100.0%	100.0%
Base *n*[a]	282	2,220	488
Premarital sex by teenage boy, in love (gamma = .23)			
Always wrong	48.4%	38.7%	26.5%
Almost always wrong	22.1	19.4	17.1
Wrong only sometimes	14.9	20.7	23.6
Not wrong at all	14.6	21.2	32.8
Column total	100.0%	100.0%	100.0%
Base *n*[a]	281	2,217	419

TABLE 2-13 (*Continued*)

Item/response	Rural area, small town	25,000 to 1 million	More than 1 million
Premarital sex by adult man, not in love (gamma = .30)			
Always wrong	67.5%	51.0%	38.4%
Almost always wrong	17.3	15.9	11.6
Wrong only sometimes	12.0	16.8	23.2
Not wrong at all	3.2	16.3	26.8
Column total	100.0%	100.0%	100.0%
Base *n*[a]	283	2,218	491
Premarital sex by adult man, in love (gamma = .32)			
Always wrong	51.4%	34.2%	20.7%
Almost always wrong	17.0	14.9	10.4
Wrong only sometimes	15.6	18.3	21.1
Not wrong at all	16.0	32.7	47.8
Column total	100.0%	100.1%	100.0%
Base *n*[a]	282	2,214	492
Premarital sex by teenage girl, not in love (gamma = .22)			
Always wrong	77.7%	68.8%	60.9%
Almost always wrong	15.2	14.9	12.4
Wrong only sometimes	6.0	11.3	14.9
Not wrong at all	1.1	5.1	11.8
Column total	100.0%	100.1%	100.0%
Base *n*[a]	282	2,222	491
Premarital sex by teenage girl, in love (gamma = .23)			
Always wrong	56.4%	47.3%	35.6%
Almost always wrong	19.1	18.1	14.6
Wrong only sometimes	13.5	17.1	21.3
Not wrong at all	11.0	17.6	28.5
Column total	100.0%	100.1%	100.0%
Base *n*[a]	282	2,220	492
Premarital sex by adult woman, not in love (gamma = .29)			
Always wrong	70.9%	56.4%	43.8%
Almost always wrong	16.7	15.4	13.0
Wrong only sometimes	9.2	15.1	20.7
Not wrong at all	3.2	13.2	22.5
Column total	100.0%	100.1%	100.0%
Base *n*[a]	282	2,220	493
Premarital sex by adult woman, in love (gamma = .30)			
Always wrong	52.3%	37.4%	24.7%
Almost always wrong	18.7	15.8	10.3
Wrong only sometimes	13.1	17.4	20.3
Not wrong at all	15.9	29.4	44.6
Column total	100.0%	100.0%	99.9%
Base *n*[a]	283	2,218	493

TABLE 2-13 (*Continued*)

Item/response	Rural area, small town	25,000 to 1 million	More than 1 million
Extramarital sex (gamma = .35)			
Always wrong	89.0%	73.2%	60.6%
Almost always wrong	6.0	15.0	16.5
Wrong only sometimes	4.6	9.8	19.1
Not wrong at all	0.4	2.1	3.9
Column total	100.0%	100.1%	100.1%
Base *n*[a]	282	2,228	492
Homosexuality without affection (gamma = .32)			
Always wrong	90.0%	79.9%	69.4%
Almost always wrong	6.4	8.5	9.9
Wrong only sometimes	2.5	6.1	10.5
Not wrong at all	1.1	5.4	10.1
Column total	100.0%	99.9%	99.9%
Base *n*[a]	281	2,197	484
Homosexuality with affection (gamma = .30)			
Always wrong	84.9%	73.0%	61.3%
Almost always wrong	7.5	8.6	9.7
Wrong only sometimes	4.7	7.3	9.3
Not wrong at all	2.9	11.2	19.7
Column total	100.0%	100.1%	100.0%
Base *n*[a]	279	2,175	483
Masturbation (gamma = .18)			
Always wrong	35.7%	28.0%	23.3%
Almost always wrong	26.3	21.9	18.6
Wrong only sometimes	28.2	31.1	31.1
Not wrong at all	9.8	19.0	27.0
Column total	100.0%	100.0%	100.0%
Base *n*[a]	266	2,158	485

[a] Excluded are 3 respondents who were noncodable with respect to current community size, as well as those who responded "don't know" or failed to answer the given item (see Table 2-1).

Summary

This chapter's overview of our findings has shown that Americans' sexual norms in 1970 were by and large conservative and that many believed they were less permissive than most of their fellow citizens. Many thought that the sexual behaviors of which they disapproved should be illegal, with "violators" to be "cured" of their aberrations or threatened with jail, although they were not

TABLE 2-14 Moral Response to Sexual Behaviors, by Religious Affiliation

Item/response	No affiliation	Reformation Protestant	Pietistic Protestant	Fundamentalist Protestant	Roman Catholic	Jewish
Prostitution						
Always wrong	27.2%	53.4%	62.3%	75.6%	51.3%	29.6%
Almost always wrong	15.4	20.5	14.1	9.9	17.2	11.3
Wrong only sometimes	27.9	14.4	16.1	9.9	19.6	28.2
Not wrong at all	29.4	11.6	7.5	4.6	11.9	31.0
Column total	99.9%	99.9%	100.0%	100.0%	100.0%	100.1%
Base *n*[a]	272	438	483	849	720	71
Premarital sex by teenage boy, not in love						
Always wrong	26.2%	52.8%	56.2%	66.7%	50.8%	31.0%
Almost always wrong	19.9	23.4	22.1	14.4	23.0	7.0
Wrong only sometimes	31.7	16.1	14.0	12.3	17.2	39.4
Not wrong at all	22.1	7.8	7.6	6.5	9.0	22.5
Column total	99.9%	100.1%	99.9%	99.9%	100.0%	99.9%
Base *n*[a]	271	436	484	845	725	71
Premarital sex by teenage boy, in love						
Always wrong	14.4%	36.7%	38.9%	49.0%	34.9%	23.9%
Almost always wrong	15.9	25.5	17.4	16.9	21.9	5.6
Wrong only sometimes	29.2	20.7	21.7	14.6	21.5	40.8
Not wrong at all	40.6	17.1	21.9	19.5	21.7	29.6
Column total	100.1%	100.0%	99.9%	100.0%	100.0%	99.9%
Base *n*[a]	271	439	483	845	722	71

TABLE 2-14 (*Continued*)

Item/response	No affiliation	Reformation Protestant	Pietistic Protestant	Fundamentalist Protestant	Roman Catholic	Jewish
Premarital sex by adult man, not in love						
Always wrong	23.6%	46.0%	55.2%	65.6%	46.9%	19.7%
Almost always wrong	12.5	18.7	13.9	12.4	18.5	9.9
Wrong only sometimes	24.7	19.8	17.0	12.1	18.0	28.2
Not wrong at all	39.1	15.5	13.9	9.9	16.6	42.3
Column total	99.9%	100.0%	100.0%	100.0%	100.0%	100.1%
Base n^a	271	439	482	845	723	71
Premarital sex by adult man, in love						
Always wrong	10.7%	30.5%	37.3%	46.3%	29.7%	8.5%
Almost always wrong	8.5	16.6	12.3	14.1	16.8	9.9
Wrong only sometimes	18.1	21.2	17.1	15.1	21.1	26.8
Not wrong at all	62.6	31.7	33.3	24.5	32.5	54.9
Column total	99.9%	100.0%	100.0%	100.0%	100.1%	100.1%
Base n^a	270	439	480	846	721	71
Premarital sex by teenage girl, not in love						
Always wrong	38.8%	68.4%	68.8%	77.6%	71.3%	48.6%
Almost always wrong	17.6	16.8	16.5	10.7	15.3	12.9
Wrong only sometimes	26.4	9.3	9.5	7.3	9.8	27.1
Not wrong at all	17.2	5.5	5.2	4.4	3.6	11.4
Column total	100.0%	100.0%	100.0%	100.0%	100.0%	100.0%
Base n^a	273	440	484	845	725	70

Premarital sex by teenage girl, in love						
Always wrong	17.7%	45.9%	45.9%	56.6%	46.5%	35.7%
Almost always wrong	14.8	22.0	18.6	13.9	20.4	10.0
Wrong only sometimes	30.6	16.4	17.8	11.7	18.1	31.4
Not wrong at all	36.9	15.7	17.8	17.7	14.9	22.9
Column total	100.0%	100.0%	100.1%	99.9%	99.9%	100.0%
Base *n*[a]	271	440	484	846	724	70
Premarital sex by adult woman, not in love						
Always wrong	25.5%	55.9%	57.5%	68.8%	55.2%	22.5%
Almost always wrong	11.1	16.0	15.6	12.7	18.1	14.1
Wrong only sometimes	26.9	15.3	14.9	9.8	15.7	29.6
Not wrong at all	36.5	12.8	12.0	8.7	10.9	33.8
Column total	100.0%	100.0%	100.0%	100.0%	99.9%	100.0%
Base *n*[a]	271	438	482	848	724	71
Premarital sex by adult woman, in love						
Always wrong	12.1%	33.3%	38.9%	49.2%	34.3%	18.3%
Almost always wrong	8.8	20.3	15.0	14.0	16.6	8.5
Wrong only sometimes	17.6	18.7	17.5	13.1	20.9	26.8
Not wrong at all	61.4	27.6	28.7	23.7	28.2	46.5
Column total	99.9%	99.9%	100.1%	100.0%	100.0%	100.1%
Base *n*[a]	272	438	481	848	723	71

TABLE 2-14 *(Continued)*

Item/response	No affiliation	Reformation Protestant	Pietistic Protestant	Fundamentalist Protestant	Roman Catholic	Jewish
Extramarital sex						
Always wrong	44.3%	74.9%	74.8%	83.7%	71.5%	45.1%
Almost always wrong	27.1	17.1	14.7	7.5	14.8	19.7
Wrong only sometimes	22.0	6.8	9.1	7.3	11.5	33.8
Not wrong at all	6.6	1.1	1.4	1.5	2.2	1.4
Column total	100.0%	99.9%	100.0%	100.0%	100.0%	100.0%
Base *n*[a]	273	438	484	854	722	71
Homosexuality without affection						
Always wrong	54.9%	80.0%	82.8%	88.8%	78.8%	45.6%
Almost always wrong	12.0	9.7	8.3	5.1	10.7	10.3
Wrong only sometimes	16.5	5.5	6.1	3.0	5.3	19.1
Not wrong at all	16.5	4.8	2.8	3.2	5.2	25.0
Column total	99.9%	100.0%	100.0%	100.1%	100.0%	100.0%
Base *n*[a]	266	434	472	846	717	68
Homosexuality with affection						
Always wrong	48.5%	72.5%	75.8%	83.7%	69.9%	39.1%
Almost always wrong	8.8	9.5	9.6	5.1	11.8	8.7
Wrong only sometimes	11.2	9.9	6.6	4.0	6.9	20.3
Not wrong at all	31.5	8.1	8.1	7.1	11.4	31.9
Column total	100.0%	100.0%	100.1%	99.9%	100.0%	100.0%
Base *n*[a]	260	433	471	840	708	69
Masturbation						
Always wrong	14.9%	20.6%	28.8%	38.4%	26.5%	10.0%
Almost always wrong	11.9	22.2	25.4	21.8	23.6	10.0
Wrong only sometimes	31.2	35.7	28.4	26.5	34.5	37.1
Not wrong at all	42.0	21.5	17.4	13.3	15.4	42.9
Column total	100.0%	100.0%	100.0%	100.0%	100.0%	100.0%
Base *n*[a]	269	423	465	822	702	70

[a] Excluded are 164 respondents with unclassifiable religious affiliations, as well as those who responded "don't know" or failed to answer the given item (see Table 2-1).

quite so intolerant of nonconjugal sexual experience among their friends, as long as it is heterosexual.

Just as these discrete percentages can be interpreted as evidence of a lack of radical sexual change in America, so too can the simple bivariate relationships introduced in the second part of the chapter. Certain relationships have been found to exist, either in sex research or in more general sociological research: older persons, for example, are more conservative than younger ones; the nonreligious are more permissive than the religiously affiliated. Thus it would be an important sign of social change if these social structural anchors of morality no longer held; that is, if these traditional relationships were sharply reduced, no longer existed, or were reversed. As nothing of this sort is evident from our data, we again feel confident in asserting the absence of far-reaching changes in sexual norms in the United States.

NOTES

1. The term *disapprove* as used here combines the responses "always wrong" and "almost always wrong."
2. When asked, "To what extent do you think homosexuality is obscene and vulgar?" 65% of our sample replied "very much" and 19% "somewhat."
3. Of our sample, 62% had *never* been personally acquainted with a male who had engaged in homosexual acts, nor 76% with such a female. For extramarital sex the figures are 17% for a male and 24% for a female; for premarital sex, 13% and 15%.
4. It should be noted that many in our sample had not experienced the behaviors they were evaluating. Thus, a substantial proportion of the respondents reported never having masturbated, never having had premarital sex, and never having had homosexual sex.
5. We consider the interview situation to be one in which respondents express public, not private, moralities because although it takes place privately, responses are made "for the record" and the interviewer is a stranger, not an intimate.
6. As noted in Appendix D, our sample overrepresents blacks. This oversampling, however, does not affect the simple bivariate relationships we present; the less-educated black respondents were somewhat more liberal than the others, but they are too few in number (5% of the total) to bias these findings.
7. Pretest items concerning these behaviors did differentiate between male and female participants; the responses were so similar regardless of participants' gender, however, that this distinction was dropped from the final interview schedule.
8. Our measure of socioeconomic status is the scale devised by Duncan (1961) from 1950 Census aggregate data on the average income and education of

persons in each Census occupational category as weighted by the North-Hatt prestige ratings.

9. How strongly people subscribe to the tenets of their particular religion may affect their sexual standards as much as does the nature of the religion itself; so we also compared our respondents on this basis, and we found those who said their religious beliefs were very strong to be a highly conservative group. On all the items except masturbation, there is an average difference of almost 37 percentage points between the strongly religious who responded "always wrong" and the least religious who did so. The gammas range from −.29 to −.45, with an average (including all measures) of −.39.

Chapter 3

Influences on Sexual Morality

In the preceding chapter we used our data for descriptive purposes. In this chapter we begin our explanatory analysis of sexual norms. So far, we have looked at single items representing particular sexual behaviors (and the conditions under which some of them occur). Our first task in this chapter is to develop a scale of general sexual morality that combines some of these items to create a parsimonious single measure for later analysis. Then we relate an array of independent variables to the general measure by means of statistical contingency tables and gamma correlation coefficients.

Our reasons for setting out our data this way, rather than proceeding directly with regression analysis, are twofold. First, because we have a national probability sample, the specific values in contingency tables represent important findings in and of themselves and are thus of interest; second, not all our data can be said to meet the assumptions required for regression techniques, such as path analysis (e.g., variables at the interval level of measurement); so gamma analysis provides for an initial approach that is conservative.[1] In the next chapter we use regression techniques to ascertain which variables remain important when others are simultaneously controlled, which variables have strong *indirect* effects even though they may exhibit weak bivariate or direct relationships, what causal sequences can be reasonably and meaningfully hypothesized among our variables, and how much variance is accounted for by many variables working together.

Beginning in this chapter, we also discuss analyses that use variables derived directly from the interview data, as well as composite variables and factors that were constructed from several items. These constructed variables and factors are described throughout the book in footnotes to the text where they are first discussed.

Measuring Sexual Morality

The discussion in Chapter 2 of items concerning individual sexual behaviors was presented mainly for descriptive purposes. In the initial stages of study and questionnaire design we had no hope of a comprehensive sexual morality measure. Ira Reiss was consulted, but we sought a more general measure of a broad spectrum of issues, while his premarital sexual permissiveness scale only pertained to heterosexual courtship (Reiss, 1967). It seemed necessary simply to ask many "wrong/not wrong" questions about a large number of sexual behaviors if we were to have a full range of data for seeing public norms, attitudes, and perceptions of homosexuality in their broader moral context.

In a first pretest of 100 cases, this approach, with a larger set of items than reported here, revealed the possibility of a Guttman scale ranging from conservative to liberal across such a broad spectrum of issues. Homosexuality was near one extreme among the most disapproved behaviors (adult sexual activity with children and parent-child sexual activity were the only items more extreme; rape was taken for granted, as a greater extreme, and hence we did not ask about it). The set of items was refined for a second pretest of 200 cases, the Guttman scale characteristics were obtained again, and the set was reduced to those items already reported, for use in the main sample survey.

Thus these items were subjected to Guttman scale analysis to derive an overall scale of sexual morality. In other words, we expected that people could be arrayed along a range from "least conservative" to "most conservative" depending on how many of the behaviors they said were always wrong. A Guttman scale is a measure for situations in which people's patterns of item responses will range along the scale in an orderly manner. In between those who disapprove of all the behaviors and those who disapprove of none of them, toward the conservative end would be people who disapproved of all but masturbation (the least widely disapproved item), and toward the liberal end would be people who disapprove of none but homosexuality (the most widely disapproved). A person who, for example, does not object to homosexuality but feels all forms of premarital sex are wrong, would not fit properly on the scale and would be considered to have a scale "error-type" pattern. For a group of items to constitute a Guttman scale, there must be very few error responses; that is, the coefficient of reproducibility must be very high, at least .92 (out of a possible 1.00).[2]

Based on the total-sample responses to the 13 individual behavior items, acceptance of homosexuality without affection clearly was the liberal end-point of our scale and forbidding masturbation was the conservative end. We hoped to come up with a scale of about 8 or 10 items, a Guttman scale guideline, so that each could be clearly discriminated from those next to it. This required changing or eliminating some of our single items as follows.

First, we noted that standards for premarital sex differ depending on whether the behavior evaluated is that of an adult or a teenager, that of a male or a female, and with or without the presence of love for one's partner. Since the latter consideration affects the extent of disapproval in every case, we decided that the scale should include one item that involved love and one that did not.[3] We could then elect to have pairs of items representing males versus females if we wanted to illustrate the influence of the traditional double standard, or pairs regarding adults versus teenagers if we were more interested in the age of the participants. Comparisons of these alternatives led us to adopt the latter course, leading to the construction of one index for adult premarital sex with love (illustrated in Tables 3-1 and 3-2) and one for teenage premarital sex without love (Tables 3-3 and 3-4). While we are aware that in doing so we lost some data concerning the fine extent to which respondents discriminate between males and females in the same activity, we feel that the age distinction was more important to preserve.[4] In any case, the resulting indices provided two discriminant points for our scale: for teenage premarital sex without affection, 54% said it is always wrong and 5% that it is not wrong at all; for adult premarital sex when the partners are in love, 33% said it is always wrong and 30% that it is not wrong at all. We thus had two items for the middle of our scale, the former

TABLE 3-1 Moral Response to Premarital Sex Among Adults in Love: Percentages Grouped for Index of Liberalism

ADULT WOMAN IN LOVE		ADULT MAN IN LOVE: Always wrong	Almost always wrong	Wrong only sometimes	Not wrong at all	Don't know	Row total	Row n
Always wrong	0	31.5	2.7	1.0	1.1	0.2	36.5	1,100
Almost always wrong	1	1.0	10.3	2.8	0.9	0.1	15.1	456
Wrong only sometimes	2[a]	0.4	0.9	13.5	2.5	0.0	17.3	522
Not wrong at all		0.3	0.3	3 1.1	4 28.7	0.0	30.4	919
Don't know	5	0.0	0.0	0.0	0.0	0.6	0.6	20
Column total		33.2	14.2	18.4	33.2	0.9		
Column n		1,004	428	554	1,004	27	Total n	3,017
							No answer	1
							Total sample	3,018

[a] The case bracketed (i.e., percentages 0.4, 0.9, 2.8, and 1.0) are scored as "pretty much wrong" in Tables 3-2 and 3-4.

TABLE 3-2 Index of Liberalism Toward Premarital Sex (Index of Moral Response to Premarital Sex Among Adults in Love)

Score[a]	*n*	Percent of total sample	Percent of applicable responses
0 Always wrong	951	31.5%	32.7%
1 Almost always wrong	422	14.0	14.5
2 Pretty much wrong[b]	150	5.1	5.2
3 Wrong only sometimes	517	17.1	17.8
4 Not wrong at all	866	28.7	29.8
5 Don't know	111	3.5	
9 No answer	1	0.0	
Total	3,018	99.9%	100.0%

[a] Index scores are shown at the left of each grouping sketched in Table 3-1.
[b] See note to Table 3-1.

to fall in mid-scale and the latter toward the conservative end (if disapproved).

Turning our attention next to the liberal end of the scale, we noted that extramarital sex and homosexuality with affection evoked about the same number of "always wrong" responses—72% and 70%, respectively. The scale analysis dictated the use of responses to homosexuality without affection (of which some 78% disapproved) as the extreme end-point of the scale, and it seemed that for the next point it would be more meaningful to retain the item concerning extramarital sex, since this is an entirely different behavior. Thus homosexuality with affection, nearly identical to extramarital sex in its strength of public disapproval, was dropped from the scale. Another item, that involving prostitution, was also dropped because it fell on the scale very near the midpoint already defined by our teenage premarital sex index. We preferred keeping this index to having only the one dealing with adults.

The resulting scale, which we refer to as the Sexual Morality Scale (SMS), is shown in Table 3-5. It has a coefficient of reproducibility by the Cornell method of .9220, which qualifies it as an adequate scale. It is considered a *quasi*-Guttman scale, since it has only five items. (Any combination of more items was found not to meet the .92 reproducibility criterion.) From the marginal distributions on the five constitutent items, it is possible to calculate a chance reproducibility of .8678. If our scale were perfect, it would have a reproducibility coefficient of 1.000; thus, a perfect

TABLE 3-3 Moral Response to Premarital Sex Among Teenagers Not in Love: Percentages Grouped for Index of Conservatism

TEENAGE GIRL, NOT IN LOVE		TEENAGE BOY, NOT IN LOVE: Always wrong	Almost always wrong	Wrong only sometimes	Not wrong at all	Don't know	Row total	Row *n*
Always wrong	**0**	51.8	9.7	4.4	1.9	0.2	68.0	2,050
Almost always wrong	**1**	1.0	8.7	3.6	1.0	0.0	14.3	434
Wrong only sometimes	**2**	0.3	0.9	8.5	1.5	0.0	11.2	337
Not wrong at all	**5**	0.2	0.1	**3** 0.5	**4** 5.0	0.0	5.8	175
Don't know		0.1	0.0	0.0	0.0	0.4	0.5	18
Column total		53.4	19.4	17.0	9.4	0.6		
Column *n*		1,609	588	513	284	20	Total *n*	3,014
							No answer	4
							Total sample	3,018

TABLE 3-4 Index of Conservatism Toward Premarital Sex (Index of Moral Response to Premarital Sex Among Teenagers Not in Love)

Score[a]	*n*	Percent of total sample	Percent of applicable responses
0 Always wrong	1,560	51.7%	54.0%
1 Almost always wrong	586	19.4	20.3
2 Pretty much wrong[b]	279	9.1	9.6
3 Wrong only sometimes	315	10.5	10.9
4 Not wrong at all	150	5.0	5.2
5 Don't know	124	4.0	
9 No answer	4	0.1	
Total	3,018	99.8%	100.0%

[a] Index scores are shown at the left of each grouping sketched in Table 3-3.
[b] See note to Table 3-1.

scale would be about 15% better than chance or 7.8% better than what we achieved.

Table 3-5 gives the scores and numbers of error responses as well as of those who fit "perfectly" into the given category—respondents who said that the given behavior and those more widely disapproved are always wrong and did not say that less-disapproved behaviors are always wrong. The Cornell method assigned error responses to a given point on the scale based on the total number of "always wrong" responses the person gave. Thus, those who scored 6 on the scale (the most liberal) include 358 who gave a response other than "always wrong" on all the constituent items and an additional 180 who, while not disapproving entirely of homosexuality without affection, did think that one of the other behaviors is always wrong. It is interesting to note that of these 180 "deviant" scores, in 136 the one always wrong behavior is extramarital sex. Similarly, among those scoring 5, in addition to the 275 "perfect" scores (people who disapproved only of homosexuality), there are 200 error responses that show different patterns of disapproval. We would like to stress that the error responses in each category of the Sexual Morality Scale do not represent absurd or meaningless statistical artifacts but rather individuals who disapproved of some sexual activities and not others in patterns that are close to the structure of our scale. The Cornell method assisted us in classifying the relative moral absolutism of our respondents as well as it can be done, given the data we had to use; and in further analyses of the SMS we include the error types as well as

TABLE 3-5 Sexual Morality Scale (SMS)

Score	Meaning of "perfect" score	Response pattern	n	Category n	Percent of total sample
1	All behaviors always wrong	00000*	417*		
				417	13.9%
2	Only masturbation not always wrong	00001*	394*		
				394	13.1
3	Masturbation and adult premarital sex with love not always wrong	00011*	333*		
		10000	10		
		01000	1		
		00100	25		
		00010	163		
				532	17.7
4	Masturbation, adult premarital sex with love, teenage premarital sex without love not always wrong	00111*	429*		
		11000	1		
		10100	1		
		10010	10		
		10001	25		
		01010	17		
		01001	13		
		00110	110		
		00101	44		
				650	21.6
5	Masturbation, adult premarital sex with love, teenage premarital sex without love, extramarital sex not always wrong	01111*	275*		
		11010	1		
		11001	2		
		10110	14		
		10101	8		
		10011	57		
		01110	37		
		01101	6		
		01011	75		
				475	15.8
6	All behaviors not always wrong	11111*	358*		
		11110	5		
		11101	2		
		11011	37		
		10111	136		
				538	17.9
Total				3,006	100.0%

NOTE. Asterisk denotes "perfect" score. Response patterns represent codes of 0 ("always wrong") or 1 ("not always wrong") for each of the five behavioral items, respectively from left to right: homosexuality without affection; extramarital sex; teenage premarital sex without love; adult premarital sex with love; masturbation.

the scale types, as assigned by the Cornell method. Finally, it should be pointed out that in category 1 of the scale—made up of people who believed that all of the behaviors in question are always wrong—there are 417 respondents, or 13.9% of the total number of 3006 (12 of the total sample did not answer one or more of the constituent items). Combined with the 394 in category 2 (13.1% of the total sample) who said that all the behaviors except masturbation are always wrong, this shows that at the time of our survey, 27% of American adults—more than one in four—were extremely conservative about sexual behaviors.

The SMS has a Kuder-Richardson alpha reliability coefficient of .583, which means that we could expect a correlation of .583 between this scale and any other sexual morality scale similarly constructed of five items. It also means that, since the square root of alpha estimates the correlation between our scale and some hypothetical "true" scale (i.e., one that would be a perfect measure), this correlation would be .764. Finally, since the square of a correlation estimates how much variance in "true" scores the measure in question could account for, we know that our scale can explain 58.3% of the variance in scores on the "true" scale.[5]

Our Sexual Morality Scale, then, describes the relative conservatism in the moral stance of our respondents. In the next section, in a beginning attempt to understand the primary sources of the sexual standards people hold, we introduce our independent variables and show how they relate to respondents' scores on the SMS.

Correlates of Sexual Morality

Independent Variables

Consideration of how sexual norms are acquired and maintained is an area in which one finds little theoretical direction. Sociology assumes that social norms are acquired in some vaguely specified way through socialization, and that they function to maintain societal stability. It pays lip service to such concepts as "folkways," "mores," "norms, and "values," yet the sociology of normative phenomena is undeveloped. (Although Reiss's [1967] theory of sexual standards has helped us somewhat, it was developed ad hoc and so shares with our work a rather open character.)[6] Our approach therefore has been ecletic and basically descriptive, attempting to isolate experiences and influences throughout a person's life that seem closely connected with moral development. Most simply, we looked at four sets of potential determinants, arranged in temporal stages in accordance with the life-cycle:

1. The environment into which a person was born, including his or her cultural milieu (e.g., hometown size), characteristics of the family of origin (e.g., presence or absence of brothers), and parental characteristics (e.g., social class); birth cohort and gender were included here as givens.
2. Early socialization experiences (e.g., parents' disciplinary attitudes, prepubertal masturbation).
3. Later socialization experiences (e.g., premarital sexual involvement, military service).
4. Current influences (e.g., present religious devoutness, marital status).

The analysis begins with 83 variables arranged in this temporal sequence (Table 3-6).

For the most part, we present findings relating to our independent variables according to the temporal stage in which they belong. For some variables, however, we found it instructive to compare childhood and current situations, and to offer a preliminary analysis here on the effect of changes in these dimensions over the respondent's lifetime. We present these comparisons following the discussion of the childhood situation rather than in the final stage (current influences), where they might properly appear; we do so to provide a more meaningful assessment of the lifetime effects of the particular variable.

Dependent Variable

Our dependent variable, of course, is the SMS. For the cross-tabulations presented, we collapsed the six categories of the scale into three (1 and 2, 3 and 4, 5 and 6) to permit easier reading of the tables. It should be remembered that each of the original categories is meaningfully distinct from its neighbors. Nonetheless, these three broader categories can also be considered meaningful groupings; for example, the "conservative" group (categories 1 and 2) are those respondents who said all behaviors, or all except masturbation, are always wrong.

TABLE 3-6 Independent Variables Examined for Correlation with the SMS

Stage 1: Early Environment Variables

- Childhood geographic region
- Childhood residence size (urban/rural)
- Birth order
- Size of family of origin
- Had older brother(s)
- Had younger brother(s)
- Had older sister(s)
- Had younger sister(s)
- Family breakup during childhood
- Age at family breakup
- Childhood religious affiliation
- Strength of religious beliefs in childhood home
- Parental religious devoutness
- Parental socioeconomic status
- Parental education level
- Parental generation
- Parental sexual permissiveness
- Father sexually strict
- Mother sexually strict
- Father masculine
- Mother masculine
- Father feminine
- Mother feminine
- Father sociable
- Mother sociable
- Father serious and moral about sex
- Mother serious and moral about sex
- Father a sexual person
- Mother a sexual person
- Father loving/hostile
- Mother loving/hostile

Stage 2: Early Socialization Variables

- Childhood sex play
- Age at first masturbation
- Age at first heterosexual experience
- Childhood sex guilt
- Guilt over heterosexual sex play
- Father predictable/unpredictable
- Mother predictable/unpredictable
- Father freedom-giving/controlling
- Mother freedom-giving/controlling
- Lifetime sexual environment

Stage 3: Later Socialization Variables

- Premarital sexual involvement
- Had premarital sex
- Frequency of premarital sex
- Positive toward premarital sex
- Negative toward premarital sex
- Respondent's education level
- Time served in military
- Age at first marriage

Stage 4: Currently Influential Variables

- Current age
- Sex
- Race
- Marital status
- Number of marriages
- Geographic region
- Community size (urban/rural)
- Religious affiliation
- Religious devoutness
- Socioeconomic status
- Number of children
- Age of oldest dependent son
- Age of oldest dependent daughter
- Respondent masculine
- Respondent feminine
- Respondent sociable
- Respondent work oriented
- Have wanted counseling or professional help
- Respondent a sexual person
- Respondent serious and moral about sex
- Respondent sexually threatened by opposite sex

In evaluating the relationships provided by our cross-tabulations, we were looking for particular groups in the population among whom the range of SMS scores diverged notably from that for the population as a whole. We defined a notable divergence as a difference of at least 10 percentage points from total-sample figures. For example, about 27% of the population scored in the conservative sector of the SMS. A group in which 38% scored conservative, then, would be an unusually conservative group.

After identifying these divergent groups (which sometimes involved more than one category of a given independent variable), we calculated the gamma coefficient for the relationship between group membership and SMS score. In this calculation, not belonging to the exceptional group was assigned a score of 0 and belonging to it, a score of 1. Gamma is an estimate of association, so that the higher its value, the stronger the relationship; we consider a gamma of less than $\pm .20$ to indicate an unremarkable association (i.e., not notably different from the general population). In the tables, we present percentages and gammas for both the divergent groups and the other respondents (the "residual" groups), so that the reader can infer the entire contingency table on which these values are based.[7] In the text, we note as well certain relationships that did not meet our 10-percentage-point criterion but were associated with a gamma of reasonable size. We did not use statistical significance as a criterion because our sample is so large; those findings that meet our criteria are significant at least at the .001 level. Finally, even though regression techniques were employed for control purposes in our work on later chapters, we did use a variety of control variables in preparing this chapter where they seem most likely to provide elaboration.

Early Environment (Stage 1) Variables

Cultural Milieu: Region. The first finding that emerges concerns the region of birth in the United States. We find that respondents who grew up on the Pacific coast were more liberal in their current sexual standards, and those from the Rockies-Southwest less so, than were those from "elsewhere," the Northeast or South and Midwest (Table 3-7). For current region of residence the relationships are not so strong. Nevertheless, as Table 2-12 suggested, people who live on the Pacific coast or in the Northeast tended to be less conservative than others.

TABLE 3-7 Percent in Selected Sociological Categories Scoring Conservative, Moderate, or Liberal on the SMS

	Percent conservative (1-2)	Percent moderate (3-4)	Percent liberal (5-6)	Base *n*	Gamma	Percent of total sample (*n* = 3,018)
Total sample	27.0	39.3	33.7	3,006	—	99.6
Childhood geographic region						
Pacific coast	16.7	36.6	46.8	186	.26	6.2
Rockies-Southwest	34.0	42.3	23.7	430	−.21	14.2
Elsewhere in the U.S.	26.9	38.9	34.3	2,234	.03	74.0
Change in geographic region						
From Northeast to Pacific coast, or vice versa	19.7	27.3	53.0	66	.29	2.2
From Midwest-South to Rockies-Southwest, or vice versa	45.0	36.7	18.3	60	−.35	2.0
Other regional mobility	24.9	41.3	33.8	429	.03	14.2
Has always lived on Pacific coast	15.5	38.1	46.4	168	.27	5.6
Has always lived in Midwest-South	36.8	39.6	23.6	815	−.28	27.0
Has always lived elsewhere in the U.S.	23.2	39.2	37.7	1,312	.15	43.5
Childhood community size						
Rural area or small town	39.0	42.2	18.8	918	−.34	30.4
Metropolitan (over 1 million)	17.5	35.4	47.1	885	.38	29.3
Other	24.9	39.9	35.2	1,197	.19	39.7
Current community size						
Rural area or small town	42.0	42.7	15.3	281	−.26	9.3
Metropolitan	14.6	38.3	47.1	493	.33	16.3
Other	27.9	39.1	33.0	2,229	.07	73.9
Change in community size						
Moved to smaller place	21.9	33.8	44.3	420	.19	13.9
Larger or same-size place	27.8	40.2	32.0	2,586	−.20	85.7
Number of siblings						
None	22.6	33.6	43.8	235	.17	7.8
One to four	23.4	37.4	39.2	1,651	.21	54.7
Five or more	33.3	43.2	23.5	1,118	−.28	37.0
Birth order						
First to sixth born	26.3	38.9	34.8	2,720	.19	90.1
Seventh or later born	33.6	42.8	23.7	283	−.19	9.4
Childhood religious affiliation						
None	13.8	32.8	53.4	58	.36	1.9
Jewish	6.6	19.7	73.7	76	.66	2.5
Other	27.8	40.3	31.9	2,756	−.33	91.3
Current religious affiliation						
None	7.3	29.2	63.5	274	.58	9.1
Fundamentalist Protestant	39.4	39.9	20.7	852	−.35	28.2
Jewish	7.2	23.2	69.6	69	.61	2.3
Other	24.6	42.2	33.2	1,648	.04	54.6

TABLE 3-7 (*Continued*)

	Percent conservative (1-2)	Percent moderate (3-4)	Percent liberal (5-6)	Base *n*	Gamma	Percent of total sample (*n*=3,018)
Change from Fundamentalist affiliation						
No change; still Fundamentalist	38.3	39.7	22.0	614	−.30	20.3
Changed to no affiliation	13.1	44.3	42.6	61	.25	2.0
Other change, or not reared as Fundamentalist	24.3	39.1	36.6	2,331	.25	77.2
Change to no religious affiliation						
Yes	7.3	30.2	62.4	245	.56	8.1
No	28.7	40.1	31.1	2,761	−.56	91.5
Parents' date of birth						
1850 or earlier	41.5	41.5	17.1	41	−.33	1.4
1851 to 1875	39.4	41.6	18.9	449	−.33	14.9
1876 to 1925	24.9	38.4	36.7	2,355	.24	78.0
After 1925	10.8	50.0	39.2	74	.23	2.5
Parents' socioeconomic status						
Upper	21.1	33.9	45.0	664	.24	22.0
Other	28.8	40.8	30.4	2,265	−.22	75.0
Parents' education						
College degree(s)	17.4	26.8	55.8	190	.36	6.3
Less than bachelor's degree	27.3	39.8	33.0	2,612	−.08	86.5
Respondent's education						
Beyond high school	18.4	20.0	61.5	320	.30	10.6
12th grade or less	28.1	41.6	30.3	2,681	−.30	88.8
Age						
Under 35	16.7	40.4	42.9	1,063	.32	35.2
35 to 64	31.0	37.9	31.2	1,501	−.14	49.7
65 or older	38.5	41.7	19.8	439	−.31	14.5
Gender						
Female	32.2	40.2	27.6	1,548	−.22	51.3
Male	21.4	38.4	40.2	1,458	.22	48.3
Race						
Black	14.0	49.4	36.5	479	.19	15.9
Not black	29.4	37.4	33.2	2,527	−.19	83.7
Marital status						
Widowed	39.3	41.6	19.1	262	−.37	8.7
Never married	14.2	34.8	51.0	198	.34	6.6
Other	26.7	39.4	33.9	2,546	.03	84.4

NOTE. The criterion for selection is a difference of at least 10 percentage points in any one of these three SMS categories between the given population category and the total sample. Where applicable, residual percentages are also given. Base *n*'s in the various parts of the table do not add up to the total-sample figure of 3,018 because 12 respondents did not answer one or more of the items in the SMS and others were noncodable with respect to certain independent variables.

We checked to see if these findings could be attributed to an urban/rural difference, since there is a relationship between region and population density. (For example, 47% of the respondents from the Midwest-South and Rockies-Southwest regions spent their childhood in rural areas, compared with 18% from the Pacific coast and 13% from the Northeast.) The results, however, show that this is not the case: strong regional effects do exist, in accord with the accepted view of a liberal Northeast and West Coast and a conservative "middle America." Evidently this effect is maintained throughout life, as the finding refers to childhood and not current region, although a substantial relationship exists between the two: except for the Pacific coast region, about 80% of our respondents reported that they still lived in the region where they grew up. Among our West Coast respondents, only 47% so reported.

With regard to those who had moved from one region of the country to another,[8] Table 3-7 shows some interesting findings despite the fact that our regional indices represent very broad categories. The most liberal respondents were those who had moved from one liberal region to the other; the most conservative ones were those reporting conservative regional mobility. Nearly as conservative were those who had not moved away from their native Midwest-South. Apparently, when one disregards newcomers to this region, it remains a basically conservative part of the country. And once again, among our "stay-at-home" respondents, those native to the Pacific coast were the most liberal.

Community Size. The second important finding relates to region. Respondents who grew up in urban areas were less conservative than those reared in small towns or rural areas (Table 3-7). These results are similar to those for size of current residence, and they remain when we control for region. Since younger persons often migrate from rural areas and small towns to larger communities, leaving older persons behind, we also controlled for age. The relationship, however, remains substantially the same, with a tendency toward slightly reduced differences for those respondents over 65. The correlation between childhood and current community of residence is .67. Rural and urban environments do originate and tend to perpetuate differing levels of conservatism in sexual morality, even among those moving elsewhere.[9] In sum, Table 3-7 shows that rural and smaller places tend to be more conservative; size of the respondent's original community had a greater effect than current residence on current sexual morality; and those who had moved between childhood and adulthood from larger to smaller places (compared to all others, who experienced no change or moved to larger places)[10] tended marginally toward liberal morality (gammas of +.19 and −.20, mirror each other, differing only owing to rounding error). This reinforces the finding that origin affects morality more than current community, which seems to reflect the persistent strength of differential early socialization patterns.

Family Characteristics. Another finding concerns the respondent's ordinal position in his or her family of origin. Respondents who were the only child in their families were more likely to be liberal than other respondents and, in general, an earlier position in the family meant more liberal current sexual norms (Table 3-7). Controlling for age and parental socioeconomic status and education does not affect these findings, which appear to contradict those of Kammeyer (1966) and of Reiss (1968), both of whom found earlier-born persons to be more conservative toward premarital sex. Reiss (1967) found only children to be most permissive, while Kammeyer found them the least so. Both investigators also found education to have a liberalizing effect. Kammeyer pointed out that if first-born (or only) children are more likely to attend college, education may even be a suppressor variable in the relationship between birth order and conservatism. On the other hand, Bell and Chaskes (1970), in their samples, found no significant relationships between family-characteristic variables (except religion) and conservatism. Finally, Swanson (1971) pointed out that Kilpatrick and Cauthen's (1969) findings, which showed later-born females to be more conservative than first-born females, could survive a more rigorous analytical method than the authors first used. Swanson suggested that apparently contradictory findings in ordinal-position studies may be due to the use of differing types of analysis. Controlling for gender and respondent's education, in any case, does not substantially affect our findings.[11]

We also find a relationship between family size and moral response. Respondents who came from small families were more liberal in their sexual norms that were those who came from larger families (Table 3-7). Controlling for age, gender, parental socioeconomic status and education, and parental generation does not affect these findings.

This seems closely related to the ordinal-position finding. It could be that respondents from larger families grew up in a less individualized milieu in which parents dealt with their children as a group, while in a smaller family children would be more likely to orient themselves quickly to adult-centered (i.e., more autonomous) values.

Religious Affiliation. We find a strong relationship between the religious affiliation of our respondents and their sexual norms. As we might expect from earlier research (see Dittes, 1969), those who were brought up as Jews or without any religious affiliation were much more liberal than respondents from Catholic or Protestant backgrounds (Table 3-7). (Here and elsewhere in our analysis, readers should bear in mind that there were only 77 Jewish respondents in our sample.) These findings remain when we control for parental socioeconomic status and education.

Comparing childhood and current religion indicates the continuing effect of religious affiliation. Table 3-7 shows that the relationship between current religion and the SMS parallels that for childhood affiliation, with the additional finding that Fundamentalist Protestants are an unusually conservative group. (Those reared as Fundamentalists were also somewhat more conservative than the sample as a whole but not by our 10% divergence criterion.) We note in this regard a strong tendency for respondents to have maintained their childhood religious affiliation. Thus, 87% of those raised as Catholics and Jews, 79% of Fundamentalist Protestants, and about 61% of the other Protestants still reported the same affiliation. In addition, 57% of those who reported no childhood religion still had none.

As current religious affiliation is associated with one's social status (see Pope, 1953), we controlled the above findings for current socioeconomic status and respondent's education. The relationship between religious affiliation and sexual norms remains unaffected, again suggesting that the moral views associated with religious creed have enduring effects on a person's own stance toward sexual behavior.

Although the majority of our respondents reported no lifetime change in religion, we looked at those who did change, especially if it was away from the most conservative or toward the most liberal groups—that is, away from Fundamentalist Protestantism[12] or toward having no religious affiliation.[13] Table 3-7 shows that a shift away from Fundamentalism is generally related to a more liberal direction, with the greatest change being among those who changed to no affiliation; and complementarily the table shows the general liberal tendency of respondents who moved from any religious affiliation to none.

Religious Devoutness. The strength of religious beliefs in the respondents's childhood home appears related to his or her current sexual norms, with those who reported a nondevout background displaying more liberal moralities (Table 3-8). This finding, however, is not nearly as strong as the religious affiliation findings just discussed, perhaps because it has more to do with respondents' parents than with respondents themselves.

TABLE 3-8 Percent in Selected Social Psychological Categories Scoring Conservative, Moderate, or Liberal on the SMS

	Percent conservative (1–2)	Percent moderate (3–4)	Percent liberal (5–6)	Base *n*	Gamma	Percent of total sample (*n* = 3,018)
Total sample	27.0	39.3	33.7	3,006	–	99.6
Religious beliefs in childhood home						
Weak or absent	17.3	38.4	44.3	341	.24	11.3
Moderately or very strong	28.2	39.5	32.4	2,655	−.23	88.0
Current religious devoutness						
Low	12.8	36.1	51.0	1,068	.50	35.4
Medium	23.1	44.8	32.1	853	.03	28.3
High	44.0	38.2	17.9	1,085	−.51	36.0
Change from childhood devoutness						
Much less devout now	12.8	34.8	52.4	290	.14	9.6
Other change or no change	29.7	39.7	30.7	2,465	−.32	81.7
Feels serious and moral about sex						
Slightly or not at all	16.8	36.5	46.8	823	.34	27.3
Moderately	24.1	40.3	35.6	1,080	.08	35.8
Very much so	37.4	40.5	22.0	1,103	−.36	36.5
Father loving/hostile						
Loving	20.2	35.9	43.9	955	.26	31.6
Somewhat or very hostile	30.7	40.8	28.5	1,860	−.25	61.6

TABLE 3-8 (*Continued*)

	Percent conservative (1–2)	Percent moderate (3–4)	Percent liberal (5–6)	Base *n*	Gamma	Percent of total sample (*n* = 3,018)
Parental sexual permissiveness						
Strict	38.5	39.1	22.4	1,064	−.36	35.3
Moderate	23.9	43.1	33.0	1,109	.04	36.7
Permissive	16.3	34.6	49.1	833	.38	27.6
Guilt over sex in childhood						
No	18.3	35.9	45.8	889	.31	29.5
Yes	30.6	40.8	28.6	2,117	−.31	70.1
Extent of lifetime sexual environment						
Narrow	39.6	42.7	17.6	1,044	−.44	33.3
Medium	25.9	39.4	34.7	907	.03	30.1
Broad	16.3	36.2	47.6	1,095	.40	36.3
Positive feelings recalled about premarital sex						
Few or none	41.1	38.2	20.7	871	−.39	28.9
Some	18.4	40.5	41.1	696	.22	23.1
Many	13.2	39.2	47.5	953	.42	31.6
Negative feelings recalled about premarital sex						
Few or none	16.4	39.6	44.0	671	.28	22.2
Some or many	27.1	39.1	33.7	1,849	−.00	61.3
Respondent a sexual person						
No	37.8	41.2	21.0	900	−.35	29.8
Yes	22.4	38.5	39.1	2,106	.35	69.8
Feels threatened in heterosexual relationships						
Very little or not at all	16.7	33.2	50.1	861	.39	28.5
Somewhat	23.8	40.1	36.1	1,075	.09	35.6
A great deal	38.4	43.5	18.1	1,070	−.43	35.5

NOTE. The criterion for selection is a difference of at least 10 percentage points in any one of these three SMS categories between the given population category and the total sample. Where applicable, residual percentages are also given. Base *n*'s in the various parts of the table do not add up to the total-sample figure of 3,018 because 12 respondents did not answer one or more of the items in the SMS and others were noncodable with respect to certain independent variables.

On the other hand, when we look at current devoutness,[14] we find that respondents with a high level of devoutness were much less liberal than those low in devoutness (Table 3-8). Indeed, current religious devoutness is the most powerful of all our final-stage variables. Controlling for age and gender does not affect this finding, but controlling for respondent's education and socioeconomic status shows that social status plays an important role in the relationship. The higher the respondent's education level and social class, the greater the relationship between current devoutness and moral stance.[15] This is especially pronounced in the case of those with college degrees, where a gamma of −.77 obtains.

Presumably, being a devout adult implies chosen adherence to traditionally stringent, religiously based moral values, while the level of childhood devoutness is less important because it is susceptible to change by intervening influences such as education. So, given that religious devoutness operates to maintain conservative sexual standards, we compared current with childhood levels.[16] Table 3-8 shows that a great decrease from childhood to current devoutness is connected with more liberal current norms. (For smaller decreases in devoutness the relationship is weaker. People who reported being *more* devout than their parents approximated total-sample distributions in their SMS scores; this group comprised some 43% of the sample.)

Parents' Generation. A strong relationship is found between parental generation[17] and sexual norms. Respondents whose parents came from earlier generations were much more conservative than those with younger parents (Table 3-7). This apparently reflects a sexual socialization more restrictive in content and delivery among earlier parental generations, representing in turn more generally restrictive sexual norms. Controlling for age of respondent, however, greatly reduces the relationship (for those under 35, gamma = .08; for ages 35–64, gamma = .15; for 65 or older, gamma = .08), suggesting that a life-cycle as well as a generational effect is in operation.

Parents' Socioeconomic Status. Respecting parental social class, we find that respondents from a higher-status background were more liberal than the rest (Table 3-7). The negative gamma for lower and middle parental socioeconomic status reflects the fact that although percentage differences are small, those respondents whose parents came from the middle stratum of society actually held the least liberal norms. (The result for respondent's own social class is weaker still, suggesting again a lifelong socialization effect; the correlation between parent and respondent socioeconomic status is .34). Controlling for parental education, we see that the relationship between parents' social class and the SMS is weakest among those whose parents had the highest level of education, stronger for those with less-educated parents. (For those with parents of less than eighth-grade education, gamma = .25; for those whose parents completed high school, gamma = .13.) This anticipates the following subsection by showing that parental education had a direct effect on respondents' norms, as well as working on those norms indirectly through parents' occupational status.

Because socioeconomic status and educational level are closely linked, the effects of parent-respondent differences on both these variables are discussed together in the following subsection.

Parents' Education. We find (Table 3-7) that the amount of education parents received has a clear effect on moral stance: the more educated the respondent's parents, the more liberal the respondent's norms. This finding, as could be expected from the analysis of single items, is replicated when we examine the respondent's own educational level. That the parents' group here consists of college graduates whereas the respondents' group includes people with any college experience may suggest that the effects of education are stronger in younger generations. (The gamma between parent and respondent education is .45.) Thus, not only do more-educated parents tend to foster liberal norms in their children, but greater participation in the educational process is liberalizing in itself as well.

Age and gender were introduced as controls for respondents' education. Gender does not produce any effects, but age does, with the relationship between education and the SMS disappearing among the oldest respondents. (For those under 35, gamma = .22; for 35–64, gamma = .21; for 65 or older, gamma = −.02).

We next examine the effect of changes in social status, as measured by respondents' education[18] and social position[19] compared with that of their parents. Since we know that education and the SMS are related, it is surprising to note little liberal increase among respondents with more education than their parents; even those at the level of greatest increase over their parents were not notably more liberal (41%, compared with 34% for the total sample). In comparing parents' and respondents' socioeconomic status, we find a similar trend, but it is weaker still. Presumably respondents who changed along these dimensions were less influenced by upwardly mobile referents than by values learned in childhood.

Parents' Attitudes. In addition to the foregoing sociological factors, we also find that parental attitudes and ensuing parent-child interaction influenced respondents' sexual norms. Those who reported that their fathers were not very serious and moral toward sex[20] were somewhat less likely to be conservative in their present sexual standards, although the relationship does not meet our 10% criterion. More notably, those respondents who said they were serious and moral about sex themselves[21] were less liberal than those who said they were not very serious and moral (Table 3-8); controlling for age and gender does not affect these findings. Like several of the preceding background-versus-current comparisons, this latter relationship is more pronounced, although its childhood roots are clear: the correlation between father serious and moral and respondent serious and moral is a substantial .50. Apparently a less liberal view of sex on the part of the father influenced the respondent and consequently generated less tolerance for unconventional kinds of sexual activity.

The relative importance of the father is seen again in a finding which, like that above, does not appear for the mother. Respondents who recalled their fathers as warm and loving[22] were more likely to hold liberal sexual norms than those whose fathers were described as more detached and hostile (Table 3-8). The father's salience on these measures could be a reflection of traditional family structure, wherein socialization is generally a matter of the mother's teaching children to uphold the father's moral standards.

We also considered how sexually permissive the respondent's parents were.[23] Respondents from relatively permissive families were much more likely to be sexually liberal than were those whose parents were relatively strict (Table 3-8). Once again the father appears to have been more important: the correlation between father strict and the SMS is .36, while that for mother strict is .31. To test for the effects of class differences in child rearing (see Kohn, 1969), we controlled this relationship for parental socioeconomic status and education, but the results remain unchanged, although the relationship is stronger for those from higher-status backgrounds (e.g., for low or middle parent socioeconomic status, gamma = .30; for upper parent SES, gamma = .47).

All the preceding findings might also be affected by the gender of the respondent. Thus we ran father serious and moral, father loving/hostile, parental sexual permissiveness, father strict, and mother strict against the SMS, this time controlling for gender. Again our results are unaffected. Finally, introducing age, parental generation, and parental religious devoutness (see note 16) as controls produces no effects.

Childhood Socialization (Stage 2) Variables

Childhood Sex Play. The findings that appear in this section have mainly to do with early sexual experiences, and the first is that respondents who frequently engaged in sex play with other children[24] were more likely to be liberal in their current sexual norms (Table 3-9). Early sexual experience apparently promotes a greater acceptance of various sexual behaviors in later life. We ran these data while holding constant age, gender, and parental

TABLE 3-9 Percent in Selected Behavioral Categories Scoring Conservative, Moderate, or Liberal on the SMS

	Percent conservative (1–2)	Percent moderate (3–4)	Percent liberal (5–6)	Base *n*	Gamma	Percent of total sample ($n = 3{,}018$)
Total sample	27.0	39.3	33.7	3,006	–	99.6
Childhood sex play						
Little or none	30.8	42.1	37.1	2,251	−.43	74.6
A great deal	15.6	31.1	53.2	755	.43	25.0
Age at first masturbation						
Under 13	17.1	32.5	50.4	557	.35	18.5
13 to 17	17.6	38.3	44.0	806	.28	26.7
18 or older	24.7	39.7	35.6	219	.05	7.3
Never masturbated	37.6	42.2	20.2	1,114	−.26	36.9
Age at first heterosexual experience[a]						
Under 13	15.4	36.5	48.1	104	.29	3.4
13 to 17	16.2	41.2	42.6	1,087	.32	36.0
18 to 21	29.4	38.7	31.8	1,046	−.07	34.7
22 or older	42.5	37.3	20.1	616	−.37	20.4
Premarital sexual involvement[a]						
Little or none	44.9	38.5	16.6	1,101	−.55	36.5
Some	24.8	44.3	30.9	839	−.01	27.8
A great deal	10.2	36.2	53.6	1,066	.57	35.3
Had premarital sex[a]						
No	43.6	38.7	17.7	1,168	−.53	38.7
Yes	16.4	39.7	43.9	1,838	.53	60.9
Frequency of premarital sex[a]						
Rarely or never	37.9	40.5	21.6	1,605	−.50	53.2
Occasionally	15.4	37.7	46.9	657	.33	21.8
Often	6.5	37.0	56.5	524	.55	17.4

NOTE. The criterion for selection is a difference of at least 10 percentage points in any one of these three SMS categories between the given population category and the total sample. Where applicable, residual percentages are also given. Base *n*'s in the various parts of the table do not add up to the total-sample figure of 3,018 because 12 respondents did not answer one or more of the items in the SMS and others were noncodable with respect to certain independent variables.

[a] Not necessarily coitus (see text).

socioeconomic status, education, and sexual permissiveness; but only age has an effect: the strength of the relationship between childhood sex play and the SMS is reduced for respondents aged 45 or more. (For respondents under 30, gamma = .37; for 30–44, gamma = .37; for 45 or older, gamma = .25). It is possible that this reflects a generational effect for the older group that is stronger than the effects of experience.

Age at First Sexual Experience. In addition to the frequency of childhood sexual experiences, the age at which they began is important. Thus, Table 3-9 shows that more liberal norms are found among respondents who experienced early masturbation and had early heterosexual experience involving orgasm (not necessarily coitus). These findings were controlled for age, gender, and parental socioeconomic status. Only gender has an effect, with the strength of the relationship between the SMS and age at first heterosexual experience being halved for females. (For males, gamma = −.43; for females, gamma = −.19.)

Childhood Sex Guilt. A relationship appears between childhood sex guilt[25] and the SMS. Respondents who felt guilty over sex in childhood were less liberal than those who felt no such guilt, regardless of whether they actually had sexual experiences at that time (Table 3-8). Controlling for gender does not affect these findings, but controlling for age does: the relationship between childhood sex guilt and current norms almost disappears among respondents aged 65 or older. (For those under 35, gamma = .26; for 35–64, gamma = .29; for 65 or older, gamma = .04.) Again we posit a generational effect.

Lifetime Sexual Environment. Table 3-8 shows that respondents with what we call a broad sexual environment[26]—those who said they had personally known people who engaged in a variety of sexual behaviors—were more liberal than those who had not had such contact. This variable is placed in the early socialization stage because awareness of others' sexual behavior can be a lifetime process, even preceding one's own sexual maturity. Thus, it could be that in the extreme case, a child who is aware of others' participation in premarital, extramarital, or homosexual sex could come to accept these behaviors as an ordinary part of life more readily than a child without such awareness. Then, in adolescence, peers often discuss their own, their parents', and other adults' sexual activities. Further, the extent to which an adult has friends or acquaintances involved in these behaviors is probably a function of early socialization.

Our finding that a broad sexual environment predisposes liberal scores on the SMS is not affected when gender is held constant, but it decreases sharply among respondents aged 65 or older and those who said they were religiously devout (e.g., for low devoutness, gamma = .42; for moderate devoutness, gamma = .40; for high devoutness, gamma = .18). Thus, for example, if people are highly devout, the sexuality of their perceived environment does not seem to play as strong a role in determining their current sexual norms.

Later Socialization (Stage 3) Variables

Premarital Sexual Experiences. This stage, which includes experiences during adolescence and early adulthood, is dominated by premarital sexual behaviors and the feelings surrounding them. Those who scored high on our premarital sexual involvement factor[27] were much more likely to hold liberal sexual norms than were respondents with negligible involvement (Table 3-9). Almost as strong are relationships involving those with some kind of premarital genital contact compared with those who did not have it, and the relative frequency of such premarital sex among those reporting it.

Feelings About Premarital Sex. Because we felt that norms regarding premarital sex might not be unidimensional, we also employed two measures separately assessing positive feelings[28] and negative feelings[29] about premarital sex that the respondent recalled from before marriage, regardless of whether he or she had premarital sexual experience. Those who scored high on the positive measure were more likely to hold liberal sexual norms than were those who reported few positive feelings (Table 3-8). Similarly, those who expressed many negative feelings were less likely to hold liberal standards than were those with low negative scores. The latter relationship, however, is much less pronounced, suggesting that positive and negative feelings toward premarital sex do indeed belong on separate continua.

The above premarital variables were run against the SMS controlling for age, race, gender, and parental sexual permissiveness. For older respondents, there is a marked and consistent reduction in the relationships between the SMS and premarital involvement, having had premarital sex, and having felt positive toward it. (For premarital sexual involvement: under 35, gamma = .50; 35–64, gamma = .50; 65 or older, gamma = .39. For premarital sex: under 35, gamma = .52; 35–64, gamma = .51; 65 or older, gamma = .38. For positive feelings: under 35, gamma = .32; 35–64, gamma = .33; 65 or older, gamma = .26.) That is, such feelings and experiences had less of a liberalizing effect in older generations.

In the case of race, for blacks the relationships are reduced between the SMS and premarital sexual involvement, frequency of premarital sex, and feeling positive toward premarital sex. (For premarital involvement: whites, gamma = .53; blacks, gamma = .34. For sexual frequency: whites, gamma = .50; blacks, gamma = .37. For positive feelings: whites, gamma = .37; blacks, gamma = .14.) This seems to be linked with blacks' somewhat greater tolerance for premarital sexual activity. Evidently the experience of premarital sex among blacks is less important in the determination of their later norms than it is for whites.

None of the above results is affected by controlling for gender or parental permissiveness, which shows that the effect of premarital sexual experiences on current sexual norms is the same for both sexes and for those from either restrictive or liberal family backgrounds.

Currently Influential (Stage 4) Variables

A number of these variables describing respondents' current situations influence the determination of sexual norms. Some of them,[30] and the effects of lifetime changes in them, have been presented earlier. We will now enumerate the other influential variables in this stage.[31]

Age. A very clear relationship obtains for age, as we might expect from the analysis of the single items: the older respondents were, the more sexually conservative were their norms (Table 3-7). Conversely, we find that younger respondents were more liberal.

Holding constant gender, race, and education does not affect these findings. One variable that does, however, is whether the respondent had dependent children under the age of 20: the relationship between age and sexual norms holds more strongly among those who did *not* have such parental responsibility. (For those with young children, gamma = −.21; for those without them, gamma = −.35.) Moreover, when we inspect some of the individual items, we find this specification especially pronounced with regard to teenage girls having premarital sex without love (for those with young children, gamma = −.21; for those without them, gamma = −.61) and to homosexuality. (For homosexuality without affection: parental responsibility gamma = −.06, no responsibility gamma = −.52; for homosexuality with affection, parental responsibility gamma = −.11, no responsibility gamma = −.50.) Thus the effects of age are modified by whether one has parental responsibilities.

This seems to suggest that when parental responsibility is absent, the effects of age—maturational and generational—are at their most powerful. Lacking children to care for, the older person is more apt to be concerned with the interests of his or her own age group and to be out of touch with the world of the young. Such persons being older, too, are subject to the conservative influences of older generations. Conversely, the young who do not have children are free of entangling responsibilities and subject to the liberalizing influences of similarly situated peers as well as current generational influences. These results are not consistent with Reiss's (1967, 1968) research on premarital sexual permissiveness. He explained his similar age findings in terms of the role position of the parent, who feels responsible for the consequences of his or her children's sexual activity, rather than in terms of generational effects. If this is true, we would expect the relationship between age and the SMS to disappear when parental responsibility is introduced as a third variable. Instead, we obtain the above specification. The difference is probably due to the concentration on premarital sex in Reiss's study, compared to the wider range of norms in ours. We would thus assume that parental responsibility, age, and maturational factors can have different effects on different norms.

Gender. Our data show females to be somewhat more sexually conservative in their moralities than males, as we might anticipate; although neither gender differs appreciably from total-sample figures, the relationship bears a gamma of −.22 with, for example, 28% of the women but 40% of the men scoring in the liberal group. This may reflect traditional sex-role differences: before marriage, it is the female who takes responsibility for the extent of a couple's sexual behaviors, and in parenthood it is she primarily who socializes the children even though, as we have shown, the father strongly determines the content of socialization. It should be reiterated that this relationship is weak, but it persists regardless of age, race, or education. In fact, this simple bivariate look at gender masks some meaningful complexities that emerge in later multivariate findings.

Race. We find that whites are likely to be more sexually conservative than blacks, with little difference apparent between the races in liberal norms (Table 3-7). However, the overall SMS measure masks some interesting findings, as shown in Chapter 2. For example, we found there that with regard to prostitution and masturbation, blacks are slightly more likely than whites to be *disapproving*. On the other hand, blacks are much more likely than whites to be permissive toward heterosexual behaviors involving love (regardless of the age or gender of those involved). These findings remain when age, gender, and socioeconomic status are controlled. Controlling for education, however, produces a specification of our findings, especially for premarital sex (Table 3-10). Among those respondents who did not finish high school, blacks were much more permissive toward these behaviors than whites were. Racial differences in sexual morality thus seem more pronounced within what has been called the "black underclass," whereas more-educated blacks seem closer to more conservative white middle-class sexual norms.

Marital Status. As we found earlier, the widowed are most likely to be conservative regarding sex, and single people (i.e., never married) are the least so (Table 3-7); similarly, never-married people are the most liberal, and the widowed are the least so. Married and divorced or separated people fall in between these two categories.[32]

Substantially the same results are found when gender is introduced as a control—males in all categories still appear more liberal than females—although there is less difference between single and divorced-separated men than there is for similarly situated women. Age is an obvious control variable but presents certain difficulties; for example, there are few widows among younger age groups. (In our sample of 3,018 there were only 19 widows under age 45.) Looking at the results for those under 45, we find that the single people were the most liberal, but not much more so than the younger

TABLE 3-10 Percent Responding "Not Always Wrong" to Selected Sexual Behaviors, by Education and Race

Activity	11th grade or less			12th grade or more			Total Sample
	White	Black	Gamma	White	Black	Gamma	
Prostitution	9.4%	6.9%	−.18	12.4%	16.8%	.03	11.2%
Premarital sex by teenage boy, not in love	6.8	10.8	.06	9.3	22.2	.15	9.5
Premarital sex by teenage boy, in love	17.0	48.8	.47	19.0	39.1	.28	22.5
Premarital sex by adult man, not in love	12.3	15.2	.12	17.9	32.8	.19	16.8
Premarital sex by adult man, in love	23.0	59.7	.55	32.6	54.5	.34	33.6
Premarital sex by teenage girl, not in love	4.0	8.0	.24	4.9	18.9	.10	5.8
Premarital sex by teenage girl, in love	12.5	42.4	.48	15.8	38.7	.31	18.8
Premarital sex by adult woman, not in love	9.0	14.5	.24	14.9	28.0	.17	13.8
Premarital sex by adult woman, in love	21.2	55.0	.51	29.5	51.6	.36	30.7
Extramarital sex	1.6	3.4	.31	1.5	8.6	.20	2.2
Homosexuality without affection	3.8	3.1	−.08	6.6	13.3	.05	5.8
Homosexuality with affection	7.9	10.6	−.01	13.1	21.7	.05	11.8
Masturbation	12.7	14.2	.04	23.7	26.4	−.03	19.5
Base *n*	964	290		1,554	185		2,993

widows. Of course, the small *N* for the widows makes interpretation of these results difficult. On the other hand, there were few never-married people among our respondents aged 45 and older—only 51 in all. Responses of these older single people do not stand out in any special way, although they are more conservative than those of any other group except the widowed. Again, the small *N* precludes a conclusive interpretation. Tentatively, however, we would suggest that age does play an important role in understanding the relationship between marital status and moral stance, but it is hard to illustrate in three-variable analysis.

Social Psychological Variables. Another group of findings involving final-stage variables are of a social psychological nature. For example, respondents who viewed themselves as being "a sexual person" were more liberal than those who did not (Table 3-8). This finding is not affected when age and gender are controlled. In addition, persons who scored high on our composite measure of feeling sexually threatened by the opposite sex[33] tended to hold more conservative norms than those who said they felt little or no threat. This finding also holds regardless of age or gender. However, when the respondents's education is introduced, we find the relationship increasing in strength. (For those with less than a high school education, gamma = .29; for high school graduation or some college, gamma = .31; for college graduation and above, gamma = .40.) So, too, do we find a change in the relationship when current religious devoutness is controlled, with a decrease in strength among the most devout. (For low devoutness, gamma = .40; for moderate devoutness, gamma = .35; for high devoutness, gamma = .24.) It appears, then, that among the more educated and less devout, feeling threatened by the opposite sex is more of an influence on their sexual norms. As these groups are generally high in their liberalism, we could speculate that this finding reflects an ambivalence toward attempts to alter traditional gender roles, which can be particularly pronounced in these segments of society.

Summary

This chapter has identified variables that appear to have been preliminary determinants of our respondents' sexual norms as reflected in our general measure, the Sexual Morality Scale or SMS.

Our findings reveal the striking fact that many variables were currently influencing our respondents just as they apparently did in childhood. Thus, most Americans at the time of our study still lived in the geographic region where they grew up, resided in the same sized community, and were affiliated with the same religion. That is not to say that change may not occur, but for change in these characteristics to be powerful enough to alter sexual norms it must be dramatic indeed—such as abandoning one's childhood religious affiliation in favor of none at all.

These continuing childhood influences, whether they be structural or social psychological (e.g., parental attitudes), emphasize the *persistence* of socialization effects, which often are undervalued in the face of current social changes that have been assumed to override them. Cultural continuity may not be as exciting a notion as sexual revolution, but it certainly seems to be a more accurate picture of events. We simply do not find evidence that in 1970 recent societal events had brought about a sweeping liberalization of public moralities. Even among the population groups we have identified as unusually liberal, about one in six people, on the average, held quite conservative norms.

These background influences do not go unchallenged, of course. Although they appear from our data to have lifelong effects in determining sexual standards, one type of variable especially seems to mitigate them—early and frequent sexual experiences. Thus respondents who had participated in childhood sex play, adolescent sexual activities, and frequent premarital sex, and who had been subject to a broad sexual environment, tended to hold more liberal sexual norms. This statement is more true for younger than for older respondents, suggesting (a) that generational effects might outweigh sexual experiences in the determination of sexual morality among the older generation and (b) that any liberalizing effects on the sexual norms of the younger generation will still take a long time to emerge.

NOTES

1. The logic of this approach was similarly explained by Empey and Lubeck (1971).

2. A coefficient of reproducibility of .92, for example, would mean that if one knew where each person scored along the scale, one could correctly predict for 92% of the people how each one scored on the items that made up the scale.
3. Of course, we could have elected to retain all the premarital sex items in an effort to replicate earlier research like Reiss's (1967), but we did not want to lose the opportunity to construct a more broadly based scale that would also have distinct points along it. "Always wrong" responses to the eight premarital sex items range from 33% to 68%, while the range encompassed by including masturbation (27% "always wrong") and homosexuality without affection (78%) is obviously greater.
4. Tables 3-1 and 3-3 show the marginal distributions for these items as well as the distribution of similar and dissimilar responses to them. Readers who are interested in the amount of data lost by combining adults and teenagers rather than males and females may wish to compare these marginals to see whether they would have decided as we did.
5. See Nunnally (1967), pp. 194–199.
6. As Reiss himself said in 1967 (10), "It should be apparent that it is necessary to begin research in the area of sexual relationships with the few *ad hoc* findings that are available and with hunches regarding what other factors are worth investigating."
7. Space limitations require that our data be presented in this abbreviated form.
8. This composite measure combines the variables childhood geographic region and current geographic region.
9. Reiss (1967) also found, in studying premarital sexual standards, that people from more-urban places and from more-liberal geographic regions are more permissive than others. These differences did not disappear when he controlled his urban/rural findings for region or when he controlled his regional findings for urbanization. He speculated that in urban areas, courtship styles are more autonomous and unmarried couples are subjected to less parental scrutiny or supervision, and that this urban style of courtship would be more prevalent in areas that are more heavily settled (such as the Northeast) and less common elsewhere (such as the South). Consequently, people accustomed to this courtship style would be more tolerant toward premarital sex.
10. This composite measure combines the variables urban/rural childhood community and urban/rural current community.
11. Controlling for gender, we find later-born respondents of both sexes to be less liberal; moreover, the relationship is much stronger for females. (For males, gamma = −.07; for females, gamma = −.20). Controlling for the respondent's education, the relationship between birth order and the SMS disappears among those who did not complete high school.
12. This composite measure combines the variables childhood Fundamentalist (a dummy variable) and current religious affiliation.
13. This composite measure combines the variables childhood religious affiliation and current affiliation. Although Jews were also liberal, all respondents who were currently Jewish had been reared as such, so this measure does not provide a category for change to Judaism.
14. This measure is a factor resulting from oblique rotation in which the constituent variables loaded in the following (descending) order: strength of current religious beliefs, current church attendance. A parallel factor for parental devoutness failed our criteria for inclusion here, but because it is constituted in the same way as current devoutness and could thus provide a sounder basis

for comparison, we used it in subsequent analyses instead of religious strength in childhood home. See note 16.

15. By comparison, Reiss (1967, 1968) found higher socioeconomic status to be associated with greater tolerance for premarital sex only in a liberal context, that is, among respondents who were also socially and politically liberal.
16. This composite measure combines the factors parental devoutness and current devoutness. Parental devoutness results from oblique rotation in which the constituent variables loaded in the following (descending) order: mother's church attendance, father's church attendance, strength of religious beliefs in childhood home.
17. This composite measure combines the variables father's age at respondent's birth and respondent's current age. (Where father's age was unknown, mother's age was substituted.)
18. This composite measure combines the variables education completed by main earner in respondent's childhood home (i.e., parental education) and education completed by respondent. Marginal distributions allow for 7 degrees of increase over parents' education, as follows: less education than parents, 12.7%; same amount, 20.4%; one category higher, 19.6%; two categories higher, 20.0%; three categories higher, 16.4%; four to seven categories higher, 10.9% (base $n = 2{,}833$).
19. This composite measure combines the variables parental socioeconomic status and respondent's socioeconomic status. Marginal distributions allow for 7 degrees of increase over parents' status: lower socioeconomic status than parents, 35.4%; same level, 23.5%; one category higher, 12.4%; two categories higher, 10.1%; three or four categories higher, 13.2%; five to seven categories higher, 5.3% (base $n = 2{,}954$).
20. This measure is a factor resulting from oblique rotation in which the constituent variables loaded in the following (descending) order: father serious about sex, father moral about sex. A parallel factor, mother serious and moral, proved less important.
21. This measure is a factor resulting from oblique rotation in which the constituent variables loaded in the following (descending) order: respondent serious about sex, respondent moral about sex.
22. This measure is a factor resulting from orthogonal equimax rotation in which the constituent variables loaded in the following (descending) order: father unreasonable/reasonable, father belittling/praising, father rejecting/accepting. A parallel factor, mother loving/hostile, failed our criteria for inclusion here.
23. This measure is a factor resulting from oblique rotation in which the constituent items loaded in the following (descending) order: mother strict in sexual matters, father strict in sexual matters.
24. This measure is a factor resulting from oblique rotation in which the constituent items loaded in the following (descending) order: no childhood sex play (a dummy variable), both homosexual and heterosexual childhood sex play, frequency of homosexual childhood sex play, frequency of heterosexual childhood sex play.
25. This measure is a factor resulting from oblique rotation in which the constituent items loaded in the following (descending) order: guilt over heterosexual sex play (a dummy variable), guilt over homosexual sex play (a dummy variable), mother punished heterosexual sex play.
26. This measure is a factor resulting from oblique rotation in which the constituent items loaded in the following (descending) order: number of women respondent has known to be involved in extramarital sex, number of men

likewise, number of women respondent has known to be involved in premarital sex, number of men likewise, number of men respondent has known to be involved in homosexual sex, number of women likewise.

27. This measure is a factor resulting from oblique rotation in which the constituent items loaded in the following (descending) order: frequency of premarital sex (including noncoital activities leading to orgasm), never had such premarital sex (a dummy variable), number of invitations to premarital sex respondent made, age at first heterosexual experience (including noncoital activities and, if applicable, marital sex), positive feelings about premarital sex (see note 28), number of invitations to premarital sex respondent received, never masturbated (a dummy variable).
28. This composite measure combines the following variables concerning premarital feelings about premarital sex, whether actually experienced or just anticipated: pleased with the physical feeling, pleased to be wanted or needed this way, happy it showed/would show I had sex appeal, happy to have finally had a full sexual experience, pleased to have this special kind of relationship with someone.
29. This composite measure combines the following variables concerning premarital feelings about premarital sex, whether actually experienced or just anticipated: fear it would cause pregnancy; guilt, shame, or embarrassment; afraid of failure as a sexual partner; disappointed in the sexual experience; feeling of disgust or filth about sex.
30. Namely, geographic region, residence size, religious affiliation, religious devoutness, socioeconomic status, educational level, and feeling serious and moral about sex.
31. We chose to treat age, sex, and race as variables currently operating on the respondent even though they are "ascribed" statuses operating throughout a person's life. In the next chapter this is recognized in treating them as exogenous variables.
32. The same relationships were reported by Reiss (1967) for premarital sexual standards.
33. This measure is a factor resulting from oblique rotation in which the constituent variables loaded in the following (descending) order (questions were asked only about the opposite sex): women/men rob men/women of their dignity or self-respect in sexual relationships; men/women can expect to get hurt sooner or later when they get sexually involved with women/men.

Chapter 4

Accounting for Sexual Morality

The Use of Path Analysis

Chapter 3 examined the correlates of respondents' sexual norms by describing the zero-order relationships between our independent variables and the Sexual Morality Scale (SMS). In this chapter we move to a more comprehensive method, path analysis, in order to address the following questions: (a) Taken altogether, how much variability in sexual morality can our system of variables account for? (b) Which among our variables are the most powerful predictors of respondents' expressed current sexual norms when other variables have been taken into account? (c) Do some apparently strong variables cease to be effective when other influences are controlled? (d) Are some variables more important in their indirect effects than in their direct effects? (e) What causal sequences seem best to account for the acquisition and maintenance of sexual norms? Our analysis proceeded as follows.

First, 83 independent variables of interest were arranged according to where they seemed to fit best in the four temporal stages explained in Chapter 3 (Table 4-1). In the analysis for this chapter, we experimented somewhat with the temporal order of these variables, since strong arguments can be made for placing certain variables in more than one stage. The following results represent what we hypothesized to be the best placement. The findings to be presented must be viewed as conditional on the soundness of these temporal sequences.

Next, these variables were related by path analysis to the SMS. Here we present a general overview of this technique so that our data can be interpreted by the nontechnical reader.

TABLE 4-1. Independent Variables Considered for the Path Analysis

Stage 1: Exogenous influences
- Sex-female
- Race-black
- Age
- Parents' generation
- High parental SES
- Low parental SES
- Reared in Northeast
- Reared in Midwest-South
- Reared on Pacific coast
- Urban childhood
- Reared on farm
- Father sociable
- Mother sociable
- Father active-energetic
- Mother active-energetic
- Father masculine
- Mother masculine
- Father feminine
- Mother feminine
- Size of family of origin
- Older brother(s)
- Younger brother(s)
- Older sister(s)
- Younger sister(s)
- Parents' education
- Reared as Fundamentalist
- Reared as Catholic
- Reared as Jewish
- No childhood religion
- Parents' devoutness
- Parental sexual permissiveness
- Father a sexual person
- Mother a sexual person

Stage 2: Early socialization influences
- Father predictable
- Mother predictable
- Father freedom-giving
- Mother freedom-giving
- Father serious and moral about sex
- Mother serious and moral about sex
- Lifetime sexual environment
- Childhood sex play
- Punished for sex play
- Childhood sex guilt
- Prepubertal masturbation
- Prepubertal coitus
- Prepubertal family breakup
- Father loving
- Mother loving

Stage 3: Later socialization influences
- Pre-adult family breakup
- Education
- Time served in military
- Positive feelings about premarital sex
- Negative feelings about premarital sex
- Premarital sexual involvement
- Premarital sex before age 25
- Never masturbated
- Age at first marriage

Stage 4: Current influences
- Number of marriages
- Currently married
- Currently divorced or separated
- Never married
- Number of children
- Age of dependent son
- Age of dependent daughter
- Current high SES
- Current low SES
- Lives in Northeast
- Lives in Midwest/South
- Lives on Pacific Coast
- Current urban residence
- Currently farming
- Is sociable
- Is serious and moral about sex
- Is a sexual person
- Is masculine
- Is feminine
- Is work-oriented
- Currently Fundamentalist
- Currently Catholic
- Currently Jewish
- No current religion
- Current devoutness
- Feels sexually threatened

NOTE: These variables are essentially the same as the 70 listed in Table 3-6. For the most part, they differ only occasionally in stage location and in that here a dichotomized "dummy" variable may be entered for more than one of the categories of a categorical variable listed once in Table 3-6.

Path analysis is a multiple regression technique for estimating the causal relationships between variables. It cannot prove causality but estimates the magnitude of the *direct* and *indirect* effects of certain variables on certain others according to a causal, temporal ordering *hypothesized* by the researcher. (Alternative temporal hypotheses would yield other results.) Further, it is assumed that these effects are *recursive*, that is, that causality moves in one direction with no "feedback" effects, and that measures of effect are due to causation (e.g., *not* due to reverse causation or intercorrelated measurement error). Thus, although we use the word *causal* repeatedly in describing our results, the reader should remember that any causal inference rests on these assumptions; in other words, the findings are sound to the extent that these hypotheses of causality, temporal order, and measurement are near enough to reality.

Relationships (or paths) between variables are evaluated by a *path coefficient* (a standardized regression coefficient, or beta weight). The size of this coefficient is an estimate of the *net* degree of change in the dependent variable, in standard units, that would result from one standard deviation unit of change in the independent variable (the greater the coefficient, the greater the change). Each beta value therefore represents the relative amount of contribution of a variable after contributions of *all others* in the causal network are taken into account; that is, the contribution of other included variables is *controlled*.

Finally, we also obtain an overall multiple correlation coefficient R^2, which shows how well one can *predict* scores on one dependent variable by combining the predictive power of all the independent variables antecedent to it in the path analytic model. R^2, with a range of 0 to 1.00, then shows the *proportion* of the variance in the dependent variable accounted for by the operation of all these independent variables. The *residual* factor in the path analysis is calculated as $\sqrt{1-R^2}$. The residual path coefficient e represents the correlation between the given dependent variable and a hypothetical measure that would help "explain" all the variance in variable that the model does not account for. Thus, the larger the value of e, the less the model tells us about the causal antecedents of the variable (and e^2 represents the proportion of unexplained variance).

This procedure then yields, for all variables except those in the final (current) stage, two separate path coefficients, or betas (β).

The beta value between a given independent variable and the main dependent variable—here, the SMS—when *all other* variables in the system are taken into account, is termed the *direct effect*. The beta value between the same pair of variables when only the independent variables in the *same or preceding stages* are taken into account, is the independent variable's *total effects* upon the SMS. In the final stage, all other variables must necessarily be taken into account, so that for the variables in this stage, there is no difference between direct and total effects. For all other independent variables, the *difference* between direct and total effects is due to the net result of *indirect* effects—a summary measure of the ways in which a given independent variable influences the main dependent variable indirectly through its influence on subsequent-stage (i.e., intervening or mediating) independent variables.

A variable's total effects also are related to Pearson's product-moment zero-order correlation—here termed *total association*—between it and the dependent variable, in that differences between the two values occur because independent variables share causality (being intercorrelated) or because of effects of variables extraneous to the system. Accordingly this difference is called *extraneous effects*.

The first rank—earliest temporal stage—of predictor variables in a path model are called *exogenous variables*, because any determinants of these variables (if indeed there are any sociopsychologically meaningful determinants of such variables as region, place, or year of birth, or gender) are antecedents of—hence outside of, exogenous to—the entire system of predictors. Consequently, in the decomposition-of-effects scheme, exogenous variables will have no "extraneous effects," except those owing to how much exogenous variables may be intercorrelated, hence share in how they affect a dependent variable.

For our preliminary analysis, the various effects of our independent variables on the SMS were decomposed (Alwin & Hauser, 1975), with calculations for decomposition tables based on the above-described logic, expressed in the following arithmetic relationships:

$$\text{Total association } (r) = \text{total effects } (\beta_T) + \text{extraneous effects } (\beta_E)$$

$$\text{Total effects } (\beta_T) = \text{direct effect } (\beta_D) + \text{indirect effects } (\beta_I)$$

The arithmetic of this system is complicated because combinations of positive and negative relationships may be involved. For example, although a direct effect is either positive or negative, indirect effects may be composite of both positive and negative influences, the sum of which may have the same or a different algebraic sign from the direct effect; so a large positive direct effect but slightly larger (net) negative indirect effects would yield total effects appearing to be negligibly negative. Similarly, large positive total effects might be combined with strong negative extraneous effects, and thus with a small total association. Of course, when there are small extraneous effects, the total effects will approximate total association, and when indirect and extraneous effects are small, the direct effect will approximate both total effects and total association.[1]

Since we had a large number of independent variables to begin with, we decided that before beginning the actual path analysis, we should develop a method of reducing their number to a parsimonious set that could be studied in more detail. We therefore ran a multiple regression with the SMS as the sole dependent variable (rather than also taking intervening independent variables as dependent with respect to those in earlier stages, as in the internal structural equations of path analysis). Our aim was to see whether the weakest, thus least important, predictors could be dismissed from further consideration.

The multiple regression on the SMS using our initial 83 variables provided a multiple correlation R of .640 and an R^2 of .409, which means that about 41% of the variance of the SMS was accounted for statistically. We reported earlier a reliability alpha of .58 for the SMS. The square root of alpha (in this case about .76) estimates the correlation between actual scale scores and theoretical *true* scores; our alpha itself estimates that 58% of our SMS score variance is the result of the variance of a theoretically pure measure of an SMS without measurement error (Nunnally, 1967:196–197). Thus an analysis that accounted totally for true SMS scores could account for 58% of our SMS scores, and the R^2 value of .41 is about three-quarters of this .58 maximum possible value.

The following variables displayed the greatest total effects in this initial run: current devoutness, premarital sexual involvement, lifetime sexual environment, sex-female, parental sexual permissiveness, race-black, and childhood sex play. Thus, some of the bivariate relationships presented in Chapter 3 retain their strength when many other influences are controlled.

The Development and Application of Predictor-Winnowing Procedures

These initial efforts at path analytic strategy relied on early examples of sociological applications that had been done for purposes of simple or complex hypothesis testing, limited to data on less than a dozen—perhaps 6 or 8—predictors to begin with (Blalock, 1964; Duncan, 1966; Schoenherr & Greeley, 1974). The predictors analyzed in such strategies were likely to be selected for inclusion quite simply, solely on theoretical grounds and/or on the basis of cutting-point criterion strengths of coefficients measuring only their zero-order and direct-effect relationships to the dependent variable in question—e.g., ±.10 or .20. Given the exploratory, descriptive, atheoretical nature of our study, searching across such a broad range of simultaneously examined potential predictors, we did not have theoretical grounds for elimination. Furthermore, we immediately realized that with such a "single shot" procedure of screening out a number of potential predictors at once on the basis of a stringent uniform beta cutting point, this could have the immediate effect of heightening some and severely lessening some of the remaining betas.

This prompted two realizations. It might then seem necessary to eliminate those with such diminished betas and, among those already eliminated, there might have been some that would have gained sufficiently increased betas, when others were eliminated, to justify their retention. In addition, considerations of meaningful and substantial indirect effects seemed to demand the examination of such indirect values before elimination of potential predictors. However, before the appearance of the Alwin and Hauser publication on "decomposition of effects" (1975) we had not seen a method of arriving at summary net (±) values of indirect effects, nor the distinction to be made between contributions via indirect effects and via "spurious" or "extraneous" effects, without the necessity of a multiplicity of hand-calculated beta-value multiplications along all possible simple and complex paths to the dependent variable. Given four or five temporal stages, with a total of 83 potential predictors to be evaluated for inclusion/exclusion as they interacted with each other in their effects on the dependent variable, the task might not be as enormous as two to the 83rd power, but not sufficiently less than that to be a practical possibility.

With the appearance of the Alwin and Hauser "effects arithmetic" it became possible to devise a method of inclusion/exclusion of potential predictors in an objective manner that we and other researchers could replicate as precisely as desired. Alwin and Hauser's arithmetic of decomposition of effects offered a simplicity of effort that would bring two features of our ideal solution to the problem of including/excluding decisions among 80 to 100 potential predictors within the range of humanly manageable possibility: (1) With a five-stage model of predictors, only five multiple regression equations would provide all the beta values needed for applying cutting-point criteria of magnitude and/or significance level to all of the five values of every potential predictor, with overnight computer results: direct and total effects, hence also net indirect effects and extraneous effects, along with zero-order correlation. (2) With the ease of this operation, it became possible to "winnow" in gradual phases, several times over, as cautiously as desired. Starting with a very modest cutting-point criterion (e.g., $p < .001$, or a beta of about $\pm .045$), and the next day carrying out a winnowing phase with slightly higher criteria, we could in four or five days (three to five phases of incremental winnowing) arrive at all those predictors highly significant with betas of at least $\pm .10$. This kind of winnowing of potential predictors yields a descriptive objective summary of the "reality" of available variables not dependent upon prior theoretical biases or wisdom (which at any rate is not always readily available).

Winnowing Predictors of Sexual Morality

When we decomposed the effects of the 83 initial variables, it was clear that many of them were unimportant, either directly or indirectly. Our next step, therefore, was to eliminate systematically these unimportant variables by devising a screening procedure, using repeated regressions, until we achieved a more parsimonious system that could be subjected to path analysis. Our screening procedure was as follows:

1. From inspection of the results of the first regression, we determined that a conservative approach would be to keep only those variables with total effects of ±.045 or more, and/or direct or indirect effects of ±.07 or more. (This prevented dropping variables with small total effects caused by large countervailing direct and indirect effects, or those lacking sizable direct effects when they have substantial total effects.) We chose to start with these modest criteria based on the level at which our most important variables were operating. It should be noted that in a few instances, in this and succeeding steps, we left in for further evaluation variables that seemed theoretically important but barely failed our criteria for inclusion.

2. After this operation, we put the surviving variables through another multistage regression on the SMS and evaluated the new effects. This time we excluded those variables that did not have total effects of at least ±.07, except where either the direct or indirect effects were at least ±.07.

3. Finally, the same procedure was carried out a third time, this time excluding variables that did not have a total effect of ±.08 or more, except where either the direct or indirect effects were ±.07 or more.

The results of our procedure left us with a set of 16 variables that we can consider essential for explaining sexual norms. These variables provided an R of .600 and an R^2 of .360. Thus, the exclusion of 67 variables resulted in the loss of 5 percentage points, from .41 to .36, losing 12% of the .41 variance accounted for by the 83 variables. This is also equivalent to losing about 8% of the .58 level of maximum variance to be explained, given the reliability level of the SMS.

The beta values resulting from this regression show how each of the 16 independent variables affects the SMS if we allow each of them to have a path to every subsequent-stage variable in the model (including the SMS), regardless of how large or small these paths might be. Accordingly we call this "fully recursive" model the *total-path model*.

To examine the relationships among the 16 variables, and thus to suggest a causal explanation of the SMS, each of the 16 except those in the first stage was considered dependent in turn, using internal structural equations. This series of separate multiple regressions yielded R and R^2 and beta weights for all the variables in earlier stages, thereby showing how these earlier variables connect to intervening ones *regardless* of their direct effects on the SMS. Thus, the path analysis showed how the *indirect* effects of the different variables are generated. In developing this *path diagram model*, we eliminated those paths between variables that did not meet a $\beta \geq \pm .08$ criterion[2] and calculated total (direct + indirect) effects[3] on the basis of those paths that remained. We were thereby able to compare effects from this *path diagram model* with those of the *total-path model* in Table 4-2 to see how robust the former would be when many paths of lesser magnitude were eliminated.

In this way we arrived at a parsimonious model that isolates the most important variables in explaining sexual norms, demonstrates the most important relationships among predictors, and, through our temporal-stage arrangement, shows how these norms are acquired and maintained throughout a person's life.

We turn now to the detailed results involving the 16 variables in our system. First we discuss the most important predictors, using the total-path model as the basis of our conclusions.

The Relative Importance of Variables in the Total-Path Model

Stage 1 Variables

As ranked by total effects, age is the most important of our exogenous variables. Almost all of its effects are indirect; that is, its power works chiefly through its influence on subsequent (later-stage) variables. Its net correlation (total effects or total association) is a negative one: the older the respondents in our 1970 study the more conservative their sexual norms. In addition, only 24% of its total association with the SMS is extraneous.

Next in importance is parental sexual permissiveness, with effects split equally between direct and indirect, although some 41% of its total association is extraneous—thus, the more permissive the parent, the more liberal the respondent.[4]

The third strongest variable is sex-female. Here it should be noted that a strong positive direct effect and large negative indirect effects counteract each other in the determination of total effects. Thus, while gender directly affects sexual attitudes according to our analysis (showing females to be more liberal than males, all other variables being equal), there is an even stronger negative indirect effect attached to being female through other variables that themselves strongly influence the SMS. Hence the net result, which in total effects shows females to be more conservative than males.

Next in this stage are two variables that are somewhat interrelated: urban childhood and reared in Midwest-South. They are of similar magnitude, although of the latter's total effects, 78% are direct rather than indirect. So in our analysis, coming from a rural background produces conservative sexual norms directly, and it does so indirectly and equally through the way it relates to other experiences. On the other hand, being reared in the Midwest or Deep South leads directly to conservative standards that are relatively unaffected by subsequent variables. Of the total association of these two exogenous variables with the SMS, about half is extraneous.

Our analysis also shows that race-black displays roughly equal direct and indirect positive effects. However, its positive total effects are combined with negative extraneous effects to yield a total association *smaller* than the total effects. Thus, whites' conservatism is more pronounced—as revealed by the size of the total effects—than it would appear to be if one looked only at the zero-order correlation.

Two variables remain in this stage. Being reared as a Fundamentalist Protestant is shown to produce conservative norms, mainly in a direct way (73% of its total effects are direct); 26% of this variable's total association with the SMS is extraneous. Having had devout parents also leads to conservatism, although in this case the influence is mainly indirect: in our analysis parental devoutness has essentially no direct effect but large negative indirect effects, mostly mediated by offspring's continuing devoutness, and some 45% of its total association is extraneous.

Stage 2 Variables

The two variables that make up our second stage are both very powerful in our total set. Lifetime sexual environment is our third most powerful variable overall, with a strong positive direct effect. Growing up in awareness of others' sexual activities is thus shown to lead directly to later holding liberal sexual norms. Some 62%

of this variable's total effects, however, are indirect; such an environment strongly exposes a person to further liberalizing experiences, which in turn affect sexual norms. About 38% of the total association between sexual environment and the SMS is extraneous.

Childhood sex play is the fifth most powerful variable overall, operating mainly directly (two-thirds of its total effects are direct). That is, having experienced sex play as a child liberalizes the sexual norms one holds in adulthood. Thirty-six percent of the total association between childhood sex play and the SMS is extraneous.

Stage 3 Variables

The strongest variable in this stage—premarital sexual involvement—is also the most powerful overall. Some two-thirds of its effects are direct and positive. (It should be remembered that the more advanced the temporal stage, the less the opportunity for variables in that stage to have indirect effects mediated by subsequent variables.) Thus, in our analysis, the more a person is involved in premarital sexual activity, the more likely the person is to develop liberal sexual norms. Premarital sexual involvement also has the largest total association of all our variables, although about 52% of it is extraneous.

Next in importance in this stage is having positive feelings about premarital sex, regardless of whether one has engaged in it. Again, the effects are mainly direct (79%) and positive. This variable also has a substantial total association with the SMS, but almost 65% of it is extraneous. Having felt positively about premarital sexual experiences thereby predisposes one to later accept liberal sexual norms.

The final variable in this stage—whether a person has ever masturbated—is one of our weakest. Ninety-three percent of its effects are direct—according to our analysis, persons who have never masturbated are most likely to be conservative in their sexual norms—and 63% of its total association with the SMS is extraneous.

Stage 4 Variables

Our method of analysis affects final-stage variables in two ways. First, placement of any variable in the final stage means by definition that no other variable can intervene between it and the SMS; hence, there will be no indirect effects. Second, the absence of indirect effects in turn means that the difference between total association and direct effects will be due entirely to extraneous effects, so that variables in this stage will display comparatively large proportions of extraneous effects.

Current devoutness is the most powerful variable in this stage, with the second greatest total effects of all our variables. Its strong negative effect shows that religiously devout persons tend to hold conservative sexual norms. Next in importance, although relatively low in overall importance among our variables, is feeling sexually threatened by the opposite sex: the more a person feels such threat, in our analysis, the more conservative are his or her norms. Finally, defining oneself as serious and moral about sex operates similarly. As expected, all three of these variables have substantial extraneous effects, amounting to 58% of the total association for feeling sexually threatened and around 50% for both current devoutness and serious and moral about sex.

At this point, then, we have isolated the most important among our total array of variables; we know that they are not spurious (i.e., cannot be explained away by other available variables); and we know that they can account for over a third of the variance in the SMS (or 60% of it, if allowing for reliability of the SMS). Our next task is to locate our set of variables within a causal network to show how they are most likely to relate to the SMS.[5]

Relationships Among Variables in the Path Diagram Model

Dropping Paths

The 83 variables with which we began represented 3,403 potential variable pairs. In the foregoing section we discussed the analysis that identified the 16 most important independent variables; but even this refined model implies 136 possible pairings (35 of which involve noncausal pairing within stages). This number is sizable enough that in assessing causal chains, it is still difficult to determine which relationships are most important.

Therefore we continued to simplify our model by dropping paths

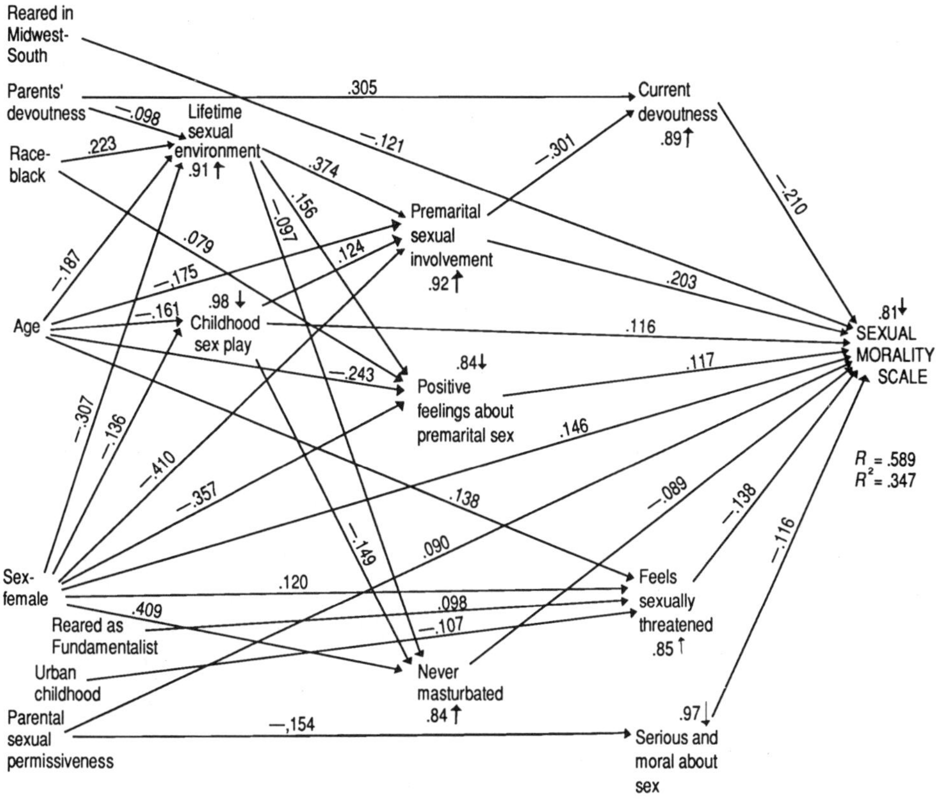

Figure 4-1 Path Diagram Model for the SMS
Note: Correlations among independent variables are given in Appendix E.

among predictors, as well as relative to the SMS, that proved insubstantial, and then examining the effects on the paths that remained. This time we used the exclusion criterion of $\beta \geq \pm .08$. This final exclusion process reduced the number of causal inferences to 35.[6] These variables provide an *R* of .589 and an R^2 of .347. Dropped paths account, therefore, for only about 1% of the variance. The resulting path diagram is shown in Figure 4-1.

Before discussing particular relationships, however, we needed to evaluate how nearly this path diagram model approximated our total-path model, which has all paths included. Therefore we calculated direct and indirect effects from the model in Figure 4-1 to compare them with the results using all paths. The comparison is presented in Table 4-2, with the path model diagram effects shown in italics.

Criteria have been suggested that allow the investigator to estimate how well two such models fit (see Mueller et al., 1977). This is fine for testing rigorous causal models. Our case, however, is a more inductive approach that allows for looser criteria and comparisons (e.g., ranking). Ranking the variables in the path diagram model by their total effects (Table 4-2) yields few important changes in the relative importance of variables. There are some of note, though. Sexual environment and urban childhood *decrease* in importance because the path diagram model does not allow for them to have direct effects (i.e., the direct path coefficient between these variables and the SMS is less than .08). In addition, the indirect effects of urban childhood diminish greatly. Parental permissiveness also decreases in importance through the loss of indirect effects, even though its direct effect has now in fact increased. On the other hand, feeling sexually threatened has *increased* in relative importance owing to an increased direct effect. Finally, although they change little in rank, both race-black and reared as Fundamentalist have lost much of their total effects, again owing to the path diagram model having eliminated their direct effects. Despite these changes, however, we feel satisfied that the model depicted in Figure 4-1 represents the most meaningful and parsimonious one our data can provide.

Even with the exclusion of weaker paths, the diagram looks complicated, because it simultaneously illustrates several separate relationships among different groups or clusters of variables, some of which operate in the direction of liberal standards and others in the direction of conservative standards. In the following sections we discuss each cluster separately in terms of the relationships among the variables it contains.

Influences Toward Liberal Sexual Norms

As we noted in Chapter 2, we found most of our respondents' norms to be stable and conservative. Concomitantly, most of the variables in our path diagram model are related to one another in ways that show how conservative values are acquired. Before passing to the description of these relationships, however, we now look at two variable clusters that illustrate the acquisition of *liberal* norms. These clusters of variables depict influences that our analysis shows

TABLE 4-2 Comparison of Effects in the Total-Path Model with Effects in the Path Diagram Model

Variable	Direct effect	Indirect effects	Total effects	Extraneous effects	Total association
Premarital sexual involvement	.147	.059	.206	.220	.426
	.203	*.085*	*.288*	*.138*	
Current devoutness	−.205	—	−.205	−.192	−.397
	−.210	—	*−.210*	*−.187*	
Lifetime sexual environment	.072	.117	.189	.116	.305
	—	*.135*	*.135*	*.170*	
Age	.040	−.213	−.173	−.057	−.230
	—	*−.146*	*−.146*	*−.084*	
Childhood sex play	.110	.055	.165	.092	.257
	.116	*.049*	*.165*	*.092*	
Parental sexual permissiveness	.080	.080	.160	.111	.271
	.090	*.018*	*.108*	*.163*	
Sex-female	.118	−.260	−.142	−.014	−.156
	.146	*−.277*	*−.131*	*−.025*	
Urban childhood	.067	.059	.126	.127	.253
	—	*.015*	*.015*	*.238*	
Reared in Midwest-South	−.096	−.027	−.123	−.083	−.206
	−.121	—	*−.121*	*−.085*	
Feels sexually threatened	−.123	—	−.123	−.188	−.311
	−.138	—	*−.138*	*−.173*	
Positive feelings about premarital sex	.097	.026	.123	.223	.346
	.117	—	*.117*	*.229*	
Race-black	.062	.053	.115	−.055	.060
	—	*.039*	*.039*	*.021*	
Is serious and moral about sex	−.110	—	−.110	−.123	−.233
	−.116	—	*−.116*	*−.117*	
Reared as Fundamentalist	−.074	−.027	−.101	−.035	−.136
	—	*−.013*	*−.013*	*−.123*	
Never masturbated	−.091	−.006	−.097	−.164	−.261
	−.089	—	*−.089*	*−.172*	
Parents' devoutness	.007	−.092	−.085	−.071	−.156
	—	*−.077*	*−.077*	*−.079*	

NOTE: Figures in the first row following each variable represent effects with all possible paths between variables. Figures in italics represent effects with only those paths surpassing exclusion criteria.

not only lead to people's holding more liberal standards; they also, by implication, are influences that the more conservative majority must have either avoided or resisted. It is interesting, therefore, that both of these groups of variables deal centrally with sexual experience—one in terms of behavior and the other in terms of feelings.

Sexual Behavior. This cluster of variables on the path diagram includes premarital sexual involvement, never masturbated, childhood sex play, and their antecedents.[7] This variable cluster shows that never having had the fairly common experience of masturbation tends to produce more conservative norms in an adult (and therefore, that having masturbated *lessens* the likelihood of conservatism); and it shows that the greater the extent of childhood sex play or premarital sexual involvement, the more liberal a person is likely to be. All three of these effects are represented by direct paths to the SMS, which means that they operate regardless of any later influences.

Three important ascribed variables—roles ascribed to cultural categories—are the basis for this cluster. For the first, age, our analysis shows that the older a person is, the less likely he or she is to have experienced childhood sex play, to have been exposed to a sexual environment, ever to have masturbated, or to have had much premarital sexual involvement or positive feelings about it. The absence of any of these both directly and indirectly fosters more conservative sexual norms. The relationship of age and the SMS through premarital sexual involvement alone represents 25% of age's indirect effects and that through childhood sex play 13%.[8]

The second ascribed variable, being female, has a similar pattern: females in our analysis are less likely than males to have engaged in childhood sex play or to have been exposed to a sexual environment. They are a *great deal* less likely to have masturbated or to have been involved in premarital sex or to have had positive feelings about it. Again, most of the indirect effects of sex-female (42%) are exercised through premarital sexual involvement, with paths through never masturbated accounting for 13% and through childhood sex play 6%. Thus, our finding is that those experiences and environmental characteristics that predispose toward liberal norms are much more common among males than females, with a resulting tendency for females to be much less sexually liberal than males. Again, we would point out that this negative effect of females' socialization overwhelms the tendency toward *greater* liberalism than males' that is shown in the positive direct effect of sex-female on the SMS.

Finally, the ascribed variable race-black in this group works solely through sexual environment and early positive feelings about premarital sex: blacks are more likely than whites to be exposed to such an environment and have such feelings, which leads indirectly to a more liberal set of sexual norms through increasing the probability of masturbation and premarital sexual involvement. The latter is the more important, however, accounting for 44% of the indirect effects of race.

Our interpretation of this cluster is that early exposure to and experiences with sexuality have a positive conditioning effect on people. They learn that sex exists, that it is pleasurable, and that any fears and apprehensions they might have had were likely exaggerated. This in turn can lead to their seeking out further sexual experiences. In sum, people with wider experience and knowledge of sex will be less likely to disapprove of or feel threatened by their own or others' sexuality.

Feelings About Sex. Complementary to the group of variables just described is one centered on the third variable in stage 3, positive feelings about premarital sex. This variable, as described in note 28 to Chapter 3, is a composite measure telling us the extent to which respondents recalled experiencing *as adolescents* various positive reactions or anticipatory feelings about premarital coitus (thus permitting both those with and those without the experience to score on the composite).[9] It is therefore contemporaneous with other early-adulthood variables and does not refer to how respondents currently rated the morality of premarital coitus.[10]

This group of variables includes many of the same measures as the "Sexual Behavior" cluster just discussed.[11] This similarity, together with the conceptual complementarity of behavior and feelings, suggests strongly that differential socialization processes engender differential feelings *and* behavior in youth, and that these feelings and behavior remain differentiated in adulthood. (We realize that in addition to socialization other factors—such as opportunity—may be influential, but we do not have data on these.)

This cluster shows that younger persons hold more liberal sexual norms than older persons, through the young's more positive evaluations of premarital sex, as the more one holds such positive feelings the more liberal are one's sexual values (19% of the indirect effects of age are transmitted this way). In addition, younger persons are more likely to be exposed to a sexual environment, which leads indirectly to more liberal sexual norms through increasing the probability of feeling positive toward premarital sex.

As regards gender, our analysis shows that females are much less likely than males to evaluate premarital sexual involvement positively, with paths involving positive feelings about premarital sex accounting for 15% of the indirect effects of sex-female.

In this cluster, race affects sexual norms only through positive feelings about premarital sex. Blacks are more likely than whites to have these feelings, which produces more liberal sexual norms. Some 23% of the indirect effects of race work this way. A causal chain from race to positive feelings is also evident through sexual environment, indicating that blacks have a more sexual environment than whites, which produces more positive feelings toward premarital sex, with consequent liberalizing effects on blacks' sexual norms. This connection, however, accounts for only 10% of the indirect effects of race.

We can therefore say that younger persons, blacks and especially males, evaluate premarital sex positively, which leads indirectly to their holding more liberal sexual norms. Blacks and males are groups more socialized toward premarital sexual experimentation and expression. Males are encouraged by their peers (and often male adults) to realize self-esteem through heterosexual exploits. Among blacks of both sexes, premarital sexual involvement is often tolerated, with parental cautions emphasizing discretion and selectivity rather than abstinence.

Other Variables. Some other independent variables express a connection with the SMS in a liberal direction. Urban childhood is one. Its sole path is a negative one to the fourth-stage variable sexually threatened. This connection tells us that the larger the town or city in which people grow up, the less likely they are to worry about being hurt or losing personal dignity in heterosexual relationships: so people with urban childhoods are indirectly more likely to be sexually liberal (and conversely, those from rural areas are more likely to feel sexually threatened and to be more conservative).

Also, having sexually permissive parents shows a liberalizing effect on adult norms. The less restrictive parents were about a respondent's sexual activity as a child, the less likely the respondent was to score high on our composite measure serious and moral about sex. This implies that less-restrictive parents raise children who, as adults, are less apt to invest sexuality with restrictive moral meanings. In addition, the direct path from parental permissiveness to the SMS shows that growing up with a comparatively liberal value system directly predisposes toward having similar values as an adult. These connections are not surprising; what does seem odd is that there is no path from parental permissiveness to either positive feelings about premarital sex or premarital sexual involvement. This may suggest that adolescents from permissive homes are *not* necessarily more likely than those strictly raised to positively evaluate or participate in premarital sex, either of which, according to our analysis, tends to liberalize adult norms.

Influences on Conservative Sexual Norms

We have already noted that, in keeping with most respondents' sexual norms being conservative, most of the relationships on our path diagram model show how conservative standards arise and persist. Inferentially, we have also surmised that conservative moral teachings are more likely to be revised in a liberal direction among those who have more extensive premarital sexual experience and/or who feel more positively toward it, as well as among those who by accident of birth belong to less restrictively socialized groups such as urban children, blacks, and males (as contrasted to rural people, whites, and females, respectively).

As pointed out, the diagram in Figure 4-1 shows ways in which such ascribed characteristics could be mitigated in their effect on a given person. For example, there is a negative path from the variable sex-female to childhood sex play and a positive one from the latter to SMS score. This means that females are less likely than males to have childhood sexual experience; it also means, however, that a female who nevertheless does pursue childhood sex play is subject to its influence toward liberal norms much as if she were male. We will now examine the ways in which, according to our analysis, more conservative norms are acquired and (at least implicitly) maintained. The underlying assumption is that since most respondents were quite conservative as adults, these influences operated without much interruption for many of them.

Religiosity. Four variables comprise the portion of the path diagram that involves the strength of religious beliefs (regardless of the particular religious affiliation).[12] Clearly this is very important in the determination of moral standards, and not unexpectedly so, given that religious devoutness popularly connotes moral conservatism. The diagram shows that respondents whose parents were highly religious were quite likely to be devout adults and thereby to hold conservative norms. In fact, current devoutness is the second strongest of all our predictors. In addition, a high level of parental devoutness leads to less awareness of the sexual environment, thence to less premarital sexual involvement. To complete the circle, premarital sexual involvement is negatively connected with current devoutness.

The effects of religiosity lie mainly in having had devout parents, who engendered current devoutness in the respondent, which in turn strongly affected sexual morality. Some 83% of the indirect effects of parental devoutness work through its influence on current devoutness. Having devout parents also is shown to reduce the probability of having an extensive sexual environment, which strongly predicts involvement in premarital sex, with both direct and indirect effects on sexual norms. The indirect effect of premarital sexual involvement, however, operates to *reduce* the influence of current devoutness, as noted earlier.

This variable cluster thus demonstrates the lasting effect of moral values and how those values operate to restrict exposure to various sexual knowledge and experiences. Further, it indicates that among those who do have premarital sexual experiences these values are weakened. Whether such people find that their religious views conflict with reality or that sexuality is more gratifying than morality, the result is a decrease in devoutness and a lessening of conservative sexual norms.

Age. The tendency for younger people to be less sexually conservative than older people is illustrated in another variable cluster.[13] The strongest indirect effects of age work through premarital sexual involvement (24% of these effects) and feeling positive about premarital sex (19%). Thus, our finding is that the older the respondent, the less the level of premarital involvement and positive feelings concerning it, and both circumstances strongly produce conservative sexual norms. Age also has other important indirect effects on sexual norms through its relationship with childhood sex play, the lack of which produces a tendency toward conservative sexual norms: the older the respondent in our study, the less likely childhood sex play was. This causal connection with the SMS accounts for 13% of the indirect effects of age. Lack of childhood sex play also is associated with lower levels of premarital sexual involvement. This chain of variables, however, accounts for only about 3% of the indirect effects of age. Far more important is the indirect effect of age through the variable feels sexually threatened: the older the respondent, the more likely he or she was to feel uneasy about heterosexual involvements and thereby to subscribe to conservative sexual norms. Since American sexual values have traditionally been conservative, it is not surprising that our older respondents were more apt to keep up this tradition. What this variable cluster tells us seems to be that it is adherence to traditional models of male-female relationships that contributes to traditional morality.

Gender. The role of gender as a key factor in differential socialization is illustrated by that portion of the path diagram connected with the variable sex-female, which shows how females are different from males in their experience of what we are calling liberalizing influences.[14] Thus, we see from the diagram that being female is related to less exposure to, or being shielded from, sexual experiences and environments that challenge adherence to conservative sexual norms. Chief among these relationships is a low level of premarital sexual involvement, which accounts for 30% of the indirect effects of being female, followed by *less* positive feelings about premarital sex, which accounts for 15%. Almost as important is never having masturbated, accounting for 13% of the indirect effects of being female. According to our analysis, females are also more likely than males to regard heterosexual sex as potentially degrading or harmful, but the connection between sex-female and feels sexually threatened involves only 6% of the indirect effects of gender. (The operation of the sex-threat variable is discussed more fully below.)

The findings here probably reflect the typical socialization of females in our culture. Compared with males, females are less likely to have masturbated and are less likely to have engaged in childhood or adolescent sexual experimentation (furthermore they report fewer positive feelings about such involvement whether or not they have experienced it). They are trained to comprehend their sexuality in terms of marriage and maternity; for example, explanations of menarche usually do not involve much sexual or contraceptive information. Believing that sexual activity is to be delayed until marriage, females tend to avoid obstacles to the prime goal of nuptial virginity (such as a tarnished reputation or an illegitimate child) by avoiding actual sexual experiences, with an accompanying conservative influence on their sexual norms.

Feeling Sexually Threatened. A final set of variables that mediate conservative influences are those that work through feeling sexually threatened by the opposite sex.[15] This variable, which denotes concern about being hurt or losing personal dignity in heterosexual relationships, directly produces conservative sexual norms. Variables that directly produce feelings of threat, in order of their importance, are being older, being female, having spent one's childhood in a rural area, and having been reared as a Fundamentalist. All these factors contain elements that could indeed lead to distrust of the opposite sex. For example, female socialization, with its discontinuity insofar as the *sexual* aspects of sexual relationships are concerned, can lead to unpreparedness and shock when faced with the realities of heterosexual relationships. The sex-role segregation that more typified older generations may have discouraged the type of intimate relationships in which a person could feel relaxed and secure. Finally, strong sex-role traditions are also characteristic of a rural or Fundamentalist upbringing. In addition, Fundamentalism teaches that woman is evil and responsible for man's fall from grace. In fact, the variables for rural and Fundamentalist upbringing operate in the model only through their connection with feels sexually threatened.

Other Variables. Our analysis shows that people raised in more conservative areas of the country—the Deep South or the Midwest, sometimes called the Bible Belt—are directly more likely to hold conservative sexual norms. Evidently the cultural effect of childhood region is lifelong regardless of anything else with which such an upbringing is associated. This can be seen clearly in two ways. First, there is no relationship between this variable and current devoutness. Having grown up in these parts of the country does not seem to have made respondents any more devout than those reared elsewhere. Second, there are no indirect paths through any of the sexual experience variables, suggesting that those who grew up in this region were not characterized by different sexual experiences than those reared elsewhere. Thus, if there are consequences of being from the Midwest or Deep South that indirectly influence sexual norms, they have not been captured by our path model.[16]

The final variable of note, being serious and moral about sex, also directly promotes conservative sexual norms. We might note that the size of the path coefficient (−.116) between the SMS and this variable would be much larger if "serious and moral" had invariably connoted "repressive" to our respondents. That it did not shows the existence of competing versions of what constitutes "morality" among the population.

Summary

In this chapter we have explored in more detail what influences the nature of sexual morality in the United States. Basically, the result of further analysis has been to confirm the evidence of the last chapter, at the same time permitting us to see how our 16 most important variables produce the effects that they do.

The path analytic techniques that we have used shows that some variables have direct effects on sexual norms; that is, they tend to bring about more conservative or more liberal morality regardless of the operation of any other variables in our model. Among these, by far the most powerful are being highly devout, which fosters conservatism, and having had considerable sexual experience before marriage, which leads to more liberal norms. The less powerful direct predictors of a conservative stance include having grown up in the South or Midwest, never having masturbated, feeling threatened in relations with the opposite sex, and describing oneself as serious and moral concerning sexual matters. Variables directly linked to liberal morality, in addition to premarital involvement, are having had sexually permissive parents, having had sex play in childhood, and having felt positively about premarital sex (through either anticipation or reaction) in youth. Of special interest in this regard is that being female also has a direct influence toward more liberal norms, but that the conservative influences of females' sexual socialization probably outweigh this effect.

Ten of the variables in our model also affect sexual norms indirectly by influencing other variables in subsequent stages of life, which in turn directly or indirectly affect people's norms. Six variables have only indirect effects: being older, having had religiously devout parents, and having been reared as a Fundamentalist Protestant indirectly produce more conservative norms; while being black, growing up in an urban area, and experiencing an open sexual environment as a child all lead toward more liberal norms. Among the rest, three—parental sexual permissiveness, childhood sex play, and premarital sexual involvement—have indirect effects of the same sign (i.e., positive-liberal) as their direct effect, so that the indirect effects enhance their intrinsic influence on sexual norms. The other one, being female, has—as mentioned—indirect effects that apparently overbalance the opposite-sign direct effect. The net result is that females, who are much less likely than males to be characterized by the sexual-experience variables that lead to more liberal values, appear in the end to be more sexually conservative than males even though considering only the direct effect of gender implies that they are less so.

The causal chains leading from one variable to the next in our path diagram model illustrate that the nature of a person's sexual norms can be accounted for by one or more of six basic characteristics: sexual behavior, sexual feelings, age, gender, religiosity, and the presence or absence of a sense of threat in heterosexual relations. Examination of various portions of the path diagram has shown us that people are socialized toward being more conservative or more liberal in their adult sexual morality according to these six dimensions. Thus, the *religiously devout* among our sample were likely to have been reared by devout parents who restricted the sexuality of their environment. Consequently they had little premarital sexual involvement, and they tended to be sexually conservative. In contrast, analysis of a group of variables based on *sexual behavior* shows that younger persons, blacks, and males are more likely to hold liberal norms as a result of their greater participation in childhood sex play, masturbation, and premarital sex. Similarly, having had *positive feelings toward premarital sex* during adolescence—which has lasting effects on adult norms—is shown to be more common among males, blacks, and younger people, all of whom are more likely to have early sexual experiences and thereby to be more liberal as adults. The influence of sexuality as one grows up is recapitulated when we look at two other groups of variables: those connected with *age* and with *gender*. Both the older respondents and the females in our sample were less likely to have had experience with liberalizing influences centering on their own and others' sexual behavior, suggesting the relatively different ways in which they were socialized. As shown in the portion of the diagram concerning *feeling threatened by the opposite sex*, these two groups of respondents, as well as those brought up in rural areas and those who had Fundamentalist Protestant parents, were likely to express sexual conservatism because of this unease, regardless of whether they had had early sexual experiences or how they felt about them.

The data presented in this chapter thus show principal ways in which relatively liberal or relatively conservative sexual norms are generated, maintained, and by implication, revised. (For example, our path model has shown that the predictive power of parental religious devoutness on current devoutness can be affected by one's participation in premarital sex.) Nevertheless, most of the predictors emerging from our analysis act so as to preserve, not alter, sexual values; this supports the finding in Chapter 2 that most people's norms are relatively stable. The question that next arises, therefore, has to do with the people who *do* report changing their sexual norms at some time between childhood and the time they were interviewed. We will explore this unusual phenomenon in the next chapter.

NOTES

1. Indirect effects can be calculated in greater detail by determining the various routes or avenues that lead from a given independent variable, through subsequent-stage independent variables, to the dependent variable; multiplying together the beta coefficients for all paths comprising such a route or avenue; and adding together the resulting products. In later phases of our analysis we report results of this method instead of simple subtraction ($\beta_T - \beta_D$).
2. All beta coefficients in the path diagram model are also statistically significant, most—because of our large sample—at .001 or better.
3. Here, indirect effects are calculated as explained in note 1.
4. The location of parental sexual permissiveness in stage 1 does raise two important issues: first, that it may itself be determined by other exogenous variables; and second, that such permissiveness may have different effects at different times.
5. In looking at this model, it should be kept in mind that path analysis *assumes*

that the relationships depicted are causal—that an earlier event must cause, not just precede, a later one—and that this causality is neither reversible nor spurious, nor due to correlated measurement error. For example, it might be argued that it is current standards that influence devoutness and not, as our model has it, the other way around. Or it could be claimed that a rural upbringing does not directly bring about a sense of sexual threat; it is just a coincidence. Thus, path analysis, although our method of choice, is not a means for making absolute or conclusive sense of our data.

6. This criterion is more conservative than that of standard errors of b. Had we used the double standard error of b, the paths retained would have had $\beta \geq \pm .04$ instead of .08.
7. Variables in this cluster provide an R of .488 and R^2 of .238.
8. The basis for this and following calculations is the path-diagram-model effects in Table 4-2.
9. For example, "[I was/would be] pleased to be wanted or needed this way," ". . . proud to know I had sex appeal," " . . . pleased with the physical feeling."
10. As it happens, the two measures are related, however. For example, the correlation between having positive feelings before marriage and current approval of premarital sex is .32 respecting teenagers not in love and .41 for adults in love ($p < .001$).
11. By themselves, these six variables produce an R of .467 and R^2 of .218.
12. By themselves, these variables would provide R = .509 and R^2 = .259.
13. By themselves, these variables would provide R = .501 and R^2 = .251.
14. By themselves, these variables would provide R = .518 and R^2 = .268.
15. By themselves, these variables would provide R = .311 and R^2 = .097.
16. A similar situation exists with the variable reared as Fundamentalist. Those brought up this way are more likely to feel threatened in relationships with the opposite sex and, thereby, to be more sexually conservative. Nevertheless, a childhood Fundamentalist affiliation is *not* related to preadult sexual experiences, to feeling currently serious and moral about sex, or to the current level of religious devoutness (the lack of the last-named connection seems definitely to contradict popular notions of Fundamentalist Protestantism).

Chapter 5

Perceived Changes in Sexual Morality

Analyses in preceding chapters have dealt with sexual norms as a continuum along which respondents are ranged on the basis of their reports at the single point in time when the interview was conducted. This has been useful for our exploration of influences on current moral stance, but focusing on one point in time implies that sexual morality is static. In reality, some people reexamine and reformulate their sexual standards at one time or another, or undergo periods of uncertainty about them, while others retain the moralities they learned in childhood. In this chapter, therefore, we explore the nature of changes in sexual morality our respondents reported having experienced over their lifetimes, examining their comparisons of their present and past norms and of their own norms and their parents'. These comparisons form the basis for index measures of perceived moral change.

We expect to find, if not a radical departure from traditional moralities, at least some evidence of the perception of gradually increasing liberality. This is suggested in our own finding that current age is a predictor of moral stance, and it has also been found by other investigators. For example, Glenn and Weaver (1979), using data gathered by NORC since the time of our survey, noted a steady increase in acceptance of premarital sex during the 1970s, although nearly half of the respondents in each of their national probability samples continued to disapprove of it (e.g., in the 1978 sample 41% said it is "always" or "almost always" wrong; see Singh, 1980). And in later national surveys of young people, premarital sex has been judged "wrong" or "immoral" by no more than one-third (Yankelovich, 1974; Gallup, 1978).

Before we proceed to our findings, however, a cautionary remark or two is in order. As a cross-sectional survey rather than a longitudinal one, our study has limitations in analyzing changes in sexual norms (or in any other characteristic that might vary over time). To use our data to study change, we must therefore make several assumptions: (a) we must believe that the phenomena of interest—in this case, respondents' moral evaluations of various kinds of sexual behavior—are stable enough that they do not measurably fluctuate from day to day; (b) for data on whether respondents' evaluations had changed, we must rely on their recollections, since we do not have actual data from earlier points in their lives; (c) similarly, we do not actually know what respondents' parents felt about the behaviors in question, only what the respondents said they *thought* their parents felt (which may, however, be more important). A further limitation is that, although as we began the study we shared the notion that a "sexual revolution" was probably in progress, we did not intend it to be a primary analytic focus of the study, and we limited interview questions addressing this issue to a minimum. This means, for example, that we have little interrelated data that can be used to check the internal consistency or reliability of responses, and that we lack a theoretically focused set of independent variables by which change can be adequately explained. Still, as most studies like this have concentrated on the young (see Victor, 1980) or have inferred change by percentage comparisons rather than directly asking about it, we may be able to shed indirect light on the continuity or discontinuity of sexual socialization.

One other important point remains. Because a person's age, as shown in Chapter 4, is important in predicting his or her sexual norms, we will be especially concerned here with the relationship between age and reported changes in sexual morality. Our study, as mentioned, was not designed primarily to investigate this relationship; therefore we have retrospective rather than longitudinal data, and while we may divide our respondents into age groups, these groups do not necessarily constitute methodologically rigorous age cohorts. Nevertheless, the data that we do have allow us to make certain inferences on the assumption that our various age groups do approximate cohorts. Such inferences might deal with three interpretations regarding age and change:

1. The *aging effect* (or maturational effect) is *longitudinal*, operating when a particular person's norms change as a function of growing older. Thus, to consider this effect we look at one individual—or age group—moving through time. A literal measure of this would require longitudinal data from repeated waves of interviewing. Basic to this consideration is that older people whose longer lives may include a greater diversity of experience, should be more likely to evince whatever effect aging has.
2. The *intergenerational effect* can be assessed with *cross-sectional* data and appears when there are differences (e.g., in changing rates of, say, certain childhood or early adult experiences across succeeding age cohorts) between the reports of older and younger people at a particular moment in time (e.g, the date of the interview). Thus, this effect can be thought of as perpendicular to the aging effect: here, we are static with respect to time but move from age group to age group as we examine our data. Underlying this approach is the supposition that if an intergenerational effect exists, differences between the very oldest and the very youngest respondents will be more marked than those between adjacent age groups.
3. There is the possibility of *period change* associated with relatively delimited historical events, such as a world war or depression, or widespread alarm about a consensual notion concerning a sexual revolution. This might appear with evidence of fairly clear disjunctures in rates at some point in time, affecting all age cohorts simultaneously.

Any of these effects may be operating, but it may be more likely that there are combinations of all three. One may augment the other if they are in the same direction (e.g., if greater age is associated with greater conservatism; or, if they operate in opposite directions, they may cancel one another, or else one may be stronger and so prevail. The following examples show how this may happen (see Glenn, 1974):

1. As people grow older, they become more conservative because their increased experience with life convinces them that society works best if individual behavior is closely constrained

(aging effect). Thus, they report more conservative values than younger people do (intergenerational effect, explained by aging effect).

2. The more rapid the pace of social change during the years of primary socialization, the less ideologically rigid a person's values are; so people who reached adulthood more recently would be more liberal than their elders (intergenerational effect). The older people might then modify their own norms in an effort to lessen dissonance, whether within their own families or between themselves and society (aging effect, explained by intergenerational effect).

3. As people grow older, they perceive themselves as having a greater investment in society—for example, through owning property, rearing children, paying taxes, and so on—and so they conform more closely to general societal norms (aging effect toward conservatism). At the same time, personal experience may suggest to them that sexual norms should be based on prudence rather than definitions of good and evil (aging effect toward liberality). Furthermore, the older people are, the less impact a single experience is likely to have on them, so that beyond a certain age any kind of change becomes unlikely (aging effect specifying certain age groups). If all three of these aging effects are operating, the result may be to suggest a limited effect, an ambiguous one, none at all, or just one of the three, if it is stronger than the other two.

4. Since most people's norms are apparently quite conservative to begin with, any change within a given age cohort, regardless of what happens with an individual respondent, is more likely to be in a liberal direction (aging effect). Thus, older people might appear *more* conservative than younger ones owing to their being born in an earlier, more conservative societal era, but their cohort as a whole may tend to become *less* conservative over time (intergenerational effect outweighing aging effect).

In examining our data on perceived changing sexual morality, we are concerned with evidence of overall (i.e., net) aging or intergenerational effects, since the data are too limited to warrant a highly complex investigation, and since we have no longitudinal data. We assume that if such an effect appears, it is important to note regardless of the possibly numerous reasons for its existence. Our criterion for identifying such an effect will be a percentage difference among age groups of at least 10%; it will be ascribed to aging if it describes a maturational or lifetime change, and to generation if it distinguishes between or specifies age groups. Again, we must emphasize that our data can reveal only *net* effects; how they are composed can only be speculated. In addition, of course, it is possible that aging or intergenerational effects can be accounted for by other variables (such as education) in the prediction of moral change. First we consider the prevalence of net aging effects.

Reported Maturational Moral Change

After asking our respondents how they evaluated premarital and extramarital sex, homosexuality, and masturbation, we asked, "Have you always felt this way [about the behavior in question], or have there been times in the past when you felt more approving or less approving?" Our basic indicator of possible aging effects is thus simple: respondents who said they had not always felt as they did at the time of the interview are considered to have changed their morality. Table 5-1 gives the distribution of responses to these questions about change in sexual norms.

This table shows, as reported in Chapter 2, that our respondents tend to perceive their sexual norms as stable. The majority said they had always felt as they did when interviewed: three-quarters claimed to have never changed their evaluation of masturbation, two-thirds said they still felt the same about premarital and extramarital sex, and 82% that they adhered to their original feelings about homosexuality (presumably harsh ones: the vast majority, it will be remembered, considered this behavior always wrong).

Among the minority who did report a lifetime change in morality, the reported change tended to be in a liberal direction. Thus, of those who said they changed their minds about masturbation or homosexuality, about seven out of eight used to be less approving of it. Somewhat fewer of those who reported a change toward premarital and extramarital sex—but a still sizable majority of 70%—used to be less approving.

Comparatively few of the respondents said they had changed their norms to a more conservative position, and even fewer that they had felt different ways at different times—sometimes less approving than currently and sometimes more so. It is on pre-

TABLE 5-1 Reports of Change in Sexual Norms

Response	Have you always felt this way about . . . masturbation?	premarital and extramarital sex?	homosexuality?
Always felt this way	73.0%	65.7%	81.6%
Used to be more approving	4.3	9.3	2.0
Used to be less approving	22.2	24.0	16.2
Have been both more and less approving than now	0.5	1.0	0.2
Column total	100.0%	100.0%	100.0%
Base *n*	2,978	3,011	3,004
No answer	40	7	14
Total sample	3,018	3,018	3,018
If change reported:			
Used to be more approving	15.8%	27.2%	11.0%
Used to be less approving	82.2	69.8	87.7
Have been more and less approving than now	2.0	3.0	1.3
Column total	100.0%	100.0%	100.0%
Base *n*	803	1,033	554
Did not change	2,175	1,978	2,450
No answer	40	7	14
Total sample	3,018	3,018	3,018

marital and extramarital sex that responses show the greatest reported change away from approval. Possible reasons for this could be that the experience of either premarital or extramarital sex may have resulted in unanticipated distress, or that becoming a parent of a teenager may have changed assumptions about the young. It should be pointed out, though, that relatively small numbers—10% of the total sample—reported either being more conservative or fluctuating. For statistical purposes, therefore, we can disregard these two responses and conclude that in the minority of the sample where change was reported, it was predominantly in a more liberal direction.[1] If we consider only the people who reported a change of some kind, there appears to be an aging effect toward becoming more liberal: for all respondents who reported change except the 2% who were over 75, more people said they became more liberal than said they became more conservative; and people tended to report only one kind of change, as the small minority reporting both kinds is the same for all age groups. In addition, there was a greater *incidence* of perceived change (of whatever kind) among younger people, so that the younger people appear as significantly less conservative (gamma = .20 for masturbation, .25 for heterosexual sex, .30 for homosexuality).

Since the Sexual Morality Scale showed masturbation to be disapproved relatively seldom, premarital and extramarital sex to be intermediate in this regard, and homosexuality to be most frequently disapproved, the question arises whether these more liberal/not more liberal data on reported change are similarly scalable. For example, if moderating one's perceived stance toward homosexuality involves greater nonconformity to prevailing moral standards, to what extent does it involve becoming more liberal toward the other behaviors as well? Cross-tabulation of these three items does suggest some evidence of scalability; among the people who said they were now more approving of masturbation, for instance, one-third—the largest number—had apparently changed their attitude only about this most-accepted behavior, whereas the greatest number of those who said they used to be less approving of homosexuality had also apparently changed their minds with respect to the other two behaviors.

From these data, therefore, we constructed an index of perceived maturational change (in the liberal direction), with those whose norms had changed only with respect to masturbation at one end of the scale and those who were more liberal on all three issues at the other end. This index, which we call the Moral Change Index (MCI), was constructed in deliberate parallel to the SMS in terms of how widely disapproved the behaviors were; the correlation between the two is .46, suggesting some basis for this parallel.

People were assigned scores based on the data in Table 5-1, with the stipulation that the index would disregard those few reporting conservative change. Thus, the people who answered "used to be more approving" to any of the questions were grouped with those who reported their norms had never changed, and all were assigned an index score of 0, indicating "no liberal change." The 30 respondents who "used to be both more and less approving," scored 1, indicating "irregular change," because ". . . less approving" does connote some kind of liberal change. The next four categories follow the sequence of behaviors in the SMS. A score of 2 was assigned to those who said they had become more liberal

TABLE 5-2 Moral Change Index (MCI)

Score	Category	*n*	Percent of total sample	Percent of those now more liberal
0	No liberal change	1,786	59.2%	—
1	Irregular change	30	1.0	2.6%
2	More liberal toward masturbation only	217	7.2	18.5
3	More liberal toward premarital and extramarital sex only	287	9.5	24.4
4	More liberal toward masturbation and toward premarital and extramarital sex	156	5.2	13.3
5	More liberal toward homosexuality only	120	4.0	10.2
6	More liberal toward homosexuality and toward either masturbation or premarital and extramarital sex	176	5.8	15.0
7	More liberal on all three issues	189	6.3	16.1
8	No answer on one or more issues	57	1.9	—
	Total	3,018	100.1%	100.1%

only toward masturbation, a score of 3 to those more liberal only toward premarital and extramarital sex, and a score of 4 to those more liberal toward both of these but not toward homosexuality. People who said they had become more liberal only toward homosexuality were assigned an index score of 5; toward homosexuality and *either* of the others, a score of 6 (they were too few to warrant two separate categories); and toward homosexuality and *both* of the others, a score of 7. (Those who did not answer one or more of the three questions were given a missing value code of 8.)

The resulting MCI is shown in Table 5-2. It is clear from inspecting the percentages in this table that there are irregularities in the scale data—for example, 35% said they had changed only respecting either nonmarital sex or homosexuality—which seem to raise questions about the validity of how we ordered the scores. Indeed, the MCI does not approach Guttman scalability as did the SMS.[2] It can also be argued that the index does not take into account what people's norms were before they thought they changed, and thus it may combine in the same category a number of individuals with quite different values.

To answer these objections, we start with our basic findings, which are that people do tend to be less condemning of masturbation, more so of homosexuality, and so forth. Therefore, we can surmise that if we could have assessed the sexual moralities of the people who reported change before that change occurred, we would have found them to be more liberal with regard to masturbation, slightly less so about nonmarital heterosexual sex, and least liberal about homosexuality, since these are the patterns we found to be most common in our sample (the majority of whom, it will be remembered, had *not* become more liberal). Thus, people who reported changing their norms about masturbation might have moved from a comparatively liberal position on that behavior to one even more so, whereas people who came to feel differently about homosexuality would probably have felt initially that it is always wrong. Regardless of what their new position was, then, the people who said they had changed their minds about homosexuality could be seen as making a more radical change, since they would most likely have been adding a qualification of some sort to what had been an absolute judgment.[3] Another way of looking at this is to point out as an example that at the time of our interview, to believe masturbation to be wrong only sometimes was to agree with 30% of one's fellow citizens, while to say the same about homosexuality was to agree with only 6%. As to the extent to which reported changes regarding homosexuality were accompanied by reported changes toward the other behaviors, this could clearly have been affected by how liberal people already were about the others. For example, a person who already felt that masturbation is wrong only sometimes and that premarital-extramarital sex is almost always wrong might not have changed opinions about these two issues even though he or she had moved from considering homosexuality always wrong to considering it almost always wrong.[4] In any case, to the extent that greater approval toward homosexuality was accompanied or preceded by less than absolute condemnation of the other two behaviors, reported liberalization with respect to homosexuality does seem to connote the greatest change.

So far, our retrospective data have shown the following:

1. Most respondents claimed that they had never changed their moral view of a given sexual behavior.

2. The few who did report a change in moral outlook generally said they had become more liberal. Some aging and intergenerational effects appear to underlie this result, but they are hard to isolate without further data.

3. This perceived liberal change proved to be less likely respecting a widely condemned behavior, such as homosexuality, than toward behaviors that are not so universally disapproved.

4. However, if a respondent had actually become more liberal toward homosexuality, it is probable, broadly speaking, that he or she had also become more liberal toward one or more other behaviors. Thus we can combine reports of change in an index (the MCI) to measure the extent of aging effects toward liberality.

Since being more liberal on the SMS is associated with having undergone a reported liberal moral change, as measured by the MCI, we may assume that people who say they have changed their morality are less likely to say a given behavior is always wrong and more likely to use one of the less extreme categories. Therefore, we next examine how evaluation of the five items that make up our Sexual Morality Scale relates to the presence or direction of perceived moral change. Table 5-3 presents these five items in cross-tabulation with reports of maturational change.

This table shows, first, that the respondents who said they had not changed their standards were most likely to be extremely conservative—to say a given behavior is always wrong—and this likelihood is greater as one reads down the table, since each successive behavior was more widely disapproved than the one preceding it. In addition, the people who said they had become more conservative were likewise apt to take an extremely conservative view. It is interesting to note that the people who reported that their norms had not changed were more likely to say a given behavior is always wrong than are those who had become more conservative. However, these differences are usually quite small, which tends to support our combining these two groups in the MCI.

Among the group that had become more liberal, it may seem surprising how many, despite their reported moderated stance, still said a given behavior is always wrong. If we eliminated the no-change group from the calculations, in fact, we would see that the more broadly disapproved a behavior is, the more likely it seems to be that a person could come to feel more liberal about it and still believe it is always wrong.[5] Only with regard to the first two behaviors—masturbation and adult premarital sex—do a small number take this position. However, it should be pointed out that only concerning these two behaviors did fewer than half of the

TABLE 5-3 Evaluation of Behaviors Comprising the SMS by Reported Moral Change

Current standards	No change	Now more conservative	Now more liberal	Irregular change
Masturbation				
Always wrong	35.8%	28.2%	3.4%	12.5%
Almost always wrong	23.8	33.1	13.0	25.0
Wrong only sometimes	26.1	30.7	44.8	62.5
Not wrong at all	14.4	8.1	38.9	0.0
Column total	100.1%	100.1%	100.1%	100.0%
Base *n*[a]	2,103	124	656	16
Premarital sex between adults, in love				
Always wrong	41.2%	36.3%	9.3%	17.2%
Almost always wrong	15.2	15.6	12.0	24.1
Pretty much wrong	5.3	5.2	4.9	0.0
Wrong only sometimes	13.8	17.0	28.8	20.7
Not wrong at all	24.6	25.9	45.0	37.9
Column total	100.1%	100.0%	100.0%	99.9%
Base *n*[a]	1,902	270	698	29
Premarital sex between teenagers, not in love				
Always wrong	61.2%	57.2%	33.3%	34.5%
Almost always wrong	18.5	20.4	24.8	31.0
Pretty much wrong	8.0	11.5	12.9	13.8
Wrong only sometimes	7.9	6.3	21.1	17.2
Not wrong at all	4.3	4.5	7.9	3.4
Column total	99.9%	99.9%	100.0%	99.9%
Base *n*[a]	1,912	269	673	29
Extramarital sex				
Always wrong	81.8%	77.1%	46.9%	51.6%
Almost always wrong	9.5	14.3	27.2	25.8
Wrong only sometimes	6.6	6.8	23.0	22.6
Not wrong at all	2.0	1.8	2.9	0.0
Column total	99.9%	100.0%	100.0%	100.0%
Base *n*[a]	1,970	280	717	31
Homosexuality without affection				
Always wrong	88.0%	63.3%	36.1%	50.0%
Almost always wrong	5.6	18.3	21.9	50.0
Wrong only sometimes	3.2	11.7	22.8	0.0
Not wrong at all	3.1	6.7	19.2	0.0
Column total	99.9%	100.0%	100.0%	100.0%
Base *n*[a]	2,418	60	474	4

[a] Excludes respondents who did not answer one or the other of these items.

total sample respond "always wrong." Therefore, it is of particular note that only one-third of those who said they had become more liberal said homosexuality without affection is always wrong, since more than double that percentage of the general sample believed this. Among the last three behaviors in the table, homosexuality is also the only one that evoked a sizable number of "not wrong at all" responses from those who had become more liberal.

We can summarize these findings as follows:

1. People who reported that they had not changed their sexual norms were more likely to be disapproving than approving of a given behavior.
2. People who claimed to have changed their norms were more likely to have become more liberal than to have become more conservative or to have vacillated in both directions.
3. People who said that they had changed their norms in either direction were more likely to take an intermediate or qualified moral stance toward a given behavior than were those who claimed their sexual norms had not changed.
4. People who said they had become more liberal approved more often of masturbation and adult premarital coitus (behaviors the general sample did not absolutely condemn) than of homosexuality, which was usually considered always wrong. This supports the assumption underlying the MCI that a perceived change with respect to a *more* widely disapproved behavior is more important than one toward a *less* widely disapproved behavior.

The MCI thus can be used as a summary measure of reported aging change in sexual standards. As we have noted, though, intergenerational effects seem to be operating more powerfully than those of aging, so we now proceed to a detailed examination of this indicator of moral change—whether respondents thought their sexual norms had altered from those held by their parents.

Reported Intergenerational Moral Change

Basic to traditional sociology is the idea that external cultural norms become "internalized" during childhood and adolescence. The mechanism of this socialization process involves the neophyte "identifying" with his or her parents and eventually learning to see the world from their point of view. If this theory is true, there must be some point in early life when a person's moral evaluations are closely congruent with those of his or her parents. Sexual norms may be something of a special case in this regard, since parents may introduce explicit teachings about sex at a later point than they do about such behaviors as theft or lying; and according to moral development theory (see Piaget, 1948; Kohlberg, 1969), older children may accept parental values less unquestioningly than younger ones do. Nevertheless, it can also be argued that even the young child senses parental sexual morality in a general permissive-restrictive context well before it is literally spelled out (if it ever is). Indeed, we can assume that most people would recall their parents' instructions about how they ought to behave sexually as primarily restrictive, regardless of whether explicit statements were involved. Therefore, we now look at how respondents compared their sexual norms with their parents', expecting to find that those who were more liberal than the general sample tended to report norms different from their parents', or conversely, that those who said they thought differently from their parents were more likely to report liberal sexual standards. Later, we will examine the extent to which any intergenerational change of this sort can be tied to social climate, either that of the "revolutionary" 1960s or the social environment of respondents' youth.

After we had ascertained respondents' current evaluations of premarital and extramarital sex and of homosexual activity, we asked, "How would you say your feelings about [the behavior in question] compare with the way your parents felt toward this when you were a child? Are you more approving or less approving than they were at that time?" To this question, respondents could also say that they felt the same as their parents, but we did not explicitly offer this response category, since to do so might bias responses in the direction of reporting no change. Table 5-4 presents responses to this question, including data for people who rejected our alternatives of more approving or less approving and claimed they felt the same as their parents did. Looking at the first column, we note that almost half of the respondents chose the response category that was not explicitly offered, saying that they felt just as their parents did about premarital and extramarital sex. Even more—about two-thirds—gave the same response regarding homosexuality. (It is interesting to note that 8% said they did not know how their parents felt about homosexuality, even though, if it was not

TABLE 5-4 Respondents' Sexual Norms Compared to Their Parents'

Response	Regarding premarital and extramarital sex			Regarding homosexuality		
	A	B	C	A	B	C
More approving than parents were	45.7%	47.1%	86.4%	25.5%	27.7%	84.4%
About the same	44.2	45.6		61.7	67.2	
Less approving than parents were	7.2	7.4	13.6	4.7	5.1	15.6
Don't know	2.9			8.1		
Column total	100.0%	100.1%	100.0%	100.0%	100.0%	100.0%
Base *n*	3,008	2,922	1,591	3,012	2,768	909
No answer	10	10	10	6	6	6
Don't know		86	86		244	244
No change from parents			1,331			1,859
Total sample	3,018	3,018	3,018	3,018	3,018	3,018

NOTE: Columns A exclude "no answer" respondents; columns B exclude "no answer" and "don't know" respondents; columns C exclude "no answer," "don't know," and "about the same" respondents.

mentioned, they might have assumed that their parents took a generally negative stance toward it.) It seems reasonable to suppose that among the 47% who were more approving than they thought their parents were regarding heterosexual sex, most of them were referring to premarital rather than extramarital relations. This supposition reflects findings from four NORC surveys subsequent to ours that showed extramarital sex continuing to be soundly condemned by large majorities of Americans (Glenn & Weaver, 1979).

Of those respondents who thought they had moved away from their parents' norms, many more said they had become more approving than more disapproving toward the given behavior. Taking into account only these respondents (the third column for each behavior), approximately 85% were more approving and 15% less approving of both nonmarital heterosexual sex and homosexual sex than they believed their parents were while they were children. This finding suggests that there is a slight intergenerational tendency toward change in sexual norms, with a few people in each generation perhaps adopting norms more liberal than those they were taught. This would imply that younger people's greater liberality—which Chapter 4 has already demonstrated—results in part from this modification of the older people's norms. This intergenerational effect seems continuous rather than a recent phenomenon (e.g., it is not a product of the postwar years) because among those who did report a change from their parents' standards, there is no relationship to current age (gamma = .03 for heterosexual sex, .07 for homosexuality). (We take a closer look at this speculation in the next subsection, "Moral Change and Age.")

The situation according to our data, then, seems to be that for most people, parental socialization has succeeded, in the sense that they adhere to standards learned in childhood, but some have modified these traditional norms and have become more liberal, so that we have a net intergenerational effect. There are two basic ways in which intergenerational change might operate. If parents' moral teachings are overwhelmed by competing influences from outside the family—such as pressure from peers or ideas gathered from popular media—people would report that although they are more liberal than their parents they have "always felt this way." On the other hand, if an aging effect toward liberality is operating too, we would expect people who are more liberal than their parents to report as well that they "used to be less approving" of the given behavior.

Cross-tabulating our measures of reported change, we find that both kinds of processes seem to have occurred. Respondents who apparently were displaying intergenerational change only—those who reported no change in their own norms—constitute 47.2% of those more liberal than their parents respecting heterosexual sex, and 46.6% of those more liberal toward homosexuality. Corresponding figures for those who did apparently change their original stance (i.e., the ones who also reported maturational change) are respectively 40.9% and 49.6%. Thus, hardly any respondents who claimed to be more liberal than their parents also said they had changed toward greater conservatism (these few people—138 respecting heterosexual sex, 26 in the case of homosexuality—evidently had an aging change in one direction that competed with intergenerational change in the other). Interestingly, any tendency for liberal aging and intergenerational effects to enhance each other is not reciprocated in the reports of the small number who said they were more *conservative* than their parents: for both kinds of behaviors the majority said they had always felt as they did currently. These people (who number fewer than 10% of the total sample) may have been taught unusually permissive morals, which they rejected in favor of a more conventional stance. In any case, among the minority who said they had departed from parental teachings, the general tendency was to have become more liberal, whether or not an aging change appears to have been involved.[6]

Our next concern, therefore, is to see whether this intergenerational liberal trend appears in a definable group of people. To the extent that the respondents who said they were more liberal than their parents about homosexuality were the same ones who felt this way about nonmarital heterosexual sex, these data should be scalable on an index of generational change. When these two measures are cross-tabulated, it appears that about half of the sample were *not* more liberal in their own minds than their parents in either respect, while some 20% were more liberal on both dimensions. People who were more approving of the heterosexual behaviors but not of homosexuality make up another one-fourth, while those who were more approving only of homosexuality are the smallest group—6%. From these data we constructed an index of Liberality Versus Parents', which takes no reported liberal change on either dimension as its conservative end-point, change respecting only the heterosexual behaviors as next most conservative (since feeling more tolerant of homosexuality is a more radical stance to take), change respecting homosexuality as the next point, and change along both dimensions as the most liberal end-point. This scale correlates with the SMS at .51.

Our next step is to compare respondents' positions on Liberality Versus Parents' with our other data about perceived change to further investigate what kind of change respondents experienced.

Table 5-5 shows the predictive value, based on our 1970 data, of knowing how people compare their own norms with their parents'. The first column of percentages shows that the more generally disapproved a given behavior, the more likely it is that people who think they are *not* more liberal than their parents will say this behavior is always wrong. Conversely, people who believe they are more liberal than their parents are more likely to give a less disapproving response, with this relationship being more pronounced when the particular behavior is less widely disapproved. Interestingly, people who report the greatest divergence from parental values (according to our scale) are more likely to approve fully of adult premarital sex than of any of the other behaviors;

TABLE 5-5 Evaluation of Behaviors Comprising the SMS by Liberality Versus Parents'

Current standards	Not more liberal than parents	More liberal, hetero. sex	More liberal, homo. sex	More liberal, both
Masturbation				
Always wrong	41.0%	21.5%	17.8%	8.5%
Almost always wrong	24.7	23.1	14.8	14.9
Wrong only sometimes	24.9	35.1	39.6	37.1
Not wrong at all	9.5	20.3	27.8	39.5
Column total	100.1%	100.0%	100.0%	100.0%
Base *n*[a]	1,386	754	169	590
Premarital sex between adults, in love				
Always wrong	52.4%	15.9%	15.8%	10.8%
Almost always wrong	15.8	14.4	22.4	9.2
Pretty much wrong	5.0	6.5	4.8	4.0
Wrong only sometimes	11.4	23.4	21.2	25.0
Not wrong at all	15.4	39.8	35.8	51.0
Column total	100.0%	100.0%	100.0%	100.0%
Base *n*[a]	1,415	738	165	575
Premarital sex between teenagers, not in love				
Always wrong	72.2%	40.6%	41.9%	29.2%
Almost always wrong	15.1	28.9	27.5	20.1
Pretty much wrong	6.7	12.1	13.2	12.5
Wrong only sometimes	4.2	12.7	10.8	25.8
Not wrong at all	1.9	5.8	6.6	12.5
Column total	100.1%	100.1%	100.0%	100.1%
Base *n*[a]	1,420	727	167	562
Extramarital sex				
Always wrong	89.4%	65.1%	64.4%	43.4%
Almost always wrong	6.2	19.3	21.3	26.1
Wrong only sometimes	3.4	13.2	10.9	26.1
Not wrong at all	1.0	2.5	3.4	4.4
Column total	100.0%	100.1%	100.0%	100.0%
Base *n*[a]	1,452	774	174	590
Homosexuality without affection				
Always wrong	93.0%	88.8%	53.6%	38.8%
Almost always wrong	3.5	6.1	17.9	21.8
Wrong only sometimes	1.7	3.1	16.7	20.2
Not wrong at all	1.7	2.0	11.9	19.2
Column total	99.9%	100.0%	100.1%	100.0%
Base *n*[a]	1,437	767	168	578

[a] Excludes respondents who did not answer one or the other of these items.

perhaps this behavior is most likely to be revaluated as one grows older. In addition, the percentage responding "always wrong" tends to decrease as the amount of perceived liberal change increases, and conversely, the more people think they have changed, the more likely they are to respond "not wrong at all." Still, the most populous cells in this table are those combining "not more liberal" and "always wrong," demonstrating once again the essential perceived stability of American sexual norms.

We can summarize our investigation of intergenerational change as follows:

1. Most respondents evaluated homosexuality as they thought their parents did, while not quite half felt as they thought their parents did toward nonmarital heterosexual sex. Since the majority did say that extramarital sex is always wrong, we may infer that people's reported divergence from parental values in this latter respect usually involved their being more tolerant of premarital sex.
2. Most of the people who thought they did not share their parents' moral views said they were more liberal, not more conservative, than their parents were.
3. These data can be scaled on a liberality index permitting degrees of reported change from parents' morality. We then see that the greater the reported change, the more approving of a given behavior respondents were currently; on the other hand, the people who claimed to agree with their parents' views were most likely to be disapproving. That the latter make up the largest group seems clear evidence of the powerful primacy of early socialization.

We have thus developed two measures that can be used to indicate various levels of perceived moral change in a liberal direction: the Moral Change Index, based on whether people think they have ever changed their views of certain behaviors (aging or maturational change); and Liberality Versus Parents', based on whether people share their parents' moral standards (intergenerational change). We examined these findings for a gender specification, since the SMS analysis suggested that one may be present, but males and females did not differ.[7] However, because Chapter 4 also showed that age is an important predictor of the SMS, we looked further into this by considering the intergenerational tendency toward more liberal norms as reflected in the age when reported change last occurred.

Reported Moral Change and Age

Respondents indicating maturational change were asked, "How long have you felt the way you do now—since what age?" (We asked for their age in an attempt to get more precise data than "oh, about ten years," the type of response we could otherwise expect.) Responses to this question as regards masturbation and homosexuality are related in Table 5-6 to respondents' age at the time of the interview.[8]

Looking first at the "Total" column (the farthest right), we note that there does not seem to be a particular five- or ten-year period that stands out as the time when these respondents thought they adopted their current moralities. About half of them mentioned the "revolutionary" 1960s, and percentages are quite a bit smaller for the years before 1946, but these two phenomena are clearly a function of respondents' age. That is, our youngest respondents—who were babies in the 1940s—had to have changed their moralities rather recently if they changed them at all. If we exclude those under 35 from these percentages, the 1960s no longer seem so important in this respect, while the postwar years become more salient. (For example, respecting masturbation, 15% had had their most recent reported moral change in 1961–1970 and 35% in 1946–1955. For homosexuality, comparable figures are 27% and 28%.) This suggests that perceived moral change may be tied to social climate—with different social climates influencing the perceptions of different age groups. Thus, our younger respondents may have been more responsive to the atmosphere of the 1960s, our oldest ones to that of the 1920s.

These data also give evidence of a steady intergenerational trend. The row "Percent who changed" shows that no matter when (or why) reported moral change may have taken place, it is more likely to have occurred the younger the respondent. There is no notable difference between adjacent age groups, but the youngest and the oldest groups do differ appreciably in the incidence of perceived maturational change.[9] Apparently, neither the 1960s nor any other decade—assuming that the social climate of youth is most influential—stood out in respondents' minds as a revolutionary time. Instead, since reported change and liberality are related (Tables

TABLE 5-6 Reported Moral Change and Perceived Moral Stability over Time

Date of most recent moral change	Age in 1970						
	Under 25	25-34	35-44	45-54	55-64	Over 64	Total
Regarding masturbation							
1966–1970	60.8%	17.6%	7.9%	4.6%	5.2%	4.9%	18.0%
1961–1965	35.8	42.2	13.2	8.4	6.5	4.9	22.4
1956–1960	1.7	30.2	27.6	19.8	7.8	8.2	19.1
1946–1955	1.7	10.1	45.4	34.4	28.6	19.7	23.0
1936–1945			5.9	29.8	26.0	16.4	10.5
1926–1935				3.1	22.1	11.5	3.8
1925 or earlier					3.9	34.4	3.2
Column total	100.0%	100.1%	100.0%	100.1%	100.1%	100.0%	100.0%
Base *n*	120	199	152	131	77	61	740
Percent who changed	33.9%	29.5%	26.8%	25.1%	20.6%	14.5%	25.4%
Age group *n*[a]	354	675	567	522	374	422	2,914
Regarding homosexuality							
1966–1970	65.3%	29.8%	12.5%	9.6%	6.8%	5.3%	26.3%
1961–1965	32.7	48.3	25.9	16.4	11.4	0.0	30.2
1956–1960	1.0	18.5	34.8	17.8	18.2	18.4	18.6
1946–1955	1.0	3.4	25.0	41.1	15.9	28.9	15.3
1936–1945			1.8	13.7	31.8	10.5	5.5
1926–1935				1.4	11.4	13.2	2.0
1925 or earlier					4.5	23.7	2.0
Column total	100.0%	100.0%	100.0%	100.0%	100.0%	100.0%	99.9%
Base *n*	98	178	112	73	44	38	543
Percent who changed	26.0%	25.8%	19.3%	13.6%	11.5%	8.8%	18.2%
Age group *n*[a]	367	691	579	538	382	434	2,991

[a] Three respondents did not give their current age, 101 did not give the age of their most recent change respecting masturbation, and 24 did not give the age of their most recent change respecting homosexuality.

5-3 and 5-5), it seems as if an aging effect toward liberality is offset by a much stronger intergenerational effect. The paucity of our data (e.g., the small *N* for those who changed regarding homosexuality, and our lack of more comprehensive measures) permit no more detailed analysis of this question. Nonetheless, these findings suggest that perceived moral change—among the minority who did report it—occurred as part of a maturational process, not directly from external social influences, except insofar as these influences reflect each generation's propensity to question the norms of its forebears. There is no evidence that respondents in any age group recalled experiencing radical change congruent with the notion of the "revolutionary" 1960s.

Reported Sexual Norms in the 1970s

If the social turmoil of the 1960s provoked radical change in American morals, our 1970 data should have reflected it. Some commentators, however, might protest that our survey is too old, that real changes in people's norms have only begun to appear in response to the social climate of the 1970s.

We are fortunate that NORC surveys subsequent to ours used some of the same questions, so that we can see whether such an argument is a valid one. Respondents in several of NORC's annual General Social Surveys taken between 1972 and 1978 were asked to rate the morality of extramarital, premarital, and homosexual sex, using the same response categories as in our own survey (Glenn & Weaver, 1979), although without specifying the degree of affection between adults engaging in premarital or homosexual sex. If our data were gathered too early to capture the perceived effects of the "sexual revolution," they ought to display markedly greater conservatism than do the later data.

Table 5-7 presents comparisons between these subsequent surveys and our own. The table reads from left to right, so that to compare the various samples, we can look down the column under the response of interest. The first column shows that extramarital sex, as mentioned earlier, continues to be considered always wrong by seven out of ten Americans, and premarital sex between adults by about a third of the population. In the latter case, though, the data can also be read as indicating a very small but persistent tendency away from conservatism, in keeping with our identifi-

TABLE 5-7 Comparison of Our 1970 Data with Data from Later National Samples

Behavior/sample year	Always wrong	Almost always wrong	Wrong only sometimes	Not wrong at all	Row total	Base *n*
Extramarital sex						
1970	72.6%	14.4	10.8	2.2	100.0%	3,006
1973	69.6	14.8	11.6	4.1	100.1	1,491
1974	74.1	11.8	11.6	2.5	100.0	1,460
1976	68.7	15.6	11.5	4.3	100.1	1,475
1977	73.0	13.6	10.1	3.2	99.9	1,510
Premarital sex between adults						
1970 (adults in love)[a]	32.7%	14.5	23.0	29.8	100.0%	2,906
1972	36.6	11.8	24.3	27.3	100.0	1,537
1974	33.0	12.7	23.6	30.7	100.0	1,429
1975	30.9	12.3	24.0	32.8	100.0	1,427
1977	31.0	9.5	23.0	36.5	100.0	1,481
1978	29.3	11.7	20.3	38.7	100.0	1,494
Homosexuality						
1970 (without affection)	79.1%	8.6	6.5	5.8	100.0%	2,964
1970 (with affection)	72.2	8.6	7.4	11.8	100.0	2,940
1973	74.3	6.7	7.8	11.2	100.0	1,417
1974	73.1	5.2	8.2	13.4	99.9	1,361
1976	70.1	6.2	7.9	15.9	100.1	1,426
1977	71.9	5.8	7.5	14.9	100.1	1,453

NOTE. The source for data from the later samples is Glenn and Weaver (1979). "Don't know" and "no answer" respondents are excluded.

[a] For comparability, we combine here our index categories "pretty much wrong" (5.2%) and "wrong only sometimes" (17.8%). See footnote to Table 3-1.

cation of an intergenerational liberal trend among a minority of people. The same seems to be true for homosexuality. Still, what appears most evident from this table is that American sexual norms have not profoundly changed throughout the 1970s, any more than they seem from our data to have done in previous decades.

Summary

This chapter's principal finding is that no matter how closely we examine our data, we can only reiterate that in 1970 most Americans did not report any change in their public moral evaluations of sexual behaviors. This holds true regardless of whether respondents were comparing their own current and past views or their views with their parents'; regardless of the particular behavior in question; and regardless of respondents' gender or age.

Among the minority who did report moral change, we found

that most claimed to be more liberal than they were before or than their parents were. This permitted the construction of two indexes—Moral Change and Liberality Versus Parents'—which could be used to assess the extent of perceived change in a liberal direction. We found that people who did report change were more likely to score at the less-conservative end of our global measure, the Sexual Morality Scale; and that when we considered how they rated individual behaviors, they were more likely to qualify their disapproval or to respond "not wrong at all" than were the nonchanging respondents, who were more likely to rate any given behavior always wrong. Furthermore, the greater the extent of reported change in a liberal direction, the less disapproving a person's response was apt to be. All these findings may seem unsurprising, but it is their consistency that permits us to use index measures in considering perceived moral change.

Among the people who reported moral change, our data show both aging and intergenerational effects (although we can look only at the *net resulting* effects, since the number of changers is too small for an elaborate analysis). Aging effects—those that emerge as a person grows older—include a tendency for people to say they became more liberal if they changed at all. Intergenerational effects—those that distinguish one age group or generation from the next—include, besides reports of change from parental norms, the greater tendency for younger people to think they have experienced liberal change and for older people to think they have changed in a conservative direction. Basically, however, our data on change show two main kinds of effects: an aging effect—people becoming more liberal as they grow older—and an even stronger intergenerational tendency whereby young people appear more liberal than older ones, presumably because of the particular social milieux in which they grew up.

Finally, we have examined our data for evidence of a "sexual revolution" in moral norms. On the basis of our findings, we cannot conclude that such a revolution was under way at or near the time of our survey in 1970. Not only did most respondents report unchanged, conservative morals; in addition, those who reported that they did change were not especially likely to have done so recently. Moreover, comparable data gathered up to 1978 show the same patterns of approval/disapproval we found.

In short, the generally conservative norms of the majority, whose moralities display neither aging nor generational change, suggest that traditional values and cultural continuity controlled contemporary American sexual norms in 1970, as they presumably did in the past.

NOTES

1. Of course, these data do not tell us *how much* more (or less) approving people have become, or *how many* successive moral changes they thought they experienced.
2. An index like the MCI, constructed by attribute-space analysis (i.e., with the expectation that people's scores on the constituent items will display a progression rather than high intercorrelation), does not admit of reliability testing by alpha.
3. It might be possible, as well, that such a person could make a bigger change regarding homosexuality than masturbation—e.g., from "always wrong" to "wrong only sometimes" would be more of a change than from "almost always wrong" to "wrong only sometimes."
4. It should also be mentioned that a person who says he or she is now more liberal about homosexuality than before might still consider it always wrong.
5. For example, a person may abandon the notion that adultery should be a criminal offense but may still believe that extramarital sex is morally wrong.
6. Controlling these data for age might show whether there is an aging effect that some respondents were too young to have experienced and that is thus obscured in our broader findings. However, this is not feasible with our data—the *N*'s are too small for meaningful interpretation.
7. For example, 25% of respondents of either sex reported a change in morality respecting masturbation (gamma = .02). Since many more males than females have ever masturbated (Kinsey et al., 1953), if experience mitigates standards, we should have expected a difference between the sexes here. Further, although females commonly begin masturbating at later ages than males, controlling for age at change likewise produces no differences. Similarly, 20% of the males and 17% of the females reported a moral change concerning homosexuality (gamma = .08). Again, age at change does not differentiate the two sexes further, even though this experience is also more common among males; for example, Kinsey et al. (1953) found that by age 15, 5% of all females but 28% of all males had had a homosexual contact.
8. We do not present data simply for reported "age at last moral change" because they can be misleading; e.g., as our questions did not provide for successive changes, we cannot infer that the age respondents gave is necessarily that at which their moralities would have become permanently stabilized.
9. In all age groups, perceived moral change is associated with more liberal norms, and those who reported change had similar standards regardless of age. Thus, young people do not seem to be making a radically different *type* of change.

Chapter 6

Premarital Sex

The study of premarital sex is one of the major research areas in the sociology of sexual behavior. Indeed, the notion of a sexual revolution is often associated with the idea that the sexual behavior of the young indicates what is happening to sexuality in the United States. We have already seen, too, the important influence of premarital experiences upon our respondents' current sexual norms. Now in this chapter we present in greater detail our data on the premarital sexual experiences of the American population in 1970.

Studies in the late 1960s and the 1970s showed an increase in the incidence of premarital sexual intercourse, especially among females (e.g., Kaats & Davis, 1970; K. Davis, 1971; Robinson et al., 1972; Bauman & Wilson, 1974). Others noted a convergence in sexual attitudes and behavior for males and females (Pope & Knudsen, 1965; Christensen & Gregg, 1970). In addition, it appears that formal engagement to marry had become a less important prerequisite for female participation in premarital coitus (Bell & Chaskes, 1970). This situation was described by Reiss (1967) as "permissiveness with affection"—young persons who are fond of each other engage in sex without necessarily planning eventual marriage. Moreover, there was some evidence that females felt less guilt or remorse about their sexual behavior than formerly (Bell & Chaskes, 1970; Christensen & Gregg, 1970). Although the preponderance of such studies dealt with college students, some of these results were supported in a random sample of females aged 15–19 (Zelnik & Kantner, 1972, 1977) and among other young, noncollege groups (Miller & Simon, 1974; Vener & Stewart, 1974).

It is not possible to compare our study to the foregoing ones because only two of them (Zelnik & Kantner, 1972, 1977) employed nationwide probability samples, and both were limited to females then aged 15–19. Moreover, we chose our variables with the particular aim of explaining sexual norms; so we do not have data on many issues of concern to previous studies of premarital sexual behavior. (For example, we do not have a measure of specific *types* of sexual behavior, such as kissing or petting as differentiated from coitus.)

On the other hand, our study does have some advantages. Being representative of the general population, it allows us to portray the premarital sexual experience of the American people at one particular time. In this way it provides a benchmark for future investigations of changing sexual patterns. As it covers a wide span of ages, our sample can also be used retrospectively to suggest the situation in past times. Finally, in terms of predicting premarital sexual behavior, we have data on a large array of variables that previous researchers have not used. In the sections that follow, we first present our data and then, by means of path analysis, attempt to predict the extent of involvement in premarital sex.

Reports of Premarital Sexual Behavior

In earlier chapters, the major variable concerning premarital sex is the composite measure premarital sexual involvement. This factor includes giving or receiving sexual propositions and engaging in coitus as well as other heterosexual sexual behaviors. As such it represents a more realistic indicator of youthful sexual experience than the ones traditionally used, incidence and/or frequency of premarital *coitus* (only), because many young people may abstain from coitus but substitute for it other equally "advanced" activities (Kinsey et al., 1948). It is this premarital sexual involvement measure that we use in our later regression analyses. For this part of the chapter, however, we use our variable premarital sexual frequency. Again, this represents an improvement over previous research emphasizing purely coital experiences, in that it measures the amount of *any type* of premarital sexual activity. The data come from a question that reads as follows: "How old were you the first time you had sexual activity with someone of the opposite sex when either you or your partner came to a sexual climax (orgasm)?" Questions then continue as to the fre-

TABLE 6-1 Reports of Premarital Sexual Experience

	Male	Female	Total sample
Incidence			
No such experience before marriage	20.6%	59.3%	41.0%
At least one experience before marriage	79.4	40.7	59.0
Column total	100.0%	100.0%	100.0%
Base *n* (ever married)	1,298	1,468	2,766
No answer	32	21	53
Never married	135	64	199
Total sample	1,465	1,553	3,018
Age at first experience			
Under 16	33.5%	19.5%	28.4%
16	16.2	16.8	16.4
17	13.8	15.4	14.4
18	14.2	15.0	14.5
19	7.1	11.3	8.6
20	4.3	6.7	5.2
21–22	5.8	9.4	7.1
23–24	2.1	2.9	2.4
25–29	2.3	2.4	2.3
30 or older	0.7	0.7	0.7
Column total	100.0%	100.1%	100.0%
Base *n*	1,005	585	1,590
No answer	58	37	95
No premarital sex	267	867	1,134
Never married	135	64	199
Total sample	1,465	1,553	3,018

NOTE. Those who had never been married—6.6% of the total sample—are excluded from data in this and following tables for two reasons: (1) in a cross-sectional survey it may confound results to include data from people whose "premarital" experiences are not complete, and (2) the social and intrapsychic meanings of sexuality may be different for the never-married minority, who have not chosen or at least lack the institutionalized regular sexual access marriage provides.

quency, number of partners, and so on, regarding these "sexual experiences." Thus, although coitus probably represents an important part of such experiences, we must again stress that our terms *premarital sex* and *premarital sexual experience* imply more than just coital experiences.[1]

Of our respondents who had ever been married, 59% said they had had at least one premarital sexual experience of the kind we have defined. Table 6-1 shows that over a quarter of these had their first such experience before they were 16, and about 60% before age 18. Premarital sex clearly begins most often in the teen years: almost 90% of these respondents reported that their first experience occurred when they were 20 or younger.

Table 6-2 shows the relationship between gender and premarital sexual experience. Such experiences are about twice as likely to have characterized males among our respondents, who were also likely to have had their first experiences earlier than females. Males also reported a higher frequency, although this relationship is much less strong than that for incidence. A stronger relationship is found for number of partners. Males were much more likely than females to have had a large number of partners: 35% of men compared to only 4% of women reported ten or more premarital sex partners. Further, about half the females had premarital sex only with their future spouses, compared to about 10% of the males. This indicates the closer association between sex and affection in the sexual experience of females as compared to males. Controlling these findings for a variety of other variables, such as prepubertal exposure to various kinds of sexuality, failed to have an effect. This seems to imply that differences in male-female sexual experience are too broad to be encompassed in any one of our variables.

Table 6-2 also shows the relationship between premarital sexual experiences and age. It is evident that these experiences were less common among older respondents, with 44% of those over 65 reporting them, compared with 74% of those under 35. In addition, such experiences began at an earlier age among current than among past generations. Younger age groups also reported a higher frequency of premarital sex, although frequency differences are less pronounced than those for incidence. When it comes to number of partners, however, the situation is reversed—those in older generations had *more* sexual partners than younger generations, while younger people were more likely to have had their premarital experiences only with their future spouses. This seems to indicate a change in premarital sexual patterns from the older one, where a small number of females were involved with a large number of males, to a contemporary pattern in which premarital sex often accompanies affectionate relationships. When these findings are controlled for gender, the relationship between age and having premarital sex only with the future spouse disappears for females (partial gamma = .02), suggesting that the younger males are con-

TABLE 6-2 Dimensions of Premarital Sexual Experience

	Gender		Age			Race		Total sample
	Male	Female	Under 35	35 to 64	65 or older	White	Black	
Had premarital sex	80.2%	42.0%	73.8%	55.7%	43.6%	56.9%	79.3%	60.4%
Base *n*	1,433	1,532	1,054	1,484	424	2,492	473	2,965
Gamma	−.70			−.30		.49		
If yes:								
Age at first experience								
Under 16	33.5%	19.0%	31.4%	26.7%	23.1%	25.6%	39.2%	28.4%
Over 18	22.1	33.8	19.5	29.9	39.9	28.4	17.9	26.3
Base *n*	1,109	621	758	797	173	1,378	352	1,730
Gamma	.29			.19		−.27		
Frequency								
Rarely ("once or twice")	22.6%	34.7%	22.2%	29.4%	35.8%	25.7%	31.6%	26.9%
Fairly often	35.8	26.3	38.2	29.9	19.0	31.3	36.6	32.4
Base *n*	1,051	574	725	730	168	1,286	339	1,625
Gamma	−.23			−.14		−.00		
Number of partners								
Only the future spouse	9.8%	47.1%	28.1%	21.7%	11.1%	24.5%	20.2%	23.6%
Ten or more	35.4	4.3	21.6	25.4	27.8	23.8	24.3	23.9
Base *n*	982	580	716	700	144	1,241	321	1,562
Gamma	−.73			.12		.00		

verging with traditional female patterns, rather than that both sexes are changing equally.

Regarding race, Table 6-2 shows that more blacks than whites had had premarital experiences and began them earlier, although there are no real differences in frequency. In general, too, we find that there are no differences by race in the number of premarital sexual partners or in whether such experiences took place solely with one's future spouse. These findings represent cultural differences between blacks and whites whereby the experience of premarital sex is more common and begins earlier in black society; circumstances of the partnerships involved, however, are apparently similar across racial lines.[2]

When broken down by other standard sociological variables, these data yield few clear findings. For example, community size is modestly related with incidence, with somewhat more of the respondents who grew up in large cities reporting that they had premarital sex compared with those from small towns or farms (gamma = .21), but there are no differences in frequency or partners. For geographic region, despite regional differences in the conservatism of prevailing sexual norms, no substantive differences appear on any of these variables. Concerning education, there are some differences between the most and the least educated. Of those who went to college, 68% reported premarital experiences, but only 50% of those who did not go beyond the eighth grade did so, and the college people reported a higher frequency, but this probably reflects the later age at marriage for the college people (i.e., a longer period of opportunity), and differences between adjacent categories are small. For parents' social class, however, there is no relationship at all. Childhood religious affiliation produces the predictable finding that premarital sex is more apt to occur, and is less apt to take place only with the future spouse, among those with no affiliation; the small number of Jews were also somewhat more likely to report partners other than their fiancés. Finally, premarital sexual experience seems unrelated to the success of marriage, as the currently married and those divorced or separated do not differ on any of these measures. (The widowed are too concentrated in the older age categories for meaningful comparison.)

Feelings About Premarital Sexual Experiences

Besides asking about actual premarital sexual behaviors, we also collected data on the feelings that can accompany these behaviors. These feelings included regret surrounding the experience as well as the data summarized in Chapter 3 as positive and negative feelings about premarital sex. Here we present data on the items used to make up these two composite measures. These data are arranged according to whether the respondent did or did not have the actual experience. In the latter case we asked what respondents thought they would have felt at the time: thus we can look for factors that may have prevented those respondents from having the actual experience.

Of course, we are dealing here with retrospective data. This means, for one thing, that respondents who did not have premarital sex may, in indicating which of several feelings they recall about it, have unconsciously justified that long-ago decision by choosing responses that would reflect their present-day morality. Such a process could help raise the proportion of negative responses, and lower that of positive responses, among the premaritally inexperienced. Therefore we take note only of the most striking differences. Furthermore, the structure of our interview requires us to assume that respondents' premarital behavior was guided (or even determined) by the norms and attitudes they held in their teens, although we cannot test this notion explicitly because we did not ask—except as the items discussed below imply—what their norms were in those days. (This question is addressed, however, in Chapter 11, where we look for indications of respondents' having behaved contrary to their moralities.) In the paragraphs below, we therefore place greater stress on the patterns contributing to positive or negative feelings in the aggregate than on responses to individual interview items.

Regret over Premarital Sex

About 40% of those who had premarital experience expressed at least some regret about it, while about 8% of the inexperienced regretted that they did *not* have the experience (Table 6-3).[3] This difference remains constant across age categories. Regarding gender, among the experienced nearly twice as many females as males

TABLE 6-3 Regret over Premarital Sex

	Gender		Age			Race		Total sample
	Male	Female	Under 35	35 to 64	65 or older	White	Black	
Had premarital sex:								
"Do you now feel strong regret, only some regret, or no regret at all . . .?"								
Strong or some regret	30.9%	55.1%	40.7%	38.9%	40.9%	40.3%	36.2%	39.5%
Base *n*	1,080	587	740	754	171	1,319	348	1,667
Gamma	.44			−.02		−.08		
Did not have premarital sex:								
"Have you ever regretted that you did not have . . .?"								
Yes	13.5%	6.7%	10.4%	7.3%	5.7%	8.2%	10.0%	8.3%
Base *n*	251	808	249	682	211	969	90	1,059
Gamma	−.37			−.20		.11		

regretted that premarital sex occurred; the reverse is true for the inexperienced, where more males than females regretted that they did not have the experience. Absolute percentages are perhaps more striking: whereas 14% of the inexperienced males regretted not having premarital sexual experience, over half of the experienced females (and 31% of the males) expressed some regret. No such differences appear for race.

Positive Feelings About Premarital Sex

For the experienced, the positive feeling remembered most often about their premarital experiences was physical pleasure, reported by almost 60% regardless of age or race (Table 6-4). The inexperienced respondents were also most likely to think this would have been a feature of premarital sex had they had it, especially the younger ones.

In terms of gender, more males than females mentioned physical pleasure regardless of whether they were experienced. The females gave equal emphasis to the pleasure received in being wanted or needed (they did not differ from the males, however, in the proportion emphasizing this feeling). Next among important feelings was the happiness in finally having had a "full" sexual experience; twice as many males reported this as females. It is interesting to note that few of either gender put much stress on the admiration of peers, sometimes thought of as an important socializing factor for males. In fact, only 17% of the males reported receiving respect from others of their sex after the experience. In addition, nearly half of the males seem to have had sex with affection, claiming that the sexual experiences signified a special relationship with the female. These two findings seem to restrict the applicability of Gagnon and Simon's (1973) theory of sexual socialization, with its emphasis on the homosocial and genital focus of early male sexuality. These findings also are not specified by social class or educational level, although there was a slight tendency for the lowest educational groups to report more feelings of respect from peers than groups at higher levels. We would note, however, that peer support seems more common among older groups, so that we might be tapping significant social changes.

As to race, blacks with premarital experience were more likely than whites to report satisfaction with having had the experience and pleasure at being wanted or needed this way, to be happy

TABLE 6-4 Positive Feelings About Premarital Sex

	Gender				Age					
	Experienced		Inexperienced		Experienced			Inexperienced		
Felt/would have felt:	Male	Female	Male	Female	Under 35	35 to 64	65 or older	Under 35	35 to 64	65 or older
Pleased with the physical feeling	68.7%	41.0%	62.2%	36.2%	61.0%	57.8%	54.8%	52.3%	41.4%	28.8%
Base *n*	1,062	590	185	636	743	739	168	218	456	146
Gamma	−.48		−.48			−.06			−.19	
Happy to have finally had a full sexual experience	49.4%	24.0%	51.1%	25.5%	40.7%	39.5%	42.6%	34.1%	29.9%	29.9%
Base *n*	1,046	579	184	639	732	729	162	217	458	147
Gamma	−.49		−.51			−.00			−.00	
Pleased to be wanted or needed this way	38.7%	42.4%	48.9%	35.5%	44.3%	37.6%	28.8%	42.9%	39.0%	30.0%
Base *n*	1,044	583	180	645	740	732	163	217	457	150
Gamma	.06		−.26			−.16			−.12	
Pleased to have this special kind of relationship with someone	44.6%	29.2%	44.2%	26.0%	43.4%	36.1%	33.3%	36.1%	29.2%	23.6%
Base *n*	1,049	585	181	646	742	731	161	219	459	148
Gamma	−.32		−.39			−.12			−.13	
Happy it showed I had sex appeal	34.6%	26.3%	42.6%	30.6%	31.0%	30.6%	36.5%	36.5%	33.6%	25.3%
Base *n*	1,043	586	183	648	739	731	167	219	461	150
Gamma	−.18		−.26			−.04			−.08	
Pleased because others of my sex respected me for it	17.4%	8.1%	28.8%	14.0%	8.3%	15.3%	21.7%	13.4%	17.2%	22.5%
Base *n*	1,047	582	184	643	735	731	161	217	458	151
Gamma	−.52		−.42			.07			.21	

TABLE 6-4 (*continued*)

	Race					
	Experienced		Inexperienced		Total sample	
Felt/would have felt:	White	Black	White	Black	Experienced	Inexperienced
Pleased with the physical feeling	58.2%	61.5%	41.4%	47.9%	58.8%	42.0%
Base *n*	1,322	330	748	73	1,652	821
Gamma	.06		.11			
Happy to have finally had a full sexual experience	38.5%	48.0%	29.8%	43.2%	40.4%	31.0%
Base *n*	1,302	323	749	74	1,625	823
Gamma	.19		.26			
Pleased to be wanted or needed this way	38.2%	47.3%	37.9%	44.0%	40.0%	38.4%
Base *n*	1,297	330	750	75	1,627	825
Gamma	.17		.10			
Pleased to have this special kind of relationship with someone	36.8%	48.5%	28.8%	42.5%	39.1%	30.0%
Base *n*	1,306	328	754	73	1,634	827
Gamma	.19		.27			
Happy it showed I had sex appeal	27.8%	46.6%	32.8%	37.8%	31.6%	33.2%
Base *n*	1,301	328	756	75	1,629	831
Gamma	.27		.07			
Pleased because others of my sex respected me for it	10.2%	29.5%	16.4%	26.0%	14.1%	17.3%
Base *n*	1,300	329	754	73	1,629	827
Gamma	.40		.25			

because it showed they had sex appeal, and to be pleased because other members of their sex respected them for it. Among the inexperienced, blacks were more likely than whites to note that they would have liked the sense of finally having had a full sexual experience and the special relationship it implied. These findings are the same for both black males and black females and presumably reflect the more accepting stance toward premarital sexuality found in black society, as we have mentioned earlier.

Considering the data in this table, what appears most striking is a general tendency for more of the premaritally experienced than of the inexperienced in a particular group to express a particular positive feeling. These differences are usually quite small, but they contribute to an overall pattern that leads us to speculate that the lack of positive anticipation may have contributed to many people's avoidance of premarital sex. This pattern seems to be eminently sensible, so the few exceptions to it are noteworthy. For example, among the youngest group of respondents, on the question of whether they thought they would have felt confirmed in their sex appeal and respected by their peers, slightly *more* of the inexperienced felt this way than the percentage of the experienced who expressed this feeling. In addition, among the males, nearly half of the inexperienced versus two-fifths of the experienced stressed pleasure in their partner's desire for them. It is possible that these findings point up a difference between sexual imagery and sexual reality. We have already noted that inexperienced males (and females too, but to a lesser extent) apparently anticipate more reinforcement from their friends than the experienced seem actually to perceive, or at least to value. Still, it must be stressed that in almost every case, fewer than half of the inexperienced groups thought they would have had *any* of these positive reactions.

Negative Feelings About Premarital Sex

Table 6-3 shows that premaritally experienced respondents more often regretted this experience than the inexperienced regretted *not* having it. The following data specify some of the feelings that can underlie regret or at least part of the ambivalence that can characterize the experience. In addition, as suggested earlier, they may help to explain why the inexperienced respondents refrained from premarital sex; for as we can see, the nine negative feelings we asked about were reported much more frequently by the inexperienced.

Chief among the negative feelings was the fear that pregnancy might ensue, with 42% of the experienced and 84% of the inexperienced reporting this fear (Table 6-5). Among the experienced this does not vary by age, but it does among the inexperienced, where this fear was more common among the *younger* respondents. Since this generation presumably had access to a wide variety of reliable contraceptives, it may be that for them the fear of pregnancy masqueraded for deeper and less articulated moral concerns, and this may go far in explaining why they did not have this experience. Fear of pregnancy also is predictably differentiated by gender: almost twice as many experienced females (over half) as males feared pregnancy. Among the inexperienced, large majorities of both sexes reported this fear. The difference between the two groups of males may reflect ignorance or stricter moral training among the inexperienced. When we compare races, the fear of pregnancy appears to have been less common among the inexperienced blacks.

Two closely allied items were next most often cited among the experienced groups: being afraid that their activities would be discovered or their reputation threatened. Twenty-four percent of the experienced, compared with many more of the inexperienced (69% and 83%, respectively), reported these two feelings. The size of this difference may suggest that people who refrained from premarital sex grew up in circumstances where one's "good name" depended on this kind of abstinence more than it did for the experienced respondents. For example, while more females than males expressed both of these concerns (although more than half of the inexperienced males did so), 89% of the inexperienced females but only 44% of the experienced ones feared for their reputations. This implies that some 56% of the experienced females were not particularly affected while growing up by the traditional emphasis on a girl's remaining "chaste" until marriage. Across age groups there are almost no differences on these measures (36% of the oldest respondents with premarital experience, compared with 22% of the youngest, worried about their reputation; elsewhere percentages are quite similar). Between the two races there are no differences at all.

Another component of a moral dimension that may have under-

TABLE 6-5 Negative Feelings About Premarital Sex

	Gender				Age					
	Experienced		Inexperienced		Experienced			Inexperienced		
Felt/would have felt:	Male	Female	Male	Female	Under 35	35 to 64	65 or older	Under 35	35 to 64	65 or older
Fear it would cause pregnancy	32.6%	57.6%	70.5%	88.1%	42.4%	41.7%	37.1%	90.5%	84.6%	73.6%
Base *n*	1,070	601	193	671	745	757	167	222	486	155
Gamma	.43		.46			−.09			−.22	
Fear of discovery	17.0%	37.3%	56.1%	72.6%	23.3%	25.4%	22.7%	71.8%	69.4%	64.7%
Base *n*	1,047	582	187	664	733	731	163	223	474	153
Gamma	.37		.32			−.04			−.06	
Fear of bad reputation	12.7%	44.2%	61.8%	89.4%	22.0%	23.3%	35.9%	83.7%	84.6%	79.0%
Base *n*	1,059	595	186	669	742	743	167	221	481	152
Gamma	.62		.64			−.05			−.02	
Fear of venereal disease	21.5%	16.3%	63.0%	58.4%	10.0%	25.8%	34.8%	56.0%	61.3%	58.4%
Base *n*	1,053	583	189	646	738	732	164	218	462	154
Gamma	−.34		−.10			.27			.09	
Guilt, shame, or embarrassment	8.9%	33.2%	69.4%	86.6%	18.0%	17.6%	15.1%	85.6%	83.7%	75.6%
Base *n*	1,056	591	193	671	740	739	166	222	485	156
Gamma	.58		.49			−.07			−.13	
Physical pain	3.1%	16.1%	15.7%	46.9%	9.7%	6.5%	4.4%	47.0%	37.3%	38.6%
Base *n*	1,049	583	178	636	742	727	161	215	453	145
Gamma	.76		.62			−.27			−.07	

Afraid of failure as a sexual partner	5.9%	10.2%	24.9%	30.2%	9.0%	6.0%	6.2%	35.3%	26.6%	27.0%
Base *n*	1,054	587	185	652	742	736	161	218	466	152
Gamma	.17		.11			−.21			−.07	
Feeling of disgust or filth about sex	4.7%	8.6%	33.9%	47.4%	5.3%	6.0%	8.6%	42.5%	42.0%	54.4%
Base *n*	1,051	583	180	644	734	735	163	219	457	147
Gamma	.29		.25			.04			.13	
Disappointed in the sexual experience	5.0%	11.5%	17.2%	35.5%	8.2%	6.2%	8.0%	35.9%	29.9%	29.9%
Base *n*	1,043	581	180	633	734	726	162	217	451	144
Gamma	.48		.42			−.03			−.06	

(*table continued on next page*)

TABLE 6-5 (*continued*)

	Race					
	Experienced		Inexperienced		Total sample	
Felt/would have felt:	White	Black	White	Black	Experienced	Inexperienced
Fear it would cause pregnancy	41.6%	41.7%	85.2%	73.1%	41.6%	84.1%
Base *n*	1,326	145	786	78	1,671	864
Gamma	.03		−.38			
Fear of discovery	23.9%	25.5%	69.3%	65.8%	24.2%	69.0%
Base *n*	1,308	321	775	76	1,629	851
Gamma	.05		−.10			
Fear of bad reputation	21.9%	12.5%	83.8%	78.9%	24.0%	83.4%
Base *n*	1,322	332	739	75	1,654	855
Gamma	.13		−.19			
Fear of venereal disease	18.2%	25.2%	59.2%	61.3%	19.6%	59.4%
Base *n*	1,310	326	760	75	1,636	835
Gamma	.18		.03			
Guilt, shame, or embarrassment	17.2%	19.3%	83.2%	77.6%	17.6%	82.8%
Base *n*	1,315	332	788	76	1,647	864
Gamma	.02		−.18			
Physical pain	5.2%	17.7%	37.6%	64.0%	7.7%	40.0%
Base *n*	1,305	325	739	75	1,632	814
Gamma	.50		.47			

Afraid of failure as a sexual partner	6.5%	11.2%	28.7%	32.0%	7.4%	29.0%
Base *n*	1,301	323	762	75	1,394	837
Gamma	.03		.05			
Feeling of disgust or filth about sex	4.4%	12.7%	43.9%	50.0%	6.1%	44.4%
Base *n*	1,301	323	748	76	1,634	824
Gamma	.16		.11			
Disappointed in the sexual experience	6.1%	12.4%	31.3%	33.8%	7.3%	31.5%
Base *n*	1,301	323	739	74	1,394	813
Gamma	.16		.03			

lain respondents' decisions about whether to engage in premarital sex is feeling guilty, ashamed, or embarrassed about it (see Mosher & Cross, 1971). Such feelings were reported by fewer than 20% of the experienced but over 80% of the inexperienced, and more often by females than by males. The idea that some people might have abstained from premarital sex because, believing it was wrong, they would have felt bad about it, seems illustrated best in the percentages for the males: only 9% of the experienced had these feelings, while 69% of the inexperienced males anticipated feeling this way. In addition, young people who have received extremely strict warnings about premarital sex may regard it with some revulsion. Thus, 44% of the inexperienced but hardly any of the experienced reported feelings of "disgust or filth about sex."

Slightly more common than the latter was concern about venereal disease. Among the experienced, this was reported more often by the oldest respondents—over one-third, compared with a tenth of those under 35—probably as a reflection of the type of partner and situation that characterized earlier patterns of this behavior. It was also cited more frequently by the inexperienced respondents (59%) than by the experienced (20%); this difference seems unlikely to reflect differences in the kind of partners who were available, as there is no age difference among the inexperienced, so it seems possible that the inexperienced groups may simply have been warned about this consequence without learning much about its prevalence or prevention.

The fear of physical pain also differentiates the two groups, with 40% of the inexperienced having anticipated it and 8% of the experienced having actually felt it. This was reported more often by females than males; 16% of the experienced females—but one-fifth as many males—said that their premarital sexual experiences were physically painful. More blacks than whites also reported that they experienced pain or supposed they would have. (Although females made up a larger proportion of the experienced blacks than they did among whites, this does not explain why more blacks experienced pain, as it occurred more often in blacks of both genders.)

Finally, given the notion that premarital sexual encounters may be furtive, hurried, or awkward, it is interesting to note that hardly any of the experienced respondents reported disappointment in the experience. Among the inexperienced, about a third had an-

TABLE 6-6 Current Sexual Enjoyment, by Premarital Sexual Experience (Percentages Finding Sexual Experience Enjoyable Just About Every Time)

	Had premarital sex	Base *n*	No premarital sex	Base *n*	Gamma
Gender					
Male	61.4%	994	51.7%	234	.20
Female	31.9	580	25.6	806	.17
Age					
Under 35	49.9	651	41.2	250	.18
35 to 64	51.6	754	28.2	585	.45
65 or older	48.8	168	28.4	204	.44
Race					
White	51.9	1,270	31.1	958	.42
Black	44.9	305	35.4	82	.18
Total sample	55.5%	1,574	31.4%	1,040	.38

ticipated feeling disappointed. In both groups disappointment was more often reported by females, but only by a small proportion—about one in ten of the premaritally experienced, for example. Having felt fear of failure as a sexual partner was similarly not common among either group of respondents, although twice as many inexperienced females as males had had this concern.

Negative feelings about premarital sex were, in summary, more characteristic of respondents who did *not* have experiences of this kind than among those who did. Differences between the two groups tend to be most marked concerning the consequences and implications of the act, permitting the inference that worries about pregnancy, a bad reputation, and so forth, coupled with feelings that premarital sex is wrong, may have led many in our inexperienced group to abstain from such encounters.

A final question is one often raised about premarital sex: To what extent do premarital sexual experiences affect later sexual adjustment. Kinsey et al. (1953) suggested that the relationship is a positive one, as did later research (Kanin & Howard, 1958). As we have data on current enjoyment of sex among our respondents, we can see if reported premarital experience affected it in any way; Table 6-6 reports these findings.

The relationship between premarital experience and postmarital sexual enjoyment appears to be substantial. Of the experienced, 55% reported currently enjoying sex just about always, compared to 31% of the inexperienced. These findings are affected by age, race, and gender, with the relationship being weaker among those under 35, blacks, and females (although for males it is not markedly stronger). This finding suggests that actually having had premarital sex is less important for postmarital sexual happiness for the younger generation and for blacks, two groups among whom it is a common experience.

Explaining Premarital Sexual Involvement

A variety of factors have been found to be associated with participation in premarital coitus (see Chilman, 1978:123–144, for a review of these factors). Among them are some on which we have data, such as race, gender, religiosity, home community during childhood—both geographic region and urban/rural—and so on. We cannot attempt to replicate these findings insofar as we do not have a measure of coital behavior per se. However, our measure of premarital sexual involvement does just as well as a measure of general sexual involvement and is at least as valid as one dealing solely with coitus. We can expect, therefore, that results of our analysis of general premarital sexual involvement should closely resemble those for studies of premarital coitus.[4]

We began our analysis with 53 independent variables,[5] which we ran against our dependent variable of premarital sexual involvement, giving us an R of .769 and an R^2 of .590. Using the same screening techniques as for the SMS (Chapter 4), we arrived at a set of 12 variables that provide an R of .757 and an R^2 of .573. In this total-path model, as ranked by total effects, sex-female is the strongest variable in the explanation of premarital sexual involvement. Next in order, but far behind, come lifetime sexual environment, positive feelings about premarital sex, and age. Sex-female works almost equally in direct and indirect ways and has virtually no extraneous effects. Lifetime sexual environment, on the other hand, exerts its effects overwhelmingly directly, and some 38% of its total association with premarital sexual involvement is extraneous. Positive feelings about premarital sex has no indirect effects because of its location in our temporal model, and about half of its total association is extraneous. Age has more indirect than direct effects—nearly twice as many—with very little extraneous association.

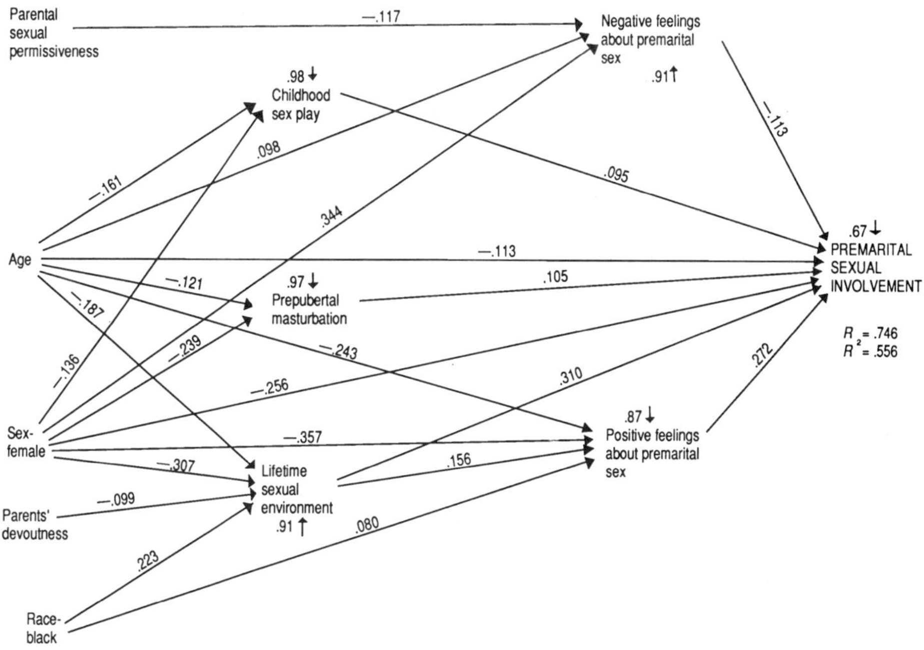

Figure 6-1 Path Diagram Model for Premarital Sexual Involvement
Note: Correlations among independent variables are given in Appendix E.

To examine the interrelationships among the variables, we constructed a path diagram (Figure 6-1) using our previously established criterion in the dropping of paths. It provides an *R* of .746 and an R^2 of .556, so that dropped paths account for less than 2% of the variance explained. Table 6-7 compares the effects of variables in this path diagram model with the effects of those in the total-path model and shows a close fit. The four strongest variables are retained in the same order with roughly the same direct and indirect effects. We do lose the variables reared on farm and never masturbated, however, as their connections to other variables do not meet our path inclusion criteria. Other variables more or less retain their rank, with the following two exceptions: parental sexual permissiveness is reduced in importance because we cannot include its direct path (which is too weak to meet our criterion) and because of a large diminution in its indirect effects; and neg-

TABLE 6-7 Comparison of Effects in the Total-Path Model with Effects in the Path Diagram Model

Variable	Direct effect	Indirect effects	Total effects	Extraneous effects	Total association
Sex-female	−.236	−.274	−.510	.001	−.509
	−.256	*−.282*	*−.538*	*.029*	
Lifetime sexual environment	.290	.045	.335	.207	.542
	.310	*.042*	*.352*	*.190*	
Positive feelings about premarital sex	.252	—	.252	.283	.535
	.272	—	*.272*	*.263*	
Age	−.080	−.124	−.204	−.002	−.206
	−.113	*−.145*	*−.258*	*.052*	
Race-black	.055	.088	.143	−.019	.124
	—	*.100*	*.100*	*.024*	
Prepubertal masturbation	.087	.031	.118	.191	.309
	.105	—	*.105*	*.204*	
Parental sexual permissiveness	.048	.061	.109	.180	.289
	—	*.013*	*.013*	*.276*	
Reared on farm	−.065	−.043	−.108	−.070	−.178
	[Does not meet diagram inclusion criteria]				
Childhood sex play	.084	.017	.101	.161	.262
	.095	—	*.095*	*.167*	
Negative feelings about premarital sex	−.099	—	−.099	−.185	−.284
	−.113	—	*−.113*	*−.171*	
Parents' devoutness	−.066	−.031	−.097	−.034	−.131
	—	*−.035*	*−.035*	*−.096*	
Never masturbated	−.066	—	−.066	−.342	−.408
	[Does not meet diagram inclusion criteria]				

NOTE: Figures in the first row following each variable represent effects with all possible paths between variables. Figures in italics represent effects with only those paths surpassing exclusion criteria.

ative feelings about premarital sex increases in importance because of an increase in its direct effect and because of the removal of reared on farm from our set of variables. Altogether, we feel justified in assuming that our path model represents the most parsimonious model for analysis of the relationships among our variables, to which we now turn.

Gender, as earlier analyses implied, relates most strongly to involvement in premarital sex. Thus, female respondents were much less likely than males to report being involved in sex before marriage. Gender also has strong indirect effects, influencing the probability of premarital sexual involvement through the way being female relates to other variables. Most powerful are those that work through positive feelings about premarital sex and account for almost 35% of the indirect effects of gender: as Table 6-4 showed, females were less likely than males to positively anticipate or evaluate premarital sex, and according to our analysis, this strongly determined their level of involvement in it. Almost as strong an intervening variable is lifetime sexual environment, which carries about 34% of the indirect effects of gender. Our finding is that females are less frequently exposed to a sexual environment than are males, and this in turn reduces the probability of their becoming involved in premarital sex. The only other important indirect path leads through feeling negative toward premarital sex and accounts for about 14% of the indirect effects of sex-female. Females are more likely to anticipate or experience negative feelings about premarital sex and hence are less likely to become very much involved in it. It can be assumed that females who do experience premarital sex have evaded whatever external controls are placed upon them; internal controls are less easy to gainsay, however, as suggested in Table 6-5, where premaritally experienced females displayed more negative feelings than their male counterparts.

Age is also an important exogenous variable. According to our analysis, the older a person is, the less likely it is that he or she has had much premarital sexual involvement. Age also has strong indirect effects, mainly through the same paths as gender: positive feelings about premarital sex and lifetime sexual environment each account for about 40% of the indirect effects of age. Thus, an older person is less likely to have anticipated or evaluated premarital sex positively or to have grown up in a sexual environment, and the absence of each of these conditions decreases the probability of premarital sexual involvement.

Among other variables of interest, race-black works mainly indirectly, and overwhelmingly so, through lifetime sexual environment (which carries almost 70% of its indirect effects). Our analysis shows that blacks are more likely than whites to report having experienced a relatively broad sexual environment, and this directly increases the level of their premarital sexual involvement. About 20% of the indirect effects of race-black work through feeling positive toward premarital sex. (This was illustrated in Table 6-4.) Blacks' greater likelihood of positively anticipating or evaluating premarital sex, then, increases the probability of their involvement in it.

We thus have a causal model showing that the structural factors of age, sex, and race are important determinants of the kinds of sexual environment a person is exposed to and the kinds of norms and attitudes he or she will apply to premarital sex, both of which affect the probability that he or she will actually become involved in it.

In a number of ways these data bear out the predictions of other studies (see Schulz et al., 1977), even though our measure of "involvement" allows for activities besides coitus. We find a high degree of premarital sexual involvement to be more common among males, younger people, blacks, or those whose parents were either low in religious devoutness or high in sexual permissiveness. The influence of peers is implied in our sexual environment factor (several studies have found higher rates of premarital coitus among young people with sexually active friends; see Walsh, 1970, 1972; Schulz et al., 1977). We do not have such frequently used measures as dating frequency, fraternity affiliation, and so on, since these are important only for the college-student sample typical of earlier studies, whereas in our national sample over three-quarters had never attended college. Given this striking difference from most "premarital" samples, with the implication that a number of different courtship styles are represented, it is still more noteworthy that in some cases our findings are similar. In addition, we find important influences in respondents' reported childhood sexual experiences and whatever feelings about sexuality their early socialization "conditioned" them to have. Taken together, the variables in our model seem to imply not so much a differential opportunity structure as differences in the inclination to act upon whatever opportunity presents itself.

Summary

Our principal measure in this chapter, premarital sexual involvement, assesses the extent to which respondents reported participating in a number of sexual activities before marriage. This permits our data to describe not only respondents who had premarital coitus but also those who avoided coitus but engaged in other, equally intimate activities. Over half of the ever-married sample did have this kind of sexual involvement before marriage, typically beginning in the late teens.

These incidence figures bear out some popular predictions. Males were more likely than females to have had such experiences, blacks more likely than whites, and younger people more likely than those from earlier generations. A higher incidence rate is also to be found among people growing up in urban areas, those with college education, and those with nonreligious parents. As to frequency, the same relationships are found for males and younger respondents; these groups also tended to report having had their first premarital experience at an earlier age, as did blacks.

We also illustrate how the circumstances of premarital sexual encounters are allied with how different groups of people interpret the meaning of sex. For example, males more often reported a number of different premarital partners, while females were much more likely to engage in premarital sex only with their eventual husbands. (This was true among both blacks and whites.) The older respondents with premarital experience tended to report more partners than did the younger ones, among whom more of the males limited their contacts to their future wives; this seems to bear out our earlier contention that the traditional double standard has become less of a prescriptive influence than it was in earlier generations.

Both respondents who had premarital sex and those who did not were asked to recall how they had felt about it at the time. Not surprisingly, the experienced respondents reported more positive feelings and fewer negative feelings than the inexperienced group. The experienced respondents were also much more likely to express regret that they had engaged in premarital sex than the inexperienced ones were to say that they regretted not having engaged in it.

Among specific feelings that the respondents with premarital experience most often recalled were those involving the immediate circumstances—physical gratification, enjoyment at being in such a close relationship, and so on. Those without experience similarly tended to report that they would probably have had these feelings. Relatively few thought that their peers' approval was or would have been an important part of their feelings. Some respondents without premarital experience mentioned that they would have felt sexually desirable if they had had such contact; the experienced ones were less likely to cite such an enhanced self-image.

The negative feeling that both experienced and inexperienced respondents most often mentioned was, predictably, the fear that pregnancy would ensue. Other social consequences—such as a loss of reputation—were next most often cited. The inexperienced group also thought they would have felt ashamed or guilty, which may reflect a moral basis for their abstinence. Negative feelings pertaining to the encounter itself—worries about sexual inadequacy, pain, or disappointment in the experience—were reported relatively seldom.

In many cases, females were less likely than males to report having had a particular positive feeling and more likely to report a particular negative one. The two genders seem to display the differential pattern anticipated by other investigators, wherein females are more concerned with the relational implications of sexual contact and males with the nature of the contact itself. Blacks' responses showed a less clear pattern; where they did differ from whites it was in putting more stress on feelings of personal satisfaction and social approval. As to differences among age groups, slight support for the contention that in earlier times premarital partnerships were different from more recent ones (e.g., the partner was more often a prostitute) can be inferred from two findings among the experienced respondents: the older ones more often worried about their reputation and about catching venereal disease.

With all these findings as background, we conducted a path analysis to see what factors might predict greater involvement in premarital sex. In this analysis, and controlling for many variables, we found the strongest predictor to be gender. According to our analysis, being female sharply limits the likelihood of one's having grown up in a sexual environment or developing a positive anticipation of premarital sex, and it also reduces the likelihood of one's having engaged in childhood masturbation or sex play. And females are much more likely than males to feel apprehension or disfavor when contemplating premarital sex. Age and race-black are also important, but they are surpassed in overall strength by lifetime sexual environment and feeling positive toward premarital sex, because the latter two have strong direct effects.

Two variables commonly appearing in other studies emerged in ours as indirect but not direct determinants of premarital sexual involvement: whether one's parents were religiously devout, which tends to limit one's awareness of a sexual environment; and whether they were sexually permissive, which tends to limit the extent of one's negative feelings about premarital sex. Another two, having grown up on a farm and never having masturbated, exhibited some effects but were too weak for inclusion in our final model. Basically, we found that people are more likely to have engaged in premarital sex if they are male, younger, and black. In addition, such people are more likely to have experienced masturbation and sex play in childhood and to have had friends or acquaintances who they knew were involved in various nonconjugal sexual activities. And predictably, we found that premarital sexual experiences are more common among people who had looked forward to having them and less common among those who had not.

Our analysis shows that blacks, males, younger people, and those from sexual environments (and indirectly, those whose parents were not especially devout) are more likely to develop positive feelings about premarital sex. Females, people whose parents were sexually strict with them, and those from earlier generations are more likely to react negatively to it. It seems, then, that relatively early influences help to determine young people's attitudes toward and participation (or not) in premarital sex.

NOTES

1. The following comment sums up the issue rather nicely: "Adolescents kiss, cling, fondle together; touch each other publicly in public places and privately in private places. They masturbate, pet above the waist, pet below the waist, and do a variety of other things sexual. Why, then, does so much of the literature reserve the term "sexually active" only for those adolescents who have engaged at least once in heterosexual intercourse?" (Society for the Study of Social Problems: Sexual Behavior Division, *Newsletter,* 1, no. 1 (Fall 1979), 2.)
2. Zelnik and Kantner (1977) showed that for unmarried females aged 15–19 during the period 1971–1976, blacks remained more experienced than whites, although relative differences had become smaller. Blacks continued to have sexual experiences at an earlier age, but there were still no differences in frequency. A change occurred over this period, however, in that blacks reported more of an increase in the number of partners than did whites.
3. When asked, "Have you ever wished that you had more of this sexual expe-

rience before marriage?" two-thirds of the premaritally experienced replied "no."

4. The analysis we are about to describe was repeated using the variable frequency of premarital sex as dependent, so as to provide a basis for replicability. (Whether people ever had premarital sex or not, as a dichotomous variable, would be less useful for path analysis.) The results were virtually the same as for the more comprehensive involvement factor, except that we could account for about 10% less of the variance in the frequency measure. This somewhat strengthens our belief that premarital sexual involvement is a superior measure.
5. Naturally we did not include the 30 variables pertaining to respondents' current situation, which comprised Stage 4 in the SMS analysis.

Chapter 7

Reactions to Homosexuality: Attitudes and Stereotypes[1]

The social psychological reaction toward homosexuality is a prime focus of our study, as we consider it crucial to understanding sexual morality in the United States. As Bell (1978) has noted, homosexuality impinges on such questions as what it means to be male or female, what can be considered sexual pathology, what the "purposes" of human sexuality are, and so forth. Thus homosexual relationships challenge the moral and emotional basis for the way our culture deals with sexuality. For this reason, any change in the social reaction toward homosexuality could indicate an important reassessment of sexual life in general. Some authors would go further, noting the peculiar role this form of sexual expression has played in Anglo-American culture, and claim that any such change would presage much wider social alterations. Consider, for example, Adam's comment (1978:42): "The common portrait [of the homosexual] retains the role of foil to ideals of health and the good. As these standards of 'official reality' evolve, the composite portrait accommodatingly adjusts in order to negatively index the norms of propriety, decency, conventionality, right."

This chapter studies this "portrait" as it emerges from the data provided by our respondents. In this way we will be able to see what is entwined within the moral meanings of homosexuality and perhaps to discover more about the operation of sexual moralities in general. For this reason we move from the concept of sexual *norms* to concepts of *attitudes* and *stereotyping*.

Attitude has many definitions, none of which is widely accepted

(Brannon, 1976). We have chosen that of Rokeach (1976:113): "An attitude is a relatively enduring organization of beliefs around an object or situation predisposing one to respond in some preferential manner." Furthermore, attitudes are seen as having three components (McGuire, 1969:155–156): a cognitive component, how the object of an attitude is perceived; an affective component, which refers to feelings or emotions toward the attitude object; and a conative component, that is, behavioral dispositions toward the attitude object. Thus we shall examine perceptions of homosexuality, feelings toward it, and what people think should be done about those who practice it.[2]

Many studies have shown that Americans hold strong attitudes regarding homosexuality. For instance, Simmons (1965) asked a sample of 134 respondents which characteristics they believed were true of homosexuals: 72% thought of homosexuals as sexually abnormal, 52% as perverted, 40% as mentally ill, 40% as maladjusted, and 29% as effeminate. Rooney and Gibbons (1966), in a study of 353 respondents from the San Francisco area, found that even in this relatively permissive city, 87% believed that homosexuals are psychologically disturbed and 69% that they are dangerous because they often try to seduce young boys. Other studies also document Americans' fear of homosexuals. A 1966 National Opinion Research Center poll of a nationwide probability sample of 946 persons 18 or older found that a third of the public believe homosexuality to be a social danger. A Harris poll in 1965 placed homosexuals third in a list of persons considered most harmful to the nation; only Communists and atheists were seen as more dangerous.[3] Steffensmeier (1970) found that two-thirds of his 373 respondents believed that homosexuality is a "sickness," 38% that it is "dangerous," and about 20% that homosexuals are "effeminate."

Studies such as these affirm that Americans disapprove of and fear homosexuality and suggest that such a reaction is associated with three commonly held beliefs about homosexuals—that they are sick, effeminate, and dangerous.

The first such belief, that homosexuals are sick, is a product of psychoanalytic theories of homosexuality that have dominated the scientific and medical literature for many years (Weinberg & Bell, 1972). Here, homosexuality is defined as a pathological deviation from the "normal" heterosexual outcome. Despite a retreat from this view by some professional organizations, a large number of psychiatrically influenced persons still hold to the older belief that homosexuality per se constitutes a mental illness.[4]

Concomitant with the belief that homosexuality is an illness is the belief that it can therefore be "cured." Thus, many persons feel that the homosexual is in need of psychotherapy. Other beliefs concerning the "cure" for homosexuality are less sophisticated, ranging from highly punitive legal measures to providing a talented partner of the opposite sex. Regardless, a significant proportion of the population obviously feels strongly that something should be done about the "problem of homosexuality."

The next belief, that male homosexuals are effeminate, is clearly based on the sex-role stereotyping that abounds in our culture. To be a "man" necessarily involves a strong and observable interest in women. A male who lacks this interest must then be less than a man, even womanish, according to such stereotyping. This belief, which equates masculinity/femininity with heterosexuality/homosexuality (see Gagnon & Simon, 1967), gains further credence from those homosexual males who fulfill the prophecy and behave in an effeminate manner. As this can be done publicly, these persons become the most visible of homosexuals and constitute a sample from which people generalize that all homosexual men are effeminate.

Finally, the belief that homosexuals are dangerous is one that people often ascribe to minority groups about which they know little (Adam, 1978). The sources of such fear are various; most common, however, is the belief that homosexuals molest children or attempt to convert them to homosexuality. Homosexuals are believed to prey on children as a result of their generally lustful and promiscuous sexuality. If people cannot control the direction of their sexual desires, this argument runs, no more can they control the objects, quantity, frequency, or anything else having to do with their sexual behavior.

Another important source of fear of homosexuals centers around the belief that homosexuality is "unnatural." Based on a theological conception of natural law and enshrined in criminal law by the sodomy statutes, this view accepts the teleology that the intention of sex is procreation, and any sexual act that cannot result in it is unnatural. This stance is consistent with genital physiology in the minds of many people. Thus, they not only have trouble conceptualizing what homosexuals do together sexually, but they also deny homosexuals the associated emotions of intimacy and love for each other (which also fits with the lustful image).

"Unnaturalness" also seems to be the basis for strong feelings of disgust toward homosexuality. Homosexuality violates the belief that there are two complementary sexes and calls into question socially defined limits to the nature of sexuality, which can be very threatening. Even more threatening, and a major reason why people recoil with disgust from homosexuality, is that many fear homosexual feelings in themselves (see Roeburt, 1963; Weinberg, 1972; Gagnon, 1977). Among men, this fear need not be explicitly sexual but can arise from concern about whether they are "masculine" enough. The fear of too close an identification in any way with a homosexual leads to aggressive feelings (San Miguel & Millham, 1976) and to an exaggerated anxiety about homosexual influence, suspicions of homosexual conspiracies or a belief that homosexuality was responsible for the downfall of civilizations, the Roman Empire, for instance.

Most of these research findings are not based on representative samples; so it is difficult to infer how widely the entire population share some of these attitudes. This chapter analyzes our 1970 data on attitudes toward and stereotyping of homosexuals in the United States. Our aim is to identify prevailing attitudes and to determine which of those attitudes predominated in the stereotyping we discovered.

The Social Reaction Toward Homosexuality

In the paragraphs below we have grouped findings according to whether they represent the cognitive, affective, or conative components of antihomosexual attitudes, corresponding to the components of content and process in stereotyping. This tripartite approach will be used again in later analyses (Chapters 8 and 9).

Homosexuality as Alien

One strong cognitive response toward homosexuals is that they are different from other people. That is, they are thought to look, act, and feel in distinctive ways. Accordingly, 37% of our respondents believed that they could recognize homosexuals by how they look. Nearly 70% agreed that homosexuals "act like the opposite

TABLE 7-1 Cognitive Beliefs About Homosexuals

Response	Homosexuals act like the opposite sex.	Homosexuals fear the opposite sex.	It is easy to tell homosexuals by how they look.	Homosexuals have unusually strong sex drives.	There is some homosexuality in everyone.
Strongly agree	22.4%	16.0%	11.9%	22.6%	9.6%
Somewhat agree	47.1	40.0	25.2	36.3	30.1
Somewhat disagree	15.9	22.4	24.8	14.8	16.3
Strongly disagree	6.9	10.9	30.2	6.6	34.2
Don't know	7.7	10.8	7.9	19.6	9.7
Column total	100.0%	100.1%	100.0%	99.9%	99.9%
Base *n*	2,990	3,002	2,998	2,999	2,998
No answer	28	16	20	19	20
Total sample	3,018	3,018	3,018	3,018	3,018

sex"; nevertheless, 56% said that homosexuals fear the opposite sex. Almost 60% agreed that homosexuals have very strong sex drives. Finally, despite this distancing from homosexuals, 40% agreed with the proposition that there is an element of homosexuality in everyone (Table 7-1).

Causes and "Cures" of Homosexuality

Equally as strong are the cognitive beliefs regarding causes of homosexuality. We asked our respondents whether they felt each of several lay and professional theories was true for various proportions of American homosexuals (ranging from "all or almost all" to "hardly any or none"). The most popular causal notion was that "young homosexuals became that way because of older homosexuals," which is consonant with the widespread fear that homosexuals seduce children (Table 7-2). About 43% of the sample believed that this theory accounts for homosexuality in more than half of all cases (nearly half of these believed that it applies to all homosexuals). The next most popular idea centers on family circumstances. Nearly 40% agreed that most homosexuals are products of "how their parents raised them" (14% believed this applies to all homosexuals). Fewer than 30% thought that more than half of all homosexuals have simply failed to attract the opposite sex. All these theories have to do with the environment; people are less inclined to consider homosexuality inherent. Forty-four percent of our respondents believed that few if any homosex-

TABLE 7-2 Cognitive Beliefs About Causes and Cures of Homosexuality

	"Causes"				"Cures"			
For what proportion of homosexuals is each statement true?	Young homosexuals become that way because of older homosexuals.	People become homosexual because of how their parents raised them.	People become homosexual because they are not attractive to the opposite sex.	Homosexuals are born that way.	Homosexuality is a sickness that can be cured.	Homosexuals can stop being homosexual if they want to.	Homosexual men can be turned into heterosexuals by women who have enough sexual skills.	Homosexual women can be turned into heterosexuals by men who have enough sexual skills.
All or almost all	18.9%	13.7%	11.7%	16.8%	38.2%	23.2%	8.9%	13.9%
More than half	24.0	25.0	18.0	13.7	24.2	17.6	16.6	20.6
Less than half	21.7	24.3	23.0	18.1	16.6	21.0	26.4	22.6
Hardly any or none	26.6	31.5	40.0	44.1	13.0	29.4	31.5	26.5
Don't know	8.8	5.4	7.3	7.4	7.9	8.7	16.7	16.5
Column total	100.0%	99.9%	100.0%	100.1%	99.9%	99.9%	100.1%	100.1%
Base *n*	3,000	2,995	2,998	3,003	2,992	2,996	2,990	2,995
No answer	18	23	20	15	26	22	28	23
Total sample	3,018	3,018	3,018	3,018	3,018	3,018	3,018	3,018

uals were "born that way," the largest response for this item. (About 30%, however, did agree that more than half of all homosexuals are innately so.)

To the extent that homosexuality may develop in response to environmental circumstances, it could be reversible in other circumstances. Thus, 62% of the respondents said that homosexuality is a curable sickness in at least half of those who practice it; almost 40% believed this to be the case for all homosexuals. But such a "cure" may be difficult to achieve. Fifty percent of the sample expressed doubt that many homosexuals could change their sexual orientation just by wanting to, and 29% doubted that any could. (As we saw in Chapter 2, some form of psychotherapy is the favored "cure" for homosexuality.) We also included two items to explore further the belief that homosexuals are merely inexperienced or incompetent with the opposite sex. About one-fourth of the respondents agreed that many homosexual men could be turned into heterosexuals by sexually skilled women, while about one-third believed that at least half of all lesbians could be "converted" by sexually skilled men.

Fear and Revulsion Toward Homosexuality

The strength of the emotional response to homosexuality (i.e., the affective component) is illustrated in further findings. Not only do people set apart homosexuals because of their "condition"; they also appear to be revolted by what they think is typical homosexual behavior. Thus, about two-thirds of our sample strongly agreed that the idea of sexual relations between persons of the same sex is "obscene and vulgar" (Table 7-3). Only 15% admitted to some disagreement with this position. Moreover, these feelings are associated with a pervasive sense of concern. Over 70% of the sample believed that there is at least some truth in the idea that homosexuals seek to become sexually involved with children. In fact, about 45% felt strongly that for this reason it is dangerous to have homosexuals as teachers or youth leaders, and 35% strongly agreed with the proposition that homosexuals frustrated in their search for partners seek out children for sexual purposes (over 70% felt this way to some degree). Further, homosexual seduction, according to many of our respondents, is not confined to children. Almost 40% believed that more than half of all homosexuals tend to corrupt their fellow workers sexually (about 23% believed that

TABLE 7-3 Fears About Homosexuals

Response	To what extent do you think homosexuality is obscene and vulgar?[a]	Homosexuals try to play sexually with children if they cannot get an adult partner.	Homosexuals are dangerous as teachers and youth leaders because they try to get sexually involved with children.	Homosexuals tend to corrupt their fellow workers sexually.[b]	If homosexual men cannot find men for partners, they try to force their attentions on women.[b]	Homosexuality is a social corruption that can cause the downfall of a civilization.	Homosexuality in itself is no problem, but what people make of it can be a serious problem.
Strongly agree	66.0%	35.3%	45.2%	22.9%	7.0%	25.2%	27.6%
Somewhat agree	18.9	36.2	29.1	15.7	11.0	23.9	28.1
Somewhat disagree	7.6	10.0	12.1	19.1	22.4	18.9	17.1
Strongly disagree	7.6	8.6	9.7	35.2	45.7	24.7	23.2
Don't know	—	9.8	4.0	7.0	13.8	7.3	3.9
Column total	100.1%	99.9%	100.1%	99.9%	99.9%	100.0%	99.9%
Base *n*	2,985	2,999	2,992	2,999	2,997	2,998	2,991
No answer	33	19	26	19	21	20	27
Total sample	3,018	3,018	3,018	3,018	3,018	3,018	3,018

[a] This item provided four response categories: "Very much," "Somewhat," "Very little," and "Not at all."

[b] These two items provided five response categories concerning how many homosexuals are like this: "All or almost all," "More than half," "Less than half," "Hardly any or none," and "Don't know."

all or nearly all do), and 18% believed that most male homosexuals will importune women if they fail to find male partners. These fears also embrace social consequences: almost half our respondents said that homosexuality can cause the downfall of a civilization. Nevertheless, more than half denied that homosexuality is by its nature a social problem, agreeing that it is only people's attitudes that make it so.

Controlling Homosexuality

That there is a clear conative dimension in antihomosexual attitudes is seen in the fact that people desire not only to "cure" homosexuality but, even more strongly, to control it. Control can take many forms; most prominently, it can have the force of law. Indeed, the majority of people in our study believed homosexuality to be a crime. Thus, 59% said there should be a law against any form of homosexual contact, and 60% agreed that this should include activities between consenting adults in private (Table 7-4). Most of those supporting legal control of homosexuality said, as mentioned earlier, that those convicted should be forced to seek treatment, but one-third preferred orthodox criminal penalties.

In addition to direct sanctions against sexual activities, social control can extend into the occupational sphere by excluding homosexuals from certain occupations, a proposition most in our study agreed with. A large majority said they would deny homosexual men the right to work at professions that carry authority and influence. More than three-quarters said they would bar such

TABLE 7-4 Approval for Legal Control of Homosexuality

Response	Any kind of homosexual act should be against the law.	Private, consensual, adult homosexuality should *not* be against the law.	Homosexuals should be fined, jailed, or imprisoned.
Agree	59.1%	35.9%	33.9%
Disagree	37.8	59.7	64.8
Don't know	3.2	4.3	1.4
Column total	100.1%	99.9%	100.1%
Base *n*	3,007	3,014	1,765
No answer	11	4	23
Total sample	3,018	3,018	1,788[a]

[a] Excludes the 1,230 who opposed outlawing homosexuality in either or both of the other two items in the table.

men from teaching, the ministry, or the judiciary, and two-thirds said they would bar them from medical practice or government service (Table 7-5). With regard to this latter concern, nearly 60% believed that more than half of all homosexuals are high security risks in government jobs. (Most of these respondents, or 43% of the entire sample, held this to be true of all or nearly all homosexuals.) An evident conclusion is that the public does not want homosexuals in positions of public responsibility, particularly when moral leadership is explicitly involved. However, most respondents accepted the notion of homosexuals working in the creative sorts of occupations they are commonly thought to prefer. On the average, 82% said it is all right for homosexual men to be florists, musicians, artists, or beauticians. Interestingly, among those who disagreed, nearly twice as many objected to a homosexual beautician (who has physical contact with clients) as to the other three occupations.

Rights of Homosexuals

The foregoing findings raise the question of the range of the conative response—for example, whether the American public would also deny homosexuals some of the rights heterosexuals take for granted. We find that many in our sample said society should be properly concerned with how homosexuals spend their leisure time, especially as regards purely recreational activities; people were more tolerant about activities with a comparatively "serious" connotation. Thus, while 47% believed homosexuals should not be allowed to form social groups (with 31% feeling strongly about this), fewer (20%) felt they should not be allowed to organize to deal with their social problems (Table 7-6). Nearly three-quarters (and 55% strongly) objected to homosexuals dancing together in public places, and 43% opposed bars serving homosexuals (27% strongly). But 80% disagreed with the notion of excluding homosexuals from membership in churches and synagogues. We also find two-thirds of the sample affirming that what consenting adult homosexuals do in private is no one else's business; this seems oddly in conflict with other data, such as those in Table 7-4, where a similar majority reported that precisely these activities ought to be not only a social but a legal concern. We suspect that responses to this item are anomalous because of the word *private* and the phrase "no one else's business," which may

TABLE 7-5 Approval for Limiting Homosexuals' Occupational Opportunities

	Would you say that homosexual men should or should not be allowed to work in the following professions?								
	Court judge	School-teacher	Minister	Medical doctor	Government official	Beautician	Artist	Musician	Florist
Should not be allowed	77.2%	76.9%	76.6%	67.7%	67.4%	28.3%	15.5%	14.8%	13.2%
Should be allowed	22.8	23.1	23.4	32.3	32.6	71.7	84.5	85.2	86.8
Column total	100.0%	100.0%	100.0%	100.0%	100.0%	100.0%	100.0%	100.0%	100.0%
Base *n*	2,957	2,974	2,970	2,961	2,954	2,969	2,960	2,974	2,972
No answer	61	44	48	57	64	49	58	44	46
Total sample	3,018	3,018	3,018	3,018	3,018	3,018	3,018	3,018	3,018

TABLE 7-6 Approval for the Rights of Homosexuals

Response	Homosexuals should be allowed to organize groups for social and recreational purposes.	Homosexuals should be allowed to organize groups to deal with their social problems.	Homosexuals should be allowed to dance with each other in public places.	Bars serving homosexuals should be permitted.	Homosexuals should *not* be allowed to join churches or synagogues.	What consenting adult homosexuals do in private is no one else's business.
Strongly agree	17.7%	41.4%	7.4%	19.6%	9.0%	38.3%
Somewhat agree	29.6	33.6	15.3	31.2	8.1	30.0
Somewhat disagree	15.9	8.4	18.2	15.9	20.4	14.1
Strongly disagree	30.9	12.4	55.3	27.5	58.8	14.2
Don't know	5.9	4.2	3.8	5.9	3.7	3.4
Column total	100.0%	100.0%	100.0%	100.1%	100.0	100.0%
Base *n*	2,992	2,992	2,996	3,002	2,990	3,002
No answer	26	26	22	16	28	16
Total sample	3,018	3,018	3,018	3,018	3,018	3,018

have evoked the traditional American ideals of self-sufficiency and respect for individuality and privacy.

Shared Responses Toward Homosexuality

At this point we have shown that our data support previous research in demonstrating the generally negative public response to homosexuality that dominates in the United States. We next consider which of the attitudes we have examined are the most important. By combining these items, we can see which of these negative attitudes were most *pervasive* among our population and which of them distinguished the most from the least negative among our respondents (as indicated by the *number* of attitudes or stereotyping components held). In this way we can develop a parsimonious measure of attitudes toward homosexuality that future investigations might attempt to replicate in assessing change in the prevalence of attitudinal patterns.

Thus, after more complex analysis (see Chapters 8 and 10), we decided to construct a Likert-type scale of about ten items from the data just discussed. We examined the distribution of responses to the individual attitude items. This inspection suggested to us that anywhere from 40% to 80% of our study population tended to take a negative view of homosexuals or to express negative judgments about them in a wide variety of ways and, therefore, that a general antihomosexual attitude, or stereotyping "gestalt," is widespread among U.S. adults. Within this majority, there seemed to be a subgroup—about 15% to 25% of the entire sample—who also consistently subscribed to a set of even more negative views (e.g., people who would not even allow homosexual men to be artists or florists). In addition, at the other extreme, a minority of perhaps 15% to 25% tended to hold few negative attitudes. Finally, between these high- and low-negative groups we expected to find a mixed or "medium-negative" group of people holding a variety of antihomosexual attitudes with no discernible pattern.

An additive measure could help demonstrate to what extent these groups of people shared the same response toward homosexuals and so could not only delineate particular antihomosexual types but also demonstrate which antihomosexual attitudes are most common. From our data, therefore, we expected to isolate three main groups: (1) low-negatives, those respondents holding few or no antihomosexual attitudes; (2) medium-negatives, those holding some antihomosexual attitudes in various combinations or patterns; and (3) high-negatives, those holding most of the antihomosexual attitudes we studied (included here would be a category of extreme-negatives, holding all the attitudes in our scale).

In preparing this index measure we selected from Tables 7-1 through 7-6 an initial pool of 23 items whose response distributions allowed for maximal variance. With Likert-type scoring, a person who scored 0 on a scale made up of these items would not express any negative attitudes; one who scored 8 would hold 8 of these attitudes; and one who scored 23 would hold all of them.

We intended that out of these 23 initial items, some would be dropped to make our additive measure as simple and reliable as possible in its substantive categories. Our next step, therefore, was to calculate Kuder-Richardson alpha coefficients of reliability both for the 23-item scale as a whole and for a scale made up of the remaining items if each one was excluded in turn. The results showed whether the alpha value would increase or decrease (i.e., whether reliability would improve or deteriorate), and if so by how much, given the exclusion of any one item in turn while the others were retained.

Accordingly, from our list of 23 attitudes we eliminated, one at a time, the 10 whose exclusion would most enhance the reliability

TABLE 7-7 Items Comprising the Antihomosexuality Attitude Index (AAI)

Interview item	Criterion response(s)	Prevalence in population ($n = 3{,}018$)
Would you say that homosexual men should or should not be allowed to work in the following professions?		
Schoolteacher	Not allowed	75.8%
Court judge	Not allowed	75.6
Minister	Not allowed	75.3
Medical doctor	Not allowed	66.4
Government official	Not allowed	65.9
[To what extent do you think homosexuality is obscene and vulgar?]	Very much	65.2
Tell how much you agree or disagree.		
Homosexuals are dangerous as teachers or youth leaders, because they try to get sexually involved with children.	Strongly agree, somewhat agree	73.5
Homosexuals try to play sexually with children if they cannot get an adult partner.	Strongly agree, somewhat agree	71.1
Homosexuals should be allowed to dance with each other in public places.	Strongly disagree	54.9
Homosexuality is a social corruption that can cause the downfall of a civilization.	Strongly agree, somewhat agree	48.8

of the measure, always on the basis of recalculated alphas. When alpha could no longer be improved upon, we used other techniques to eliminate 3 more items, leaving us with 10.[5] We thus arrived at a parsimonious index of negative attitudes toward homosexuals. This index, which we refer to as the Antihomosexuality Attitude Index (AAI), has an alpha reliability of .87 and is shown in Table 7-7.

Since these are the items that our index designates as summarizing the nature of Americans' attitudes toward homosexuality, it is notable that no more than a quarter of our sample can be estimated *not* to have shared any of them. In fact, as Table 7-8 shows, some who did not hold a given one of these attitudes did subscribe to at least one other, so that among the entire sample only 6% appear to have been free of all the antihomosexual attitudes in the index. That this general negativism persists, despite suggestions to the contrary by popular media, has also been dem-

TABLE 7-8 Distribution of Scores on the AAI

Number of attitudes held	*n*	Percent of total sample	Subgroup total
0	180	6.0%	Low-negative: 19.2% (578)
1	132	4.4	
2	137	4.5	
3	129	4.3	
4	128	4.2	Medium-negative: 27.5% (833)
5	179	5.9	
6	203	6.7	
7	323	10.7	
8	417	13.8	High-negative: 53.2% (1,607)
9	607	20.1	
10	583	19.3[a]	
Total	3,018	99.9%	

[a] This group, a subcategory of the "high-negatives," we refer to as the "extreme-negatives."

onstrated in national studies with more recent data than ours (see Nyberg & Alston, 1976–77). It also bears remarkable agreement with the "homosexuality is always wrong" component of the SMS.

Our new measure allows us, first, to delineate the major types of antihomosexual respondents as defined by the *number* of such attitudes they hold. The sample distribution percentages in Table 7-8 show that some 19% of the respondents held no more than 3 of the 10 attitudes: this is the group of low-negatives we expected. At the opposite end of the scale, another 19% held all 10 attitudes: these are the extreme-negatives we referred to earlier. That the majority of the sample held antihomosexual attitudes is shown in that 53% (including the extreme-negatives) held 8 or more of the 10 attitudes, to constitute that category we refer to as high-negatives. Finally, some 28% held from 4 to 7 of the 10 attitudes in the AAI; these are the medium-negatives who were less antihomosexual than the majority.

Proceeding further along these lines, Table 7-9 shows which attitudes are most and least likely to characterize these groups of respondents. It shows that those who held few or no antihomosexual attitudes—the low-negatives—still harbored considerable fear that homosexuals will molest children (for example, among those who held only 1 out of the 10 attitudes, 35% agreed with one or the other of the two items referring to children). In fact, the two attitudes reflecting homosexuals' putative involvement with

TABLE 7-9 Percent in AAI Population Groups Sharing Attitudes Toward Homosexuality

Attitude	Low-negative	Medium-negative	High-negative[a]	Gamma
Homosexual men should not be allowed to work as:				
Court judge	11.8%	74.8%	99.1%	.79
Schoolteacher	6.6	77.8	99.8	.84
Minister	10.7	75.9	98.3	.80
Medical doctor	5.7	53.9	94.8	.90
Government official	9.0	55.0	92.1	.86
Homosexuals are dangerous as teachers or youth leaders	21.8	64.7	96.9	.85
Lonely homosexuals approach children.	27.9	61.3	91.7	.76
Homosexuality is very obscene and vulgar.	20.2	52.1	88.2	.76
Definitely forbid homosexual dancing.	14.0	42.6	76.0	.71
Homosexuality endangers civilization.	9.5	28.4	73.4	.77

[a] Includes the extreme-negative subgroup, who are not presented in a separate column because all of them subscribe to all the items in the AAI.

children stand out as among the most commonly held in each of our categories, with as many as one-quarter feeling this way among those we call the low-negatives. Excluding from this calculation those holding none of these attitudes, about a third of the low-negatives subscribed to this idea.

Another finding for the low-negatives is that a fifth of them felt that homosexuality is "very" obscene and vulgar. This shows that even the least negative population group can often experience a visceral, negative response to homosexuality. No matter what their cognitive beliefs may be, a strong emotional response still operates among many in this group.

The fear that homosexuals constitute a threat to children is even more evident when we look at those respondents we have called medium-negatives (where two-thirds felt this way) and high-negatives (where the figure is 92% to 97%). Despite these large proportions, however, it is not these particular attitudes that prevailed most among these two groups. Rather, the most common attitude was that homosexual men should not be judges, teachers, or ministers (held by an average of 76% for these 3 items among the medium-negatives and 99% for the high-negatives). In addition, among the high-negative group, 95% and 92% said they would deny homosexuals jobs as medical doctors and government officials, respectively. The strongest response expressed by both high- and medium-negatives was to favor denying homosexuals jobs as schoolteachers, which seems closely connected with the belief that homosexuals are dangerous to children.

The extreme-negative subgroup (one-third of the high-negatives) does not appear separately in Table 7-9 because they all held all of the ten attitudes. Excluding them from the calculations, however, does not materially change the relative prevalence of these attitudes among the other high-negatives.

Conclusion

This chapter begins the section of the book on the social reaction toward homosexuality—an important issue to understand, because attitudes toward homosexuality involve so many factors that operate in sexual norms in general. Our data illustrate that such attitudes are wide-ranging, fitting well along the cognitive, affective, and conative dimensions of attitude theory. These attitudes are overwhelmingly negative (supporting findings from previous research with more limited samples); based on our sample, only 6% of the public did not share them in 1970. Furthermore, certain negative attitudes are clearly pervasive in the sense that they were most likely to be held even by respondents with few antihomosexual attitudes. Two such attitudes are that homosexuals constitute a danger toward children and that homosexuality is obscene and vulgar. Among more strongly antihomosexual respondents there was, in addition, a genuine consensus that homosexual men should be excluded from positions of authority.

These findings warrant some further comments. It seems evident to us that the desire to deny homosexuals authoritative jobs is based on two things: (1) the moral stance that homosexuality is wrong and that those in high social positions should be of good moral rectitude because these are leadership positions; and (2) the belief that if homosexuals had these jobs, they would be placed in positions of great power, allowing them to spread "homosexual influence" throughout society. In addition, it would follow that if they are generally lacking in moral character, homosexuals would be unable to do an effective job in these occupations. In any case, they are considered to be vulnerable to bribery and blackmail and to be poor security risks. These beliefs and fears, then, account for the fact that homosexuals are generally refused clerical ordination, that there is concern about their supposed inordinate influence in government and the military (Suggs & Marshall, 1971; Tripp, 1975), and that they are in fact denied jobs and careers because it is said they are a security risk (Williams & Weinberg, 1971).

The danger homosexuals are thought to pose to children involves some similar reasoning. Not only is there a belief in an excessive sexuality of homosexuals and that it requires younger as well as older partners; it is also held that homosexuals actively seek converts to their life-styles. Young people are seen as especially vulnerable, so that any possibility of homosexuals occupying positions of authority over children, where they might act as role models, is actively opposed.

Whether everyone who holds that homosexuals constitute a danger to children bases this attitude on the role-model rationale is open to question. We are faced with the apparent anomaly that even among those we call low-negatives, the attitude most often shared with progressively more negative groups was the fear that homosexuals are dangerous to children. Perhaps this belief among those otherwise unwilling to generalize reflects a lack of knowledge about homosexuality: even relatively "liberal" or tolerant people may draw the line where their children are concerned. "Better safe than sorry" may seem a reasonable maxim in these circumstances, even among those who do not fear homosexuality in other areas of their lives.

Thus, the findings of our study represent not merely some interesting academic facts; they also clearly show that antihomosexual attitudes are widespread and probably will continue to produce bitter political battles. The findings show, furthermore, that our 1970 data were not inaccurate in failing to illustrate the extreme liberalism that was thought to characterize the time. On the basis of what we have learned about the support for sexual attitudes (described in Chapter 4), we can see that there exists in the United States a remarkably stable, conservative structure of public sexual morality.

NOTES

1. The work described in this and the following three chapters was initially derived from a factor analysis that focused on "the structure of public attitudes and perceptions of homosexuality" (Klassen and Levitt, 1974). We had previously constructed around three core concepts—"primary traits," "secondary traits," and "normative prescriptions"—a model of stereotyping that seemed to offer a reasonably good fit between the reported factors and these components. Equally important, the model seemed to match the public images of homosexuals reflected in our substantive data. Later we discovered that an attitudinal model built on cognitive, affective, and behavioral components might be congruent with the stereotyping model, and the results already produced. Although we will continue to refer to stereotyping, the results presented in our chapters on homosexuality are reported primarily in the terminology of our later attitudinal model. It may be useful, therefore, to describe briefly our original model of stereotyping.

   This model of stereotyping is viewed as a perceptual subsystem, a form of typification (Schutz, 1964). This subsystem involves a dynamic clustering of a number of primary traits, secondary traits, and normative prescriptions, a complex gestalt attributed by perceivers to members of a social category—in this case, homosexual persons.

   This version of stereotyping postulates that the ascription of primary traits to a person arises from the perceiver's propensity to generalize about members of a social category (see Lippman, 1922; Krech & Crutchfield, 1948; Asch,

1952; Lindzey, 1954; Schellenberg, 1970; Secord & Backman, 1974). Applications of primary traits to incumbents of a given category depend on that category's perceived social salience and on one's personal familiarity with its members: whether its incumbents are believed to be readily identified; whether they are seen as significantly "different from the rest of us"; and whether their defining characteristics can be altered.

According to this model, as applied to causal path analysis, ascription of primary traits leads in the perceptual process to a variety of secondary trait elements—attributions with evaluative implications—that describe sources of fear or favor toward category members. Finally, the dynamics of primary and secondary traits lead to normative prescriptions, behavioral norms expressing how people may or may not act toward the incumbents of the category and how the incumbents are required to behave.

Applying the model to the case in hand suggests that certain beliefs about homosexuals, for example, that they can be easily identified or that they are not like the rest of us, are important primary traits. These and similar primary traits then give rise to secondary traits like the conviction that homosexuals are a threat to children, that they are vulnerable to blackmail, and they corrupt society's morals. These secondary traits would, in turn, induce a set of normative constraints that would curtail the civil rights of homosexuals and severely limit their occupational choices.

2. In this model, sexual standards are considered to fall under the cognitive dimension. However, there do appear to be some conceptual problems here. As Rokeach (1976:121) has said, "Is a positive or negative preference due to the fact that the attitude object or situation is affectively liked or disliked, or because it is cognitively evaluated as good or bad?" We follow Rokeach in agreeing that the preferential response usually involves both and that analysis of such a response requires looking at the interaction between them. This interaction is especially evident in our culture because (as we have seen) people often strongly moralize about sexuality. We feel angry or hurt when we learn of a spouse's infidelity because it violates our moral values about sexual exclusivity. On the other hand, that infidelity is socially penalized can make an extramarital affair all the more exciting for the participants. Emotions and morality, therefore, are highly related in our attitudes toward sex; of course, the role of *unconscious* emotions on morality has long been a tenet of faith among many social psychologists (see Adorno et al., 1950).
3. The NORC poll was described in *Drum* 25 (August 1967). The results of the Harris poll appeared in the *Washington Post,* 27 September 1965, as reported in *The Challenge and Progress of Homosexual Law Reform* (San Francisco: 1968), p. 68.
4. Organizations that have abandoned this view include the Group for the Advancement of Psychiatry (in 1966), the Mental Health Association (1970), the American Psychological Association (1972), and the American Psychiatric Association (1973). Perhaps the last is the most notable because of psychiatrists' traditional commitment to psychoanalytic theory.
5. Each of the 13 items was cross-tabulated with each of the others to see whether people tended to score alike on each item in the pair and whether each pairing produced a particular distribution—for example, we looked for cases in which 40% to 60% of the population agreed with both of the items and about 20% disagreed. We also cross-tabulated individual items with the 13-item scale score as a whole to assess the contribution of each to "deviant" scores.

Chapter 8

The Structure of Antihomosexual Attitudes[1]

At the end of the last chapter we examined attitudes toward homosexuality to see which ones our 1970 respondents were most likely to hold in common. In this chapter we explore another aspect of the social reaction toward homosexuality—the extent to which antihomosexual attitudes are structured; that is, whether these attitudes cluster together in some meaningful way.

By the late 1970s, a good deal of work had focused on the structure of antihomosexual attitudes; most of it employed the technique of factor analysis to isolate one or more underlying variables or "factors" from a variety of intercorrelated indices (e.g., Millham et al., 1976; Fennessey, 1977; Ward, 1977). However, we feel that the unrepresentative samples and lack of theoretical direction in this work have been major drawbacks in elucidating the structure of antihomosexual attitudes. We hope to rectify these deficiencies in the analysis that follows.

Discovering the Structure of Antihomosexual Attitudes

As with previous studies, factor analysis of individual attitude items is the major technique in our search for structure among antihomosexual attitudes. Factor analysis is a statistical technique that shows how individual variables tend to cluster together to express or measure a certain, more general kind of phenomenon. Each one of these conceptually distinct clusters of items, or factors, can subsequently be used as a single variable in place of the five or six that go to make it up. The use of factor variables thus organizes and summarizes a large array of information and minimizes the complexity of analyzing the data involved.[2]

An initial attempt at factor analysis of our 1970 data (Klassen & Levitt, 1974) involved subjecting our array of items on homosexuality to a single-universe factor analysis. The results yielded seven separately distinct factors, of which the four strongest involved what we call the denial of authoritative jobs, allowing stereotypic jobs, denial of social freedoms, and the belief that homosexuals are apt to molest children or fellow workers. Other factors reflected the notions that homosexuals are susceptible to "cure" by the right heterosexual partner, act in identifiable ways, and are products of an abnormal environment. At first it seemed to us that these different factors could be grouped to correspond to the three stereotyping stages: primary and secondary traits, and normative prescriptions. Subsequently, it appeared to us that these three stereotyping stages could be considered the equivalent of the cognitive, affective, and conative components of the attitude model discussed in Chapter 7.

Our next step, reported in what follows, was to classify the same items into these three stages or dimensions representing the three components. We then factor analyzed items *within* each of these domains. All of the items in a given stage or dimension were allowed to play a part in each of the resulting factors, although some played a relatively weak part and could not be considered really a constituent of the factor. Thus, to use our factors in subsequent analyses, we applied a criterion for inclusion. Each item had to have a structure-matrix loading of at least ±.400 to be considered a meaningful part of the factor in which it appeared, and each factor was required, in final form, to have a reliability alpha of .60. Only the items meeting this criterion were run again in a second analysis forcing a single-factor structure for each of the six factors we ultimately obtained. The factor-score coefficients from this procedure were used in computing respondents' scores on the particular factor.[3]

The factors that eventually emerged are shown in Table 8-1, where they are also compared to the results of the earlier factor analysis. They fit the three-dimensional model of attitudes as follows:

1. Cognitive dimension. Four factors emerged among items classed in this component. In the first one, the constituent items are "Homosexual men can be turned into heterosexuals by women who have enough sexual skills" and "Homosexual women can be turned into heterosexuals by men who have enough sexual skills." Accordingly, we named this factor "heterosexual sex cure." The second factor, "voluntary cure," consists of the items "Homosexuals can stop being homosexual if they want to" and "Homosexuality is a sickness that can be cured." The third factor also includes two items, "Homosexuals act like the opposite sex" and "It is easy to tell homosexuals by how they look"; this factor is called "homosexuals identifiable." Finally, a fourth cognitive factor is made up of "Homosexuals are born that way," reversed (i.e., meaning that they are *not*), and "People become homosexuals because of how their parents raised them"; we designated this factor "environmental cause."

TABLE 8-1 Comparison of Results in Single-Universe and Three-Domain Factor Analyses

Dimension/factor/item	Three-dimensional analysis: single-factor loading	Single-universe analysis: Factor Number	Single-universe analysis: Loading
I: COGNITIVE DIMENSION			
Heterosexual sex cure (alpha = .794)			
Homosexual men can be turned into heterosexuals by women who have enough sexual skills.	.808	5	.741
Homosexual women can be turned into heterosexuals by men who have enough sexual skills.	.808	5	.707
Voluntary cure (alpha = .657)			
Homosexuality is a sickness that can be cured.	.695	6	.658
Homosexuals can stop being homosexual if they want to.	.695	6	.580
Homosexuals identifiable (alpha = .436)			
Homosexuals act like the opposite sex.	.527	7	.566
It is easy to tell homosexuals by how they look.	.527	7	.487
Environmental cause (alpha = .208)			
(Homosexuals are born that way.)	(−.340)	7	−.261
(People become homosexual because of how their parents raised them.)	(.340)	6	.264

TABLE 8-1 (*continued*)

Dimension/factor/item	Three-dimensional analysis: single-factor loading	Single-universe analysis Factor Number	Loading
Homosexuality is distorted heterosexuality (alpha = .720)			
Homosexual women can be turned into heterosexuals by men who have enough sexual skills.	.795	5	.707
Homosexual men can be turned into heterosexuals by women who have enough sexual skills.	.777	5	.741
If homosexual men cannot find men for partners, they try to force their attentions on women.	.540	5	.544
Homosexuals can stop being homosexuals if they want to.	.484	6	.580
(People become homosexual because they are not attractive to the opposite sex.)	(.340)	5	.349
II: AFFECTIVE DIMENSION			
Homosexuals are dangerous (alpha = .780)			
Homosexuals are dangerous as teachers or youth leaders, because they try to get sexually involved with children.	.812	4	.657
Homosexuals try to play sexually with children if they cannot get an adult partner.	.756	4	.568
Homosexuals tend to corrupt their fellow workers sexually.	.608	4	.546
Homosexuality is a social corruption that can cause the downfall of a civilization.	.607	4	.483
Homosexuals are a high security risk for government jobs.	.482	4	.495
(Homosexuals have unusually strong sex drives.)	(.385)	7	.332
Homosexuality is abhorrent (alpha = .687)			
To what extent do you think homosexuality is obscene and vulgar?	.649	3	.405
There is some homosexuality in everyone.	−.555	3	−.447
Homosexuality in itself is no problem, but what people make of it can be a serious problem.	−.515	3	−.521

TABLE 8-1 (*continued*)

Dimension/factor/item	Three-dimensional analysis: single-factor loading	Single-universe analysis: Factor Number	Single-universe analysis: Loading
III: CONATIVE DIMENSION			
Deny authoritative jobs (alpha = .890)			
Would you say that homosexual men should or should not be allowed to work in the following professions?			
Court judge	−.844	1	−.790
Schoolteacher	−.823	1	−.756
Minister	−.814	1	−.754
Medical doctor	−.746	1	−.650
Government official	−.718	1	−.647
Allow stereotypic jobs (alpha = .839)			
Would you say that homosexual men should or should not be allowed to work in the following professions?			
Florist	.802	2	.796
Musician	.797	2	.801
Artist	.763	2	.772
Beautician	.688	2	.675
Deny freedoms (alpha = .759)			
Homosexuals should be allowed to organize groups for social and recreational purposes.	−.756	3	−.645
Bars serving homosexuals should be permitted.	−.640	3	−.553
What consenting adult homosexuals do in private is no one else's business.	−.636	3	−.611
Homosexuals should be allowed to organize groups to deal with their social problems.	−.556	3	−.547
Homosexuals should be allowed to dance with each other in public places.	−.516	3	−.502

NOTE: Parentheses denote an item which, although it has a loading of ±.400 or more in the analysis involving all items in the domain, loaded less strongly when the items passing this criterion were forced into a single-factor structure.

Although all these factors seem to reflect different kinds of "objective" beliefs that may underlie people's reactions to homosexuals as a social category, the latter two—"homosexuals identifiable" and "environmental cause"—are statistically weak, with reliability alphas of only .44 and .21, respectively. Thus, we concluded that the items that make them up are less useful in identifying cognitive clusters than are those in the first two factors. This means that while "homosexuals identifiable" and "environmental cause" are meaningful elements in the global response to homosexuality, we could not make confident inferences about the ways in which, as composite measures, they would relate to other variables. We thus repeated the factor analysis for the cognitive dimension, leaving out the items that made up these two factors. In this reanalysis, one factor emerged that was reliable enough to meet our criterion (alpha ≥ .60). The constituent items are "Homosexual women can be turned into heterosexuals by men who have enough sexual skills"; "Homosexual men can be turned into heterosexuals by women who have enough sexual skills"; "If homosexual men cannot find men for partners, they try to force their attentions on women"; and "Homosexuals can stop being homosexual if they want to." This combination suggests that underlying the perception of homosexuality is the belief that homosexuals are really heterosexuals whose sexual orientation has gone astray; hence, we designated this factor "Homosexuality is distorted heterosexuality."

2. *Affective dimension.* A two-factor structure occurs in this secondary-trait affective attribution dimension. The first factor to emerge has five constituent items: "Homosexuals are dangerous as teachers or youth leaders, because they try to get sexually involved with children"; "Homosexuals try to play sexually with children if they cannot get an adult partner"; "Homosexuals tend to corrupt their fellow workers sexually"; "Homosexuality is a social corruption that can cause the downfall of a civilization"; and "Homosexuals are a high security risk for government jobs." Although it entails obviously cognitive elements, this factor is clearly dominated by an affective component, in this case fear or apprehension of homosexuals. We therefore called it "Homosexuals are dangerous."

The second factor in the affective component consists of the items "Homosexuality is obscene and vulgar"; "There is an element of homosexuality in everyone" (reversed, hence denied); and "Homosexuality in itself is no problem, but what people make of it can be a serious problem" (also reversed, i.e., in the factor this item has the meaning that homosexuality per se *is* a problem). This factor definitely taps an affective response, reflecting, we believe, repugnance or revulsion toward homosexuals; it is named "Homosexuality is abhorrent."

3. Conative dimension. For this dimension, the computations yielded a structure containing three factors. The first is composed of items expressing the willingness to prohibit homosexual men from working as a court judge, school teacher, minister, medical doctor, or government official. Thus, the factor was called "Deny authoritative jobs."[4]

Items in the second factor load so as to reflect *approval* for homosexual men to work as florists, musicians, artists, or beauticians. We called this one "Allow stereotypic jobs."

The third factor along this dimension is designated "Deny freedoms." Its constituent items are "Homosexuals should be allowed to organize groups for social and recreational purposes"; "Bars serving homosexuals should be permitted"; "What consenting adult homosexuals do in private is no one else's business"; "Homosexuals should be allowed to organize groups to deal with their social problems"; and "Homosexuals should be allowed to dance with each other in public places." All these items are reversed, meaning that the factor represents disagreement with the various notions.

This procedure of dividing items into three separate dimensions in line with a conceptual model is unusual in factor analytic work. It seemed important, therefore, to compare the results obtained using this theoretically focused method with the results from our earlier factor analytic work, which utilized the more traditional approach. We thus compared the six factors derived from the three-dimensional method with the seven that had emerged originally. We find, as shown in Table 8-1, that there are more similarities than differences between the two groups of factors. In the original analysis, the first factor that emerged is the same as the one we now call "Deny authoritative jobs"; not only do the two factors contain the same items, but the items load in exactly the same order. Similarly, the second factor of the original seven appears once more as "Allow stereotypic jobs," with a close correspondence among the constituent items. Since our separating the individual items into three dimensions or components did not allow for them to emerge in order of overall strength (as they do in a single-universe procedure), it is notable that these two factors, which were the strongest in the original structure, have the highest alpha values of the six factors in the three-dimensional analysis.

The third factor in the original structure had to do with limiting homosexuals' social freedoms and with feelings of revulsion toward homosexuality. In the three-dimensional analysis, these items were split into two groups since social freedoms have to do with the conative component and feelings toward homosexuals with the affective. However, we find that this third factor reappears first constituting the factor "Deny freedoms," with the rest of the items forming "Homosexuality is abhorrent," again with a close correspondence in loading values.

The fourth original factor, reflecting the view that homosexuals are threatening to society, is nearly identical to the other affective-dimension factor, "Homosexuals are dangerous," and the fifth similarly reappears as "Homosexuality is distorted heterosexuality." The sixth and seventh factors in the original structure, because they appeared late in the structure, are somewhat weaker than those already mentioned; in the three-dimensional analysis, we find that for the most part they are replicated in our own weakest factors, the ones we discarded in favor of the sole cognitive factor about distorted heterosexuality.

It seems, then, that dividing our items into three separate dimensions or components produces results that are strikingly similar to those obtained when all the items were factor analyzed together. The strongest of those original factors were resurrected intact; the weaker ones do not show perfect correspondence but appear in the new analysis in a fashion that reflects their original weakness. In short, we feel assured that forcing the factor analysis to fit the three-component model rather than allowing freer clustering provides a secure basis for our results. Whether we force our variables to fit the components of the model or factor analyze a general pool of items, the results show clearly enough that in the case of antihomosexual attitudes, three components, with subcomponents, appear to organize the data quite well, whether viewed as general attitudes or as stereotypes.

The Distribution of Antihomosexual Attitudes

The six factors obtained from our factor analysis provide convenient summary measures of attitudes toward homosexuality. In this section we briefly examine how these attitudes are distributed across standard sociological variables (here, the six factors were simply dichotomized to produce dependent variables for tabular presentation).[5]

Age. The older people are, the more likely they are to hold highly negative attitudes toward homosexuals. They are especially likely to believe that homosexuals are dangerous and to be unwilling to permit homosexuals to take jobs stereotypically associated with them (Table 8-2). These relationships were examined introducing education and parental responsibility as controls. Controlling for education does not affect our findings, but parental responsibility affects two: among those *with* such responsibility, the relationship between age and "Homosexuals are dangerous" or "Deny authoritative jobs" was substantially reduced (partial gamma = .17 and .09, respectively); in other words, people's scores were less related to their age. These two measures included items dealing with children, so this finding could be expected. Age considerations seem to play a lesser role, however, in determining whether or not a person feels that homosexuality is abhorrent.

Gender. As we saw previously, men and women differ little in their moral standards toward homosexuality. We now find a similar situation when attitudes in general are examined. The largest difference is that women were more likely than men to consider homosexuality abhorrent.

Race. Table 8-2 shows that black respondents were more likely than whites to accept the notion of homosexuality as distorted heterosexuality. At the same time, blacks were less likely than whites to deny homosexual men the right to authoritative occupations. Other differences between the races are quite small.

Education. Education has strong effects on people's attitudes toward homosexuality. The less education people have, the more likely they are to hold highly negative attitudes toward homosexuality. Note, however, that education has much less effect on feelings of abhorrence toward homosexuals. Similarly, the less educated among our respondents were much more punitive in their reaction than the more educated, especially in their refusal to allow stereotypic jobs. These results are not affected when the age of our respondents is taken into consideration.

Marital status. Differences in attitudes toward homosexuality held by respondents with differing marital statuses were small but consistent, with the widowed most likely to hold high-negative

TABLE 8-2 Percent in Selected Population Categories Agreeing with Attitudes Toward Homosexuality[a]

	Homosexuality is distorted heterosexuality.	Homosexuals are dangerous.	Homosexuality is abhorrent.	Deny authoritative jobs.	Allow stereotypic jobs.	Deny freedoms.	Base *n*
Age							
Under 35	40.7	43.2	50.4	46.2	75.5	44.0	1,067
35 to 64	48.1	56.6	53.2	53.1	65.8	48.9	1,508
65 or older	60.0	74.3	60.0	63.9	43.4	58.6	400
Gamma	.21	.34	.14	.23	−.34	.20	
Gender							
Male	48.6	54.7	48.2	53.6	63.8	48.0	1,465
Female	46.0	54.3	57.9	51.0	67.9	49.0	1,553
Gamma	−.05	−.01	.21	−.04	.10	.03	
Race							
White	45.0	54.0	54.0	54.5	65.2	49.7	2,536
Black	59.3	57.1	49.2	40.5	71.0	42.3	482
Gamma	.28	.06	−.10	−.29	.09	−.14	
Education							
Less than 12th grade	60.1	67.2	54.8	59.3	51.8	54.5	1,260
High school–some college	39.3	49.7	56.2	51.5	72.8	46.9	1,432
College graduation	32.4	25.2	34.0	28.4	91.3	30.5	321
Gamma	−.38	−.44	−.17	−.29	.50	−.28	
Marital status							
Married	45.2	53.4	53.8	53.3	66.9	49.1	2,344
Widowed	61.2	70.0	62.7	62.0	50.6	56.7	263
Divorced or separated	55.2	55.2	49.1	40.1	70.8	42.5	212
Single	45.2	46.2	37.7	39.7	70.4	37.2	199

Community size							
Rural area or small town	51.6	61.2	59.7	73.6	72.2	57.8	1,180
25,000 to 1,000,000	43.5	51.5	51.8	62.6	81.9	45.3	1,339
Metropolitan	47.2	46.4	41.3	52.4	83.5	35.1	496
Gamma	−.09	−.19	−.21	−.28	.24	−.28	
Geographic region							
Northeast	43.3	48.3	47.5	48.8	72.5	42.0	1,289
Rockies-Southwest	49.2	55.7	55.8	57.0	54.8	54.0	400
Midwest-South	54.1	65.6	61.2	60.3	57.5	59.5	946
Pacific Coast	41.8	46.5	49.6	39.2	76.5	37.6	383
Religious affiliation							
None	33.6	35.0	30.7	25.2	81.4	26.3	274
Reformation Protestant	39.4	47.4	55.1	57.2	69.1	49.8	428
Pietistic Protestant	50.7	58.6	54.0	53.2	63.3	48.9	485
Fundamentalist Protestant	48.7	65.5	66.3	64.8	55.5	63.0	825
Roman Catholic	43.6	50.8	51.7	52.0	70.2	46.1	729
Jewish	33.8	23.9	26.8	31.0	91.5	22.5	71
Total sample	47.2	54.5	45.1	45.8	68.1	49.7	3,018

[a] "Agreeing" is defined as scoring above the mean for the given factor.

attitudes and single persons least likely to do so. The results remain substantially the same when we control for age.

Residence. Respondents from various-sized communities did not differ much in whether they were likely to see homosexuality as distorted heterosexuality. However, large differences appear concerning "Homosexuality is abhorrent" and "Homosexuals are dangerous." The smaller the community in which respondents lived, the greater the likelihood that they would see homosexuals as abhorrent and dangerous. This no doubt accounts for the strong punitive reaction on the part of those from smaller communities, who were much more likely to deny homosexuals occupational and social freedoms. Controlling for age and education does not affect the overall results, but two specifications emerge: among both the young and the more educated, the relationship is stronger with respect to "Homosexuality is abhorrent" and to "Deny authoritative jobs" (for age, partial gamma = −.35 and −.31, and for education, −.36 and −.38, respectively). This shows, we feel, where important changes in attitudes toward homosexuality can be found: among the well-educated urban young.

Region. Consistent patterns in attitudes toward homosexuality emerge when respondents from different regions of the country are compared. Those from the South and Midwest were most likely, and those from the Pacific states least likely, to hold highly negative attitudes toward homosexuality. There is an average difference of 18% between Southern-Midwestern and Pacific respondents across the six measures. It should be noted that respondents from the Northeast were quite similar to those from the Pacific states in their scores on these items, while those from the Southwest and Rockies were much like the southerners and midwesterners in showing a greater likelihood of holding high-negative attitudes toward homosexuality. Introducing community size as a control does not substantially alter these results.

Religious background. Definite patterns and large differences appear in attitudes toward homosexuality when we examine the religious affiliation of our respondents. Fundamentalist Protestants were most likely and Jews least likely to hold high-negative attitudes. On the first three measures, there is an average difference of 32% between these two groups. Pietistic Protestants came close to Fundamentalists in their attitudes (except regarding abhorrence), and those with no religious affiliation scored almost as liberally as Jews. Thus Fundamentalists were, as might be expected, the most punitive toward homosexuals and Jews the least so. There is one slight inconsistency in that those with no affiliation were the group least likely to deny homosexuals authoritative jobs, but they differed from Jews by only 5% on this measure. The other two Protestant groups were similar in the extent of their punitiveness but, as before, not as punitive as the Fundamentalists. All these findings were examined holding socioeconomic status constant, but the relationships remain unchanged.

As mentioned earlier, Ward (1977) showed that stereotyping homosexuals does not cut across demographic lines but that different groups stereotype in different ways. Our results suggest that this is also the case for attitudes in general toward homosexuality, but with the important exception that there is little variance across demographic groups when it comes to feeling that homosexuality is abhorrent.

Developing a Global Antihomosexuality Measure

The previous chapter presented a simple reliable summary measure of negative attitudes toward homosexuality (the AAI) in connection with illustrating which attitudes are most pervasive. However, that measure is based on a pool of 23 items selected after submitting all of the 35 attitudinal items to factor analysis as reported in this chapter; it is not the most *comprehensive* overall measure our data can provide for analyzing antihomosexual attitudes in general. The question that next arose in connection with our factor analytic work was whether any of the factors we derived might combine to form a superfactor, or factor-of-factors, that would provide a more adequate measure of general negativism toward homosexuality. This would meet the need for a primary dependent variable to analyze, paralleling the SMS analysis.

One concern at this point was whether such a superfactor would be a sensible and meaningful measure or whether it might be just the artifactual product of statistical manipulations. Consequently, we tried several alternative procedures. If the results turned out to be quite similar, use of a factor-of-factors might seem justified; if they seemed to depend on which procedure was used, we would have to be much less satisfied with this step in our analysis.

Since we wanted a superfactor that would enhance the natural intercorrelation among the various factors, we used oblique rotation in a factor analysis that involved the nine antihomosexuality factors described above; that is, we included the four cognitive factors that first emerged, rather than the single distorted heterosexuality factor from the revised analysis. Our reasoning was that although two of these factors, as mentioned earlier, were too weak to stand alone as separate measures, using them in the new factor analysis did allow a fuller array of individual items to be represented, and they might form part of a factor of sufficient reliability. We duplicated this procedure using the individual items rather than the factors they had made up to see whether this affected the results. Finally, for further comparison, we used equimax and varimax orthogonal rotation in factor analyses of both the various factors and the individual items. The results of these different analyses are shown in Table 8-3.

In all these alternative procedures, a three-factor structure emerged that was quite similar regardless both of whether individual items or factors were used and of the kind of rotation employed in the procedure. Several features of our results should be pointed out:

1. (a) The first factor to emerge, and therefore a dimension of major import, comprises willingness to deny homosexuals authoritative jobs or social freedoms, coupled with feelings of fear and disgust toward them.

(b) The second factor combines the perception of homosexuality as distorted heterosexuality plus, again, most of the items dealing with fear of homosexuals.

(c) The third factor consists of the propensity to allow homosexuals to take stereotypic jobs. By implication, this factor identifies an especially hostile subgroup in the population, just as it did in earlier analyses.

2. The two weakest cognitive dimension factors do not have strong loadings in any of the three superfactors, either when they are entered as factors or when the individual constituent items are used. This strengthens our impression that these particular items are less important in understanding negative attitudes toward homosexuality.

3. Since oblique rotation commonly yields higher loadings than an orthogonal method, it is striking that the various loadings are

not too different from one another. It appears, then, that we have defined several important dimensions of antihomosexual attitudes, since the results are not affected very much by the particular procedure employed.

It appears also that the belief that homosexuals are dangerous is pivotal in understanding these negative attitudes, because the factor "Homosexuals are dangerous" is connected both to the denial of freedoms and authoritative jobs and to the idea of homosexuality as distorted heterosexuality.

If we are to use one of these three superfactors as a global measure, the first one seems to be the best choice. the second factor does not deal with the conative dimension of attitudes toward homosexuals, a salient component of such negative feelings in general. The third factor, while it is the least complex and easiest to understand, pertains to a minority of those who hold negative attitudes and thus would be less useful in predicting these attitudes among most of the public. In addition, of course, the first factor is the strongest of the three, since it emerged first in the analysis.

We named this first factor the Multidimensional Antihomosexuality Factor (MAF); its constituent items are those with loadings under "Factor 1" in Table 8-3. The MAF has an alpha reliability of .82 and represents responses by 2,736 people, or 90.7% of our sample (282 did not answer one or more of the individual constituent items). Because of its scope and validity, we use the MAF in the regression analysis in Chapter 10, where we attempt to explain why people hold the attitudes toward homosexuality that respondents indicated.

It should be pointed out that the MAF is not analogous as a scale to the Sexual Morality Scale (SMS), which does present some problems. The SMS has six empirically meaningful scores, or points along the scale, that range from most to least conservative and specify in terms of individual items exactly what each score means. The MAF also has a range of available scores, but they are calculated according to the strength each of the individual constituent items contributed in constructing the factor. Thus they cannot be readily translated into empirical terms. For example, two respondents could have approximately the same score on the MAF even though they may have given different responses to the original items, as long as the combination of responses worked

TABLE 8-3 Three-Factor-Structure Loadings Comparing the Use of Factors and Individual Items and Three Methods of Rotation

	Factor 1			Factor 2			Factor 3		
Factor/item[a]	OBQ	EQX	VMX	OBQ	EQX	VMX	OBQ	EQX	VMX
Heterosexual sex cure				.645	.638	.636			
Heterosexual women can cure homosexual men.				.672	.677	.681			
Heterosexual men can cure homosexual women.				.752	.750	.753			
Lonely homosexual men attack women.				.533	.521	.524			
Voluntary cure				.648	.633	.628			
Homosexuals can stop being homosexual.				.515	.503	.503			
Homosexuality is a curable illness.				.415	.403	.398			
Homosexuals identifiable									
Homosexuals act like opposite sex.									
Homosexuals are recognizable by their looks.									
Homosexuals fear opposite sex.									
Environmental cause									
Parents create homosexuals.									
Homosexuals are born that way.									
Homosexuals are dangerous	.695	.513	.548	.437	.351	.336			
Homosexual teachers seduce children.	.668	.584	.607	.447	.396	.377			
Lonely homosexuals approach children.	.579	.506	.624	.440	.403	.385			
Homosexuals corrupt fellow workers.	.472	.378	.343	.489	.445	.436			
Homosexuality can destroy civilization.	.555	.452	.482	.415	.364	.351			
Homosexuals are high security risks.	.440	.385	.401						
Homosexuals have strong sex drive.									

Homosexuality is abhorrent	.719	.695	.704						
Homosexuality is obscene and vulgar.	.620	.571	.587						
Homosexuality itself is not a problem.	−.485	−.488	−.496						
There is some homosexuality in everyone.	−.413	−.392	−.403						
Deny authoritative jobs	.716	.641	.659						
Court judge	.737	.713	.726						
Schoolteacher	.770	.740	.755						
Minister	.739	.714	.728						
Medical doctor	.712	.658	.681						
Government official	.668	.621	.642						
Allow stereotypic jobs							.412	.387	.335
Florist							.781	.774	.762
Musician							.777	.766	.751
Artist							.745	.734	.719
Beautician							.678	.654	.625
Deny freedoms	.795	.793	.798						
Allow homosexual social groups.	−.573	−.503	−.531						
Private homosexuality is no one's business.	−.538	−.526	−.536						
Allow gay bars.	−.537	−.464	−.494						
Allow homosexual problem-solving groups.	−.531	−.464	−.491						
Allow homosexuals to dance together.	−.526	−.536	−.538						
Allow homosexuals to join churches.									

NOTE: The three methods of rotation are abbreviated as follows: OBQ = oblique; EQX = orthogonal equimax; VMX = orthogonal varimax. Loadings are not given when a factor or item had loadings of less than ±.400 in all three methods.

[a] Item content is given verbatim in Table 10-1.

TABLE 8-4 Multidimensional Antihomosexual Factor/Antihomosexual Attitude Index

	AAI group				
			High-negative		
MAF score[a]	Low-negative	Medium-negative	High-negative	Extreme negative	(Row *n*)
0–2	93.1%	14.9%	0.0%		(566)
3–6	6.9	71.0	20.6		(861)
7–11	0.0	14.1	79.4		(1,309)
Column total	100.0%	100.0%	100.0%		
Base *n*	492	723	1,521		
Gamma = .94					
0–2	93.1%	14.9%	0.0%	0.0%	(566)
3–5	6.9	56.7	11.0	0.3	(550)
6–8	0.0	27.8	67.7	35.0	(1,043)
9–11	0.0	0.6	21.3	64.6	(557)
Column total	100.0%	100.0%	100.0%	99.9%	
Base *n*	492	723	947	574	
Gamma = .89					

[a] For cross-tabulation, standard MAF scores were grouped in 12 integer codes (0–11) that reflect their natural factor-score distributions. These codes are combined in the first part of the table so as to provide, as nearly as possible, that respondents be distributed as they are in the established AAI categories. In the second part of the table, MAF codes are grouped arbitrarily so that each of the four rows includes 3 of the 12 codes.

out to be close arithmetic equivalents. In addition, we know that those who scored highest on the MAF were the most negative toward homosexuality, but we would not know exactly how to describe the feelings of people who scored around the midpoint—were they half as negative in their feelings, or one-third less negative, than the people at the top? What does "half as negative" really mean? As well as this problem of interpretation, an associated difficulty with the MAF is that it is almost impossible for others to replicate our results because of the complex process by which the measure was developed.[6]

The MAF becomes more understandable, however, in conjunction with our subsequent development of the AAI, presented in Chapter 7. It can be seen that the MAF does resemble the AAI in the items that both measures include. This accounts for the high correlation of .87 between them. In relating the MAF and the AAI we can see, further, that by knowing in which group a respondent fell on the AAI—low, medium, or high-negative—we could predict with a fair degree of accuracy how he or she would score on the MAF. Table 8-4 shows that when the two measures are cross-tabulated (with people trichotomized on the MAF according to whether their standard scores were relatively low, medium, or high), they yield a gamma of .94. If there are four subgroups (dividing the AAI high-negatives into the most extreme and the remainder and grouping MAF scores in four categories instead of three), the gamma is .89. Table 8-4 takes and AAI as the independent variable in this cross-tabulation and the MAF as dependent, thus showing that AAI scores can predict those on the MAF. The result is quite a high concordance with, for example, 93% of the low-negatives scoring in the lowest category of the MAF and none of them in the highest.

The correlation matrix in Appendix E shows how the MAF and the factors comprising it relate to one another and to other variables of interest. For example, education, religiosity, age, and early sexual experience show relatively strong associations to the MAF. These associations reflect the relationships in Table 8-2, suggesting that the MAF does serve as a meaningful and useful summary measure of negative attitudes toward homosexuality.

Summary

This chapter has analyzed the structure of antihomosexual attitudes, that is, the ways in which various attitudes hang together or cluster along meaningful dimensions. Our methodological approach was factor analysis of the individual attitude items introduced in the previous chapter. This analysis was guided primarily by that part of attitude theory positing that attitudes can be organized along three dimensions—the cognitive, affective, and conative. Although it has been claimed that such a distinction is unwarranted by empirical research, the results of our factor analysis do show that attitudes toward homosexuality can be arranged along these three dimensions. Next, the distribution of the various clusters of attitudes across traditional sociological variables was presented to show which social groupings are associated with holding one particular attitude more than another. Earlier research that purported to show that stereotyping homosexuals does not cut across demographic lines was supported in the case of general attitudes toward homosexuality as well. Finally, the factors that we developed were combined to form a factor-of-factors, the MAF, to serve in our further analyses. The results of this exercise reaffirmed both our earlier findings in this chapter and the utility of the AAI measure constructed in the previous chapter.

NOTES

1. The term *homophobia* was coined years ago, probably jointly by Smith (1971) and Weinberg (1972) to denote an antihomosexuality position. Since then, a generation of writers of human sexuality texts have followed Smith and Weinberg in this usage, evidently blind to its inaccuracy (e.g., Hyde, 1979; Crooks & Baur, 1980; Rathus, 1983; Harmatz & Novak, 1983; Knox, 1984; Masters, Johnson & Kolodny, 1985; Allgeier & Allgeier, 1988; Denny & Quadagno, 1988—the list is not comprehensive). Several scales for the measurement of "homophobia" (Smith, 1971; Hudson & Ricketts, 1980) have probably helped to solidify the position in the literature of this erroneous hellenism.

   "Homo" = "sameness" and "phobia" = "fear" literally translate into "fear of sameness," a generic expression that could have reference to a myriad of phenomena. A more accurate term would be *homosexphobia*, a designation suggested at one time by Levitt & Klassen (1974). Ironically, some of the authors who have perpetuated the Smith-Weinberg error have also cited Levitt & Klassen (1974) as evidence (e.g., Harmatz & Novak, 1983; Allgeier & Allgeier, 1988; Denney & Quadagno, 1988).

   The Levitt-Klassen term corrects part of the error but it does not address the assumption that antihomosexuality is a phobic response, a conclusion that lacks convincing support. For this reason, the word homosexphobia has been abandoned in this volume and is replaced throughout by the unimpeachable expression, *antihomosexuality*.
2. Traditionally, factor analysis involves the assumption that all the items involved constitute a single reality or universe, and that the relationship between each item and every other item will determine the makeup of the factors that emerge. If these factors are to be statistically *inter*dependent, so that relationships between the various items are to be preserved in the analysis as much as possible, the researcher will probably choose to use what is called *oblique rotation* in the procedure. On the other hand, if the various factors are to be generated so as to force them to be as independent from one another as possible, the researcher will select what is called an "orthogonal" method of rotation. The latter course was adopted, since all the items had roughly similar content—that is, attitudes toward homosexuality—and we wanted to see whether factors would emerge consisting of meaningfully distinct clusters.
3. Another point to consider in deciding whether a given factor constitutes a good substitute for the constituent items has to do with when it emerges in the computation, if there is more than one factor in the structure. The loadings of items on the first factor in the structure mainly reflect how they are intercorrelated. This first factor will absorb as much of the variance in its constituent items as is statistically possible, but some residual variance will be left over to be absorbed in subsequent factors. Thus, when these same items

appear in the second factor, the loadings they have there may have something to do with intercorrelations but will also represent unabsorbed variance left over from the first factor. In the third factor, one may expect residual variance to have a still greater effect, and so on throughout the structure. This can mean that factors later in the structure may be less reliable measures than the first one. Consequently, we required that for our factors to be useful as individual measures, each must bear a Kuder-Richardson reliability alpha of at least .60. All of the six factors we finally used met this criterion. Correlations among all these factors and the original interview items are given in Appendix E.

4. Even though pretesting determined that the public tends to condemn homosexuality among females as readily as that among males, the items about homosexuals' occupations specify "men" because traditionally "masculine" occupations are generally deemed more respected and consequential than "feminine" ones.
5. Note that as our factors are comprised only of items reflecting negative attitudes toward homosexuality, they measure *degrees* of negativism rather than its presence or absence. Strictly speaking, therefore, our findings refer to the correlates of low-negative or high-negative attitudes toward homosexuality.
6. For example, replication would involve beginning with the same 35 items and subjecting them to the same kind of factor analysis in the same arbitrarily assigned domains; further, any eventual superfactor would bear little resemblance to our MAF unless it emerged from the same empirical results—the same response distributions to the items, the same intercorrelations, the same factor loadings, etc.

Chapter 9

The Dynamics of Antihomosexual Attitudes

In the preceding chapter we showed how antihomosexual attitudes cluster together and fall along the three dimensions indicated by attitude theory in general. This chapter looks at the question of how these dimensions or components of attitudes are connected to one another—that is, how the cognitive, affective, and conative dimensions interrelate to produce specific attitudes. Thus we attempt to illuminate the functioning of antihomosexual attitudes by discovering the dynamics that underlie such reactions.

As noted in Chapters 7 and 8, earlier studies have investigated antihomosexual attitudes and their clustering. When it comes to relationships among the components of attitudes, however, we have little or no previous work to guide us. In the field of sexuality there have been only a few studies that have considered the relationship between "attitudes" (usually sexual norms) and sexual behaviors (see Christensen, 1966; Christensen & Gregg, 1970; Athanasiou, 1973). While such research is certainly intriguing, it does not provide much of a theoretical guide, especially in our case, which involves a specific attitude object. For this reason we begin by offering a simple model of the dynamics of antihomosexual attitudes, which can be readily tested.

A Dynamic Model of Attitudes Toward Homosexuality

First, it is believed that a certain group of people (for example, "homosexuals") share a number of common characteristics that distinguish them from others and that in combination identify and define them as a meaningful social category. These characteristics can be relatively neutral and "informative" (e.g., "Male homosexuals are artistically inclined,") or even positive (e.g., "Male homosexuals are more sensitive than other males"). In the main, however, more emphasis is put on negative attributes thought to characterize the category (e.g., "Male homosexuals are suffering from some kind of mental illness"). Whatever the case, the group is cognitively perceived as a social category and is attributed characteristics claimed to typify all members of that social category. Thus Ward (1977) and Staats (1978) showed how homosexuals are perceived in a stereotypical way. Indeed, Chapter 7 of this book shows that in 1970 large portions of the U.S. population held such attributes to be true of most or all homosexuals.

Categorizing or typing persons is a necessary way of dealing with the social world and often functions to ensure smooth social interactions. However, when such categorizing is based mainly upon attributing negative characteristics to a group, a strong emotional response is likely to accompany the cognition, so that social distance or awkward interaction characterizes relationships with persons perceived as members of that group. That is, particular emotions are linked to the cognitive belief that members of a social category have distinctive characteristics. It follows, then, that as the category "homosexual" is typified by negative attributes, the emotional response is usually negative—some people feel antipathy toward homosexuals ranging from derision directed toward an effeminate type to disgust and revulsion at the thought of two members of the same sex having sex together. To extend our previous example, the cognitive belief that homosexuals are sick is usually followed by fear over their supposed unpredictability or sexual threat and/or disgust at their sexual behavior.

Given a perception and an emotional reaction, it further follows that people often hold behavioral dispositions toward homosexuals. As we have seen, these dispositions cover a wide range, from simple avoidance to punitive treatment. Probably most people would prefer to avoid homosexuals, although our research shows that a sizable portion of the population would support harsher treatment. Thus, to complete our example, if male homosexuals are thought to be mentally ill, as evidenced by the things they do sexually, then they should be forced into some kind of treatment and kept out of positions in society where they might influence the young.

Our theoretical model therefore operates as follows: in the case of homosexuals, cognitively attributed characteristics give rise to certain emotional reactions that engender specific behavioral prescriptions. Now, it could be that cognitions produce behavioral prescriptions without producing emotional reactions as an intervening step; or that emotional reactions engender behavioral prescriptions by themselves, with little cognition involved; or maybe the process is reversed in certain ways. In a later section we test these alternatives to see if they fit our data better. In the case of homosexuality, however, we feel that the first model captures most accurately the dynamic process involved in antihomosexual attitudes. Since our factor analysis in the preceding chapter showed that these attitudes apparently fall along cognitive, affective, and conative dimensions, it should be possible to test our model, and we turn to this next.

Testing the Model

Path analytic procedures, it will be remembered, are useful for demonstrating the ways in which a group of independent variables work together to influence scores on a dependent variable. In addition to showing the relative importance of each independent variable in predicting (or accounting for) scores on the dependent variable, the path diagram shows ways in which an independent variable may be influenced by others antecedent to it and in turn may influence those that intervene between it and the dependent variable, thereby indirectly influencing the latter. This procedure usually involves a model that groups independent variables according to temporal stages. For example, the model we used in the path analytic examination of the SMS in Chapter 4 included four temporal stages: influences operating at the time of the respondent's birth, during early childhood, in adolescence and early adulthood, and finally, at the time of the interview. A path analytic test of our model of attitudes toward homosexuality requires some departure from this temporal arrangement.

First, the three dimensions in the model are all seen as operating currently—in the respondent's adulthood. Thus the operation of attitudes represents progress not through time but through social psychological stages.

Second, the model leads us to expect that the influence of cog-

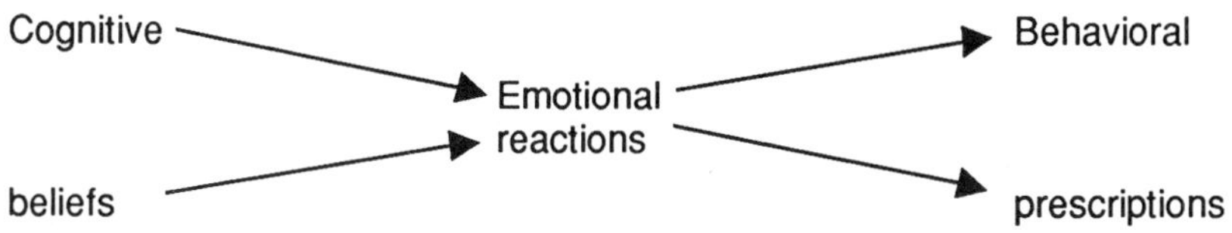

Figure 9-1 A Dynamic Model of Attitudes Toward Homosexuality

nitive beliefs will operate mainly through emotional reactions, with little or no *direct* influence on behavioral prescriptions. In terms of path analysis, we would expect that a diagram with cognitive beliefs in the first stage, emotional reactions in the second, and a behavioral prescription as the dependent variable would not have a statistically strong path from the first stage to the dependent variable. Usually in path analysis, a direct path from an independent variable earlier than the last stage is theoretically interesting; here such a path would tend to contradict our model.

Our theoretical model is outlined in Figure 9-1; the path analysis scheme that we used to test the model is shown in Figure 9-2, which names the factors we used. Note that each of the three different behavioral prescription factors is used in turn as the dependent variable, namely, "Deny authoritative jobs," "Deny freedoms," and "Allow stereotypic jobs." The emotional reaction dimension includes our two factors reflecting affective states— "Homosexuals are dangerous" and "Homosexuality is abhorrent." Cognitive beliefs are represented by the sole factor, "Homosexuality is distorted heterosexuality."[1]

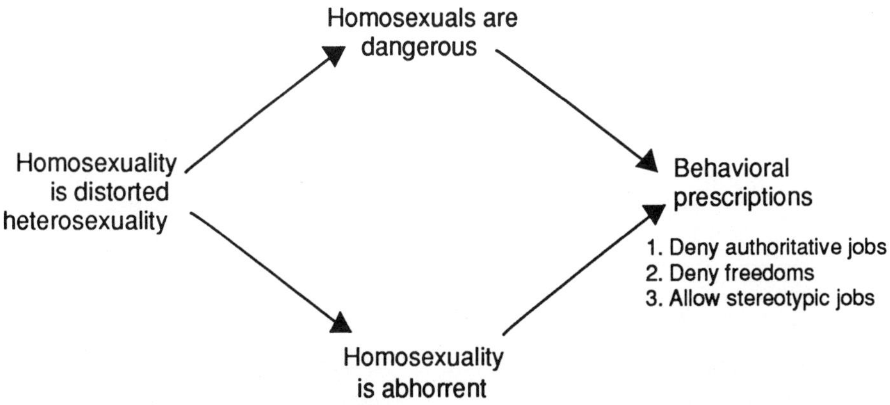

Figure 9-2 Path Analysis Scheme for Testing the Model in Figure 9-1

Proscribing Authoritative Jobs

Figure 9-3 and Table 9-1 show the system with the factor "Deny authoritative jobs" as the dependent variable to be explained. In support of our model, no direct path appears between the cognitive belief factor "Homosexuality is distorted heterosexuality" and the dependent variable. (As the table shows, this path would have a beta value of .053, which is too weak to be substantively meaningful.) Instead, cognitive beliefs indirectly influence the disposition to deny authoritative jobs to homosexual men by affecting the likelihood that people with these beliefs will feel that homosexuals are dangerous and homosexuality is abhorrent. For all its simplicity, this system, with an R of .667 and an R^2 of .445, does reasonably well in explaining how people come to deny such jobs to homosexual men. Of particular note is the part played by "Homosexuals are dangerous." This variable has the strongest total

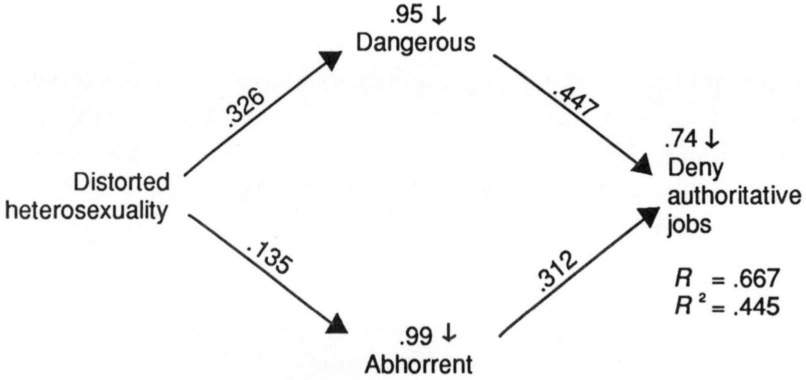

Figure 9-3 Path Diagram Model for "Deny Authoritative Jobs"

TABLE 9-1 Effects of Variables in the "Deny Authoritative Jobs" Model

Variable	Direct effect	Indirect effects	Total effects	Extraneous effects	Total association
Distorted heterosexuality	.053	.188	.241	−.035	.206
Homosexuals are dangerous	.447	—	.447	.148	.595
Homosexuality is abhorrent	.312	—	.312	.164	.476

effects (.447) and also the highest total association with "Deny authoritative jobs." Such a connection is quite reasonable: the fear of homosexuals—which includes notions that they try to get involved sexually with children and can undermine society—strongly influences people's idea that homosexuals should not be allowed to teach school, or be in the position to judge, counsel, or otherwise influence the lives of others as they would if they were judges, doctors, ministers, or government officials. Apparently, the fear that a homosexual man in such a position might misuse his authority or influence is stronger than the notion that he is unfit for it because his sexual orientation renders him repugnant.

It is also noteworthy that the cognitive belief factor "Homosexuality is distorted heterosexuality" has a stronger connection with "Homosexuals are dangerous" than with "Homosexuality is abhorrent." These relationships are unaffected by the choice of dependent variable, so they are the same in each of the three systems. We should therefore expect that in each system, "Homosexuality is distorted heterosexuality" will exert a greater proportion of its indirect effects through "Homosexuals are dangerous" than through "Homosexuality is abhorrent." In the present system, 78% of the indirect effects of "distorted heterosexuality" work through "Homosexuals are dangerous." Thus the latter effects the propensity to deny authoritative jobs through its role as a mediator of the influence of "distorted heterosexuality," as well as directly. It should be pointed out, however, that "Homosexuality is abhorrent," while weaker, also has a sizable effect.

Proscribing Social Freedoms

This system, with the factor "Deny freedoms" as the dependent variable, is presented in Figure 9-4 and Table 9-2. In terms of explanatory power, it is nearly as strong as the preceding one, with an R of .641 and an R^2 of .411. Here, too, the direct path from "Homosexuality is distorted heterosexuality" is too weak to warrant inclusion in the diagram. This time, however, the notion of "Homosexuality is abhorrent" is the stronger of the two second-stage variables, to the extent that even though it is not as strongly connected with "distorted heterosexuality" as is "Homosexuals are dangerous," it carries about the same proportion of the indirect effects of "distorted heterosexuality."

Again the dynamics of this system seem clear. If homosexuals

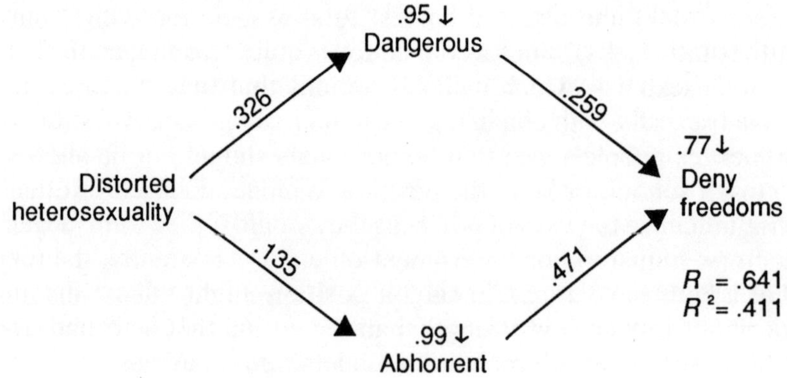

Figure 9-4 Path Diagram Model for "Deny Freedoms"

TABLE 9-2 Effects of Variables in the "Deny Freedoms" Model

Variable	Direct effect	Indirect effects	Total effects	Extraneous effects	Total association
Distorted heterosexuality	.019	.148	.167	.005	.172
Homosexuals are dangerous	.259	—	.259	.224	.483
Homosexuality is abhorrent	.471	—	.471	.123	.594

are to be denied authoritative jobs for fear that they might abuse such positions, they are to be denied various social freedoms because the thought of what they might otherwise do—for example, dance with one another—is disgusting. The contribution of "Homosexuals are dangerous" can be interpreted in light of some of the other individual items that make up the factor "deny freedoms." For example, it may be seen as dangerous for homosexuals to form groups to deal with their social problems because in so doing they might achieve a socially disruptive amount of political power.

In both this system and the previous one, the three-dimensional model of attitudes seems adequately supported. Both systems achieve a satisfactory degree of explanatory power with the variables used. In both, cognitive beliefs lead to emotional reactions rather than directly to the behavioral proscription in question. The cognitive belief factor "Homosexuality is distorted heterosexuality" connects more strongly with "Homosexuals are dangerous" in apparent reflection of threat people feel when confronted by what they view to be an aberration they do not understand. That a homosexual is believed to be a heterosexual manqué also leads to feelings of disgust about homosexual preferences and practices, but not quite so strongly. Clearly, these feelings of threat or disgust are in turn responsible for people's desire to deny homosexuals certain occupational and social freedoms. It is interesting, however, to note that different emotions appear to operate in producing different outcomes in this process. This lends additional support for the path analytic three-dimensional model because it further specifies how attitudes toward particular social objects can operate differentially.

Proscribing Stereotypic Jobs

As pointed out earlier, the factor "Allow stereotypic jobs" works in a different way from the two just discussed. There was reasonably strong majority consensus among our respondents that certain authoritative jobs and certain social freedoms should be denied homosexual men. However, most of our respondents did *not* want to deny them access to traditionally "gay" jobs; thus this factor seems to identify a distinctive minority who are especially hostile toward homosexuals. Since our interest is in examining the mechanisms involved in negative attitudes toward homosexuals, we coded this factor so that in the path analysis it could be used to predict the inclination to deny instead of allow these stereotypic jobs. (For this reason we refer to it as "*Deny* stereotypic jobs.") This means that relatively few of the respondents are being "predicted" in this system, so with less variance to explain, there may be less explanatory power—that is, a lower R^2—and perhaps other differences as well.

Figure 9-5 and Table 9-3 bear out these expectations. The system has an R of .375 and an R^2 of .141, which is quite low. In addition, there is a direct path to "Deny stereotypic jobs" from the cognitive belief factor "Homosexuality is distorted heterosexuality." The latter exerts fully 89% of its indirect effects through "Homosexuals are dangerous," which also has a direct effect three times as strong as the one for "Homosexuality is abhorrent." In fact, the latter is relatively unimportant in this system, so little so that if it is eliminated entirely, the R^2 is only slightly reduced—to

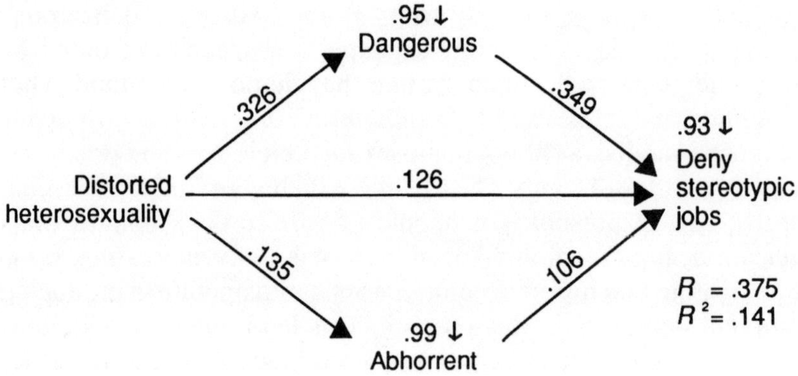

Figure 9-5 Path Diagram Model for "Deny Stereotypic Jobs"

TABLE 9-3 Effects of Variables in the "Deny Stereotypic Jobs" Model

Variable	Direct effect	Indirect effects	Total effects	Extraneous effects	Total association
Distorted heterosexuality	.126	.128	.154	.062	.216
Homosexuals are dangerous	.349	—	.349	−.025	.324
Homosexuality is abhorrent	.106	—	.106	.109	.215

.137—meaning that this variable explains less than one-half of one percent of the variance in "Deny stereotypic jobs."

It appears, then, that the propensity to prohibit homosexual men's working as florists, artists, musicians, or beauticians is based mostly on fear, and to a much lesser extent on believing that they are perverse heterosexuals—in short, that they are dangerous individuals. Given the substance of these results, as applied to an extreme minority of the sample, these findings do not seem to seriously call into doubt the general "fitness" of our model.

The results of these three tests of our dynamic model of attitudes appear to support our assertions as to the operation of negative attitudes toward homosexuals, as they did in the original use of the stereotyping concept. To further examine the model we looked for groups of respondents that varied considerably from the general sample in the way they reacted to homosexuality to see if the model would still apply. Since Table 8-2 showed that education is strongly related to antihomosexual attitudes, we chose to divide respondents on this basis for a subpopulation test of the model.

A Subpopulation Application of the Model

Although our analysis of general sexual norms (Chapter 4) did not identify educational level as a principal determinant, findings in Chapter 8 suggested that education does influence attitudes toward homosexuality. It might be expected, for example, that educational experiences can involve exposure to both individuals and information that can change how a person reacts to supposed "deviants." Thus, it makes sense that our highly educated respondents displayed a pattern of stereotyping somewhat different from that for the less educated. At the same time, dividing our respondents into subgroups would allow us to see how generally applicable the three-component attitudinal model might be.

Here is how our subpopulation test of the model proceeded. Based on the information in Table 8-2, we repeated the three foregoing path analyses, first for respondents who had not completed high school and then for those who had (this divides our sample roughly in half). The resulting path models are shown in Figures 9-6, 9-7, and 9-8. In these diagrams we give the unstandardized path coefficient (*b*) rather than beta, since these are subsample data; therefore, while the general shape of the models is comparable to the total-sample models presented previously, the path sizes are not. We shall look instead at the *relative* strength of the various relationships displayed in the diagrams.

Deny Authoritative Jobs. Figure 9-6 shows, first of all, that unlike the case for the total sample (and for the more educated), among respondents with less than twelfth-grade education the feeling that homosexuality is abhorrent seems not to have been tied to any cognitive beliefs. These less educated respondents also may have based a desire to bar homosexual men from professions of authority directly upon the notion that homosexuality is distorted heterosexuality, regardless of the respondents' emotional response to homosexuality. However, this connection is not as strong as those between feeling fear or abhorrence toward homosexuals and the denial of authoritative jobs. For both education subgroups, as for the total sample, fear of homosexuals appears to be more important in engendering this denial than is a feeling of abhorrence toward them.

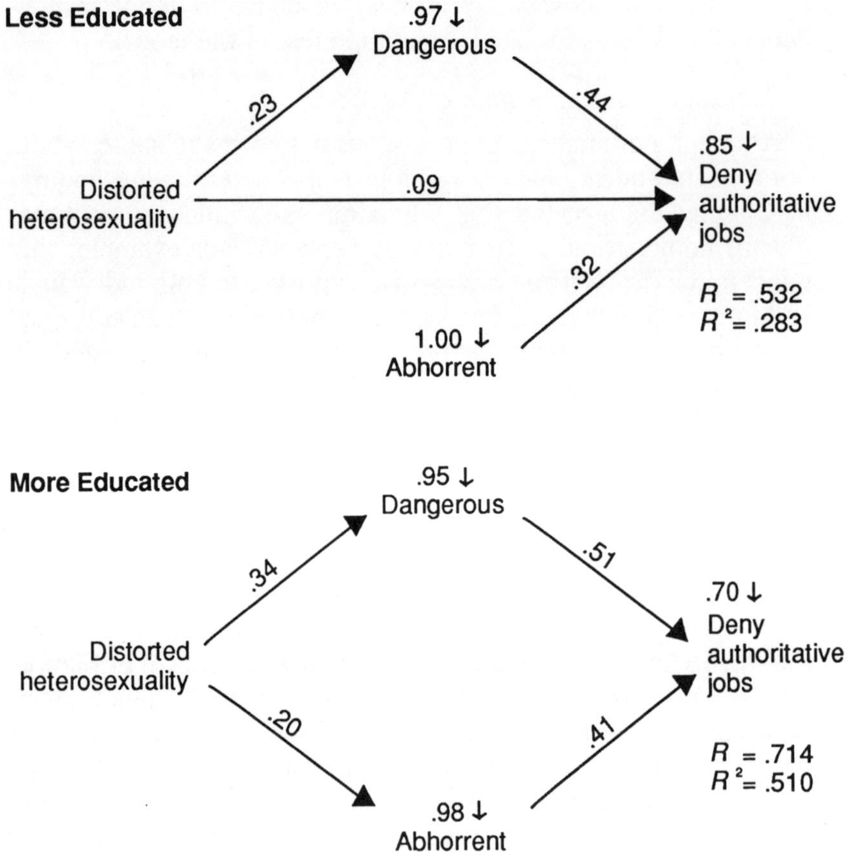

Figure 9-6 Path Diagram Models for "Deny Authoritative Jobs" in Educational-Level Subsamples

Deny Freedoms. The model works about equally well for the two education groups when it comes to restricting homosexuals' social freedoms (Figure 9-7). As noted earlier, being disgusted by what homosexuals may do in their leisure time seems to be the principal determinant of wanting to limit their social involvements, and this is so regardless of educational level.

Deny Stereotypic Jobs. As Figure 9-8 shows, predicting this less common attitude is more difficult with our data, just as we saw in Figure 9-5 for the total sample. Among both the less and the more educated, fear of homosexuals is the strongest predictor, and there is a direct path from "Homosexuality is distorted heterosexuality,"

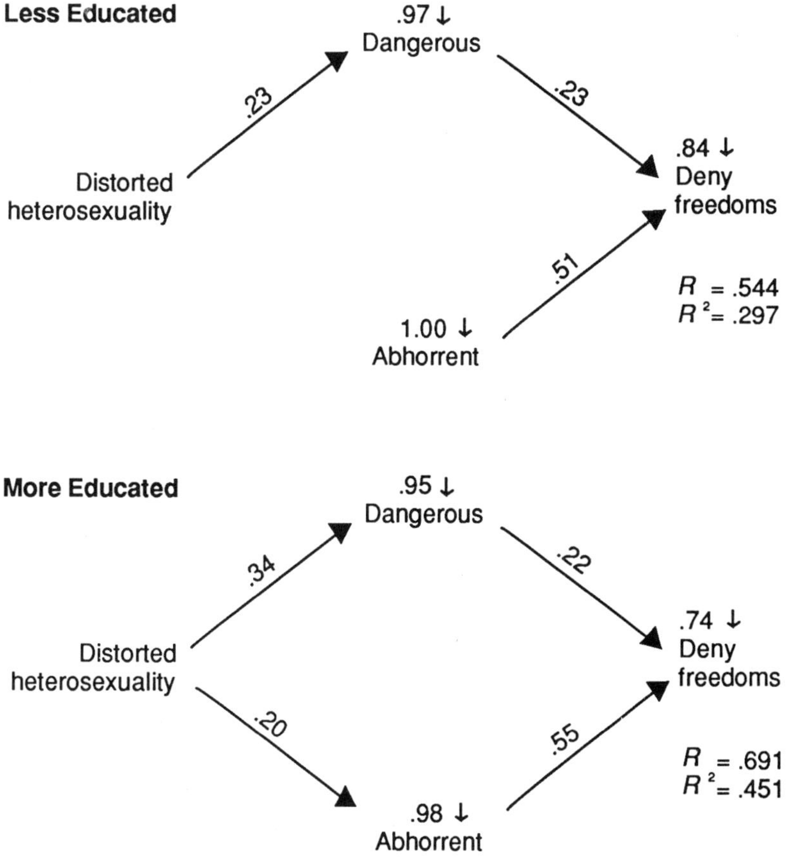

Figure 9-7 Path Diagram Models for "Deny Freedoms" in Educational-Level Subsamples

in violation of the theoretical premise that cognitions influence behavioral responses only through engendering emotional reactions. It is a relatively small path, though, thus indicating the primacy of emotions.

Conclusions. For all three conative factors, we note that the R^2—hence, the explanatory power—is apparently higher for the more-educated respondents. For the first two, the more-educated R^2 is also a bit higher than that for the population at large. The three-part attitudinal model thus seems less applicable to those with relatively little education. Their feelings of abhorrence toward homosexuals appear to be reflexive rather than the product

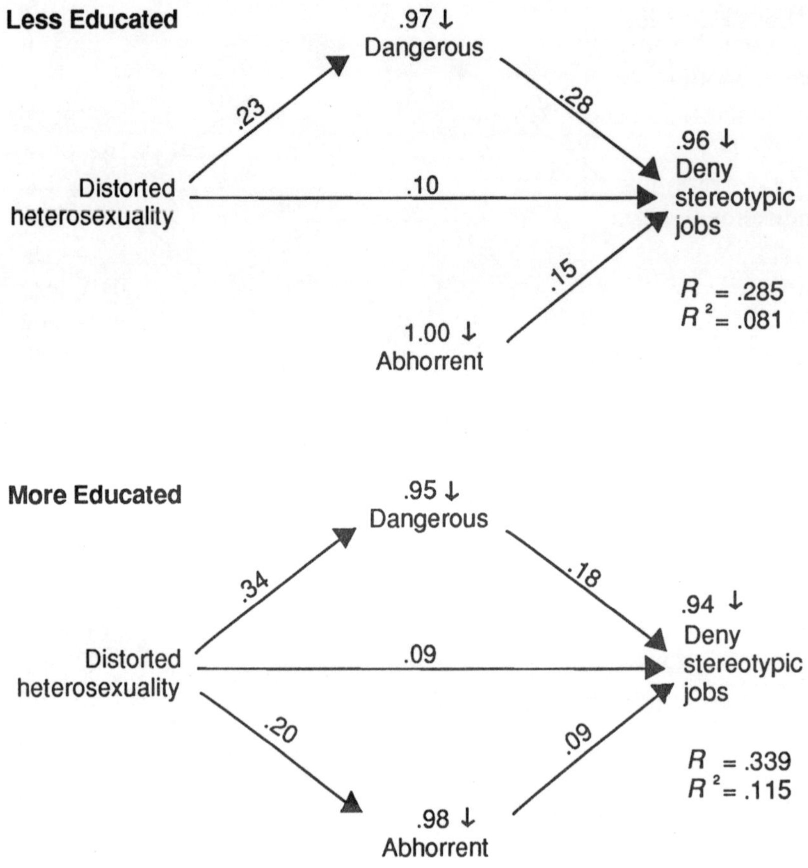

Figure 9-8 Path Diagram Models for "Deny Stereotypic Jobs" in Educational-Level Subsamples

of cognition, and their inclinations to restrict homosexuals' occupational or social freedom cannot be accounted for with this model as well as they can among those with more education. Perhaps the educational process serves to organize the operation of attitudes as the three-component theory predicts, while among the less-educated segment of the population (42% of our respondents did not finish high school) the sources and operation of attitudes are less definable or predictable. The situation may also involve a partially artifactual effect, if education tends to stimulate a greater variance of tolerance, compared to less among the less educated. This may account in part for the difficulty previous investigators have had in trying to test the utility of the tripartite concept. Nonetheless, these results do not seriously sabotage our basic model. For example, the role of cognition is stronger in influenceing emotions than in influencing behavior, and in many respects the two subpopulations are similar to the total sample. Thus, subpopulation applicability does seem to be a feature of the model.

As we pointed out earlier, it is possible to argue that the dimensions of attitudes operate in a different sequence from the one we have used so far. While the subpopulation test just described seems to support the model in Figure 9-1, a comparison with alternative sequences is clearly in order as well. These tests are described in the following section.

Testing Alternative Models

Although the model we have been using seems valid and responsible, it is at variance with the conclusions of some investigations of attitudes toward other social objects and situations. For example, we interpreted people's willingness to deny authoritative jobs to homosexual men as arising from feelings of fear and abhorrence, which in turn were influenced by thinking of homosexuality as distorted heterosexuality. But it might also be possible that people develop cognitive beliefs in the process of accounting for their emotional reactions; in path analytic terms, this would require that our affective-component factors ("Homosexuals are dangerous" and "Homosexuality is abhorrent") should come in the first stage and precede instead of follow the cognitive factor "Homosexuality is distorted heterosexuality." Or it could be hypothesized that people who vote in support of removing homosexual teachers do so because they feel that homosexuality is threatening or disgusting, and then arrange their cognitions in keeping with this action; this hypothesis would mean that "Homosexuality is distorted heterosexuality" ought to be the dependent variable, with "Deny authoritative jobs" intervening between it and the two affective variables. Accordingly, we ran additional path analyses with our six attitudinal variables in all the alternative sequences possible.[2]

Feelings Influencing Thinking and Behavior. Our results do not support the notion that the emotional response to homosexuality underlies both beliefs about it and behavioral dispositions. When the cognitive factor "Homosexuality is distorted heterosexuality" is placed so as to intervene between the affective factors ("Homosexuals are dangerous," "Homosexuality is abhorrent") and either "Deny authoritative jobs" or "Deny freedoms," it becomes too weak statistically (beta = .06 and −.02, respectively) to have a part in the model at all. This shows that these behavioral reactions arise directly from emotional reactions. When the dependent variable is "Deny stereotypic jobs"—a situation, it will be remembered, involving relatively few respondents—it is "Homosexuality is abhorrent" that drops out of the model (beta = .07). With all three dependent variables, there is some loss in explained variance, as the R^2 is reduced when independent variables are dropped; and since our factor analyses (Chapter 8) did confirm the importance of all six factors in describing the dimensions of antihomosexuality, a model set that does not make use of them all seems inferior to the main one. Further, the failure of "Homosexuality is abhorrent" to connect meaningfully with the cognitive belief that homosexuals are perverted heterosexuals is strange insofar as the main models do contain this path when cognition is allowed to precede emotion. This strengthens our assumption that cognitive beliefs are psychologically antecedent to emotional reactions; to put it another way, "objective" cognitions do not mediate the tendency for people to act in keeping with their emotions, except when the action is unusually punitive toward homosexuals (i.e., denying them relatively uninfluential jobs).

Cognitions as the Result of Behavior. It has been suggested (see Festinger, 1957) that if people behave in ways that conflict with what they believe, they may rearrange their cognitions to accord with their behavior. We tested this hypothesis in several ways. First, we took the three behavioral factors as independent variables, with our cognitive factor dependent. In this preliminary test, no path appeared from "Deny authoritative jobs" to "Homosexuality is distorted heterosexuality"; thus it cannot be asserted that people develop the latter notion in defense of such denial. This suggests a problem with this analytic sequence since "Deny authoritative jobs" is our strongest factor and thus might be expected to relate well with the others; this factor also happens to measure a particularly salient behavioral disposition (e.g., see page 192). We obtained a low R^2 (.055) for this abbreviated model, which reflects the omission of the affective factors. We proceeded to add these—"Homosexuals are dangerous" and "Homosexuality is abhorrent"—to the model, first as the second or intervening stage. Our speculation here was that if behavior alone cannot clearly be shown to affect thinking, an emotional response to the situation may be required. The resulting analysis shows, as before, that feeling "Homosexuality is abhorrent" does not lead to thinking "Homosexuality is distorted heterosexuality," and the former factor therefore does not belong in this model. "Deny authoritative jobs" acquires a *negative direct* path, meaning that people who espouse this denial are thereby likely *not* to believe that homosexuals are failed heterosexuals, but it has *positive indirect* effects through "Homosexuals are dangerous," which also mediates all the effects of "Deny Freedoms" and about a third of those of "Deny stereotypic jobs." The five behavioral and emotional factors together can account only for about 14% of the variance in "Homosexuality is distorted heterosexuality," which together with the difficulty in interpreting the role of "Deny authoritative jobs" suggests that this is not a very good model.

When emotions are allowed to precede behaviors in the model, as our analyses thus far suggest they should, the results are similarly confusing. Here, feelings of abhorrence toward homosexuals influence denying them authoritative jobs (as in the main model), but since the latter variable maintains its negative connection to cognition, the effects of "Homosexuality is abhorrent" are also negative—that is, the model says that people who feel homosexuality is disgusting are unlikely to decide that it is a perverted form of "normal" sex. This is a puzzling inference. Thus, taking cognition as either the direct or indirect outcome of behavior does not seem to be the best use for our data.

These experiments do not cast doubt on cognitive dissonance theory per se, however. If the development of post hoc cognitions happens relatively seldom, the process could not be precisely depicted in a path analysis that uses data from many people who did not experience such dissonance. Our results suggest, rather, that forming cognitions to accord with past behavior is not the usual case respecting antihomosexual attitudes.

Emotional Response as the Final Result. Finally, it could be supposed that cognitions take up a small part of conscious regard, that behavior can be transitory, and that both are more readily changeable than emotional reactions, which are more powerful, reflexive, and enduring. (We saw some evidence of this in Chapter 7, where the low-negative people were more likely to exhibit emotional negativism than other kinds of antihomosexuality.) First we tried putting our behavior-disposition variables in the first stage and the cognitive factor ("Homosexuality is distorted heterosexuality") second. The results show that when "Homosexuals are dangerous" is the dependent variable, all four of the others have paths to it, and denial of stereotypic jobs and of freedoms also have small indirect effects through the cognitive factor. This model has an R of .692 and an R^2 of .479, comparable to those for the main models. When "Homosexuality is abhorrent" is the dependent variable, two of the others—the cognitive one and that concerning stereotypic jobs—have very weak connections and drop out of the model; these play so little part that when they are excluded from calculation, the R of .650 and R^2 of .422 remain the same to the third decimal place.

When the behavioral factors concerning denial of jobs and freedoms are placed in the second stage and preceded by "Homosexuality is distorted heterosexuality," the resulting models are slightly improved (although R and R^2 are as before because the same variables are used). In the model for "Homosexuals are dangerous," all the possible paths among the different variables are substantively significant ($\beta \geq \pm .08$, $p < .001$). In that for "Homosexuality is abhorrent," the cognitive variable stays in this time because it has indirect connections to the dependent variable via "Deny authoritative jobs" and "Deny freedoms."

In short, this experiment shows that our cognitive and behavioral factors can account for nearly half of the variance in feeling either fear or disgust toward homosexuals. But this "success" is mainly statistical. The models suggest that emotions can be demonstrated as the direct consequence of behavior, and this is sensible enough if the emotions concerned are in process associated with actions, such as guilt or satisfaction would be. However, that does not seem to be the case here. The first model, for example, suggests that fear of homosexuals arises from denying them certain "rights," and this seems reasonable only if we are considering fear of reprisal, which is not included in our "dangerous" factor. Thus, we infer that while it is statistically useful to treat emotions as the result of both behaviors and cognitions, care must be taken to make sure that the analytic outcome makes theoretical sense.

We summarize this section, therefore, by noting that our main models, which are based upon traditional attitude theory, seem to be the most workable way of demonstrating how antihomosexual attitudes operate. Alternative versions do not improve upon the explanatory power of the original scheme and are difficult to interpret sensibly. At best they may demonstrate uncommon exceptions to the cognitive-affective-conative principle.

Summary

This chapter has dealt with the relationships among the cognitive, emotional, and conative dimensions of attitudes toward homosexuality. Noting that there is little or no theoretical guidance on this matter, we further examined the theoretical model of the dynamics of antihomosexual attitudes, which states that cognitive beliefs about homosexuals lead to certain emotional reactions that engender various behavioral prescriptions. A path analytic test of this model suggests that there is some validity to it. In the first instance, the cognitive belief that homosexuals are distorted heterosexuals leads to the denial of authoritative jobs to homosexuals only indirectly and mainly through feelings of danger. Next, homosexuals are denied social freedoms through the fear they arouse, but even more so through the feelings of abhorrence engendered by seeing them as perverted heterosexuals. The model did not do so well in predicting whether homosexuals should be denied stereotypic jobs, but this was for methodological rather than theoretical reasons. We tested the applicability of the model by examining whether it fit the attitudinal dynamics of people with little education (a strongly antihomosexual group) as compared to those who had at least finished high school. The model was somewhat more successful for the more-educated half of the sample; among the others, abhorrence toward homosexuals appeared unconnected to cognitions. However, for the most part the model did operate for both groups as it did for the entire sample, suggesting that it may fit a wide variety of subpopulations. Finally, rearranging the sequence of variables in the model failed to produce a superior alternative.

NOTES

1. It will be remembered that the analysis described in Chapter 8 originally yielded four cognitive factors. Two of these were statistically unreliable. A subsequent analysis excluding the items in those two weak factors produced the single factor pertaining to distorted heterosexuality. We use this single factor in the first stage of our model because of its superior reliability (alpha = .72). However, to test the validity of this choice we also tried using the original four cognitive factors. In this test we obtained results virtually identical to those using the single factor "Homosexuality is distorted heterosexuality."
2. These additional analyses did not include testing whether the six factors were assigned properly to the various dimensions—e.g., it might be questioned whether thinking of homosexuals as unsuccessful heterosexuals and denying them social freedoms are really part of the same social psychological phenomenon—for two reasons. First, the factor analytic tests of this question (described in Chapter 8) supported the constitution of the three path analytic stages we use. Second, the path analytic procedure itself implicitly tests it by permitting all variables an equal chance to influence (i.e., to have a path to) the dependent variable.

Chapter 10

Explaining Attitudes Toward Homosexuality

In the preceding two chapters we have been looking at the structure and dynamics of antihomosexual attitudes and stereotypes, and we have demonstrated useful ways to measure them. This chapter considers how much we can account for variations in antihomosexuality among our respondents, that is, for why some persons' antihomosexual attitudes are stronger, more comprehensively stereotypic than others'.

Certain psychological factors have been shown to relate to antihomosexual attitudes. Smith (1971) found the "homophobic" individual to be status conscious, authoritarian, and sexually rigid. MacDonald et al. (1972) demonstrated that negative attitudes toward homosexuality were associated with support of the double standard for sex in general. Dunbar, Brown, and Amoroso (1973) found that Canadian antihomosexual respondents were intolerant of certain heterosexual practices, had greater guilt over their own sexual feelings, and held stronger sex-role stereotypes. Their findings were further replicated among Brazilian and West Indian subjects (Dunbar, Brown, & Vuorinen, 1973; Brown & Amoroso, 1975). MacDonald and Games (1974) found that negative attitudes toward homosexuals are associated with lack of support for equality between the sexes, with an authoritarian personality, and with particular elements of authoritarianism such as intolerance of ambiguity and cognitive rigidity.

Even though all of the above work used student samples, empirical studies such as these suggest some conclusions. First, antihomosexual attitudes may be related to problems with gender role (MacDonald et al., 1972). Laner and Laner (1979) noted that so-called homophobia is more strongly directed at gender-anomalous ("hypo-" and "hypermasculine") homosexual men than at more conventional ones. This negativism should hold especially true among groups that share narrowly defined sex-role stereotypes. For example, Dunbar, Brown, and Vuorinen (1973) demonstrated strong antihomosexual feelings among Brazilian respondents who subscribe firmly to the notion of "machismo."

Second, antihomosexual attitudes are related to authoritarianism. The authoritarian personality defends against unwanted sexual impulses through repressing them; such impulses may be transformed into hostility toward a minority group. Berry and Marks (1969), for example, showed a relationship between guilt about sex and disapproval of homosexuality. Furthermore, with their concern for social stability and intolerance of ambiguity, authoritarians are more likely to disapprove of a group they perceive as deviant with regard to many conventional social and sexual patterns. San Miguel and Millham (1976) found that males who are intolerant of homosexuals react more aggressively toward a homosexual whom they perceive as similar to themselves in certain personality characteristics. (When the comparison is with a heterosexual male, greater perceived similarity produces *less* aggressive behavior.) San Miguel and Millham interpreted this finding in terms of the personal threat induced by the comparison (although whether it is due to a vulnerable sexual identity could not be ascertained.)

Third, antihomosexual attitudes are associated with intolerance toward sexual variation in general. Dunbar, Brown, and Amoroso (1973) found this phenomenon to be proof of Churchill's (1967) assertion that prejudice against homosexuals is consistent with a sex-negative culture like that of North America. They note, however, that this relationship is not overly strong, suggestng that antihomosexuality may be a specific stance in itself. Brown (1952), in a cross-cultural comparison of sexual mores, showed that societies more tolerant toward heterosexual behavior of various kinds tend also to be tolerant of homosexual behavior; and Reiss (1964) noted that sexual restrictiveness in America applies both to homosexuality and heterosexuality. Nyberg and Alston (1976–77) also showed that attitudes toward homosexuality are part of attitudes toward sex in general.

Sociological work on antihomosexual attitudes focuses on their sources in social structure.[1] In his functional theory, K. Davis (1971) viewed antihomosexual attitudes as maintaining the family and sexual bargaining system. Marcuse (1955) and Reich (1969) suggested that homosexuality, which is not tied to a family system and thus is associated with promiscuity, is disapproved because it becomes a distraction from work in a capitalist society. Plummer (1975) theorized that homosexuality is threatening because it is an anomaly that disrupts the category system of society, especially the belief that the family is a natural social arrangement and that sexual categories admit of only two, male and female. Lehne (1976) developed a theory by which so-called homophobia has the function of supporting norms of male sex-role behavior. It is not homosexuality per se that is the real threat, he argues, but potential changes in male sex-role definition. Homophobia thus is used to force conformity to the male role and is better seen as controlling all men, not just homosexual males.

We find a consistency between such theorizing and the research data presented previously. Homosexuality is disapproved because it is seen as socially disruptive. It has no place in a society that values heterosexual family life and supports sex-role definitions that maintain traditional family stability. Accordingly, sociological research on those who are intolerant of homosexuals shows such persons to share conservative social characteristics. For example, the following variables seem to be operative:

Religion. Kinsey et al. (1953) ascribed the source of antihomosexual attitudes to the Judeo-Christian tradition. Thus, persons who are religiously devout show the least tolerant attitudes toward homosexuals. Lehne (1976), however, noted that individuals who cite the Bible in support of their antihomosexual positions often ignore other biblical injunctions (e.g., dietary laws), showing that they interpret the Bible literally but selectively. This kind of religious teaching characterizes those who are more orthodox or fundamentalist—and who have been observed to be the most antihomosexual. Such individuals not only interpret the Bible literally but may often occupy a marginal social position and so use antihomosexual attitudes to claim moral and social superiority. Nyberg and Alston (1976–77) demonstrated in a national probability sample the importance of religion, especially religious affiliation, in determining attitudes toward homosexuality.

Education. Kitsuse (1962) showed that the response toward homosexuality is not globally negative but that education plays an important role in mediating attitudes. These results have been supported by Simmons (1965), Rooney and Gibbons (1966), Lumby (1976), Nyberg and Alston (1976–77), Jenkins (1977), and Ward (1977), all of whom found less negative responses to homosexuals among the more highly educated.

Social status. Farrell and Morrione (1974) found lower-status respondents to define fewer groups as deviant, to be less discriminating in their responses to behaviors and persons they define as deviant, but to react more negatively toward those so defined. In addition, lower-status homosexuals perceived less acceptance from members of their own social class than did upper-status homosexuals (as was also found by Weinberg & Williams, 1975a). Farrell and Morrione theorized that this is because there is a stronger dichotomization of sex roles in lower social strata; consequently, lower-status persons are more likely to apply strong sanctions toward homosexuals. Indeed, they found that lower-class homosexuals more often resemble homosexual stereotypes (e.g., effeminacy among males). This, they suggest, represents an attempt by lower-status homosexuals to resolve the cognitive dissonance between their sexual behavior and the strong expectations surrounding the male role among the lower classes.

Age. Rooney and Gibbons (1966) noted slightly more tolerance of homosexuality among younger persons, as did Jenkins (1977) and Ward (1977), but Simmons (1965) found no such relationship. Nyberg and Alston (1976–77) did find this relationship, but showed that city size and education explain most of its variance. They concluded that antihomosexual attitudes are not a generational matter but a function of one's social environment.

Gender. Rooney and Gibbons (1966) found males to be somewhat less antihomosexual than females. Simmons (1965), however, found no gender differences in attitudes toward homosexuality, nor did Ward (1977). Millham et al. (1976) found gender differences with regard to the particular stereotype of homosexuals that is held and as to whether the homosexual was male or female.

Other determinants. Very little data exist concerning other social-background predictors of antihomosexual attitudes. Nyberg and Alston (1976–77) did find more liberal attitudes among respondents from larger towns and cities, which is in line with some of our own findings already presented in Chapter 8.

We did not design our study to test specific theories of attitudes toward homosexuals but tried instead to tap a broad array of potential determinants, including many of those just discussed, both directly and indirectly. For example, we included variables that would describe sexually restrictive family backgrounds and that would reflect the sexual experience, sexual rigidity, and gender-role characteristics of the respondent, as well as those that might indicate conservatism in the respondent's social environment. In setting up our investigation of antihomosexual predictors, we also included those variables that our previous analysis of the Sexual Morality Scale had shown to be importantly related to sexual norms.

We have already shown the extent of antihomosexual attitudes in American society in 1970 and mapped some of their demographic characteristics. Now we are in a position to determine the most important variables in accounting for such attitudes and the causal ways in which those variables operate.[2] To do so we shall use as the dependent variable our global antihomosexuality scale, the Multidimensional Antihomosexual Factor or MAF (described in Chapter 8), which combines the three dimensions of antihomosexual attitudes and is the most extensive measure our data can provide.[3] We now turn to this analysis.

Accounting for Antihomosexuality

As we did in explaining sexual norms, we first consider the variance explained by our independent variables and which of them are the most important when other influences have been controlled. Following this, we attempt to provide a parsimonious model of how people come to adopt and maintain attitudes toward homosexuality. In other words, our analysis proceeds similarly to that of the SMS, with the added benefit that we know more about the operation of some of our variables from the SMS analysis.

First, all variables of interest—the same 83 as those used for the SMS analysis—were arranged according to their temporal stages. Then these variables were related directly to the MAF to ascertain the total effects (and their direct and indirect components) of each independent variable on the dependent variable.

The 83 variables provided an *R* of .603 and an R^2 of .364. In this initial analysis, the following variables displayed the greatest total effects: childhood sex play, race-black, lifetime sexual environment, reared as Jewish, urban childhood, parents' education, and current devoutness. As in the case of the SMS, sex-female had both a strong negative direct effect (i.e., in the direction of less intolerancc) and strong positive indirect effects, the two nearly canceling each other to provide apparently small positive total effects.

Next, we performed successive screening procedures to reduce the number of variables toward a parsimonious model. Here we used the same procedures as in our analysis of the SMS, excluding variables that did not meet criterion levels of total effects or direct and indirect effects over three successive screenings (see pages 93–94). This resulted in a set of 17 variables we considered essential for the explanation of the MAF. These variables provide an *R* of .566 and an R^2 of .320. Thus the exclusion of 66 variables results in the loss of 4 percentage points in variance explained, from 36% to 32%, which is 12% less variance than was accounted for by all 83 variables.

Finally, from these 17 variables in our total-path model we constructed a path diagram to examine the relationships among our variables and so suggest a causal explanation of the MAF. Again, we used the same criteria for dropping paths of low value from this diagram as we did for the SMS (see page 98). From this *path diagram model* we calculated total (direct + indirect) effects, which we compared to those of the *total-path model* to see how robust it would be when many paths of lesser magnitude are eliminated.

We turn now to the detailed results involving the seventeen variables in our final system. First, in the next section, we discuss which are the most important predictors in our system, using the total-path model as the basis for our conclusions—that is, we consider the effects of the 17 predictors allowing all possible paths between them.

The Relative Importance of Variables in the Total-Path Model

Stage 1 Variables

As ranked by total effects, urban childhood, parents' education, and race-black are the most important of our exogenous variables.

The first two work both directly and indirectly on the MAF (while race is primarily direct in its effects), with 49% and 38%, respectively, of their total association being extraneous. Reared as Jewish also has strong total effects, of which 80% are direct, and having grown up in the Midwest or Deep South similarly has a strong direct effect. Parental sexual permissiveness operates almost equally directly and indirectly, with 48% of its total association extraneous. Age and sex-female have relatively smaller effects on the MAF than they do on the SMS, although sex-female shows the same characteristic of countervailing large direct and indirect effects. The weakest of our first-stage variables is reared as Fundamentalist, with mostly indirect effects. The effects of all these variables suggest that less negativism toward homosexuals is to be found among blacks, people with highly educated or permissive parents, Jews, and the young, while those who grew up in rural areas, in the South or Midwest, or in a Fundamentalist family are more likely to have high-negative attitudes.

Stage 2 Variables

Two very powerful variables comprise our second stage: childhood sex play, the second most powerful variable overall, and lifetime sexual environment, the fourth most powerful. Both operate in the direction of low-negative attitudes. Childhood sex play has mainly direct effects—over 80% of its total effects are direct. The effects of sexual environment operate both directly and indirectly; a greater proportion of them are direct here than for the SMS. Of the total associations of these two variables with the MAF, 29% and 38%, respectively, are extraneous.

Stage 3 Variables

Of the two variables active in this stage, one—respondent's education—does not appear in the SMS system. However, 57% of its total association with the MAF is extraneous. The other variable in this stage is premarital sexual involvement, which is important in all our analyses. Here, though, it is eighth in strength among all the variables, as compared with being the strongest for the SMS. As in the SMS analysis, about half of its association with the MAF is taken up by extraneous effects. These variables work to reduce the negativism of antihomosexual attitudes.

Stage 4 Variables

Current devoutness dominates this stage, as it does the entire system, being our most important variable. This variable is also the second most important one in the explanation of the SMS. Another important variable in this stage is feels sexually threatened, fifth in importance in the MAF system, compared to its tenth ranking in the explanation of the SMS; half of the effects of this variable are extraneous. Currently Fundamentalist is the other variable in this stage. One of our weaker predictors, it still merits inclusion by our criteria, with a direct (total) effect of .09, but 53% extraneous effects. The three final-stage variables denote characteristics that tend to foster a greater amount of negativism toward homosexuals.

Relationships Among Variables in the Path Diagram Model

The foregoing effects of these 17 variables, as mentioned earlier, were calculated on the basis of all possible relationships among them (a "fully recursive" model). To reduce the picture to the most important kinds of interaction among them, we developed a path diagram model (as with the SMS) by dropping out relatively unimportant relationships or paths. Again we used the inclusion criterion of beta$\geq \pm .08$, and again we lost less than 1% of the explained variance owing to our omissions. The resulting path diagram is shown in Figure 10-1.[4]

Table 10-1 compares the direct and indirect effects calculated from the path diagram in Figure 10-1 with those of the total-path model (i.e., the one with all possible paths left in). The path diagram model yields an R^2 of .312, compared with .320 for the total model. From Table 10-1 we can see that there is a close correspondence between the two models. Two departures, however, warrant comment: first, urban childhood is reduced in importance in the path diagram model. This is partially due to its losing some of its indirect effects through the omission of weaker paths. Second, respondent's education and age increase in importance. In the path diagram model, education has a much greater direct effect, and its indirect effects have also increased. For age, our path diagram model criteria do not allow for a direct effect on the MAF,

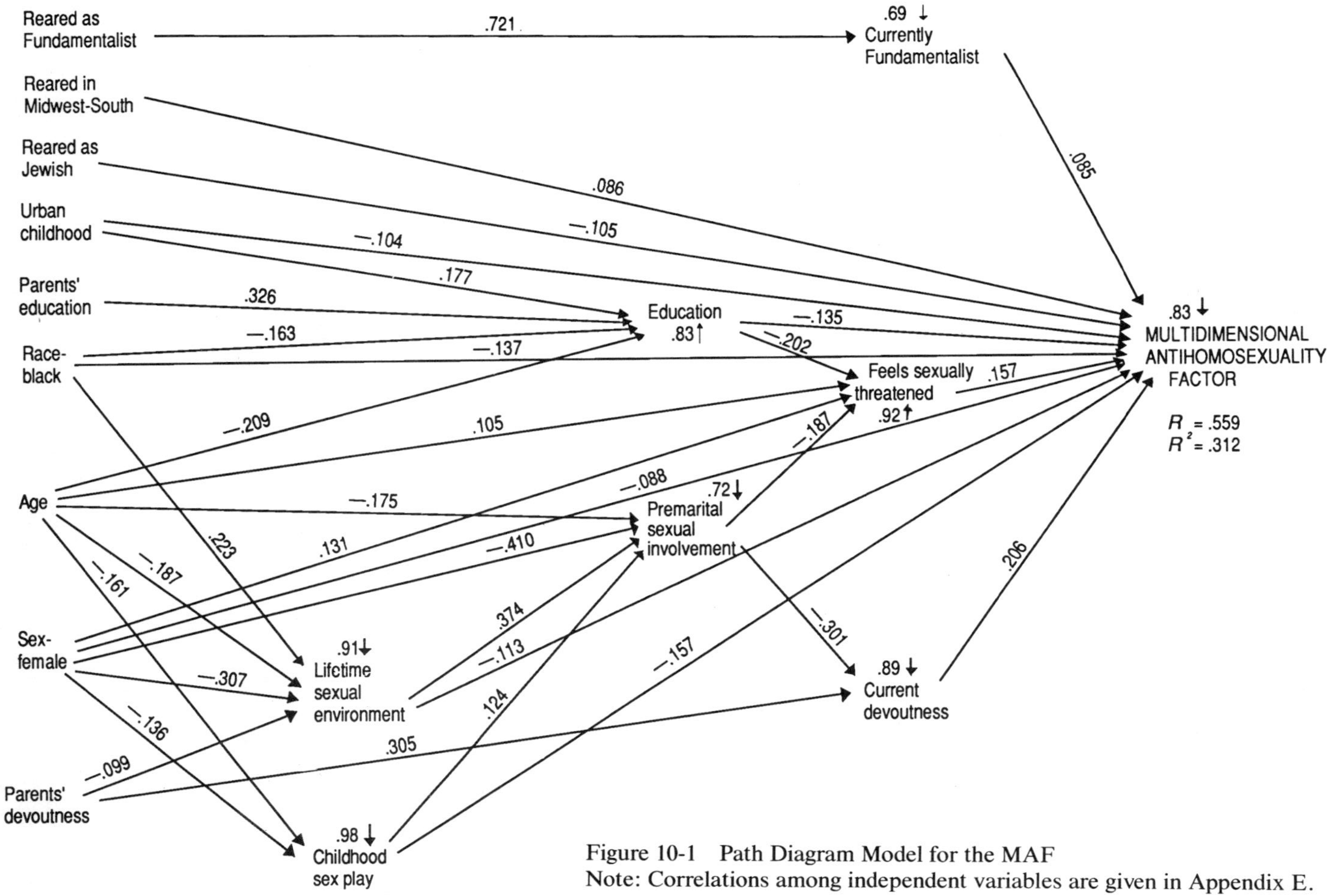

Figure 10-1 Path Diagram Model for the MAF
Note: Correlations among independent variables are given in Appendix E.

TABLE 10-1 Comparison of Effects in the Total-Path Model with Effects in the Path Diagram model

Variable	Direct effect	Indirect effects	Total effects	Extraneous effects	Total association
Current devoutness	.187 *.206*	— —	.187 *.206*	.143 *.124*	.330
Childhood sex play	−.148 *−.157*	−.031 *−.012*	−.179 *−.169*	−.072 *−.082*	−.251
Urban childhood	−.094 *−.104*	−.061 *−.030*	−.155 *−.134*	−.148 *−.169*	−.303
Lifetime sexual environment	−.086 *−.113*	−.063 *−.034*	−.149 *−.147*	−.090 *−.092*	−.239
Feels sexually threatened	.148 *.157*	— —	.148 *.157*	.152 *.143*	.300
Race-black	−.134 *−.137*	−.009 *−.005*	−.143 *−.142*	.070 *.069*	−.073
Parents' education	−.069 —	−.072 *−.054*	−.141 *−.054*	−.087 *−.174*	−.228
Premarital sexual involvement	−.065 —	−.067 *−.091*	−.132 *−.091*	−.155 *−.196*	−.287
Reared as Jewish	−.107 *−.105*	−.024 —	−.131 *−.105*	−.064 *−.090*	−.195
Respondent's education	−.104 *−.135*	−.108 *−.032*	−.122 *−.167*	−.159 *−.114*	−.281
Parental sexual permissiveness	−.052	−.051	−.103	−.094	−.197
	[Does not meet diagram inclusion criteria]				
Reared in Midwest-South	.082 *.086*	.013 —	.095 *.086*	.099 *.108*	.194
Age	−.013 —	.108 *.121*	.095 *.121*	.105 *.079*	.200
Currently Fundamentalist	.093 *.085*	— —	.093 *.085*	.104 *.112*	.197
Reared as Fundamentalist	−.020 —	.087 *.061*	.067 *.061*	.058 *.064*	.125
Parents' devoutness	−.009 —	.075 *.077*	.066 *.077*	.064 *.053*	.130
Sex-female	−.117 *−.088*	.150 *.125*	.033 *.037*	.002 *−.002*	.035

NOTE: Figures in the first row following each variable represent effects with all possible paths between variables. Figures in italics represent effects with only those paths surpassing exclusion criteria.

while the total model does have a small one of a sign different from the indirect effect; thus, in the total model the total effects of age are smaller. In addition, in the path diagram model the indirect effects of age have increased.

One final note in this comparison: our path diagram criteria prevent parental permissiveness from being included as a variable in our path diagram model. While the total-path model includes this variable, suggesting that it is important in explaining antihomosexual attitudes, its direct and indirect paths are too small individually for any of them to meet our inclusion criteria. This means that although parental sexual permissiveness does affect how intolerant of homosexuals a person becomes, this effect is probably too diffuse to be graphically illustrated in a path diagram.

As in the case of the SMS, our final diagram is a complicated one because it includes relationships among different clusters of variables, some of which operate on attitudes toward homosexuality in a more negative and some in a less negative way. In the following sections we discuss each such cluster separately.

Influences on Low-Negative Attitudes Toward Homosexuality

As noted in Chapter 7, most Americans in 1970 were quite negative in their attitudes toward homosexuality. In looking at what accounts for these attitudes we first consider those variables that produce *low* negative attitudes toward homosexuality. The reverse side of this interpretation, of course, is that these variables represent influences that our high-negative respondents have *not* experienced.

Sexual Behavior. This cluster of variables is very similar to the one isolated in the SMS analysis.[5] Except for never masturbated, it has all the same variables, although the lack of a direct path from premarital sexual involvement to the MAF means that current devoutness and feels sexually threatened are included to establish a nexus for the premarital variable. In this group of variables, both childhood sex play and lifetime sexual environment have direct effects on the MAF, so that the more sexual experience in childhood and greater awareness of the sexual environment, the less negative a person's attitudes toward homosexuality are likely to be.

There is no such direct effect for lifetime sexual environment on the SMS, suggesting that a greater awareness of others' sexual activity can have more influence on person's attitudes toward homosexuality, unlike the case for general sexual norms. Another very important difference from the SMS analysis is that there, greater premarital sexual involvement is shown directly and powerfully to influence overall sexual norms. In the case of attitudes toward homosexuality, however, such experience has a weaker, indirect effect; it acts to reduce religious devoutness and, less strongly, to minimize feelings of threat surrounding heterosexual involvements.

The ascribed variables age, sex-female, and race-black are the basis for this cluster just as they are for the SMS, and they operate in similar ways. Thus, younger age increases the likelihood of childhood sex play, more awareness of the sexual environment, and premarital sexual involvement, all of which either directly or indirectly engender less negative attitudes toward homosexuality. Age, however, does not exert most of its influence through premarital sexual involvement as it does with the SMS; this time it is childhood sex play (carrying about 21% of the indirect effects of age) and sexual environment (about 17%) that are the most important mediating influences.

Gender has the same pattern in both analyses, with females less likely than males to have engaged in childhood sex play or to have been exposed to a sexual environment. They are also a great deal less likely to have been involved in premarital sex, but the absence of a direct path from this variable to the MAF means that it is less important in mediating the indirect effects of gender than in the SMS analysis. Nonetheless, it still carries 30% of the total indirect effects of gender, being outweighed in importance only by lifetime sexual environment, which accounts for 36%. (As before, we note that females' overall tendency to be more negative toward homosexuality—considering total effects—is composed of a *less* negative direct effect counterbalanced by *more* positive—net antigay—indirect effects, suggesting again that it is these socialization influences that result in females' being overall less tolerant of homosexuality than are males.)

Finally, unlike in the SMS analysis, race has a strong direct effect on the MAF, meaning that blacks are less likely than whites to hold strong antihomosexual attitudes. As with the SMS, the indirect effects of race-black work solely through sexual environment, blacks being more likely than whites to have had such an environment. Since sexual environment has a direct path to the MAF, this implies that most of the liberalizing effects of being black arise from subcultural differences rather than particular sexual experiences.

Our interpretation of this cluster of variables is that early and continuous exposure to sexuality in general is a prerequisite to a low-negative stance toward homosexuality. Actual premarital heterosexual experiences indirectly influence such a stance, but it appears that even considerable involvement of this kind is of limited relevance; that is, there is no direct effect. Presumably this is because few people can link homosexuality to anything about their premarital heterosexual experiences, so that attitudes toward homosexuality remain compartmentalized.

Education. This cluster of variables is not part of the SMS model, as education surprisingly did not appear in our final model explaining general sexual norms.[6] Education affects the MAF both directly and indirectly through the variable feels sexually threatened. Thus, more-educated people are likely to hold low-negative attitudes toward homosexuality and in addition to feel less threatened by the opposite sex, which also lessens antihomosexuality. (Some 20% of the total effects of education are exerted indirectly in this latter way.) The determinants of educational level seem clear. People who are white, relatively young, from an urban background, or, especially, children of well-educated parents, are likely to attain high levels of education themselves, which leads to a less negative stance toward homosexuality. Being black is associated with a lower level of education, but this is offset, as we have seen, by a strong direct effect between race-black and the MAF in the opposite direction, as well as by the indirect effects of experiencing a more extensive sexual environment. Finally, as in the preceding cluster, we should note that in addition to predicting a lower level of education, age relates positively to feels sexually threatened, with older persons being more apt to report this feeling.

Many variables may contribute to the determination of sexual norms in general, as these standards tend to reflect a person's basic life-style and philosophy. Homosexuality, however, is something someone may avoid learning about; if learning occurs, as we have argued, it is generally negative and unlikely to be challenged unless a person attains a relatively high level of formal education, which can act to produce a more tolerant stance toward the world in general. Again, we emphasize the compartmentalization of homosexuality as an object of attention.

Other Variables. Two other independent variables express a connection with the MAF in a low-negative direction: urban childhood and reared as Jewish. Urban childhood has a direct connection: having been brought up in a large city predisposes a person to hold less negative attitudes toward homosexuality. This is an important relationship; urban childhood is one of our strongest variables and exerts most (78%) of its effects directly. (We have already mentioned its indirect effects through education.) This indicates that such a childhood probably prepares a person to readily accept a more heterogeneous collection of people as part of the social scene. Homosexuality as a visible urban phenomenon is also notable here. This may explain, as well, why urban childhood does not have a direct effect on the SMS, where its influence is more diffused.

The final variable, reared as Jewish, does not appear at all in the SMS analysis. This variable directly affects the probability of holding low-negative attitudes toward homosexuality. Such a background is likely to produce more tolerant attitudes in general, low-negative attitudes toward minorities being a by-product.

Influences on High-Negative Attitudes Toward Homosexuality

The clusters of variables just discussed illustrate factors associated with relatively limited antihomosexual attitudes. As noted, the reverse of these variables (e.g., little sexual experience or knowledge, restricted education) should produce stronger antihomosexual attitudes. We turn now to clusters of variables that are closely connected with the acquisition and maintenance of these more extreme antihomosexual attitudes.

Religiosity. Included in this cluster of variables is current devoutness, the most powerful predictor of attitudes toward homosexuality in our total system.[7] Our finding is that the more religiously devout (regardless of religious affiliation) people are, the more likely they are to hold highly negative attitudes toward homosexuality. We also see the strong relationship between being currently devout and having had devout parents (which accounts for 82% of the latter's indirect effects). Parental devoutness also has smaller indirect effects: those with devout parents are less likely to have experienced a broad sexual environment, which contributes directly to holding less antihomosexual attitudes as well as to other consequences through increasing the probability of premarital sexual involvement.

Another set of variables is included in this cluster. Our analysis shows that having grown up in a Fundamentalist family strongly determines whether someone is currently a Fundamentalist, which increases the likelihood of holding highly negative attitudes toward homosexuality. (The variable currently Fundamentalist does not appear in our analysis of the SMS.)

These findings illustrate that the traditional religious underpinning of highly antihomosexual attitudes is still very much alive. This is seen most clearly in the case of Fundamentalist Protestants who, as we have seen (Chapter 8), are very likely to hold extreme antihomosexual attitudes and to target homosexuals for punishment. Moreover, the power of religious socialization is evident not only here but in the case of general sexual norms too. (We should note in conclusion that as is the case for the SMS, premarital sexual involvement leads to a decrease in current devoutness, although not to abandoning a Fundamentalist affiliation; nor are Fundamentalist adolescents less likely to participate in premarital sex.)

Age. This cluster operates along much the same lines as in the case of the SMS.[8] All of the effects of age are again indirect, although this time education, and not premarital sexual involvement, is the most important mediating influence, transmitting about 23% of its total indirect effects.

Apparently, older generations have less formal education than younger generations and therefore fewer opportunities to modify their attitudes toward homosexuality. Beyond this, age operates through the restriction of sexual experiences and the maintenance of feelings of sexual threat among older generations, as in the SMS analysis: some 58% of the indirect effects of age are transmitted through the three early sexuality variables and another 14% through sexual threat.

Gender. We have already noted that gender operates as in the case of the SMS, with the important difference that no direct path runs between premarital sexual involvement and the MAF.[9] Here, the most important effects of being female are mediated by sexual environment (36% of the indirect effects of sex-female work through this single path). It apparently is the restricted sexual environment of females, compared with other causal chains, that has the greatest influence on their accepting high-negative attitudes toward homosexuality. Next in importance (18% of indirect effects) is the indirect effect of gender through childhood sex play, which further reduces females' experience with sexuality. Again our interpretation is the same as for the SMS; that is, if a woman's own sexual experiences and knowledge are limited, it is not surprising that she can muster little understanding for those whose sexuality is unconventional. As support for this we note the direct effect of gender on the MAF, which suggests that if females' experience with sexuality had been more extensive, their negative attitudes toward homosexuality might be less extreme than they are, and indeed notably less so than males'.

Feels Sexually Threatened. A final cluster of variables that mediate high-negative attitudes toward homosexuality work through feeling sexually threatened by the opposite sex.[10] This cluster also appears in the SMS analysis, but with important differences. In that analysis, all determinants of such sexual threat are from exogenous or first-stage variables—age, gender, urban childhood, and reared as Fundamentalist—suggesting the continuity of such feelings over the life span. For the MAF, we still find age and gender affecting feels sexually threatened, with older persons and females most likely to feel this way. However, the other two variables have been replaced by two different ones, education and premarital sexual involvement, both third-stage variables. Thus, less education and less premarital sexual experience increase the likelihood of feeling suspicious about relationships with the opposite sex, with a consequent increase in negative attitudes toward homosexuality. We have already interpreted the role of age and sex-female on feels sexually threatened in terms of probable sex-role segregation and differential experiences (Chapter 4). For people lacking education, life may involve distrust and fear of the unfamiliar, which could be extended to the opposite sex. This is especially seen in Rainwater's (1964) study of lower-class (presumably less-educated) couples, where strict sex-role segregation in other spheres of social life led to a lack of intimacy in their sexual lives (see also Rubin, 1976). The relationship between premarital sexual involvement and feels sexually threatened also is new in the MAF analysis. It is probably best understood in light of the *lack* of a direct relationship between premarital sexual involvement and the MAF. There is a strong connection between premarital experience and the SMS, and we have argued that actual involvement in sexuality is a relevant issue in a person's choice of sexual norms. But the SMS included judgment of the morality of premarital sex. For the MAF we infer that heterosexual experience is not directly relevant to homosexuality and thus does not directly affect attitudes toward homosexuals. Rather, the effects are *indirect* and operate in two ways. The first, twice as important as the second, is to reduce the level of devoutness, a causal connection also appearing in the SMS and discussed previously. The second indirect route is to reduce feelings of threat from the opposite sex. That is, in the determination of attitudes toward homosexuality, experiencing premarital sex also works by reducing distrust between the sexes, which we propose also confirms the sense of gender identity. Such security apparently reduces the need to distance oneself from unconventional sexual styles by adopting a defensive stance—for example, by espousing antihomosexual attitudes. As MacDonald et al. (1972:161) suggest, "preservation of the masculine-feminine dichotomy may be threatened by the homosexual, whom we believe to be feminine when male (pansy, fairy, etc.) and masculine when female (butch, etc.). Accordingly, we may condemn the homosexual in order to reduce sex role confusion."

Other Variables. Having grown up in the Midwest or Deep South is the remaining factor directly influencing high-negative attitudes toward homosexuality. A similar direct relationship also exists between this variable and the SMS. Thus it appears that the cultural tradition of this area not only produces conservative sexual norms in general but also high-negative attitudes toward homosexuality in particular.

Conclusion

Chapter 4's analysis of the acquisition and maintenance of general sexual norms, as measured by the Sexual Morality Scale (SMS) yielded results that were in many cases similar to those we obtained in this chapter, where the Multidimensional Antihomosexuality Factor (MAF) is the variable of interest. This is somewhat unexpected, as the MAF deals only with one kind of sexual behavior—the one we found to be most widely disapproved by American society—and it deals not simply with whether that behavior is right or wrong but also with what the consequences of being homosexual ought to be (as well as what is to be expected of homosexuals). That there is a marked similarity between overall sexual norms and this more complex measure of attitudes toward homosexuality suggests that many Americans typify people according to their sexual proclivities—at least in this particular instance—and morally evaluate them with little regard for individual characteristics.

Our global antihomosexuality measure includes the extent to which people agree that homosexuals are distorted heterosexuals, are disgusting and dangerous, and should be denied responsible jobs and social freedoms. Respondents' scores on the MAF take into account how similarly they scored on the various constituent items, so it is not possible to generalize about them except very broadly; nevertheless it seems reasonable to define a high score on the MAF as agreeing with all these different ideas—that is, subscription to the perversion and reprehensibility of homosexuals, and to the need for their suppression—with a lower score connoting less complete espousal of this global attitude.

Using this interpretation we find, as mentioned above, strong parallels between the SMS and MAF analyses. Thus we conclude that people whose general sexual norms are most disapproving tend also to be those who express the firmest negative attitudes toward homosexuality. (The correlation between SMS and MAF scores is .55.) Our findings show that these people tend to have had little premarital acquaintance with sexuality, their own or others'. In addition, they are likely to be religiously devout and to come from backgrounds associated with conservatism and from rural areas and/or the South or Midwest; their parents were likely little educated, strict, and devout, and perhaps Fundamentalist Protestants. By contrast, Jews, blacks, and our younger respondents are notably less negative in their attitudes toward homosexuality.

We hasten to point out here that we are not simply combining all of our separate predictors to form a composite picture of the especially antihomosexual respondent: to do so would be to assume that the individual determinants we have cited are all highly interrelated, which is not necessarily true. However, our findings do permit us to infer that the extent of people's negativism toward homosexuals can be estimated if we know several different sorts of things about them, such as their early sexual behavior, their education, their religiosity, their age, their gender, and how much suspicion they attach to heterosexual relationships. That is, the effects of childhood and adolescent sexual experience and of comparatively high levels of education tend to reduce the otherwise lasting influence of antihomosexual attitudes learned in childhood, which our path diagram suggests are closely connected with a strong religious commitment. Our analytic model thus presupposes that people are in fact taught these attitudes when they are quite young (as evidenced by direct paths to the MAF from a number of our "early" variables). If contemporary children are learning different values, the model does not apply so well to them. However, so many of our respondents in 1970 (78%) said that homosexuality is "always wrong" that it seems unlikely they would teach their children otherwise. This again seems in contrast to the SMS, where there are fewer direct paths. General sexual norms thus are the result of many mediated influences, whereas attitudes toward homosexuality, once learned in early life, retain their influence relatively unshaken by subsequent experiences.

One interesting feature of our model is the extent to which a person's perception of heterosexuality seems to influence how he or she feels about homosexuality. We find this to be especially true regarding sexual *feelings*. Regarding behaviors, a heterosexual variable powerful in explaining the SMS (premarital sexual involvement) notably does not affect antihomosexuality directly. Our indicator of sexual feelings, feels sexually threatened (by the opposite sex), shows that people who anticipate hurt or loss of self-respect in heterosexual relationships feel especially negative toward homosexuals. Perhaps, since this sense of threat is reduced among the sexually experienced, this implies fear of sexual experience as well as the meaning of that for a person's sense of gender. Since sexual threat is also reduced among the more educated, it may imply as well greater readiness to condemn people who are different. Thus, even though attitudes toward homosexuality are not *directly* related to premarital sexual experiences because of the specific lack of relevance between them—"compartmentalization" in our phrase—our model suggests that compartmentalization is not a completely sufficient explanation because of the *indirect* effects of having sexual experiences prior to marriage.

Finally, our model notes that males and females cannot be distinguished in the degree of their antihomosexuality. This is because females are much less likely to have those sexual experiences that *reduce* antihomosexuality (and thereby are *indirectly* more likely to be devout), but at the same time they begin by being directly *less* negative than males. This direct path from sex-female to the MAF may mean that young girls receive less parental warning about homosexuals than boys do: perhaps parents see homosexuality as less of a threat to their daughters than to their sons.

We can conclude by reiterating that the antipathy of most of our respondents toward homosexuals seems clearly to spring from the teachings of childhood, which tend to persist unless one's lifestyle becomes more sexually liberal than that of one's parents or formal education leads one to seriously question the beliefs and values learned while growing up. For example, religion—although, apparently, *not* the so-called Judeo-Christian tradition, in that Jews appear relatively tolerant in our model—and religious involvement, as well as other elements of a conservative childhood, seem to have lasting effects, some of which appear relatively impervious to modification. It is as if Americans' attitudes toward homosexuality occupy a compartment separate from the one for ideas about other kinds of sex. Though not perfectly watertight, this compartment is less likely to be breached by life experiences than is the case for sexual morality in general. Clearly, our findings are consistent with many of the theoretical expectations surveyed earlier. Although we can only hint at the particular dynamics involved, we have no doubt that homosexuality stirs the deepest of fears and negative feelings when Americans consider human sexuality.

NOTES

1. A great deal of work on antihomosexual attitudes, however, has also been generated in connection with modern sociological work on the behavior of homosexuals. Rather than dealing with etiological questions about the "cause" of homosexuality, the modern perspective is more interested in questions concerning the homosexual's adaptations to a hostile social environment (Wein-

berg & Williams, 1975a). Thus, Plummer (1975) argued that homosexuals must be studied as responsive actors in a particular social context whose self-perceptions derive from cultural interpretations. Clearly the influence of this "interactionist" perspective calls for more information about the exact nature of antihomosexual reactions.

2. To maximize the number of valid cases, the sample for this analysis includes 279 respondents who reported one or a few homosexual contacts and 29 others (1% of the total) with frequent homosexual experiences. Excluding these respondents would make little difference in most of the relationships shown in Figure 10-1; current devoutness and childhood sex play do lose some strength, however, with a corresponding loss of 4% in variance explained.
3. We have noted elsewhere (page 205, n.5) that while the MAF, in terms of its extent and complexity, is the best global measure to be derived from our data, it is not readily replicable because it is based on the statistical relations between the various distributions of responses that our particular respondents provided. Consequently we conducted the same path analytic procedures we are about to describe with the simple Likert-type Antihomosexual Attitude Index (pages 176–181) as dependent. The results were quite similar to those for the MAF, except that we could not account for as much variance in the AAI, obtaining R^2 of .210 in the total-path model and .183 in the path diagram model (compared with .320 and .312 for the MAF). This suggests the inferiority of the AAI as a comprehensive measure.
4. We should note once again (see page 84, n.5) that our use of path analysis limits us to assuming one-way causality in the relationships shown in the model. Thus, this technique precludes conflicting interpretations, e.g., that the extent of premarital involvement and the sexuality of one's environment are mutually reinforcing, or that any connection between a Jewish background and a less antihomosexual feeling is spurious.
5. By themselves these variables produce $R = .481$ and $R^2 = .231$.
6. By themselves these variables produce $R = .433$ and $R^2 = .188$.
7. By themselves these variables produce $R = .398$ and $R^2 = .158$.
8. By themselves these variables produce $R = .407$ and $R^2 = .165$.
9. By themselves these variables produce $R = .411$ and $R^2 = .169$.
10. By themselves these variables produce $R = .365$ and $R^2 = .133$.

Chapter 11

Reactions to Norm Violators[1]

Now that we have examined the social reaction toward homosexuality, we consider our respondents' social reactions, this time in relation to a wider range of sexual behaviors—the propensity to sanction those who violate sexual norms. Some persons' reactions are simply informal sanctions—for example, they express the desire to avoid associating with violators. Others' reactions also include supporting formal sanctions; for example, they might approve of laws against the undesired behavior. As described in Chapter 2, our 1970 data show the propensity to sanction violators of sexual norms to be quite widespread in the United States. In this chapter we explore what the determinants of such a propensity may be.

Freud (1930) suggested that it is "self-punitive" anxiety that produces moral action in the form of sanctions. Others (Adorno et al., 1950; Stern, 1962; Hoffman & Saltzstein, 1967) have claimed, in addition, that such self-punitiveness can be directed outward; thus the moralistic are insecure about the effectiveness of their own internal controls, so that they exaggerate the value of external authority and project their own "unwanted" impulses onto members of various out-groups.

Another tradition in psychology considers moral judgment to be more developmental and cognitive. Piaget (1948), for example, describes persons as moving through two broad stages of moral development. The first, moral realism, is where rules are seen as all-powerful, perfect, and sacred *reality*; thus, those who disobey are totally wrong, regardless of the circumstances, and must be punished. The second stage, autonomous reality, is where rules no longer are seen as absolute and actions are judged as relative. The philosophy of "an eye for an eye" as a response to rule-breakers is replaced by one of restitution in kind. Kohlberg (1969) divides each of Piaget's stages into three levels to show how moral development goes hand in hand with cognitive development. The majority of the adult population are assumed to be at Kohlberg's Stage 4, however, which is characterized by a law-and-order orientation—actions are moral if permitted by those in authority; rules continue to be seen as fixed and sacred and rule breakers as deserving of punishment.

Sociological approaches to understanding sanctioning behavior hold that the response to rule violators is determined by people's position in the social structure. Thus Lipset (1959b) explains the greater authoritarianism of the working class in terms of their life situations of uncertainty and deprivation. Class, status, and power figure prominently among sociological explanations. Becker (1963) introduced the term *moral entrepreneur* to define those rule creators characterized by crusading zeal who stand to increase their status if their crusade is successful. Douglas (1970) has argued that moral evaluations constitute a "zero-sum game" in which one group can only upgrade its social status by degrading others. A widely cited work in this genre is that of Ranulf (1938), who described moral indignation as "disguised resentment" characteristic of an "economically and psychologically thwarted" lower middle class.

Mixed in with stratification is the issue of religiosity. Bell (1966) said that religion has been the major social agency for defining American morality. Bellah (1964) saw this role to be growing, noting an increasing differentiation between religious and other facets of society, so that the church is now expected to minister to narrowly defined religious needs, among them the need to provide a moral stance for its membership. This would appear to be the case regardless of affiliation. Herberg (1960) argued that all three major faiths basically preach the same gospel—the "American way of life," or what Bellah (1967) referred to as the "civil religion." Thus religious involvement rather than faith is important: those who are most involved in religion are most committed to the "American way of life." They are more likely, therefore, to take a public stance against those who violate their moral rules.

Because sex figures prominently among the issues that the religious conceive of as moral, it follows that religious involvement gives the devout the necessary credentials (a public moral stance) for taking a public stance of sanctioning those who violate traditional sexual morality.

This is not to say that within-faith differences are unimportant. Kelley (1971) describes thc basic groupings of Protestant denominations as liberal or conservative, the former being more tolerant of differing theological views and more liberal on social issues than the latter. Further, Lipset (1964) indicates that conservative denominations are likely to have a predominantly lower-class membership (see also Boisen, 1955). Goode (1966) notes that lower-status church members view their participation as "sentimental," with the consequence that they are more likely to apply sanctions for perceived moral violations among their fellow members (e.g., "churching," or excommunication). In this way, then, in religious groups that stress sentiment there will be more emphasis on taking a public moral stance to signify one's claim to membership. This should also be reinforced by the social-class position of these religious participants. The relationship between social class, religious affiliation, and religiosity is also found among Jews, with the Orthodox/Reformed distinction corresponding to the Conservative/Liberal among Protestants. Among Catholics there is a similar split but not as important (Roche, 1968). This is because Catholics have not separated into different denominations, and sanctions are applied by the clergy and not the church membership. The Catholic hierarchy is authoritarian and nonpermissive regarding sexual morality; recent changes in Catholic doctrine beginning with Vatican II are notable for their inflexibility toward sexual matters.

However, people's behavioral intentions (how they would treat moral violators) are not always congruent with their moral standards, and their actual behaviors are probably even less so. Research on the relationship between attitudes and actions consistently has shown a low correlation between the two (Deutscher, 1973). This should not be surprising, because behaviors are dependent on social situations. For example, people may fail to see any association between words and deeds; thus they deny the logic that an attitude implies a certain behavior. Actions may also not follow attitudes on the grounds of simple expedience. People will act in ways contrary to their moral norms if doing so enhances their interests.

This is quite evident in politics. A politician may personally approve of, say, abortion and sex education yet to retain political office may vote against measures supporting them. In fact, most of us, finding ourselves in concrete situations that involve other people, may suppress our private norms in favor of group expectations and the desire to conform. Clearly, then, we cannot infer attitudes from actions unless we know the particular situation in which persons are acting. Among others, Ehrlich (1969) has specifically outlined some of the intervening variables that occur between attitudes and behaviors.

Since we are studying *public* norms, and ones that deal with a very volatile issue, we should expect considerable incongruity between these moral attitudes and *private* moralities and behavior. We begin our investigation by comparing sexual norms with behavioral *intentions* regarding the propensity to sanction. We realize, of course, that intentions are not behaviors and that we are really comparing two attitudes. We compare attitudes and behaviors later; however, we believe this prior analysis does provide some important information.

Sexual Norms and the Propensity to Sanction

To see how closely avowed behavioral intentions agreed with norms, we asked our respondents how they judged the morality of a given sexual behavior, how they would react to the discovery that a good friend had been engaging in it (an informal sanction), and whether it should be illegal (a formal sanction). The data provide three indexes of the propensity to sanction, one concerning premarital sex, one extramarital sex, and one homosexuality.[2]

Theoretically, several possible outcomes could be expected: first, *perfect negative congruence*, wherein the respondent would say that the behavior in question is always wrong, it ought to be against the law, and he or she would have nothing more to do with a friend who had engaged in it. With *perfect positive congruence*, responses would be that the behavior is not wrong at all, it would not affect friendship, and it should not be outlawed. In between could be many types of incongruity; for example, a respondent might consider the behavior morally wrong but be willing to forgive it in a friend while at the same time supporting a law against it.

The available variables allow 48 logical combinations or types of incongruity, taking into account all the possible response categories. To simplify the analysis, we dichotomized the "friendship" variable into "still be friends, no problem" versus all other responses, together connoting "problem with friendship." The variable concerning the morality of the behavior had to be dichotomized in two different ways—"always wrong" versus all other responses and "not wrong at all" versus all other responses—in order for the analysis to delineate both of the types of perfect congruity described above.[3] This resulted in the elimination of many potential groupings, since a given respondent could not be allowed membership in more than one group. In addition, one group had very few people in it so it was combined with the group most similar to it (see Type 5 below). Eventually we were able to identify eight groups, which include six types of incongruity:

Type 1—Negative Congruity. Always wrong; problem with friendship; should be illegal.

Type 2—Incongruity. Always wrong; should be illegal; but no problem with friendship.

Type 3—Incongruity. Problem with friendship; should be illegal; but not always wrong.

Type 4—Incongruity. Not always wrong; no problem with friendship; but should be illegal.

Type 5—Incongruity. Problem with friendship; but should not be illegal. (This group contains all possible responses concerning morality because very few people who say that the particular behavior is not wrong at all also indicate a problem with friendship.)

Type 6—Incongruity. No problem with friendship; should not be illegal; but always wrong.

Type 7—Incongruity. No problem with friendship; should not be illegal; but "almost always" or "sometimes" wrong (i.e., the residual group of respondents who do not fit in Type 6 or Type 8).

Type 8—Positive Congruity. Not wrong at all; no problem with friendship; should not be illegal.

Table 11-1 presents the distribution of respondents in these eight groups for each of the three behaviors being considered. Two things seem immediately apparent: first, behavioral intentions are *not* always congruent with the morality on which they are supposedly based; second, the extent of incongruity varies with the particular behavior.

TABLE 11-1 Congruent and Incongruent Morality-Sanction Responses

Type	Always wrong	Not wrong at all	Problem with friendship	Should be illegal	Premarital sex	Extramarital sex	Homosexuality
1	Yes	(No)[a]	Yes	Yes	13.8%	32.0%	49.2%
2	Yes	(No)	No	Yes	5.5	15.6	5.2
3	No	(Yes)	Yes	Yes	5.5	2.1	5.8
4	No	(Yes)	No	Yes	5.7	3.2	1.1
5	(Any response)[b]		Yes	No	11.0	15.1	23.5
6	Yes	(No)	No	No	7.8	13.5	4.1
7	No	No	No	No	38.5	16.7	6.9
8	(No)	Yes	No	No	12.3	1.9	4.1
			Column total		100.1%	100.1%	99.9%
			Base *n*		2,730	2,926	2,821
			Don't know, no answer		288	92	197
			Total sample		3,018	3,018	3,018

[a] The variable concerning the "wrongness" of the behavior was dichotomized in two different ways (see text). Parentheses indicate the dichotomy that was *not* used in defining this group; at least some group members did, however, give the response in parentheses, in that it is implicit in the criterion response.

[b] This group has no criterion response concerning "wrongness" because of the small number who responded "not wrong at all."

Regarding premarital sex, for example, about one-quarter of the respondents expressed "perfect" congruity between morality and propensity to sanction (Type 1 plus Type 8). Even more, 39%—the largest number—were Type 7: they thought premarital sex is wrong in some circumstances but opposed either informal or formal sanctions against it. This response reflects the position that there are conditions under which premarital sex is morally acceptable; as we have seen, a position taken increasingly among those whose sexual norms are changing (Chapter 5). It is possible to claim that if we include the Type 7 group with the Type 8, the response toward premarital sex does in fact show a considerable amount of consistency at the liberal end of the scale.

Regarding extramarital sex, nearly one-third of the sample were Type 1, the perfect negative group, while hardly any fell into Type 8, the perfect positives. This reflects the wide moral disapproval of extramarital sex. Among the incongruity types, no particular group stands out as especially numerous; one interesting combination, though, is Types 6 and 7—people who, despite rating extramarital sex as wrong at least sometimes, hesitated to apply any sanctions; these were about as numerous as the Type 1 people. In contrast, people who would oppose a law against extramarital sex but would invoke less formal sanctions (Type 5) were only half as numerous (as it happened, *nobody* in this group said extramarital sex is not wrong at all). Perhaps extramarital sex, though morally deplorable to many, appears—unlike premarital sex—to be an exclusively adult activity in which others should not interfere.

Homosexuality is the behavior that evoked the most congruity, with nearly half the respondents saying that it is always wrong, ought to be illegal, and is incompatible with friendship. Another one-fourth (Type 5) said they would not legislate against it but still thought it would be difficult to remain friends with a homosexual. This response reflects the fear of personal closeness described earlier and underlines again that moral acceptance of homosexuality does not necessarily mean emotional acceptance and that the affective response toward homosexuality is the most important of its attitudinal constituents.

In an attempt to locate these different response types within the sample, we cross-tabulated the three indexes against the variables that earlier analyses identified as important influences on sexual attitudes. As expected, perfect negative congruity—Type 1—tends to characterize people who have been subject to such conservatizing influences as being female, being white, having had sexually strict parents, being devout, having had little or no premarital sex, or feeling sexually threatened by the opposite sex. Generally, as one moves down the list of various types of incongruity, each subsequent type reflects less of these conservatizing influences than the type preceding it. This is particularly true for premarital sexual involvement. Finally, and as also expected, perfect positive congruity—Type 8—represents people who have been least subject to conservatizing influences, again, especially those who have had considerable premarital sexual experience. We should note, however, that although this does imply a certain pattern underlying these response sets, the variables we used in cross-tabulation do not differentiate very well between the different types of incongruity. This is particularly true concerning extramarital sex, which might be expected in light of the ambivalent response to this behavior.

Sexual Norms and Sexual Behavior

Another approach to the question of congruity is to use a measure of actual sexual behavior, in this case whether one ever ex-

TABLE 11-2 Percent Evaluating Premarital Sexual Behaviors "Always Wrong," by Premarital Sexual Experience and Gender

	Premarital experience			No premarital experience		
Circumstances	Male	Female	Total	Male	Female	Total
Teenage boy, not in love	38.7	51.1	43.1	74.1	69.2	70.4
Base *n*	1,172	656	1,828	282	883	1,165
Gamma	−.23			.01		−.50
Teenage boy, in love	25.2	29.3	26.7	52.3	55.6	54.8
Base *n*	1,170	658	1,828	281	883	1,164
Gamma	−.12			−.10		−.50
Adult male, not in love	34.5	45.1	38.3	71.9	68.9	69.6
Base *n*	1,170	661	1,831	281	883	1,164
Gamma	−.23			.07		−.53
Adult male, in love	21.4	21.7	21.5	52.9	52.5	52.6
Base *n*	1,169	660	1,829	280	882	1,162
Gamma	−.07			.00		−.55
Teenage girl, not in love	50.7	69.6	57.5	81.1	86.7	85.3
Base *n*	1,173	658	1,831	281	886	1,167
Gamma	−.36			−.20		−.61
Teenage girl, in love	31.6	35.5	33.0	60.6	69.0	67.0
Base *n*	1,172	657	1,829	282	886	1,168
Gamma	−.11			−.19		−.56
Adult female, not in love	36.1	52.9	42.2	74.8	77.5	76.9
Base *n*	1,169	662	1,831	282	885	1,167
Gamma	−.32			−.07		−.61
Adult female, in love	22.6	24.1	23.2	54.1	59.0	57.8
Base *n*	1,170	660	1,830	281	886	1,167
Gamma	−.10			−.12		−.58

perienced premarital sex, and compare it to respondents' sexual norms regarding this behavior. The problem here, of course, is that a respondent's sexual norms are *current* ones, whereas the behavior happened at some time in the past. Nonetheless the exercise is instructive in that it can show the patterns whereby sexual experiences determine specific sexual norms (we know this is the case because of the influential role the variable premarital sexual involvement plays on the SMS). Table 11-2 presents our detailed results.

Looking first at figures for males and females together (the percentages in the two "Total" columns), we see that those who did not have premarital sex were more likely to say that a given premarital sexual behavior is always wrong than were those who had had premarital sex. The gammas (far right "Total" column) range from −.50 to −.61, the relationship being strongest with reference to females (teenagc or adult) who have premarital sex when they are not in love. The most disapproval (in terms of absolute percentages) was expressed by both groups toward teenage girls in this situation, and the least disapproval toward adult males who have premarital sex when they are in love.

When these data are broken down by gender, a consistent pattern emerges—notable gender differences are found only among those who experienced premarital sex and only for the four items in which love is absent. We find that the experienced females were more likely than the males to disapprove of premarital sex without love for either gender and at any age. This suggests that the actual experience of premarital sex for females competes with socialization effects (the emphasis on conjoining sex and love) in determining their sexual norms, rather than that their norms reflect some hypocrisy or denial. We might thus expect guilt or shame to accompany females' premarital experiences more than for males, although this would be attenuated by our earlier finding that love accompanies many of their premarital sexual experiences. Table 11-3 supports this notion: among those who had premarital sex, 23% of the females reported feeling considerable guilt, shame, or embarrassment, compared to only 9% of the males. Those who did *not* have any premarital experience also show a gender difference in the same direction on the question of how they thought they would have felt had they had premarital sex. This finding seems to accord with that of Christensen and Gregg (1970), who noted in a 1968 sample that females with premarital coital experience were less likely than males to approve of premarital coitus when love is involved; that is, females were more likely than males to violate their own moral norms in having premarital sex. In any case, our data indicate that not only do moral norms act strongly to control sexual behavior, but that guilt and shame do sometimes accompany the violation of these norms and do so more often for women than for men.

TABLE 11-3 Guilt over Premarital Sex, by Premarital Sexual Experience and Gender

	Male	Female	Total
PREMARITAL EXPERIENCE			
"Guilt, shame, or embarrassment" felt . . .			
Strongly	8.7%	23.4%	17.4%
Somewhat	35.8	43.7	38.6
Not at all	55.5	33.0	44.0
Column total	100.0%	100.1%	100.0%
Base *n*	1,056	591	1,647[a]
NO PREMARITAL EXPERIENCE			
"Quite sure you would have felt . . . guilt, shame, or embarrassment"			
Yes, would have felt	69.4%	86.7%	82.9%
No; would not have felt	30.6	13.3	17.1
Column total	100.0%	100.0%	100.0%
Base *n*	193	671	864[a]

[a] The 507 respondents (17% of the total sample) not represented in this table include 151 who had premarital sex and 303 who did not, and did not answer this particular question, as well as 53 who did not indicate whether they had had premarital sexual experience.

Determinants of the Propensity to Sanction

So far our analysis has suggested that some people exhibit a discrepancy between their moral evaluation of a given sexual behavior and their inclination to sanction those who engage in it. Part of this discrepancy, or incongruity as we have called it, arises from our having combined in the same measure both formal and informal kinds of sanctions: a number of respondents chose one kind but not the other. On the other hand, some responses are perfectly congruent, with people who said they absolutely condemn the behavior on moral grounds also saying they would drop a friend who was involved in it and that it should be against the law, but so far we do not know to what extent these are the same people regardless of the behavior in question.

Our next step, therefore, is to make up two new measures, to be used in path analysis, that emphasize the type of sanction to be invoked rather than the particular behavior. The first, which we call the Maintenance of Friendship Scale (MFS), is made up of the items that asked about effects on friendship. The second scale, called the Sexual Suppression Scale (SSS), is made up of the items that asked whether there should be laws against the three behaviors.[4] The two measures have an intercorrelation of .44, reflecting some respondents' choice of one kind of sanction but not the other. As to the relationship with sexual norms, the MFS correlates with the SMS at .44, and the SSS-SMS correlation is −.53. Thus, maintaining friendship correlates with liberal morality, and supporting sex laws with conservative morality. These moderate correlations are evidence that people sometimes but not always act in accord with their norms and attitudes.

Before considering the results of our path analyses, note that we do not have measures of all the determinants of the propensity to sanction that, as noted in the beginning of this chapter, others have suggested. However, the data do cover most of the important ones—social class, religious affiliation, and religiosity—directly, and some others indirectly—for example, parental permissiveness in the case of self-punitiveness and actual sexual experiences for the sexually thwarted. Moreover, Table 11-1 shows some consistency between the type of sexual norms held and the propensity to sanction, with those evincing the strongest disapproval being the most punitive. Thus one might expect that our success in predicting the propensity to sanction violators of sexual norms would closely parallel the prediction of sexual norms in general, especially in the similarity of variables included in the model.

Our procedure in analyzing these two scales is the same as earlier—beginning with 83 independent variables and gradually reducing their number in successive winnowings to arrive at a parsimonious model. We first discuss the analysis of the MFS.

Maintaining Friendship

The initial 83 variables produced an R^2 of .317; the final total-path model contains 10 predictors that yield $R = .502$ and $R^2 = .252$. Thus, these 10 variables can account for a quarter of the variance in the MFS, while the 73 that were dropped would have explained only 7% more. From Table 11-4 and the diagram in Figure 11-1 we can see that as predicted, the model emerging to explain informal sanctions is quite similar to the one in Chapter 4 explaining general sexual norms. This is important, as it suggests that a general conservative-liberal pattern underlies attitudes toward sexuality regardless of the particular level or substratum. Before turning to the path diagram model, note that three variables

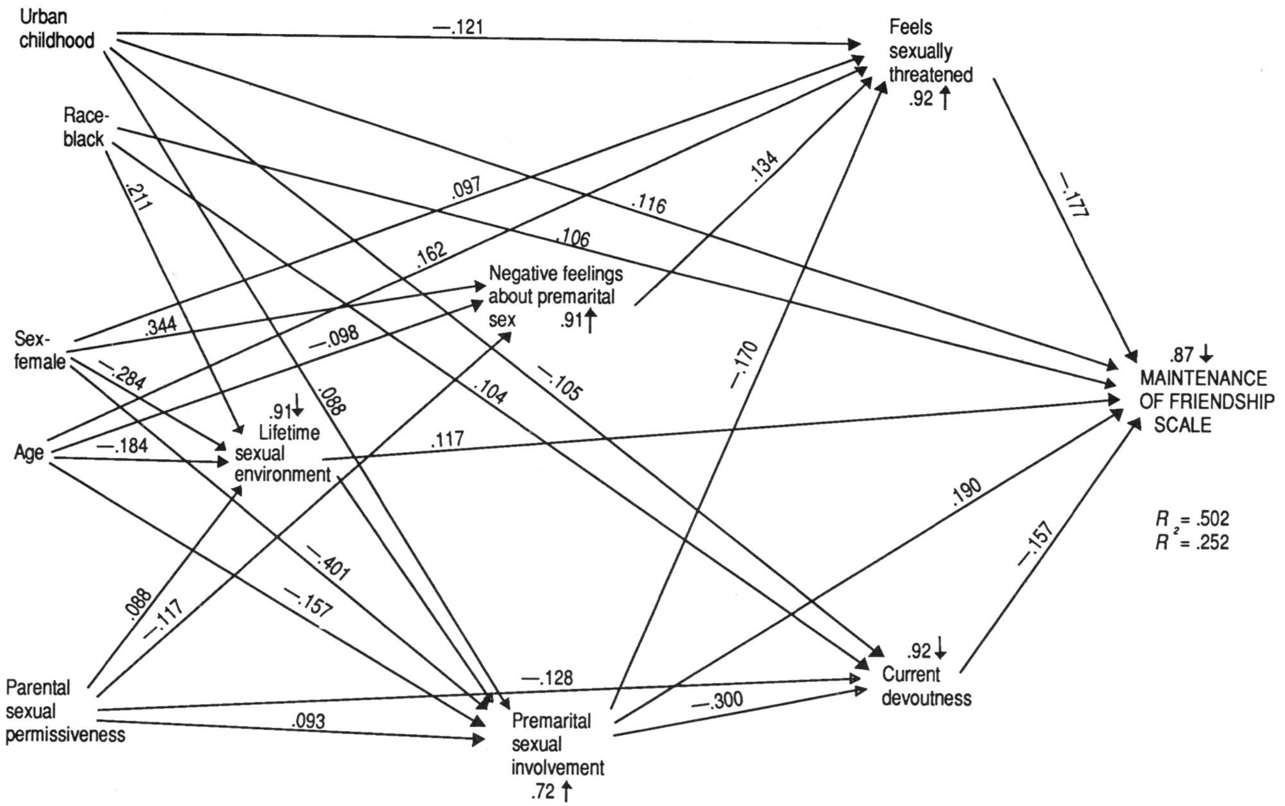

Figure 11-1 Path Diagram Model for the MFS
Note: Correlations among independent variables are given in Appendix E.

TABLE 11-4 Comparison of Effects on the MFS in the Total-Path Model with Effects in the Path Diagram Model

Variable	Direct effect	Indirect effects	Total effects	Extraneous effects	Total association
Premarital sexual involvement	.154 *.190*	.063 *.077*	.217 *.267*	.176 *.126*	.393
Lifetime sexual environment	.109 *.117*	.099 *.101*	.208 *.218*	.110 *.100*	.318
Sex-female	.000 —	−.193 *−.194*	−.193 *−.194*	−.013 *−.012*	−.206
Urban childhood	.103 *.116*	.068 *.061*	.171 *.177*	.047 *.041*	.218
Feels sexually threatened	−.157 *−.177*	— —	−.157 *−.177*	−.149 *−.129*	−.306
Current devoutness	−.145 *−.157*	— —	−.145 *−.157*	−.152 *−.140*	−.297
Age	−.049 —	−.089 *−.113*	−.138 *−.113*	−.040 *−.065*	−.178
Parental sexual permissiveness	.065 —	.073 *.067*	.138 *.067*	.086 *.157*	.224
Race-black	.114 *.106*	.022 *.030*	.136 *.136*	.000 *.000*	.136
Negative feelings about premarital sex	−.077 —	−.024 *−.024*	−.101 *−.024*	−.098 *−.175*	−.199

NOTE: Figures in the first row following each variable represent effects with all possible paths between variables. Figures in italics represent effects with only those paths surpassing exclusion criteria.

do appear in our total-path model that were strangers to our SMS analysis: age of dependent son, age of dependent daughter, and number of children. These variables reflect the fact that the protection of children is an important concern when it comes to sexual matters. We saw this vividly in the case of homosexuality. It is apparent here that these concerns underlie sexual nonconformity in general, especially as friendship may make the family vulnerable to unwanted sexual intrusions. This needs to be mentioned here, as Figure 11-1 includes none of these three variables: the last two do not survive path inclusion criteria and the first does not fit meaningfully into the causal nexi of a temporal model and was therefore dropped.

As to the path diagram model, we see from Table 11-4 that just as dropping many independent variables made relatively little difference in its explanatory power (R^2), dropping weak paths does not notably affect the strength of most of the final 10 predictors. The most powerful, premarital sexual involvement, increases in both its direct and indirect effects when lesser paths are eliminated. Accordingly, our finding is that people with extensive sexual experience are more likely to remain friends with others engaged in unconventional kinds of sex, both directly and because they are less likely to feel sexually threatened or religiously devout—relationships we have seen before. The second strongest predictor, lifetime sexual environment, exerts about 46% of its total effects through the various connections of premarital sexual involvement; the rest are direct.

In this model, being female is the third strongest predictor, with indirect/total effects of −.194, the bulk of which operate through females' reduced premarital sexual involvement. Sex-female does not display here its earlier pattern of countervailing direct and indirect effects (with resulting low total effects). Instead the model says only that females are more willing than males to invoke this kind of informal sanction. The absence of any direct "liberal" effects suggests that females are more concerned than males with avoiding persons they consider immoral.

The fourth of our 10 predictors is another exogenous variable, urban childhood. Our analysis shows that people who grew up in large cities are more willing than those from rural areas to tolerate a friend's unconventional sexual behavior. This is expressed through a direct path to the MFS, which represents about two-thirds of urban childhood's total effects of .177, suggesting that rural moralities are less flexible, as we have seen before. Of course, in rural and small town communities, relationships are more visible, and reputation less hidden, less possible to guard. This is underscored by two indirect paths which, because of "competition" from other variables not present here, did not appear in models for the SMS (Chapter 4) or MAF (Chapter 10). These paths show that people from urban areas are prone to greater premarital sexual involvement and less current devoutness. The reverse is thereby also true: people who grew up in small towns or the country are more devout and less premaritally experienced.

The next two variables, in order of strength, are the only two from our final (current) stage—feels sexually threatened and current devoutness. Both act directly against the maintenance of friendship with an "immoral" person, for readily understandable reasons. People who feel uneasy in encounters with the opposite sex will probably also feel some discomfort in associating with a person violating sexual norms. And people who are religiously devout may feel bound by the teachings of their sect to exclude that person from further friendship. These two variables are of only moderate strength, however, with respective direct/total effects of −.177 and −.157.

The next three predictors occur in the exogenous (first) stage of our model. Seventh out of the 10 in overall strength is age. Age's total effects are smaller in the model that includes only the strongest paths than they would be if all paths were permitted, because in the former model its direct path of −.049 is too small to appear, but its remaining connections are ones we have seen before, with older people appearing more likely to be sexually threatened in a heterosexual context, to have looked negatively upon premarital sex as teenagers, and to have experienced little sexual contact before marriage. Hence older people's overall greater reluctance (total effects of −.113) to accept unconventional sexual behavior in their friends.

Parental sexual permissiveness is next strongest (that is, third weakest) in terms of its overall strength in the model allowing all paths. Like urban childhood, it displays some interesting—and theoretically predictable—connections that did not appear in our earlier, less parsimonious models. In addition to being exposed to a more sexual environment, as we have seen before, children of sexually permissive parents are less apt to be currently devout, both directly and through having had more premarital sex; these two paths transmit two-thirds of the total effects of parental sexual permissiveness. (A negligible influence works through negative feelings about premarital sex.) The operation of a permissive background therefore affects both sexuality and religiosity in this model.

Another variable affecting the propensity to invoke personal sanctions is race. Of the effects of race-black, 78% are direct and most of the rest work through lifetime sexual environment, connections that together suggest that blacks' greater acceptance of sexually unconventional friends may simply reflect that among blacks, some of the behaviors in the MFS—premarital sex, for example—are just not so "unconventional." It is interesting to note that the indirect effects of race-black include as well a *negative* component which, like others we have mentioned, did not appear in earlier models: blacks are more likely than whites to be religiously devout. In the MFS model, these three paths from race-black—to sexual environment, current devoutness, and the MFS itself—together produce total effects of .136, which is the same as the total association.

The weakest of our 10 variables is having had negative feelings about premarital sex. Such feelings in adolescence, according to the model, help to engender feelings of apprehension toward the opposite sex in adulthood. This unsurprising connection is the only way in which such negative feelings are shown to influence the MFS. Its total effects of −.024 reflect that a potential direct path was too small to include. It should also be noted that 88% of this variable's association with the MFS is taken up by extraneous effects, suggesting that its function in our model is as a mediator of the indirect effects of earlier-stage predictors.

Briefly, then, what this model seems to show is that the same sort of characteristics that we have already shown to help predict a conservative stance, either in overall sexual norms (the SMS) or in attitudes toward homosexuality (the MAF), also help to predict a tendency among respondents to avoid friendship with people who have violated accepted sexual norms.

Support for Laws

The 83 variables that we screened for our path analysis of the SSS produced an initial R^2 of .329. In subsequent screenings, their number was reduced to only 8, which yield an R of .405 and an R^2 of .164; when only substantively significant paths are allowed to appear, the R^2 is .162. Thus the model shown in Figure 11-2 and Table 11-5, while notable for its parsimony, does not explain very much of the variance in the SSS.[5]

What is striking about this model is that the predictors in it are by now very familiar ones. All of them appear in the final models for the MFS, the SMS, and the MAF. This seems to further support our basic contention that there are certain fundamental influences upon American sexual norms and attitudes.

In the SSS path diagram model, the strongest predictor is premarital sexual involvement, with a direct effect of −.149 and total effects of −.214. Other variables that directly contribute to people's approval of laws against unconventional sex include feeling

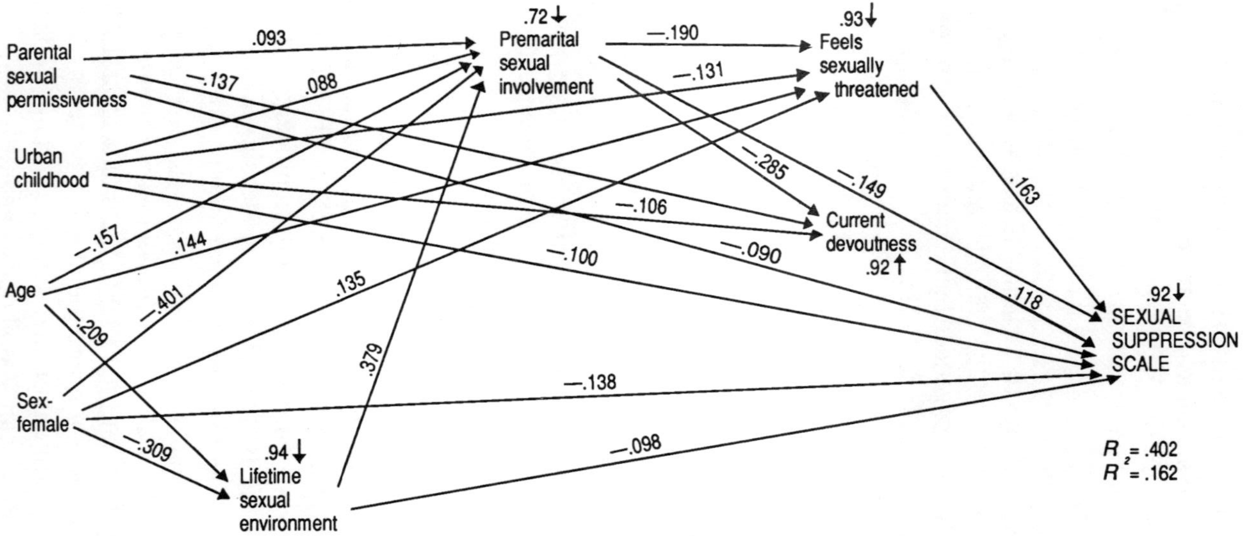

Figure 11-2 Path Diagram Model for the SSS
Note: Correlations among independent variables are given in Appendix E.

TABLE 11-5 Comparison of Effects on the SSS in the Total-Path Model with Effects in the Path Diagram Model

Variable	Direct effect	Indirect effects	Total effects	Extraneous effects	Total association
Premarital sexual involvement	−.138 *−.149*	−.057 *−.065*	−.195 *−.214*	−.109 *−.090*	−.304
Lifetime sexual environment	−.094 *−.098*	−.078 *−.081*	−.172 *−.179*	−.034 *−.027*	−.206
Feels sexually threatened	.157 *.163*	— —	.157 *.163*	.183 *.177*	.340
Urban childhood	−.093 *−.100*	−.055 *−.053*	−.148 *−.153*	−.104 *−.099*	.252
Parental sexual permissiveness	−.085 *−.090*	−.056 *−.036*	−.141 *−.126*	−.065 *−.080*	−.206
Age	.049 —	.089 *.094*	.138 *.094*	.076 *.120*	.214
Current devoutness	.116 *.118*	— —	.116 *.118*	.157 *.155*	.273
Sex-female	−.123 *−.138*	.150 *.163*	.027 *.025*	.013 *.015*	.040

NOTE: Figures in the first row following each variable represent effects with all possible paths between variables. Figures in italics represent effects with only those paths surpassing exclusion criteria.

sexually threatened, being devout, growing up in a rural area, and having had a narrow sexual environment or sexually strict parents. Sex-female also has a direct effect of −.138 (less likely than males to be legalistically punitive, all else being equal) and even larger indirect effects of the opposite sign, resulting in total effects of .025. In fact, all of the variables in the model except for age—which has lower total effects than any other predictor except sex-female—have direct paths to the SSS. We interpret this to mean that the extremely conservative attitudes that are expressed by the willingness to invoke formal sanctions of this kind are quite basic and therefore can be impervious to later influences.

The diagram suggests that premarital sexual involvement, the most powerful predictor—people with more early sexual experience being less likely to support legal control of sexuality—is, as other models have illustrated, less common among females, people from earlier generations, and those with a relatively asexual environment. In addition, with the smaller number of competing variables that this model permits, there are two paths to premarital sexual involvement that do not appear in the SMS or MAF models:

from parental sexual permissiveness and from urban childhood. These two variables also are shown to lessen the extent of current devoutness.

Thus the SSS model, even though it does not explain very much about how people become proponents of laws against unconventional sex, seems to underscore the presence of a combination of factors that influence the liberal/conservative extent of people's sexual norms and attitudes. We seem to be identifying the people who show no discrepancy between their moralities and their approval of formal sanctions, since the predictors are those we have already shown to account for the most conservative stance. That many people are in fact "incongruent" in their morality and propensity to sanction is reflected in the low R^2 of the SSS model and the not very large correlations (Appendix E) between our "sanctioning" variables and the more global SSS and MAF.

Summary

This chapter has examined an important aspect of the behavioral component of moral attitudes: people's propensity to sanction violators of sexual norms. We considered two kinds of sanctions, informal and formal. With respect to the former, we asked respondents how they would react if a good friend had participated in nontraditional kinds of sex (premarital, extramarital, or homosexual activities); our measure of formal sanctions was whether respondents felt any of these sexual behaviors should be against the law.

When we compared responses to these questions with how respondents morally evaluated the given behavior, we found some respondents to be "congruent" in their moral attitudes, approving of both kinds of sanctions if they thought the behavior is always wrong, or of neither kind if they thought the behavior is not wrong at all. Many, however, appeared to be "incongruent," displaying the often-noted discrepancy between words and deeds (actually, in this case, between what they *said* they believed and what they *said* they would do). For example, some who thoroughly disapproved of the behavior in question and agreed that it ought to be illegal said they would tolerate it (or at least not make an issue of it) in a good friend. Others said they would not associate with people who were "immoral" but opposed the notion of treating them as criminals. This implies that having people rate a behavior on a scale ranging through various degrees of "wrongness" is insufficient by itself if we are to fully describe the liberality or conservatism of American sexual norms. That so many people give "incongruent" responses further suggests that there are different types of sexual conservatism. On the one hand are people who would exclude certain norm violators from friendship but would not want these norms to have the force of law. These people seem to comprehend morality as an individual concern, but they are cautious enough to avoid associating with people they consider deviant (perhaps wanting to protect their children from them). On the other hand are people who do approve of "legislating morality." Those in this group who would not have problems with "immoral" friends may feel that if an act is defined as wrong both morally and legally, people who engage in it need the compassion, guidance, and good example a friend could provide. (Or it could be that they cannot conceive of their friends as behaving in such a way.) Those who accept both kinds of sanctions can be more clearly thought of as expressing a deeply rooted, reflexive, rather than contemplative, conservative morality.

Exploring this line of thought further, we find first that the same group of predictors that previous analyses (Chapters 4, 6, 10) isolated appear again in our "explanations" of the propensity to invoke either informal or formal sanctions. This strengthens our conviction that certain identifiable variables—for example, religiosity, lack of early experiences with sexuality, and socialization factors associated with being older or rural or from sexually strict homes—underlie a general conservatism in sexual attitudes regardless of which dimension we are examining. The notion introduced in the previous paragraph, that there may be two kinds of conservatism operating simultaneously, is not necessarily contradicted by the similarity of these models. Instead, we infer that some support for it lies in the way these predictors do a much better job of accounting for informal than for formal sanctions. If willingness to invoke both kinds of sanctions characterizes roughly the same individuals, the explanatory levels of the two models ought to be alike. Thus it seems that even though the predictors are about the same, they are describing *two separate processes*. Since it is approval for laws that is harder to account for, it seems reasonable to suppose that the people being "predicted" in this model constitute an especially rigid subgroup of conservatives. This may seem a difficult inference, based on the data we have presented here (although Chapter 7 did suggest that there is an extreme subgroup, the minority who would deny "stereotypic" jobs to homosexual men).

NOTES

1. This chapter is based on the dissertation of Robert E. Dergitz (1976).
2. Unfortunately, we cannot make up a similar scale regarding prostitution—the behavior our respondents were most willing to outlaw (page 21)—since we did not ask how they would react to a good friend's acting as or visiting a prostitute. This was one of many important questions omitted to keep the interview short.
3. Based on findings presented in Chapter 2, three composite measures were prepared as constituent items for these indexes after the fashion illustrated in Tables 3-1 through 3-4. The first combines responses to our various questions concerning the morality of premarital sex under different circumstances: always wrong, 40.8%; almost always wrong, 11.4%; pretty much wrong, 14.7%; wrong only sometimes, 21.0%; not wrong at all, 12.0% (base n = 2,804). A second variable combines the two questions concerning the morality of homosexuality: always wrong, 72.1%; almost always wrong, 8.6%; pretty much wrong, 3.5%; wrong only sometimes, 7.6%; not wrong at all, 8.1% (base n = 2,934). The third combines the two questions concerning the effect upon friendship if a good friend had been engaging in homosexual activity: not want to have anything more to do with that person, 38.0%; still be in touch, but no longer be friends, 20.5%; stay friends, but it would be a problem, 26.1%; still be friends, no problem, 15.3% (base n = 2,965). (As explained in the note to Table 3-1, the response "pretty much wrong" is a composite category.)
4. Marginal distributions for the MFS are no problem, 18.7%; problem with one behavior, 29.8%; problem with two behaviors, 21.5%; problem with all three, 30.0% (base n = 2,980). For the SSS they are no laws, 24.1%; one behavior should be outlawed, 21.9%; two should be, 23.2%; all three should be, 30.8% (base n = 3,003). The MFS has a reliability alpha of .79, and the SSS one of .73.
5. In this analysis, age of dependent son and age of dependent daughter were also initially in the final model. However, the latter variable had strong *negative* total/direct effects, apparently meaning that the closer a girl is to age 20, the *less* likely her parents are to support these laws. We suspect that these highly intercorrelated variables (r = .55) were dividing up the available effects of parental responsibility, thereby yielding an artifactual rather than valid finding. When we substituted for them a single variable that did not specify the gender of the oldest child, this proved to be true: parental responsibility displayed very low positive effects that were too weak for it to be included in the final model.

Chapter 12

Sexual Morality and Contemporary Society

Our data have shown that the patterns of sexual morality in the United States in 1970 tended to be quite conservative. The findings do not support the contention that a "sexual revolution" had occurred in 1970 or is occurring now in the United States. They do suggest a continuity in sexual norms that appears remarkable in its consistency and persistence.

The determinants of people's sexual norms and attitudes also seem to be relatively clear.[1] Many of the important predictors identified by our analyses reflect a strong pluralism—multiple sources and reinforcers of morality—in our social life, a pluralism that a number of sociologists have assumed no longer holds. Thus, for example, Wilensky (1964:180) wrote, "we may assume that the influence of mass education, the media, and the centralized state will in the long run overcome the influence of variations in work, religion, age and locality as sources of cultural values . . . and we can expect mass culture in both Europe and America to penetrate structures more or less insulated from it."[2]

Our investigation, however, shows that factors such as region, locality, and religion remain important forces in sustaining sexual norms and attitudes regardless of their direction (e.g., having grown up in the Midwest or Deep South has a lifelong effect in creating conservative sexual norms; having had a Jewish childhood has similar effects in producing liberal attitudes toward homosexuality). Moreover, the importance of factors such as age, race, education, and gender further attest to the strength of traditional socializing influences in the determination of moral values.

On one level, results such as these are not surprising; it could be said that predictors of liberal and conservative norms, values, and attitudes, are well-known from previous research in other areas. On the other hand, these results are remarkable given the drastic changes in our society after World War II, changes that most commentators insist must have altered American sexual patterns. Thus, television, penicillin, the Pill, the bikini, rock 'n' roll, affluence, suburbanization, and so on, were all thought to have tremendous effects on sexuality. Apparently, though, these effects have been limited. Speaking of young people (where change has been thought to be especially pronounced), Gagnon and Simon (1970:113) commented on such expectations:

> What was expected was that young people, when the constraints on freedom of all sorts were released, would do what adults thought they might do (but also would not have): go out and have a sexual ball. The problem is that sex is not a beast lurking ready to lunge out and run amok if but one chain is removed from it. . . . Sex is only realized and sexual arousal only occurs in social situations which are designed to elicit sexual responses. . . . What this means is that without creating a learning situation in which sex could be given a new connection to other aspects of social life there is no good reason to expect any change.

Our argument is that for the U.S. population as a whole, few new "learning situations" have arisen to provide strong competition for the old, familiar ones. Rather, traditional structures of meaning have remained powerful and continue to provide the social context of sexuality for most Americans. This is not to say that no competing sets of norms have emerged or that commitment to traditional moralities is necessarily strong. As we argue later, such traditional meanings serve a variety of motives.

Our data strongly suggest that we should deal with traditional influences first. Among those it is evident that religion continues to be a major source of sexual morality. The particular influence of Judeo-Christian culture on sexual norms comes from certain interpretations of the Bible (especially when it is taken literally, as by Fundamentalists) and the idea of "natural law" (especially important to Roman Catholic doctrine). The result is a perspective on sexuality that emphasizes restraint. For example, early Christianity taught the virtues of celibacy and the condemnation of the flesh, with sex being seen as carnal, sinful, and inferior to all things of the spirit. Thus woman is inherently evil insofar as she lures man toward the sexual and away from God. Correspondingly, the noblest achievement for women is virginity. Both the Hebrews of biblical times and the theology of the Middle Ages, as exemplified by Aquinas, viewed man as having a "proper nature" or divinely intended purpose. This doctrine of "natural law" reinforced the view of sex as evil, as only sex with a procreative intent, that is sex in marriage, could be acceptable. In sum, as one commentator has said (Chamberlain, 1975:75), "at about the time the Church began to emerge as the formative institution in the West, its attitudes toward sexuality were formed around the twin pillars of sexuality as evil but justified in marriage by procreation. There was no intrinsic value to sexuality."

Moreover, the "natural" was seen only as biological (the obvious "natural" result of coitus was children). Furthermore, the natural was equated with the "normal" and thus quite easily with the "moral." Heterosexual, monogamous sexuality became the norm, chastity the ideal, and nonprocreative sex "unnatural" or "perverse." In the United States, these religious views were extended by sects such as the Puritans, who saw sexual desires as manifestations of a "fall from grace" and restricted sex to marriage and procreation. Sex and morality thus became intertwined in our thinking, so that the word "morality" inevitably connotes "sexual morality." The interrelation of social, moral, and sexual norms has been described by Cory (1956:428):

> More than any other power, the United States was founded on traditions of Puritanism. The concept of sex as a necessary evil, an ugly pursuit, enjoyed by man because of the devil incarnate in the flesh, was taught by the early cultural leaders of this country. The varying and diverse elements that made up the American melting pot vied with one another to appear before the masses as pure and good, one group not to be outdone by another in the antisexual repudiation of physical desire. Thus the struggle of the Protestant Puritans to maintain a rigid and self avowedly virtuous ban on all things sexual was strengthened by the several minorities that found conformance the road to acceptance and possible integration into American life.[3]

Religious views such as these formed the basis of our most powerful institutions and have had a tremendous influence on American culture.[4] For example, the law enshrines the belief that certain sexual acts are "crimes against nature" and criminalizes them in our penal codes. Our vocabulary of sexual morality uses marriage as a criterion, so that we speak of premarital and extramarital sex. So too do natural law notions of sexuality articulate, if not help determine, commonsense ideas about sexuality shared by most people in our culture. Sexuality, it is believed, is a naturally occurring phenomenon that expresses nature's plan by following the dictates of the body. Gagnon and Simon (1973:5) have succinctly described this view:

> It is perhaps startling to consider that when we think about the sexual, nearly our entire imagery is drawn from the physical activities of bodies. Our sense of normalcy derives from organs being placed in legitimate orifices. We have allowed the organs, the orifices and the gender of the actors to personify or embody or exhaust nearly all the meanings that exist in the sexual situation.

It is difficult, therefore, for those raised in this culture not to react to sex as having its own unfolding logic, so that people do "what comes naturally." This means, then, that even today our thinking about sexual morality is based on the perceived naturalness of behavior. Ironically, this restricts the realm of moral choice, as nature cannot or should not be interfered with. The perception of sex as "natural" (or otherwise), of course, operates as an important force in sustaining conservative sexual norms. It also accounts for the feelings and emotions engendered by sexual acts that are seen as unnatural even by people with no theological training. Nowhere is this more clearly demonstrated than in our findings for homosexuality. Homosexuality is often seen as an unnatural act par excellence in that it is neither tied to marriage nor results in procreation nor involves opposite-sex partners or conventional gender roles. Thus, our data show that strong feelings of disgust and abhorrence toward homosexuality underlie people's attitudes toward it and cut across demographic lines, being common even among the most liberal respondents. Sexual moralities, then, do not arise only from cognitive beliefs; they are also squarely based on feelings. Thus we should heed Durkheim's (1951:315) caution that although social life is structured by rules, "beneath all these maxims are actual living sentiments summed up by these formulae but only as in a superficial envelope. The formulae would awake no echo if they did not correspond to definite emotions and impressions scattered through society."

In our religiously influenced culture, then, it is no surprise that fear, disgust, abhorrence (and their correlates of fascination, temptation, and attraction) underlie many widely held sexual norms. (This does not mean that rational arguments cannot also be given for many of them, as we point out further on.) Thus one legacy of so-called Puritanism is expressed in an inability to deal candidly with sex—in the euphemisms, double entendres, innuendos, "locker-room" humor, and guilty pleasures that are so evident throughout our society.

The relationship of emotion, sexuality, and morality is also seen in the reaction toward sexual violators where, as our data show, punitiveness is more characteristic of the morally conservative. Though psychological reasons may be involved, we consider Ranulf's (1938) argument a more socially relevant explanation.[5] Ranulf called attention to what he labeled "middle-class moral indignation," which is based on resentment rather than direct gain. Middle-class people engage in "disinterested punishment" of others because their precarious status permits them no chance to indulge in the evasions of norms available to those of more secure status, such as either aristocrats or the disreputable poor.

This idea highlights the point that traditionally in this culture, sexual restraint has been seen as an index of social worth, such that eschewing the sexual increases moral status. Thus many contemporary social conflicts that create strong feelings are a strange mixture of sex and politics. It is no accident that important political and moral issues often involve conflicts over sex education, abortion, homosexual civil rights, and so forth. An impressive demonstration of this was provided by Zurcher et al. (1971) in their study of an antipornography movement. This movement operated as a moral crusade, serving the need of certain persons to defend or enhance the prestige of their life-style against the threats of others. Pornography became a symbol through which this conflict was fought. Members of the movement, for example, were often unable to define what pornography was, and many had never seen or read it. All they "knew" was that persons who supported it had life-styles they strongly disapproved of, styles opposite to theirs, which (though often marginal) they saw as a "model of the legitimate and dominant definition of respectability" (1971:231).

The movement thus was able to demonstrate publicly that this style of life was alive and not at all powerless, thereby reinforcing it.[6]

We turn now to two important anchors of conservative sexual norms that exhibit a widespread influence throughout our analytic models: age and gender. Older people are more conservative than younger people because they come from more conservative generations. That is, they grew up in times when conservative influences like religion were more powerful than they are today. Moreover, they were less subject to experiences that might have caused a change in those norms. This is not to say that older persons have not changed; in fact, though few of our respondents reported moral change, among those who did we find older persons being *more* liberal than younger persons who had not changed. This maturational effect is outweighed by a larger generational effect, however, so that older persons represent the bearers of traditional moralities for our society. Traditional influences, of course, are passed on not only through the socialization process but also because older persons usually have positions of greater authority and power.

Our findings for gender sensitize us to what exactly was transmitted from the past. Clearly, the general experiences of females have limited their sexual experiences, the prime determinant of less conservative sexual norms.

The sheltering of females from sexual experiences has been a prominent feature of our male-dominated culture, in which women were once considered the exclusive private sexual property of the men to whom they were married (and before marriage the property of their fathers, acting in trust for the future husbands). Many of our sexual norms are rooted in such beliefs. Rape, for example, was until recently seen in terms of one man violating the property rights of another. Prohibitions of premarital sex and emphasis on virginity likewise can be seen as efforts to preserve the market value of females. Historically, then, challenges to these traditional property arrangements have met with strong opposition.[7] Today, male-female relationships are more likely to involve a different economic arrangement, one in which the male protects and supports the female in return for exclusive sexual rights and domestic obligations. Unrestricted female sexual independence would destroy this traditional bargain and all the institutions that it fosters. Thus a fundamental change in gender relationships would ensue, involving a diminution of the power traditionally exercised by males. Support for traditional sexual morality, then, operates to support traditional gender roles.[8] Females have often complied with this system in that, ideally, it does provide rewards such as security, leisure, and status. Perhaps it is for this reason that females tend to be more conservative than males in their sexual norms. Beyond this, however, is the fact that for many women, the traditional gender role system has appeared to be the *only* available source of rewards. In their eyes, then, it is true that violations of sexual norms do constitute a threat to the family—given one particular family system.[9]

It should be no surprise, then, that the feminist movement arouses such strong opposition. Its demands for a change in power relationships between men and women would mean radical social change in sexual institutions. This further explains why the maintenance of gender-role definitions ranks high among conservative concerns. We see some hint of this in our finding that feeling sexually threatened by the opposite sex is a strong determinant of conservative sexual norms and that this feeling is related to such conservative influences as age, being female, and having been raised as a Fundamentalist. The whole issue is well demonstrated in our finding that removing the socializing effects of being female (the indirect effects of our variable sex-female) would result in a reversal of the traditional relationship, with females holding less conservative sexual standards than males (the direct effect of the same variable).[10] We tend to agree, then, with Coleman's (1966:217) proposition that "the rigidity of premarital sex codes varies inversely with female dominance in the determination of family status. Where females are more dominant, that is where the system is more matriarchal, the sex codes will be less rigid, than when the female's ultimate status depends on the status of her husband."[11] We should note that our findings regarding race are also consistent with Coleman's theory. Race as a variable particularly distinguishes the premarital sexual experiences of our respondents. Thus, compared to whites, black respondents were much more tolerant regarding premarital sexual norms, a tolerance reflected in their higher incidence of such behavior and their more positive appraisal of it. This is partly explained by the greater equality between males and females among blacks, itself a consequence of economic discrimination whereby black males have found it more difficult to obtain employment than do black females. If the black male has had little power in determining the female's future status, therefore, he has also been less able to establish sexual norms advantageous to himself.

Along with feminism the second great challenge to traditional sexual norms has been the homosexual movement. Homosexuality represents a supreme challenge to all the sexual institutions. It is not tied to the family because it does not involve procreation (thus making it the classic unnatural act); involving partners of the same sex, it also represents a challenge to conventional gender definitions. Consequently, homosexual relationships are more varied, involving a range of relational forms, some that the larger society considers deviant, such as impersonal sex (Humphreys, 1970; Weinberg & Williams, 1975b). Additionally, many homosexuals consider sex in itself intrinsically good and celebrate this in subcultural forms that many heterosexuals find offensive. Small wonder, then, that highly negative attitudes toward homosexuality are strongly related to conservative influences. Indeed, the models we derived for explaining general sexual norms and attitudes toward homosexuality are similar. The major differences show that these influences are lifelong in the case of homosexuality and are less mediated by other variables. These attitudes furthermore seem much more impervious to other influences in that, of all behaviors we examined, norms regarding homosexuality were the ones that changed least frequently. Perhaps this should be expected, since a widespread change in moral views toward homosexuality would indicate that the normative and emotional basis of sexual institutions had become seriously weak. This is not the case. Instead, although homosexuality has been made a political issue in many parts of the country, the demands of homosexuals at the time of our study were frequently soundly rejected. These defeats seem to illustrate Durkheim's observation on the social utility of misbehavior. Opposition to homosexuality has allowed a large section of society to draw the line against what it will approve. Thus Safire (1978) has warned that resistance to homosexual demands should not necessarily be seen as a crusade of the radical right or even a civil rights issue. Rather, the issue, as often put forward by homosexuals themselves, is between tacit toleration and outright approval. Most people apparently care little what is done in private but will not give public approval to a behavior they believe immoral. That is, there is a strong belief that certain moral norms are worth asserting. Such conflicts will not readily disappear in the future: disapproval of homosexuality, as our results show, is unlikely to abate. This disapproval may, in fact, be strengthened by current tactics that compare homosexuals to racial minorities and claim for them a protected status requiring special legislation. Such tactics have been interpreted by many commentators (Greenfield, 1978; Leo, 1979) as tantamount to asking for legislation to protect a widely disliked life-style. The more approval is asked for, the more likely it will be opposed, because the majority of Americans will not, we believe, evaluate traditional life-styles and their sexual institutions as anything but morally appropriate.

In summary, we can say that in 1970 a strong strain of traditionalism regarding sexual morality still permeates American society. This is represented by what we might call the old conservatives in our society. These people not only hold conservative sexual norms but also believe in their theological underpinnings. They believe in the sanctity of the family, which should be based on clear gender role definitions wherein the male retains his dominance. They tend to be absolute and literal in their moral judgments, conceptualizing the world in moral blacks and whites and responding punitively to violators. They are also likely to come from groups and sectors in our society that are segregated from more cosmopolitan influences. In our data, these old conservatives are represented by those from older generations, females, the devout, those from Fundamentalist or small-town backgrounds, and so forth. Old conservatives have influence far greater than their numbers because of a situation of "pluralistic ignorance" (O'Gorman, 1988) regarding sexual moralities, wherein people rarely make their sexual standards public. Gagnon (1967:20–21) described how this sustains traditional views:

> The privatization of sexual consensus means that no one can be sure of the behavior of others, and this insecurity is accompanied by a belief that statements that differ from the conventional norms will be taken as evidence of sexual deviation. The only system of values that can be evoked in a time of sexual controversy is the most conservative. . . . This lack of consensus makes it very difficult for a body of disinterested opinion about sexuality to exist.

It is difficult to estimate how large a group share the characteristics of old conservatism as we have defined it. Some 19% of our 1970 sample held all 10 anti-homosexual attitudes in our Antihomosexuality Attitude Index (AAI), and about 25% were in categories 1–2 (the most conservative) on the SMS. It could be estimated, therefore, that old conservatives constitute about a fifth to a quarter of the population.[12]

Adherence to conservative sexual standards is widespread in American society, and we have isolated some of the most important predictors of such a moral stance. As our results show, however, there is a considerable amount of "variance" that we are unable to explain. We believe that our models do a good job of explaining the old conservative stance but that there is also a great deal of sexual conservatism in the United States that derives from sources other than the ones we have measured. There are intriguing indications of this throughout our data, for instance, the ambivalence in the propensity to sanction shown by many respondents. This suggests to us that many Americans hold conservative sexual norms for reasons different from the traditional ones. Since we do not have data on this, what follows is necessarily speculative.

Moralities are always intertwined with social structures in basic ways. This is the position of the best-known approach to norms and values in sociology—functionalism—which sees normative phenomena as meeting requisites of social systems, as illustrated by K. Davis's (1971) well-known explanation of sexual norms in terms of their function in (a) supporting the formation and continuance of families and (b) regulating competition over the sexual accessibility of persons.[13]

Basically, such a position—that rules have functions for society—can be a useful way of looking at things. For example, the reproductive consequences of unrestricted sexuality still remain despite our contraceptive technologies; witness teenage pregnancy rates, which account for some of our premarital sex codes. Furthermore, the persistent social need to bear and rear children (unless completely met by artificial insemination, sperm banks, embryo transplantation, etc.) means that rules concerning certain areas of sexuality will always remain. Other sex rules seem more to fit the "regulation of competition" function that Davis suggests. Sprey (1976:374), for example, commented on a situation in which sexuality is not tied to reproductive aims:

Even under circumstances in which individuals would be totally free to dispose of their sexuality as they see fit, the community at large must be responsible to protect them against fraud and force. Furthermore, the linkages of sexuality with other social spheres—economics, politics, and entertainment, to mention only a few—may also be expected to require a variety of types of social intervention, affecting the degree of autonomy of sexual behavior.

Such reasoning as this draws attention to the *pragmatic* aspects of sexual norms. We assert that for many persons, contemporary social changes have made traditional, absolutist, religiously based moral reasoning appear inappropriate to the realities of the modern world. It is beyond the scope of this book to outline these changes, but we can summarize their effects as weakening traditional structures of meaning.[14] At odds with the traditional external sources of moral norms but with a pragmatic need to orient themselves within a system of moral meanings, some Americans have sought to construct their own moralities from a variety of available resources—Freudian psychology, Eastern religions, the human potential movement, and so on. These new moralities have often been disappointing, however. Lacking institutional support, they hardly restrain in any way and seem inchoate; being overly intellectualized, they often have little practical relevance. Thus, though many people have become dissatisfied with traditional morality, there seems to be nothing to take its place and, because of the prevailing "pluralistic ignorance," few others with whom to conduct the search. (Many other Americans, of course, have rejected "new moralities" out of hand because often they are presented by groups or persons considered socially deviant or politically suspect.)

This situation we refer to as "sexual anomie." Anomie, as a concept, was introduced to society by Durkheim, who held different views of what it meant throughout his life (Marks, 1974). In general, according to Giddens (1978:107) his use "assimilates two discrete senses in which aims are unrealizable." First, there are no restraints on appetites, which leads to normlessness or lack of meaning in life; second, aspirations cannot be met in a particular society by following the rules, which leads to deviant adaptations. We will use the term mainly in its former sense to indicate a lack of normative guidelines.[15]

Given that many Americans have increasingly found themselves in a situation where they have felt an absence of moral guidelines for sexual conduct, it is our contention that their response has tended to be the practical adoption of simplistic codes that minimize the anxieties produced by the necessities of undirected choice. We do not claim that this is a new insight or theory. For example, in summarizing many studies of social and political conservatism, Wilson (1973:261–262) said,

> Conservative attitudes serve a defensive function. They arise as a means of simplifying, ordering, controlling, and rendering more secure, both the *external* world (through perceptual processes, stimulus preferences, etc.) and the *internal* world (needs, feelings, desires, etc.). Order is imposed upon inner needs and feelings by subjugating them to rigid and simplistic external codes of conduct (rules, laws, morals, duties, obligations, etc.), thus reducing conflict and averting the anxiety that would accompany awareness of the freedom to choose among alternative modes of action.

Our explanation is less psychological; we do not assume some sexual beast that must be repressed but rather emphasize the anxiety arising from being unable to locate oneself within some structure of meaning in order for sexuality to be expressed at all.

These new codes are, on the surface, similar to what we have called traditional morality. The important difference is that the principles underlying such codes are not religious values, as in the case of the old conservatives, but pragmatic considerations. That is, with no viable alternatives, it seemed socially and psychologically useful to adopt rules that at least meshed with traditional sexual institutions and therefore appeared "workable."[16] This is not to say that traditional morality is not pragmatic too (as functionalism shows it to be), but rather that the new codes involve no theological or external underpinning that needs to be blended with utility in the adoption of such rules.[17] What we have, then, are norms in search of values, a situation that further exacerbates the feelings of anomie produced by reactions to these norms in the first place.

Though sexual conservatism is as prevalent as in the past, we submit that it is now fed by different sources. Previously, conservative values were always *imposed from without* by society and were supported by most of its social institutions. Today, this is no longer always true; our society has become increasingly anomic with regard to sexuality, so that a variety of value positions compete, each receiving different amounts of institutional support. Thus, acceptance of conservative values is increasingly likely to *evolve from within* as a response to such uncertainty and lack of direction. A national survey conducted for *Time* magazine in 1977 showed, as do our own earlier data, not only that traditional conservative sexual values received widespread support among Americans but also that over 60% of those surveyed felt "morally confused" over sex. Gagnon (1977:26, 31) has referred to such changes as follows:

> What has happened in the last few years . . . has been a far more individual perspective on sexuality. It is not sexuality in the service of some larger set of purposes, but rather sexuality in terms of individual preference. Sex is justified by what an individual wants to do. . . . [However,] in plans based on individualism, it is difficult to decide what is right or correct, not only for other people but also for the self; this situation is typical of the 1960's and 1970's.

This, we believe, is what lies at the heart of the notion of a "sexual revolution": not that "anything goes" or that unrestricted sexual freedom is to be preferred, but that our society has a number of sexual norms from which to choose, with none of them strongly preferred as *the* best. For many people, the problem then becomes *how to choose*, in that no guidelines are offered by which one alternative can be compared with another. The result is that many accept conservative values because they are workable, hallowed by time, and socially respectable. Will (1977:92) illustrated this: "a society swept by the trendy thought that 'liberation' from 'mere' conventions is an inherent good soon finds that its values have been reduced to desiccated concepts like 'change' and 'free choice of life styles.' But especially in such a society many people want a few rocks to cling to in the rip tide that washes away old moral moorings."

People who adopt conservative sexual norms as a reaction to sexual anomie we refer to as the new conservatives. This group holds many of the standards held by the old conservatives but in a less absolute or literal way, because they have rejected the theological basis of those norms. They are more likely to adopt a "situational ethic"—to look beyond the sexual act itself in considering its moral qualities. Accordingly, they are less punitive toward violators of sexual norms and may be willing to tolerate certain behaviors that they are reluctant to try themselves or to provide with social acceptance. A crucial difference between the two sexual conservatisms is that old conservatism has a great deal of institutional support—for example from the churches—whereas the new does not: in fact, owing to the widespread pluralistic ignorance regarding sex, the new conservative is likely to feel alone. New conservatives are characterized in our data by respondents from more open, cosmopolitan backgrounds, such as urban dwellers with higher education and greater sexual experience (e.g., a broad awareness of sexual environment). It is difficult to estimate how large a group the new conservatives are because they share many characteristics with the old. We suggest that this group corresponds to those in categories 3–4 on the SMS, which represents some 40% of the sample population. This, however, is a conservative estimate. Adding category 5 would raise the number to slightly over half the population, which might be more accurate.[18]

It is important to note that in the 1970s, sexual anomie has also played a role in sustaining the old conservative position. The upheaval of the 1960s, much of which was a revolt against traditional ways of doing things, resulted in new vigor for traditionalists who often saw in these disruptions the fulfillment of their prophecies. Encouraged, too, by the fragmentation of the opposition and the increasing support of many who were shocked by the social turbulence, the old conservatives fought back. Traditional sexual morality was vigorously reasserted. Political radicals were stereotyped as sexually depraved and sex became a symbol around which many battles could be fought; abortion, homosexual civil liberties, the Equal Rights Amendment are all sex-related issues. On these issues the old conservatives find they can do better than on many non-sex-related ones, because they benefit from the absence of a cohesive prosex movement and the pervasive pluralistic ignorance in the population. We predict, therefore, that America will remain as conservative as ever in its sexual norms, as sexual anomie will not abate. The sources of conservatism have undergone a change, however, so that factors producing the new conservatism may become as strong as those that produced the old.

If our analysis is correct, then, public moral stance and private moral commitment stand in an uneasy relationship to each other. This conclusion can be schematized as shown in Figure 12-1.

Type 1 people publicly support traditional morality with great

		PUBLIC MORAL STANCE	
		Supports traditional sexual morality	Does not support traditional sexual morality
PRIVATE MORAL BELIEFS	Believes in traditional sexual morality	(1) Old Conservatives (low anomie)	(3) Conventional Liberals (high anomie)
	Does not believe in traditional sexual morality	(2) New Conservatives (high anomie)	(4) Moral Radicals (low anomie)

Figure 12-1 Relationships Between Public and Private Moralities

fervor because their support springs from strong private moral beliefs. There is institutional expression and group support of these private beliefs, so that public and private moralities are one and are often complemented by behavior. Such consistency means that sexual anomie is low. These people are the ones we refer to as old conservatives, whom we estimate at about 20% or 25% of our sample.

Type 4 people openly discard a public stance of sexual respectability, and their private beliefs (and often behaviors) are consistent with this. A contemporary example would be someone who has "come out of the closet" to stand publicly as an overt homosexual. His or her private moral commitment and sexual behavior deviate from traditional norms but are consistent with his or her public moral stance. This type, representing people highly committed to their "sexual deviance," whom we call moral radicals, is empirically small but growing. Its consistency between public and private moralities means that this type is characterized by low sexual anomie. Type 4 moral radicals could be typified by category 6 on the SMS, where none of the behaviors in the scale was rated "always wrong." This would be 18% of the sample. But this seems to us too high and artificially inflated by the choice of response categories; that is, it would not distinguish between people who responded "almost always wrong" and those saying "not wrong at all" (though the former response does imply that the given behavior is permissible in some circumstances). A better indicant is the 6%

of the sample that was free from antihomosexual stereotypes, as measured by the AAI.

Type 2 people publicly support traditional sexual morality but privately do not subscribe to the traditional values underlying such beliefs. That is, they may adopt the conventional stance, but only because conformity seems socially expedient, not because they are deeply committed to it. Such lack of commitment can result in behaviors not in accord with traditional morality. People in this category are mainly those we have called the new conservatives. We see sexual anomie as high for all type 2 people, who we have suggested comprise about half the sample.[19]

Type 3 people also show an inconsistency between public and private faces, this time by not supporting traditional sexual morality in public yet privately holding moralities (and behaving) in accord with such values. This type includes those who present themselves as sexually liberal in public but are privately reluctant to practice the behavior that they support. They often take their public stance in an attempt to be perceived as sexual sophisticates. This characterizes many male "radicals" who claim that they support sexual freedom but draw the line at accepting homosexuality and treat women in a most traditional way. Another case exemplifies the difference between many young people of the 1970s and their parents. Parents often publicly profess sexual norms that are more conservative than their private moralities and behaviors—they are type 2 people. Young people, however, are often type 3. Publicly, they may hold norms that are more (fashionably) liberal than their private moralities and behavior, sometimes because they have accepted the myth of the sexual revolution, sometimes because to espouse a less liberal public stance would invite ridicule from their peers. This can result in their engaging in sexual behavior when they would rather not. Finally, we would note that type 3 inconsistency between public and private faces probably reflects increasing tolerance, so that many type 3 people represent what we call conventional liberals (as opposed to the unconventional ones of type 4). As can be imagined, types 2 and 3 overlap, the latter group having their tolerance challenged when confronted by actual situations and retreating to the pragmatism of the new conservatives. Nonetheless, though we suggest that sexual anomie is relatively high for type 3 people, it is less so than that for type

2's. We estimate that type 3, conventional liberals, could include as much as 20% of the population.

Change in sexual norms among some people has occurred, as our data show. In fact, although the number of people involved is small, our analysis revealed that the least conservative people on the SMS tended to have reached this stance through changing their original morality, rather than being people who received unusually liberal moral training. It follows that anything that works counter to conservatizing influences can act as a possible agent of change in sexual norms and attitudes. Such developments could represent new "learning situations" that might challenge traditional moral meanings. One clear example is a high level of education, which reduces the extent of antihomosexual attitudes. What our data seem to show most consistently, however, is that sexual experience per se acts as a strong predictor of liberal sexual norms and attitudes. Why is unclear; there are probably several different processes at work. One is the opportunity to compare *actual* sexual behavior with the reality stipulated by a moral point of view. This could underlie our finding that premarital sexual experience reduces religious devoutness and thus moderates conservative sexual norms. Probably more important as a process is that sexual experience itself acts as a strong positive conditioner (the positive aspect of premarital sex most widely recalled was physical pleasure); this process may be at work even—we may infer—among those behaving discordantly with their moralities. Such people may seek further gratifying experiences, discarding those moralities that hinder their search. Actual sexual experience, then, in and of itself creates the most powerful of new learning situations. We do not say that becoming sexually active is always a positive experience (although apparently for most people it is), but that those who do react positively appear less likely to adopt norms and attitudes that disapprove of similar experiences for others. A third process, less directly sexual in a personal, physical sense, is exposure to what we have called a sexual environment. This is the knowledge a person has of the sexual behavior of his or her acquaintances. Such a social context can provide the moral meanings for the quantity and character of sexual acts. That is, this environment provides a normalizing backdrop to sexuality, so that certain acts and conditions do not stand out as "deviant" and produce a sense of moral shock.

Our data show that sexual environments and experiences are less likely to occur among people from certain backgrounds, such as those with highly devout parents. There are other background characteristics that increase the likelihood of sexual environments and experience and their liberalizing influences. Three of these stand out. First, being male in our culture is a status that is often confirmed by sexual prowess. Young men are encouraged to explore their sexuality and are rewarded for sexual success (while women are sanctioned for the same activity) and are less likely to be "protected" from knowledge about sex. Consequently males tend to be more liberal. Second, blacks are more likely than whites to have frequent and enjoyable youthful sexual experiences. This is presumably because black culture provides a sexual environment largely free from the particular antisexual influences that typify white majority culture, and in black culture also, sex-role equality is more widespread. Such a background is more conducive to liberal sexual norms. The final important background characteristic is age. For a variety of reasons, current generations appear to be exposed to broader sexual environments and more sexual experiences than do older generations.

Not all background features that produce liberal sexual norms and attitudes have to work through sexual experiences and environments, though these appear to be the most important mediators. Other learning environments clearly exist. One is growing up in an urban locale, which directly reduces antihomosexual attitudes and indirectly does so in being related to educational achievement. Urban people also tend to feel less distrusting of involvements with the opposite sex. Rather than encouraging the positive conditioning of individual experiences, then, urban backgrounds appear to exert influence by providing a learning environment that includes a wide variety of life-styles within what is routinely tolerated. Rural environments, in contrast, provide few examples of diversity and reward conventionally conservative behaviors.

On a more personal level, our data show that for a small number of people, having had sexually permissive parents can produce similar effects. This permissiveness fosters liberal sexual norms directly and through leading people to regard themselves as less serious and moral about sex. Thus, this kind of parental socialization influences people to extend to others the tolerance experienced at home and to be personally less prone to absolutist judgments. Permissiveness can lead to tolerance, then; but this is not to say that tolerance necessarily brings about permissiveness. A parent can teach tolerance of differences without encouraging them.

It is evident that—apart from certain experiences, sexual or educational—factors that would promote change away from the dominant morality are not readily available. Obviously, such ascribed statuses as age, race, and gender cannot be changed. Cultural meanings associated with ascribed statuses can be transformed, but not necessarily in ways disruptive of traditional morality; for example, upwardly mobile blacks become more conservative. So too may changes toward sex-role equality produce in males a family-centeredness and reevaluation of sexuality that can lead to a less liberal bias in their sexual norms. Other variables such as parental permissiveness seem to relate to cyclical swings in child-rearing ideologies that typify different generations (Bronfenbrenner, 1958) and are related to major historical factors. This is true too of changes in religious devoutness, but with less dramatic fluctuation. Our study seems to show a tendency in 1970 toward increasing devoutness: nearly half of our respondents considered themselves to be more devout than their parents. At present such increases seem more prevalent among Fundamentalist than mainstream denominations. Change in a liberal direction would most likely have to involve transformations in social structure that are relatively long-term in nature. In our data these points of change are represented by age, urbanism, and education. Generational change seems to go in a liberal direction and to be cumulative, but large-scale social phenomena like wars or economic depressions can upset the steadiness of any such trend. Urbanization continues, yet may reach a point where urban problems become so great as to undermine traditional urban tolerance. Increasing educational levels seem most likely to determine future changes, if education retains its popularity and declining birth rates do not impoverish educational systems. Even here, though, such changes may be limited to reducing misinformation about certain acts, homosexuality, for example, or extending tolerance to other acts, such as premarital sex among adults. And this is not a certainty for two reasons that our data have shown. First, quite a number of young, urban, or highly educated respondents do hold traditionally conservative norms. More important, many sexual norms and attitudes are based on feelings rather than cognitions.

That our 1970 data generally show great stability in sexual norms is thus understandable if our models have isolated the most important variables, because these variables are and have been unlikely to fluctuate very much over so short a span as a few decades. Revolutionary changes in sexual mores, so often proclaimed, would require revolutionary changes in total social structure. We doubt that there was a radical change in the social structure of the United States in the 1970s and, public impressions notwithstanding, we found there and then no systematic evidence of a revolutionary change in sexual norms.

NOTES

1. This compares interestingly with the lack of theories to make sense of such data. As Lukes (1973:432) has commented, "It is astonishing how little attention has been given to such questions [of morality] in twentieth century sociology and social anthropology. Indeed it is not an exaggeration to say that the sociology of morality is the great void in contemporary social science."
2. A similar belief concerning the homogenization of sexual attitudes and behaviors was asserted by DeLora and Warren (1977:542–543) and criticized with empirical data on social class by Weinberg and Williams (1980).
3. Bell (1966) states that we should not overestimate the influence of the Puritans because that ignores other nearly contemporaneous sects, for example Methodists, Baptists, and Calvinists. Also, the American South was not as influenced by Puritanism as the North, so that a double standard arose there much earlier than in the North. Southern male chivalry protected white females but permitted men sexual access to black females.
4. K. Davis (1971:318) notes that sexual morality is difficult to enforce, so that societies have often used their most powerful weapons to control the sex lives of their members. This implies a religious link, as it can result in ". . . the elevation of the sex mores to the sacred realm, where they are surrounded with mystery and imbued with deep moral significance." In this way, sex becomes part of the sacred order of the cosmos, integrated with other powerful supernatural beliefs. Not all commentators see the development of sexual moralities as influenced by religion in a direct way. Van Ussel (1969), for example, considers sexual repression a result of socioeconomic changes and the church a vehicle rather than a cause of such changes. Haeberle (1977) says that religion per se was important up through the Middle Ages but after that more secular, external factors were of greater influence.
5. Some psychologists see the formulation of sexual attitudes and standards as the result of repressed emotions (see Adorno et al., 1950). Persons who are authoritarian have been found to project their own unacceptable sexual impulses onto another group toward which they behave punitively. An example

is given by Brown (1965:502): "Projection [has] a functional role in the southern white man's sexual use of Negro women. If one can believe that Negro women are inherently sexual and promiscuous, then one can believe that they seduce a man against his better impulses." While some individuals may indeed project in this way, we believe the sociological account described in the text to be more generally applicable.

6. Emotions and sexual norms are not only linked through threats to social status; there are more direct relationships. Our society emphasizes the relationship of sex and love, conjoining strong feelings of personal attraction, romanticism, and sexuality, so that not only does love justify sex but sex is a prime criterion of the demonstration of love. Also, since sex is a social relationship, our society "connects eroticism with affection, trust, dependence, esteem, aggression, distrust, jealousy, and envy" (K. Davis, 1971:316).
7. Supporting these arrangements was an associated belief—that in the absence of controls, females would be sexually voracious. This picture is unwittingly supported by some feminist writers (e.g., E. Davis, 1971; Sherfey, 1972) who claim, often on the basis of a simplistic interpretation of modern work on sexual response or a dubious archeology, that females are indeed much more sexual than males who, fearing such appetites, have suppressed women's sexuality in their own interest.
8. Studying sexual behaviors and norms in a variety of societies, Stephens (1971) found that females' sexual behavior is more closely constrained the more that gender roles approach a dominant-submissive polarity, and that such constraints are relaxed in societies where gender roles are egalitarian.
9. This situation is carried to extremes in Latin American societies with the cult of "marianismo," wherein the very suffering that females experience provides them a secondary gain in that it indicates their special grace as victims, a status they use to create power over males (Stevens, 1973).
10. Emphatically, though, we do not ascribe male-female differences entirely to socialization. For example, in societies where both genders receive the same sexual socialization, males still appear more interested and active than females. The ubiquity of such phenomena points to a substantial psycho-biological influence as well (see Hagen, 1979).
11. This account has been commented on by Reiss (1967). He emphasizes more the autonomy of courtship roles, however. Both Reiss and Coleman have been criticized by Eckhardt (1971), the former for tautological reasoning and the latter for incomplete theorizing.
12. It is possible to choose other cutting points, of course. For example, 53% of the sample population held 8 of the 10 attitudes on the AAI, which would expand the number of old conservatives. On the other hand, category 1 of the SMS, which includes only those who viewed all the behaviors in that scale as always wrong, takes in 14% of the population, which would reduce the number.
13. There are, of course, various brands of functionalism (see Turner, 1978). For some functionalist approaches to sexual morality see Goethals (1971), Broude (1975), and Davenport (1978), who sums up the basic position of most who take this approach (1978:161–162): "The culture of sex is anchored in two directions. In one direction, it is moored to the potentialities and limitations of biological inheritance. In the other direction, it is tied to the internal logic and consistency of the total culture. As one sector of culture changes, all of the other sectors that articulate must undergo adjustment."
14. There appears to be some agreement that the changing economic system of

society has had the most powerful effect on sexuality; e.g., Bell (1976) has reasoned that sexual restraint, as a product of subsistence economy—"prudence in a world of scarcity"—underlay the morality of early Puritan America and is being replaced by the "prodigality in abundance" ethic of contemporary consumer capitalism. Analyses that share similar assumptions have been provided by Van Ussel (1969), Haeberle (1977), and Wilson et al. (1977). It is interesting that in the twentieth century the notion of a sexual revolution only arises in affluent Western societies (see Cameron, 1976).

15. Durkheim's account is worth quoting at length, especially as it deals with sex (1951:271):

"The lot of the unmarried man is different. As he has the right to form attachment wherever inclination leads him, he aspires to everything and is satisfied with nothing. This morbid desire for the infinite which everywhere accompanies anomy may as readily assail this as any other part of our consciousness; it very often assumes a sexual form which was described by Musset. When one is no longer checked, one becomes unable to check one's self. Beyond experienced pleasures one senses and desires others; if one happens almost to have exhausted the range of what is possible, one dreams of the impossible; one thirsts for the nonexistent. How can the feelings not be exacerbated by such unending pursuit? For them to reach that state, one need not even have infinitely multiplied the experiences of love and lived the life of Don Juan. The humdrum existence of the ordinary bachelor suffices. New hopes constantly awake, leaving a trail of weariness and disillusionment behind them. How can desire, then, become fixed, being uncertain that it can retain what it attracts; for the anomy is two-fold. Just as the person makes no definitive gift of himself, he has definitive title to nothing. The uncertainty of the future plus his own indeterminateness, therefore, condemns him to constant change."

16. Such pragmatism need not be utterly rational, however. Witness that even among relatively tolerant respondents, the belief that homosexuals molest children continued to be held.

17. That is, we do not see our respondents as passive "cultural dopes" (Garfinkel, 1967). Though many people do take on a set of norms handed down by the culture (the old conservatives, for example), many others are actively engaged in constructing their own moralities. Even old conservatives can quarrel over different interpretations of a code they all accept (hence the rise of sectarian movements).

18. "New" and "old" conservatives, as we have defined them, do not exhaust the variety of conservatives in America. Another group that should be mentioned are also known as new conservatives but are quite different from those we have given the same name. This group is composed of intellectuals who are ardently opposed to the "adversary culture" of the 1960s and are pessimistic about change (especially its unintended consequences), wary of ideologies, and concerned with reinvigorating American institutions (see Steinfels, 1979).

19. All members of this type need not be considered hypocrites. Some surely are—e.g., the politician who condemns homosexuality and is later arrested for homosexual sex in a public restroom. Others, however, may believe in their public stance but be unable to live it in their private lives, such as a woman whose husband threatens to leave her if she will not engage in sexual activities she finds distasteful. It is the lack of commitment to traditional value structures among the new conservatives that indicates hypocrisy is not the issue.

Appendices

Appendix A

History and Design of the Study

This study is a product of the late 1960s, a time in which many hitherto disregarded segments of our society were demanding social change and could no longer be ignored. One such segment was the homosexual population, which is probably the most widely despised and harshly treated of all the sexual minorities. In recognition of this, the Director of the National Institute of Mental Health (NIMH), Stanley Yolles, established the NIMH Task Force on Homosexuality in 1967 in an effort to meet the mental health needs of homosexuals. It soon became apparent that before any concrete proposals could be made, extensive research was required into the social and psychological situation of homosexual people. NIMH thus funded a variety of research projects on homosexuality. The Institute for Sex Research (ISR) was the recipient of two large grants, one to study the social and psychological adjustment and developmental experiences of homosexual men and women (Bell & Weinberg, 1978; Bell et al., 1981) and another that became the basis for this work.

The Task Force concluded that the major source of homosexuals' problems lay in the heterosexual majority's negative reaction toward them. But how widespread this reaction was, which groups it mainly typified, and how deep it ran were questions that could not be answered from the present state of knowledge. And these questions were crucially important. More and more homosexuals were challenging social and legal conventions and claiming that their sexual preference was not a just basis for denying them access to education, employment, military service, preferred living arrangements, and so on. Homosexuals had become an important social group whose situation required official notice, for whom official policies would have to be made. How could this be done without understanding the public's attitudes and reactions toward homosexuality?

Jack Wiener, Project Officer and Assistant Chief of the NIMH Center for Studies of Mental Health and Social Problems, was instructed to explore the possibility of a national survey. This brought him to the Institute for Sex Research, both because of the Institute's reputation for careful, methodical research and because Paul Gebhard, its director, was also a member of the Task Force. Initially the Institute thought of purchasing a small part of a larger national survey. For example, at that time one could contract with the National Opinion Research Center (NORC) at the University of Chicago, a prominent survey research organization, to have a series of questions included in one of their periodic "amalgam" surveys using national samples of 1,500 adults at the rate of $1,000 per minute of interviewing time, or $60,000 for an entire one-hour national interview. Later, however, we realized that the scope of the data we needed would necessitate a survey of our own. Central to this decision was our conviction that data on the public reaction to homosexuality would be fully meaningful only if they could be compared to similar data on other behaviors such as premarital and extramarital sex, masturbation, prostitution, and so on.

Thus what had originally been conceived as a study of the social context of one particular kind of social behavior became a more general study of American sexual norms and attitudes. To keep the length of the interview manageable, we decided to ask only about norms and attitudes concerning sexual behaviors that were relatively prevalent sexual outlets (e.g., premarital intercourse, masturbation), were considered to be relatively serious social problems (e.g., prostitution, homosexuality), or were generally accepted as universally taboo (e.g., incest, sex with children). Therefore we included no questions, for example, about voyeurism, exhibitionism, transvestism, or sex with animals. Subsequently, items about incest and child molesting were dropped, as pretest data (see Appendix C) showed such high disapproval that little variance existed to be accounted for.[1]

We must emphasize that from the outset this research was intended to be primarily *descriptive*. There was no particular overall theoretical framework that guided the study. Rather, we chose basic sociological and psychological variables that in the past had shown strong correlations with attitudes and values. In addition, we included questions reflecting the generally accepted assumptions of the disciplines—on, for example, the effects of the character of the relationship an individual has with his or her parents, which taps the Freudian notion of superego development. Finally, we inquired extensively into respondents' own sexual experiences. Not only did we believe that sexual experiences influence sexual norms and attitudes (an assumption rarely explored in previous research); we also felt there was a possibility that with a representative sample, we might obtain a reasonably accurate depiction of the sexual history of the American population. Our study was an opportunity to see if we could obtain, in a national sample survey, the kind of data that Kinsey collected with his cluster sampling of volunteer informants. At the same time, of course, we felt that special methods must be devised for collecting such sensitive data (see Appendix B).

The emphasis of the study, nonetheless, remained the discovery of public attitudes toward homosexuality, so this topic accounted for the most detailed questions. Our proposal to NIMH listed several of the things that we hoped to find out with our study:

What perceptions and information about homosexuality are held among the public; how widely are they held?

How many people display contradictions or inconsistencies in their views of homosexuality?

To what extent, and in what ways, is homosexuality seen as a threat to the social order?

How common is the desire for strong negative sanctions against homosexuals?

How widely is homosexuality viewed as pathological, and to what extent as "curable"?

What do most people see as the etiology of homosexuality—is it voluntary or not? It is brought about by experiences in childhood or later in life?

To what extent are people willing to accept the integration of homosexuals into society and their participation in social institutions?

In what ways are homosexual females viewed differently from males?

What are the correlates of negative views toward homosexuality?

With the backing of a major federal agency and the opportunity to conduct a broad survey about sexuality, we had to ensure that the data we collected would be of the highest quality. To this end we contracted the NORC to gather the information for us. Working in partnership with NORC, we were assured that we would have well-trained interviewers, thorough pretesting of our instruments, and an accurately drawn sample. Still, because we would be asking such intimate questions, special preparation was required in all three respects. It is to these matters that we turn in the three appendices that follow.

NOTES

1. At one point we also planned to include questions on exposure to and attitudes toward erotic material, at the request of the Commission on Obscenity and Pornography. However, problems of timing intervened, and these plans fell through.

Appendix B

Training the NORC Field Supervisors[1]

One of the primary tasks of this project was the development of a useful questionnaire that would allow the collection of valid and reliable data. But it was also clear that the data collection procedure itself would be a crucial factor in achieving our research goals. No matter how careful the attention to the research problems, how skillful the construction of the questionnaire, or how sophisticated the data analysis, the outcome of the study would depend ultimately on the quality of the mechanism by which the data were gathered. Therefore we worked closely with the NORC administrators to exercise as much quality control as possible over the interviewing procedures.

Before the first pretest, letters describing the study, defining its goals, and suggesting possible problems were sent to NORC interviewers throughout the nation. The interviewers were encouraged to write back to ask us questions or to comment on being involved in sex research. More important, they were urged to take on pretest interviewing only if they were reasonably certain that they would feel comfortable doing so. After the two pretests (detailed in the following appendix), interviewers completed a questionnaire in which they were asked to identify problem questions and to make general suggestions and comments.

Although the analysis of these reports did not indicate really serious difficulties, it was clear that all was not well. Some interviewers were bothered by "a few of the questions—those intimate ones." Others said that the interviewing was "rough,"; they felt "drained after some of the interviews" and had "a certain concern" for themselves. Still others, in the words of one, "found the subject somewhat embarrassing, especially when interviewing the opposite sex." They described some respondents as reluctant, suspicious, even hostile, and occasionally doubted that their respondents had been truthful: "I never saw women with so many children and no spouse where premarital sex was not involved."

The problems suggested by these pretest reports were underscored when some respondents were reinterviewed to establish the reliability of the study data (see Appendix C). While some of these respondents indicated that the original interviews had been carried out in a matter-of-fact, easy manner, others thought that the NORC interviewers had been under stress, nervous, and eager to finish the ordeal. The NORC field staff, it seemed clear, would have to be specially prepared for the main survey.

It was also clear that interview training beyond what NORC always provides for major national surveys would be exceedingly expensive. To reduce costs and still provide a small-group setting in which each interviewer would be able to work out the problems he or she anticipated, we decided on a two-step plan. We would meet with interviewers' field supervisors, who would then pass on their training to their field interviewing staffs.

The plan called for a three-day training session. The first day would be devoted to upgrading general interviewing skills, and the activities of the other two days would directly address the problems connected with our own study of sexual attitudes and behaviors. This sequence would permit the participants to get to know each other and develop some rapport, so that by the time the sensitive problems connected with our particular project were introduced, they could discuss them more easily. Activities for the first day were planned by NORC; the other two days we planned ourselves, subject to NORC approval.[2]

Before proceeding with specific plans, we defined the problems that needed to be dealt with. The first problem—explaining how to use the questionnaire—was largely technical. Since this was a professional interviewing staff, we anticipated no real difficulty. A second problem—the need to ensure that NORC's predominantly female, middle-class interviewers would know the language lower-class respondents used for such behaviors as masturbation and homosexuality—was more complex. Language patterns differ among geographic areas, and since this survey was to be conducted throughout the nation, these differences needed to be discussed. The most difficult problem, the one that really dictated the necessity for the training session, was anxiety among interviewers about being involved in sex research. We expected that many interviewers would feel anxious even if they did not frankly say so, and we planned activities to help counter this anxiety. We hoped that these activities would enable the supervisors to deal with any personal concerns and also that they would exemplify training techniques that could easily be adapted for the interviewers themselves.

As noted, our plan was to move from less to more sensitive areas. For example, the first day would be devoted to general NORC problems, followed by an informal social gathering. The second day would begin with a discussion of sex research and the need for responsible studies in the field. After giving a brief description of Kinsey's pioneering work and other investigations by the Institute, we would spend most of the day going over the questionnaire with the group. This item-by-item examination would allow us and the supervisors to anticipate any problems that might arise in the interviews, other than those already covered. That evening, and all the third day, would be spent confronting particular problems arising from the content of our study.

During this last day and a half, we would have to be able to deal openly and thoroughly with whatever concern might arise. Because time would be at a premium, we wanted to overcome quickly the participants' natural reticence so that they could talk freely about their attitudes toward sex and sex research. Here we planned exercises and activities that we called "negative practice interviews," "structured conversations," and "role-modeling working trios." In addition, we would include a discussion about sex norms.

The purpose of the negative practice interview was to help allay interviewers' fear of saying the wrong thing. The members of the group would pair off and simulate interviews in which the person playing the interviewer's role would deliberately try to make every conceivable thing go wrong, thus meeting head-on any fears of awkwardness or embarrassment.

The structured conversation activity also involved working in pairs. Those playing the part of interviewers would be asked to explain their involvement in sex research to their partners, variously cast as the interviewer's husband, mother, clergyman, and so forth. We hoped that these conversations might put into words ideas and attitudes that could then be discussed with the entire group.

The training activity that ultimately proved most useful was the working trio exercise. One person in each trio played the role of interviewer. Another was the respondent, using a script that indicated how a particular kind of person might actually reply. The third member acted as observer, keeping notes so that a useful discussion of the ensuing interaction could take place. We held three practice interviews so that everyone could play all three parts.

We used another exercise to deal with the problem of semantics. The participants would be asked to write answers to questions they might be asked during the interview, like "What does 'masturbation' mean?" or "Just what do those lesbians do together?" A discussion based on these written answers would give us the opportunity to point out that vernacular expressions using "four-letter words" are the only sexual terms many people know. Such persons might use "four-letter words" as factual, not profane.

Another aspect of our planning was to keep things easy and informal; a schoolroom atmosphere was to be carefully avoided. We would provide mimeographed handouts to describe each activity or discussion so the participants would not be distracted or inhibited by taking notes. We also felt that the NORC administrative staff should not attend the discussions designed to deal with fears about being involved in sex research. We wanted to handle these discussions and activities entirely by ourselves, since NORC field supervisors might avoid discussing (or even admitting) their concerns in front of their own supervisors.

After we had worked out these preliminary plans, we sent NORC a copy for their approval. An immediate difficulty arose: the NORC administrators were uneasy about our plan to conduct some training sessions by ourselves. They did not want their people to receive any instructions that they could not observe. Eventually, though, we were able to persuade them that observers could inhibit the participants' candor—and to assure them that we were not planning an "encounter weekend."

NORC scheduled three separate three-day training sessions, since we had asked that the number of participants be limited. Although we had, of course, intended that the sessions be uniformly conducted and otherwise similar, their character was markedly different. The first session especially differed from the later two. To some extent this was because more people attended: it had 20 participants, while only 16 came to either of the other two sessions. This difference sounds small, but the first three-day session had a certain "large-group" feeling, hence a more impersonal atmosphere.

There were other differences as well. We did not formally classify participants in one session or another on the basis of how long they had worked for NORC or of whether they worked in urban, suburban, or rural areas. It appeared, however, that a larger proportion of those who attended the first session had long-standing personal and professional relationships with the NORC Chicago staff. This group may not really have been more experienced and confident than other interviewers, but they gave the impression of sophistication and professional assurance. Indeed, they seemed to feel that most of the scheduled training was unnecessary, that as professionals, they and their staffs were quite able to conduct successful interviews on any imaginable subject.

Finally, of course, the first session differed from the second and third because it *was* the first. No matter how detailed the planning or how clearly envisioned the goals and problems, a certain amount of clumsiness and fumbling was probably inevitable. The first session, then, apparently served as a "shake-down cruise" that allowed the NORC and Institute staffs to work through difficulties and disagreements so that the other two sessions could proceed more smoothly.

Differences among the three sessions were clearest during the meetings that treated the issues of attitudes and feelings about sex and being involved in sex research. Whether it was a matter of our inexperience or the participants' attitude that the training was unnecessary, the initial meeting between the first group and the Institute staff did not turn out well. Rather than accepting the planned exercises as techniques that could be used in local training sessions, the supervisors acted offended and persisted in an extended defense of their interviewers' abilities. This meeting ended rather abruptly, but afterward the communication barrier did seem to open. In the lobby, the bar, the halls, and some of the supervisors' rooms, the participants began to talk about their worries, fears of embarrassment or misunderstanding, and apprehensions about the survey. Institute staff members were involved in these discussions, each one with different groups, and though all this was unplanned, it seemed to serve the purpose of the training session.

In all three training sessions, the activities of the final day went smoothly. The exercise dealing with definitions of sexual terms was followed by a general, candid discussion of how to make the questions clear to all kinds of respondents. The working trio exercise was particularly useful in stimulating serious consideration of the many problems the interviewers might encounter in the field.

For the other two training sessions, we decided to eliminate the negative practice interview and structured conversation exercises, and the initial meeting between the supervisors and Institute staff was considerably less difficult. We opened the introductory evening session with a talk about the pretest interviewers' experiences. We made clear that many interviewers with years of experience had found it disturbing to administer our questionnaire. Demonstrating the need for training in this indirect way seemed to make a difference.

Since the training-session concept was experimental, we made several efforts to assess its results. At the end of the sessions, the participants rated each of the training activities on a four-point scale from "very helpful" to "not helpful" and answered two open-ended questions, "How useful was the first day's training at NORC?" and "In general, do you think the last two days were useful?" After they had finished conducting their own sessions with the local interviewers, the supervisors were asked to respond to a more elaborate schedule of questions. This questionnaire asked again how helpful each activity had been, whether they had considered it for use in local training, whether they had actually used it (and if so, for how long), and whether, if called on to do another briefing, they would use it again and if not, why not. We also asked whether supervisors had been offended, insulted, or embarrassed during the Chicago meetings and whether their sense of competence and self-confidence had been shaken. Finally, we asked for suggestions for future sessions.

All the activities except the negative practice interview and structured conversation exercises were rated as either very helpful or helpful by a large majority of the participants. Five activities (NORC's two sessions on sampling, the introduction to the study, the item-by-item consideration of the questionnaire, and the trio exercise) were assigned the highest rating by over half the participants in all three training sessions.

Since the atmosphere of the different sessions had varied, we tested responses for statistically significant differences. We found that the first group rated NORC's morning seminar on sampling as more helpful than did those in the second training session. The third group differed from the other two in rating role modeling by staff and role playing in trios more highly: no one in this group said these activities were somewhat or not helpful, but several supervisors in the first and second groups gave these activities low ratings.

Dichotomized as "very helpful" versus the other three responses, the data revealed a slightly larger number of significant differences in the intergroup comparisons. Chi-square values indicate that the three groups made significantly different evaluations of the afternoon seminar on sampling, the discussion of sexual norms, the provision of handouts so note-taking was unnecessary, and the exercise of writing term definitions.

The assessments made in Chicago were necessarily limited to a supervisor's notion of how useful the training had been personally and of how *potentially* useful it could be in local training. The later questionnaire, then, would measure how useful the training sessions had *actually* proved to be. The results indicated that the supervisors considered the Chicago experience generally quite useful in preparing interviewers for the study.

Not all the training activities were found equally helpful, however. The sampling seminar, which had been highly rated at the end of the Chicago sessions, proved less useful in local training than did the activities related directly to the study. And the "optional briefing techniques"—the exercises presented by the Institute staff—were rated more highly after the local training sessions than they had been in Chicago.

The item-by-item discussion of the questionnaire received the lion's share of time spent in the local training groups. Over half of the local one-day training sessions had devoted at least three hours to this activity, and more than a quarter spent over four hours going over the questionnaire. The working-trio exercise was the activity used next most often, taking up one to three hours in over half of the local training sessions.

As mentioned above, the optional briefing techniques that we introduced were rated more highly after the local training was completed. The value of these training techniques varied according to the size of the local session, however. Supervisors who trained only one interviewer rated this kind of training less helpful after the local sessions than they had rated it in Chicago, while supervisors who trained larger numbers of interviewers reversed the ratings. In Chicago, 20% of the supervisors who trained more than five interviewers rated the optional briefing techniques as very helpful; after completion of local training, 50% did so.

Over half of the 39 supervisors who responded to the second questionnaire answered our request for suggestions with comments about the specifics of the Chicago sessions. Some thought that individual supervisors should have had the opportunity to privately discuss local problems with NORC or project staff members; others said there should have been less planned activity and more informal discussion. Many had no suggestions but commented favorably on the way the meetings had been planned and conducted.

Almost all of these remarks were positive. "The meetings were of incalculable help," said one participant. "Far more helpful than I thought," another wrote. Reflecting an initial skepticism, a third supervisor commented, "They proved to me that although I know my field work, there are areas in a sex study about which I had little knowledge." Illustrating that in at least one case we got across our idea that the field staff had a crucial role to play, a fourth supervisor noted, "I do not wish to be anonymous—you have made me feel that what I think is important."

While we tried to measure our results as best we could in such ways, this was merely an applied investigation. We have no way to comprehensively evaluate these training sessions; there is no way to tell for certain whether or not better interviews, providing higher-quality data, actually resulted. Nevertheless, it is clear that the supervisors who attended the sessions did regard them as useful.

The most important effect of the training sessions may have been nonspecific. We are fairly certain that the participants learned how to use our questionnaire and how to teach their interviewers to do so. We think that perhaps they also learned how to react (by not reacting) when a respondent's vocabulary of sexual terms was limited to four-letter words. They might have grown more comfortable about asking people they had never met what they thought about sex. But most of all, we believe that they learned in Chicago that the members of the Institute staff were concerned about them and their attitudes and feelings; and this knowledge may have favorably affected the outcome of the survey.

NOTES

1. This appendix was written by Jan Shipps.
2. We were assisted in this by Anthony Banet, at that time Associate Professor of Psychiatry at the Indiana University School of Medicine. A clinical psychologist who is accredited as a group trainer in laboratory education by the International Association of Applied Social Scientists, he has conducted numerous workshops and encounter and sensitivity sessions for many different groups.

Appendix C

Pretesting the Interview[1]

Before we conducted the 1970 survey, we did two pretests with smaller samples. This pretesting was necessary for several reasons. First, as discussed in Appendix B, we needed to find out how difficult it was for the NORC interviewers to ask questions that were much more intimate than they were used to. By the same token, we wanted to find out if any questions would be especially hard for the respondents to answer because, for instance, of ambiguity in wording or the respondent's embarrassment or inability to remember.[2] We planned to use a number of questions new to national survey research, and we needed to see if they might be technically dispensable once the data were gathered, for example, because they provided so little variance in responses that they would not be useful to analyze or because they appeared redundant with responses to a similar question. We also needed to find out how long it would take to administer the questionnaire in actual interviews. Because we would be billed for the interviewers' time, we wanted to keep the interviews short enough to be financially feasible and yet long enough to yield a comprehensive data base. Finally, by repeating pretest interviews with some respondents, we would be able to check on the reliability of our questions—if people tended to answer them the same way each time, it would indicate that the data we were getting were stable and thus amenable to analysis.

The First Pretest

The first pretest was carried out during November and December 1969 with a fairly random nationwide sample of 100 adults (80 selected by block quota, 20 by acquaintance referrals). Most of the 17 pretest interviewers commented favorably on the experience, and the NORC pretest report stated,

The acceptance of this study on the part of our staff, and of the public, has been quite good. The refusal rate seems no higher than normal, and does not relate to the subject matter but rather to the usual "too busy," "not interested," and "just leaving for the store." None of the interviewers has reported any dramatic incident, and definite hostility was apparent in only one area.

The hostility mentioned refers to two Indiana-based NORC interviewers. They accepted pretest assignments as a favor to their local supervisor but strongly objected to the subject matter. The Chicago NORC office did not know this; NORC policy is never to give assignments to interviewers who have objections.

The reports of the 17 interviewers showed that the two Indiana interviewers and one other seriously questioned the feasibility of a survey of this nature; another suspected that her respondents had not reported their sexual experience truthfully. The other 13 matter-of-factly described how well the interviewing went (and 4 were quite enthusiastic about their respondents' interest and cooperation). While a number of respondents felt uneasy or shy in answering questions about their sexual experience, all but a handful overcame this reluctance. This handful included 6 males and 4 females who would not give their age at first masturbation, and 3 females who would not answer questions about same-sex experience. Furthermore, even interviewers anticipating a hostile reception—characteristic of certain neighborhoods to which they were assigned—reported that respondents were friendly and appreciated the importance of such a study about sex.

We were primary concerned in this pretest with two questions: whether responses to some items might prove so negative that there would be too little variability for analysis, and whether there might be either so many refusals to answer or so much denial of experiences that sexual experience data would be unreliable or invalid. However, neither of these concerns appeared warranted from our findings. There was ample variation in the evaluative data, ranging from highs of about 90% judging that sex between a child and adult is "always wrong," down to only about one-third considering premarital intercourse to be "always wrong." In general, between one-third and two-thirds gave this response to such questions as these.[3]

The second concern—about getting valid and reliable sexual experience data—did not appear problematic either. Of the 49 male respondents, only 4 reported never having masturbated (6 withheld answers). Of the 51 females, 23 responded "never" (4 did not answer). These gender-specific proportions are close to what we could expect, so our concern was with those who refused to respond. However, it appeared that a disproportionate number of refusals occurred with the Indiana interviewers who objected to asking such questions. The others who withheld responses, among the 90 interviews elsewhere in the nation, included some who apparently could just not remember how old they were when they first masturbated.

When we asked for age at first heterosexual experience, some respondents apparently thought that we meant only premarital intercourse, although we intended that age at marriage be reported here if that was the first occasion. Thus, only 1 never-married person answered "never," but so did 3 males and 9 females who were married. Of the 49 males, all 7 who had never married reported heterosexual experience, and of the 42 ever-married males 7 (counting the 3 who seem to have misunderstood) reported no premarital sex. Among the 51 females, one of the 5 who had never married reported no heterosexual experience, and 25 (including the 9 who apparently misunderstood) of the rest reported no premarital experience.

Assuming that some married persons did deny opposite-sex experience because they misunderstood this question, the first pretest results were very satisfying in this regard. With all but one of the 12 never-married persons, over 80% of ever-married males, and over 45% of ever-married females reporting premarital experience, we were within the range of what one might expect of an adult sample ranging in age from 20 to 75.

Aside from the question of reported sexual experience, it was also reassuring to find that this loosely applied block quota sampling technique resulted in 10% of the females and 14% of the males never having been married. These percentages are close to independently estimated parameters of the never married and are crucially related to the chances of including in a national sample persons who have extensive involvement in homosexual experience.

Regarding sexual activity with someone of the same sex, we expected 1 or 2 of the 100 persons to be currently involved in homosexuality. However, the less than rigorous sampling procedures for this first pretest provided little basis for such hope. Our findings were thus satisfactory. Of the 49 males in the sample, 3 reported minimal homosexual experience (i.e., 3 or more partners, over 4 to 11 years, "occasionally" or "fairly often"). Of the 51 females, 3 did not answer these items and 3 did report varying amounts of same-sex experience. Two of these had had no such experience since ages 10 and 16 respectively, but the other reported "occasional" homosexual contact between ages 25 and 30, with 2 different partners.

Reliability of the First Pretest[4]

There were reasons to feel unsure about whether the NORC interviewers could get reliable responses on such sensitive matters as respondents' sexual behavior and attitudes. Therefore, as a precaution, we planned follow-up interviews with 25 of the 100 respondents in the first pretest. We conducted these interviews ourselves (to allow respondents to comment on the NORC interviewer they had had) within six weeks after the original interview. We used a structured questionnaire containing some items from the pretest schedule and additional inquiries about the respondents' reaction to the original interview. If responses to the two interviews tended to be alike, we could infer that the main survey data would be reasonably reliable.

Because of our plan for reinterviews, the first pretest questionnaire ended with the question,

This is the first phase of a large survey which is going to be conducted all over the country during the next few months. Members of the study staff at Indiana University may therefore want to talk with some of the people who have been interviewed concerning their impressions about the survey and the questionnaire, and any objections they may have. Would you be willing to have one of the staff members call on you some time in the near future for such a discussion?

Since 76 of the 100 respondents answered "yes" to this question, we anticipated no difficulty in obtaining 25 for follow-up. Based on their age, sex, marital status, and occupation, we selected people to be reinterviewed so as to obtain a fairly heterogeneous subsample.

As it happened, we were unable to reach 9 of our choices, so in the end, 16 respondents were reinterviewed—7 males and 9 females, ranging in age from 21 to 56. Of these, 12 were married, 3 had never been married, and one was currently separated; 8 lived in Chicago, 4 in Indianapolis, and 4 in a rural county in Nebraska.

We made preliminary telephone calls to arrange our visits. During these calls we told the respondents that some of the questions from the pretest questionnaire would be asked again. They were assured, however, that there was no need to try to remember what they had said originally, since the purpose of the second interview was "to see whether the questions are clearly worded so that they always mean the same thing." A letter confirming the appointment described what the interview would be like:

One part of the visit will be to find out whether the questions we are using are worded well enough that they always mean the same thing to people when they are asked. Another part of the visit will be about what kinds of questions were hard to answer. The third part of the visit is to see what general feelings and ideas you have about the interview, and to answer any questions you or other members of your household may want to ask about our study. You really do *not* need to make any preparation for my visit. It does *not* depend on your remembering any details of the interview.

This letter also explained that the person conducting the second interview would have no way of knowing what the respondent had said in the original interview, so that it would be impossible for the interviewer to inquire about it. At the beginning of the reinterview, the respondent was again told "not to think about how you answered the questions in the other interview."

These repeated instructions not to try to recall earlier responses were given to minimize respondents' efforts to force agreement between the two interviews. We were more interested in discovering technical problems such as ambiguity in the wording of questions or failure to provide adequate response categories. Moreover, it probably served to put respondents at ease, thereby enhancing the validity of responses.

The reinterview schedule contained 48 items that were identical to those in the first pretest questionnaire. They covered a wide range of topics, but none in areas that we suspected would be subject to change in the interval between the two interviews. The degree of agreement between interview and reinterview that might be considered acceptable reliability should vary according to the nature of the questions: nonsexual background items would be expected to display the most agreement, questions requiring distant recollection should have the least agreement, and items dealing with current attitudes should fall somewhere in between.

Table C-1 compares the two sets of responses. For some items, the

TABLE C-1 Agreement Between Pretest and Reinterview Responses

Item	Degree of agreement	r_{11}	No answer in pretest (*N*)	Base *N*
Nonsexual background				
Age at last birthday	69%	.93	0	16
Education completed	81	.88	0	16
Ever married	100	1.00	0	16
Number of children	85	.93	0	13
Current marital status	100	1.00	0	16
Sexual circumstances and feelings				
Ever had sex education	88%	.71	0	16
Knows persons with premarital sex experience	94	.97	0	16
Knows persons with homosexual experience	87	.77	1	16
Has received heterosexual overtures	100	1.00	0	16
Has made heterosexual overtures	94	.88	0	16
Has received homosexual overtures	100	1.00	0	16
Has been labeled homosexual	94	.00	0	16
Has thought he or she might be homosexual	100	.00	0	16
Might enjoy homosexual sex	92	.00	2	16

TABLE C-1 (*continued*)

Item	Degree of agreement	r_{11}	No answer in pretest (*N*)	Base *N*
Might enjoy heterosexual sex	100	1.00	0	16
Exposure to sexual phenomena				
Number of acquaintances with premarital sex	73%	.88	1	16
Knew any homosexuals before age 11	100	1.00	0	7
Knew any homosexuals while age 11–13	86	.00	0	7
Knew any homosexuals while age 14–16	100	1.00	0	7
Knew any homosexuals while age 17–19	57	.17	0	7
Knew any homosexuals after age 19	83	.00	1	7
Number of years he or she has known homosexuals	0	.67	0	7
Number of homosexuals around respondent's age	17	.57	1	7
Sociosexual opportunities				
Number of heterosexual overtures received	25%	.65	4	16
Number of heterosexual overtures declined	23	.76	3	16
Number of heterosexual overtures made	29	.98	2	9
Number of heterosexual overtures made and turned down	14	.99	2	9
Number of homosexual overtures received	20	.84	1	6
Number of homosexual overtures declined	33	.74	2	6
Age at first sexual experiences				
Age at first masturbation	25%	.98	7	16
Age at first heterosexual experience	58	.98	4	16
Age at first homosexual experience	81	.43	1	16
Extent of sexual experience				
Number of premarital heterosexual partners	27%	.90	0	11
Number of homosexual partners[a]	0	.00	0	1
Sexual attitudes				
Morality of premarital sex	50%	.78	0	16
Should premarital sex be illegal	81	.30	0	16
Always felt this way about premarital sex	56	.33	0	16
Comparison with parents' view of premarital sex	81	.83	0	16
Children with heterosexual sex play should remain friends	85	.43	0	16
Children with homosexual sex play should remain friends	75	.23	0	16
What parent should do if child masturbates	67	.67	0	16
What parent should do if child engages in heterosexual sex play	56	.33	0	16
What parent should do if child engages in homosexual sex play	63	.51	0	16
Has sex generally been enjoyable	94	.00	0	16

[a] This question was to be asked only if the respondent did give an age at first experience (previous section of the table). There is no agreement because the one respondent in this situation in the reinterview had reported no homosexual experience in the original interview.

percentage of agreement is a more revealing indicator of reliability, while for others the correlation coefficient (r_{11}) provides a more accurate evaluation. For example, there was more than 30% disagreement on the simple item of age ("what was your age on your last birthday?"), but the correlation between the responses obtained on interview and reinterview is .93, and disagreement is due to people whose birthdays fell between interview and reinterview. On the other hand, the item "Have you ever thought you might be homosexual?" yielded 100% agreement but a correlation of zero, because everyone gave the same response ("no").

The findings in Table C-1 can be summarized in the following way. Of 832 possible points of agreement or disagreement between interview and reinterview in the 16 questionnaires, 208, or 25%, were disagreements. The degree of agreement is substantially greater for items requiring only a yes or no response, usually at least 85%. Items requiring exact numerical statements about past events, such as "how many people . . ." or "how old were you when . . ." evoke the lowest degree of exact agreement. It is noteworthy, however, that the correlation between such estimates is often satisfactorily high, even when the percentage of agreement is quite low. And, as Table C-2 shows, if these data are transposed into more general response categories such as 0 to 2, 3 to 5, and so on, the agreement between interview and reinterview improves.

An important aspect of this test-retest reliability comparison has to do with the number of "don't know" or "no answer" responses recorded by the NORC interviewers to questions for which "don't know" was not a permissible answer. There were 32 such instances in the first interviews but none in the reinterviews, so that all of these 32 instances represent

TABLE C-2 Reducing Disagreement by Combining Responses

Item	Actual test-retest disagreements: Uncombined[a]	Actual test-retest disagreements: Combined[a]	Resulting reduction in disagreements
Number of years respondent has known homosexuals	9 (100%)	5 (56%)	4 (44%)
Number of homosexuals around respondent's age	8 (89%)	7 (78%)	1 (11%)
Number of heterosexual overtures received	13 (81%)	12 (75%)	1 (6%)
Number of heterosexual overtures made	7 (78%)	5 (56%)	2 (22%)
Number of homosexual overtures received	5 (83%)	4 (67%)	1 (17%)

[a] "Uncombined" refers to the responses actually given in the interview, i.e., the respondent had to give the exact number. "Combined" means that these responses were grouped in categories, e.g. 0 to 2, 3 to 5, etc.

disagreements. Since there were 592 possible points of this kind of disagreement, NORC interviewers failed to obtain information in 5.4% of instances.

There is, of course, no objective way to determine whether such a percentage should be regarded as high or low. The same applies to the 25% overall degree of test-retest disagreement. Our eventual conclusion was that the degree of agreement was high enough to warrant cautious optimism about the reliability of data to be obtained in the main survey, and low enough to indicate an urgent need for special steps to increase it in the main survey.

Changes in the Wording of the Interview

Reinterviewing gave us a good opportunity to determine how well the questionnaire worked from a technical standpoint. We found that several items needed clarification. The question about number of children, for example, had to specify that it did not refer to adoptions or stepchildren. The phrase "not necessarily as friends" had to be added to queries about having known persons who had premarital sex. Items asking for comparisons between respondents' and their parents' attitudes needed it made clear that we meant whoever had brought up the respondent if the biologic parents did not. Minor changes were made in several other general background and evaluative items.

Some of the questions about sexual experience also needed altering. The queries about sexual advances made to the respondent were made more explicit, the first being changed to read, "Have there been times when someone . . . *clearly* proposed or attempted sexual relations with you," and we added that we meant only situations in which the respondent had to make a definite decision about it. The phrase "not as a joke" was added to the question of whether anyone had ever suggested that the respondent might be homosexual or lesbian. The qualification clause in the item about whether homosexual sex offers any possibility of enjoyment was changed from "if state laws and your own morality did not apply" to "if there were no question of right or wrong." Finally, we added the definition "make [one]self come to a sexual climax" to items about masturbation, a word many respondents apparently did not know.

Questions About Sexual Experience

One important advantage of reinterviewing was that it allowed us to directly observe respondents' reactions to questions about personal sexual experience. We already knew from the pretest interviewers' reports that many of them thought these questions embarrassed the respondents, especially concerning masturbation. Our reinterviewing experiences led us to agree, especially when we noted that 4 of the 16 people said "yes" when asked if any of the questions had forced them to "avoid telling the whole story about what was asked." In addition, when we met with several of the NORC staff members who had worked on the pretest, they pointed out not only that respondents were sometimes uncomfortable answering personal questions but also that the interviewers were sometimes embarrassed to ask them. Taking all these things into account, we decided that it might be better to experiment with a self-administered supplement to gather sexual experience data.

General Evaluation of the Interview

Two questions about the original NORC interviewer were included at the end of the reinterview. One asked if the interviewer had any trouble managing the interview. Only 1 of the 16 reinterviewed people said "yes, very much"; everyone else responded "no, not at all." The other item asked if the interviewer's own sexual attitudes had been apparent from the way the questions were asked; only 2 of the 16 thought this was the case.

Responses to these two questions thus seemed to indicate that the pretest was, in the main, carried out smoothly and effectively by the NORC interviewers. However, when we chatted with the respondents after the reinterview, we found that this was not always true. Some said that although the interviewer had no trouble with the technical details of the questionnaire, there were times when she seemed fairly uncomfortable with its content. Of course, an interviewer's uneasiness could easily have been communicated to respondents.

The reinterviewing process, then, left us with the feeling that some of NORC's interviewers were not totally at ease participating in a survey about sex, as was borne out in their written reports and in our meeting with the NORC staff. Indeed, interviewer anxiety was a matter of such concern that we decided to conduct special training sessions for the main survey (see Appendix B).

In general, we found that most people enjoyed being interviewed. For example, no one said yes to a question asking whether any item in the questionnaire caused resentment or anger. By and large, our informal discussions with respondents also reflected this positive attitude. There were a few negative feelings, however. Three respondents said that the interview made them remember things they would rather forget. Two others said that it aroused feelings of guilt. One said that at least once during the interview he had been sorry that he agreed to it. Another thought that some of the questions were designed to trap him.

In conclusion, then, while this reinterviewing was undertaken primarily for the purpose of evaluating data reliability, it served several other ancillary purposes. We discovered a number of technical problems with the questionnaire. We were able to see for ourselves how respondents reacted to questions about their own sexual experience. We got some indication of the way the original interviews had been conducted by the NORC people. And we formed an overall impression of how people will react to the survey research approach when the subject of the interview is sex. Several major changes in our handling of the second pretest and the main survey resulted.

The Second Pretest

Our second pretest was done in May 1970 with a national sample of 200. Three major tasks were to be accomplished. The two most important consisted of finding ways to reduce the length of the interview, while at the same time including sufficient questions on all the things we considered essential, so that we could arrive at a final questionnaire with an average interview time of 90 minutes. A third task was to experiment with a self-administered booklet on sexual experience, to compare resulting data with that obtained by face-to-face interviewing.

Reducing the Length of the Interview

The following agreement was negotiated with NORC: our project staff would cut the 2-hour, 2-minute questionnaire of the first pretest down to less than 90 minutes; in turn, NORC would forgo the conventional final pretest designed to approximate the interview length planned for the main survey, allowing us to add up to 40 minutes' worth of new material for pretesting.

We used several approaches to reduce interview time. The major approach was to identify areas in the questionnaire that were time-consuming primarily because we were asking for so much detail. For example, we dropped several questions about the sex and birth order of respondents' children, substituting more general inquiries. The greatest reduction of this nature lay in eliminating many questions about erotic materials, an area of less than central interest to us.[5]

In addition, we accomplished reduction by examining groups of related items. Some items in such a group were dropped because they were almost always answered in the same way as others in the group, so that they did not seem to be supplying new information. We also had groups of items in various parts of the questionnaire that we hoped could be used for multiple-item measurement (scaling). From such groups we deleted items that were ambiguous or did not appear to function in the scaling procedure as we had intended. In the end, we retained roughly 85 minutes of the first pretest questionnaire. Thus, we could add new questions constituting 40 to 45 minutes of extra interviewing time.

Estimating Interview Time

For the first pretest, the questionnaire had been divided into 13 sections of varying length, and interviewers had recorded the exact time at which each section was completed. This time-recording enabled us to reliably calculate seconds-per-item throughout the questionnaire. These calculations predicted the length of the second pretest with considerable precision.

We anticipated, as mentioned above (85 minutes plus 40 or 45 minutes), an average interview duration of 2:05 or 2:10 hours. When the second pretest was completed, we found that the actual averages were 2:05 among those interviewed with a self-administered booklet for sexual experience questions and 2:02 for face-to-face interviewing throughout the questionnaire. Thus we and NORC were both confident that we could come up with a final instrument that really would average the 90 minutes allotted to the 3,000 interviews of the main survey.

Experimenting with the Self-Administered Booklet

As indicated, in the second pretest we compared face-to-face interviewing with self-administered booklet methods for reporting sexual experience. Half of the 200 respondents were randomly assigned to using the 12-page booklet, and half were to be asked the same questions face-to-face. In nine cases, respondents in the latter group showed a clear preference for use of the booklet and were accommodated by the interviewers. In six cases, "booklet" respondents had trouble reading, so the interviewers asked the questions aloud. Thus, 103 respondents filled out the booklet and 97 were in the face-to-face group.

A comparison of the two methods of data collection suggested that some "face-to-face" respondents showed a subjective reaction to the interviewer. This seemed to involve reluctance to admit experiences about which they felt guilt or embarrassment and, on the part of males interviewed by females, defense of a conventional masculine image (i.e., less willingness to report homosexual experience and possibly some exaggeration of heterosexual experience). A defensive reaction also appeared among the "booklet" respondents, who more often left some questions unanswered; but at the same time they reported more sexual experience than the other group. On the other hand, the face-to-face situation allowed interviewers to press for answers from reluctant respondents, but when they did, the respondents seemed more likely to deny having had the experience in question. This pattern was complicated by the fact that much of the failure to answer occurred in the last 2 pages of the 12-page booklet, which had a very packed—and therefore formidable-looking—format of questions. Thus, if we took care to improve the format in the main survey, we might reduce the no-answer problem, and the self-administered booklet could be the method of choice.

In addition, some of the 30 interviewers in the second pretest indicated that respondents were generally more at ease in using the self-administered booklet and also, at least implicitly, that they themselves preferred it. While none of them complained of obscenity or "prurient interest" in the questionnaire (as 3 first-pretest interviewers had done), 5 indicated some embarrassment and another 4 thought the respondents needed more privacy. A substantial minority (13) reported enjoying this study less than other NORC surveys. Thus, if both interviewers and respondents felt uneasy with the face-to-face method, the booklet seemed better to use. In short, four major considerations presented themselves:

1. Substantially more respondents—especially among males—reported sexual experience (sometimes two or three times as high a percentage) in the privacy of the self-administered booklet, as compared with answering an interviewer.
2. Interviewers more frequently sensed uneasiness and lack of candor when respondents were required to answer face-to-face.
3. Having to ask for self-reports of sexual experiences caused some discomfort for a minority of the interviewers.
4. Respondents more frequently failed to answer questions in the self-administered booklet.

All but the last of these considerations suggested that the self-administered booklet would be better to use. Still, we could examine respondents who failed to answer booklet questions for distinctive characteristics, as revealed elsewhere in the interview. Consequently, both Institute and NORC staff agreed that the self-administered booklet, in a somewhat shortened version, should be used in the main survey.

Development of the Final Questionnaire

Since the second pretest took, as predicted, an average of 125 minutes to administer, we needed to shorten the questionnaire again to reduce the average time to 90 minutes. This was an overriding consideration in developing the final instrument. In general, we used the methods and kinds of reasoning described earlier to cut 15 minutes from the part of the questionnaire that had survived the first pretest. Substantial reductions occurred basically in two areas.

First, as mentioned previously, items concerning erotic materials were most tenuous, since we would not get financial support for this part of the study. Having determined that time pressures must prevail, we dropped the remaining items in this area.

The other large reduction occurred in the lengthy lists of items about attitudes toward homosexuals and homosexuality. Some items that had previously distinguished between male and female homosexuals were combined (i.e., reference to gender was dropped), since the pretest respondents tended not to make such distinctions in their own attitudes. Other items were eliminated on the basis of similarity or on judgments of research relevance. In the end, these lists were reduced roughly by half.

By the end of the second pretest, we were able to evaluate the wording and format of questions about sexual norms. For example, in the pretesting, we made age (under 20 and 20 or older) and gender distinctions regarding the moral acceptability of masturbation. However, in the final questionnaire these distinctions were dropped in favor of a single question about masturbation in general. A single question of this kind also proved sufficient for prostitution, for extramarital sex, and for homosexual activity (although here we did retain affectional distinctions).

In the area of premarital sex, we originally had questions distinguishing among three age groups (teenagers, young adults, and older adults) and in terms of affection, relational commitment, and gender. Pretest data showed that some of these distinctions made little or no difference, so we eliminated these. The age distinction was reduced to teenager versus adult. The affection distinction—whether or not the people were in love—was retained, but we dropped commitment in the form of engagement to marry. Thus, in the final survey the 18 questions about the morality of premarital sex were reduced to 8.

We had originally wanted to assess moral evaluations of sexual behaviors so universally disapproved that responses to such items could serve as an anchor point in a scale measure of sexual morality. Both pretests therefore included questions about adults initiating sexual contact with children—their own and, in the first pretest, someone else's. But the pretest data on the one hand belied the "universal taboo" proposition, with 91% to 94% (i.e., not 100%) responding "always wrong" to these questions. On the other hand, for statistical purposes the less than 10 percent giving other responses leaves so little variance to be explained that these items would not be analytically useful. Consequently they were omitted from the final questionnaire.

Finally, we cut out 20 minutes by reducing material added and tested for the first time in the second pretest. Since this material involved about 40 minutes of interview time, we used the same approaches as before to shorten each of these additional sections by half. Thus, we had taken out 35 minutes altogether, leaving for the main survey the required average of 90 minutes' interviewing time.

Comparisons Among Samples

Table C-3 presents data on moral evaluations of every kind of sexual behavior for which we have at least two different samplings. Actually, of the 14 different behaviors included, all except the parent-child sex item are based on three samples: the first pretest ($N = 100$), the second pretest ($N = 200$), and the main national survey sample ($N = 3,018$). As just explained, the parent-child item had to be excluded from the main survey. While in our main analyses of these data only those of the main survey were used, all of these data have played a role in decisions regarding data reliability, soundness of sampling methods, and possibilities of sample bias.

In this table, the percentage distribution of responses in each of the three samples reads from left to right. We can see how the three groups of respondents differ by reading down any of the columns for a particular response. For clarity, we will limit our comparisons to the most extreme responses, "always wrong" (the first column in the table) and "not wrong at all" (the fourth column).

Looking down these columns, we can see that in most cases, differences among the three samples are very small, ranging over no more than 10 percentage points. Thus these data cannot be said to be overly subjective or "soft"—unreliable and subject to vicissitudes of mood or situation. The table shows that, at least for the period of the year that elapsed between first pretest and main survey, there is considerable reliability and stability in the standards being tapped.

Two items, however, do show appreciable differences: those evaluating prostitution and extramarital sex. Compared with respondents in the main survey, those in the first pretest were less likely to rate prostitution as always wrong (57% vs. 43%), although responses in the other categories are distributed similarly. Regarding extramarital sex, there is an even greater difference: 72% in the main survey but 44% in the first pretest said it is always wrong; conversely, 17% of the first pretest but just 2% of the main survey said extramarital sex is not wrong at all. Furthermore, even though differences between those two samples are otherwise too slight to be notable, it does appear throughout that the first-pretest respondents tended to be a little less conservative in their responses than either of the other two samples.

We view this tendency as evidence of the difficulties with the first pretest mentioned earlier, especially the sampling employed. We know that although the first pretest, involving 100 interviews, was done according to national sampling specifications, NORC was somewhat lenient about the degree to which some of their interviewers met those specifications. Some of the interviewers were extremely uncomfortable with the sexual content of the questionnaire, so much so that a few got permission to find friends or use referrals of friends to fill their assigned quotas. Apparently these referrals tended to be somewhat liberal people, whose own attitudes would be less likely to add to the interviewer's discomfort. If so, first-pretest responses might be somewhat more liberal overall. We do not claim to understand why this should be more pronounced for the items on prostitution or extramarital sex; perhaps it is due to sampling error, or just to chance.

The second-pretest respondents tended not to differ importantly from the other two samples. Generally they fall in between the others, responding slightly less liberally than the first pretest and slightly less conservatively than the main sample. The only exception is, again, in responses of "always wrong" to extramarital sex, where this tendency appears as a definite difference (of 14 percentage points in either direction). However, as in the main survey, hardly any of the second-pretest respondents say it is not wrong at all.[6]

What can we infer from these comparisons? Bearing in mind that for the most part there are no real differences among the three samples, just fairly consistent but small trends, we can conclude that there seems to be a relationship between the quality of sampling and the quality of resulting data. We have already indicated that sampling methods in the first pretest were less than rigorously applied. There was no such flaw in the sampling of the second pretest; however, as described in Appendix B, we took special pains to enhance the quality of the sampling for the main survey. That is, differences between the second pretest and the main survey may be ascribed to the special training program for NORC field supervisors, which was intended to encourage in the interviewers greater than usual tact and understanding in dealing with respondents and a strong commitment to the success of the project. We wanted them to be comfortable and at ease with their work, given the difficulties of securing and conducting interviews with sensitive content. According to the data in Table C-3, this effort seems to have been successful. As to the slight extent that the main survey respondents are more conservative, it is possible that this extra training enabled interviewers to get cooperation from extremely conservative respondents who might otherwise have refused.

Later Evaluation of Data Quality

One additional kind of comparison can be made in assessing the quality of our sampling: comparison with a later survey. NORC does a General Social Survey annually as part of the National Data Program for the Social Sciences, funded by the National Science Foundation. Since these annual surveys involve samples just like ours, data from them will be

TABLE C-3 Reports of Sexual Norms in Pretests and Main Survey

Behavior	Always wrong	Almost always wrong	Wrong only sometimes	Not wrong at all	Don't know[a]	Row total	Base *N*
Masturbation							
First pretest	21.0%	19.0	25.0	28.0	7.0	100.0%	100
Second pretest	21.5%	21.0	33.5	22.0	2.0	100.0%	200
Main survey	26.9%	21.0	29.8	18.8	3.5	100.0%	3,018
Prostitution							
First pretest	43.0%	17.0	23.0	17.0	0.0	100.0%	100
Second pretest	46.5%	20.5	21.0	11.0	1.0	100.0%	200
Main survey	57.1%	14.8	16.3	11.1	0.7	100.0%	3,018
Extramarital sex							
First pretest	44.0%	17.0	22.0	17.0	0.0	100.0%	100
Second pretest	58.0%	25.5	12.5	3.5	0.5	100.0%	200
Main survey	72.3%	14.3	10.8	2.2	0.5	100.1%	3,018
Homosexuality with affection							
First pretest	68.0%	9.0	7.0	15.0	1.0	100.0%	100
Second pretest	72.0%	8.0	8.0	10.5	1.5	100.0%	200
Main survey	70.3%	8.4	7.2	11.5	2.6	100.0%	3,018
Homosexuality without affection							
First pretest	74.0%	10.0	7.0	8.0	1.0	100.0%	100
Second pretest	81.5%	9.0	3.5	5.5	0.5	100.0%	200
Main survey	77.7%	8.4	6.4	5.7	1.8	100.0%	3,018
Parent-child sex							
First pretest	91.0%	5.0	1.0	0.0	3.0	100.0%	100
Second pretest	92.5%	3.5	3.0	0.5	0.5	100.0%	200
Main survey			[not asked; see text]				
Premarital sex by teenage girl, not in love							
First pretest	59.0%	7.0	23.0	11.0	0.0	100.0%	100
Second pretest	60.5%	18.5	12.5	7.5	1.0	100.0%	200
Main survey	67.9%	14.4	11.3	5.8	0.7	100.1%	3,018

Premarital sex by teenage girl, in love							
First pretest	44.0%	11.0	21.0	23.0	1.0	100.0%	100
Second pretest	40.0%	19.5	22.0	17.5	1.0	100.0%	200
Main survey	45.9%	17.5	17.3	18.6	0.7	100.0%	3,018
Premarital sex by teenage boy, not in love							
First pretest	51.0%	11.0	20.0	16.0	2.0	100.0%	100
Second pretest	50.0%	18.0	19.5	10.0	2.5	100.0%	200
Main survey	53.3%	19.5	17.0	9.4	0.8	100.0%	3,018
Premarital sex by teenage boy, in love							
First pretest	34.0%	14.0	19.0	31.0	2.0	100.0%	100
Second pretest	33.5%	20.0	22.5	21.0	3.0	100.0%	200
Main survey	37.3%	19.1	20.4	22.3	0.8	99.9%	3,018
Premarital sex by adult woman, not in love							
First pretest	55.0%	6.0	16.0	23.0	0.0	100.0%	100
Second pretest	48.5%	17.0	16.5	16.5	1.5	100.0%	200
Main survey	55.3%	15.0	15.3	13.7	0.7	100.0%	3,018
Premartial sex by adult woman, in love							
First pretest	35.0%	11.0	21.0	33.0	0.0	100.0%	100
Second pretest	26.5%	16.5	18.5	36.0	1.0	100.0%	200
Main survey	36.4%	15.1	17.3	30.5	0.7	100.0%	3,018
Premarital sex by adult man, not in love							
First pretest	44.0%	9.0	21.0	26.0	0.0	100.0%	100
Second pretest	41.5%	18.5	20.5	18.5	1.0	100.0%	200
Main survey	50.1%	15.2	17.2	16.7	0.8	100.0%	3,018
Premarital sex by adult man, in love							
First pretest	29.0%	9.0	23.0	39.0	0.0	100.0%	100
Second pretest	24.5%	16.0	19.5	38.0	2.0	100.0%	200
Main survey	33.3%	14.2	18.4	33.3	0.9	100.1%	3,018

[a] Includes "no answer" because of the small *n* involved. For example, among the main survey respondents, 106 are in this column for masturbation; of these, 102 are people who did not know how to judge the morality of masturbation, and only 4 are people who failed to answer.

directly comparable to ours, provided that the questions and response categories are the same. We have already noted in Chapter 5 that in the years 1972 through 1978, the moral evaluation of various sexual behaviors closely resembled what we have found ourselves (see Table 5-7, page 134). Thus, in representative samples the same degrees of liberalism and conservatism continue to appear.

For example, in our own survey, about 12% said that homosexuality in the presence of "special affection" is not wrong at all. In 1973, three years later, 11% of 1,417 respondents (who were not offered any qualification respecting the relationship) said homosexuality is not wrong at all; this response was also given by 13% of a sample of 1,361 in 1974, by 16% of 1,426 in 1976, and by 15% of 1,453 in 1977. These percentage differences are so small as to permit the inference that our own data are satisfactorily valid. In fact, Table 5-7 reveals distributions so nearly identical that one might be tempted to disregard that our survey asked about affection between the partners while the others did not. We would rather take this into account by making an observation about the experience of being interviewed. When respondents are asked a question that involves no qualification and must consider choosing a response as absolute as "always wrong," it may be implicit to them that they must privately consider any qualifications before answering. This would suggest that some of the later respondents made allowances for whatever qualification came to mind; a loving relationship must surely be one of the most important anyone might think of. Speculative though this may be, it does imply that we might expect a closer agreement between the subsequent data and the 1970 item specifying love than between the former and the 1970 item stipulating no affection, where only 6% said "not wrong at all."

We can consider the foregoing differences of a few percentage points to be virtually no differences only if we are dealing with truly representative samples that can accurately depict diversity and similarity in the general public. In the following appendix we describe our own sample and show why it is satisfactory in this regard. The final interview schedule and respondents' answers classified by gender appear in Appendix F.

NOTES

1. This appendix was written by Jan Shipps.
2. The questionnaires used in the two pretests that we describe are not fully reproduced here. The final interview schedule appears in Appendix F.
3. As in the main 1970 survey, questions about the morality of sexual behaviors on both pretests allowed four responses (as well as "don't know"): "always

wrong," "almost always wrong," "wrong only sometimes," and "not wrong at all."

4. The reinterviewing program was not primarily concerned with the *validity* of the questionnaire. A number of items allowing cross-checking were included in the schedule to provide for an assessment of validity. In addition, the training program described in Appendix B was designed to enhance validity by creating a relaxed and confident interview situation.
5. At one point the President's Commission on Obscenity and Pornography had offered to underwrite this part of the survey, but in the end they were unable to do so. Since the questions we had included on this topic in anticipation of possible funding would have increased the interview time, necessitating additional financial support, we excluded some from the second pretest and, ultimately, all from the final interview.
6. We do not have data to ascertain whether experience with extramarital sex may have affected evaluations of it in any of the three samples.

Appendix D

The Sample

The way in which particular individuals are selected to be respondents in a survey—that is, the sample design—is crucial in a study like ours, where the aim is to achieve a probability sample representative of the adult population of the United States. Such representativeness means that every adult should have an equal chance of being interviewed and that each person chosen represents, in proportion, thousands of others with the same sociological characteristics (e.g., age, education, geographic region). Thus, with a representative sample the researcher can generalize findings to the population at large. In this appendix we describe how our sample of 3,018 was drawn and then compare it with national Census data collected the same year to see how closely representative it is.

Probability sampling is a complicated and expensive technique. Therefore, as indicated earlier, we subcontracted this part of our work to the National Opinion Research Center (NORC). In an initial stage, NORC's national probability sampling procedure has involved listing the states and parts of each state with a count of their populations, so that geographically defined primary sampling units (PSUs), all with chances of inclusion equal to their proportion of the nation's population, can be randomly selected on the basis of the necessary sampling interval. A PSU may consist of part or all of a city or part or all of a county, depending, again, on each's population. Then within the PSU, sample segments are defined, with known population characteristics, to provide a basis for a national master sample. This enables NORC sampling design to select blocks of a city or rural mail routes at random to constitute a final sample for a given survey. The advantage of our employing NORC for our sampling was that the hardest part of the job was already done: they had established PSUs (73 metropolitan areas and 61 less urbanized or rural counties) where local residents had already been trained and were working as professional interviewers under NORC supervision.

For the purposes of our sample survey needs, there are basically two alternative choices for probability sampling at this "block" or "route" level: using "call-backs" and using "quotas" (Sudman, 1967). With call-backs, the interviewer is told exactly how to select dwellings and persons within them, on a random basis, and to look for respondents and, if no one is home, to keep trying. This maximizes both the random and the representative qualities of the sample. With quotas, the technique chosen for this study, the interviewer is told where to begin (e.g., at the northwest corner of the block) and how many men or women of whatever particular characteristics or "sampling parameters" to interview.[1] If the people in the first house refuse or are not home, the interviewer simply continues on throughout the neighborhood until the quotas are filled.

The advantage of using quotas instead of call-backs is economy. Interviewers must be paid for their time in the field whether they are actually interviewing or just canvassing; the data come in more slowly with call-backs (since it may take many calls to secure one interview), so that initial processing may be spread over a much longer time, and the interviewing staff must be paid regardless of the outcome. On the other hand, there is the problem of sample bias—the extent to which the eventual sample is really not representative. Unknown, uncontrolled bias is present in either kind of sample but is harder to estimate and is greater in a quota sample. However, this risk of greater bias is reported to be generally negligible for all but the most precision-oriented surveys. We did not consider this degree of precision as paramount for our study; rather, a primary concern was having enough cases for elaborate cross-classification.

Our choice of quota over call-back sampling, then, was based on cost, time, and quality considerations. Field expenses would be only half as much as if call-backs were used, time in the field would be shorter, and we felt that quota sampling would provide a sample of adequate quality for the analyses we intended.

The size of our final sample—3,018 adults—was also dictated by our analytic requirements. It was decided that for a 95% level of confidence (i.e., reproducibility), our sample must consist of approximately 1,500 males and 1,500 females to narrow the margin of error to less than one percent in estimation of a parameter of 4 percent. To judge how representative our final sample of 3,018 adults was, we present comparisons between our data and data from the 1970 Census. Strict comparability is not always possible because of Census classification schemes we could not reproduce with our data; for example, we had few respondents below the age of 21.[2] Thus we had proportionately fewer persons in the youngest categories than the Census did.

We do not report on the statistical significance of the differences between our sample and Census data. Because of sample sizes, very small percentage differences will be statistically significant. Thus we comment only on differences that might illustrate a trend or that are at least 5% in magnitude.[3]

Age, Sex, and Race

Tables D-1 and D-2 compare our 1970 NORC sample with 1970 Census data for age, sex, and racial categories. For males there appears to have been a good fit, except in the case of underrepresented middle-aged black males. For females, the fit was less neat, with oversampling of young nonblacks and undersampling of both blacks and nonblacks over 65. The last column of each table shows that when age is disregarded, our sample had proportionately fewer white males and females and proportionately more black males and females. Overall, about 9% of the population age 25 and older in 1970 were black, yet blacks comprise almost 16% of our NORC sample.[4]

The bottom rows of Tables D-1 and D-2 reflect the sex ratio within the races. Among nonblacks, although females slightly outnumbered males in both samples, in the Census figures this difference was greater. For blacks, however, in the NORC sample there were more males than females, but the Census data reversed this proportion. (Census sex ratios are given in Table D-3). Thus, apart from the black-versus-white proportions, males of both races were overrepresented.

Finally, looking at age groups among blacks (the last column), the bias in our sample can be seen more clearly. For black females our NORC sample approximated Census data except in the case of those aged 45–64, where we oversampled. For black males, we had more in each category than shown by Census data, especially in the youngest age group. Thus we can say that with regard to age, sex, and race, our NORC sample was somewhat biased in that we oversampled young black males.

Urban-Rural Differences

Many studies of sexual behavior and attitudes have neglected that part of the population that lives and works outside of urban and suburban areas. We were interested in including these persons as representatively as possible. Tables D-4 through D-6 compare "farm" and "nonfarm" respondents on the basis of current occupation and of current residence. Although in most cases the latter basis provided a closer fit, the bias in

TABLE D-1 Males 25 and Older, Age by Race, 1970

Age	Black		Not black		Total		Percent black	
	Census	NORC	Census	NORC	Census	NORC	Census	NORC
25–44	49.1%	51.2%	44.7%	43.6%	45.1%	44.8%	10.0	18.1
45–64	36.5	31.1	38.8	35.3	38.6	34.7	8.6	14.2
65 and older	14.4	17.7	16.5	21.1	16.3	20.6	8.1	13.7
Total	100.0%	100.0%	100.0%	100.0%	100.0%	100.1%	8.9	15.9
Base N^a	4,719	209	46,837	1,109	51,556	1,318	51,556	1,318
					Female	1,328		1,328
					Under 25	369		369
					NA, age	3		3
					Total NORC sample	3,018		3,018
Percent male	45.8	50.6	47.5	49.6	47.4	49.8		
Base N^a	10,089	413	98,112	2,228	109,311	2,641		
					Other race	5		
					Under 25	369		
					NA, age	3		
					Total NORC sample	3,018		

[a] 1970 Census *N*'s are given in 000's.

TABLE D-2 Females 25 and Older, Age by Race, 1970

Age	Black		Not black		Total		Percent black	
	Census	NORC	Census	NORC	Census	NORC	Census	NORC
25–44	49.0%	53.9%	41.6%	51.9%	42.3%	52.2%	11.4	15.9
45–64	35.4	37.3	37.8	34.7	37.6	35.1	9.2	16.3
65 and older	15.7	8.8	20.6	13.4	20.1	12.7	7.7	10.7
Total	100.1%	100.0%	100.0%	100.0%	100.0%	100.0%	9.5	15.4
Base N^a	5,670	204	52,069	1,124	57,739	1,328	57,739	1,328
					Male	1,318		1,318
					Under 25	369		369
					NA, age	3		3
					Total NORC sample	3,018		3,018
Percent female	54.2	49.4	52.5	50.4	52.6	50.2		
Base N^a	10,089	413	98,112	2,228	109,311	2,641		
					Other race	5		
					Under 25	369		
					NA, age	3		
					Total NORC sample	3,018		

[a] 1970 Census *N*'s are given in 000's.

TABLE D-3 Basis for Age-Race-Sex Distributions in 1970 Census Data

Age	Black		Not black	
	Sex ratio	*N* (000's)	Sex ratio	*N* (000's)
25–44	83.6 M	2,317.77	97.0 M	20,957.23
	100.0 F	2,776.23	100.0 F	21,638.77
Base *N* (000's)		5,094		42,596
45–64	85.9 M	1,722.80	92.2 M	18,169.92
	100.0 F	2,006.20	100.0 F	19,707.08
Base *N* (000's)		3,729		37,877
65 and older	76.4 M	678.08	71.9 M	7,709.91
	100.0 F	887.92	100.0 F	10,723.09
Base *N* (000's)		1,566		18,433

NOTE: These figures exclude *Statistical Abstracts* data for Alaska and Hawaii.

our NORC sample tended to remain regardless of how "farm" was defined. One exception was among the youngest (21–24) group of "farm" respondents: undersampling appears in all three tables for the occupation criterion but not for that using place of residence, which increases the size of the "farm" population. In contrast, the oldest "farm" males appear oversampled more in terms of occupation than in terms of residence. Bias is more consistent in the larger, "nonfarm" group. Here, the oversampling is among females aged 25–34, while females 65 and older are underrepresented, as are the youngest group of "nonfarm" males.

Altogether, then, bias in the NORC sample appears to have involved interviewing too many elderly farm males and young nonfarm females, and too few young nonfarm males and elderly nonfarm females. These differences between NORC and Census data tend, however, not to be great.

Education

Tables D-7 and D-8 show the educational experience of our sample compared with Census data. Taking whites and other nonblack respondents first, the total column shows that we somewhat overrepresented those with at least some college education. Looking further into the table we see that this was especially so for the groups aged 25–44, the largest discrepancy being for the 30–34 age group. The data in Table D-9 suggest that this bias was especially present among females.

For blacks in our sample, a similar bias occurred, with an oversampling of those with college education. The biggest difference, again, is to be found among those aged 30–34. This age category seems particu-

TABLE D-4 U.S. Population 21 and Older, Age by Farm/Nonfarm, 1970

	Farm			Nonfarm			Total	
Age	Census	NORC: farming as occupation	NORC: farm as residence size	Census	NORC: farming as occupation	NORC: farm as residence size	Census	NORC
21–24	8.5%	2.2%	9.3%	13.1%	10.3%	10.1%	12.9%	10.0%
25–34	13.0	13.0	18.9	20.1	24.7	24.2	19.8	23.7
35–44	18.0	15.1	16.1	18.3	20.6	20.3	18.3	19.9
45–54	21.2	20.5	18.9	18.3	18.7	18.3	18.4	18.4
55–64	20.4	21.1	16.4	14.5	12.6	12.7	14.7	13.0
65 and older	19.0	28.1	20.4	15.8	13.0	14.4	15.9	15.0
Total	100.1%	100.0%	100.0%	100.1%	99.9%	100.0%	100.0%	100.0%
Base *N*[a]	5,906	185	280	120,204	2,585[b]	2,660[c]	126,110	2,940
							Under 21	75
							NA, age	3
							Total NORC sample	3,018

[a] 1970 Census *N*'s are given in 000's.

[b] Excluded are 24 respondents with military occupations, 110 with no main earner, and 36 noncodable with respect to occupation.

[c] Included are 3 respondents noncodable with respect to residence size.

TABLE D-5 Males 21 and Older, Age by Farm/Nonfarm, 1970

	Farm			Nonfarm			Total	
Age	Census	NORC: farming as occupation	NORC: farm as residence size	Census	NORC: farming as occupation	NORC: farm as residence size	Census	NORC
21–24	8.9%	0.9%	7.9%	13.5%	9.5%	9.2%	13.2%	9.1%
25–34	12.3	13.1	18.6	20.9	22.7	22.4	20.5	22.0
35–44	17.2	14.0	15.0	18.9	19.3	19.1	18.8	18.7
45–54	20.5	17.8	18.6	18.6	18.9	18.2	18.7	18.3
55–64	21.3	21.5	15.7	14.4	12.7	13.0	14.7	13.2
65 and older	19.9	32.7	24.3	13.8	16.9	18.1	14.1	18.7
Total	100.1%	100.0%	100.1%	100.1%	100.0%	100.0%	100.0%	100.0%
Base *N*[a]	3,016	107	140	56,721	1,282	1,310	59,737	1,450
							Female	1,490
							Under 21	75
							NA, age	3
							Total NORC sample	3,018

[a] 1970 Census *N*'s are given in 000's.

TABLE D-6 Females 21 and Older, Age by Farm/Nonfarm, 1970

	Farm			Nonfarm			Total	
Age	Census	NORC: farming as occupation	NORC: farm as residence size	Census	NORC: farming as occupation	NORC: farm as residence size	Census	NORC
21–24	8.0%	3.8%	10.7%	12.8%	11.1%	10.9%	12.6%	10.9%
25–34	13.8	12.8	19.3	19.4	26.7	26.1	19.1	25.4
35–44	18.8	16.7	17.1	17.8	21.9	21.5	17.9	21.1
45–54	21.8	24.4	19.3	17.9	18.6	18.4	18.1	18.5
55–64	19.4	20.5	17.1	14.5	12.5	12.4	14.8	12.8
65 and older	18.1	21.8	16.4	17.5	9.1	10.8	17.5	11.3
Total	99.9%	100.0%	99.9%	99.9%	99.9%	100.1%	100.0%	100.0%
Base N[a]	2,890	78	140	63,484	1,303	1,350	66,374	1,490
							Male	1,450
							Under 21	75
							NA, age	3
							Total NORC sample	3,018

[a] 1970 Census *N*'s are given in 000's.

TABLE D-7 Blacks 20 and Older, Education by Age, 1970

	20–24		25–29		30–34		35–44		45–54		55 and older		Total[a]	
Education level	Census	NORC	Census	NORC	Census	NORC	Census	NORC	Census	NORC	Census	NORC	Census	NORC
4 grades or less	1.6%	0.0%	2.5%	0.0%	3.3%	0.0%	7.1%	5.0%	12.4%	15.7%	34.2%	39.3%	15.1%	14.9%
5–7 grades	3.8	3.1	4.7	6.3	9.8	3.0	12.7	14.0	20.0	18.0	26.3	20.6	16.7	13.9
8th grade	3.9	3.1	5.6	2.1	4.6	6.1	10.9	11.0	15.2	13.5	13.9	10.3	11.2	9.5
Some high school	25.7	32.3	31.3	31.3	32.3	36.4	27.8	33.0	23.3	24.7	12.5	14.0	23.3	26.6
High school graduation	42.4	41.5	39.0	41.7	37.6	30.3	29.4	21.0	19.8	14.6	7.7	6.5	23.4	19.8
Some college	19.3	16.9	9.8	12.5	7.8	18.2	7.0	12.0	5.5	10.1	2.5	6.5	5.9	11.2
B.A. or more	3.3	3.1	7.3	6.3	4.6	6.1	5.2	4.0	3.8	3.4	2.9	2.8	4.5	4.1
Total	100.0%	100.0%	100.0%	100.2%	100.0%	100.1%	100.1%	100.0%	100.0%	100.0%	100.0%	100.0%	100.1%	100.0%
Base *N*[a]	1,826	65	1,453	48	1,198	66	2,347	100	2,128	89	2,962	107	10,089	410
													Not black	2,231
													Under 20	38
													20–24	331
													NA, age	3
													NA, education	5
													Total NORC sample	3,018

[a] Excluding those under 25. [b] 1970 Census *N*'s are given in 000's.

TABLE D-8 Nonblacks 20 and Older, Education by Age, 1970

	20–24		25–29		30–34		35–44		45–54		55 and older		Total[a]	
Education level	Census	NORC	Census	NORC	Census	NORC	Census	NORC	Census	NORC	Census	NORC	Census	NORC
4 grades or less	0.8%	0.0%	0.9%	0.0%	1.4%	0.7%	2.2%	2.3%	2.7%	1.6%	8.4%	4.9%	4.3%	2.5%
5–7 grades	1.9	1.9	2.2	2.3	3.3	1.8	5.4	3.7	6.5	5.5	14.6	13.0	8.3	6.6
8th grade	2.8	1.9	4.0	3.9	5.2	1.8	8.1	7.5	11.7	12.0	23.7	25.0	13.6	12.8
Some high school	12.0	12.4	15.1	17.7	15.8	16.2	17.4	17.6	17.9	22.0	16.0	19.9	16.5	19.0
High school graduation	43.1	41.0	44.7	37.6	44.5	41.0	41.8	36.0	39.9	33.9	22.1	18.7	35.1	30.9
Some college	30.0	34.2	15.5	22.5	13.6	17.3	11.5	15.7	10.6	15.5	7.7	12.2	10.6	15.7
B.A. or more	9.5	8.6	17.5	16.1	16.3	21.0	13.7	17.2	10.6	9.5	7.9	6.3	11.7	12.5
Total	100.1%	100.0%	99.9%	100.1%	100.1%	99.8%	100.1%	100.0%	99.9%	100.0%	100.4%	100.0%	100.1%	100.0%
Base N^b	13,767	266	12,060	311	10,154	271	20,674	483	21,170	451	35,164	715	99,222	2,231
													Black	410
													Under 20	38
													20–24	331
													NA, age	3
													NA, education	5
													Total NORC sample	3,018

[a] Excluding those under 25. [b] 1970 Census N's are given in 000's.

TABLE D-9 U.S. Population 25 and Older, Education by Race and Sex, 1970

	Black				White				Both races				Total	
	Male		Female		Male		Female		Male		Female			
Education Level	Census	NORC	Census	NORC	Census	NORC	Census	NORC	Census	NORC	Census	NORC	Census	NORC
4 grades or less	18.6%	19.8%	12.1%	9.9%	4.5%	3.4%	3.9%	1.5%	5.9%	6.0%	4.7%	2.8%	5.3%	4.4%
5–7 grades	16.0	15.9	17.3	11.8	8.8	7.7	7.8	5.6	9.4	9.0	8.8	6.6	9.1	7.8
8th grade	11.1	5.3	11.3	13.8	13.9	12.4	13.4	13.3	13.6	11.3	13.1	13.3	13.4	12.3
Some high school	21.9	25.6	24.5	27.6	14.1	17.8	17.3	20.3	16.1	19.0	18.0	21.4	17.1	20.2
High school graduation	22.2	18.4	24.4	21.2	30.9	28.2	39.0	33.5	30.1	26.6	37.5	31.7	34.0	29.2
Some college	5.7	11.6	6.0	10.8	11.3	15.1	10.1	16.3	0.8	14.5	9.7	15.4	10.2	15.0
B.A. or more	4.6	3.4	4.4	4.9	15.0	15.4	8.6	9.5	14.1	13.5	8.2	8.8	11.0	11.2
Total	100.1%	100.0%	100.0%	100.0%	98.5%	100.0%	100.1%	100.0%	100.0%	99.9%	100.0%	100.0%	100.1%	100.1%
Base N^a	4,619	207	5,470	203	46,606	1,107	51,506	1,124	51,784	1,314	57,527	1,327	109,310	2,641
													Under 25	369
													NA, race	3
													NA, education	3
													NA, both	2
													Total NORC sample	3,018

[a] 1970 Census N's are given in 000's.

TABLE D-10 U.S. Population 21 and Older, Age by Geographic Locale, 1970

Age	New England		Mid-Atlantic		East North Central		West North Central		South Atlantic	
	Census	NORC	Census	NORC	Census	NORC	Census	NORC	Census	NORC
21–24	10.3%	8.8%	9.3%	10.7%	10.3%	11.6%	10.0%	8.7%	11.2%	10.8%
25–34	19.3	19.7	19.1	24.7	20.5	23.3	19.2	18.7	20.8	23.6
35–44	18.2	24.5	18.9	23.6	19.0	21.1	17.7	17.6	18.9	15.4
45–54	19.3	16.3	19.8	18.4	19.2	19.2	18.0	22.1	18.5	18.8
55–64	15.4	18.4	16.1	12.9	15.0	13.4	15.6	14.2	14.8	11.8
65 and older	17.5	12.2	16.8	9.6	15.9	11.3	19.6	18.7	15.8	19.5
Total	100.0%	99.9%	100.0%	99.9%	99.9%	99.9%	100.1%	100.0%	100.1%	99.9%
Base *N*[b]	7,267	147	23,294	559	23,296	558	9,808	289	18,516	415
Percent of total U.S. population	6.0	5.0	19.1	19.0	19.6	19.0	8.0	9.8	15.2	14.1

Age	East South Central		West South Central		Mountain		Pacific[a]		Total	
	Census	NORC	Census	NORC	Census	NORC	Census	NORC	Census	NORC
21–24	10.6%	7.9%	11.1%	7.8%	11.6%	14.4%	11.2%	8.6%	10.5%	10.0%
25–34	20.2	24.5	20.8	26.3	21.8	22.1	21.6	26.3	20.5	23.7
35–44	18.5	19.4	18.9	16.5	19.4	27.9	19.0	18.5	18.8	19.9
45–54	18.2	14.4	18.0	18.2	18.5	14.4	19.0	17.2	18.9	18.4
55–64	15.6	13.7	15.1	12.9	14.2	11.5	14.2	11.3	15.2	13.0
65 and older	16.8	20.1	16.2	18.2	14.6	9.6	15.1	18.1	16.4	15.0
Total	100.0%	100.0%	100.1%	99.9%	100.1%	99.9%	100.1%	100.0%	100.3%	100.0%
Base *N*[a]	7,557	139	11,359	357	4,764	104	15,593	372	122,084	2,940
Percent of total U.S. population	6.2	4.7	9.3	12.1	3.9	3.5	12.8	12.7		
									Under 21	75
									NA, age	3
									Total NORC sample	3,018

[a] Excluding Alaska and Hawaii. [b] 1970 Census *N*'s are given in 000's.

larly prone to error in the sense that we also seem to have undersampled both blacks in this group who had gone no further than elementary school and those who had graduated from high school. Again, Table D-9 shows that both these errors were more likely to involve females than males; thus, we had somewhat undersampled black females who did not complete elementary school and oversampled black females with college experience (the differences between black males and females are not particularly large, however).

The total columns in Table D-9 allow us to put the results this way: we had more college-educated respondents, both males and female, than the Census showed; but the discrepancy involving females was greater than that for males.

Geographic Region

In a truly "national" sample, every region of the country needs to be adequately represented. Table D-10 shows the results of our sampling to be in virtual accord with Census data. Moreover, the very small differences that occurred are likely due to NORC's sampling quota assignments being based on the population distributions of record for the years before 1970. With respect to age, most categories seem to have adequately represented the given region; oversampling to a modest degree was generally confined to ages 25–44, which appear to have been slightly too numerous in the NORC sample as a whole.

Marital Status

Tables D-11 and D-12 show the marital status distributions for males and females, respectively. What is immediately striking in both cases is the underrepresentation of the single (never married) and the overrepresentation of the married for the age category 20–24. This should not be construed as sampling error but as a result of sampling categories. To compare our sample to Census data, we had to use the *Statistical Abstracts* age category 20–24. Our sample, however, was intended to be of adults 21 and older, with persons under 21 included only if they were heads of household (see note 2). Therefore, we should not have had any single 20-year-olds in our sample. This necessarily reduces numbers in our category Single/20–24 and increases those for Married/20–24.

Other discrepancies regarding marital status occurred at the other end of the age range. For males, we underrepresented those 75 years and older who were single (never married) and overrepresented widowers between 65 and 74. For females, we underrepresented those 65 and older

TABLE D-11 Males 20 and Older, Marital Status by Age, 1970

Marital status	20–24 Census	20–24 NORC	25–29 Census	25–29 NORC	30–34 Census	30–34 NORC
Married[a]	43.6%	57.4%	77.9%	83.3%	87.4%	86.8%
Divorced	1.1	0.7	2.3	1.4	2.9	3.3
Widowed	0.0	0.0	0.1	0.0	0.1	0.6
Never married	55.2	41.8	19.7	15.2	9.6	9.4
Total	99.9%	99.9%	100.0%	99.9%	100.0%	100.1%
Base *N*[b]	7,787	141	5,232	138	6,861	181

Marital status	35–44 Census	35–44 NORC	45–54 Census	45–54 NORC	55–64 Census	55–64 NORC
Married[a]	89.3%	91.9%	87.2%	90.2%	85.6%	84.4%
Divorced	2.9	4.1	3.6	3.4	3.0	3.1
Widowed	0.6	1.1	1.6	2.3	3.9	5.2
Never married	7.2	3.0	7.6	4.2	7.6	7.3
Total	100.0%	100.1%	100.0%	100.1%	100.1%	100.0%
Base *N*[b]	11,090	271	11,031	265	8,672	192

Marital status	65–74 Census	65–74 NORC	75 and older Census	75 and older NORC	Total Census	Total NORC
Married[a]	77.6%	77.2%	61.5%	62.6%	78.8%	82.2%
Divorced	2.9	4.3	1.5	3.6	2.7	3.2
Widowed	11.0	16.0	30.4	33.7	3.6	5.3
Never married	8.5	2.7	6.6	0.0	14.9	9.3
Total	100.0%	100.2%	100.0%	99.9%	100.0%	100.0%
Base *N*[b]	5,770	188	2,548	83	58,991	1,459
					Female	1,518
					Under 20	38
					NA, age	3
					Total NORC sample	3,018

[a] Includes informal or legal separation, for comparability with *Statistical Abstracts* data. About 5% of the married NORC males were separated but not divorced from their wives.
[b] 1970 Census *N*'s are given in 000's.

who were married, especially those 75 and older, with a corresponding oversampling of older widows.

It should be noted, though, that these differences involve quite small *N*'s. For example, the oversampling of widowed females means that the NORC sample included 10 too many.

Occupational Status

This was perhaps the most difficult dimension on which to compare

TABLE D-12 Females 20 and Older, Marital Status by Age, 1970

	20–24		25–29		30–34	
Marital status	Census	NORC	Census	NORC	Census	NORC
Married[a]	61.5%	83.7%	84.7%	88.3%	88.3%	90.5%
Divorced	2.3	4.2	4.3	5.4	4.6	4.5
Widowed	0.3	0.5	0.3	0.5	0.8	2.5
Never married	35.9	11.6	10.7	5.9	6.4	2.5
Total	100.0%	100.0%	100.0%	100.1%	100.1%	100.0%
Base *N*[b]	8,305	190	7,374	222	5,215	157
	35–44		**45–54**		**55–64**	
Marital status	Census	NORC	Census	NORC	Census	NORC
Married[a]	86.9%	89.8%	82.0%	83.3%	67.3%	69.1%
Divorced	5.4	6.4	4.9	5.1	4.5	4.7
Widowed	2.5	2.9	8.1	10.2	21.3	21.5
Never married	5.2	1.0	4.9	1.5	6.8	4.7
Total	100.0%	100.1%	99.9%	100.1%	99.9%	100.0%
Base *N*[b]	11,798	314	11,930	275	9,755	191
	65–74		**75 and older**		**Total**	
Marital status	Census	NORC	Census	NORC	Census	NORC
Married[a]	45.4%	39.0%	20.9%	8.7%	71.3%	78.5%
Divorced	3.0	5.7	1.3	4.3	4.1	5.2
Widowed	43.7	52.0	70.5	78.3	14.2	12.1
Never married	7.9	3.3	7.4	8.7	10.4	4.2
Total	100.0%	100.0%	100.1%	100.0%	100.0%	100.0%
Base *N*[b]	8,395	123	3,140	46	65,912	1,518
					Male	1,459
					Under 20	38
					NA, age	3
					Total NORC sample	3,018

[a] Includes informal or legal separation, for comparability with *Statistical Abstracts* data. About 5% of the married NORC females were separated but not divorced from their husbands.
[b] 1970 Census *N*'s are given in 000's.

our sample with Census data, for two reasons. First, the Census data included persons 16 years and older, whereas our sample had mostly 21 and older; the few who were younger than 21 were not an adequate sample of the age group 16–21 (see note 2). This age group was also a source of bias because of the type of jobs associated with persons this young—their jobs may be temporary, for example those taken during school vacations, or they may be entry-level jobs that do not reflect where the young people will finally end up in the labor force. The second reason involves the females in our sample. NORC procedure is to collect oc-

TABLE D-13 U.S. Population 16 and Older, Occupation by Sex of Main Earner, 1970

	Male		Female		Total	
Occupation	Census	NORC	Census	NORC	Census	NORC
White-collar						
Professional and technical	14.0%	14.2%	14.5%	18.7%	14.2%	15.0%
Manager, proprietor, official	14.2	12.9	4.5	8.4	10.5	12.2
Sales	5.6	5.5	7.1	4.5	6.2	5.3
Clerical	7.1	6.0	34.5	15.3	17.4	7.5
(Subtotal)	(40.9)	(38.6)	(60.6)	(46.9)	(48.3)	(40.0)
Blue-collar						
Craftsman, foreman	20.1	23.8	1.1	6.4	12.9	21.3
Operative	19.6	17.5	14.5	15.5	17.7	17.2
Non-farm laborer	7.3	6.4	0.5	3.9	4.7	6.0
(Subtotal)	(47.0)	(47.7)	(16.1)	(26.2)	(35.3)	(44.5)
Service	6.7	6.4	21.7	24.1	12.4	9.3
Farm	5.3	7.3	1.8	2.8	4.0	6.6
Total	99.9%	100.0%	100.2%	100.0%	100.0%	100.4%
Base *N*[a]	48,960	2,368	29,667	465	78,627	2,839
					Military	28
					No main earner	113
					NA, occupation	38
					Total NORC sample	3,018

[a] 1970 Census *N*'s are given in 000's.

cupational information on the "head of household." Usually this means that if a male is in the household, he is taken as its head. Those NORC females who are "head of household" are thus a very selective group, comprised of the never married, divorced, and widowed. This is quite different from Census procedure, which is to collect occupational data on females with jobs regardless of whether they are heads of household, in order to represent the total labor force.

Despite these difficulties, Table D-13 shows less discrepancy between our NORC sample and Census data than might be expected; there seems to have been no great differences for males. Among females, however, it is apparent that we underrepresented white-collar workers (especially clerical) and overrepresented blue-collar workers.

Table D-14 introduces race as a factor and is more detailed in listing occupations, since we may expect less bias here. Among both whites and blacks we undersampled white-collar workers (especially, again,

TABLE D-14 U.S. Population 16 and Older, Occupation by Race of Main Earner, 1970

Occupation	Black Census	Black NORC	Not black Census	Not black NORC	Total Census	Total NORC
White-collar						
Professional and technical	4.7%	4.0%	9.3%	13.0%	8.8%	11.6%
Medical and other health	1.6	1.8	2.3	1.3	2.2	1.3
Teaching (noncollege)	2.9	1.1	3.2	2.2	3.2	2.0
Manager, proprietor, official	3.5	4.9	11.4	13.5	10.5	12.2
Retail sales	1.6	0.2	4.0	0.6	3.7	0.6
Other sales	0.5	0.9	2.6	5.5	2.4	4.8
Stenographer, secretary, receptionist	2.3	0.4	4.7	1.3	4.4	1.2
Other clerical	10.9	5.4	13.2	6.5	13.0	6.3
(Subtotal)	(28.0)	(18.7)	(50.7)	(43.9)	(48.2)	(40.0)
Blue-collar						
Carpenter	0.7	0.7	1.1	2.6	1.1	2.3
Mechanic, repairman	2.6	4.9	3.7	4.5	3.6	4.6
Foreman	0.9	1.6	2.0	2.3	1.9	2.1
Other craft	4.1	9.8	6.6	12.5	6.3	12.1
Driver, delivery	4.1	6.7	3.1	4.6	3.2	4.9
Other operative	19.6	23.7	13.9	10.1	14.5	12.3
Nonfarm laborer	10.3	14.3	4.1	4.4	4.8	6.0
(Subtotal)	(42.3)	(61.7)	(34.5)	(41.0)	(35.4)	(44.3)
Farm						
Farmer, farm manager	1.0	1.6	2.4	6.3	2.2	5.6
Farm foreman, farm laborer	2.9	0.7	1.6	1.0	1.7	1.0
(Subtotal)	(3.9)	(2.3)	(4.0)	(7.3)	(3.9)	(6.6)
Service						
Bar, restaurant	3.4	2.2	2.8	1.3	2.9	1.4
Protective services	0.9	0.9	1.3	2.4	1.3	2.1
Private household	7.7	4.0	1.3	0.5	2.0	1.1
Other service	14.0	9.8	5.4	3.7	6.3	4.6
(Subtotal)	(26.0)	(16.9)	(10.8)	(7.9)	(12.5)	(9.2)
Total	100.2%	99.6%	100.0%	100.1%	100.0%	100.1%
Base *N*[a]	8,455	447	70,182	2,392	78,627	2,839
					Military	28
					No main earner	113
					NA, occupation	38
					Total NORC sample	3,018

[a] 1970 Census *N*'s are given in 000's.

clerical workers) and oversampled blue-collar workers (especially among the Other craft and Foreman categories). As we explained above, these differences most likely were confined to females.

Conclusion

In general we feel that our 1970 sample was representative enough to permit accurate general statements about the population of the United States in that year. Most of the discrepancies were not of a magnitude to cause great concern. Compared with Census data, our sample did have proportionately more blacks, college females, young marrieds, and female blue-collar workers than the population at large, and fewer older females, young poorly-educated blacks, and female white-collar workers. These differences, however, were statistically controlled in our analyses. And in light of our major findings, it is interesting to note that among variables that appeared as important influences on sexual norms, having had more blacks, more highly educated respondents, and fewer older females ought to have biased the sample in a *liberal* direction. It seems likely, then, that any sample bias does not interfere with our major conclusion that American sexual norms tend to be stably conservative.

NOTES

1. Our quotas, based on Census data already available for sampling segments, were age for males, so that we had males under 30 and males 30 and over, and labor-force status for females, so that we had females who were employed and females who were not employed.
2. We intended originally to include no one under 21; however, NORC permitted interviews with people this young if they were "heads of household" (and so, presumably, adult in their outlook). Thus our youngest respondents were not only fewer in number than in the Census, but also quite unlike others in their age cohort in other respects. Since our youngest respondents were probably *not* representative, then, they were excluded from most of the comparisons with Census data.
3. The source for Census data in the following tables is the U.S. Census Bureau's *Statistical Abstracts of the United States,* 92nd edition (1971).
4. According to a report in *Time* (March 31, 1980), about 2.5% of the population did not get counted in the 1970 Census—about 1.9% of all whites and 7.7% of all blacks, especially urban blacks. Extrapolating from the figures in Tables D-1 and D-2, this suggests that the proportion of blacks in the 1970 population was perhaps one-half of one percent greater than these tables show.

Appendix E

Correlations Among Major Variables of Interest

This appendix presents (with decimal points omitted) the Pearsonian product-moment correlations among variables used in the major analyses of this book. Because of the size of the sample, significance levels are not given; most correlations of ± .04 or more are statistically significant. The first part lists 93 independent variables and our 17 principal dependent variables; the second part lists correlations underlying the factor analytic work in Chapter 8.

PART I Major Ordinal Independent and Dependent Variables

	Sex-female	Race-black	Age	Parents' generation	High parental SES	Low parental SES	Parental SES	Parents professional	Reared in Northeast	Reared in Midwest-South	Reared on Pacific Coast	Urban childhood	Reared on farm	Father sociable	Mother sociable	Mother active	Father not sexual	Mother not sexual	Father masculine
Sex-female		−00	−12	10	01	00	01	02	01	01	−01	02	00	03	01	−01	01	02	−19
Race-black			−04	07	−16	25	−21	−06	−16	08	−04	−00	08	−08	−08	−00	10	−07	−05
Age				−83	−13	−00	−01	−08	−04	06	−08	−22	27	07	−04	16	−08	11	02
Parents' generation					11	02	−03	05	07	−09	07	23	−28	−06	03	−15	09	−11	−03
High parental SES						−20	72	44	06	−13	04	21	−31	08	06	−05	02	−02	09
Low parental SES							−58	−10	−05	02	03	02	−07	−06	−07	03	04	−01	−06
Parental SES								41	−01	−01	01	−02	10	09	08	−03	01	−01	12
Parents professional									03	−07	03	11	−15	06	04	−04	02	−01	06
Reared in Northeast										−36	−14	25	−24	02	02	−03	01	01	−04
Reared in Midwest-South											−17	−30	32	−01	−01	04	−01	01	−01
Reared on Pacific Coast												05	−05	−03	02	−06	−01	−02	−02
Urban childhood													−58	05	04	−10	02	−01	−05
Reared on farm														−02	−01	08	−04	−01	03
Father sociable															26	07	10	−05	10
Mother sociable																19	01	16	04
Mother active																	00	−10	09
Father not sexual																		−38	08
Mother not sexual																			−05
Father masculine																			
Mother masculine	−08	−00	02	−03	−00	−02	−00	02	02	−04	−00	02	−01	07	14	27	01	−01	21
Father feminine	−02	10	−12	10	01	02	−01	02	−02	−01	−03	−00	−01	−01	−05	−04	10	−04	14
Mother feminine	−06	09	−23	20	05	−01	02	04	−00	−05	02	07	−07	−05	04	−10	10	−09	16
Number of siblings	−02	17	21	−28	−22	06	−11	−12	−11	13	−04	−28	27	−08	−11	07	03	−03	03
Older brother(s)	−03	06	08	−22	−08	01	−02	−04	−03	05	−03	−14	11	−01	−02	07	00	−00	03
Younger brother(s)	00	05	07	00	−07	−00	−02	−01	−05	06	−01	−12	10	−04	−03	02	06	−05	01
Older sister(s)	−04	07	09	−22	−10	03	−05	−05	−05	07	−04	−10	13	−03	−06	04	−03	02	00
Younger sister(s)	00	02	05	01	−08	02	−05	−06	−04	03	−00	−10	10	−03	−05	−02	04	−02	−01
Parents' education	06	−15	−29	26	38	−10	34	35	05	−12	09	24	−25	13	12	−08	01	−05	08
Reared Fundamentalist	00	31	−03	04	−15	08	−11	−09	−27	24	−01	−20	16	−09	−11	02	07	−05	01
Reared as Catholic	03	−18	−06	06	02	−01	−06	−06	26	−18	−01	22	−16	03	00	00	−03	03	−05
Reared as Jewish	−02	−07	−00	01	06	−03	04	04	15	−10	−02	22	−09	02	02	−04	00	−00	−02
No childhood religion	−05	−05	−00	01	03	−00	02	03	−02	00	04	01	00	−02	−01	−04	−03	03	01
Parents' devoutness	−02	17	14	−15	−04	00	02	−02	−06	07	−12	−12	13	10	09	12	−04	00	04
Parents permissive	−23	−04	−16	15	08	−00	00	01	05	−08	05	15	−13	00	06	−08	07	−08	−04

Father controlling	04	−00	−00	−00	00	−02	01	00	−02	01	−02	−04	02	−10	−05	−04	−02	02	18
Mother controlling	07	08	02	−01	−05	03	−05	−01	−01	03	−03	−03	02	−02	−06	03	−03	08	−06
Father predictable	−03	−10	12	−12	00	−05	04	−02	01	02	−04	−06	07	09	02	09	−04	01	07
Mother predictable	−04	−02	12	−11	−01	−05	04	−01	−04	04	−03	−08	10	04	06	13	00	−04	04
Father serious & moral	09	−10	04	−08	06	−05	09	03	−04	04	−01	−04	02	09	05	10	11	−10	09
Mother serious & moral	08	−14	04	−07	07	−08	08	02	−01	01	−03	−01	−02	08	08	15	08	−14	08
Father loving	03	02	12	−12	−02	−02	01	−00	−02	04	−07	−05	06	18	06	14	01	−04	−06
Mother loving	−04	01	12	−12	−04	00	−02	−04	−04	05	−06	−08	−08	05	11	19	04	−13	10
Childhood broken home	03	17	02	02	−09	17	−15	−04	−07	04	−01	00	−06	−02	−06	−01	01	05	−04
Childhood sex play	−12	−01	−14	12	07	−02	02	08	−00	−04	02	08	−11	03	04	−03	−01	−02	01
Sex play punished	−10	06	−04	05	02	01	00	02	−06	03	02	00	−04	00	−01	−05	05	00	03
Early masturbation	−22	−06	−09	09	07	−02	04	05	−01	−03	02	09	−09	−03	02	−04	04	−07	04
Early coitus	−12	08	−04	04	−01	06	−03	00	−02	−01	00	04	−02	−04	−03	−01	04	−03	01
Childhood sex guilt	−03	−08	−18	17	07	04	03	06	−00	−02	05	07	−12	01	02	−04	00	−01	−00
Sexual environment	−28	22	−17	17	04	03	−00	06	−03	00	03	09	−07	−03	00	−02	13	−09	10
Preadult broken home	04	19	02	02	−08	17	−15	−03	−06	04	−01	00	−06	−02	−05	−01	02	04	−06
Had sex education	08	00	−33	28	16	−04	08	13	03	−10	11	17	−18	07	07	−07	06	−08	02
Education completed	00	−20	−34	29	32	−13	24	21	10	−11	07	30	−28	12	18	−10	02	−02	04
More ed. than pars.	−07	−03	04	−06	−12	03	−13	−19	03	04	−03	01	01	−04	03	01	00	03	−06
Military service	−53	−04	−01	03	02	−02	−01	−02	06	−07	02	06	−08	00	01	−02	05	−04	12
Pos. to premar. sex	−37	12	−23	22	09	00	01	06	03	−10	07	13	−14	00	03	−06	06	−12	08
Neg. to premar. sex	38	04	−12	08	−03	02	−02	00	−04	05	−02	−06	05	03	−01	−00	−02	04	−08
Premar. sex. involve.	−51	12	−21	20	09	00	01	07	03	−09	05	16	−18	−02	03	−07	12	−10	12
Premar. sex. freq.	−40	15	−26	24	08	00	02	08	03	−09	06	14	−17	−03	03	−09	09	−09	09
Had premarital sex	−35	14	−25	23	05	01	−01	08	03	−08	06	11	−13	−03	00	−09	08	−08	08
Never masturbated	45	01	06	−06	−05	00	−03	−08	−00	06	−03	−06	07	01	−02	01	−02	04	−02
Age first married	−39	−08	34	−30	07	−07	10	04	08	−09	−01	02	01	10	08	04	−05	02	09
Number of marriages	04	07	23	−16	−07	04	−05	−04	−10	10	−00	−06	07	−01	−05	05	01	02	−01
Currently married	−06	−14	−14	14	03	−02	00	01	02	−02	03	05	−08	05	04	−05	03	−03	−02
Divorced, separated	05	02	02	−01	−03	02	−02	−01	01	01	00	−00	01	−00	−03	03	−00	02	03
Never married	−10	04	−18	11	05	00	01	02	03	−05	02	04	−04	−04	01	−03	−01	−03	00
Number of children	06	07	18	−11	−11	04	−06	−09	−01	07	−04	−13	14	−04	−07	02	−00	03	00
Age of oldest boy	−03	07	65	−45	−14	06	−09	−07	−01	05	−07	−07	13	04	−08	04	−00	06	01
Age of oldest girl	−10	02	64	−41	−11	02	−08	−03	−02	04	−12	−10	09	03	−06	04	02	04	06
Current high SES	00	−15	−08	07	25	−11	22	15	06	−10	04	17	−15	08	08	−04	01	−03	04
Current low SES	04	21	06	−04	−10	16	−12	−04	−03	04	−05	−06	08	−08	−05	03	−03	−01	−04
Higher SES than pars.	−01	−02	−03	05	−31	33	−52	−15	05	−06	02	13	−18	01	00	−02	01	01	−05
Lives in Northeast	01	−08	−03	05	03	−02	−03	01	78	−34	−13	22	−21	02	−00	−02	00	00	−04
Lives Midwest-South	02	02	04	−07	−10	−01	02	−06	−29	73	−13	−27	29	00	00	03	−02	02	01
Lives Pacific Coast	−02	−04	01	−02	04	−03	03	03	−15	−04	60	01	00	−01	01	−02	02	−01	−02
Urban residence	−00	21	−06	08	07	07	−04	07	−19	02	47	−17	−26	−01	−02	−08	03	−02	−02
Urban mobility	−02	19	17	−17	−15	04	−01	−05	−21	13	−03	−58	36	−06	−05	02	00	−02	03
Lives on farm	−05	−07	14	−14	−09	−01	04	−06	−12	24	−01	−24	31	03	03	03	−04	05	01

PART I (*continued*)

	Sex-female	Race-black	Age	Parents' generation	High parental SES	Low parental SES	Parental SES	Parents professional	Reared in Northeast	Reared in Midwest-South	Reared on Pacific Coast	Urban childhood	Reared on farm	Father sociable	Mother sociable	Mother active	Father not sexual	Mother not sexual	Father masculine
Moved away from farm	06	12	13	-14	-18	-04	06	-09	-13	10	-01	-31	57	-05	-04	04	-00	-02	02
Sociable	10	-03	-11	07	06	-05	07	03	06	-04	-04	10	-06	23	22	05	04	-06	05
Serious & moral	11	-06	02	-04	01	-03	02	01	-03	03	-01	-04	-01	04	02	08	13	-12	06
Not a sexual person	11	-06	29	-26	-11	02	-05	-07	-05	08	-03	-12	14	-04	-08	02	-29	31	-05
Masculine	-21	-02	-00	-00	04	-01	02	03	02	-05	-01	03	-03	05	07	07	06	-05	38
Feminine	11	02	-28	23	08	00	01	04	-00	-03	04	10	-11	-05	01	-03	10	-07	07
Work-oriented	-20	10	18	-17	-07	01	-05	-04	-03	-00	-03	-03	04	01	-01	17	01	-02	10
Fundamentalist	04	27	01	00	-15	-09	-10	-08	-25	24	-04	-23	18	-08	-10	03	05	-04	00
Change from Fund.	-07	-14	-01	01	08	-06	06	04	12	-12	06	13	-11	04	05	-03	-03	01	01
Catholic	05	-18	-07	06	02	00	-05	-05	26	-16	-03	20	-14	03	01	02	-03	03	-04
Jewish	-01	-07	00	00	06	-03	04	05	13	-10	-02	21	-09	04	03	-03	02	-02	-00
No current religion	-13	-01	-06	04	07	-02	05	07	00	-05	10	06	-07	-06	-04	-08	-03	04	-02
Change to no religion	-11	02	-06	04	06	-02	04	06	01	-05	07	05	-07	-05	-03	-06	-01	02	-02
Current devoutness	18	08	14	-14	-08	02	-04	-08	-08	11	-11	-17	15	06	04	10	00	-02	02
Decreasing devoutness	-14	-05	-03	00	04	-01	04	06	03	-05	03	03	-03	01	01	00	-02	03	00
Sexually threatened	21	04	20	-18	-10	02	-04	-06	-07	10	-08	-19	16	04	-06	08	-06	08	-00
Sexual Morality Scale	-16	06	-23	22	13	03	03	10	15	-21	08	25	-22	01	03	-09	06	-05	-01
Liberal. Vs. Parents'	-07	-02	-22	19	11	09	04	08	09	-12	05	20	-17	-01	02	-09	01	01	00
Moral Change Index	-00	-08	-22	19	13	08	06	10	08	-13	11	22	-18	02	05	-09	00	00	-01
Heterosexual cure	-04	10	12	-13	-10	-08	-08	-07	-08	05	-04	-13	12	-01	-03	07	-03	-01	04
Voluntary cure	-04	08	10	-10	-11	-09	-07	-06	-09	09	-04	-16	12	-01	-03	09	-02	01	04
Hs identifiable	01	18	02	-03	-11	03	-11	-09	03	03	-05	-03	03	-04	-06	02	02	-00	01
Family cause	-03	06	20	-17	-10	-00	-05	-07	-00	05	-04	-08	09	-00	-04	05	-03	02	-02
H is distorted HT	-05	14	15	-15	-13	06	-09	-08	-10	08	-05	-16	15	-02	-05	09	-03	01	04
Hs are dangerous	-03	02	27	-25	-19	06	-11	-13	-11	17	-11	-27	24	-01	03	-14	03	-08	-04
H is abhorrent	10	-06	11	-10	-11	-02	-03	-11	-11	16	-07	-22	16	01	-00	07	-00	-01	01
Deny authorit. jobs	02	-11	14	-15	-12	-01	-06	-09	-05	13	-08	-22	15	01	-02	07	-02	05	01
Allow stereo. jobs	07	00	-22	21	13	-03	05	08	10	-14	05	23	-22	04	07	-05	08	-07	-03
Deny freedoms	02	-06	15	-15	-12	-01	-03	-10	-09	17	-10	-27	21	-02	-04	06	-08	-07	02
Antihomosexual factor	04	-07	20	-20	-16	-00	-06	-13	-10	19	-12	-30	23	00	-03	11	-04	06	02
Maint. of friendship	-21	14	-18	17	04	06	-05	04	10	-13	08	22	-18	-00	02	-04	08	-07	01
Sexual suppression	04	00	21	-20	-18	02	-10	-13	-13	18	-09	-25	22	-03	-07	07	-08	06	02
Opposed to sex educ.	-01	-04	28	-25	-16	02	-08	-11	-12	12	-09	-23	20	-02	-05	12	-03	04	04

	Mother masculine	Father feminine	Mother feminine	Number of siblings	Older brother(s)	Younger brother(s)	Older sister(s)	Younger sister(s)	Parents' education	Reared as Fundamentalist	Reared as Catholic	Reared as Jewish	No childhood religion	Parents' devoutness	Parents permissive	Father controlling	Mother controlling	Father predictable	Mother predictable
Education completed	04	−05	04	−37	−16	−15	−17	−16	45	−20	01	12	−00	−07	14	−08	−06	05	−00
More ed. than pars.	03	−03	−03	02	05	−03	04	−03	−61	01	03	06	−03	−01	−00	−02	02	03	04
Military service	07	−00	07	−06	−02	−04	−02	−02	02	−04	01	−00	05	−03	18	−01	−03	00	01
Pos. to premar. sex	07	08	16	−11	−06	−03	−05	−05	11	−03	−01	04	03	−03	21	−01	−02	−09	−08
Neg. to premar. sex	00	06	04	02	02	−01	01	−01	−03	04	−00	−02	−06	04	−18	06	08	−03	−09
Premar. sex. involve.	07	10	17	−11	−05	−06	−03	−03	10	−01	−03	05	06	−13	29	−05	−04	−07	−06
Premar. sex. freq.	05	10	16	−11	−06	−04	−03	−05	12	−02	−03	03	06	−13	25	−04	−04	−07	−07
Had premarital sex	05	08	12	−09	−05	−03	−02	−04	10	−01	−03	02	06	−12	22	−04	−01	−08	−08
Never masturbated	−07	−08	−11	06	01	03	00	04	−08	−01	02	−02	−05	03	−19	04	07	03	03
Age first married	04	−07	−06	−00	−01	−00	01	−01	−00	−15	06	07	04	09	05	−02	−04	08	09
Number of marriages	03	00	−03	07	00	04	03	01	−11	12	−07	−07	−00	−01	−10	04	06	−03	−04
Currently married	01	02	04	−06	−03	00	−04	−01	02	−04	05	−01	01	−03	01	01	−01	−02	−01
Divorced, separated	01	06	−02	−01	00	−02	02	−01	02	03	−02	−00	−00	−02	01	01	03	−05	−02
Never married	−01	−01	04	−04	02	−07	−01	−03	07	−03	00	05	02	−02	10	−04	−04	02	02
Number of children	03	−00	−04	16	08	05	06	06	−14	05	02	−04	−02	02	−04	05	06	−01	−00
Age of oldest boy	−04	−07	−15	07	02	03	04	07	−20	00	−00	−00	−04	10	−14	01	−00	06	08
Age of oldest girl	−01	−03	−14	06	02	−02	08	−03	−18	02	−05	−01	−01	06	−08	02	03	06	05
Current high SES	02	−06	−02	−20	−08	−10	−10	−09	26	−15	02	05	−01	−04	05	−05	−04	02	−00
Current low SES	−04	01	01	09	03	06	04	06	−13	08	−02	−04	−01	03	−06	03	03	−02	−03
Higher SES than pars.	03	−03	−04	−09	−02	−07	−03	−05	−02	−05	05	03	−02	−06	05	−06	−00	−02	−02
Lives in Northeast	−00	−02	−01	−07	−02	−04	−02	−04	01	−24	25	17	−02	−04	05	01	−01	−01	−04
Lives Midwest-South	−02	−01	−04	10	04	03	05	03	−08	17	−14	−09	00	06	−08	02	03	03	03
Lives Pacific Coast	−02	−02	01	−02	−02	−00	−03	02	05	−02	−04	−03	05	−12	02	−01	02	−02	−00
Urban residence	00	06	06	−06	−03	−01	−01	03	08	−03	10	13	−02	−01	06	03	00	−07	−04
Urban mobility	−01	05	−02	23	11	12	09	08	−18	17	−13	−10	−03	12	−11	07	04	−00	04
Lives on farm	02	−03	−05	07	04	03	05	02	−05	−01	−06	−04	01	06	−04	−04	−02	04	03
Moved away from farm	−02	01	−01	17	06	06	06	08	−18	16	−10	−05	−02	06	−10	04	04	03	05
Sociable	08	01	07	−08	−03	−02	−02	−01	08	−09	08	03	−04	06	−01	−03	01	01	00
Serious & moral	08	01	04	00	02	−01	−01	−01	−03	04	00	−07	−05	05	−16	04	04	07	08
Not a sexual person	−05	−08	−15	11	04	02	06	03	−13	01	−04	00	−02	07	−13	01	03	04	02

PART I (*continued*)

	Mother masculine	Father feminine	Mother feminine	Number of siblings	Older brother(s)	Younger brother(s)	Older sister(s)	Younger sister(s)	Parents' education	Reared as Fundamentalist	Reared as Catholic	Reared as Jewish	No childhood religion	Parents' devoutness	Parents permissive	Father controlling	Mother controlling	Father predictable	Mother predictable
Mother masculine		11	11	−01	03	−02	03	−06	−02	−03	05	−00	−02	07	−00	−12	19	04	−01
Father feminine			37	02	02	01	−02	03	−03	08	02	01	00	−00	01	01	−05	−14	−02
Mother feminine				−02	−01	03	−03	03	04	05	01	02	01	−02	05	04	−05	−07	−14
Number of siblings					44	37	43	38	−31	18	−01	−10	−04	14	−17	15	06	−02	03
Older brother(s)						−07	33	−04	−16	07	00	−04	−05	11	−07	03	01	02	03
Younger brother(s)							−07	28	−09	09	01	−03	00	04	−08	10	09	−02	−00
Older sister(s)								−06	−16	05	−01	−03	−04	06	−03	01	−01	00	03
Younger sister(s)									−11	08	03	−06	−00	04	−07	10	05	−06	−02
Parents' education										−18	−03	05	03	−05	12	−05	−06	01	−03
Reared as Fundamentalist											−34	−10	−08	08	−09	06	07	−00	04
Reared as Catholic												−09	−08	13	−02	03	02	−02	−05
Reared as Jewish													−02	−10	08	−03	−03	01	−01
No childhood religion														−23	05	−02	−02	−05	−00
Parents' devoutness															−23	03	08	13	11
Parents permissive																−24	−17	−10	−08
Father controlling																	26	−12	−04
Mother controlling																		−01	−16
Father predictable																			24
Mother predictable																			
Father serious & moral	04	−05	−01	00	02	−00	02	01	08	03	−02	−03	−01	08	−21	04	03	17	08
Mother serious & moral	06	−02	−04	−03	−01	−02	−01	−03	07	02	00	−00	−01	07	−16	02	05	14	15
Father loving	10	−12	−11	−00	06	−06	03	−05	−00	03	−00	−01	−06	20	−04	−41	−00	43	17
Mother loving	−09	−01	−07	06	04	−03	05	−02	−05	06	−06	−02	−05	13	−04	−02	−42	16	47
Childhood broken home	02	04	−04	−04	−03	−06	01	−08	−03	09	−02	−05	−04	−08	00	01	08	−05	−08
Childhood sex play	02	05	06	−10	−02	−06	−05	−08	11	−03	−00	02	03	−04	11	−04	−02	−04	−04
Sex play punished	01	04	07	−00	−00	01	−02	00	02	09	−05	−04	02	00	01	03	05	−02	−06
Early masturbation	04	04	08	−09	−03	−05	−04	−05	07	−00	−02	00	03	−07	12	−01	−01	−04	−01

Early coitus	04	02	05	02	−00	00	01	02	−01	05	−04	−01	00	−00	05	−02	−01	−04	−03
Childhood sex guilt	−00	04	07	−14	−05	−03	−05	−07	10	−04	−01	01	04	−09	07	−03	−01	−03	−07
Sexual environment	08	11	16	−03	−01	−04	00	−03	07	08	−09	01	02	−08	17	−02	−02	−09	−08
Preadult broken home	02	04	−03	−04	−04	−07	00	−07	−03	09	−03	−03	−03	−09	01	02	09	−09	−08
Had sex education	02	05	10	−17	−09	−06	−08	−06	22	−07	−00	04	−00	−02	06	−05	−03	−03	−03
Respondent masculine	39	16	21	−02	00	00	−02	02	00	−04	05	04	−02	05	02	04	−00	02	00
Respondent feminine	16	39	45	−05	01	−03	−02	−04	04	03	04	01	−01	−09	01	05	03	−13	−11
Work-oriented	08	−02	−01	11	05	04	05	05	−12	04	01	−01	−02	14	−06	−00	04	09	08
Fundamentalist	−04	06	03	18	09	08	08	07	−16	72	−31	−09	−04	08	−12	05	09	03	06
Change from Fund.	04	−04	00	−12	−07	−04	−08	−02	10	−37	13	04	03	−09	10	−03	−07	−07	−03
Catholic	05	02	−00	−02	−01	01	−01	02	−01	−31	82	−09	−03	10	−03	04	02	−02	−05
Jewish	−01	−00	02	−09	−05	−02	−03	−05	06	−09	−09	91	−01	−08	07	−03	−03	01	−00
No current religion	−01	−00	04	−09	−04	−03	−05	00	06	−03	−05	02	20	−14	12	−02	−05	−07	−04
Change to no religion	−01	−00	03	−07	−02	03	−03	00	04	01	−01	03	−27	−03	10	−01	−04	−05	−04
Current devoutness	03	−00	−03	14	08	04	06	03	−12	10	06	−12	−16	34	−24	04	08	10	09
Decreasing devoutness	01	00	02	00	03	−00	01	01	06	00	06	−02	−03	44	01	−01	01	01	−01
Sexually threatened	02	06	−02	16	06	08	08	07	−14	12	−05	−09	−02	12	−19	06	04	−01	02
Sexual Morality Scale	02	04	10	−17	−09	−07	−07	−06	18	−14	08	13	07	−16	27	−06	−08	−10	−10
Liberal. Vs. Parents'	04	06	09	−13	−05	−07	−05	−07	14	−11	04	08	−00	−09	14	−01	−01	−05	−10
Moral Change Index	03	05	10	−16	−08	−07	−08	−05	18	−10	03	09	02	−11	14	−01	−02	−06	−09
Heterosexual cure	04	03	−00	15	04	08	06	06	−12	10	−03	−05	−02	08	−09	02	02	−04	02
Voluntary cure	04	04	−00	13	05	07	06	05	−13	12	−05	−06	−05	08	−06	02	05	00	03
Hs identifiable	−00	07	07	09	07	01	04	04	−13	08	03	−05	−02	08	−07	04	02	−04	−04
Family cause	−02	−07	−04	11	04	03	06	05	−15	06	−02	−06	−02	07	−06	−01	02	02	01
H is distorted HT	04	04	01	19	05	09	08	07	−17	12	−04	−06	−03	09	−10	03	02	−03	03
Hs are dangerous	04	02	05	22	11	08	−08	08	−23	14	−06	−16	−06	14	−18	03	02	02	05
H is abhorrent	−03	−01	−05	15	07	07	06	05	−15	12	−02	−16	−03	09	−17	03	04	06	06
Deny authorit. jobs	01	−03	−06	11	07	04	04	05	−18	06	−02	−15	−03	08	−13	−01	−02	04	00
Allow stereo. jobs	−01	−00	07	−20	−11	−06	−10	−06	17	−10	06	07	00	−08	12	−05	−00	−01	−03
Deny freedoms	−01	−01	−04	18	09	08	08	06	−18	12	−06	−14	−03	11	−16	06	04	04	06
Antihomosexual factor	−00	−01	−06	21	10	08	08	07	−23	12	−04	−19	−04	13	−20	03	04	05	05
Maint. of friendship	02	01	06	−13	−07	−06	−04	−07	10	−07	03	10	03	−11	22	−05	−06	−05	−07
Sexual suppression	−01	02	−02	24	10	10	12	10	−23	15	−05	−12	−05	12	−21	06	06	02	05
Opposed to sex educ.	02	00	−03	18	12	07	08	07	−23	10	−05	−12	−03	13	−19	05	04	05	05

PART I (*continued*)

	Father serious & moral	Mother serious & moral	Father loving	Mother loving	Childhood broken home	Childhood sex play	Sex play punished	Early masturbation	Early coitus	Childhood sex guilt	Sexual environment	Preadult broken home	Had sex education	Education completed	More ed. than parents	Military service	Positive to premar. sex	Negative to premar. sex	Premar. sex. involvement
Father serious & moral		49	11	08	-04	-03	-00	-00	-02	-02	-06	-06	05	06	-02	-02	-08	01	07
Mother serious & moral			06	10	-04	00	02	02	-04	01	-07	-04	03	10	02	-01	-06	-01	-08
Father loving				26	-04	-09	-07	-06	-04	-08	-11	-06	00	-02	-01	-06	-07	-02	-12
Mother loving					-08	-06	-06	-04	-02	-09	-08	-08	-02	-07	-00	-00	-06	-04	-09
Childhood broken home						-01	-00	01	06	-03	06	86	-06	-12	-04	-00	-02	03	03
Childhood sex play							28	18	10	72	18	-01	10	17	04	13	16	-03	26
Sex play punished								14	10	32	12	-01	04	04	02	11	11	00	17
Early masturbation									24	18	18	00	07	12	04	22	18	-12	31
Early coitus										05	16	07	-02	-02	-00	10	08	-09	22
Childhood sex guilt											13	-02	12	18	05	10	16	07	21
Sexual environment												07	08	10	01	23	32	-16	54
Preadult broken home													-07	-13	-05	-00	04	-01	04
Had sex education														33	04	01	10	10	04
Education completed															39	14	13	-02	17
More ed. than parents																10	-00	01	03
Military service																	25	-20	39
Positive to premar. sex																		-08	55
Negative to premar. sex																			-28
Premar. sex. involve.																			
Premar. sex. freq.	-06	-08	-12	-09	04	25	14	27	20	21	46	05	10	15	00	28	56	-24	88
Had premarital sex	-06	-06	-11	-10	01	20	11	24	17	21	40	03	09	12	-02	26	54	-17	71
Never masturbated	03	04	06	03	03	-21	-13	-37	-10	-18	-24	05	-06	-11	-03	-30	-31	18	-41
Age first married	02	03	04	07	-09	02	01	03	00	-02	01	-10	-04	12	11	29	08	-16	16
Number of marriages	02	-01	-00	-05	07	-07	01	-01	03	-05	07	07	-11	-18	-02	00	-05	02	-01
Currently married	02	02	-01	-04	-06	01	02	05	00	06	-07	-06	07	10	06	10	02	-05	02
Divorced, separated	-03	-02	-05	-05	06	02	02	-01	01	04	11	05	-02	-02	-04	-04	-00	03	01
Never married	-04	-03	-01	03	00	08	01	04	05	02	06	-00	02	09	00	02	11	-02	13
Number of children	-02	-05	-02	-01	05	-06	02	-03	-01	-06	-05	05	-10	-20	-03	-06	-11	01	-16
Age of oldest boy	-00	-02	04	09	03	-01	03	-02	-03	-04	-07	04	-14	-12	12	08	-15	-09	-13
Age of oldest girl	02	02	01	02	03	02	08	-01	00	-02	01	02	-18	-16	07	09	-10	-09	-03
Current high SES	06	10	-01	-04	-05	08	-00	07	-03	08	01	-05	17	38	06	05	03	-04	08
Current low SES	-01	-02	00	02	05	-05	-01	-05	03	-07	00	06	-07	-25	-07	-11	-01	04	-04

Higher SES than pars.	-02	01	-01	-03	06	05	-01	04	01	05	-00	06	06	18	19	07	-00	-01	04
Lives in Northeast	-06	-03	-01	-03	-04	-01	-06	-04	-02	-02	-04	-04	01	04	02	04	03	-04	02
Lives Midwest-South	04	02	05	03	02	-04	01	-04	-03	-03	-02	00	-11	-10	02	-08	-10	04	-10
Lives Pacific Coast	02	01	-07	-06	01	03	05	05	02	06	02	03	09	07	01	05	03	-00	04
Urban residence	-01	-01	-04	-03	10	04	04	06	05	01	12	10	09	11	01	06	13	-03	16
Urban mobility	03	01	00	05	09	-04	04	-04	01	-06	02	08	-09	-20	01	01	-01	03	-02
Lives on farm	-04	-04	05	02	-05	-04	-03	-05	-04	-05	-08	-06	-09	-12	-05	-05	-08	03	-14
Moved away from farm	07	03	03	05	-02	-06	-02	-05	01	-07	-02	-01	-08	-13	08	-04	-07	03	-07
Sociable	03	05	06	-01	-06	02	00	-00	-02	03	04	-06	12	17	04	-02	02	03	02
Serious & moral	36	38	06	06	00	-07	-03	-03	-02	-03	-13	00	03	02	04	-02	-12	04	-15
Not a sexual person	-06	-08	05	05	01	-12	-06	-14	-07	-12	-25	01	-14	-19	-01	-14	-26	13	-31
Masculine	04	05	-03	-01	-04	04	04	10	07	02	16	-04	05	10	07	16	14	-09	18
Feminine	01	03	-14	-15	03	07	06	09	02	09	15	03	09	07	01	-03	10	12	12
Work-oriented	03	02	12	08	02	-04	01	-02	01	-06	04	00	-06	-11	04	11	03	-10	05
Fundamentalist	04	03	05	08	07	-04	07	-02	03	-05	-04	05	-06	-22	-01	-05	-07	06	-07
Change from Fund.	-03	-04	-06	-09	00	04	-03	03	-00	04	02	02	01	12	00	05	09	-07	11
Catholic	-01	-01	00	-05	-03	-03	-05	-04	-06	-02	-10	-04	00	01	02	-00	-05	-01	-06
Jewish	-01	-00	00	00	-05	02	-04	00	-00	-00	01	-04	04	11	03	00	04	-02	04
No current religion	-04	-04	-12	-09	01	10	-00	10	07	06	16	05	01	07	00	07	12	-07	22
Change to no religion	-03	-03	-10	-06	03	08	-01	08	07	04	15	06	01	07	02	05	11	-04	18
Current devoutness	09	08	18	12	-02	-13	-03	-13	-07	-10	-23	-05	-03	-10	04	-12	-22	14	-34
Decreasing devoutness	00	-01	01	-03	-02	08	04	06	06	02	12	-00	00	03	-04	08	15	-07	18
Sexually threatened	00	-02	05	05	04	-13	-05	-14	-04	-12	-17	05	-12	-27	-08	-18	-26	21	-31
Sexual Morality Scale	-14	-11	-14	-12	00	26	10	19	07	20	30	01	14	22	00	12	35	-14	43
Liberal. Vs. Parents'	-05	-02	-13	-13	-00	18	09	13	06	17	25	00	13	21	02	09	27	-08	31
Moral Change Index	-07	-04	-11	-15	-00	20	08	13	01	24	19	01	15	26	03	05	20	-02	21
Heterosexual cure	-04	-05	02	07	04	-06	-02	-05	03	-08	-03	03	-11	22	-05	-04	-05	05	-08
Voluntary cure	02	-02	06	03	03	-09	-04	-06	00	-09	-09	04	-09	-17	-01	-03	-10	03	-12
Hs identifiable	-02	-04	03	01	04	-10	02	-06	03	-10	02	05	-06	-20	-03	-00	01	05	-01
Family cause	-03	-04	09	06	02	-11	-05	-05	-03	-12	-09	-03	09	-21	-01	-02	-03	-03	-06
H is distorted HT	-06	07	03	07	04	-09	-01	-09	03	-10	-05	04	-14	-28	-06	-05	-07	07	-10
Hs are dangerous	03	-02	12	11	03	-18	-01	-10	00	-14	-14	02	-17	-33	-03	-03	-18	06	-22
H is abhorrent	11	09	11	11	-01	-24	-10	-11	-06	-16	-22	-03	-09	-19	-01	-08	-21	08	-26
Deny authorit. jobs	02	01	10	07	01	-17	-05	-08	-02	-11	-20	00	-08	-18	03	-02	-16	05	-21
Allow stereo. jobs	06	10	-06	-08	-04	10	02	11	03	12	14	-04	15	29	06	08	13	-04	18
Deny freedoms	01	01	08	10	01	-19	-07	-08	-04	-15	-21	00	-12	-22	00	-05	-22	06	-25
Antihomosexual factor	05	03	12	12	01	-25	-07	-11	-04	-18	-24	-00	-14	-28	00	-05	-23	08	-29
Maint. of friendship	-06	-06	-07	-08	02	15	06	14	08	11	32	04	07	17	03	15	28	-20	39
Sexual suppression	02	02	09	12	02	-20	-03	-13	-05	-19	-21	02	-14	-33	-04	-08	-23	13	-30
Opposed to sex educ.	06	05	09	11	02	-14	-03	-08	-01	-12	-15	00	-17	-27	01	-05	-20	07	-22

PART I (*continued*)

	Premar. sex. frequency	Had premarital sex	Never masturbated	Age first married	Number of marriages	Currently married	Divorced, separated	Never married	Number of children	Age of oldest boy	Age of oldest girl	Current high SES	Current low SES	Higher SES than parents	Lives in Northeast	Lives in Midwest/South	Lives on Pacific Coast	Urban residence	Urban mobility
Premar. sex. freq.		83	−36	09	−01	04	−00	11	−17	−18	−12	06	−03	03	01	−10	04	14	−02
Had premarital sex			−32	03	−00	06	−00	07	−10	−16	−10	04	−03	04	01	−08	03	13	00
Never masturbated				−17	03	−09	02	−06	04	00	−02	−07	05	−05	00	06	−04	−07	−00
Age first married					15	21	−04	[a]	−22	06	10	11	−05	04	08	−08	01	05	03
Number of marriages						05	07	−55	05	10	11	−04	00	02	−10	08	06	02	08
Currently married							−39	−50	−02	−05	−02	11	−19	13	−00	−00	01	−07	−11
Divorced, separated								−06	−03	02	01	−02	02	−02	−01	01	02	04	04
Never married									[a]	00	05	−03	06	−06	05	−05	00	03	−03
Number of children										40	37	−10	06	−03	00	07	−02	−06	07
Age of oldest boy											55	−03	01	05	00	01	−04	−02	05
Age of oldest girl												−06	−03	04	−02	04	−06	−04	07
Current high SES													−28	54	02	09	05	10	−07
Current low SES														−29	−00	−00	−00	03	09
Higher SES than parents															03	−07	02	07	−06
Lives in Northeast																−34	−21	09	−13
Lives in Midwest/South																	−23	−25	04
Lives on Pacific Coast																		08	06
Urban residence																			43
Urban mobility																			
Lives on farm	−12	−09	04	06	−00	04	−02	−04	12	09	06	−18	−04	−06	−13	28	−03	−36	−09
Moved away from farm	−08	−06	06	−03	07	−10	01	−00	03	05	02	05	08	−05	−09	04	04	04	37
Sociable	03	01	02	00	−03	04	02	−04	−06	−09	−12	08	−09	03	06	−03	−06	03	−07
Serious and moral	−15	−12	08	−04	03	08	−05	−08	04	02	03	07	−02	05	−05	03	01	−01	03

Not a sexual person	−29	−25	16	02	−01	−21	02	04	06	09	07	−10	07	−05	−06	08	−02	−09	05
Masculine	13	10	−16	06	01	04	00	−01	−01	01	06	07	−08	06	−00	−07	02	02	−02
Feminine	13	11	−05	−15	02	06	03	−02	−05	−03	−11	02	02	01	−02	−04	03	06	−05
Work-oriented	01	−00	−09	11	07	−04	02	−02	−00	12	08	−05	02	−01	−01	−04	03	07	10
Fundamentalist	−07	−05	02	−15	11	−04	02	−06	04	−03	−00	−15	08	−07	−24	20	−03	−04	19
Change from Fund.	10	05	−04	09	−03	01	00	06	−03	05	03	09	−03	03	11	−12	07	01	−13
Catholic	−06	−05	04	05	−08	06	−02	−02	04	−02	−05	02	−01	04	26	−12	−07	06	−14
Jewish	03	02	−02	07	−05	−00	00	03	−03	−00	−02	05	−05	02	16	−08	−03	11	−10
No current religion	19	15	−12	02	−01	−06	03	12	−08	−04	−03	02	−01	−00	−02	−08	13	07	−01
Change to no religion	16	12	−10	00	−01	−06	03	10	−07	−02	−02	02	−00	01	−00	−08	11	07	01
Current devoutness	−32	−26	18	−13	02	06	−06	−12	10	11	08	−03	01	−00	−07	15	−13	−12	07
Decreasing devoutness	16	13	−11	04	−01	−07	04	07	−04	−00	01	00	−00	−02	03	−10	05	08	04
Sexually threatened	−30	−25	16	−01	08	−07	04	−06	09	07	10	−13	07	−09	−08	10	−05	−08	11
Sexual Morality Scale	40	35	−26	02	−08	−01	03	11	−13	−12	−10	11	−04	07	13	−21	08	19	−08
Liberal. Vs. Parents'	30	27	−17	−03	−06	−02	03	08	−09	−14	−11	11	−05	04	07	−12	05	13	−08
Moral Change Index	22	20	−14	−03	−07	02	02	08	−07	−08	−12	18	−08	09	07	−16	12	11	−12
Heterosexual cure	−07	−07	01	00	05	−07	01	−02	07	02	04	−11	06	−04	−04	04	−03	−03	10
Voluntary cure	−11	−11	06	−01	06	−04	−00	−04	05	03	04	−10	05	−04	−05	06	−03	−09	08
Hs identifiable	−00	−01	06	−04	06	−03	03	−03	04	02	−00	−11	08	−05	05	02	−06	06	09
Family cause	−06	−05	06	01	04	−03	−01	−02	03	08	09	−14	06	−06	−03	05	−05	−06	03
H is distorted HT	−10	−09	03	01	−06	−07	01	−02	07	03	06	−13	10	−07	−05	06	−04	−06	11
Hs are dangerous	−23	−18	09	01	10	02	−04	−11	09	12	09	−19	05	−09	−10	16	−09	−16	11
H is abhorrent	−26	−21	19	−05	05	03	−02	−11	05	00	−01	−13	02	−07	−10	16	−06	−17	07
Deny authorit. jobs	−21	−16	10	−03	05	06	−03	−10	08	06	05	−11	01	−04	−07	15	−10	−19	04
Allow stereo. jobs	16	14	−04	−03	−07	05	00	04	−08	−10	−06	15	−08	09	09	−14	07	15	−09
Deny freedoms	−25	−20	11	−03	05	03	−05	−09	09	06	06	−12	03	−07	−09	21	−12	−20	09
Antihomosexual factor	−29	−23	16	−03	08	04	−03	−12	10	07	06	−16	04	−08	−11	21	−12	−22	10
Maint. of friendship	36	29	−20	03	00	00	03	07	−10	−04	−03	07	−02	09	11	−16	08	19	−04
Sexual suppression	−30	−25	17	−02	06	−03	−01	−07	11	09	07	−19	09	−09	−11	18	−08	−14	12
Opposed to sex educ.	−24	−21	09	02	07	−02	−01	−06	11	13	10	−14	04	−04	−11	13	−06	−13	11

[a] Uncomputable.

PART I (*continued*)

	Lives on farm	Moved away from farm	Sociable	Serious and moral	Not a sexual person	Masculine	Feminine	Work-oriented	Fundamentalist	Change from Fundamentalist	Catholic	Jewish	No current religion	Change to no religion	Current devoutness	Decreasing devoutness	Sexually threatened	Sexual Morality Scale	Liberality Vs. Parents'
Lives on farm		−47	−03	−05	10	01	−05	−02	−02	03	−05	−04	−03	−03	06	−02	06	−13	−12
Moved away from farm			−03	05	07	−04	−04	05	17	−10	−09	−05	−04	−03	09	−02	09	−11	−05
Sociable				10	−18	15	05	06	−06	−00	10	04	−12	−10	14	−08	−04	03	07
Serious and moral					−16	11	07	12	06	−05	01	−05	−13	−11	21	−10	09	−23	−12
Not a sexual person						−14	−21	−03	04	−03	−03	00	−07	−06	08	−02	22	−23	−18
Masculine							18	18	−04	06	03	04	01	02	00	03	−03	08	08
Feminine								−12	00	03	02	−00	06	06	−06	01	−01	10	12
Work-oriented									05	−01	01	01	−06	−05	12	02	08	−06	−06
Fundamentalist										−72	−33	−09	−18	−16	22	−10	14	−20	−14
Change from Fundamentalism											15	03	32	30	−23	13	−09	14	08
Catholic												−09	−18	−16	13	−04	−03	05	01
Jewish													−05	−05	−09	−03	−08	11	06
No current religion														89	−54	34	−10	22	13
Change to no religion															−46	35	−09	18	13
Current devoutness																−56	20	−40	−26
Decreasing devoutness																	−06	20	14
Sexually threatened																		−31	−24
Sexual Morality Scale																			49
Liberality Vs. Parents'																			
Moral Change Index	−09	−09	05	−13	−15	06	14	−10	−16	11	02	08	14	13	−25	13	−20	46	43
Heterosexual cure	07	06	−01	00	08	02	−01	10	09	−04	−04	−04	−07	−06	12	−04	21	−12	−10
Voluntary cure	05	07	−03	−06	09	−01	−04	11	13	−07	−06	−06	−08	−06	13	−04	15	−21	−16
Hs identifiable	−03	03	03	02	−01	02	01	08	08	−04	03	−05	−04	−03	06	−00	15	−08	−05
Family cause	06	02	−02	−03	10	−05	−10	08	05	−01	−02	−05	−03	−02	04	01	10	−10	−12
H is distorted HT	09	07	−04	−00	12	00	−02	13	13	−06	−05	−05	−09	−07	13	−04	26	−15	−15
Hs are dangerous	13	11	−01	09	18	00	−09	14	20	−12	−04	−13	−18	−15	25	−09	33	−42	−31
H is abhorrent	08	08	03	20	11	−06	−07	07	18	−12	01	−13	−23	−21	29	−17	22	−49	−34
Deny authorit. jobs	10	05	01	13	10	−02	−07	06	12	−09	01	−12	−20	−18	23	−12	21	−38	−24
Allow stereo. jobs	−14	−07	07	03	−17	02	09	−10	−15	10	04	06	09	09	−11	03	−23	26	17
Deny freedoms	12	09	−03	11	18	−04	−08	08	18	−12	−02	−12	−20	−18	29	−14	22	−48	−34
Antihomosexual factor	13	10	01	17	17	−04	−10	12	20	−13	−01	−16	−25	−23	33	−16	30	−55	−39
Maint. of friendship	−13	−08	02	−13	−22	08	03	−01	−12	08	01	08	18	16	−30	15	−31	44	29
Sexual suppression	10	11	−05	10	22	−05	−05	13	22	−14	−02	−11	−18	−15	27	−12	34	−53	36
Opposed to sex educ.	14	07	−02	15	18	01	−06	09	17	−10	−03	−11	−15	−13	25	−10	31	−39	−30

	Heterosexual cure	Voluntary cure	Hs identifiable	Family cause	H is distorted HT	Hs are dangerous	H is abhorrent	Deny authoritative jobs	Allow stereotypic jobs	Deny freedoms	Antihomosexual factor	Maintenance of friendship	Sexual suppression scale	Opposed to sex education
Moral Change Index	−12	−18	−13	−14	−15	−36	−41	−32	18	−37	−46	26	−36	−30
Heterosexual cure		42	13	−01	97	32	12	13	−18	15	22	−12	24	24
Voluntary cure			11	−09	52	28	20	20	−17	23	28	−14	26	16
Hs identifiable				10	16	33	14	16	−10	08	22	−05	15	14
Family cause					−00	13	09	08	−09	05	11	−08	13	15
H is distorted HT						37	15	17	−24	19	27	−15	29	28
Hs are dangerous							48	61	−35	48	79	−32	46	47
H is abhorrent								52	−22	59	81	−38	40	32
Deny authoritative jobs									−32	51	83	−32	38	33
Allow stereotypic jobs										−37	−39	24	−38	−23
Deny freedoms											80	−38	47	33
Antihomosexual factor												−43	53	45
Maintenance of friendship													−45	−27
Sexual suppression scale														37

PART II Attitudes Toward Homosexuality

	Act like opposite sex	Afraid of opposite sex	Distinctive appearance	Strong sex drives	H in everyone	Seduced by older Hs	Parents create H	Are HT "failures"	Born that way	Can be cured	Can stop voluntarily	HT women cure H men	HT men cure H women	Obscene and vulgar	May approach children	Dangerous as teachers	H men attack women	May destroy civilization	People make the problem
Act like opp. sex		20	28	21	-10	09	-00	08	08	10	09	08	11	15	22	22	11	15	-05
Afraid of opp. sex			11	12	-01	12	07	10	-00	11	04	08	08	11	17	18	04	14	-03
Distinctive appearance				18	-06	11	-03	15	13	05	08	08	12	11	20	22	13	17	02
Strong sex drives					-09	10	-05	15	12	12	09	15	16	21	31	27	19	25	-05
H in everyone						-07	15	-03	-07	-09	-09	-03	-06	-37	-23	-24	-05	-20	28
Seduced by older Hs							08	16	-10	13	18	19	23	15	20	23	16	19	-11
Parents create H								07	-12	07	-00	03	03	-11	-09	-09	02	-05	04
Are HT "failures"									05	11	17	22	23	11	12	13	30	12	05
Born that way										-09	-09	03	01	01	08	08	16	02	10
Can be cured											49	23	32	22	16	20	16	20	-11
Can stop voluntarily												35	40	17	17	19	26	23	-05
HT women cure H men													66	14	17	18	41	18	02
HT men cure H women														19	23	22	39	26	02
Obscene and vulgar															37	43	17	39	-34
May approach children																71	20	44	-20
Dangerous as teachers																	19	50	43
H men attack women																		21	03
May destroy civilization																			-28
People make problem																			

Security risks	12	14	09	16	−11	15	−01	07	03	17	13	08	14	23	31	35	11	27	−21
Corrupt fellow workers	18	15	21	28	−15	20	−05	21	13	19	21	23	32	30	39	43	28	39	−28
No gay judges	10	10	10	18	−26	14	−09	08	01	18	14	07	12	40	39	43	09	33	−28
No gay teachers	13	11	11	18	−26	15	−09	08	02	21	12	07	14	44	46	56	10	38	−31
No gay ministers	14	11	09	16	−29	15	−09	10	00	17	13	06	13	44	39	44	10	36	−29
No gay doctors	11	12	10	22	−25	15	−11	10	03	16	10	10	14	43	39	45	14	37	−28
No government jobs	12	07	09	15	−21	14	−07	08	06	14	10	06	11	34	37	42	10	32	−25
Gay beauticians O.K.	−04	−09	−10	−18	17	−08	10	−13	06	−13	−16	−15	−19	−24	−25	−31	−21	−32	16
Gay artists O.K.	−03	−04	−12	−10	11	−07	06	−11	−06	−11	−15	−12	−17	−14	−16	−23	−18	−23	09
Gay musicians O.K.	−03	−05	−12	−11	13	−08	05	−10	−06	−11	−15	−09	−15	−16	−15	−22	−15	−23	13
Gay florists O.K.	−02	−02	−09	−09	11	−08	03	−10	−05	−10	−14	−11	−15	−13	−12	−20	−16	−21	08
No H rec. groups	02	05	04	19	−28	15	−09	08	−02	19	18	12	14	40	28	35	14	39	−35
No problem groups	−01	−01	07	04	−19	09	−10	05	−10	04	13	06	09	24	17	23	10	27	−26
No H dancing	07	05	07	10	−28	13	−05	03	−05	16	09	02	05	41	27	33	01	29	−32
No bars for Hs	03	04	06	11	−27	12	−09	09	−00	15	16	08	13	38	25	30	11	34	−31
No Hs in churches	07	06	16	12	−11	10	−08	13	05	06	13	11	12	18	19	23	17	28	−11
H nobody's business	−06	−05	−08	−13	28	−13	10	−06	02	−15	−16	−08	−11	−37	−25	−32	−10	−38	47
Heterosexual cure	10	10	11	17	−05	23	04	24	03	31	42	91	91	19	23	23	45	24	02
Voluntary cure	11	11	07	12	−11	18	04	16	−10	86	86	33	41	22	19	22	24	23	−09
Hs identifiable	80	80	80	24	−10	12	02	14	12	09	11	10	14	16	26	27	14	19	−02
Family cause	−05	−05	−11	−11	15	12	75	01	−75	11	06	00	01	−08	−11	−11	−09	−05	−03
H is distorted HT	12	12	13	20	−06	26	03	37	04	34	53	87	89	20	24	24	60	27	02
Hs are dangerous	25	27	26	42	−26	27	−09	18	10	24	24	23	31	47	83	90	27	66	−29
H is abhorrent	14	14	08	17	−71	15	−14	06	−00	20	15	08	13	84	38	43	10	40	−67
Deny authorit. jobs	14	14	12	22	−31	18	−11	10	01	21	14	08	15	49	48	55	12	42	−35
Allow stereo. jobs	−02	−04	−13	−14	15	−09	07	−12	−07	−13	−18	−13	−20	−19	−20	−28	−21	−29	13
Deny freedoms	05	05	08	26	−36	17	−12	09	−04	20	20	11	15	50	34	43	14	47	−47
Antihomosexual factor	18	14	17	29	−51	24	−14	13	02	27	23	16	24	72	62	70	21	60	−55

	High security risks	Corrupt fellow workers	No gay judges	No gay teachers	No gay ministers	No gay doctors	No gays in government jobs	Gay beauticians O.K.	Gay artists O.K.	Gay musicians O.K.	Gay florists O.K.	No H recreational groups	No H problem-solv. groups	No H dancing	No bars for Hs	No Hs in churches	H nobody's business	Heterosexual cure	Voluntary cure
High security risks		45	36	32	27	27	47	−20	−13	−17	−13	19	15	18	21	13	−21	12	17
Corrupt fellow workers			32	32	31	34	35	−34	−23	−25	−24	25	21	20	28	24	−28	30	23
No gay judges				68	68	61	65	−29	−18	−20	−19	34	18	36	33	14	−29	11	18
No gay teachers					70	61	57	−31	−21	−21	−19	38	20	37	32	16	−31	12	19
No gay ministers						61	54	−28	−20	−21	−18	36	21	36	33	18	−31	11	17
No gay doctors							55	−38	−25	−26	−24	38	22	34	33	18	−34	13	15
No government jobs								−33	−23	−27	−25	31	21	30	31	16	−28	09	14
Gay beauticians O.K.									57	54	53	−30	−26	−16	−30	−25	32	−19	−17
Gay artists O.K.										58	60	−23	−23	−12	−23	−24	26	−16	−14
Gay musicians O.K.											67	−24	−24	−14	−24	−24	27	−13	−14
Gay florists O.K.												−20	−23	−13	−22	−23	21	−14	−13
No H rec. groups													47	38	46	19	−46	15	21
No problem groups														22	32	22	−39	08	09
No H dancing															41	11	−32	05	14
No bars for Hs																19	−41	11	17
No Hs in churches																	−19	14	10
H nobody's business																		−10	−18
Heterosexual cure																			42
Voluntary cure																			
Hs identifiable	13	24	12	15	14	12	13	−09	−09	−09	−07	04	04	09	05	14	−08	13	11
Family cause	−03	−12	−06	−07	−06	−09	−07	10	07	06	06	−02	−07	−02	−06	−09	05	01	09
H is distorted HT	14	33	13	13	13	14	11	−21	−18	−15	−16	17	10	05	14	18	−12	97	50
Hs are dangerous	53	66	48	56	48	50	48	−37	−26	−26	−23	39	26	34	36	28	−38	30	27
H is abhorrent	25	29	43	44	47	44	36	−26	−16	−19	−15	46	30	46	43	18	−48	12	20
Deny authorit. jobs	40	39	89	87	86	79	76	−37	−25	−26	−24	42	24	42	39	19	−36	13	20
Allow stereo. jobs	−18	−31	−25	−27	−25	−32	−31	74	83	86	87	−29	−28	−16	−29	−29	31	−18	−17
Deny freedoms	26	34	42	44	44	45	39	−38	−30	−31	−27	86	63	58	73	25	−72	15	23
Antihomosexual factor	45	52	71	74	71	68	62	−43	−30	−32	−28	66	44	56	59	28	−60	22	28

	Family cause	H is distorted HT	Hs are dangerous	H is abhorrent	Deny authoritative jobs	Allow stereotypic jobs	Deny freedoms	Antihomosexual factor
Hs identifiable	−10	15	31	14	16	10	08	22
Family cause		−00	−12	−09	−08	−09	−05	−11
H is distorted HT			33	15	17	24	19	27
Hs are dangerous				48	60	32	48	79
H is abhorrent					52	22	59	83
Deny authorit. jobs						32	51	39
Allow stereo. jobs							37	80
Deny freedoms								80

Appendix F

Interview Questionnaire and Response Distributions

In this appendix we reproduce the questions that were actually asked our respondents and show what proportion of the males, of the females, and of the total sample gave each of the available responses. Questions that were not asked everyone are preceded by a notation in brackets to this effect; our comments about the coding or response distribution of a particular question appear, as necessary, in footnotes. Some parts of questions are given in parentheses to show where it was necessary for the interviewer to choose a word or phrase best suited to the particular respondent. For example, everyone was asked who the main wage earner was in the household. Subsequent questions have the phrase "main earner" in parentheses, indicating that here the interviewer said "you," "he," "she," or whatever was appropriate.

The section of the questionnaire identified as Sexual History included items in a self-administered booklet given to the respondent near the end of the interview. Interviewers handed over the booklet with these instructions: "In order to make a true evaluation of this entire survey, it is important to know something about people's experience. We would greatly appreciate your filling out this booklet, which is, of course, confidential. I will give you an envelope in which you, yourself, will seal the completed booklet. The answers from all sorts of people are really needed for statistical purposes."

The percentages that we give may add to slightly more or less than 100.0 owing to rounding. When, for a question asked of all respondents, we show responses for fewer than 1,465 males or 1,553 females (resulting in a total-sample *N* of less than 3,018), the "missing" respondents either failed to answer or gave noncodable responses.

	Males	*Females*	*Total*
1. First of all, have you ever taken part in any other survey about sexual attitudes or behavior?	(*N* = 1,464)	(*N* = 1,552)	(*N* = 3,016)
No	97.5%	97.8%	97.3%
Yes	2.5	2.2	2.3
[IF NO:] 2. Have you heard of any other surveys about sexual attitudes or behavior?	(*N* = 1,428)	(*N* = 1,518)	(*N* = 2,946)
No	58.8%	67.3%	63.2%
Yes	41.2	32.7	36.8
[IF YES to Q.1 or Q.2:] 2A. In general, do these surveys seem to you to be entirely good and respectable, entirely bad, partly good and partly bad, or do you feel you don't know enough about them to have an opinion?	(*N* = 614)	(*N* = 515)	(*N* = 1,129)
Entirely bad	2.0%	2.1%	2.0%
Partly good and partly bad	27.7	27.2	27.5
Good and respectable	37.1	36.5	36.8
Don't know	33.2	34.2	33.7

DEMOGRAPHIC CHARACTERISTICS (SEE ALSO Q. 27–29, 35, 36, 39, 100–102)

	Males	*Females*	*Total*
3. Now, we have some general questions about yourself. What was your age on your last birthday?[1]	(*N* = 1,465)	(*N* = 1,550)	(*N* = 3,015)
16–19	0.4%	2.1%	1.3%
20–24	9.6	12.3	11.0
25–29	9.4	14.3	11.9
30–34	12.4	10.1	11.2
35–44	18.5	20.3	19.4
45–54	18.1	17.7	17.9
55–64	13.1	12.3	12.7
65 or older	18.5	10.9	14.6
4. What is the highest grade or year of school you have completed?	(*N* = 1,461)	(*N* = 1,552)	(*N* = 3,013)
Less than eighth grade	13.8%	8.1%	10.8%
Eighth grade	10.3	11.7	11.0
Some high school	18.5	21.3	19.9
High school diploma or equivalent	27.7	34.0	30.9
Some college	16.4	16.8	16.6
Bachelor's degree	7.8	5.3	6.5
Postgraduate college work	5.5	2.8	4.1
5. Have you ever been on active duty for military training or service for two consecutive months or more?	(*N* = 1,452)	(*N* = 1,551)	(*N* = 3,003)
No	50.8%	99.2%	75.4%
Yes	49.2	0.8	24.6

	Males	*Females*	*Total*
[IF YES:]			
5A. What was your total time on active duty?	(*N* = 715)	(*N* = 13)	(*N* = 728)
Less than two years	22.0%	30.8%	22.1%
Two to four years	55.4	61.5	55.5
More than four years	22.7	7.7	22.4
[IF served in military:]			
5B. In what branch of the service was that?[2]	(*N* = 723)	(*N* = 14)	(*N* = 737)
Army	54.6%	42.9%	54.4%
Navy	19.4	42.9	19.8
Air Force	15.4	14.3	15.3
Marine Corps	6.1	0.0	6.0
Coast Guard	1.5	0.0	1.5
National Guard	3.0	0.0	3.0
Air National Guard	0.0	0.0	0.0
6. Are you currently married, widowed, divorced, separated, or never married?	(*N* = 1,465)	(*N* = 1,553)	(*N* = 3,018)
Currently married	80.3%	75.2%	77.6%
Widowed	5.3	11.9	8.7
Divorced	3.1	5.1	4.1
Separated	2.0	3.7	2.8
Single, never married	9.2	4.1	6.5
[IF ever married:]			
6A. What was your age when first married?	(*N* = 1,324)	(*N* = 1,482)	(*N* = 2,806)
Under 16	0.0%	5.1%	2.7%
16–19	16.2	42.3	30.0
20–24	47.5	40.8	43.9
25–29	24.7	8.9	16.4
30 or older	11.6	2.9	7.0
6B. How many children have you had? This refers to live births, not adoptions or stepchildren.)	(*N* = 1,302)	(*N* = 1,454)	(*N* = 2,756)
None	16.6%	11.2%	13.8%
One	17.2	15.8	16.5
Two	24.3	27.0	25.7
Three	15.7	18.7	17.3
Four	11.4	11.4	11.4
Five or more	14.7	15.9	15.3
6C. How many marriages have you had?	(*N* = 1,325)	(*N* = 1,483)	(*N* = 2,808)
One	80.4%	82.1%	81.3%
Two	16.4	15.1	15.8
Three or more	3.2	2.7	3.0
7. Do you have any parental (or guardian) responsibility for any children under the age of 20?	(*N* = 1,459)	(*N* = 1,548)	(*N* = 3,007)
No	51.8%	39.0%	45.2%
Yes	48.2	61.0	54.8

	Males	*Females*	*Total*
[IF YES:]			
7A. What was the age of the oldest boy on his last birthday?	(*N* = 703)	(*N* = 944)	(*N* = 1,647)
Under 6	18.1%	20.6%	19.5%
6–11	21.9	21.6	21.7
12–15	15.4	15.1	15.2
16–19	19.5	18.1	18.7
No sons (but has daughters)	25.2	24.6	24.8
7B. And the age of the oldest girl?	(*N* = 704)	(*N* = 940)	(*N* = 1,644)
Under 6	18.5%	23.0%	21.0%
6–11	20.5	24.1	22.6
12–15	20.7	15.0	17.5
16–19	17.2	14.1	15.5
No daughters (but has sons)	23.2	23.7	23.5
8. Who is this household's main earner?	(*N* = 1,460)	(*N* = 1,551)	(*N* = 3,011)
Male (respondent or spouse)	89.5%	66.1%	77.4%
Female (respondent or spouse)	2.8	25.1	14.3
Neither respondent nor spouse	5.2	3.9	4.5
No main earner	2.5	4.9	3.8
[IF household has a main earner:]			
9. What kind of work (does/did) (main earner) normally do?[3]			
[Type of work]	(*N* = 1,413)	(*N* = 1,454)	(*N* = 2,867)
Professional, technical, and kindred	13.3%	16.3%	14.9%
Manager, administrator (non-farm)	13.0	11.1	12.0
Sales worker	5.6	5.0	5.3
Clerical and kindred	7.2	7.6	7.4
Craftsman and kindred	21.7	20.0	20.9
Armed forces	0.8	1.1	1.0
Operative (non-transport)	11.7	12.6	12.1
Transport equipment operative	5.9	3.9	4.9
Laborer (non-farm)	6.6	5.3	5.9
Farmer, farm manager	6.5	4.5	5.5
Farm foreman, farm laborer	1.1	0.9	1.0
Service worker (not private household)	6.2	10.0	8.1
Private household worker	0.4	1.7	1.0
[Occupational prestige]	(*N* = 1,416)	(*N* = 1,455)	(*N* = 2,871)
Cleaner, attendant, laborer	9.5%	10.0%	9.7%
Child-care worker, factory worker	13.1	14.0	13.5
Hairdresser, file clerk, bus driver	14.1	13.9	14.0
Mechanic, bricklayer, meter reader	11.2	10.6	10.9
Farmer, firefighter, stenographer	17.4	15.4	16.4
Buyer, electrician, musician	11.7	12.6	12.2
Programmer, social worker, librarian	14.7	13.9	14.3
Higher-prestige occupations	8.4	9.8	9.1
[Industrial classification]	(*N* = 1,403)	(*N* = 1,448)	(*N* = 2,851)
Agriculture, forestry, fisheries	8.6%	6.7%	7.7%
Mining, construction	8.1	7.9	8.0
Manufacturing, durable goods	16.0	14.1	15.1

	Males	*Females*	*Total*
Manufacturing, non-durable goods	11.0	11.3	11.2
Business and professional services	21.2	26.0	23.6
Transportation, communication, utilities	10.3	7.5	8.9
Wholesale and retail trade	10.1	11.4	10.8
Finance, insurance, real estate	2.9	3.3	3.1
Public administration	11.7	11.7	11.7
10A. Who was the main wage earner for your family most of the time before you were 16?	(*N* = 1,465)	(*N* = 1,551)	(*N* = 3,016)
Respondent's father	86.8%	82.3%	84.5%
Respondent's mother	7.1	10.4	8.8
Someone else	4.7	5.6	5.1
No main earner	1.4	1.7	1.6
[IF childhood household had main earner:]			
10B. What kind of work did (main earner) do while you were growing up?[3]			
[Type of work]	(*N* = 1,430)	(*N* = 1,505)	(*N* = 2,935)
Professional, technical, and kindred	5.9%	7.0%	6.5%
Manager, administrator (non-farm)	10.1	11.1	10.6
Sales worker	3.9	2.9	3.4
Clerical and kindred	3.1	3.3	3.2
Craftsman and kindred	19.9	17.5	18.7
Armed forces	0.3	0.3	0.3
Operative (non-transport)	12.8	12.2	12.5
Transport equipment operative	3.8	4.7	4.3
Laborer (non-farm)	6.4	5.6	6.0
Farmer, farm manager	23.2	22.9	23.1
Farm foreman, farm laborer	3.3	3.8	3.5
Service worker (not private household)	5.5	6.2	5.9
Private household worker	1.7	2.5	2.1
[Occupational prestige]	(*N* = 1,433)	(*N* = 1,508	(*N* = 2,941)
Cleaner, attendant, laborer	11.4%	11.3%	11.3%
Child-care worker, factory worker	12.5	14.1	13.3
Hairdresser, file clerk, bus driver	13.2	10.5	11.8
Mechanic, bricklayer, meter reader	8.9	9.2	9.0
Farmer, firefighter, stenographer	31.9	31.8	31.9
Buyer, electrician, musician	7.3	7.0	7.1
Programmer, social worker, librarian	10.2	10.8	10.5
Higher-prestige occupations	4.7	5.3	5.0
[Industrial classification]	(*N* = 1,427)	(*N* = 1,492)	(*N* = 2,919)
Agriculture, forestry, fisheries	26.9%	27.4%	27.2%
Mining, construction	11.0	9.6	10.3
Manufacturing, durable goods	11.6	12.3	12.2
Manufacturing, non-durable goods	8.8	8.6	8.7
Business and professional services	17.9	18.6	18.3
Transportation, communication, utilities	7.7	7.4	7.5
Wholesale and retail trade	9.0	9.0	9.0
Finance, insurance, real estate	1.5	1.5	1.5
Public administration	5.7	5.7	5.7

	Males	*Females*	*Total*
11A. Approximately how old was your father when you were born?	(*N* = 1,394)	(*N* = 1,485)	(*N* = 2,879)
Under 20	2.0%	2.9%	2.5%
20–24	18.4	19.5	19.0
25–29	23.6	24.6	24.1
30–34	22.8	20.9	21.8
35–39	15.3	16.2	15.8
40–44	9.3	7.5	8.4
45 or older	8.5	8.3	8.4
11B. And about how old was your mother at that time?	(*N* = 1,411)	(*N* = 1,508)	(*N* = 2,919)
Under 20	11.1%	14.2%	12.7%
20–24	27.0	29.8	28.5
25–29	25.0	25.9	24.1
30–34	16.8	16.4	16.6
35–39	12.3	8.4	10.4
40–44	5.2	5.3	5.3
45 or older	1.6	1.2	1.5
12A. In what country was your father born?	(*N* = 1,460)	(*N* = 1,543)	(*N* = 3,003)
United States	79.7%	81.3%	80.6%
Canada or Great Britain	4.9	4.4	4.6
Western or Southern Europe	8.6	7.3	8.0
Central or Eastern Europe	5.3	5.5	5.3
Latin America	1.2	1.4	1.3
Elsewhere	0.3	0.3	0.3
12B. In what country was your mother born?	(*N* = 1,442)	(*N* = 1,534)	(*N* = 2,976)
United States	82.5%	84.5%	83.5%
Canada or Great Britain	4.4	3.8	4.1
Western or Southern Europe	7.1	5.8	6.5
Central or Eastern Europe	4.8	4.7	4.7
Latin America	0.9	1.0	0.9
Elsewhere	0.3	0.2	0.2
[IF either parent foreign-born:]			
12C. In what country were you born?	(*N* = 351)	(*N* = 352)	(*N* = 703)
United States	79.5%	78.1%	78.7%
Canada or Great Britain	5.1	8.2	6.7
Western or Southern Europe	8.5	7.4	8.0
Central or Eastern Europe	4.8	3.1	4.0
Latin America	2.0	3.1	2.6
Elsewhere	0.0	0.0	0.0
[IF respondent foreign-born:]			
12D. Were you brought up mostly in (country of birth), or mostly in the United States?[4]	(*N* = 74)	(*N* = 80)	(*N* = 154)
In country of birth	60.8%	76.2%	67.5%
In the United States	39.2	23.8	32.5

	Males	*Females*	*Total*
[IF born and/or reared in U.S.:]			
12E. In what state (or U.S. territory or possession) were you mostly brought up before age 16?[5]	(*N* = 1,465)	(*N* = 1,553)	(*N* = 3,018)
New England	4.6%	5.1%	4.9%
Mid-Atlantic	17.3	17.5	17.4
East North Central	17.7	17.1	17.4
West North Central	11.3	10.6	11.0
South Atlantic	15.1	14.0	14.5
East South Central	8.0	6.9	7.4
West South Central	11.4	13.8	12.6
Mountain	3.5	3.2	3.3
Pacific	6.6	5.9	6.2
U.S. territories or possessions	1.3	1.9	1.5
Outside the United States	3.1	3.9	3.6
13. Were you brought up mostly on a farm, in a small town, in a small city, in a medium-sized city, or a large city?[6]	(*N* = 1,464)	(*N* = 1,548)	(*N* = 3,012)
On a farm	32.4%	28.9%	30.6%
Small town (under 25,000)	26.8	29.2	28.0
Small city (under 100,000)	11.4	12.2	11.8
Medium-sized city (under 1,000,000)	15.4	15.2	15.3
Large city	14.1	14.4	14.2
14. Up to the time you were 16 years old, did you always live together with both of your *real* parents? If you or your father or mother were absent from home for *more than a year,* such as in the Armed Forces, a hospital or other institution, your answer should be "No."	(*N* = 1,461)	(*N* = 1,549)	(*N* = 3,010)
No	24.8%	29.1%	27.1%
Yes	75.2	70.9	72.8
[IF NO:]			
14A. What happened?	(*N* = 362)	(*N* = 450)	(*N* = 812)
Parent(s) died	57.2%	47.6%	51.8%
Parents divorced or separated	29.3	38.0	34.1
Other parental absence	2.8	2.4	2.6
Respondent was absent	4.1	3.1	3.6
Respondent was adopted	0.6	0.2	0.4
Other living arrangement	6.1	8.7	7.5
14B. How old were you when this happened?	(*N* = 357)	(*N* = 439)	(*N* = 796)
Under 6	46.8%	49.2%	48.1%
6–11	35.3	31.4	33.2
12–15	17.9	19.4	18.7
14C. Did this result in permanent separation, or did you later live with both *real* parents again, before you were 16?[7]	(*N* = 366)	(*N* = 452)	(*N* = 818)
Temporary separation	5.7%	6.4%	6.1%
Permanent separation	94.3	93.6	93.9

	Males	*Females*	*Total*
[IF permanent:]			
14D. Between the age when this happened and when you became 16 years old, with whom did you live *most* of the time?	(*N* = 343)	(*N* = 421)	(*N* = 764)
Mother (not remarried)	37.3%	40.4%	39.0%
Mother and stepfather	17.5	18.3	17.9
Father (not remarried)	9.6	8.1	8.8
Father and stepmother	8.5	7.6	8.0
Other relative(s)	12.5	14.0	13.4
Non-related person(s)	14.6	11.6	13.0

PATERNAL CHARACTERISTICS[8]

Now we'd like to have some description of your father.

[IF father permanently absent:]

15. These next questions should describe the man who *served* as your father, and *lived* in the same place as you. This could be your real father, or someone else if your real father was deceased or absent so early that you had little or no experience with him as your father. Which of these will you be describing—your real father, your adoptive father, your stepfather, a grandfather or uncle, an older brother or brother-in-law, or some other male person?[9]	(*N* = 1,465)	(*N* = 1,553)	(*N* = 3,018)
Real father	85.6%	83.5%	84.5%
Stepfather or adoptive father	5.1	5.4	5.2
Male relative	3.4	4.1	3.8
Some other male person	0.6	0.5	0.5
No father or father surrogate	5.3	6.6	6.0

16. Thinking of him at the time you were growing up, not only as a father, but as a man in general, how much was each of the following words true of him? Just give me one of the answers on this card. For example, the first word is "aggressive." How much was this word true of your father? Would you say very much, pretty much, somewhat, very little, or not at all?

Aggressive	(*N* = 1,372)	(*N* = 1,424)	(*N* = 2,796)
Not at all	4.4%	7.8%	6.1%
Very little	11.3	19.9	15.7
Somewhat	22.7	22.3	22.5
Pretty much	25.1	23.8	24.4
Very much	35.9	24.9	30.3
Don't know	0.7	1.3	1.0
Cool	(*N* = 1,367)	(*N* = 1,436)	(*N* = 2,803)
Not at all	10.2%	19.4%	14.9%
Very little	15.1	17.8	16.5
Somewhat	25.3	23.1	24.1
Pretty much	27.0	21.9	24.4
Very much	21.7	17.2	19.4
Don't know	0.8	0.7	0.8

	Males	Females	Total
Dreamy	(N = 1,371)	(N = 1,437)	(N = 2,808)
Not at all	40.0%	42.9%	41.5%
Very little	33.6	26.4	30.0
Somewhat	13.4	15.5	14.5
Pretty much	6.6	7.9	7.3
Very much	5.3	6.3	5.8
Don't know	0.9	1.1	1.0
Emotional	(N = 1,376)	(N = 1,434)	(N = 2,810)
Not at all	13.7%	16.0%	14.9%
Very little	27.8	26.6	27.2
Somewhat	28.5	25.8	27.1
Pretty much	16.9	15.7	16.3
Very much	12.2	15.6	14.0
Don't know	0.9	0.3	0.6
Foresighted	(N = 1,373)	(N = 1,431)	(N = 2,804)
Not at all	9.0%	12.9%	11.0%
Very little	14.3	15.0	14.7
Somewhat	22.6	19.2	20.8
Pretty much	28.2	26.2	27.2
Very much	24.7	25.4	25.1
Don't know	1.2	1.2	1.2
Impulsive	(N = 1,372)	(N = 1,433)	(N = 2,805)
Not at all	21.8%	26.9%	24.4%
Very little	29.5	30.2	29.9
Somewhat	22.8	19.0	20.9
Pretty much	13.3	12.0	12.7
Very much	10.8	10.3	10.6
Don't know	1.7	1.5	1.6
Shrewd	(N = 1,376)	(N = 1,442)	(N = 2,818)
Not at all	13.4%	22.8%	18.2%
Very little	16.0	19.5	17.7
Somewhat	22.1	20.5	21.3
Pretty much	25.4	18.6	22.0
Very much	22.6	17.5	20.0
Don't know	0.5	1.2	0.8
Submissive	(N = 1,338)	(N = 1,407)	(N = 2,745)
Not at all	22.1%	24.4%	23.3%
Very little	29.0	27.4	28.2
Somewhat	27.1	26.4	26.8
Pretty much	10.9	12.9	12.0
Very much	7.1	6.1	6.6
Don't know	3.7	2.8	3.2
Tough	(N = 1,382)	(N = 1,449)	(N = 2,831)
Not at all	15.8%	26.9%	21.5%
Very little	16.9	20.5	18.7
Somewhat	21.1	20.2	20.6
Pretty much	21.9	14.8	18.3
Very much	24.3	17.2	20.7
Don't know	0.1	0.3	0.2

	Males	*Females*	*Total*
Warm	(*N* = 1,381)	(*N* = 1,446)	(*N* = 2,827)
Not at all	2.9%	3.5%	3.2%
Very little	10.2	8.4	9.3
Somewhat	19.9	15.3	17.5
Pretty much	30.2	26.0	28.0
Very much	36.7	46.3	41.6
Don't know	0.1	0.5	0.3

Now we'd like you to fill out a sheet which contains some word pairs that can be used to describe people. There are instructions at the top of the page, but I will be happy to help you get started.[10]

17. Read each of the following pairs of words and think *what kind of parent* your father (father substitute) was *to you,* while you were growing up. For example, using the first word-pair, if you feel that he was very, very unreasonable toward you at that time, you would check the box closest to the word "Unreasonable." If you feel that he was very, very reasonable toward you, check the box closest to the word "Reasonable." If you feel that he was somewhere in between, check one of the other boxes, according to how reasonable or unreasonable you think he was. Check one of the boxes for each word-pair below.

Unreasonable/reasonable	(*N* = 1,381)	(*N* = 1,438)	(*N* = 2,819)
Relatively unreasonable	14.9%	18.1%	16.5%
Moderate	26.2	23.4	24.7
Relatively reasonable	59.0	58.5	58.8
Controlling/freedom-giving	(*N* = 1,383)	(*N* = 1,439)	(*N* = 2,822)
Relatively controlling	45.6%	49.3%	47.5%
Moderate	26.2	25.2	25.7
Relatively freedom-giving	28.2	25.4	26.8
Rejecting/accepting	(*N* = 1,384)	(*N* = 1,435)	(*N* = 2,819)
Relatively rejecting	18.4%	18.3%	18.3%
Moderate	32.2	25.2	28.6
Relatively accepting	49.4	56.6	53.1
Forbidding/permitting	(*N* = 1,381)	(*N* = 1,438)	(*N* = 2,819)
Relatively forbidding	33.2%	35.8%	34.5%
Moderate	38.6	36.5	37.5
Relatively permitting	28.3	27.7	28.1
Strict/liberal	(*N* = 1,383)	(*N* = 1,439)	(*N* = 2,822)
Relatively strict	55.9%	55.2%	55.5%
Moderate	24.5	26.4	25.5
Relatively liberal	19.6	18.3	19.0
Belittling/praising	(*N* = 1,384)	(*N* = 1,439)	(*N* = 2,823)
Relatively belittling	19.4%	18.1%	18.8%
Moderate	38.0	29.3	33.5
Relatively praising	42.7	52.5	47.7

	Males	*Females*	*Total*
18. Using the boxes in the same way, would you describe your father (or father substitute) as mostly unpredictable and inconsistent in disciplining you, or was he mostly predictable and consistent in disciplining you while you were growing up?	(*N* = 1,378)	(*N* = 1,427)	(*N* = 2,805)
Relatively unpredictable	13.3%	16.7%	15.1%
Moderate	21.4	19.3	20.3
Relatively predictable	65.2	64.0	64.6
19A. And now we'd like to ask you how much the following describe your father in social matters, while you were growing up. Again, just give me one of the answers on the card.			
Liking get-togethers, parties	(*N* = 1,381)	(*N* = 1,440)	(*N* = 2,821)
Not at all	15.8%	15.6%	15.7%
Very little	24.3	21.1	22.7
Somewhat	17.7	14.4	16.0
Pretty much	22.1	20.9	21.5
Very much	20.2	27.9	24.1
Don't know	0.0	0.0	0.0
Avoiding meetings, crowds	(*N* = 1,382)	(*N* = 1,441)	(*N* = 2,823)
Not at all	30.2%	35.9%	33.1%
Very little	29.7	26.6	28.1
Somewhat	19.8	16.9	18.3
Pretty much	11.1	11.7	11.4
Very much	9.1	9.0	9.0
Don't know	0.0	0.0	0.0
Joining organizations, groups	(*N* = 1,381)	(*N* = 1,444)	(*N* = 2,825)
Not at all	24.0%	29.2%	26.6%
Very little	29.6	27.8	28.7
Somewhat	19.8	17.9	18.9
Pretty much	15.9	13.5	14.7
Very much	10.6	11.6	11.1
Don't know	0.0	0.0	0.0
Having trouble getting along with people	(*N* = 1,384)	(*N* = 1,447)	(*N* = 2,831)
Not at all	63.6%	67.0%	65.3%
Very little	26.7	20.7	24.0
Somewhat	6.4	7.1	6.7
Pretty much	2.1	2.7	2.4
Very much	1.2	2.4	1.8
Don't know	0.0	0.0	0.0
Worrying about disapproval by others	(*N* = 1,371)	(*N* = 1,435)	(*N* = 2,806)
Not at all	46.1%	51.6%	48.9%
Very little	30.1	25.2	27.5
Somewhat	14.8	13.5	14.1
Pretty much	5.3	5.2	5.2
Very much	3.8	4.5	4.1
Don't know	0.0	0.0	0.0

	Males	*Females*	*Total*
19B. How much do the following describe the life of your father in general, as you remember it from when you were growing up?			
Easygoing	(*N* = 1,386)	(*N* = 1,446)	(*N* = 2,832)
Not at all	5.8%	8.6%	7.2%
Very little	12.0	10.7	11.4
Somewhat	22.4	20.3	21.4
Pretty much	27.5	28.5	28.0
Very much	32.3	31.8	32.0
Don't know	0.0	0.0	0.0
Full of energy	(*N* = 1,385)	(*N* = 1,447)	(*N* = 2,832)
Not at all	1.3%	1.6%	1.4%
Very little	3.0	5.4	4.2
Somewhat	11.2	12.2	11.7
Pretty much	26.9	25.4	26.2
Very much	57.5	55.4	56.4
Don't know	0.0	0.0	0.0
Headstrong	(*N* = 1,381)	(*N* = 1,442)	(*N* = 2,823)
Not at all	9.9%	11.0%	10.4%
Very little	17.5	16.9	17.2
Somewhat	19.3	20.0	19.7
Pretty much	21.4	20.0	20.7
Very much	31.9	32.2	32.0
Don't know	0.0	0.0	0.0
Active	(*N* = 1,383)	(*N* = 1,446)	(*N* = 2,829)
Not at all	0.7%	1.0%	0.8%
Very little	3.8	5.1	4.5
Somewhat	11.4	10.7	11.1
Pretty much	27.4	26.2	26.8
Very much	56.6	57.0	56.8
Don't know	0.0	0.0	0.0
19C. How much do the following describe your father in sexual matters, while you were growing up?			
Moral about sex	(*N* = 1,382)	(*N* = 1,442)	(*N* = 2,824)
Not at all	3.0%	2.8%	2.9%
Very little	6.4	4.4	5.3
Somewhat	13.1	10.9	12.0
Pretty much	22.8	15.5	19.1
Very much	49.1	62.0	55.7
Don't know	5.6	4.4	5.0
Serious about sex	(*N* = 1,378)	(*N* = 1,436)	(*N* = 2,814)
Not at all	3.9%	2.9%	3.4%
Very little	7.1	5.8	6.5
Somewhat	14.3	12.8	13.5
Pretty much	25.3	22.1	23.7
Very much	41.4	48.2	44.8
Don't know	8.0	8.1	8.0

	Males	*Females*	*Total*
A sexual person	(*N* = 1,373)	(*N* = 1,438)	(*N* = 2,811)
Not at all	14.6%	17.5%	16.1%
Very little	20.5	17.5	19.0
Somewhat	27.3	25.5	26.4
Pretty much	17.3	19.1	18.2
Very much	12.5	12.7	12.6
Don't know	7.7	7.6	7.7
Avoiding sex	(*N* = 1,376)	(*N* = 1,443)	(*N* = 2,819)
Not at all	36.5%	40.8%	38.7%
Very little	27.1	23.5	25.2
Somewhat	14.8	14.6	14.7
Pretty much	6.4	5.8	6.1
Very much	6.4	6.5	6.4
Don't know	8.8	8.9	8.8
19D. How masculine would you say your father was, while you were growing up?	(*N* = 1,378)	(*N* = 1,438)	(*N* = 2,816)
Not at all	0.4%	0.6%	0.5%
Very little	1.8	2.5	2.2
Somewhat	10.6	10.3	10.4
Pretty much	28.7	25.6	27.1
Very much	58.3	60.8	59.6
Don't know	0.1	0.1	0.1

MATERNAL CHARACTERISTICS[11]

Now we'd like to have some description of your mother.

[IF mother permanently absent:]

20. These next questions should describe the woman who *served* as your mother, and *lived* in the same place as you. This could be your real mother, or someone else if your real mother was deceased or absent so early that you had little or no experience with her as your mother. Which of these will you be describing—your real mother, your adoptive mother, your stepmother, a grandmother or aunt, an older sister or sister-in-law, or some other female person?[12]	(*N* = 1,465)	(*N* = 1,553)	(*N* = 3,018)
Real mother	92.1%	91.9%	92.0%
Stepmother or adoptive mother	2.8	2.8	2.8
Female relative	3.6	4.2	3.9
Some other female person	0.4	0.4	0.4
No mother or mother surrogate	1.2	0.8	1.0

21. Thinking of her at the time you were growing up, not only as a mother, but as a woman in general, how much was each of the following words true of her? Just give me one of the answers on this card. For example, the first word is "aggressive." How much was this word true of your mother? Would you say very much, pretty much, somewhat, very little, or not at all?

	Males	Females	Total
Aggressive	(*N* = 1,434)	(*N* = 1,524)	(*N* = 2,958)
Not at all	6.7%	11.3%	9.1%
Very little	16.4	16.9	16.7
Somewhat	19.6	20.1	19.9
Pretty much	24.3	20.8	22.5
Very much	32.0	29.7	30.8
Don't know	1.0	1.2	1.1
Cool	(*N* = 1,436)	(*N* = 1,529)	(*N* = 2,965)
Not at all	9.6%	17.7%	13.8%
Very little	15.7	19.5	17.7
Somewhat	24.1	24.7	24.4
Pretty much	27.6	18.9	23.1
Very much	22.1	18.9	20.4
Don't know	0.8	0.4	0.6
Dreamy	(*N* = 1,436)	(*N* = 1,535)	(*N* = 2,971)
Not at all	27.1%	32.8%	30.1%
Very little	28.6	26.4	27.4
Somewhat	24.0	22.0	23.0
Pretty much	12.6	10.1	11.3
Very much	6.5	7.8	7.2
Don't know	1.3	0.8	1.1
Emotional	(*N* = 1,439)	(*N* = 1,532)	(*N* = 2,971)
Not at all	7.9%	9.6%	8.8%
Very little	15.6	17.4	16.6
Somewhat	26.0	23.0	24.5
Pretty much	25.5	24.7	25.1
Very much	24.6	24.9	24.7
Don't know	0.3	0.3	0.3
Foresighted	(*N* = 1,439)	(*N* = 1,520)	(*N* = 2,959)
Not at all	8.5%	9.1%	8.9%
Very little	13.1	11.6	12.3
Somewhat	24.3	23.9	24.1
Pretty much	32.3	27.9	30.0
Very much	20.6	26.5	23.6
Don't know	1.3	1.0	1.1
Impulsive	(*N* = 1,427)	(*N* = 1,525)	(*N* = 2,952)
Not at all	18.0%	24.8%	21.5%
Very little	30.0	32.1	31.1
Somewhat	27.3	21.2	24.2
Pretty much	15.3	11.1	13.1
Very much	8.3	9.8	9.1
Don't know	1.1	1.0	1.1
Shrewd	(*N* = 1,437)	(*N* = 1,528)	(*N* = 2,965)
Not at all	13.9%	23.2%	18.7%
Very little	17.9	18.5	18.2
Somewhat	24.2	22.4	23.3
Pretty much	23.7	16.8	20.1
Very much	19.6	18.2	18.9
Don't know	0.8	0.9	0.8

	Males	*Females*	*Total*
Submissive	(*N* = 1,409)	(*N* = 1,507)	(*N* = 2,916)
Not at all	13.1%	16.9%	15.1%
Very little	22.7	23.5	23.1
Somewhat	36.0	32.2	34.0
Pretty much	16.3	15.7	15.9
Very much	9.2	9.4	9.3
Don't know	2.8	2.3	2.6
Tough	(*N* = 1,440)	(*N* = 1,536)	(*N* = 2,976)
Not at all	28.8%	36.5%	32.8%
Very little	22.0	21.3	21.6
Somewhat	19.4	16.7	18.0
Pretty much	16.1	12.4	14.2
Very much	13.7	12.9	13.3
Don't know	0.0	0.1	0.1
Warm	(*N* = 1,446)	(*N* = 1,538)	(*N* = 2,984)
Not at all	1.0%	1.7%	1.4%
Very little	2.5	4.3	3.4
Somewhat	10.7	11.9	11.3
Pretty much	27.7	23.8	25.7
Very much	58.0	58.3	58.1
Don't know	0.1	0.0	0.1

And now we'd like you to fill out the sheet of word pairs for your mother.[13]

22. Read each of the following pairs of words and think *what kind of parent* your mother (or mother substitute) was *to you,* while you were growing up. For example, using the first word-pair, if you feel that she was very, very unreasonable toward you at that time, you would check the box closest to the word "Unreasonable." If you feel that she was very, very reasonable toward you, check the box closest to the word "Reasonable." If you feel that she was somewhere in between, check one of the other boxes, according to how unreasonable or reasonable you think she was. Check one of the boxes for each word-pair below.

Unreasonable/reasonable	(*N* = 1,440)	(*N* = 1,532)	(*N* = 2,972)
Relatively unreasonable	19.5%	23.5%	21.6%
Moderate	34.5	28.9	31.6
Relatively reasonable	46.0	47.7	46.8
Controlling/freedom-giving	(*N* = 1,440)	(*N* = 1,527)	(*N* = 2,967)
Relatively controlling	48.6%	54.4%	51.6%
Moderate	29.2	26.9	28.0
Relatively freedom-giving	22.2	18.7	20.4
Rejecting/accepting	(*N* = 1,438)	(*N* = 1,527)	(*N* = 2,965)
Relatively rejecting	22.3%	24.6%	23.4%
Moderate	39.5	32.4	35.6
Relatively accepting	38.3	43.0	40.7
Forbidding/permitting	(*N* = 1,438)	(*N* = 1,523)	(*N* = 2,961)
Relatively forbidding	44.6%	49.2%	47.0%
Moderate	35.9	31.6	33.7
Relatively permitting	19.3	19.2	19.3

	Males	Females	Total
Strict/liberal	(*N* = 1,439)	(*N* = 1,528)	(*N* = 2,967)
Relatively strict	62.0%	64.7%	63.4%
Moderate	22.9	21.6	22.2
Relatively liberal	15.0	13.8	14.4
Belittling/praising	(*N* = 1,438)	(*N* = 1,530)	(*N* = 2,968)
Relatively belittling	22.3%	26.5%	24.5%
Moderate	39.0	31.2	34.9
Relatively praising	38.8	42.3	40.6

23. Using the boxes in the same way, would you describe your mother (or mother substitute) as mostly unpredictable and inconsistent in disciplining you, or was she mostly predictable and consistent in disciplining you when you were growing up?

	Males	Females	Total
	(*N* = 1,418)	(*N* = 1,502)	(*N* = 2,920)
Relatively unpredictable	21.2%	26.1%	23.7%
Moderate	39.9	31.6	35.7
Relatively predictable	38.8	42.3	40.6

24A. And now, how much do the following describe your mother in social matters, while you were growing up?

	Males	Females	Total
Liking get-togethers, parties	(*N* = 1,441)	(*N* = 1,538)	(*N* = 2,979)
Not at all	13.5%	12.2%	12.8%
Very little	15.3	14.8	15.0
Somewhat	17.7	14.3	15.9
Pretty much	26.6	24.6	25.6
Very much	26.9	34.1	30.6
Don't know	0.0	0.0	0.0
Avoiding meetings, crowds	(*N* = 1,441)	(*N* = 1,538)	(*N* = 2,979)
Not at all	32.2%	36.5%	34.4%
Very little	32.8	25.9	29.2
Somewhat	18.3	18.1	18.2
Pretty much	10.8	11.0	11.0
Very much	6.0	8.5	7.3
Don't know	0.0	0.0	0.0
Joining organizations, groups	(*N* = 1,437)	(*N* = 1,538)	(*N* = 2,975)
Not at all	24.8%	30.0%	27.5%
Very little	27.1	25.2	26.2
Somewhat	19.6	19.0	19.3
Pretty much	16.6	14.0	15.3
Very much	11.8	11.8	11.8
Don't know	0.0	0.0	0.0
Having trouble getting along with people	(*N* = 1,442)	(*N* = 1,538)	(*N* = 2,980)
Not at all	65.3%	68.5%	66.9%
Very little	25.7	21.0	23.3
Somewhat	6.0	6.9	6.4
Pretty much	1.5	1.7	1.6
Very much	1.6	2.0	1.8
Don't know	0.0	0.0	0.0

	Males	*Females*	*Total*
Worrying about disapproval by others	(*N* = 1,440)	(*N* = 1,536)	(*N* = 2,976)
Not at all	36.7%	38.5%	37.6%
Very little	24.5	22.3	23.4
Somewhat	20.8	19.3	20.1
Pretty much	10.1	10.9	10.5
Very much	7.8	9.0	8.5
Don't know	0.0	0.0	0.0

24B. How much do the following describe the life of your mother in general, as you remember it from when you were growing up?

	Males	*Females*	*Total*
Easygoing	(*N* = 1,444)	(*N* = 1,539)	(*N* = 2,983)
Not at all	4.0%	7.5%	5.8%
Very little	9.7	12.2	11.0
Somewhat	21.9	22.0	22.0
Pretty much	29.9	25.8	27.8
Very much	34.5	32.5	33.5
Don't know	0.0	0.0	0.0
Full of energy	(*N* = 1,443)	(*N* = 1,539)	(*N* = 2,982)
Not at all	1.0%	1.2%	1.1%
Very little	2.7	3.6	3.2
Somewhat	10.5	11.9	11.2
Pretty much	30.8	26.3	28.5
Very much	55.0	57.1	56.1
Don't know	0.0	0.0	0.0
Headstrong	(*N* = 1,444)	(*N* = 1,538)	(*N* = 2,982)
Not at all	15.0%	18.3%	16.7%
Very little	24.4	19.9	22.1
Somewhat	22.9	22.3	22.6
Pretty much	17.7	17.8	17.7
Very much	20.0	21.7	21.0
Don't know	0.0	0.0	0.0
Active	(*N* = 1,443)	(*N* = 1,540)	(*N* = 2,983)
Not at all	0.9%	1.2%	1.0%
Very little	3.9	4.0	4.0
Somewhat	11.4	12.9	12.2
Pretty much	30.6	27.4	28.9
Very much	53.2	54.5	53.9
Don't know	0.0	0.0	0.0

24C. How much do the following describe your mother in sexual matters, while you were growing up?

	Males	*Females*	*Total*
Moral about sex	(*N* = 1,437)	(*N* = 1,537)	(*N* = 2,974)
Not at all	2.4%	1.8%	2.1%
Very little	4.8	3.6	4.2
Somewhat	11.7	7.2	9.4
Pretty much	19.5	15.7	17.6
Very much	56.5	67.5	62.2
Don't know	5.1	4.0	4.6

	Males	*Females*	*Total*
Serious about sex	(*N* = 1,436)	(*N* = 1,535)	(*N* = 2,971)
Not at all	3.0%	3.4%	3.2%
Very little	5.2	4.6	4.9
Somewhat	14.3	13.2	13.8
Pretty much	26.4	22.8	24.5
Very much	44.1	50.7	47.5
Don't know	7.0	5.3	6.1
A sexual person	(*N* = 1,433)	(*N* = 1,536)	(*N* = 2,969)
Not at all	14.8%	18.3%	16.6%
Very little	20.9	20.7	20.8
Somewhat	30.1	27.5	28.7
Pretty much	15.3	17.5	16.4
Very much	10.3	9.5	9.9
Don't know	8.7	6.5	7.6
Avoiding sex	(*N* = 1,432)	(*N* = 1,531)	(*N* = 2,963)
Not at all	26.3%	29.1%	27.7%
Very little	24.2	25.3	24.8
Somewhat	22.3	19.0	20.6
Pretty much	8.6	9.0	8.8
Very much	7.2	9.5	8.4
Don't know	11.5	8.0	9.6
24D. How feminine would you say your mother was, while you were growing up?	(*N* = 1,427)	(*N* = 1,531)	(*N* = 2,958)
Not at all	0.9%	1.0%	1.0%
Very little	4.7	3.9	4.3
Somewhat	16.0	12.6	14.3
Pretty much	32.4	28.5	30.4
Very much	46.0	54.0	50.1
Don't know	0.0	0.0	0.0

PERSONALITY CHARACTERISTICS

These next questions are about you.

25. Thinking of yourself *now,* how much are each of the following words true for you? Again, tell me one of the answers from the card.

	Males	*Females*	*Total*
Aggressive	(*N* = 1,446)	(*N* = 1,529)	(*N* = 2,975)
Not at all	3.2%	7.0%	5.1%
Very little	9.8	14.8	12.3
Somewhat	23.8	29.8	26.9
Pretty much	37.2	28.6	32.8
Very much	26.1	19.8	22.9
Don't know	0.0	0.0	0.0
Cool	(*N* = 1,455)	(*N* = 1,542)	(*N* = 2,997)
Not at all	4.8%	13.9%	9.5%
Very little	11.7	19.0	15.4
Somewhat	33.0	33.9	33.5
Pretty much	31.7	20.7	26.0
Very much	18.8	12.5	15.6
Don't know	0.0	0.0	0.0

	Males	*Females*	*Total*
Dreamy	(*N* = 1,455)	(*N* = 1,550)	(*N* = 3,005)
Not at all	21.5%	19.9%	20.7%
Very little	22.2	20.0	21.1
Somewhat	26.9	29.9	28.5
Pretty much	16.7	16.4	16.5
Very much	12.6	13.8	13.2
Don't know	0.0	0.0	0.0
Emotional	(*N* = 1,455)	(*N* = 1,543)	(*N* = 2,998)
Not at all	9.1%	5.1%	7.1%
Very little	18.0	12.4	15.1
Somewhat	31.5	25.8	28.6
Pretty much	24.3	26.7	25.6
Very much	17.0	29.9	23.6
Don't know	0.0	0.0	0.0
Foresighted	(*N* = 1,446)	(*N* = 1,525)	(*N* = 2,971)
Not at all	7.2%	8.0%	7.6%
Very little	9.4	12.1	10.8
Somewhat	30.0	29.1	29.6
Pretty much	33.1	31.7	32.3
Very much	20.3	19.1	19.7
Don't know	0.0	0.0	0.0
Impulsive	(*N* = 1,435)	(*N* = 1,527)	(*N* = 2,962)
Not at all	12.3%	12.6%	12.5%
Very little	24.7	22.8	23.7
Somewhat	31.9	32.0	32.0
Pretty much	20.3	18.2	19.2
Very much	10.7	14.4	12.6
Don't know	0.0	0.0	0.0
Shrewd	(*N* = 1,446)	(*N* = 1,528)	(*N* = 2,974)
Not at all	10.7%	20.2%	15.6%
Very little	18.7	25.9	22.4
Somewhat	36.3	31.9	34.0
Pretty much	22.5	14.5	18.4
Very much	11.8	7.6	9.7
Don't know	0.0	0.0	0.0
Submissive	(*N* = 1,391)	(*N* = 1,500)	(*N* = 2,891)
Not at all	15.0%	12.3%	13.6%
Very little	27.0	21.3	24.1
Somewhat	37.4	41.7	39.6
Pretty much	14.7	17.5	16.2
Very much	5.9	7.3	6.6
Don't know	0.0	0.0	0.0
Tough	(*N* = 1,459)	(*N* = 1,548)	(*N* = 3,007)
Not at all	15.8%	28.7%	22.5%
Very little	23.4	28.8	26.2
Somewhat	30.2	23.6	26.8
Pretty much	19.9	12.1	15.9
Very much	10.6	6.7	8.6
Don't know	0.0	0.0	0.0

	Males	*Females*	*Total*
Warm	(*N* = 1,462)	(*N* = 1,551)	(*N* = 3,013)
Not at all	0.8%	0.3%	0.5%
Very little	3.4	1.9	2.7
Somewhat	24.0	15.8	19.8
Pretty much	38.8	42.2	40.6
Very much	33.0	39.8	36.5
Don't know	0.0	0.0	0.0

26A. How much do the following describe you in social matters?

	Males	*Females*	*Total*
Liking get-togethers, parties	(*N* = 1,465)	(*N* = 1,552)	(*N* = 3,017)
Not at all	9.5%	6.4%	7.9%
Very little	16.1	9.4	12.7
Somewhat	20.3	16.8	18.5
Pretty much	26.6	26.5	26.5
Very much	27.5	40.9	34.4
Don't know	0.0	0.0	0.0
Avoiding meetings, crowds	(*N* = 1,463)	(*N* = 1,549)	(*N* = 3,012)
Not at all	35.1%	38.7%	37.0%
Very little	27.5	25.2	26.3
Somewhat	18.5	18.8	18.7
Pretty much	11.9	10.3	11.1
Very much	7.0	7.0	7.0
Don't know	0.0	0.0	0.0
Joining organizations, groups	(*N* = 1,461)	(*N* = 1,547)	(*N* = 3,008)
Not at all	20.1%	20.2%	20.1%
Very little	27.9	26.0	26.9
Somewhat	24.1	21.8	22.9
Pretty much	16.8	17.9	17.4
Very much	11.2	14.1	12.7
Don't know	0.0	0.0	0.0
Having trouble getting along with people	(*N* = 1,464)	(*N* = 1,552)	(*N* = 3,016)
Not at all	62.0%	63.6%	62.8%
Very little	31.0	29.0	30.0
Somewhat	5.4	5.7	5.6
Pretty much	1.0	0.7	0.8
Very much	0.7	1.0	0.8
Don't know	0.0	0.0	0.0
Worrying about disapproval by others	(*N* = 1,463)	(*N* = 1,552)	(*N* = 3,015)
Not at all	44.1%	36.2%	40.0%
Very little	23.0	22.7	22.9
Somewhat	19.5	24.9	22.3
Pretty much	8.5	9.0	8.8
Very much	4.8	7.2	6.0
Don't know	0.0	0.0	0.0

26B. How much do the following describe how you live your life in general?

	Males	Females	Total
Easygoing	(N = 1,465)	(N = 1,551)	(N = 3,016)
Not at all	2.4%	3.1%	2.8%
Very little	5.9	5.9	5.9
Somewhat	23.1	25.7	24.4
Pretty much	38.0	38.5	38.2
Very much	30.7	26.8	28.7
Don't know	0.0	0.0	0.0
Full of energy	(N = 1,464)	(N = 1,550)	(N = 3,014)
Not at all	1.6%	1.9%	1.7%
Very little	5.7	7.0	6.4
Somewhat	19.2	23.2	21.3
Pretty much	36.6	36.0	36.3
Very much	36.9	31.9	34.3
Don't know	0.0	0.0	0.0
Headstrong	(N = 1,463)	(N = 1,549)	(N = 3,012)
Not at all	11.6%	12.0%	11.8%
Very little	16.6	19.4	18.1
Somewhat	28.9	29.4	29.2
Pretty much	21.3	21.0	21.1
Very much	21.6	18.2	19.9
Don't know	0.0	0.0	0.0
Active	(N = 1,463)	(N = 1,550)	(N = 3,013)
Not at all	1.0%	0.8%	0.9%
Very little	5.1	4.3	4.7
Somewhat	12.3	15.9	14.2
Pretty much	37.2	37.4	37.3
Very much	44.4	41.5	42.9
Don't know	0.0	0.0	0.0
26C. How much do the following describe you in sexual matters?			
Moral about sex	(N = 1,458)	(N = 1,545)	(N = 3,003)
Not at all	3.1%	1.7%	2.4%
Very little	6.7	4.1	5.3
Somewhat	18.7	12.7	15.6
Pretty much	29.5	28.3	28.9
Very much	42.1	53.1	47.8
Don't know	0.0	0.0	0.0
Serious about sex	(N = 1,457)	(N = 1,546)	(N = 3,003)
Not at all	4.0%	2.9%	3.4%
Very little	4.7	5.0	4.9
Somewhat	15.6	12.2	13.8
Pretty much	29.3	25.6	27.4
Very much	46.5	54.3	50.5
Don't know	0.0	0.0	0.0
A sexual person	(N = 1,436)	(N = 1,550)	(N = 2,966)
Not at all	8.4%	12.5%	10.6%
Very little	10.4	14.0	12.3
Somewhat	33.2	30.7	31.9
Pretty much	27.2	27.5	27.3
Very much	20.8	15.4	18.0
Don't know	0.0	0.0	0.0

	Males	Females	Total
Avoiding sex	(*N* = 1,451)	(*N* = 1,539)	(*N* = 2,990)
Not at all	50.3%	42.0%	46.1%
Very little	28.9	29.7	29.3
Somewhat	12.5	16.9	14.8
Pretty much	4.5	5.1	4.8
Very much	3.7	6.3	5.1
Don't know	0.0	0.0	0.0
Frank with women in sex talk	(*N* = 1,458)	(*N* = 1,545)	(*N* = 3,003)
Not at all	12.9%	8.3%	10.6%
Very little	13.6	10.7	12.1
Somewhat	18.6	14.8	16.6
Pretty much	25.0	29.4	27.2
Very much	30.0	36.8	33.5
Don't know	0.0	0.0	0.0
Frank with men in sex talk	(*N* = 1,459)	(*N* = 1,544)	(*N* = 3,003)
Not at all	9.2%	27.7%	18.7%
Very little	9.3	18.2	13.9
Somewhat	16.7	17.7	17.2
Pretty much	27.6	19.7	23.5
Very much	37.2	16.8	26.7
Don't know	0.0	0.0	0.0

26D. How much do the following describe how you go about work situations?

	Males	Females	Total
Work done on time	(*N* = 1,465)	(*N* = 1,553)	(*N* = 3,018)
Not at all	0.6%	3.0%	1.9%
Very little	1.8	5.1	3.5
Somewhat	6.8	14.6	10.8
Pretty much	33.2	34.9	34.1
Very much	57.5	42.4	49.7
Don't know	0.0	0.0	0.0
Work neat, well-organized	(*N* = 1,465)	(*N* = 1,553)	(*N* = 3,018)
Not at all	0.7%	2.1%	1.4%
Very little	2.5	4.8	3.6
Somewhat	10.4	18.7	14.7
Pretty much	34.8	36.5	35.6
Very much	51.6	37.9	44.5
Don't know	0.0	0.0	0.0
Putting off work till later	(*N* = 1,463)	(*N* = 1,550)	(*N* = 3,013)
Not at all	36.0%	28.2%	32.0%
Very little	30.6	28.9	29.7
Somewhat	21.6	28.4	25.1
Pretty much	7.7	7.9	7.8
Very much	4.2	6.6	5.4
Don't know	0.0	0.0	0.0
Hard-working	(*N* = 1,465)	(*N* = 1,553)	(*N* = 3,018)
Not at all	1.8%	1.5%	1.7%
Very little	1.9	3.3	2.7
Somewhat	12.0	16.4	14.2
Pretty much	32.5	35.5	34.1
Very much	51.8	43.2	47.4
Don't know	0.0	0.0	0.0

	Males	*Females*	*Total*
Worry about your ability, work quality	(*N* = 1,464)	(*N* = 1,551)	(*N* = 3,015)
Not at all	25.8%	21.7%	23.6%
Very little	17.8	18.1	17.9
Somewhat	19.4	20.9	20.2
Pretty much	16.3	17.8	17.0
Very much	20.8	21.6	21.2
Don't know	0.0	0.0	0.0

DEMOGRAPHIC CHARACTERISTICS (SEE ALSO Q. 3–14, 35, 36, 39, 100–102)

27. Counting yourself as one, how many children altogether were there in your family when you were growing up, including stepchildren or adopted children?	(*N* = 1,465)	(*N* = 1,551)	(*N* = 3,016)
One	7.6%	8.0%	7.8%
Two	12.8	13.9	13.4
Three	15.0	17.4	16.2
Four	15.5	13.5	14.5
Five	11.2	10.6	10.9
Six	9.3	7.9	8.6
Seven	5.9	7.8	6.9
Eight	5.7	6.2	6.0
More than eight	16.9	14.7	15.8
[IF more than one:]			
27A. What number were you in the order of their birth, starting with the eldest?[14]	(*N* = 1,353)	(*N* = 1,427)	(*N* = 2,780)
Eldest	24.8%	28.4%	26.7%
Second-born	23.4	24.8	24.1
Third-born	16.0	15.7	15.8
Fourth-born	12.1	10.2	11.1
Fifth-born	7.6	6.2	6.9
Sixth- or later-born	16.1	14.7	15.4
[IF not an only child:]			
28A. Did you have any older brothers?	(*N* = 1,348)	(*N* = 1,421)	(*N* = 2,769)
No	42.9%	46.0%	44.5%
Yes	57.1	54.0	55.5
[IF YES:]			
28A(1). How many of your older brothers were still living at home when you were 12?	(*N* = 770)	(*N* = 767)	(*N* = 1,537)
None	13.0%	14.0%	13.5%
One	49.0	51.1	50.0
Two	24.3	22.9	23.6
Three or more	13.7	12.0	12.9
[IF not an only child:]			
28B. Did you have any younger brothers?	(*N* = 1,339)	(*N* = 1,413)	(*N* = 2,752)
No	42.8%	42.3%	42.6%
Yes	57.2	57.7	57.4

	Males	*Females*	*Total*
[IF YES:]			
28B(1). How many of your younger brothers had reached the age of 12 or older before you left home?	(*N* = 766)	(*N* = 813)	(*N* = 1,579)
None	14.6%	18.9%	16.9%
One	54.3	51.3	52.8
Two	20.2	19.3	19.8
Three or more	10.9	10.5	10.5
[IF not an only child:]			
29A. Did you have any older sisters?	(*N* = 1,346)	(*N* = 1,420)	(*N* = 2,766)
No	43.7%	47.9%	45.8%
Yes	56.3	52.1	55.2
[IF YES:]			
29A(1). How many of your older sisters were still living at home when you were 12?	(*N* = 758)	(*N* = 740)	(*N* = 1,498)
None	15.2%	20.1%	17.6%
One	50.4	52.0	51.2
Two	20.2	19.1	19.8
Three or more	14.3	8.8	11.5
[IF not an only child:]			
29B. Did you have any younger sisters?	(*N* = 1,340)	(*N* = 1,406)	(*N* = 2,746)
No	43.4%	42.5%	42.9%
Yes	56.6	57.5	57.1
[IF YES:]			
29B(1). How many of your younger sisters had reached the age of 12 or older before you left home?	(*N* = 759)	(*N* = 809)	(*N* = 1,568)
None	17.1%	17.7%	17.4%
One	49.3	48.3	48.8
Two	19.6	22.1	20.9
Three or more	13.9	11.9	12.9

GENDER CHARACTERISTICS

30. Children sometimes hear stories about their parents—either father or mother—wishing that a child had been born a boy instead of a girl, or a girl instead of a boy. Do you know of any possibility that this was how your father felt when you were born?	(*N* = 1,378)	(*N* = 1,445)	(*N* = 2,823)
No	97.0%	87.4%	92.1%
Yes	3.0	12.6	7.9

31. Was there any sign while you were growing up, that your father would have preferred it if you had been a (opposite sex)? For example:

	Males	*Females*	*Total*
31A. In how he treated you, or played with you?	(*N* = 1,378)	(*N* = 1,442)	(*N* = 2,820)
No	99.3%	92.9%	96.0%
Yes	0.7	7.1	4.0
31B. In how he wanted you to dress?	(*N* = 1,377)	(*N* = 1,441)	(*N* = 2,818)
No	99.6%	98.5%	99.1%
Yes	0.4	1.5	0.9
[IF YES to either Q.31A or 31B:]			
31C. How old were you by the time he no longer treated you this way (or felt this way)?	(*N* = 14)	(*N* = 98)	(*N* = 112)
Under six	14.3%	11.2%	11.6%
6–11	35.7	23.5	25.0
12–15	21.4	28.6	27.7
16–19	14.3	24.5	23.2
20 or older	14.3	12.2	12.5
32. Do you know of any possibility that your mother wished you had been a (opposite sex) when you were born?	(*N* = 1,439)	(*N* = 1,530)	(*N* = 2,969)
No	94.6%	94.6%	94.6%
Yes	5.4	5.4	5.4
33. Was there any sign, while you were growing up, that your mother would have preferred it if you had been a (opposite sex)? For example:			
33A. In how she treated you, or played with you?	(*N* = 1,439)	(*N* = 1,533)	(*N* = 2,972)
No	98.1%	99.0%	98.6%
Yes	1.9	1.0	1.4
33B. In how she wanted you to dress?	(*N* = 1,443)	(*N* = 1,533)	(*N* = 2,976)
No	98.4%	99.3%	98.9%
Yes	1.6	0.7	1.1
[IF YES to either Q.33A or 33B:]			
33C. How old were you by the time she no longer treated you this way (or felt this way)?	(*N* = 39)	(*N* = 20)	(*N* = 59)
Under six	28.2%	15.0%	23.7%
6–11	28.2	15.0	23.7
12–15	17.9	15.0	16.9
16–19	20.5	30.0	23.7
20 or older	5.1	25.0	11.9
34A. How often have you felt you would have been happier as a (opposite sex)? Would you say often, sometimes, rarely, or never?			

	Males	*Females*	*Total*
	(*N* = 1,463)	(*N* = 1,545)	(*N* = 3,008)
Never	93.4%	70.0%	81.4%
Rarely	4.9	13.5	9.3
Sometimes	1.4	11.4	6.5
Often	0.3	5.2	2.8
34B. How often have you felt more like a (opposite sex)?	(*N* = 1,464)	(*N* = 1,544)	(*N* = 3,008)
Never	97.1%	85.8%	91.3%
Rarely	2.2	7.0	4.7
Sometimes	0.5	5.4	3.1
Often	0.1	1.8	1.0
34C. How often have you felt you would prefer to wear (opposite sex)'s clothes?	(*N* = 1,463)	(*N* = 1,544)	(*N* = 3,007)
Never	98.6%	84.0%	91.1%
Rarely	1.2	6.5	3.9
Sometimes	0.2	6.2	3.3
Often	0.1	3.3	1.7

DEMOGRAPHIC CHARACTERISTICS (SEE ALSO Q. 3–14, 27–29, 39, 100–102)

35. What is the highest grade or year of school completed by the main wage earner during your childhood?	(*N* = 1,355)	(*N* = 1,458)	(*N* = 2,813)
Less than eighth grade	41.5%	34.9%	38.1%
Eighth grade	20.3	20.4	20.4
Some high school	11.3	13.3	12.3
High school diploma or equivalent	14.8	16.6	15.7
Some college	5.7	7.7	6.7
Bachelor's degree	3.5	4.3	3.9
Postgraduate college work	3.0	2.9	3.0
36. In what religion were you mostly brought up, until you were about 16 years old?[15]	(*N* = 1,465)	(*N* = 1,553)	(*N* = 3,018)
Philosophical-rationalist	0.1%	0.0%	0.0%
General Protestant	3.3	3.0	3.1
Reformation Protestant	18.4	15.3	16.8
Pietistic Protestant	20.0	21.8	20.9
Fundamentalist Protestant	29.1	29.7	29.5
Roman Catholic	23.0	25.8	24.5
Eastern Orthodox	0.4	0.5	0.5
Jewish	2.9	2.3	2.6
Other non-Christian	0.3	0.1	0.2
No religious preference	2.6	1.3	1.9

CHILDHOOD DEVOUTNESS

37A. Up to the time you were 16 years old, did your father (father substitute) usually attend religious services once a week or more, more than once a

	Males	*Females*	*Total*
month but not weekly, about once every month or two, several times a year, about once a year or less, or not at all?	(*N* = 1,371)	(*N* = 1,436)	(*N* = 2,807)
Not at all	16.1%	21.1%	18.7%
About once a year or less	11.0	9.7	10.3
Several times a year	10.6	10.8	10.7
About once every month or two	8.0	5.4	6.6
More than once a month but not weekly	10.8	10.7	10.8
Once a week or more	43.5	42.3	42.9
37B. And how about your mother (mother substitute)—did she usually attend church services once a week or more, more than once a month but not weekly, about once every month or two, several times a year, about once a year or less, or not at all?	(*N* = 1,431)	(*N* = 1,525)	(*N* = 2,956)
Not at all	7.6%	8.7%	8.2%
About once a year or less	5.0	5.3	5.2
Several times a year	9.6	10.6	10.1
About once every month or two	7.4	6.0	6.7
More than once a month but not weekly	14.3	13.8	14.0
Once a week or more	56.0	55.5	55.8
38. Look at this card and tell me which phrase best describes how strongly religious beliefs were felt in your home while you were growing up.	(*N* = 1,462)	(*N* = 1,546)	(*N* = 3,008)
Against or rejecting religion	0.5%	0.1%	0.3%
Not strongly at all	5.6	4.9	5.2
Not so strongly	6.0	5.7	5.9
Moderately	27.7	27.2	27.4
Strongly	20.0	21.7	20.9
Very strongly	40.2	40.4	40.3

DEMOGRAPHIC CHARACTERISTICS (SEE ALSO Q. 3–14, 27–29, 35, 36, 100–102)

39. What is your religious preference *at this time*?[16]	(*N* = 1,465)	(*N* = 1,553)	(*N* = 3,018)
Philosophical-rationalist	0.8%	0.4%	0.6%
General Protestant	4.6	4.3	4.4
Reformation Protestant	14.3	14.9	14.6
Pietistic Protestant	16.0	16.1	16.1
Fundamentalist Protestant	26.4	30.1	28.3
Roman Catholic	22.0	26.2	24.2
Eastern Orthodox	0.1	0.3	0.2
Jewish	2.5	2.2	2.4
Other non-Christian	0.2	0.1	0.2
No religious preference	13.0	5.4	9.1

	Males	*Females*	*Total*
CURRENT DEVOUTNESS			
[IF religious preference given:]			
40. How often do you attend religious services?	(N = 1,275)	(N = 1,467)	(N = 2,742)
Not at all	13.2%	7.8%	10.3%
About once a year or less	12.0	7.3	9.5
Several times a year	17.2	14.0	15.5
About once every month or two	9.2	9.1	9.1
More than once a month but not weekly	13.3	18.5	16.1
Once a week or more	35.1	43.3	39.5
41. How strongly do you feel about your religious beliefs now? Just give me one of the answers from the card.	(N = 1,463)	(N = 1,552)	(N = 3,015)
Against or rejecting religion	2.5%	0.8%	1.7%
Not strongly at all	7.6	4.3	5.9
Not so strongly	7.0	5.7	6.4
Moderately	27.8	23.6	25.6
Strongly	22.3	25.6	24.0
Very strongly	32.8	39.9	36.5
PARENTAL SEXUAL PERMISSIVENESS[17]			
42A. How strict or permissive would you say your father was toward you, about sexual matters—very strict, somewhat strict, somewhat permissive, or very permissive?	(N = 1,349)	(N = 1,408)	(N = 2,757)
Very strict	33.1%	55.3%	44.4%
Somewhat strict	30.3	25.6	27.9
Neither strict nor permissive	14.1	9.4	11.7
Somewhat permissive	15.4	7.2	11.2
Very permissive	7.1	2.6	4.8
42B. And how about your mother being strict or permissive toward you about sexual matters?	(N = 1,416)	(N = 1,519)	(N = 2,935)
Very strict	39.9%	60.3%	50.5%
Somewhat strict	31.4	25.0	28.1
Neither strict nor permissive	12.4	5.9	9.0
Somewhat permissive	11.9	6.6	9.2
Very permissive	4.3	2.2	3.2

ATTITUDES TOWARD BLACKS[18]

43. As I read each of the following statements about Negroes, tell me which of the answers listed on this card comes closest to the way you feel. First, I won't associate with Negroes if I can help it. How true is this for you—very true, somewhat true, somewhat untrue, or very untrue?

	Males	*Females*	*Total*
43A. I won't associate with Negroes if I can help it.	(*N* = 1,226)	(*N* = 1,303)	(*N* = 2,529)
Very untrue	47.6%	51.8%	49.7%
Somewhat untrue	20.6	21.5	21.1
Somewhat true	18.5	17.5	18.0
Very true	12.8	8.6	10.6
Don't know	0.5	0.6	0.6
43B. Some of our best citizens come from the Negroes.	(*N* = 1,225)	(*N* = 1,304)	(*N* = 2,529)
Very untrue	6.0%	3.9%	4.9%
Somewhat untrue	10.2	9.4	9.8
Somewhat true	39.9	39.0	39.4
Very true	41.6	45.6	43.6
Don't know	2.2	2.1	2.2
43C. I suppose Negroes are all right, but I've never liked them.	(*N* = 1,225)	(*N* = 1,302)	(*N* = 2,527)
Very untrue	51.1%	61.2%	56.3%
Somewhat untrue	26.0	22.7	24.3
Somewhat true	14.6	10.8	12.6
Very true	7.3	4.3	5.8
Don't know	1.0	1.0	1.0
43D. Negroes should be regarded as any other group.	(*N* = 1,226)	(*N* = 1,303)	(*N* = 2,529)
Very untrue	4.4%	3.5%	3.9%
Somewhat untrue	5.6	4.6	5.1
Somewhat true	21.2	17.7	19.4
Very true	67.9	73.5	71.0
Don't know	0.8	0.7	0.8
43E. I have no particular love or hatred for Negroes.	(*N* = 1,218)	(*N* = 1,303)	(*N* = 2,521)
Very untrue	8.2%	9.7%	9.0%
Somewhat untrue	6.7	8.1	7.4
Somewhat true	27.2	25.6	26.4
Very true	56.8	55.5	56.1
Don't know	1.0	1.1	1.0

ATTITUDES TOWARD JEWS[19]

44. As I read each of the following statements about Jewish people, tell me which of the answers listed on this card comes closest to the way you feel. First, I won't associate with Jewish people if I can help it. How true is this for you—very true, somewhat true, somewhat untrue, or very untrue?

44A. I won't associate with Jewish people if I can help it.	(*N* = 1,416)	(*N* = 1,510)	(*N* = 2,926)
Very untrue	71.4%	75.7%	73.6%
Somewhat untrue	14.9	14.0	14.4
Somewhat true	7.3	5.6	6.4
Very true	4.3	2.1	3.2
Don't know	2.0	2.6	2.3

	Males	*Females*	*Total*
44B. Some of our best citizens come from the Jewish people.	(*N* = 1,416)	(*N* = 1,507)	(*N* = 2,923)
Very untrue	2.1%	1.8%	2.0%
Somewhat untrue	4.0	4.4	4.2
Somewhat true	33.4	29.5	31.4
Very true	57.2	59.7	58.5
Don't know	3.3	4.7	4.0
44C. I suppose Jewish people are all right, but I've never liked them.	(*N* = 1,415)	(*N* = 1,508)	(*N* = 2,923)
Very untrue	64.5%	73.1%	69.0%
Somewhat untrue	20.1	15.9	18.0
Somewhat true	9.1	6.4	7.7
Very true	3.9	1.9	2.8
Don't know	2.4	2.6	2.5
44D. Jewish people should be regarded as any other group.	(*N* = 1,416)	(*N* = 1,510)	(*N* = 2,926)
Very untrue	3.0%	2.2%	2.6%
Somewhat untrue	2.8	1.0	1.8
Somewhat true	14.1	12.1	13.0
Very true	78.9	83.9	81.5
Don't know	1.3	0.8	1.0
44E. I have no particular love or hatred for Jewish people.	(*N* = 1,408)	(*N* = 1,504)	(*N* = 2,912)
Very untrue	12.2%	14.0%	13.1%
Somewhat untrue	7.0	7.3	7.2
Somewhat true	20.7	17.9	19.2
Very true	58.5	58.8	58.6
Don't know	1.6	2.1	1.8

FEELINGS ABOUT PROSTITUTION

45. Now I'd like to ask whether *you* believe certain sexual behaviors are right or wrong. For example, do you feel that prostitution—that is, a woman selling herself to men—is always wrong, almost always wrong, wrong only sometimes, or not wrong at all? Give me the answer listed on this card which is best for you.	(*N* = 1,464)	(*N* = 1,547)	(*N* = 3,011)
Not wrong at all	16.9%	5.7%	11.1%
Wrong only sometimes	21.7	11.2	16.3
Almost always wrong	15.6	14.0	14.8
Always wrong	44.9	68.6	57.1
Don't know	1.0	0.4	0.7
46. Do you think there should or should not be a law against prostitution?	(*N* = 1,465)	(*N* = 1,520)	(*N* = 2,985)
Should not be a law	43.4%	26.7%	34.8%
Should be a law	54.7	71.2	63.2
Don't know	1.9	2.1	2.0

	Males	*Females*	*Total*
[IF should be a law:]			
46A. If a woman is guilty of prostitution and it's her first conviction, which action on the card should be taken?	(*N* = 796)	(*N* = 1,105)	(*N* = 1,901)
Assigned to a rehabilitation or treatment program	47.7%	63.9%	57.1%
Put on probation	35.2	21.4	27.2
Given a lesser punishment like jail or a fine	9.5	7.0	8.0
Given a prison term of at least a year	6.0	6.5	6.3
Don't know	1.5	1.2	1.3
46B. If a man is guilty of going to a prostitute and it's his first conviction, which action on the card should be taken?	(*N* = 784)	(*N* = 1,089)	(*N* = 1,873)
Assigned to a rehabilitation or treatment program	32.7%	41.8%	38.0%
Put on probation	41.8	33.1	36.8
Given a lesser punishment like jail or a fine	14.4	13.5	13.9
Given a prison term of at least a year	6.1	7.3	6.8

FEELINGS ABOUT PREMARITAL SEX

	Males	*Females*	*Total*
47A. If a teenage boy, 16 to 19, has sexual intercourse with a girl he doesn't love, would you say that is always wrong, almost always wrong, wrong only sometimes, or not wrong at all? Which of the answers on the card comes closest to the way you feel?	(*N* = 1,465)	(*N* = 1,550)	(*N* = 3,015)
Not wrong at all	13.8%	5.3%	9.4%
Wrong only sometimes	20.9	13.4	17.0
Almost always wrong	19.4	19.6	19.5
Always wrong	45.2	61.0	53.3
Don't know	0.8	0.7	0.7
47B. And how about if he loves her?	(*N* = 1,465)	(*N* = 1,552)	(*N* = 3,017)
Not wrong at all	29.0%	16.0%	22.3%
Wrong only sometimes	23.0	18.0	20.4
Almost always wrong	16.9	21.2	19.1
Always wrong	30.2	44.1	37.3
Don't know	1.0	0.7	0.8
48A. How do you feel about an unmarried adult man having sexual intercourse with a woman he does not love? Again, give me the answer on the card which best expresses how you feel.	(*N* = 1,465)	(*N* = 1,544)	(*N* = 3,009)
Not wrong at all	22.9%	10.8%	16.7%
Wrong only sometimes	20.3	14.3	17.2
Almost always wrong	14.4	16.0	15.2
Always wrong	41.4	58.3	50.1
Don't know	1.0	0.6	0.8

	Males	*Females*	*Total*
48B. And how about if he loves her?	(*N* = 1,465)	(*N* = 1,542)	(*N* = 3,007)
Not wrong at all	40.9%	26.1%	33.3%
Wrong only sometimes	18.6	18.1	18.4
Almost always wrong	12.2	16.0	14.2
Always wrong	27.2	39.0	33.3
Don't know	1.1	0.7	0.9
49A. And what about a teenage girl, 16 to 19, having intercourse with a boy she does not love? What is your opinion in that case?	(*N* = 1,465)	(*N* = 1,550)	(*N* = 3,015)
Not wrong at all	9.9%	1.9%	5.8%
Wrong only sometimes	16.0	6.8	11.3
Almost always wrong	17.1	11.9	14.4
Always wrong	56.2	79.1	68.0
Don't know	0.8	0.4	0.6
49B. And how about if she loves him?	(*N* = 1,465)	(*N* = 1,551)	(*N* = 3,016)
Not wrong at all	25.1%	12.6%	18.6%
Wrong only sometimes	20.3	14.4	17.3
Almost always wrong	16.9	18.1	17.5
Always wrong	36.9	54.4	45.9
Don't know	0.8	0.5	0.6
50A. How about an unmarried adult woman having sexual intercourse with a man that she does not love? Look at the card and tell me your answer.	(*N* = 1,464)	(*N* = 1,552)	(*N* = 3,016)
Not wrong at all	20.7%	7.1%	13.7%
Wrong only sometimes	23.0	10.7	15.4
Almost always wrong	14.9	15.1	15.0
Always wrong	43.2	66.8	55.3
Don't know	0.9	0.3	0.6
50B. And how about if she loves him?	(*N* = 1,464)	(*N* = 1,546)	(*N* = 3,010)
Not wrong at all	38.5%	22.9%	30.5%
Wrong only sometimes	19.0	15.8	17.3
Almost always wrong	13.1	16.9	15.1
Always wrong	28.5	43.9	36.4
Don't know	0.9	0.5	0.7
51. All things considered, do you think there should or should not be a law against sexual intercourse between unmarried adults?	(*N* = 1,464)	(*N* = 1,551)	(*N* = 3,015)
Should not be a law	73.2%	64.7%	68.8%
Should be a law	24.8	32.2	28.6
Don't know	2.0	3.1	2.6

52. If you found out that an unmarried person who is a good friend of yours recently had sexual intercourse with another unmarried person, what effect would this have on your friendship? Would you not want to

	Males	*Females*	*Total*
have anything more to do with that person; still be in touch, but no longer be friends; stay friends, but it would be a problem; or still be friends, no problem?	(*N* = 1,442)	(*N* = 1,542)	(*N* = 2,984)
Not want to have anything more to do with that person	2.6%	3.2%	2.9%
Still be in touch, no longer be friends	3.3	6.4	4.9
Stay friends, but it would be a problem	17.7	26.0	22.0
Still be friends, no problem	75.6	63.8	69.5
Don't know	0.8	0.6	0.7
53A. How many men have you known, not necessarily as friends, who had sexual intercourse (with women) before they were married? Ten or more, five to nine, or only a few—less than five?[20]	(*N* = 1,465)	(*N* = 1,552)	(*N* = 3,017)
None, or don't know	5.1%	20.3%	12.9%
A few—less than 5	16.7	28.9	23.0
Several—5 to 9	9.3	11.0	10.1
Many—10 or more	60.3	30.7	45.1
Some, but don't know how many	8.6	9.1	8.9
53B. How many women have you known, not necessarily as friends, who had sexual intercourse (with men) before they were married? Ten or more, five to nine, or only a few—less than five?[20]	(*N* = 1,461)	(*N* = 1,552)	(*N* = 3,013)
None, or don't know	11.8%	18.5%	15.3%
A few—less than 5	24.4	33.0	28.8
Several—5 to 9	12.7	14.0	13.3
Many—10 or more	42.6	26.3	34.2
Some, but don't know how many	8.5	8.2	8.4
54A. Do you think the religious group which means the most to you, even if you *do not associate* with that group, feels that sexual intercourse between unmarried adults is always wrong, almost always wrong, wrong only sometimes, or not wrong at all?	(*N* = 1,456)	(*N* = 1,551)	(*N* = 3,007)
Not wrong at all	2.3%	1.4%	1.9%
Wrong only sometimes	8.0	6.7	7.3
Almost always wrong	13.0	11.2	12.1
Always wrong	73.5	78.3	76.0
Don't know	3.2	2.4	2.8
54B. How about most mental health experts—psychiatrists and psychologists? How do they feel about it?	(*N* = 1,460)	(*N* = 1,551)	(*N* = 3,011)
Not wrong at all	17.1%	12.8%	14.9%
Wrong only sometimes	34.7	36.2	35.4
Almost always wrong	17.2	19.5	18.4
Always wrong	16.4	15.0	15.7
Don't know	14.6	16.6	15.6

	Males	Females	Total
54C. And how do courts and the law stand on sexual intercourse between unmarried adults?	(N = 1,460)	(N = 1,546)	(N = 3,006)
Not wrong at all	11.4%	11.4%	11.4%
Wrong only sometimes	23.6	20.7	22.1
Almost always wrong	19.3	17.9	18.6
Always wrong	36.9	32.6	34.7
Don't know	8.8	17.4	13.2
54D. Most young people—how would they feel?	(N = 1,461)	(N = 1,551)	(N = 3,012)
Not wrong at all	43.6%	40.6%	42.0%
Wrong only sometimes	34.1	37.9	36.1
Almost always wrong	11.6	11.6	11.6
Always wrong	6.5	5.9	6.2
Don't know	4.2	4.1	4.2
54E. And most university professors—how would they feel?	(N = 1,460)	(N = 1,549)	(N = 3,009)
Not wrong at all	23.4%	22.1%	22.7%
Wrong only sometimes	36.6	35.1	35.8
Almost always wrong	16.2	17.0	16.6
Always wrong	11.6	11.9	11.8
Don't know	12.3	13.9	13.1

FEELINGS ABOUT EXTRAMARITAL SEX

	Males	Females	Total
55A. And now, would you look at the card again, and tell me which answer applies if a married person has sexual intercourse with someone other than the marriage partner?	(N = 1,463)	(N = 1,553)	(N = 3,016)
Not wrong at all	3.6%	0.8%	2.2%
Wrong only sometimes	12.9	8.8	10.8
Almost always wrong	16.9	11.9	14.3
Always wrong	66.2	78.2	72.3
Don't know	0.5	0.3	0.4
55B. Do you think there should or should not be a law against a husband or wife having sexual intercourse with some other person?	(N = 1,464)	(N = 1,552)	(N = 3,016)
Should not be a law	48.8%	43.9%	46.3%
Should be a law	49.5	53.9	51.7
Don't know	1.8	2.3	2.0
[IF should be a law:]			
55B(1). Which action listed on the card should be taken with them?	(N = 710)	(N = 833)	(N = 1,543)
Assigned to a rehabilitation or treatment program	33.5%	41.8%	38.0%
Put on probation	37.6	30.0	33.4
Given a lesser punishment like jail or a fine	15.1	11.6	13.2
Given a prison term of at least a year	10.8	12.0	11.5
Don't know	3.0	4.8	4.0

	Males	*Females*	*Total*
56. If you found out that a married person who is a good friend of yours recently had sexual intercourse outside of marriage, what effect would this have on your friendship? Would you not want to have anything more to do with that person; still be in touch, but no longer be friends; stay friends, but it would be a problem; or still be friends, no problem?	(*N* = 1,464)	(*N* = 1,553)	(*N* = 3,017)
Not want to have anything more to do with that person	4.8%	6.6%	5.7%
Still be in touch, no longer be friends	6.2	12.4	9.4
Stay friends, but it would be a problem	27.7	38.9	33.4
Still be friends, no problem	60.5	41.3	50.6
Don't know	0.9	0.9	0.9
57A. How many married men have you known, not necessarily as friends, who had sexual intercourse with someone other than their wives while they were married? Ten or more, five to nine, or only a few—less than five?[20]	(*N* = 1,464)	(*N* = 1,552)	(*N* = 3,016)
None, or don't know	10.3%	23.7%	17.2%
A few—less than 5	32.1	43.0	37.7
Several—5 to 9	14.5	10.4	12.4
Many—10 or more	36.2	16.4	26.0
Some, but don't know how many	6.9	6.4	6.7
57B. How many married women have you known, not necessarily as friends, who had sexual intercourse with someone other than their husbands while they were married? Ten or more, five to nine, or only a few—less than five?[20]	(*N* = 1,463)	(*N* = 1,551)	(*N* = 3,014)
None, or don't know	20.6%	28.1%	24.5%
A few—less than 5	35.3	44.6	40.0
Several—5 to 9	12.8	9.3	11.0
Many—10 or more	24.8	12.0	18.2
Some, but don't know how many	6.5	6.0	6.2

58. Now I'd like to know how you think the following institutions or groups of people we mentioned before feel about sexual intercourse between people who are married but not to each other. Just tell me which answer on the card you think is true for each of them.

58A. First, the religious group that means most to you. How would they feel about it?	(*N* = 1,456)	(*N* = 1,551)	(*N* = 3,007)
Not wrong at all	0.4%	0.2%	0.3%
Wrong only sometimes	2.7	1.4	2.0
Almost always wrong	6.9	6.5	6.7
Always wrong	87.6	91.0	89.3
Don't know	2.3	1.0	1.6

	Males	*Females*	*Total*
58B. Most mental health experts—psychiatrists, psychologists?	(N = 1,459)	(N = 1,553)	(N = 3,012)
Not wrong at all	5.8%	5.2%	5.4%
Wrong only sometimes	25.9	24.3	25.1
Almost always wrong	29.1	31.7	30.4
Always wrong	29.2	28.1	28.6
Don't know	10.1	10.8	10.4
58C. And how do courts and the law stand on intercourse by married persons outside of marriage?	(N = 1,462)	(N = 1,553)	(N = 3,015)
Not wrong at all	2.3%	3.0%	2.7%
Wrong only sometimes	12.2	12.3	12.2
Almost always wrong	20.3	18.4	19.3
Always wrong	59.5	56.7	58.1
Don't know	5.7	9.6	7.7
58D. Most young people?	(N = 1,462)	(N = 1,552)	(N = 3,014)
Not wrong at all	25.6%	23.6%	24.6%
Wrong only sometimes	32.7	32.5	32.6
Almost always wrong	21.5	23.4	22.5
Always wrong	15.1	16.4	15.8
Don't know	5.1	4.1	4.6
58E. Most university professors?	(N = 1,459)	(N = 1,553)	(N = 3,012)
Not wrong at all	12.7%	11.8%	12.3%
Wrong only sometimes	30.0	31.3	30.6
Almost always wrong	24.5	24.0	24.2
Always wrong	20.6	19.1	19.8
Don't know	12.1	13.8	13.0
59A. You've said how you feel now about premarital and extramarital sexual behavior. Have you always felt this way about these matters, or have there been times in the past when you felt more approving or less approving?	(N = 1,459)	(N = 1,552)	(N = 3,011)
Used to be less approving	23.8%	24.1%	23.9%
Always felt this way	63.5	67.7	65.7
Used to be more approving	11.7	7.1	9.3
Have been both more and less approving than now	1.0	1.1	1.0
59B. How do your feelings about these things compare with the way your parents—or whoever brought you up—felt about this when you were a child? Would you say that you are generally more approving or less approving than they were at that time?[21]	(N = 1,460)	(N = 1,548)	(N = 3,008)
Less approving than parents	7.7%	7.6%	7.2%
About the same as parents	40.4	47.9	44.2
More approving than parents	49.5	42.2	45.8
Don't know	3.4	2.4	2.8

	Males	*Females*	*Total*
59C. Do you feel that you are more approving or less approving than most of your friends?[21]	(*N* = 1,465)	(*N* = 1,549)	(*N* = 3,014)
Less approving than friends	26.6%	29.3%	28.0%
About the same as friends	51.4	53.1	52.2
More approving than friends	18.6	14.8	16.6
Don't know	3.5	2.7	2.9
59D. As compared to most adults in the United States, would you say you are more approving or less approving about these matters than they are?[21]	(*N* = 1,465)	(*N* = 1,549)	(*N* = 3,014)
Less approving than most adults	34.3%	45.5%	40.0%
About the same as most adults	32.7	30.9	32.0
More approving than most adults	26.8	17.5	22.0
Don't know	6.2	6.1	6.1

FEELINGS ABOUT HOMOSEXUALITY (SEE ALSO Q. 94–98)

	Males	*Females*	*Total*
60A. What is your opinion about physical acts between two persons of the same sex for the purpose of sexual stimulation, when they have no special affection for each other? Do you think that is always wrong, almost always wrong, wrong only sometimes, or not wrong at all?	(*N* = 1,463)	(*N* = 1,553)	(*N* = 3,016)
Not wrong at all	7.9%	3.5%	5.7%
Wrong only sometimes	7.6	5.3	6.4
Almost always wrong	9.0	8.0	8.4
Always wrong	73.9	81.5	77.8
Don't know	1.6	1.7	1.7
60B. And if they love each other?	(*N* = 1,458)	(*N* = 1,551)	(*N* = 3,009)
Not wrong at all	14.5%	8.7%	11.5%
Wrong only sometimes	7.8	6.8	7.2
Almost always wrong	8.6	8.3	8.5
Always wrong	66.8	74.0	70.5
Don't know	2.3	2.3	2.3
60C. Aside from how you *feel* about it, do you think there should or should not be a law against any sex acts between persons of thc same sex?	(*N* = 1,459)	(*N* = 1,548)	(*N* = 3,007)
Should not be a law	37.1%	38.4%	37.7%
Should be a law	60.2	58.0	59.1
Don't know	2.7	3.6	3.2

[IF should be a law:]

60C(1). Should they be given a prison term of at least a year, given a lesser punishment like jail or a fine, put on probation with threat of jail if probation is

	Males	*Females*	*Total*
violated, or assigned to a rehabilitation or treatment program for help?	(*N* = 873)	(*N* = 892)	(*N* = 1,765)
Assigned to a rehabilitation or treatment program	59.7%	69.7%	64.8%
Put on probation	14.7	10.2	12.4
Given a lesser punishment like jail or a fine	8.2	6.6	7.4
Given a prison term of at least a year	15.9	12.2	14.0
Don't know	1.5	1.2	1.4

61. You've said how you feel now about sex acts between persons of the same sex. Have you always felt this way, or have there been times when you were more approving or less approving?	(*N* = 1,455)	(*N* = 1,549)	(*N* = 3,004)
Used to be less approving	17.3%	15.2%	16.2%
Always felt this way	80.0	83.0	81.6
Used to be more approving	2.6	1.5	2.0
Have been both more and less approving than now	0.1	0.3	0.2

[IF not always felt this way:]

61A. How long have you felt the way you do now—since what age?	(*N* = 282)	(*N* = 262)	(*N* = 544)
14 or younger	2.8%	3.1%	2.9%
15–19	20.6	18.3	19.5
20–24	22.7	24.4	23.5
25–29	18.4	21.4	19.9
30–34	14.2	16.4	15.3
35–44	11.7	8.8	10.3
45 or older	9.6	7.6	8.6

62. How would you say your feelings about sex relations between persons of the same sex compare with the way your parents felt toward this when you were a child? Are you more approving, or less approving than they were at that time?[21]	(*N* = 1,462)	(*N* = 1,550)	(*N* = 3,012)
Less approving than parents	5.8%	3.7%	4.7%
About the same as parents	60.0	63.4	61.7
More approving than parents	27.6	23.5	25.5
Don't know	6.6	9.5	8.1

63. Two states have laws which *do not forbid sex acts* between persons of the same sex, if done in complete privacy between consenting adults. Do you approve or disapprove of such a law?	(*N* = 1,463)	(*N* = 1,551)	(*N* = 3,014)
Disapprove	59.1%	60.3%	59.7%
Approve	36.6	35.3	35.9
Don't know	4.3	4.4	4.3

	Males	Females	Total
64. If you found out that a woman who is a good friend of yours had recently been engaging in sex acts with another woman, what effect would this have on your friendship? Would you not want to have anything more to do with her; still be in touch with her, but no longer be friends; stay friends, but it would be a problem; or still be friends, no problem?	(*N* = 1,463)	(*N* = 1,550)	(*N* = 3,013)
Not want to have anything more to do with her	31.0%	40.3%	35.8%
Still be in touch, no longer be friends	11.1	19.2	15.3
Stay friends, but it would be a problem	28.0	28.4	28.2
Still be friends, no problem	28.5	10.8	19.4
Don't know	1.3	1.4	1.4
65. And if you found out that a man who is a good friend of yours had recently been engaging in sex acts with another man, what effect would this have on your friendship? Would you not want to have anything more to do with him; still be in touch with him, but no longer be friends; stay friends, but it would be a problem; or still be friends, no problem?	(*N* = 1,465)	(*N* = 1,552)	(*N* = 3,017)
Not want to have anything more to do with him	38.2%	42.7%	40.5%
Still be in touch, no longer be friends	12.0	17.3	14.7
Stay friends, but it would be a problem	26.1	24.1	25.1
Still be friends, no problem	22.7	14.4	18.5
Don't know	1.0	1.5	1.3
66. The way people feel about these things is sometimes influenced by people they may have known. Have you ever been personally acquainted with any men or boys—not necessarily as friends—who engaged in sex acts with other males?	(*N* = 1,447)	(*N* = 1,553)	(*N* = 3,000)
No, or don't know	55.5%	69.8%	62.1%
Yes	44.5	30.2	36.9
[IF YES:]			
66A(1). Did you know any before you were age 13?	(*N* = 644)	(*N* = 462)	(*N* = 1,106)
No	84.2%	93.1%	87.9%
Yes	15.8	6.9	12.1
66A(2). When you were about 13, 14, 15, or 16?	(*N* = 642)	(*N* = 461)	(*N* = 1,103)
No	67.0%	78.3%	71.7%
Yes	33.0	21.7	28.3

	Males	*Females*	*Total*
66A(3). When you were about 17, 18, or 19?	(*N* = 642)	(*N* = 460)	(*N* = 1,102)
No	40.8%	59.1%	48.5%
Yes	59.2	40.9	51.5
66A(4). After age 20?	(*N* = 649)	(*N* = 462)	(*N* = 1,111)
No	10.2%	8.9%	9.6%
Yes	89.8	91.1	90.4
66B. During how many years of your life altogether have you been personally acquainted with such men or boys?	(*N* = 658)	(*N* = 479)	(*N* = 1,137)
One year or less	11.2%	13.6%	12.0%
More than one, less than 5 years	17.9	24.6	20.8
At least 5, less than 10 years	13.4	19.6	16.0
10 or more years	57.4	42.2	51.0
66C. Thinking of all these men or boys that you have known, how many were the same age as you—within a year older or younger?	(*N* = 634)	(*N* = 456)	(*N* = 1,090)
None of them	37.5%	54.4%	44.6%
One or two	29.0	29.6	29.3
Three to five	18.5	11.0	15.3
Six to ten	7.1	3.5	5.6
11 to 25	5.8	0.9	3.8
More than 25	2.1	0.7	1.5
66D. How many were more than a year older?	(*N* = 637)	(*N* = 463)	(*N* = 1,100)
None of them	23.7%	38.0%	29.7%
One or two	32.7	35.2	33.7
Three to five	22.8	17.3	20.5
Six to ten	11.5	6.0	9.2
11 to 25	6.8	3.2	5.3
More than 25	2.7	0.2	1.6
66E. How many were more than a year younger?	(*N* = 622)	(*N* = 459)	(*N* = 1,081)
None of them	50.3%	56.9%	53.1%
One or two	23.2	26.1	24.4
Three to five	12.9	9.8	11.6
Six to ten	8.2	4.6	6.7
11 to 25	4.2	2.2	3.3
More than 25	1.3	0.4	0.9
66F. About how many is that altogether?	(*N* = 653)	(*N* = 472)	(*N* = 1,125)
One or two	27.1%	45.3%	34.8%
Three to five	24.0	29.0	26.1
Six to ten	24.0	13.6	19.6
11 to 25	12.4	8.1	10.6
More than 25	12.4	4.0	8.9

	Males	*Females*	*Total*
67. And have you ever been personally acquainted with any women or girls—not necessarily as friends—who engaged in sex acts with other females?	(*N* = 1,455)	(*N* = 1,543)	(*N* = 2,998)
No, or don't know	75.9%	76.2%	76.1%
Yes	24.1	23.8	23.9
[IF YES:]			
67A(1). Did you know any before you were age 13?	(*N* = 350)	(*N* = 366)	(*N* = 716)
No	93.4%	92.1%	92.7%
Yes	6.6	7.9	7.3
67A(2). When you were about 13, 14, 15, or 16?	(*N* = 350)	(*N* = 366)	(*N* = 716)
No	79.1%	78.4%	78.8%
Yes	20.9	21.6	21.2
67A(3). When you were about 17, 18, or 19?	(*N* = 350)	(*N* = 362)	(*N* = 712)
No	58.6%	60.0%	59.4%
Yes	41.4	40.0	40.6
67A(4). After age 20?	(*N* = 355)	(*N* = 361)	(*N* = 716)
No	6.5%	15.2%	10.9%
Yes	93.5	84.8	89.1
67B. During how many years of your life altogether have you been personally acquainted with such women or girls?	(*N* = 350)	(*N* = 375)	(*N* = 725)
One year or less	6.0%	19.5%	13.0%
More than one, less than 5 years	22.3	25.1	23.7
At least 5, less than 10 years	18.0	19.7	18.9
10 or more years	53.7	35.7	44.4
67C. Thinking of all these women or girls that you have known, how many were the same age as you (within a year older or younger)?	(*N* = 336)	(*N* = 359)	(*N* = 695)
None of them	39.3%	52.1%	45.9%
One or two	27.1	35.4	31.4
Three to five	19.6	8.9	14.1
Six to ten	8.0	2.8	5.3
11 to 25	4.5	0.8	2.6
More than 25	1.5	0.0	0.7
67D. How many were more than a year older?	(*N* = 340)	(*N* = 365)	(*N* = 705)
None of them	37.6%	41.4%	39.6%
One or two	25.6	39.7	32.9
Three to five	19.1	12.6	15.7
Six to ten	12.1	4.9	8.4
11 to 25	4.4	1.1	2.7
More than 25	1.2	0.3	0.7

	Males	Females	Total
67E. How many were more than a year younger?	(N = 340)	(N = 363)	(N = 703)
None of them	42.6%	64.5%	53.9%
One or two	26.2	22.3	24.2
Three to five	17.9	9.4	13.5
Six to ten	7.6	2.8	5.1
11 to 25	4.4	0.6	2.4
More than 25	1.2	0.6	0.9
67F. About how many is that altogether?	(N = 352)	(N = 371)	(N = 723)
One or two	31.5%	56.6%	44.4%
Three to five	26.1	23.5	24.8
Six to ten	19.9	11.9	15.8
11 to 25	14.5	7.3	10.8
More than 25	8.0	0.8	4.3

68. I'd like to know how you think the institutions or groups of people we've mentioned before feel about sex acts between persons of the same sex. Just tell me which answer on the card you think is true for each of them.

	Males	Females	Total
68A. First, the religious group that means most to you.	(N = 1,455)	(N = 1,551)	(N = 3,006)
Not wrong at all	0.8%	0.5%	0.6%
Wrong only sometimes	2.6	2.1	2.4
Almost always wrong	5.9	5.5	5.7
Always wrong	87.0	89.6	88.4
Don't know	3.6	2.3	3.0
68B. Most mental health experts—psychiatrists, psychologists.	(N = 1,461)	(N = 1,552)	(N = 3,013)
Not wrong at all	5.4%	5.4%	5.4%
Wrong only sometimes	20.0	20.5	20.2
Almost always wrong	24.2	24.5	24.4
Always wrong	40.5	39.3	39.9
Don't know	9.9	10.3	10.1
68C. And how do courts and the law stand on sex between persons of the same sex?	(N = 1,459)	(N = 1,549)	(N = 3,008)
Not wrong at all	2.1%	2.5%	2.3%
Wrong only sometimes	9.3	9.5	9.4
Almost always wrong	23.1	21.1	22.1
Always wrong	59.3	58.2	58.7
Don't know	6.2	8.7	7.5
68D. Most young people?	(N = 1,458)	(N = 1,548)	(N = 3,006)
Not wrong at all	10.6%	12.3%	11.5%
Wrong only sometimes	25.9	23.8	24.9
Almost always wrong	27.0	26.6	26.8
Always wrong	29.8	29.0	29.4
Don't know	6.7	8.3	7.5

	Males	*Females*	*Total*
68E. Most university professors?	(*N* = 1,458)	(*N* = 1,550)	(*N* = 3,008)
Not wrong at all	7.3%	7.2%	7.3%
Wrong only sometimes	22.9	21.0	21.9
Almost always wrong	26.8	25.6	26.2
Always wrong	31.9	32.4	32.1
Don't know	11.0	13.7	12.4
68F. Your medical doctor?	(*N* = 1,461)	(*N* = 1,549)	(*N* = 3,010)
Not wrong at all	3.6%	3.3%	3.5%
Wrong only sometimes	13.1	9.7	11.4
Almost always wrong	18.4	18.0	18.2
Always wrong	53.0	56.0	54.5
Don't know	11.8	13.0	12.4

FEELINGS ABOUT MASTURBATION

	Males	*Females*	*Total*
69. How many American woman would you think have masturbated—made themselves come to a sexual climax—either as children or after they were grown up—at least once in their lives? Would you say all, most, some, or none?	(*N* = 1,463)	(*N* = 1,553)	(*N* = 3,016)
None	2.6%	4.8%	3.7%
Some	41.8	49.3	45.7
Most	31.9	25.8	28.8
All	10.8	8.4	9.6
Don't know	12.9	11.6	12.2
70. And how many American men would you think have masturbated—made themselves come to a sexual climax—either as children or after they were grown up—at least once in their lives? Would you say all, most, some, or none?	(*N* = 1,463)	(*N* = 1,553)	(*N* = 3,016)
None	1.6%	2.1%	1.8%
Some	29.3	32.4	30.9
Most	39.4	33.2	36.2
All	24.2	23.9	24.0
Don't know	5.5	8.5	7.0
71. Do you feel that masturbation is always wrong, almost always wrong, wrong only sometimes, or not wrong at all?	(*N* = 1,462)	(*N* = 1,552)	(*N* = 3,014)
Not wrong at all	21.5%	16.2%	18.8%
Wrong only sometimes	30.2	29.4	29.8
Almost always wrong	20.1	21.8	21.0
Always wrong	25.5	28.4	27.0
Don't know	2.6	4.1	3.4

72. Have you always felt this way about masturbating, or have there been times

	Males	*Females*	*Total*
when you were more approving or less approving?	(*N* = 1,451)	(*N* = 1,527)	(*N* = 2,978)
Used to be less approving	19.6%	24.6%	22.2%
Always felt this way	73.2	72.9	73.0
Used to be more approving	6.5	2.1	4.3
Have been both more and less approving than now	0.6	0.5	0.5
[IF not always felt this way:]			
72A. How long have you felt the way you do now—since what age?	(*N* = 361)	(*N* = 380)	(*N* = 741)
14 or younger	5.5%	3.2%	4.3%
15–19	31.6	19.5	25.3
20–24	24.4	28.7	26.6
25–29	11.6	16.8	14.3
30–34	8.0	14.2	11.2
35–44	12.5	10.3	11.3
45 or older	6.4	7.4	6.9
73. And now I'd like to ask you how you think the institutions or groups of people we've mentioned before feel about masturbation. Which answer on the card do you think is true for each of them.?			
73A. First, the religious group that means most to you.	(*N* = 1,456)	(*N* = 1,550)	(*N* = 3,006)
Not wrong at all	3.6%	4.1%	3.9%
Wrong only sometimes	8.9	9.7	9.3
Almost always wrong	14.9	15.2	15.1
Always wrong	67.0	63.0	64.9
Don't know	5.7	7.9	6.9
73B. Most mental health experts—psychiatrists, psychologists.	(*N* = 1,461)	(*N* = 1,551)	(*N* = 3,012)
Not wrong at all	17.4%	18.8%	18.1%
Wrong only sometimes	29.2	29.3	29.2
Almost always wrong	20.5	21.5	21.0
Always wrong	24.1	20.1	22.0
Don't know	8.8	10.4	9.6
73C. Most young people.	(*N* = 1,460)	(*N* = 1,550)	(*N* = 3,010)
Not wrong at all	29.8%	27.3%	28.5%
Wrong only sometimes	34.9	31.3	33.0
Almost always wrong	17.4	18.7	18.1
Always wrong	11.8	12.5	12.2
Don't know	6.2	10.2	8.2
73D. Most university professors.	(*N* = 1,462)	(*N* = 1,551)	(*N* = 3,013)
Not wrong at all	19.7%	18.3%	19.0%
Wrong only sometimes	30.4	30.2	30.3
Almost always wrong	17.9	19.4	18.7
Always wrong	19.2	16.2	17.7
Don't know	12.8	15.9	14.4

	Males	*Females*	*Total*
73E. Your medical doctor.	(*N* = 1,462)	(*N* = 1,551)	(*N* = 3,013)
Not wrong at all	17.1%	15.0%	16.0%
Wrong only sometimes	25.6	24.0	24.8
Almost always wrong	16.1	18.5	17.4
Always wrong	30.7	28.3	29.5
Don't know	10.4	14.2	12.3

SEX EDUCATION

74. Have you ever taken sex education as a regular course, or been taught about sex in a course like gym, personal hygiene, or physical education?	(*N* = 1,465)	(*N* = 1,553)	(*N* = 3,018)
No	76.9%	69.1%	72.8%
Yes, part of another course	10.4	14.4	12.5
Yes, a regular course	12.7	16.5	14.7

[IF YES:]

74A. In this sex education, were you taught anything about masturbation? If so, were you taught that it was always wrong, sometimes wrong, not wrong at all, or was nothing said about it being right or wrong?	(*N* = 335)	(*N* = 476)	(*N* = 811)
Not taught about it	48.1%	67.2%	59.3%
Nothing said about it being wrong	15.5	13.0	14.1
Taught that it was not wrong at all	8.7	5.7	6.9
Taught that it was sometimes wrong	12.5	7.6	9.6
Taught that it was always wrong	15.2	6.5	10.1
74B. And what were you taught about sexual intercourse before marriage?	(*N* = 336)	(*N* = 475)	(*N* = 811)
Not taught about it	35.7%	41.7%	39.2%
Nothing said about it being wrong	18.8	9.9	13.6
Taught that it was not wrong at all	6.0	1.1	3.1
Taught that it was sometimes wrong	15.2	8.4	11.2
Taught that it was always wrong	24.4	38.9	32.9
74C. What about sex between persons of the same sex—homosexuality?	(*N* = 337)	(*N* = 477)	(*N* = 814)
Not taught about it	55.5%	63.7%	60.3%
Nothing said about it being wrong	9.2	8.4	8.7
Taught that it was not wrong at all	0.9	0.4	0.6
Taught that it was sometimes wrong	4.2	3.4	3.7
Taught that it was always wrong	30.3	24.1	26.7

75. Many opinions have been expressed recently—some for and some against sex education in the schools—and I'd like to know whether you agree or disagree with these statements. Again, just give me the best answer on the card.

	Males	*Females*	*Total*
75A. In a democracy, schools should not teach sexual morality to children because not all parents want the same standards for their children.	(*N* = 1,457)	(*N* = 1,545)	(*N* = 3,002)
Strongly disagree	25.9%	26.0%	26.0%
Somewhat disagree	21.7	21.7	21.7
Somewhat agree	26.4	29.9	28.2
Strongly agree	23.7	21.2	22.4
Don't know	2.3	1.2	1.7
75B. The public has just as much right to require teenagers to take a sex information course as it does to require courses in grammar or American history.	(*N* = 1,459)	(*N* = 1,544)	(*N* = 3,003)
Strongly disagree	20.8%	18.6%	19.7%
Somewhat disagree	15.7	16.6	16.2
Somewhat agree	28.1	30.1	29.1
Strongly agree	33.4	33.4	33.4
Don't know	1.9	1.4	1.6
75C. Teaching sex information in schools without teaching sexual morality can only lead to loose morals.	(*N* = 1,456)	(*N* = 1,542)	(*N* = 2,998)
Strongly disagree	21.6%	20.4%	21.0%
Somewhat disagree	19.2	19.6	19.4
Somewhat agree	23.1	24.3	23.7
Strongly agree	33.8	34.0	33.9
Don't know	2.3	1.8	2.0
75D. Communists are trying to use sex education to weaken the morals of our children.	(*N* = 1,458)	(*N* = 1,545)	(*N* = 3,003)
Strongly disagree	36.8%	36.8%	36.8%
Somewhat disagree	15.6	16.2	15.9
Somewhat agree	18.4	18.1	18.3
Strongly agree	20.4	17.4	18.9
Don't know	8.6	11.5	10.1
75E. Usually those who don't believe in sex information for children are the ones who have personal problems about sex.	(*N* = 1,456)	(*N* = 1,544)	(*N* = 3,000)
Strongly disagree	17.4%	16.6%	17.0%
Somewhat disagree	16.8	18.0	17.4
Somewhat agree	35.6	34.7	35.1
Strongly agree	24.0	25.3	24.6
Don't know	6.3	5.5	5.9

FEELINGS ABOUT CHILDREN'S SEX PLAY

76. As you know, most children engage in sex play, or exploration, at least once or twice while they are growing up, either with other youngsters or by themselves. If a young person does this alone and

	Males	Females	Total
comes to a climax, it is generally called masturbation. Suppose as 12- or 13-year-old child masturbates. Which one of the statements on this card comes closest to your opinion of what a parent should do?	(*N* = 1,447)	(*N* = 1,529)	(*N* = 2,976)
Ignore it, not a problem	8.2%	6.8%	7.5%
Discuss it but not discourage child	33.4	33.2	33.3
Discourage it but not forbid child	22.8	28.0	25.5
Forbid it but not punish child	24.0	23.1	23.6
Punish the child	10.4	7.7	9.0
Don't know	1.1	1.2	1.2
77A. Suppose a boy and a girl about 12 or 13 years old engage in sex play together to come to a sexual climax. Do you think they should or should not be allowed to still be friends and playmates?	(*N* = 1,449)	(*N* = 1,537)	(*N* = 2,986)
Should not	44.8%	55.5%	50.3%
Should	53.1	41.4	47.1
Don't know	2.1	3.1	2.6
77B. Which one of the statements on the card comes closest to your opinion of what a parent should do in such a situation?	(*N* = 1,432)	(*N* = 1,512)	(*N* = 2,944)
Ignore it, not a problem	1.7%	0.5%	1.1%
Discuss it but not discourage child	20.1	19.9	20.0
Discourage it but not forbid child	16.6	16.1	16.4
Forbid it but not punish child	41.1	43.1	42.1
Punish the child	19.3	18.9	19.1
Don't know	1.1	1.4	1.3
78A. What about two children of the same sex, about 12 or 13 years old—if they engage in sex play together to come to a sexual climax. Do you believe they should or should not be allowed to still be friends and playmates?	(*N* = 1,454)	(*N* = 1,540	(*N* = 2,994)
Should not	58.7%	62.4%	60.6%
Should	39.1	34.7	36.9
Don't know	2.1	2.9	2.5
78B. Which one of the statements on the card comes closest to your opinion of what a parent should do in such a situation?	(*N* = 1,430)	(*N* = 1,512)	(*N* = 2,942)
Ignore it, not a problem	1.5%	0.4%	0.9%
Discuss it but not discourage child	14.5	16.5	15.6
Discourage it but not forbid child	15.0	16.3	15.6
Forbid it but not punish child	40.2	41.6	40.9
Punish the child	27.6	23.6	25.5
Don't know	1.3	1.6	1.4

	Males	*Females*	*Total*
SEXUAL EXPERIENCE (SEE ALSO Q.A–R, FOLLOWING Q.82)			
79. (Before you were married,) did *anyone* of the opposite sex ever clearly (invite, if male; propose or attempt, if female) sexual relations with you, whether or not any sex resulted? That means having to decide yes or no.	(*N* = 1,450)	(*N* = 1,548)	(*N* = 2,998)
No	37.4%	31.1%	34.2%
Yes	62.6	68.9	65.8
[IF YES:]			
79A. How many (men/women) made such advances (before you were married)? Persons with whom no sex resulted count as well as those with whom it did.	(*N* = 907)	(*N* = 1,066)	(*N* = 1,973)
One	7.2%	17.1%	12.6%
Two	13.5	18.4	16.1
Three	14.6	16.0	15.4
Four	8.4	11.3	9.9
Five to nine	25.9	19.0	22.2
10 to 19	16.5	11.0	13.5
20 or more	13.9	7.2	10.3
79B. Did sex relations ever result from any of these advances?	(*N* = 910)	(*N* = 1,060)	(*N* = 1,970)
No	28.4%	64.8%	48.0%
Yes	71.6	35.2	52.0
80. (Before you were married,) were there any times when *you* (proposed or attempted, if male; invited, if female) sexual relations with someone of the opposite sex, whether or not any sex resulted?	(*N* = 1,445)	(*N* = 1,546)	(*N* = 2,991)
No	30.7%	89.5%	61.1%
Yes	69.3	10.5	38.9
[IF YES:]			
80A. With how many (men/women) did this happen (before you were married)?	(*N* = 1,001)	(*N* = 163)	(*N* = 1,164)
One	6.0%	43.6%	11.3%
Two	9.7	23.3	11.6
Three	10.0	11.0	10.1
Four	9.9	4.9	9.2
Five to nine	24.0	9.8	22.0
10 to 19	19.0	4.9	17.0
20 or more	21.5	2.5	18.8
80B. Did sex relations ever result from any of these advances?	(*N* = 1,009)	(*N* = 164)	(*N* = 1,173)
No	15.4%	33.5%	17.9%
Yes	84.6	66.5	82.1

	Males	*Females*	*Total*
81. Have there been times when someone of the *same* sex clearly proposed or attempted sexual relations with you, whether or not any sex resulted?	(*N* = 1,458)	(*N* = 1,551)	(*N* = 3,009)
No	62.6%	90.6%	77.0%
Yes	37.4	9.4	23.0
[IF YES:]			
81A. With how many persons did this happen—including any times that resulted in sexual relations?	(*N* = 545)	(*N* = 146)	(*N* = 691)
One	33.6%	64.4%	40.1%
Two	18.3	18.5	18.4
Three	12.8	7.5	11.7
Four	7.5	2.7	6.5
Five to nine	16.9	4.1	14.2
10 to 19	5.7	2.1	4.9
20 or more	5.1	0.7	4.2
81B. (Was this/were these) person(s) (mostly) older or (mostly) younger than you?[22]	(*N* = 544)	(*N* = 144)	(*N* = 688)
Mostly younger	5.0%	6.2%	5.2%
Same age and younger	2.9	5.6	3.5
Mostly same age	4.0	7.6	4.8
Same age and older	15.4	23.6	17.2
Mostly older	68.2	54.9	65.4
Can't say, all different ages	4.4	2.1	3.9
81C. How many persons of the *same* sex made sexual advances to you and nothing came of it sexually?	(*N* = 541)	(*N* = 147)	(*N* = 688)
None	6.8%	8.8%	7.3%
One	32.3	62.6	38.8
Two	16.6	18.4	17.0
Three	11.5	3.4	9.7
Four	7.8	1.4	6.4
Five to nine	16.3	3.4	13.5
10 to 19	5.0	1.4	4.2
20 or more	3.7	0.7	3.1
81D. When persons of the same sex made sexual advances to you, did sex (ever) occur?	(*N* = 539)	(*N* = 146)	(*N* = 685)
No	85.0%	85.6%	85.1%
Yes	15.0	14.4	14.9

ATTITUDES TOWARD HETEROSEXUAL RELATIONSHIPS

82. Now, thinking about sexual relationships in general, there are some beliefs that such relationships have unpleasant, unfortunate, or even tragic results. As I read the following statements, tell me whether you feel it is almost always true, often true, sometimes true, or rarely or never true.

	Males	*Females*	*Total*
[IF MALE:]			
82A. Men can expect to get hurt sooner or later when they get sexually involved with women.	(*N* = 1,460		(*N* = 1,460)
Rarely or never true	15.9%		15.9%
Sometimes true	37.8		37.8
Often true	21.0		21.0
Almost always true	25.3		25.3
82B. Women rob men of their dignity and self-respect in sexual relationships.	(*N* = 1,459)		(*N* = 1,459)
Rarely or never true	49.8%		49.8%
Sometimes true	27.3		27.3
Often true	11.0		11.0
Almost always true	11.9		11.9
[IF FEMALE:]			
82C. Women can expect to get hurt sooner or later when they get sexually involved with men.		(*N* = 1,546)	(*N* = 1,546)
Rarely or never true		10.3%	10.3%
Sometimes true		30.4	30.4
Often true		21.8	21.8
Almost always true		37.5	37.5
82D. Men rob women of their dignity and self-respect in sexual relationships.		(*N* = 1,540)	(*N* = 1,540)
Rarely or never true		30.5%	30.5%
Sometimes true		28.4	28.4
Often true		15.1	15.1
Almost always true		26.0	26.0

SEXUAL HISTORY (SEE ALSO Q.79–81)[23]

	Males	*Females*	*Total*
A. When you were a child, before your body developed sexually, did you ever have playmates, brothers or sisters, or anyone else who had any kind of sex play or sex games with you? This idea of "sex play" does not require that sexual parts of one child touched the sexual parts of another; it *does mean* that sexual parts of one child were touched by another child.	(*N* = 1,442)	(*N* = 1,514)	(*N* = 2,956)
No	53.3%	65.1%	59.3%
Yes	46.7	34.9	40.7
[IF YES:]			
A(1). Was the sex play with children of your own sex, of the opposite sex, or of both sexes?	(*N* = 673)	(*N* = 528)	(*N* = 1,201)
Only of my own sex	6.8%	21.6%	13.3%
Only of the opposite sex	42.2	35.6	39.3
Of both sexes	51.0	42.8	47.3

	Males	*Females*	*Total*
[IF same-sex sex play:]			
B(1). Did you have sex play with children of the same sex fairly often, only sometimes, or only once or twice?	(*N* = 367)	(*N* = 334)	(*N* = 701)
Only once or twice	67.6%	74.9%	71.0%
Only sometimes	25.6	18.9	22.4
Fairly often	6.8	6.3	6.6
B(2). When you had sex play with children of the same sex, did you usually feel very guilty, somewhat guilty, or not at all guilty?	(*N* = 358)	(*N* = 327)	(*N* = 685)
Not at all guilty	29.6%	15.3%	22.8%
Somewhat guilty	41.9	39.1	40.6
Very guilty	28.5	45.6	36.6
B(3). When your mother found out about your sex play with children of the same sex, what did she do?[24]	(*N* = 363)	(*N* = 332)	(*N* = 695)
She never found out	68.9%	69.9%	69.4%
She did nothing	11.3	13.9	12.5
She scolded and threatened me	9.6	6.9	8.3
She cut back my privileges	3.6	2.7	3.2
She punished me physically	5.0	6.0	5.5
Some combination of these	1.7	0.6	1.2
B(4). When your father found out about your sex play with children of the same sex, what did he do?[24]	(*N* = 365)	(*N* = 331)	(*N* = 696)
He never found out	68.2%	75.5%	71.7%
He did nothing	14.5	17.8	16.1
He scolded and threatened me	7.4	2.1	4.9
He cut back my privileges	4.9	2.1	3.6
He punished me physically	4.1	1.8	3.0
Some combination of these	0.8	0.6	0.7
[IF opposite-sex sex play:]			
C(1). Did you have sex play with children of the opposite sex fairly often, only sometimes, or only once or twice?	(*N* = 611)	(*N* = 392)	(*N* = 1,003)
Only once or twice	50.2%	77.0%	60.7%
Only sometimes	39.1	18.6	31.1
Fairly often	10.6	4.3	8.2
C(2). When you had sex play with children of the opposite sex, did you usually feel very guilty, somewhat guilty, or not at all guilty?	(*N* = 606)	(*N* = 392)	(*N* = 998)
Not at all guilty	36.5%	17.1%	28.9%
Somewhat guilty	47.0	36.7	43.0
Very guilty	16.5	46.2	28.2

	Males	*Females*	*Total*
C(3). When your mother found out about your sex play with children of the opposite sex, what did she do?[24]	(*N* = 608)	(*N* = 392)	(*N* = 1,000)
She never found out	62.3%	68.1%	64.6%
She did nothing	13.2	12.5	12.9
She scolded and threatened me	11.7	9.4	10.8
She cut back my privileges	4.3	2.3	3.5
She punished me physically	7.6	7.1	7.4
Some combination of these	1.0	0.5	0.8
C(4). When your father found out about your sex play with children of the opposite sex, what did he do?[24]	(*N* = 611)	(*N* = 394)	(*N* = 1,005)
He never found out	64.5%	71.6%	67.3%
He did nothing	20.0	20.3	20.1
He scolded and threatened me	6.1	2.5	4.7
He cut back my privileges	3.9	1.8	3.1
He punished me physically	4.4	2.8	3.8
Some combination of these	1.1	1.1	1.1
D. How old were you the first time you made yourself come to a sexual climax? (This is called masturbation.)	(*N* = 1,330)	(*N* = 1,377)	(*N* = 2,707)
Under six	0.4%	0.7%	0.6%
6 to 10	0.7	5.7	7.7
11 to 15	58.0	12.9	35.1
16 to 20	14.6	10.0	12.2
21 to 29	1.2	4.0	2.6
30 or older	0.2	0.8	0.5
Have never masturbated	15.9	65.8	41.3
[IF ever masturbated:]			
D(1). Which of these is the *main* explanation of how you first learned this?	(*N* = 1,099)	(*N* = 474)	(*N* = 1,573)
Reading a book or pamphlet	5.1%	11.2%	6.9%
Someone explained how	24.7	10.8	20.5
Saw how someone else did it	11.6	2.5	8.8
Someone of the same sex helped	3.5	3.0	3.4
Someone of the opposite sex helped	7.4	12.2	8.8
It just happened without learning	47.8	60.3	51.6
E. How old were you the first time you had sexual activity with someone of the opposite sex, when either you or your partner came to a sexual climax? (If the first time was when you got married, please give your age at that time.) This includes other sexual activity, as well as intercourse, if one of you had a climax (orgasm).	(*N* = 1,393)	(*N* = 1,510)	(*N* = 2,903)
Ten or younger	2.7%	0.6%	1.6%
11 to 15	24.0	9.7	16.6
16 to 19	42.9	47.1	45.1
20 to 24	18.3	32.5	25.7
25 to 29	7.5	7.0	7.2
30 or older	3.3	1.8	2.5
Never	1.2	1.5	1.3

	Males	*Females*	*Total*
[IF ever heterosexual sex:]			
E(1). What was your partner's age?	(*N* = 1,269)	(*N* = 1,335)	(*N* = 2,604)
Ten or younger	2.3%	0.2%	1.3%
11 to 15	21.6	1.9	11.5
16 to 19	45.1	23.1	33.9
20 to 24	19.0	46.5	33.1
25 to 29	6.7	19.2	13.1
30 or older	5.2	9.0	7.1
E(2). Did you ever have this experience before you were married?	(*N* = 1,433)	(*N* = 1,532)	(*N* = 2,965)
No	19.8%	58.0%	39.6%
Yes	80.2	42.0	60.4
[IF YES:]			
F(1). Was there a period of time, before marriage, when you had this experience fairly often, occasionally, or rarely—maybe once or twice?	(*N* = 1,051)	(*N* = 574)	(*N* = 1,625)
Rarely—maybe once or twice	22.6%	34.7%	26.9%
Occasionally	41.6	39.0	40.7
Fairly often	35.8	26.3	32.4
F(2). With about how many *persons* altogether did you have this sexual experience before you were married? (If it happened with your husband or wife before you were first married, this counts as one person, too.)	(*N* = 982)	(*N* = 580)	(*N* = 1,562)
One	15.8%	60.2%	32.3%
Two	10.5	17.2	13.0
Three	9.7	8.6	9.3
Four	7.4	4.5	6.3
Five to Nine	21.2	5.2	15.2
10 to 20	28.2	4.0	19.2
21 to 49	4.3	0.3	2.8
50 or more	3.0	0.0	1.9
F(2)a. Did you have this experience *only* with a person you later married?	(*N* = 1,122)	(*N* = 625)	(*N* = 1,747)
No—other partner(s) as well	91.4%	56.3%	78.9%
Yes—only with future spouse	8.6	43.7	22.1
F(3). Do you now feel strong regret, only some regret, or no regret at all about having this sexual experience with someone of the opposite sex before being married?	(*N* = 1,080)	(*N* = 587)	(*N* = 1,667)
No regret at all	69.1%	44.8%	60.5%
Only some regret	22.5	33.9	26.5
Strong regret	8.4	21.3	13.0
F(4). Have you ever wished that you had more of this sexual experience before marriage?	(*N* = 1,058)	(*N* = 585)	(*N* = 1,643)
No	58.1%	82.1%	66.6%
Yes	41.9	17.9	33.4

	Males	*Females*	*Total*
F(5). Thinking back to the earliest of these experiences, please indicate whether you remember having each of the following feelings very strongly, somewhat, or not at all.			
F(5)a. Fear it would cause pregnancy (whether you are male or female).	(*N* = 1,326)	(*N* = 345)	(*N* = 1,671)
Not at all	22.4%	25.8%	23.1%
Somewhat	36.0	32.5	35.3
Very strongly	41.6	41.7	41.6
F(5)b. Fear of bad reputation.	(*N* = 1,059)	(*N* = 595)	(*N* = 1,654)
Not at all	60.6%	24.7%	47.7%
Somewhat	26.7	31.1	28.3
Very strongly	12.7	44.2	24.0
F(5)c. Pleased with the physical feeling.	(*N* = 1,062)	(*N* = 590)	(*N* = 1,652)
Not at all	8.2%	21.0%	12.8%
Somewhat	23.1	38.0	28.4
Very strongly	68.7	41.0	58.8
F(5)d. Physical pain.	(*N* = 1,049)	(*N* = 583)	(*N* = 1,632)
Not at all	89.3%	49.7%	75.2%
Somewhat	7.6	34.1	17.1
Very strongly	3.1	16.1	7.7
F(5)e. Pleased to be wanted or needed this way.	(*N* = 1,044)	(*N* = 583)	(*N* = 1,627)
Not at all	17.9%	16.5%	17.4%
Somewhat	43.4	41.2	42.6
Very strongly	38.7	42.4	40.0
F(5)f. Guilt, shame, or embarrassment.	(*N* = 1,056)	(*N* = 591)	(*N* = 1,647)
Not at all	55.5%	23.4%	44.0%
Somewhat	35.6	43.5	38.4
Very strongly	8.9	33.2	17.6
F(5)g. Afraid of failure as a sexual partner.	(*N* = 1,054)	(*N* = 587)	(*N* = 1,641)
Not at all	66.8%	59.3%	64.1%
Somewhat	27.3	30.5	28.5
Very strongly	5.9	10.2	7.4
F(5)h. Happy it showed I had sex appeal.	(*N* = 1,043)	(*N* = 586)	(*N* = 1,629)
Not at all	23.5%	31.6%	26.4%
Somewhat	41.9	42.2	42.0
Very strongly	34.6	26.3	31.6
F(5)i. Disappointed in the sexual experience.	(*N* = 1,043)	(*N* = 581)	(*N* = 1,624)
Not at all	80.2%	56.6%	71.7%
Somewhat	14.9	31.8	20.9
Very strongly	5.0	11.5	7.3

	Males	*Females*	*Total*
F(5)j. Happy to have finally had a full sexual experience.	(*N* = 1,046)	(*N* = 579)	(*N* = 1,625)
Not at all	14.0%	38.2%	22.6%
Somewhat	36.6	37.8	37.0
Very strongly	49.4	24.0	40.4
F(5)k. Feeling of disgust or filth about sex.	(*N* = 1,051)	(*N* = 583)	(*N* = 1,634)
Not at all	79.9%	67.9%	75.6%
Somewhat	15.4	23.5	18.3
Very strongly	4.7	8.6	6.1
F(5)l. Fear of venereal disease.	(*N* = 1,051)	(*N* = 583)	(*N* = 1,634)
Not at all	79.9%	67.9%	75.6%
Somewhat	15.4	23.5	18.3
Very strongly	4.7	8.6	6.1
F(5)m. Pleased because others of my sex respected me for it.	(*N* = 1,047)	(*N* = 582)	(*N* = 1,629)
Not at all	51.5%	79.6%	61.5%
Somewhat	31.1	12.4	24.4
Very strongly	17.4	8.1	14.1
F(5)n. Pleased to have this special kind of relationship with someone.	(*N* = 1,049)	(*N* = 585)	(*N* = 1,634)
Not at all	15.1%	28.9%	20.0%
Somewhat	40.3	41.9	40.9
Very strongly	44.6	29.2	39.1
F(5)o. Fear of discovery.	(*N* = 1,047)	(*N* = 582)	(*N* = 1,629)
Not at all	42.8%	26.5%	37.0%
Somewhat	40.2	36.3	38.8
Very strongly	17.0	37.3	24.2
F(5)p. Unhappy because partner felt sad or angry.	(*N* = 1,027)	(*N* = 572)	(*N* = 1,599)
Not at all	66.2%	78.8%	70.7%
Somewhat	27.3	14.3	22.6
Very strongly	6.5	6.8	6.6
F(5)q. Happy because of partner's sexual enjoyment.	(*N* = 1,041)	(*N* = 587)	(*N* = 1,628)
Not at all	13.7%	17.0%	14.9%
Somewhat	33.8	37.8	35.3
Very strongly	52.4	45.1	49.8
[IF NO premarital sex:]			
G(1). Have you ever regretted that you did not have any sexual experience with someone of the opposite sex before you were married?	(*N* = 251)	(*N* = 808)	(*N* = 1,059)
No	86.5%	93.3%	91.7%
Yes	13.5	6.7	8.3

	Males	*Females*	*Total*
G(2). If you *had* engaged in sexual intercourse before you were married, which of the following feelings are you quite sure you would have felt, and which would you probably have not felt at all?			
G(2)a. Fear it would cause pregnancy (whether you are male or female).	(*N* = 193)	(*N* = 671)	(*N* = 864)
Not felt	28.5%	11.8%	15.5%
Felt	71.5	88.2	84.5
G(2)b. Fear of bad reputation.	(*N* = 186)	(*N* = 669)	(*N* = 855)
Not felt	37.1%	10.3%	16.1%
Felt	62.9	89.7	83.9
G(2)c. Pleased with the physical feeling.	(*N* = 185)	(*N* = 636)	(*N* = 821)
Not felt	37.3%	63.2%	57.4%
Felt	62.7	37.8	42.6
G(2)d. Physical pain.	(*N* = 178)	(*N* = 636)	(*N* = 814)
Not felt	83.1%	52.5%	59.2%
Felt	16.9	47.5	40.8
G(2)e. Pleased to be wanted or needed this way.	(*N* = 180)	(*N* = 645)	(*N* = 825)
Not felt	50.6%	63.7%	60.9%
Felt	49.4	36.3	39.1
G(2)f. Guilt, shame, or embarrassment.	(*N* = 193)	(*N* = 671)	(*N* = 864)
Not felt	30.6%	13.3%	17.1%
Felt	69.4	86.7	82.9
G(2)g. Afraid of failure as a sexual partner.	(*N* = 185)	(*N* = 652)	(*N* = 837)
Not felt	74.1%	69.2%	70.3%
Felt	25.9	30.8	29.7
G(2)h. Happy it showed I had sex appeal.	(*N* = 183)	(*N* = 648)	(*N* = 831)
Not felt	56.3%	68.8%	66.1%
Felt	43.7	31.2	33.9
G(2)i. Disappointed in the sexual experience.	(*N* = 180)	(*N* = 633)	(*N* = 813)
Not felt	81.7%	63.8%	67.8%
Felt	18.3	36.2	32.2
G(2)j. Happy to have finally had a full sexual experience.	(*N* = 184)	(*N* = 639)	(*N* = 823)
Not felt	47.8%	74.2%	68.3%
Felt	52.2	25.8	31.7
G(2)k. Feeling of disgust or filth about sex.	(*N* = 180)	(*N* = 644)	(*N* = 824)
Not felt	65.0%	52.3%	55.1%
Felt	35.0	47.7	44.9

	Males	Females	Total
G(2)l. Fear of venereal disease.	(*N* = 189)	(*N* = 646)	(*N* = 835)
Not felt	36.5%	41.3%	40.2%
Felt	63.5	58.7	59.8
G(2)m. Pleased because others of my sex respected me for it.	(*N* = 184)	(*N* = 643)	(*N* = 827)
Not felt	70.1%	85.4%	82.0%
Felt	29.9	14.6	18.0
G(2)n. Pleased to have this special kind of relationship with someone.	(*N* = 181)	(*N* = 646)	(*N* = 827)
Not felt	54.7%	73.4%	69.3%
Felt	45.3	26.6	30.7
G(2)o. Fear of discovery.	(*N* = 187)	(*N* = 664)	(*N* = 851)
Not felt	42.8%	27.1%	30.6%
Felt	57.2	72.9	69.4

[IF ever married:]

H. Thinking back to your first sexual experiences with your husband/wife right after you were married, please indicate which of the following feelings you felt very strongly, somewhat, or not at all.

	Males	Females	Total
H(1). Fear it would cause pregnancy (whether you are male or female).	(*N* = 1,124)	(*N* = 1,324)	(*N* = 2,448)
Not at all	64.6%	64.9%	64.7%
Somewhat	23.1	20.5	21.7
Very strongly	12.3	14.6	13.5
H(2). Pleased with the physical feeling.	(*N* = 1,128)	(*N* = 1,321)	(*N* = 2,449)
Not at all	5.0%	14.1%	9.9%
Somewhat	17.6	35.8	27.4
Very strongly	77.5	50.1	62.7
H(3). Physical pain.	(*N* = 1,100)	(*N* = 1,297)	(*N* = 2,397)
Not at all	86.4%	51.0%	67.2%
Somewhat	10.2	36.3	24.3
Very strongly	3.5	12.7	8.5
H(4). Pleased to be wanted or needed this way.	(*N* = 1,104)	(*N* = 1,304)	(*N* = 2,408)
Not at all	6.6%	8.7%	7.7%
Somewhat	23.9	26.8	25.5
Very strongly	69.5	64.5	66.8
H(5). Guilt, shame, or embarrassment.	(*N* = 1,110)	(*N* = 1,301)	(*N* = 2,411)
Not at all	86.1%	76.6%	81.0%
Somewhat	10.1	17.1	13.7
Very strongly	3.8	6.3	5.1
H(6). Afraid of failure as a sexual partner.	(*N* = 1,098)	(*N* = 1,303)	(*N* = 2,401)
Not at all	70.2%	62.0%	65.8%
Somewhat	22.9	29.2	26.3
Very strongly	6.9	8.7	7.9

	Males	*Females*	*Total*
H(7). Happy it showed I had sex appeal.	(*N* = 1,101)	(*N* = 1,302)	(*N* = 2,403)
Not at all	15.9%	20.2%	18.2%
Somewhat	34.4	36.8	35.7
Very strongly	49.7	43.0	46.1
H(8). Disappointed in the sexual experience.	(*N* = 1,170)	(*N* = 1,341)	(*N* = 2,511)
Not at all	86.8%	68.0%	76.7%
Somewhat	9.8	23.2	16.9
Very strongly	3.4	8.8	6.3
H(9). Happy to have finally had a full sexual experience.	(*N* = 1,158)	(*N* = 1,324)	(*N* = 2,482)
Not at all	14.2%	18.4%	16.4%
Somewhat	23.7	29.8	27.0
Very strongly	62.0	51.8	56.6
H(10). Feeling of disgust or filth about sex.	(*N* = 1,153)	(*N* = 1,325)	(*N* = 2,478)
Not at all	91.1%	86.9%	88.8%
Somewhat	5.6	9.7	7.8
Very strongly	3.4	3.3	3.3
H(11). Pleased to have this special kind of relationship with someone.	(*N* = 1,164)	(*N* = 1,333)	(*N* = 2,497)
Not at all	8.8%	11.6%	10.4%
Somewhat	18.0	23.2	20.8
Very strongly	73.1	65.2	68.9
H(12). Unhappy because partner felt sad or angry.	(*N* = 1,146)	(*N* = 1,312)	(*N* = 2,458)
Not at all	78.9%	86.1%	82.8%
Somewhat	14.4	8.6	11.3
Very strongly	6.7	5.3	6.0
H(13). Happy because of partner's sexual enjoyment.	(*N* = 1,171)	(*N* = 1,339)	(*N* = 2,510)
Not at all	6.4%	8.9%	7.8%
Somewhat	20.7	18.8	19.7
Very strongly	72.9	72.3	72.6
I. What was your age the first time you had sexual experience with someone of the *same sex,* when either you or your partner came to a sexual climax? This includes persons of the same sex helping each other masturbate.	(*N* = 1,192)	(*N* = 1,288)	(*N* = 2,480)
7 or younger	0.8%	0.7%	0.8%
8 to 10	2.2	0.9	1.5
11 to 15	7.6	1.1	4.2
16 to 19	3.9	3.3	3.5
20 to 24	2.0	2.8	2.4
25 to 29	0.7	0.4	0.5
30 or older	0.3	0.1	0.2
Never	82.6	90.8	86.8

	Males	*Females*	*Total*
[IF ever homosexual sex:]			
J(1). What was your first partner's age at the time of your first experience?	(*N* = 188)	(*N* = 87)	(*N* = 275)
7 or younger	6.4%	12.6%	8.4%
8 to 10	9.6	19.5	12.7
11 to 15	44.7	12.6	34.5
16 to 19	15.4	17.2	16.0
20 to 24	10.1	19.5	13.1
25 to 29	3.7	13.8	6.9
30 or older	10.1	4.6	8.4
J(2). What was your age the last time you had this experience?	(*N* = 174)	(*N* = 79)	(*N* = 253)
7 or younger	2.9%	8.9%	4.7%
8 to 10	8.6	22.8	13.0
11 to 15	41.3	12.7	33.2
16 to 19	20.1	15.2	18.6
20 to 24	12.0	16.5	13.4
25 to 29	3.4	3.8	3.6
30 or older	11.5	17.7	13.4
J(2)a. Did you have this experience only once?	(*N* = 184)	(*N* = 88)	(*N* = 272)
No—more than once	76.6%	62.5%	72.1%
Yes, only once	23.4	37.5	27.9
[IF more than one homosexual experience:]			
J(3). Was there a period of time when you had this experience fairly often, occasionally, or rarely, or did it happen only twice?	(*N* = 137)	(*N* = 48)	(*N* = 185)
Only twice	19.0%	25.0%	20.5%
Rarely	27.7	20.8	25.9
Occasionally	35.0	22.9	31.9
Fairly often	18.2	31.2	21.6
J(4). Altogether, with about how many persons did you have this experience?	(*N* = 126)	(*N* = 49)	(*N* = 175)
Always the same partner	17.5%	51.0%	26.9%
Two different partners	35.7	20.4	31.4
Three partners	14.3	12.2	13.7
Four to six partners	18.3	6.1	14.9
Seven to nine partners	2.4	6.1	3.4
10 to 20 partners	9.5	2.0	7.4
More than 20 partners	2.4	2.0	2.3
J(5). Please give a general idea of their ages.	(*N* = 154)	(*N* = 69)	(*N* = 223)
All more than a year *younger*	3.9%	2.9%	3.6%
All my age or younger	3.2	2.9	3.1
All about my own age	30.5	23.2	28.3
All my age or older	22.7	26.1	23.8
All more than a year *older*	26.6	42.0	31.4
Can't say, all different ages	13.0	2.9	9.9

	Males	*Females*	*Total*
[IF any homosexual experience:]			
K(1). Thinking about the earliest of these experiences, which of the following feelings did you feel strongly, somewhat, or not at all?			
K(1)a. Fear of bad reputation.	(*N* = 176)	(*N* = 80)	(*N* = 256)
Not at all	42.6%	40.0%	41.8%
Somewhat	26.1	27.5	26.6
Very strongly	31.3	32.5	31.6
K(1)b. Pleased with the physical feeling.	(*N* = 174)	(*N* = 80)	(*N* = 254)
Not at all	24.1%	32.5%	26.8%
Somewhat	46.0	42.5	44.9
Very strongly	29.9	25.0	28.3
K(1)c. Physical pain.	(*N* = 170)	(*N* = 77)	(*N* = 247)
Not at all	78.8%	77.9%	78.5%
Somewhat	17.6	11.7	15.8
Very strongly	3.5	10.4	5.7
K(1)d. Feeling of being wanted or needed this way.	(*N* = 168)	(*N* = 78)	(*N* = 246)
Not at all	65.5%	56.4%	62.6%
Somewhat	19.6	19.2	19.5
Very strongly	14.9	24.4	17.9
K(1)e. Guilt, shame or embarrassment.	(*N* = 173)	(*N* = 80)	(*N* = 253)
Not at all	31.8%	30.0%	31.2%
Somewhat	35.3	26.2	32.4
Very strongly	32.9	43.8	36.4
K(1)f. Disappointed in the sexual experience.	(*N* = 169)	(*N* = 78)	(*N* = 247)
Not at all	41.4%	44.9%	42.5%
Somewhat	40.2	32.1	37.7
Very strongly	18.3	23.1	19.8
K(1)g. Happy to have finally had a full sexual experience.	(*N* = 170)	(*N* = 79)	(*N* = 249)
Not at all	61.2%	54.4%	59.0%
Somewhat	21.2	21.5	21.3
Very strongly	17.6	24.1	19.7
K(1)h. Feeling of disgust or filth about sex.	(*N* = 168)	(*N* = 78)	(*N* = 246)
Not at all	53.0%	43.6%	50.0%
Somewhat	29.8	29.5	29.7
Very strongly	17.3	26.9	20.3
K(1)i. Fear of venereal disease.	(*N* = 171)	(*N* = 79)	(*N* = 250)
Not at all	73.1%	73.4%	73.2%
Somewhat	15.2	11.4	14.0
Very strongly	11.7	15.2	12.8

	Males	*Females*	*Total*
K(1)j. Pleased to have this special kind of relationship with someone.	(*N* = 170)	(*N* = 76)	(*N* = 246)
Not at all	57.1%	50.0%	54.9%
Somewhat	25.9	27.6	26.4
Very strongly	17.1	22.4	18.7
K(1)k. Fear of discovery.	(*N* = 172)	(*N* = 77)	(*N* = 249)
Not at all	26.2%	26.0%	26.1%
Somewhat	38.4	24.7	34.1
Very strongly	35.5	49.4	39.8
K(1)l. Unhappy because partner felt sad or angry.	(*N* = 172)	(*N* = 79)	(*N* = 251)
Not at all	80.8%	74.7%	78.9%
Somewhat	13.4	13.9	13.5
Very strongly	5.8	11.4	7.6
K(1)m. Happy because of partner's sexual enjoyment.	(*N* = 169)	(*N* = 76)	(*N* = 245)
Not at all	57.4%	48.7%	54.7%
Somewhat	24.9	27.6	25.7
Very strongly	17.8	23.7	19.6
K(2). Has anyone ever found out about your experience with someone of the same sex, not counting people who have had sexual activity with someone of the same sex?	(*N* = 168)	(*N* = 80)	(*N* = 248)
No	69.6%	82.5%	73.8%
Yes	30.4	17.5	26.2
K(3). Please indicate whether each of the following people has either known or suspected that you have had experience with someone of the same sex.			
K(3)a. Has your father known or suspected?	(*N* = 166)	(*N* = 81)	(*N* = 247)
Has known	7.8%	4.9%	6.9%
Has suspected	10.2	7.4	9.3
Neither	81.9	87.6	83.8
K(3)b. Has your mother known or suspected?	(*N* = 169)	(*N* = 81)	(*N* = 250)
Has known	5.9%	4.9%	5.6%
Has suspected	13.6	13.6	13.6
Neither	80.5	81.5	80.8
K(3)c. Has a brother or sister known or suspected?	(*N* = 153)	(*N* = 74)	(*N* = 227)
Has known	17.0%	16.2%	16.7%
Has suspected	11.1	9.5	10.6
Neither	71.9	74.3	72.8

	Males	*Females*	*Total*
K(3)d. Has a boss, someone you worked *for,* known or suspected?	(*N* = 170)	(*N* = 81)	(*N* = 251)
Has known	4.1%	2.5%	3.6%
Has suspected	4.1	3.7	4.0
Neither	91.8	93.8	92.4
K(3)e. Has someone you worked *with* known or suspected?	(*N* = 169)	(*N* = 81)	(*N* = 250)
Has known	8.9%	2.5%	6.8%
Has suspected	9.5	4.9	8.0
Neither	81.7	92.6	85.2
K(3)f. Have any male friends with whom you had no sex known or suspected?	(*N* = 169)	(*N* = 82)	(*N* = 251)
Have known	17.8%	7.3%	14.3%
Have suspected	13.0	7.3	11.2
Neither	69.2	85.4	74.5
K(3)g. Have any female friends with whom you had no sex known or suspected?	(*N* = 171)	(*N* = 82)	(*N* = 253)
Have known	12.9%	9.8%	11.9%
Have suspected	14.0	8.5	12.3
Neither	73.1	82.7	75.9
L. If there was no question of right or wrong, would you say that sex with a person of the *same sex* offers you any possibility of enjoyment?	(*N* = 1,337)	(*N* = 1,455)	(*N* = 2,792)
No	85.8%	90.2%	88.1%
Yes	14.2	9.8	11.9
M. Does sex with a person of the *opposite sex* offer you any possibility of enjoyment? Any possibility of enjoyment, including love, affection, marriage, should be counted as "yes" here.	(*N* = 1,352)	(*N* = 1,452)	(*N* = 2,804)
No	11.8%	14.3%	13.1%
Yes	88.2	85.7	86.9
[IF YES to both:] N. Does sex with a person of the opposite sex offer you more, less, or about the same amount of enjoyment as sex with a person of the same sex?	(*N* = 151)	(*N* = 106)	(*N* = 257)
Opposite sex more enjoyable	80.1%	85.8%	82.5%
About the same	9.3	8.5	8.9
Same sex more enjoyable	10.6	5.7	8.6
O. Has anyone ever suggested, not as a joke, that you might be homosexual or lesbian?	(*N* = 1,316)	(*N* = 1,440)	(*N* = 2,756)
No	95.1%	96.9%	96.0%
Yes	4.9	3.1	4.0

	Males	*Females*	*Total*
[IF YES:]			
O(1). How old were you the first time this happened?	(*N* = 60)	(*N* = 40)	(*N* = 100)
Ten or younger	1.7%	2.5%	3.0%
11 to 15	23.3	17.5	20.0
16 to 19	35.0	42.5	38.0
20 to 24	20.0	17.5	19.0
25 to 29	1.7	15.0	7.0
30 or older	18.3	5.0	13.0
O(2). How many different persons suggested that you might be homosexual or lesbian?	(*N* = 46)	(*N* = 33)	(*N* = 79)
One	26.1%	48.5%	35.4%
Two	32.6	21.2	27.8
Three	15.2	12.1	13.9
Four	4.3	3.0	3.8
Five to nine	13.0	12.1	12.7
Ten or more	8.7	3.0	6.4
P. Have you ever thought that you might be homosexual or lesbian?	(*N* = 1,370)	(*N* = 1,473)	(*N* = 2,843)
No	96.9%	98.0%	97.3%
Yes	3.1	2.0	2.7
[IF YES:]			
P(1). How old were you the first time you felt this way?	(*N* = 41)	(*N* = 25)	(*N* = 64)
Ten or younger	7.3%	4.0%	4.5%
11 to 15	19.5	28.0	24.2
16 to 19	24.4	36.0	28.8
20 to 24	24.4	20.0	22.7
25 to 29	7.3	12.0	9.4
30 or older	17.1	0.0	6.2
Q. Have you ever been afraid you might become homosexual or lesbian?	(*N* = 1,362)	(*N* = 1,466)	(*N* = 2,828)
No	97.0%	97.7%	97.3%
Yes	3.0	2.3	2.7
[IF YES:]			
Q(1). How old were you the first time you felt this way?	(*N* = 35)	(*N* = 29)	(*N* = 64)
Ten or younger	5.7%	10.3%	6.2%
11 to 15	20.0	27.5	25.0
16 to 19	42.9	31.0	38.0
20 to 24	11.4	20.7	15.6
25 to 29	8.6	10.3	9.4
30 or older	11.4	0.0	6.2

R. Has sexual experience been enjoyable for you just about every time, most of the time, part of the time, or rarely or never? This includes *any* sexual

	Males	*Females*	*Total*
experience—same sex, other sex, and masturbation should be counted.	(*N* = 1,342)	(*N* = 1,423)	(*N* = 2,765)
Rarely or never	0.9%	2.9%	1.9%
Part of the time	5.4	19.9	12.9
Most of the time	34.4	49.2	42.0
Just about every time	59.2	28.0	43.2

PSYCHOLOGICAL ADJUSTMENT[25]

83. As I read the following list of conditions which trouble some people, for each one please tell me whether it is true, or not true for you. If it is true, is it often a problem for you, sometimes a problem, or is it true for you but not at all a problem?

	Males	*Females*	*Total*
83A. Shortness of breath even when not exercising or working hard.	(*N* = 1,463)	(*N* = 1,551)	(*N* = 3,014)
Not true	77.6%	70.8%	74.1%
True, but not a problem	10.1	12.8	11.5
Sometimes a problem	8.2	12.8	10.6
Often a problem	4.1	3.6	3.8
83B. Your heart beating hard.	(*N* = 1,463)	(*N* = 1,552)	(*N* = 3,015)
Not true	79.1%	68.2%	73.5%
True, but not a problem	11.7	15.7	13.8
Sometimes a problem	6.6	13.1	10.0
Often a problem	2.6	2.9	2.8
83C. Strangers looking at you critically.	(*N* = 1,460)	(*N* = 1,550)	(*N* = 3,010)
Not true	88.6%	79.5%	83.9%
True, but not a problem	7.1	10.6	8.9
Sometimes a problem	3.6	8.0	5.8
Often a problem	0.8	1.9	1.4
83D. Nervousness, being irritable, fidgety, tense.	(*N* = 1,464)	(*N* = 1,546)	(*N* = 3,010)
Not true	53.1%	31.5%	42.0%
True, but not a problem	23.4	27.4	25.5
Sometimes a problem	18.9	30.8	25.0
Often a problem	4.6	10.3	7.5
83E. Trouble getting to sleep or staying asleep.	(*N* = 1,463)	(*N* = 1,551)	(*N* = 3,014)
Not true	68.9%	56.7%	62.6%
True, but not a problem	11.8	10.3	11.0
Sometimes a problem	13.5	21.5	17.7
Often a problem	5.8	11.5	8.8
83F. Having to be on guard with people who are more friendly than you expected.	(*N* = 1,462)	(*N* = 1,551)	(*N* = 3,013)
Not true	79.5%	78.9%	79.2%
True, but not a problem	10.8	9.9	10.3
Sometimes a problem	8.5	9.4	9.0
Often a problem	1.2	1.9	1.5

	Males	*Females*	*Total*
83G. Cold sweats.	(*N* = 1,460)	(*N* = 1,550)	(*N* = 3,010)
Not true	91.7%	88.5%	90.1%
True, but not a problem	3.8	4.5	4.2
Sometimes a problem	3.8	5.2	4.5
Often a problem	0.8	1.8	1.3
83H. Hands trembling enough to bother you.	(*N* = 1,463)	(*N* = 1,551)	(*N* = 3,014)
Not true	90.7%	88.3%	89.5%
True, but not a problem	3.9	4.2	4.0
Sometimes a problem	3.9	5.7	4.8
Often a problem	1.5	1.8	1.7
83I. Wondering what hidden reason another person may have for doing something nice for you.	(*N* = 1,462)	(*N* = 1,552)	(*N* = 3,014)
Not true	78.8%	81.4%	80.1%
True, but not a problem	13.2	11.0	12.0
Sometimes a problem	6.9	6.3	6.6
Often a problem	1.1	1.4	1.2
83J. Headaches, or pains in the head.	(*N* = 1,461)	(*N* = 1,550)	(*N* = 3,011)
Not true	73.2%	53.5%	63.1%
True, but not a problem	14.9	19.1	17.0
Sometimes a problem	8.8	18.7	13.9
Often a problem	3.1	8.7	6.0

84. And now, would you tell me whether each of the following conditions is true or not true for you. If it is true, is it ever a serious problem, or not at all serious?

	Males	*Females*	*Total*
84A. Do you feel weak all over much of the time?	(*N* = 1,461)	(*N* = 1,549)	(*N* = 3,010)
No	89.0%	85.0%	87.0%
Yes, but not a problem	6.8	10.9	8.9
Yes, a serious problem	4.1	4.1	4.1
84B. Do you have periods of days or weeks when you can't take care of things because you can't get going?	(*N* = 1,462)	(*N* = 1,550)	(*N* = 3,012)
No	79.9%	67.4%	73.4%
Yes, but not a problem	15.9	27.4	21.8
Yes, a serious problem	4.2	5.3	4.8
84C. Do you suddenly feel hot all over, every so often?	(*N* = 1,462)	(*N* = 1,546)	(*N* = 3,008)
No	90.4%	73.6%	81.7%
Yes, but not a problem	8.6	22.7	15.9
Yes, a serious problem	1.0	3.7	2.4
84D. Do you ever have periods of such great restlessness that you cannot sit long in a chair?	(*N* = 1,458)	(*N* = 1,548)	(*N* = 3,006)
No	65.8%	66.0%	65.9%
Yes, but not a problem	29.5	29.3	29.4
Yes, a serious problem	4.7	4.7	4.7

	Males	*Females*	*Total*
84E. Do you have trouble with acid or sour stomach several times a week?	(*N* = 1,461)	(*N* = 1,549)	(*N* = 3,010)
No	78.6%	77.5%	78.0%
Yes, but not a problem	15.1	15.7	15.4
Yes, a serious problem	6.4	6.8	6.6
84F. Do you lack a good memory; is it not all right?	(*N* = 1,454)	(*N* = 1,544)	(*N* = 2,998)
No	81.2%	73.4%	77.2%
Yes, but not a problem	15.8	23.3	19.6
Yes, a serious problem	3.0	3.3	3.1
84G. Do you have a fullness or clogging in your head or nose much of the time?	(*N* = 1,459)	(*N* = 1,547)	(*N* = 3,006)
No	82.1%	78.6%	80.3%
Yes, but not a problem	13.5	15.3	14.4
Yes, a serious problem	4.4	6.1	5.3
84H. Do you have personal worries that get you down physically, make you physically ill?	(*N* = 1,463)	(*N* = 1,547)	(*N* = 3,010)
No	87.5%	76.1%	81.7%
Yes, but not a problem	8.5	15.7	12.2
Yes, a serious problem	4.0	8.1	6.1
84I. Do you feel that nothing ever turns out the way you want it to?	(*N* = 1,463)	(*N* = 1,548)	(*N* = 3,011)
No	77.1%	72.5%	74.7%
Yes, but not a problem	20.4	22.7	21.6
Yes, a serious problem	2.5	4.8	3.7
84J. Do you feel it is safer to trust nobody?	(*N* = 1,460)	(*N* = 1,549)	(*N* = 3,009)
No	81.8%	83.8%	82.8%
Yes, but not a problem	16.0	12.5	14.2
Yes, a serious problem	2.3	3.7	3.0
84K. Do you sometimes feel you can't help wondering if anything is worthwhile any more?	(*N* = 1,459)	(*N* = 1,548)	(*N* = 3,007)
No	73.8%	72.2%	73.0%
Yes, but not a problem	23.6	23.7	23.6
Yes, a serious problem	2.6	4.1	3.4
84L. Do you sometimes feel somewhat apart or alone, even among friends?	(*N* = 1,460)	(*N* = 1,545)	(*N* = 3,005)
No	69.4%	59.1%	64.1%
Yes, but not a problem	27.5	36.4	32.0
Yes, a serious problem	3.2	4.5	3.9
84M. Do you feel your way of doing things is apt to be misunderstood by others?	(*N* = 1,459)	(*N* = 1,547)	(*N* = 3,006)
No	57.4%	61.5%	59.5%
Yes, but not a problem	38.9	32.8	35.8
Yes, a serious problem	3.7	5.6	4.7

	Males	*Females*	*Total*
84N. Are you the worrying type—a worrier?	(*N* = 1,457)	(*N* = 1,547)	(*N* = 3,004)
No	64.0%	43.8%	53.6%
Yes, but not a problem	29.5	39.8	34.8
Yes, a serious problem	6.5	16.4	11.6
84O. Do people say all kinds of things about you behind your back?	(*N* = 1,437)	(*N* = 1,531)	(*N* = 2,968)
No	84.8%	87.8%	86.4%
Yes, but not a problem	13.3	10.1	11.7
Yes, a serious problem	1.9	2.1	2.0
84P. Have you ever had trouble with your health or your work because of drinking?	(*N* = 1,462)	(*N* = 1,551)	(*N* = 3,013)
No	95.6%	99.1%	97.4%
Yes, but not a problem	2.3	0.5	1.3
Yes, a serious problem	2.2	0.5	1.3
84Q. Has your family ever had arguments with you because of your drinking?	(*N* = 1,462)	(*N* = 1,550)	(*N* = 3,012)
No	87.3%	97.9%	92.8%
Yes, but not a problem	9.7	1.6	5.5
Yes, a serious problem	3.0	0.5	1.7
85. Have you had fainting spells—several times, a few times, or never?	(*N* = 1,462)	(*N* = 1,550)	(*N* = 3,012)
Never	88.7%	73.1%	80.7%
A few times	9.2	22.0	15.8
Several times	2.1	4.9	3.6
86. Would you say your appetite is poor, fair, good, or too good?	(*N* = 1,462)	(*N* = 1,551)	(*N* = 3,013)
Poor	2.4%	3.0%	2.7%
Fair	17.8	15.5	16.6
Good	54.4	44.9	49.5
Too good	25.4	36.6	31.2
87. In general, would you say that most of the time you are in very low spirits, low spirits, good spirits, or very good spirits?	(*N* = 1,460)	(*N* = 1,550)	(*N* = 3,010)
Very low spirits	1.5%	2.1%	1.8%
Low spirits	4.1	5.6	4.9
Good spirits	74.9	75.3	75.1
Very good spirits	19.5	17.0	18.2
88. During the past month, how often have you felt any of the following feelings—often, sometimes, rarely, or never?			
88A. On top of the world.	*N* = 1,462)	(*N* = 1,550)	(*N* = 3,012)
Never	19.4%	18.5%	18.9%
Rarely	18.2	18.6	18.4
Sometimes	41.5	41.8	41.7
Often	20.9	21.1	21.0

	Males	*Females*	*Total*
88B. Particularly excited or interested in something.	(*N* = 1,459)	(*N* = 1,550)	(*N* = 3,009)
Never	9.1%	7.6%	8.3%
Rarely	12.5	11.6	12.0
Sometimes	48.7	48.8	48.7
Often	29.7	32.0	30.9
88C. Pleased about having accomplished something.	(*N* = 1,458)	(*N* = 1,549)	(*N* = 3,007)
Never	5.3%	4.5%	4.9%
Rarely	5.8	5.4	5.6
Sometimes	45.0	45.5	45.3
Often	43.9	44.6	44.3
89. How was your physical health this past year—very poor, poor, fair, good, or excellent?	(*N* = 1,460)	(*N* = 1,550)	(*N* = 3,010)
Very poor	2.5%	2.8%	2.7%
Poor	3.8	5.2	4.5
Fair	15.5	21.0	18.3
Good	47.4	47.9	47.7
Excellent	30.8	23.0	26.8
90. Taking things all together, how would you say you are feeling these days—very happy, pretty happy, not too happy, or very unhappy?	(*N* = 1,461)	(*N* = 1,545)	(*N* = 3,006)
Very unhappy	1.6%	2.1%	1.9%
Not too happy	8.1	9.8	9.0
Pretty happy	55.9	59.7	57.9
Very happy	34.4	28.3	31.2
91. How often have you felt you should or you really wanted to go to a professional—such as a clergyman, a medical doctor, psychiatrist, psychologist, or social worker—about a personal or emotional problem of your own? Has that been often, sometimes, rarely, or never?	(*N* = 1,456)	(*N* = 1,542)	(*N* = 2,998)
Never	74.2%	55.8%	64.7%
Rarely	14.1	19.6	17.0
Sometimes	9.4	18.6	14.1
Often	2.3	6.0	4.2
92. How many such professionals have you gone to?	(*N* = 1,456)	(*N* = 1,542)	(*N* = 2,998)
None	82.6%	70.8%	76.5%
One	10.4	17.5	14.0
Two	3.8	6.7	5.3
Three or more	3.2	5.0	4.2
[IF any professional visits:]			
92A(1). Was any of these professionals a medical doctor?	(*N* = 240)	(*N* = 422)	(*N* = 662)
No	37.1%	33.6%	34.9%
Yes	62.9	66.4	65.1

	Males	*Females*	*Total*
92A(2). A clergyman?	(*N* = 230)	(*N* = 416)	(*N* = 646)
No	65.2%	60.3%	62.1%
Yes	34.8	39.7	37.9
92A(3). A social worker?	(*N* = 227)	(*N* = 393)	(*N* = 620)
No	89.9%	90.1%	90.0%
Yes	10.1	9.9	10.0
92A(4). A psychiatric social worker, psychologist, psychiatrist, analyst?	(*N* = 240)	(*N* = 414)	(*N* = 654)
No	56.7%	61.6%	59.8%
Yes	43.2	38.4	40.2
[IF any professional visits OR desire for professional help with no visits:]			
92B(1). When you (felt you wanted/went to get) professional help, was that related to problems of what is right or wrong in sexual matters?	(*N* = 349)	(*N* = 630)	(*N* = 979)
No	90.8%	87.3%	88.6%
Yes	9.2	12.7	11.4
92B(2). Sexual inadequacy—impotence or frigidity?	(*N* = 350)	(*N* = 630)	(*N* = 980)
No	93.7%	91.0%	91.9%
Yes	6.3	9.0	8.1
92B(3). Sexual frustration, or control of your sexual urges?	(*N* = 348)	(*N* = 629)	(*N* = 977)
No	93.7%	92.7%	93.0%
Yes	6.3	7.3	7.0
92B(4). Breakup of a sexual relationship—marriage, or someone you loved?	(*N* = 350)	(*N* = 630)	(*N* = 980)
No	84.9%	81.1%	82.4%
Yes	15.1	18.9	17.6
92B(5). Homosexuality?	(*N* = 349)	(*N* = 628)	(*N* = 977)
No	97.7%	99.0%	98.6%
Yes	2.3	1.0	1.4
93A. Have you ever seriously considered committing suicide?	(*N* = 1,461)	(*N* = 1,548)	(*N* = 3,009)
No	95.2%	91.2%	93.2%
Yes	4.8	8.8	6.8
[IF YES:]			
93B. How many times have you really attempted suicide?	(*N* = 66)	(*N* = 132)	(*N* = 198)
Never	63.6%	45.5%	51.5%
Once	24.2	37.1	32.8
Twice	9.1	10.6	10.1
Three or more times	3.0	6.8	5.6

	Males	*Females*	*Total*
93C. What was your age the first time you seriously considered or actually attempted suicide?	(*N* = 68)	(*N* = 133)	(*N* = 201)
15 or younger	8.8%	12.0%	10.9%
16 to 19	26.5	28.6	27.9
20 to 24	19.1	23.3	21.9
25 to 29	14.7	12.8	13.4
30 to 34	4.4	9.8	8.9
35 to 44	10.3	8.3	9.0
45 or older	16.2	5.3	9.0
93D. And what was your age the last time you seriously considered or actually attempted it?	(*N* = 66)	(*N* = 127)	(*N* = 193)
15 or younger	1.5%	3.9%	3.1%
16 to 19	24.2	22.8	23.3
20 to 24	21.2	20.5	20.7
25 to 29	16.7	16.5	16.6
30 to 34	3.0	17.3	12.4
35 to 44	12.1	11.0	11.4
45 or older	21.2	7.9	12.4
93E(1). Were any of these (suicide attempts/considerations of suicide) related to your concern with what is right or wrong in sexual matters?	(*N* = 67)	(*N* = 132)	(*N* = 199)
No	89.6%	89.4%	89.4%
Yes	10.4	10.6	10.6
93E(2). Sexual inadequacy—impotence or frigidity?	(*N* = 67)	(*N* = 132)	(*N* = 199)
No	94.0%	93.9%	94.0%
Yes	6.0	6.1	6.0
93E(3). Sexual frustration, or control of your sexual urges?	(*N* = 67)	(*N* = 132)	(*N* = 199)
No	92.5%	93.2%	93.0%
Yes	7.5	6.8	7.0
93E(4). Breakup of a sexual relationship—marriage or someone you loved?	(*N* = 68)	(*N* = 134)	(*N* = 202)
No	72.1%	64.2%	66.8%
Yes	27.9	35.8	33.2
93E(5). Homosexuality?	(*N* = 67)	(*N* = 132)	(*N* = 199)
No	97.0%	99.2%	98.5%
Yes	3.0	0.8	1.5

	Males	Females	Total
ATTITUDES TOWARD HOMOSEXUALITY (SEE ALSO Q. 60–68)			
94. To what extent do you think homosexuality is obscene and vulgar—very much, somewhat, very little, or not at all?	(N = 1,450)	(N = 1,535)	(N = 2,985)
Not at all	8.8%	6.5%	7.6%
Very little	9.1	6.1	7.6
Somewhat	18.7	19.0	18.9
Very much	63.4	68.3	66.0
95. I'm going to read a list of statements about homosexuals. For each one, tell me whether you think it is true for all or almost all of these people, more than half, less than half, or for hardly any or none of them. Just give me an answer from this card.			
95A. Young homosexuals become that way because of older homosexuals.	(N = 1,454)	(N = 1,546)	(N = 3,000)
True of hardly any or none	26.6%	26.6%	26.6%
True of less than half	21.6	21.9	21.7
True of more than half	22.7	25.2	24.0
True of all or almost all	20.6	17.3	18.9
Don't know	8.5	9.1	8.8
95.B Homosexuals are born that way.	(N = 1,457)	(N = 1,546)	(N = 3,003)
True of hardly any or none	43.4%	44.8%	44.1%
True of less than half	18.1	18.1	18.1
True of more than half	13.5	13.8	13.6
True of all or almost all	18.3	15.3	16.7
Don't know	6.7	8.1	7.4
95C. People become homosexual because they are not attractive to the opposite sex.	(N = 1,454)	(N = 1,546)	(N = 2,998)
True of hardly any or none	41.1%	38.8%	40.0%
True of less than half	23.3	22.8	23.0
True of more than half	17.5	18.5	18.0
True of all or almost all	11.3	12.0	11.7
Don't know	6.8	7.8	7.3
95D. People become homosexual because of how their parents raised them.	(N = 1,453)	(N = 1,542)	(N = 2,995)
True of hardly any or none	31.4%	31.6%	31.5%
True of less than half	25.4	23.3	24.3
True of more than half	24.6	25.4	25.0
True of all or almost all	13.4	14.1	13.7
Don't know	5.2	5.6	5.4
95E. If homosexual men cannot find men for partners, they try to force their attentions on women.	(N = 1,453)	(N = 1,544)	(N = 2,997)
True of hardly any or none	45.6%	45.9%	45.7%
True of less than half	23.9	21.0	22.4
True of more than half	10.6	11.5	11.0
True of all or almost all	7.1	6.9	7.0
Don't know	12.9	14.7	13.8

	Males	*Females*	*Total*
95F. Homosexual men can be turned into heterosexuals by women who have enough sexual skills.	(*N* = 1,452)	(*N* = 1,538)	(*N* = 2,990)
True of hardly any or none	30.7%	32.3%	31.5%
True of less than half	26.4	26.4	26.4
True of more than half	17.4	15.7	16.6
True of all or almost all	9.8	7.9	8.9
Don't know	15.6	17.6	16.7
95G. Homosexuals can stop being homosexual if they want to.	(*N* = 1,456)	(*N* = 1,540)	(*N* = 2,996)
True of hardly any or none	26.2%	32.5%	29.4%
True of less than half	21.4	20.6	21.0
True of more than half	18.7	16.6	17.6
True of all or almost all	25.0	21.5	23.2
95H. Homosexuality is a sickness which can be cured.	(*N* = 1,449)	(*N* = 1,543)	(*N* = 2,992)
True of hardly any or none	14.2%	11.9%	13.0%
True of less than half	15.2	18.0	16.6
True of more than half	24.4	24.0	24.2
True of all or almost all	39.5	37.0	38.2
Don't know	6.6	9.0	7.9
95I. Homosexuals are a high security risk for government jobs.	(*N* = 1,452)	(*N* = 1,539)	(*N* = 2,991)
True of hardly any or none	18.5%	23.5%	21.1%
True of less than half	11.7	12.5	12.1
True of more than half	16.1	15.9	15.7
True of all or almost all	48.3	39.0	43.5
Don't know	5.4	9.0	7.3
95J. Homosexuals tend to corrupt their fellow workers sexually.	(*N* = 1,455)	(*N* = 1,544)	(*N* = 2,999)
True of hardly any or none	33.4%	37.0%	35.2%
True of less than half	19.1	19.2	19.1
True of more than half	16.2	15.2	15.7
True of all or almost all	25.5	20.5	22.9
Don't know	5.8	8.2	7.0
95K. Homosexual women can be turned into heterosexuals by men who have enough sexual skills.	(*N* = 1,455)	(*N* = 1,540)	(*N* = 2,995)
True of hardly any or none	25.6%	27.3%	26.5%
True of less than half	22.3	22.9	22.6
True of more than half	20.8	20.4	20.5
True of all or almost all	15.3	12.5	13.9
Don't know	15.9	16.9	16.4

96. Now these statements are sometimes made about homosexuals, both men and women. For each one, tell me how much you agree or disagree.

	Males	*Females*	*Total*
96A. Homosexuals have unusually strong sex drives.	(*N* = 1,454)	(*N* = 1,545)	(*N* = 2,999)
Strongly disagree	7.9%	5.4%	6.6%
Somewhat disagree	13.8	15.8	14.8
Somewhat agree	37.0	35.7	36.3
Strongly agree	24.8	20.6	22.6
Don't know	16.5	22.5	19.6
96B. Homosexuals are afraid of the opposite sex.	(*N* = 1,457)	(*N* = 1,545)	(*N* = 3,002)
Strongly disagree	12.4%	9.6%	10.9%
Somewhat disagree	22.9	21.9	22.4
Somewhat agree	39.4	40.5	40.0
Strongly agree	15.2	16.7	16.0
Don't know	10.2	11.3	10.8
96C. Homosexuals act like the opposite sex.	(*N* = 1,450)	(*N* = 1,540)	(*N* = 2,990)
Strongly disagree	7.4%	6.4%	6.9%
Somewhat disagree	16.3	15.5	15.9
Somewhat agree	48.2	46.2	47.2
Strongly agree	21.6	23.1	22.4
Don't know	6.6	8.8	7.7
96D. Bars serving homosexuals should be permitted.	(*N* = 1,458)	(*N* = 1,544)	(*N* = 3,002)
Strongly disagree	28.0%	27.0%	27.5%
Somewhat disagree	15.1	16.7	15.9
Somewhat agree	30.9	31.4	31.2
Strongly agree	21.0	18.2	19.6
Don't know	5.0	6.7	5.9
96E. Homosexuals should be allowed to dance with each other in public places.	(*N* = 1,454)	(*N* = 1,542)	(*N* = 2,996)
Strongly disagree	54.3%	56.3%	55.3%
Somewhat disagree	16.8	19.5	18.2
Somewhat agree	17.1	13.5	15.3
Strongly agree	8.9	6.1	7.4
Don't know	2.9	4.7	3.8
96F. It is easy to tell homosexuals by how they look.	(*N* = 1,455)	(*N* = 1,543)	(*N* = 2,998)
Strongly disagree	30.1%	30.3%	30.2%
Somewhat disagree	25.6	24.2	24.8
Somewhat agree	25.0	25.3	25.1
Strongly agree	12.4	11.4	11.9
Don't know	6.9	8.8	7.9
96G. Homosexuals should not be allowed to be members of churches or synagogues.	(*N* = 1,449)	(*N* = 1,541)	(*N* = 2,990)
Strongly disagree	57.8%	59.8%	58.8%
Somewhat disagree	20.5	20.3	20.4
Somewhat agree	8.6	7.5	8.1
Strongly agree	10.1	7.9	9.0
Don't know	2.9	4.5	3.7

	Males	*Females*	*Total*
96H. There is an element of homosexuality in everyone.	(*N* = 1,453)	(*N* = 1,545)	(*N* = 2,998)
Strongly disagree	30.7%	37.5%	34.2%
Somewhat disagree	15.5	17.1	16.3
Somewhat agree	33.7	26.7	30.1
Strongly agree	12.4	7.0	9.6
Don't know	7.7	11.7	9.7
96I. Homosexuals should be allowed to organize groups for social and recreational purposes.	(*N* = 1,451)	(*N* = 1,541)	(*N* = 2,992)
Strongly disagree	30.9%	31.0%	30.9%
Somewhat disagree	15.9	15.8	15.9
Somewhat agree	29.1	30.0	29.6
Strongly agree	19.4	16.2	17.7
Don't know	4.8	6.9	5.9
96J. Homosexuality is a social corruption which can cause the downfall of a civilization.	(*N* = 1,455)	(*N* = 1,543)	(*N* = 2,998)
Strongly disagree	25.7%	23.8%	24.7%
Somewhat disagree	18.6	19.2	18.9
Somewhat agree	23.4	24.4	23.9
Strongly agree	26.5	24.0	25.2
Don't know	5.8	8.6	7.3
96K. Homosexuals are dangerous as teachers or youth leaders, because they try to get sexually involved with children.	(*N* = 1,450)	(*N* = 1,542)	(*N* = 2,992)
Strongly disagree	9.7%	9.6%	9.7%
Somewhat disagree	12.0	12.2	12.1
Somewhat agree	29.0	29.2	29.1
Strongly agree	46.0	44.4	45.2
Don't know	3.2	4.7	4.0
96L. Homosexuals try to play sexually with children if they cannot get an adult partner.	(*N* = 1,455)	(*N* = 1,544)	(*N* = 2,999)
Strongly disagree	8.9%	8.3%	8.6%
Somewhat disagree	10.2	9.8	10.0
Somewhat agree	36.9	35.6	36.2
Strongly agree	35.7	35.0	35.3
Don't know	8.3	11.3	9.8
96M. Homosexuals should be allowed to organize groups to deal with their social problems.	(*N* = 1,450)	(*N* = 1,542)	(*N* = 2,992)
Strongly disagree	14.0%	10.9%	12.4%
Somewhat disagree	9.0	7.9	8.4
Somewhat agree	34.1	33.1	33.6
Strongly agree	39.7	43.1	41.4
Don't know	3.3	5.0	4.2

	Males	Females	Total
96N. What consenting adult homosexuals do in private is no one else's business.	(*N* = 1,457)	(*N* = 1,545)	(*N* = 3,002)
Strongly disagree	14.6%	13.8%	14.2%
Somewhat disagree	13.7	14.4	14.1
Somewhat agree	29.4	30.7	30.0
Strongly agree	39.3	37.3	38.3
Don't know	3.1	3.8	3.4
96O. Homosexuality in itself is no problem, but what people make of it can be a serious problem.	(*N* = 1,449)	(*N* = 1,542)	(*N* = 2,991)
Strongly disagree	21.9%	24.6%	23.3%
Somewhat disagree	15.7	18.4	17.1
Somewhat agree	29.5	26.8	28.1
Strongly agree	29.4	25.9	27.6
Don't know	3.6	4.2	3.9
97. Would you say that homosexual men should, or should not be allowed to work in the following professions?			
Artist	(*N* = 1,438)	(*N* = 1,522)	(*N* = 2,960)
Should not be allowed	17.1%	14.0%	15.5%
Should be allowed	82.9	86.0	84.5
Beautician	(*N* = 1,442)	(*N* = 1,527)	(*N* = 2,969)
Should not be allowed	30.2%	26.4%	28.3%
Should be allowed	69.8	73.6	71.7
Medical doctor	(*N* = 1,438)	(*N* = 1,523)	(*N* = 2,961)
Should not be allowed	66.0%	69.3%	67.7%
Should be allowed	34.0	30.7	32.3
Florist	(*N* = 1,447)	(*N* = 1,525)	(*N* = 2,972)
Should not be allowed	16.0%	10.4%	13.1%
Should be allowed	84.0	89.6	86.8
Government official	(*N* = 1,435)	(*N* = 1,519)	(*N* = 2,954)
Should not be allowed	69.1%	65.7%	67.4%
Should be allowed	30.9	34.3	32.6
Musician	(*N* = 1,445)	(*N* = 1,529)	(*N* = 2,974)
Should not be allowed	16.5%	13.2%	14.8%
Should be allowed	83.5	86.8	85.2
Court judge	(*N* = 1,442)	(*N* = 1,515)	(*N* = 2,957)
Should not be allowed	77.1%	77.3%	77.2%
Should be allowed	22.9	22.7	22.8
School teacher	(*N* = 1,445)	(*N* = 1,529)	(*N* = 2,974)
Should not be allowed	75.8%	78.0%	76.9%
Should be allowed	24.2	22.0	23.1
Minister	(*N* = 1,444)	(*N* = 1,526)	(*N* = 2,970)
Should not be allowed	74.9%	78.2%	76.6%
Should be allowed	25.1	21.8	23.4

98. As I read each of the following statements about homosexual men, look at the card and tell me how true it is for you.

	Males	*Females*	*Total*
98A. I won't associate with these people if I can help it.	(*N* = 1,456)	(*N* = 1,540)	(*N* = 2,996)
Very untrue	8.4%	9.7%	9.1%
Somewhat untrue	7.5	11.2	9.4
Somewhat true	21.4	22.9	22.2
Very true	62.7	56.1	59.3
98B. I think some of our best citizens come from this group.	(*N* = 1,415)	(*N* = 1,474)	(*N* = 2,889)
Very untrue	38.5%	34.0%	36.2%
Somewhat untrue	23.2	28.7	26.0
Somewhat true	25.5	26.2	25.9
Very true	12.8	11.1	11.9
98C. I suppose they are all right, but I've never liked them.	(*N* = 1,430)	(*N* = 1,493)	(*N* = 2,923)
Very untrue	14.8%	16.6%	15.7%
Somewhat untrue	14.3	20.7	17.6
Somewhat true	32.4	32.1	32.2
Very true	38.5	30.6	34.5
98D. I think they should be regarded as any other group.	(*N* = 1,447)	(*N* = 1,526)	(*N* = 2,973)
Very untrue	29.4%	31.1%	30.3%
Somewhat untrue	21.3	24.1	22.7
Somewhat true	26.0	25.8	25.9
Very true	23.3	18.9	21.1
98E. I have no particular love or hatred for this group.	(*N* = 1,447)	(*N* = 1,524)	(*N* = 2,971)
Very untrue	11.7%	9.3%	10.5%
Somewhat untrue	12.0	12.6	12.3
Somewhat true	35.4	36.8	36.1
Very true	40.9	41.3	41.1

This is all of our questions. Thank you very much for your time and help. Members of our study staff may want to talk with some of the people who have been interviewed concerning their impressions about the survey and the questionnaire, and any objections or suggestions they may have.

	Males	*Females*	*Total*
99. Would you be willing to have one of our staff members call on you some time in the near future for such a discussion?	(*N* = 1,440)	(*N* = 1,506)	(*N* = 2,946)
No	30.7%	34.5%	32.6%
Yes	69.3	65.5	67.4

DEMOGRAPHIC CHARACTERISTICS (SEE ALSO Q.3–14, 27–29, 35, 36, 39)[26]

	Males	*Females*	*Total*
100. Respondent's sex.	(*N* = 1,465)	(*N* = 1,553)	(*N* = 3,018)
Male	100.0%	0.0%	48.5%
Female	0.0	100.0	51.5
101. Respondent's race.	(*N* = 1,465)	(*N* = 1,553)	(*N* = 3,018)
White	83.5%	83.3%	83.4%
Black	16.1	15.8	15.9
Other	0.4	0.9	0.7

	Males	*Females*	*Total*
102. Respondent's residence location.			
City size[27]	(N = 1,464)	(N = 1,551)	(N = 3,015)
Farm	9.6%	9.2%	9.4%
Small town (under 25,000)	29.6	29.9	29.7
Small city (under 100,000)	14.7	16.7	15.7
Medium-size city (under 1,000,000)	29.6	27.8	28.7
Large city	16.5	16.4	16.5
Geographic area	(N = 1,465)	(N = 1,553)	(N = 3,018)
New England	5.0%	5.0%	5.0%
Mid-Atlantic	18.5	19.1	18.8
East North Central	18.8	19.1	19.0
West North Central	9.9	9.7	9.8
South Atlantic	14.5	13.9	14.2
East South Central	4.6	4.9	4.7
West South Central	11.7	13.1	12.4
Mountain	3.8	3.2	3.5
Pacific	13.2	12.2	12.7

NOTES

1. In setting up sampling parameters for our survey, the National Opinion Research Center (NORC) intended to include no one under age 21, unless he or she qualified as a "head of household." The 75 respondents who are under 21 are therefore not representative of their age cohort in the general population.
2. If the respondent named more than one branch, the one in which he or she had served the longest—including being called to duty while on reserve—was coded.
3. If the respondent's first answer was vague, the interviewer probed as necessary: "What (does/did/do) (he/she/you) actually do? What (does/did) that firm or agency actually make or do?"
4. As responses to question 12C indicate, 149 respondents (plus one more who did not answer 12C) were born outside the United States. The total-sample *N* of 154 for this question includes a few of those born in the United States who were reared elsewhere.
5. Foreign-born respondents are included among those responding "outside the United States."
6. The category "small town" includes living in a rural area but not on a farm. Respondents who grew up in suburbs adjacent to a metropolitan area were considered for coding purposes to have been reared in the city of which their hometown was a suburb.
7. Respondents who reported parental death were not asked this question; "permanent" was coded automatically.
8. Questions 16–19 were not asked of respondents who did not name a father figure in Question 15.
9. Respondents who reported an intact family or a temporary separation were not asked this question; "real father" was coded automatically.
10. Questions 17 and 18 were self-administered. Thus, the questions themselves and the available response categories were read by the respondent, not spoken by the interviewer.

11. Questions 21–24 were not asked of respondents who did not name a mother figure in Question 20.
12. Respondents who reported an intact family or a temporary separation were not asked this question; "real mother" was coded automatically.
13. Questions 22 and 23 were self-administered. Thus, the questions themselves and the available response categories were read by the respondent, not spoken by the interviewer.
14. If the respondent was a twin, his or her co-twin was not counted in coding birth order.
15. Examples of religious denominations assigned to these categories are as follows: Philosophical-rationalist—intellectually based, a universal group, "not really a church," "for all the people," mysticism, Zen, humanism, etc.; General Protestant—nondenominational or multidenominational, community church, Christian Science, Unitarian-Universalist, Latter Day Saints, Jehovah's Witnesses, etc.; Reformation Protestant—Presbyterian, Episcopal, Lutheran (except Wisconsin or Missouri synods or Free), Congregational, Evangelical & Reformed, etc.; Pietistic Protestant—Methodist (except Free), United Brethren, Mennonite, Quaker, American or German Baptist, Disciples of Christ, etc.; Fundamentalist Protestant—Lutheran (Wisconsin or Missouri synod or Free), Church of the Nazarene, Free Methodist, Church of Christ, Church of God, Baptist (except American or German), Salvation Army, Pentecostal, Assembly of God, Apostolic or Holiness Church, etc.
16. Categories are illustrated in note 17.
17. For Questions 42A and 42B, the response category "neither strict nor permissive" was not offered, but was coded if the respondent said that the parent in question had been effectively neutral in this regard.
18. Questions 43A–E were not asked of black respondents.
19. Questions 44A–E were not asked of Jewish respondents.
20. The response "some, but don't know how many" was not offered, but was coded when respondents insisted that they could not estimate the number.
21. The response "about the same" was not offered, but was coded if the respondent volunteered it.
22. The three "same age" categories were not offered, but were coded if the respondent's replies indicated that they were most accurate.
23. Sexual history questions are lettered A–R rather than being numbered continuously with the rest because they were self-administered, not read aloud by the interviewer. The booklet containing these questions was filled out by the respondent after Question 82 and before the interviewer resumed with Question 83. Space limitations preclude our reproducing here the entire text of the booklet with all its instructions to respondents.
24. On this question, respondents could mark as many responses as applied; hence the category "some combination of these."
25. This section marks the conclusion of self-administered questions and the resumption of questions being read aloud by the interviewer.
26. Data in this section were recorded by the interviewer later, not asked of respondents.
27. The category "small town" includes living in a rural area but not on a farm. Respondents living in suburbs adjacent to a metropolitan area were considered for coding purposes to be residents of the principal city.

Bibliography

Adam, Barry D. 1978. *Inferiorization and everyday life*. New York: Elsevier North-Holland.
Adorno, Theodor W., Else Frenkel-Brunswik, Daniel J. Levinson, and R. Nevitt Sanford. 1950. *The authoritarian personality: Studies in prejudice*. New York: Harper & Brothers.
Allgeier, A.R. and E.R. Allgeier. 1988. *Sexual interactions*, 3rd ed. Lexington, Mass.: D.C. Heath.
Alwin, Duane F., and Robert M. Hauser. 1975. The decomposition of effects in path analysis. *American Sociological Review* 40:37–47.
Asch, Solomon E. 1952. *Social psychology*. Englewood Cliffs, N.J.: Prentice-Hall.
Athanasiou, Robert. 1973. A review of public attitudes on sexual issues. In *Contemporary sexual behavior: Critical issues in the 1970's*, eds. Joseph Lubin and John Money, 361–90. Baltimore: Johns Hopkins University Press.
Athanasiou, Robert, Phillip Shaver, and Carol Tavris. 1970. Sex. *Psychology Today* 4(2):39–52.
Bartell, Gilbert D. 1971. *Group sex: A scientist's eyewitness report on the American way of swinging*. New York: P. H. Wyden.
Bauman, Karl E., and Robert R. Wilson. 1974. Sexual behavior of unmarried university students in 1968 and 1972. *Journal of Sex Research* 10:327–33.
Becker, Howard S. 1963. *Outsiders: Studies in the sociology of deviance*. New York: Free Press.
Bell, Alan P. 1973. *Adolescent sexuality in contemporary America: A review. SIECUS Report* 2(1):1, 3.
———. 1978. Gay life and human liberation: A perspective. *SIECUS Report* 6(6):2.
Bell, Alan P., and Martin S. Weinberg. 1978. *Homosexualities: A study of diversity among men and women*. New York: Simon & Schuster.

Bell, Alan P., Martin S. Weinberg, and Sue Kiefer Hammersmith. 1981. *Sexual preference: Its development among men and women*. Bloomington: Indiana University Press.

Bell, Daniel. 1975. *The cultural contradictions of capitalism*. New York: Basic Books.

Bell, Robert R. 1966. *Premarital sex in a changing society*. Englewood Cliffs, N.J.: Prentice-Hall.

Bell, Robert R., and Leonard Blumberg. 1959. Courtship intimacy and religious background. *Marriage and Family Living* 21:356–60.

Bell, Robert R., and Jay B. Chaskes. 1970. Premarital sexual experiences among coeds, 1958 and 1968. *Journal of Marriage and the Family* 32:81–84.

Bell, Robert R., and Lillian Silvan. 1970. "Swinging": The sexual exchange of marriage partners. Paper read at the meeting of the Society for the Study of Social Problems, Washington, D.C.

Bellah, Robert. 1964. Religious evolution. *American Sociological Review* 29:358–74.

———. 1967. Civil religion in America. *Daedalus* 96:1–21.

Berry, David F., and Philip A. Marks. 1969. Antihomosexual prejudice as a function of attitude toward own sexuality. *Proceedings of the American Psychological Association* 4:573–74.

Blalock, Hubert M., Jr. 1961. *Causal inferences in nonexperimental research*. Chapel Hill: University of North Carolina Press.

Boisen, Anton T. 1955. *Religion in crisis and custom: A sociological and psychological study*. New York: Harper & Brothers.

Brannon, Robert. 1976. Attitudes and the prediction of behavior. In *Social psychology: An introduction*, eds. Bernard Seidenberg and Alvin Snadowsky. New York: Free Press.

Broadbent, D. E. 1977. The hidden pre-attentive processes. *American Psychologist* 32:109–18.

Broderick, Carlfred B. 1966. Socio-sexual development in a suburban community. *Journal of Sex Research* 2:1–24.

Bronfenbrenner, Urie. 1958. Socialization and social class through time and space. In *Readings in social psychology*, 3rd ed., eds. Eleanor E. Maccoby, Theodore W. Newcomb, and Eugene L. Hartley, 400–25. New York: Holt.

Broude, Gwen J. 1975. Norms of premarital sexual behavior: A cross-cultural study. *Ethos* 3:381–402.

Brown, Julia S. 1952. A comparative study of deviations from sexual mores. *American Sociological Review* 17:135–46.

Brown, Marvin, and Donald M. Amoroso. 1975. Attitudes toward homosexuality among West Indian male and female college students. *Journal of Social Psychology* 97:163–68.

Brown, Roger. 1965. *Social psychology.* New York: Free Press.

Cameron, J. M. 1976. Sex in the head: From machismo to mutuality: Essays on sexism and woman-man liberation. *New York Review*, May 13, 19–28.

Cannon, Kenneth L., and Richard Long. 1971. Premarital sexual behavior in the sixties. *Journal of Marriage and the Family* 33:36–49.

Chamberlain, Gary. 1975. Column. *Critic* 33:16–17, 74–80.

Chesler, Phyllis. [1972] 1973. *Women and madness.* New York: Avon Books.

Chilman, Catherine S. 1978. *Adolescent sexuality in a changing American society: Social and psychological perspectives.* Bethesda, Md.: U.S. Dept. of Health, Education, and Welfare.

Christensen, Harold T. 1966. Scandinavian and American sex norms: Some comparisons, with sociological implications. *Journal of Social Issues* 22:60–75.

Christensen, Harold T., and George R. Carpenter. 1962. Value-behavior discrepancies regarding premarital coitus in three western cultures. *American Sociological Review* 27:66–74.

Christensen, Harold T., and Christina F. Gregg. 1970. Changing sex norms in America and Scandinavia. *Journal of Marriage and the Family* 32:616–27.

Churchill, Wainwright. 1967. *Homosexual behavior among males: A cross-cultural and cross species investigation.* New York: Hawthorn Books.

Cochran, William G., Frederick Mosteller, and John W. Tukey. 1954. Statistical problems of the Kinsey Report. Washington, D.C.: The American Statistical Association.

Coleman, James S. 1966. Female status and premarital sexual codes. *American Journal of Sociology* 72:217.

Cory, Donald Webster. 1956. *Homosexuality: A cross-cultural approach.* New York: Julian Press.

Crooks, R. and K. Baur. 1980. *Our sexuality.* Menlo Park, Cal.: Benjamin/Cummings.

Dargitz, Robert E. 1976. Propensity to sanction selected forms of deviant sexual behavior. Ph.D. diss., Indiana University, Bloomington.

Davenport, William H. 1978. Sex in cross-cultural perspective. In *Human sexuality in four perspectives*, ed. Frank A. Beach, 115–63. Baltimore: Johns Hopkins University Press.

Davis, Elizabeth Gould. 1971. *The first sex.* New York: Putnam.

Davis, James A. 1975. Communism, conformity, cohorts, and categories: American tolerance in 1954 and 1972–73. *American Journal of Sociology* 81(3):491–513.

Davis, Kingsley. 1971. Sexual behavior. In *Contemporary social prob-*

lems, 3rd ed., eds. Robert K. Merton and Robert Nisbet, 313–60. New York: Harcourt Brace Jovanovich.

Degler, Karl N. 1979. *At odds: Women and the family in America from the revolution to the present*. New York: Oxford University Press.

DeLora, Joann S., and Carol A. B. Warren. 1977. *Understanding sexual interaction*. Boston: Houghton Mifflin.

Denfeld, Duane, and Michael Gordon. 1974. The sociology of mate swapping; or, the family that swings together clings together. In *Beyond monogamy: Recent studies of sexual alternatives in marriage*, eds. James R. Smith and Lynn G. Smith, 68–83. Baltimore: Johns Hopkins University Press.

Denney, N.W. and D. Quadagno. 1988. *Human sexuality*. St. Louis: Times Mirror/Mosby.

Deutscher, Irwin. 1973. *What we say/what we do: Sentiments and acts*. Glenview, Ill.: Scott, Foresman.

Dittes, James E. 1969. Psychology of religion. In *Handbook of social psychology*, 2nd ed., eds. Gardner Lindzey and Elliot Aronson, vol. 5, 602–59. Reading, Mass.: Addison-Wesley.

Douglas, Jack D. 1970. *Deviance and respectability: The social construction of moral meanings*. New York: Basic Books.

Dunbar, John, Marvin Brown, and Donald M. Amoroso. 1973. Some correlates of attitudes toward homosexuality. *Journal of Social Psychology* 89:271–79.

Dunbar, John, Marvin Brown, and Sophie Vuorinen. 1973. Attitudes toward homosexuality among Brazilian and Canadian college students. *Journal of Social Psychology* 90:173–83.

Duncan, Otis Dudley. 1961. A socio-economic index for all occupations. In *Occupations and social status*, ed. Albert J. Reiss, Jr., 109–38. Glencoe, Ill.: Free Press.

———. 1966. Path analysis: Sociological examples. *American Journal of Sociology* 72(1):1–16.

Durkheim, Émile. 1951. *Suicide: A study in sociology*. Trans. John A. Spaulding and George Simpson. New York: Free Press.

Eckhardt, Kenneth W. 1971. Exchange and sexual permissiveness. *Behavior Science Notes* 1:1–18.

Ehrlich, Howard J. 1969. Attitudes, behavior, and the intervening variables. *American Sociologist* 4:29–34.

Empey, Lamar T., and Steven G. Lubeck. 1971. *Explaining delinquency*. Lexington, Mass.: D. C. Heath.

Engels, Friedrich. [1894] 1902. *The origin of the family, private property, and the state*. Chicago: Charles H. Kerr.

Farrell, Ronald A., and Thomas J. Morrione. 1974. Social interaction and stereotypic responses to homosexuals. *Archives of Sexual Behavior* 3:425–42.

Fay, Robert E., Charles F. Turner, Albert D. Klassen, and John H. Gagnon. 1989. Prevalence and patterns of same-gender sexual contact among men. *Science* 243:338–48.

Fennessey, Alice. 1977. *An exploration of the domain of attitudes toward homosexuality.* Ph.D. diss., Columbia University. Ann Arbor, Mich.: University Microfilms.

Festinger, Leon. 1954. A theory of social comparison processes. *Human Relations* 7:117–40.

———. 1957. *A theory of cognitive dissonance.* Evanston, Ill.: Row, Peterson.

Firestone, Shulamith. 1970. *The dialectics of sex*: The Case for Feminist Revolution. New York: Bantam.

Fisher, Seymour. 1973. *The female orgasm.* New York: Basic Books.

Foucault, Michel. 1978. *The history of sexuality.* Vol. 1; *An introduction.* Trans. Robert Hurley. New York: Pantheon.

Friedan, Betty. 1963. *The feminine mystique.* New York: Dell.

Freud, Sigmund. [1920] 1955. Beyond the pleasure principle. *Standard edition. Vol. 18*, 3–64. London: Hogarth Press.

Freud, Sigmund. [1930] 1962. *Civilization and its discontents.* Trans. James Strachey. New York: W. W. Norton.

Gagnon, John H. 1967. Sexuality and sexual learning in the child. In *Sexual deviance*, eds. John H. Gagnon and William Simon, 15–42. New York: Harper & Row.

———. 1977. *Human sexualities.* Glenview, Ill.: Scott, Foresman.

Gagnon, John H., and William Simon. 1967. *Sexual deviance.* New York: Harper & Row.

——— and ———. 1970. Prospects for change in American sexual patterns. *Medical Aspects of Human Sexuality* 4:100–17.

——— and ———. 1973. *Sexual conduct: The social sources of human sexuality.* Chicago: Aldine.

Gallup, George. 1978. Premarital sex is no sin to most teens. Associated Press.

Garfinkel, Harold. 1967. *Studies in ethnomethodology.* Englewood Cliffs, N.J.: Prentice-Hall.

Giddens, Anthony. 1978. *Durkheim.* London: Fontana.

Gilmartin, Brian G. 1974. Sexual deviance and social networks: A study of social, family, and marital interaction patterns among co-marital sex participants. In *Beyond monogamy: Recent studies of sexual alternatives in marriage*, eds. James R. Smith and Lynn G. Smith, 291–323. Baltimore: Johns Hopkins University Press.

Glenn, Norval D. 1967. Massification versus differentiation: Some trend data from national surveys. *Social Forces* 46:172–80.

———. 1974. Aging and conservatism. *Annals of the American Academy of Political and Social Sciences* 415:176–86.

Glenn, Norval D., and Jon P. Alston. 1967. Rural-urban differences in reported attitudes and behavior. *Southwestern Social Science Quarterly* 47:381–400.

Glenn, Norval D., and J. L. Simmons. 1967. Are regional cultural differences diminishing? *Public Opinion Quarterly* 31:176–93.

Glenn, Norval D., and Charles N. Weaver. 1979. Attitudes toward premarital, extramarital, and homosexual relations in the U.S. in the 1970s. *Journal of Sex Research* 15:108–18.

Glock, Charles Y., and Rodney Stark. 1966. *Christian beliefs and anti-Semitism*. New York: Harper & Row.

Goethals, George W. 1971. Factors affecting rules regarding premarital sex. In *Studies in the sociology of sex*, ed. James M. Henslin. New York: Appleton-Century-Crofts.

Goldsmith, Sadja. 1973. Adolescent sexuality in contemporary America: A review. *SIECUS Report* 2:11–12.

Goode, Erich. 1966. Social class and church participation. *American Journal of Sociology* 72:102–11.

Goode, Erich, and Richard R. Troiden. 1974. *Sexual deviance and sexual deviants*. New York: Morrow.

Greene, Bob. 1975. Beyond the sexual revolution. *Newsweek*, Sept. 29, 13.

Greenfield, Jeff. 1978. Why is gay rights different from all other rights? *Village Voice* 23(6):1, passim.

Greer, Germaine. 1970. *The female eunuch*. London: MacGibbon and Kee.

Haeberle, Erwin J. 1977. Historical roots of sexual oppression. In *The sexually oppressed*, eds. H. L. Gochros and J. S. Gochros, 3–27. New York: Association Press.

Hagen, Richard. 1979. *The bio-sexual factor*. Garden City, N.Y.: Doubleday.

Haims, Lawrence J. 1973. *Sex education and the public schools: A multidimensional study for the 1970s*. Lexington, Mass: Lexington Books.

Herberg, Will. 1960. *Protestant, Catholic, Jew*. 2nd ed. Garden City, N.Y.: Doubleday Anchor.

Hite, Shere. 1976. *The Hite report: A nation-wide study of female sexuality*. New York: Macmillan.

Hoffman, Martin L., and Herbert D. Saltzstein. 1967. Parent discipline and the child's moral development. *Journal of Personality and Social Psychology* 5:45–57.

Hudson, W.W. and W.A. Ricketts. 1980. A strategy for the measurement of homophobia. *Journal of Homosexuality* 5:357–72.

Humphreys, Laud. 1970. *Tearoom trade: Impersonal sex in public places*. Chicago: Aldine.

Hunt, Morton. 1974. *Sexual behavior in the 1970's*. New York: Dell.

Hyde, J.S. 1979. *Understanding human sexuality*. New York: McGraw-Hill.

Jenkins, David Price. 1977. *Demographic variations in societal response to homosexuality*. Ed.D. diss., State University of New York at Albany. Ann Arbor, Mich.: University Microfilms.

Kaats, Gilbert R., and Keith E. Davis. 1970. The dynamics of sexual behavior of college students. *Journal of Marriage and the Family* 32:390–99.

Kammeyer, Kenneth. 1966. Birth order and the feminine sex role among college women. *American Sociological Review* 31:508–15.

Kanin, Eugene J., and David H. Howard. 1958. Postmarital consequences of premarital sex adjustments. *American Sociological Review* 23:556–62.

Kasun, Jacqueline. 1979. Turning children into sex experts. *The Public Interest* 55:3–14.

Kelley, Dean M. 1971. *Why conservative churches are growing*. New York: Harper & Row.

Kilpatrick, Dean G., and Nelson R. Cauthen. 1969. The relationship of ordinal position, dogmatism, and personal sexual attitudes. *Journal of Psychology* 73:115–20.

Kinsey, Alfred C., Wardell B. Pomeroy, and Clyde E. Martin. 1948. *Sexual behavior in the human male*. Philadelphia: Saunders.

Kinsey, Alfred C., Wardell B. Pomeroy, Clyde E. Martin, and Paul H. Gebhard. 1953. *Sexual behavior in the human female*. Philadelphia: Saunders.

Kitsuse, John I. 1962. Societal reaction to deviant behavior: Problems of theory and method. *Social Problems* 9:247–56.

Klassen, Albert D. 1982. The undersocialized conception of woman. Paper presented at the annual meeting of the Midwest Sociological Society, Des Moines, Iowa.

Klassen, Albert D., and Eugene E. Levitt. 1974. A search for structure in public attitudes and perceptions of homosexuality: 1970 national survey by the Institute for Sex Research. Paper read at the meeting of the American Anthropological Association, Mexico, D.F.

Klassen, Albert D., Colin J. Williams, Eugene E. Levitt, Laura Rudkin-Miniot, Heather Miller, and Sushama Gunjal. 1989. Trends in premarital sexual behavior. In *AIDS, sexual behavior, and IV drug use*, eds. Charles F. Turner, Heather G. Miller, and Lincoln E. Moses, 548–67. Washington, D.C.: National Academy Press.

Knox, D. 1984. *Human sexuality: the search for understanding*. St. Paul: West Publishing.

Kohlberg, Lawrence. 1969. *Stages in the development of moral thought and action*. New York: Holt.

Kohn, Melvin L. 1969. *Class and conformity: A study in values*. Homewood, Ill.: Dorsey.

Kretch, David, and Richard S. Crutchfield. 1948. *Theory and problems of social psychology.* New York: McGraw-Hill.

Kuhn, Thomas S. 1962. *The structure of scientific revolutions*. Chicago: University of Chicago Press.

Laner, Mary Riege, and Roy H. Laner. 1979. Personal style or sexual preference? Why gay men are disliked. *International Review of Modern Sociology*.

Lehne, Gregory K. 1976. Homophobia among men. In *The forty-nine percent majority: The male sex role*, eds. Deborah S. David and Robert Brannon, 66–88. Reading, Mass.: Addison-Wesley.

Leo, John. 1979. Homosexuality: Tolerance vs. approval. *Time*, Jan. 8, 48, 51.

Levitt, Eugene E., and Albert D. Klassen. 1973. Public attitudes toward sexual behaviors: The latest investigation of the Institute for Sex Research. Paper presented at the annual meeting of the American Orthopsychiatric Association, New York.

Levitt, Eugene E., and Albert D. Klassen. 1974. Public attitudes toward homosexuality: Part of the 1970 survey by the Institute for Sex Research. *Journal of Homosexuality* 1(1). Reprinted in Martin P. Levine, ed. 1979. *Gay men: The sociology of male homosexuality*, 21–35. New York: Harper & Row.

Lewis, Robert A., and Wesley R. Burr. 1975. Premarital coitus and commitment among college students. *Archives of Sexual Behavior* 4:73–79.

Lindzey, Gardner, and Elliot Aronson, eds. 1969. *The handbook of social psychology.* 2nd ed. Reading Mass.: Addison-Wesley.

Lippmann, Walter. 1922. *Public opinion*. New York: Free Press.

Lipset, Seymour Martin. 1959a. Some social requisites of democracy. *American Political Science Review* 53:69–105.

———. 1959b. Democracy and working-class authoritarianism. *American Sociological Review* 24:482–501.

———. 1964. Religion and politics in the American past and present. In *Religion and social conflict*, eds. Robert Lee and Martin E. Marty, 69–126. New York: Oxford University Press.

Luckey, Eleanore B., and Gilbert Nass. 1969. A comparison of sexual attitudes and behavior in an international sample. *Journal of Marriage and the Family* 31:364–79.

Lukes, Steven. [1972] 1973. *Émile Durkheim, his life and work: A historical and critical study.* New York: Penguin.

Lumby, Malcolm E. 1976. Homophobia: The quest for a valid scale. *Journal of Homosexuality* 2:39–47.

MacDonald, A. P., and Richard G. Games. 1974. Some characteristics of those who hold positive and negative attitudes toward homosexuals. *Journal of Homosexuality* 1:9–27.

MacDonald, A. P., Jim Huggins, Susan Young, and Richard A. Swanson. 1972. Attitudes toward homosexuality: Preservation of sex morality or the double standard? *Journal of Consulting and Clinical Psychology* 40:161.

Malinowski, Bronislaw. [1925] 1948. *Magic, science, and religion and other essays*. Garden City, N.Y.: Doubleday.

Marcus, Steven. 1966. *The other Victorians*. New York: Basic Books.

Marcuse, Herbert. 1955. *Eros and civilization: A philosophical inquiry into Freud*. Boston: Beacon Press.

Marks, Stephen R. 1974. Durkheim's theory of anomie. *American Journal of Sociology* 80:329–63.

Masters, William H., and Virginia E. Johnson. 1966. *Human sexual response*. Boston: Little, Brown.

Masters, William H., Virginia E. Johnson, and Robert J. Levin. 1975. *The pleasure bond: A new look at sexuality and commitment*. New York: Bantam.

Masters, William H., Virginia E. Johnson, and Robert C. Kolodny. 1982. *Human sexuality.* Boston: Little, Brown.

McGuire, William J. 1969. The nature of attitudes and attitude change. In *The handbook of social psychology*, 2nd ed., eds. Gardner Lindzey and Elliot Aronson, vol. 3, 136–314. Reading, Mass.: Addison-Wesley.

Miller, Patricia Y., and William Simon. 1974. Adolescent sexual behavior: Context and change. *Social Problems* 22:58–76.

Millham, Jim, Christopher L. San Miguel, and Richard Kellogg. 1976. A factor-analytic conceptualization of attitudes toward male and female homosexuals. *Journal of Homosexuality* 2:3–10.

Mirande, Alfred M. 1968. Reference group theory and adolescent sexual behavior. *Journal of Marriage and the Family* 30:572–77.

Mosher, Donald L., and Herbert Cross. 1971. Sex guilt and premarital sexual experiences of college students. *Journal of Consulting and Clinical Psychology* 36:27–32.

Mueller, John H., Karl F. Schuessler, and Herbert L. Costner. 1977. *Statistical reasoning in sociology.* 3rd ed. Boston: Houghton Mifflin.

National Institute of Mental Health Task Force on Homosexuality: Final report and background papers, ed. John M. Livingood. 1972. Washington, D.C.: U.S. Department of Health, Education, and Welfare.

Nunn, Clyde Z., Harry J. Crockett, Jr., and J. Allen Williams, Jr. 1978. *Tolerance for nonconformity.* San Francisco: Jossey-Bass.

Nunnally, Jum C. 1967. *Psychometric theory.* New York: McGraw-Hill.

Nyberg, Kenneth L., and Jon P. Alston. 1976–1977. Analysis of public attitudes toward homosexuality. *Journal of Homosexuality* 2:99–107.

O'Gorman, Hubert J. 1988. Pluralistic ignorance and reference groups: The case of ingroup ignorance. In *Surveying Social Life: Papers in Honor of Herbert Hyman*, ed. Hubert J. O'Gorman, 145–73. Middletown, Conn.: Wesleyan University Press.

Pareto, Vilfredo. 1935. *The Mind and Society.* New York: Harcourt, Brace.

Pervin, Lawrence A. 1978. *Current controversies and issues in personality.* New York: Wiley.

Petras, John W. 1973. *Sexuality in society.* Boston: Allyn & Bacon.

———. 1978. *The social meaning of human sexuality.* 2nd ed. Boston: Allyn & Bacon.

Piaget, Jean. 1948. *The moral judgment of the child.* Trans. Marjorie Gabain. Glencoe, Ill.: Free Press.

Plummer, Kenneth. 1975. *Sexual stigma: An interactionist account.* London: Routledge.

Pope, Hallowell, and Dean D. Knudsen. 1965. Premarital sexual norms, the family, and social change. *Journal of Marriage and the Family* 27:314–23.

Pope, Liston. 1953. Religion and the class structure. In *Class, status and power: A reader in social stratification*, eds. Reinhard Bendix and Seymour Martin Lipset, 316–23. Glencoe, Ill.: Free Press.

Rainwater, Lee. 1964. Marital sexuality in four cultures of poverty. *Journal of Marriage and the Family* 26:457–66.

Ranulf, Svend. 1938. *Moral indignation and middle class psychology: A sociological study.* Copenhagen: Leven & Munksgaard.

Rathus, S.A. 1983. *Human sexuality.* New York: Holt.

Reich, Wilhelm. 1969. *The sexual revolution: Toward a self-governing character structure.* 4th rev. ed. New York: Farrar, Straus & Giroux.

Reiss, Ira L. 1964. *Premarital sexual standards in America.* New York: Free Press.

———. 1967. *The social context of premarital sexual permissiveness.* New York: Holt.

———. 1968. How and why America's sex standards are changing. *Trans-Action* 5(4):26–32.

———. 1973. *Heterosexual relationships inside and outside of marriage.* Morristown, N.J.: General Learning Press. 1–29.

———. 1976. *Family systems in America.* 2nd ed. Hinsdale, Ill.: Dryden.

Rich, Adrienne. 1976. *Of woman born: Motherhood as experience and institution.* New York: Norton.

Robinson, Ira E., Karl King, and Jack O. Balswick. 1972. The premarital sexual revolution among college females. *Family Coordinator* 21:189–94.

Roche, Douglas J. 1968. *The Catholic revolution.* New York: McKay.

Roeburt, John. 1963. *Sex-life and the criminal law: A new book.* New York: Belmont Books.

Rokeach, Milton. 1976. *Beliefs, attitudes, and values: A theory of organization and change.* San Francisco: Jossey-Bass.

Rooney, Elizabeth A., and Don C. Gibbons. 1966. Social reactions to "crimes without victims." *Social Problems* 13:400–10.

Rubin, Lillian Breslow. 1976. *Worlds of pain: Life in the working-class family.* New York: Basic Books.

Safire, William. 1978. Toleration or outright approval? New York Times News Service.

San Miguel, Christopher L., and Jim Millham. 1976. The role of cognitive and situational variables in aggression toward homosexuals. *Journal of Homosexuality* 2:11–27.

Schachter, Stanley. 1964. The interactions of cognitive and physiological determinants of emotional state. In *Advances in experimental social psychology*, ed. Leonard Berkowitz, 49–80. New York: Academic Press.

Schellenburg, James A. 1970. *An introduction to social psychology.* New York: Random House.

Schoenherr, Richard A., and Andrew M. Greeley. 1974. Role commitment processes and the American Catholic priesthood. *American Sociological Review* 39(3):407–26.

Schulz, Barbara, George Bohrnstedt, Edgar F. Borgatta, and Robert R. Evans. 1977. Explaining premarital sexual intercourse among college students. *Social Forces* 56:148–65.

Schutz, Alfred. 1964. *Collected papers II: Studies in social theory.* The Hague: Martinus Nijhoff.

Secord, Paul F., and Carl W. Backman. 1974. *Social psychology.* 2nd ed. New York: McGraw-Hill.

Sherfey, Mary Jane. 1972. *The nature and evolution of female sexuality.* New York: Random House.

Simmons, J. L. 1965. Public stereotypes of deviants. *Social Problems* 13:223–32.

Simon, William, Alan S. Berger, and John H. Gagnon. 1972. Beyond anxiety and fantasy: The coital experience of college youths. *Journal of Youth and Adolescence* 1:203–22.

Singh, B. K. 1980. Trends in attitudes toward premarital sexual relations. *Journal of Marriage and the Family* 42:387–93.

Smith, Kenneth T. 1971. Homophobia: A tentative personality profile. *Psychological Reports* 29:1091–94.

Smith, Lynn G., and James R. Smith. 1974. Co-marital sex: The incorporation of extramarital sex into the marriage relationship. In *Beyond monogamy: Recent studies of sexual alternatives in marriage*, eds. James R. Smith and Lynn G. Smith, 84–102. Baltimore: Johns Hopkins University Press.

Somerville, Rose. 1971. Family life and sex education in the turbulent sixties. *Journal of Marriage and the Family* 33:11–35.

Sorensen, Robert. 1973. *Adolescent sexuality in contemporary America: Personal values and sexual behavior ages thirteen to nineteen*. Tarrytown, New York: World.

Sorokin, Pitirim A. 1956. *The American sex revolution*. Boston: Porter Sargent.

Sprey, Jetse. 1976. On the institutionalization of sexuality. In *The social psychology of sex*, ed. Jacqueline P. Wiseman, 371–85. New York: Harper & Row.

Staats, Gregory R. 1978. Stereotype content and social distance: Changing views of homosexuality. *Journal of Homosexuality* 4:15–27.

Staples, Robert. 1972. The sexuality of black women. *Sexual Behavior* 2(6):4–15.

Steffensmeier, Darrell J. 1970. *Factors affecting reactions toward homosexuals*. Ph.D. diss., Iowa University. Ann Arbor, Mich.: University Microfilms.

Steinfels, Peter. 1979. The reasonable right. *Esquire*, Feb. 13, 24–30.

Stephens, William N. 1971. A cross-cultural study of modesty and obscenity. In *Technical report of the Commission on Obscenity and Pornography*. Vol. 9, 405–51. Washington, D.C.: U.S. Government Printing Office.

Stern, G. 1962. Environments for learning. In *The American college*, ed. N. Sanford, 690–773. New York: Wiley.

Stevens, Evelyn P. 1973. Machismo and marianismo. *Society* 10:57–63.

Sudman, Seymour. 1967. *Reducing the cost of surveys*. Chicago: Aldine.

Suggs, Robert C., and Donald S. Marshall. 1971. Anthropological perspectives on human sexual behavior. In *Human sexual behavior; variations in the ethnographic spectrum*, eds. Robert C. Suggs and Donald S. Marshall, 218–43. New York: Basic Books.

Swanson, Blair. 1971. Note on the relationship of ordinal position, dogmatism, and personal sexual attitudes. *Journal of Psychology* 77:213–15.

Tavris, Carol, and Susan Sadd. 1977. *The* Redbook *report on female sexuality: 100,000 married women disclose the good news about sex*. New York: Delacorte.

Terman, Lewis M. 1948. Kinsey's *Sexual behavior in the human male:* Some comments and criticisms. *Psychological Bulletin* 45:443–59.

Tripp, C. A. 1975. *The homosexual matrix.* New York: McGraw-Hill.

Turner, Jonathan H. 1978. *The structure of sociological theory.* Rev. ed. Homewood, Ill.: Dorsey.

Van Ussel, J. 1969. Socio-economische grondslagen van de seksuele moraal. *Tijdschrift voor Sociale Wetenschoppen* 14(2):155–206.

Vener, Arthur M., and Cyrus S. Stewart. 1974. Adolescent sexual behavior in Middle America revisited: 1970–1973. *Journal of Marriage and the Family* 36:728–35.

Victor, Jeffrey S. 1980. *Human sexuality: A social psychological approach.* Englewood Cliffs, N.J.: Prentice-Hall.

Wallin, Paul. 1949. An appraisal of some methodological aspects of the Kinsey Report. *American Sociological Review* 14:197–210.

Walsh, Robert H. 1970. *A survey of parents' and their own children's sexual attitudes.* Ph.D. diss., Iowa University. Ann Arbor, Mich.: University Microfilms.

———. 1972. The generation gap in sexual beliefs. *Sexual Behavior* 2(1):4–10.

———. 1978. Sexual attitudes, standards and behavior: A current assessment. In *The new sex education: The sex educator's resource book,* ed. Herbert A. Otto, 294–312. Chicago: Association Press.

Ward, Russell A. 1977. Typifications of homosexuals: A replication and extension. Paper read at the meeting of the American Sociological Association, Chicago.

Weinberg, George. 1972. *Society and the healthy homosexual.* New York: St. Martin's Press.

Weinberg, Martin S. 1971. Sex and the sexual revolution. Unpublished manuscript, Institute for Sex Research, Indiana University.

Weinberg, Martin S., and Alan P. Bell. 1972. *Homosexuality: An annotated bibliography.* New York: Harper & Row.

Weinberg, Martin S., and Colin J. Williams. [1974] 1975a. *Male homosexuals: Their problems and adaptations.* Rev. ed. New York: Penguin.

——— and ———. 1975b. Gay baths and the social organization of impersonal sex. *Social Problems* 23:124–36.

——— and ———. 1980. Sexual embourgeoisment? Social class and sexual activity: 1938–1970. *American Sociological Review* 45:33–48.

Wilensky, Harold L. 1964. Mass society and mass culture: Interdependence or independence? *American Sociological Review* 29:173–97.

Will, George F. 1977. How far out of the closet? *Newsweek,* May 30, 92.

Willets, F. K., R. C. Bealer, and D. M. Crider. 1973. Leveling of attitudes in mass society: Rurality and traditional morality in America. *Rural Sociology* 38:36–45.

Williams, Colin J., and Martin S. Weinberg. 1971. *Homosexuals and the military: A study of less than honorable discharge.* New York: Harper & Row.

Wilson, Glenn D. 1973. *The psychology of conservatism.* New York: Academic Press.

Wilson, Sam, Bryan Strong, Leah Miller Clarke, and Thomas Johns. 1977. *Human sexuality: A text with readings.* St. Paul, Minn.: West.

Wrong, Dennis H. 1966. The oversocialized conception of man in modern sociology. *American Sociological Review* 26(2):183–93.

Yankelovich, Daniel. 1974. *The new morality: A profile of American youth in the 1970's.* New York: McGraw-Hill.

Zelnik, Melvin, and John F. Kantner. 1972. Sexuality, contraception, and pregnancy among young unwed females in the United States. In *Demographic and social aspects of population growth*, eds. Charles F. Westhoff and Robert Parke, Jr., 357–74. Washington, D.C.: U.S. Government Printing Office.

——— and ———. 1977. Sexual and contraceptive experience of young unmarried women in the United States, 1966 and 1971. *Family Planning Perspectives* 9(2):55–71.

Zurcher, Louis A., Jr., George Kirkpatrick, Robert G. Cushing, and Charles K. Bowman. 1971. The anti-pornography campaign: A symbolic crusade. *Social Problems* 19:217–38.

Index